ECONOMIC GROWTH IN PREWAR CHINA

USSR

HEILUNGKIANG

• Harbin

MONGOLIA

KIRIN

Changchun

CHAHAR

LIAONING

JEHOL

• Mukden

NINGSIA   SUIYUAN   • Kalgan   Ying-kou •
                                                                Antung
                        Tatung •   • Peking   • Dairen
                        Paoting ⊙   • Tientsin
                        HOPEH
                                                          • Chefoo
                    ⊙ Taiyuan
                    SHANSI
                         • Yenan   ⊙ Tsinan   • Tsingtao
        ⊙ Lanchow   SHANTUNG
        KANSU   Wei   River
                          Loyang Kaifeng
                • Sian   KIANGSU
        SHENSI   HONAN   JAPAN
                                        ANHWEI
        SZECHWAN   Nanking ⊙
                        Yangtze HUPEH   Hofei •
        ⊙ Chengtu   • Ichang • Hankow   Wuhu• Tai Lake • Shanghai
        Chungking •   River Anking ⊙ Soochow
                              Tungting   Hangchow ⊙
                              Lake Yochow Poyang   • Ningpo
                                    Changsha Lake
                                        • Nanchang CHEKIANG
                        Hsiang-tan   KIANGSI   • Wenchow
        KWEICHOW   HUNAN
                    ⊙
        YUNNAN | Kweiyang   • Foochow
        ⊙ Kunming   Kweilin ⊙   FUKIEN
                                                        Taipei •
                        KWANGSI |
                        Wuchow \ KWANGTUNG   • Amoy   TAIWAN
                    • Mengtze   River
                        Nanning   • Canton   • Swatow
        Hanoi •   • Pakhoi   Hong Kong
        FRENCH   Macao
        INDO-CHINA
                            Hainan
                            Island
        SIAM

- - - Provincial boundary
⊙ Provincial capital
• Other cities

0   500 Mi
N
0   500 Km

Map 1. China, ca. 1930.
Source: Based on John K. Fairbank and Albert Feuerwerker, eds., *The Cambridge History of China*: vol. 13: *Republican China, 1912–1949, part 2* (Cambridge, 1986), 5 and Albert Hermann, *An Historial Atlas of China* (Chicago, 1966).

ECONOMIC GROWTH IN PREWAR CHINA

THOMAS G. RAWSKI

UNIVERSITY OF CALIFORNIA PRESS
BERKELEY   LOS ANGELES   OXFORD

University of California Press
Berkeley and Los Angeles, California

University of California Press, Ltd.
Oxford, England

The University of California Press gratefully
acknowledges support from the China Publication
Subventions program.

Library of Congress Cataloging-in-Publication Data

Rawski, Thomas G., 1943–
  Economic growth in prewar China / Thomas G. Rawski.
    p. cm.
  Bibliography: p.
  Includes index.
  ISBN 0-520-06372-4 (alk. paper)
    1. China—Economic conditions—1912–1949. I. Title. II. Title:
Economic growth in prewar China.
HC427.8.R384 1989   88-7834
338.951—dc19   CIP

Printed in the United States of America
1   2   3   4   5   6   7   8   9

In Fond Remembrance of
Alexander Eckstein (1915–1976)
Who Loved to Learn

Contents

Tables, Figures, and Maps

Figures

Maps

Notes to the Reader

Romanization of Chinese and Japanese

The romanization of Chinese and Japanese follows G. William Skinner, ed., *Modern Chinese Society: An Analytical Bibliography*, vol. 1, *Publications in Western Languages, 1644–1972* (Stanford, 1973), 1:lviii–lx.

Abbreviations

The following abbreviations are used in the tables:

. . . indicates that relevant data are not available.

--indicates amounts that are not relevant or amounts that are negligible.

1914–21 indicates a passage of time: "output grew during 1914–21."

1914/18 indicates a time interval that is used for analytic purposes as a single point: "the economy grew at 2 percent annually between 1914/18 and 1931/36."

Weights and Measures

Weight

All tonnage figures are in metric tons.

Except as noted, 1 picul or *tan* = 133.33 pounds; 16.53 piculs = one metric ton; 1 picul = 100 catties.

Volume

Marine cargo capacity is converted at 10 *koku* = 1 ton (Table 4.5).

Area

1 mou or mu = 0.1647 acre = 0.0666 hectare.

Currency units

The term "dollar" refers to Chinese silver dollars unless otherwise specified. The term *tael* refers to various silver units of account employed in China prior to 1932. The *Hai-kuan* or (Haikwan) *tael* used by China's Maritime Customs administration was converted into Shanghai *tael*s at a standard rate of 100 *Hai-kuan tael*s = 111.40 Shanghai *tael*s. $100 exchanged for 72 Shanghai *tael*s, so one *Hai-kuan tael* was equivalent to $1.55.

Sources: Liang-lin Hsiao, *China's Foreign Trade Statistics, 1864–1949* (Cambridge, 1974), 297; Eduard Kann, *The Currencies of China*, 2d ed. (Shanghai, 1927), 84, 171; Ta-chung Liu and Kung-chia Yeh, *The Economy of the Chinese Mainland: National Income and Economic Development, 1933–1959 (Princeton, 1965),* xv; *Namboku Manshū no shuyō kaikō kakō* (Dairen, 1927), 101.

Acknowledgments

I could never have completed this volume without the generous cooperation and support of numerous individuals and institutions. Ramon Myers, Dwight Perkins, and Evelyn Rawski offered commentary and advice on every aspect of my research over a period of twelve years. The National Fellowship Program of the Hoover Institution provided an ideal research environment that allowed me to assemble disconnected ideas into a coherent structure. Additional financial support came from the Social Sciences and Humanities Research Council of Canada, the Connaught Senior Fellowship Program at the University of Toronto, and the University Center for International Studies at the University of Pittsburgh.

Sherman Cochran, Andrew Nathan, and Nicholas Lardy reviewed the initial draft with insight and care. Loren Brandt and Thomas Gottschang offered numerous suggestions along with data and references to expedite improvements. Among the many researchers who supplied me with information and ideas, I am particularly grateful to Chang Chung-li, S. H. Chou, Robert Dernberger, Ding Richu, Lloyd Eastman, Scott Eddie, Liu Foding, Shigeru Ishikawa, Barry Naughton, Penelope Prime, Peter Schran, Terry Sicular, G. William Skinner, Tim Wright, Wu Chengming, and Shu-jen Yeh. While all scholarship builds on earlier research, my tattered copies of works by the late Ta-chung Liu and by Kung-chia Yeh display my extreme debt to their diligence and vision.

I have also benefited from the bibliographic, linguistic, and technical expertise of staff members, librarians, and students at the University of Toronto, Stanford University, the University of

Pittsburgh, and research libraries on several continents, including Patricia Bennett, David M. Brown, Alice S. Y. Chan, David T. L. Chang, Fu-mei Chen, Ch'en Ch'iu-k'un, Francine Dennis-McCauley, Teresa Hsieh, William Jaeger, C. W. Keng, C. Y. Kuo, Thomas Kuo, Robert Manson, Steve McGurk, Emiko Moffitt, Della Sinclair, Mark Tam, Anna L. U, Sharon Wetzel, and Lisa Woo. Sheila Levine, Jay Plano, and Betsey Scheiner guided my manuscript through the production process with style and grace.

This book is dedicated to the late Alexander Eckstein, who did not live to see the outcome but was always ready to encourage an ambitious but confused young scholar.

Introduction

This is a study of economic growth in China during the half-century preceding World War II. I focus on the development of the modern sector, which is defined to include economic activities based on products, materials, technologies, and institutional arrangements taken or adapted from foreign models. Cotton textile factories, rail or steamship transport, and western-style commercial banking will serve as typical examples of modern-sector operations. Economic growth in prewar China, achieved in the face of extreme political and economic uncertainty, produced significant results, whose size and impact resembled contemporaneous developments in other fast-growing economies, including Japan's.

The effects of economic change extended far beyond the cities in which the modern banks and factories clustered. Strong complementarities between old and new forms of enterprise meant that modern-sector growth strengthened long-established traditional sectors of China's economy. Modern-sector innovations centered in China's coastal cities brought significant improvement to the economic lives of the nation's enormous populace, so much so that the national average level of per capita real output and consumption rose considerably between World War I and the outbreak of the Pacific War in 1937. This study seeks to delineate both the extent and the limits of growth and structural change in China's prewar economy, to investigate the relationship between the modern and the inherited sectors, and to consider the impact of prewar developments on the shape of China's economy in the postwar period of Communist leadership.

The beginnings of modern growth in China's economy can be
traced to the 1890s when three major sources of new economic
patterns—transport by rail and steamship, factory industry, and
commercial banking—first attained significant dimensions. The
entrepreneurial initiative for these innovations came in varying degrees from the Chinese government, Chinese businessmen, and
the foreign community.

Economic growth in prewar China spread outward from two
areas: the Kiangnan region centered on the dynamic metropolis of
Shanghai and the Manchurian region linked with the industrial and
transport centers of Shenyang (Mukden), An-shan, Pen-hsi, Ying-
k'ou (Newchwang), and Dairen in the southeastern portion of what
is now Liaoning province. Shanghai was among the original treaty
ports, which were opened by force of arms to Western commercial
activity in the 1840s. Favored by its location at the mouth of the
Yangtze River, the main artery of China's domestic commerce,
Shanghai had become one of the world's largest ports even before
the expansion of trade and manufacturing that followed the partial
suspension of Chinese sovereignty under the nineteenth-century
treaty system.[1] Shanghai's commercial and industrial development
rested almost exclusively in the hands of private business, both
Chinese and foreign. From the start, the great metropolis drew on
its intimate ties with the traditional economy to obtain investable
funds as well as materials, labor, and markets.

Manchuria developed under a combination of private initiative
and foreign governmental influence, first from Russia and then,
following Russia's defeat in the Russo-Japanese War of 1904–5,
from Japan. A large mining and metallurgy complex grew up
during the 1920s and 1930s, but remained oriented toward the
economy of Japan rather than China. At the same time, the existence of virgin lands and the expansion of transport facilities by the
Chinese and Japanese governments attracted waves of migrants
from North China and encouraged the vibrant expansion of the
Manchurian farm economy.

New forms of economic activity spread along several paths from
the urban centers of Kiangnan and southern Manchuria. Major
trading centers that served as collection points for Chinese export

1. Rhoads Murphey, *Shanghai: Key to Modern China* (Cambridge, 1953), 58–59.

products or materials destined for factories in Shanghai, Dairen, or other large cities gradually began to develop their own industries. Their extensive trade links stimulated the growth of transport, communication, and financial enterprise as well. The expansion of factories and the deepening of transport networks spawned new demands for electric utilities, repair works, and other ancillary facilities so that by the 1920s centers like Hankow, Harbin, Changsha, and Kunming, while lagging far behind Shanghai or Tientsin, nonetheless boasted a considerable range of modern-sector activity. Similar changes occurred on a smaller scale in lesser urban centers.

The spread effects of industrialization also affected the immediate environs of major growth centers. This was particularly evident in the Lower Yangtze region near Shanghai, an area with a long history of commercial farm and handicraft production. With easy access to the markets and resources of the great metropolis, the whole Kiangnan area gradually developed into a beehive of industrial activity. As increasing numbers of rural workers were drawn into modern-sector employment, areas like Wu-chin, Wu-sih, Ningpo, and Ch'ang-chou became ever more closely integrated with the industrial and commercial economy of Shanghai. Similar developments occurred in the hinterlands surrounding other centers of modern-sector activity in both China proper and Manchuria, although the Japanese orientation of the largest industrial, mining, and financial operations in Manchuria attenuated the local spread effects of economic growth in the northeast.

In addition to these developments, which resulted primarily from the efforts of profit-seeking individuals in China proper and a combination of private and (largely foreign) public initiative in Manchuria, Chinese officials also fostered the spread of new economic activities. Public-sector entrepreneurship, a central feature of China's postwar economy, is also visible before 1937. The efforts of reform-minded Ch'ing officials to develop arsenals, steamship lines, railways, mines, cotton mills, ironworks, modern schools, and a variety of other new enterprises are familiar from a multitude of historical studies. Bureaucratic entrepreneurship continued under the Republic that succeeded the Ch'ing dynasty in 1912, particularly in the fields of transport, heavy industry, and banking. During the Nanking decade (1928–37), the central government de-

voted considerable planning and effort to the creation of state industries, the expansion of China's road and rail network, and currency unification.[2] A striking instance of official entrepreneurship
occurred in landlocked Shansi province, where Yen Hsi-shan, a
military figure whose forces controlled the province from 1911 to
1949, sponsored a development program that included new railroads, civilian and military industrial plants, and banks and was
even formulated in terms of five- and ten-year plans.[3] Other provincial military regimes supported a variety of projects directed
toward increasing the production of militarily useful items or of
taxable trade goods, but only Shansi's efforts brought discernible
and lasting changes in a regional economic structure.

Private and official entrepreneurs confronted formidable obstacles in attempting to extend the ambit of modern growth beyond
the initial centers of development. Constraints limiting the spread
of economic growth in China included China's immense size, the
strength and persistence of inherited economic patterns, political
instability and fragmentation, and a long list of shocks that acted as
general disincentives to investment.

In any country or region, growth begins somewhere, not everywhere. Economic momentum spreads outward from initial growth
poles to encompass a gradually increasing fraction of the population
and producing units. When most economic agents are drawn into
the growth process, development takes on a national rather than a
regional character. Although a large nation may, on a per capita
basis, have as many resources available to spur this transition as a
smaller community, the need for greater numbers of people to recognize the benefits of new economic modes is likely to retard the
spread of industrialization even if, as in China, there is a considerable degree of ethnic, cultural, and linguistic homogeneity.

Many historical accounts attest to the forceful visual impact of
modernization. In small nations, first-hand acquaintance with new
technologies, products, or materials can spread quickly. E. A. Wrig-

2. The hitherto neglected history of state industries is recounted by William C.
   Kirby, "Kuomintang China's 'Great Leap Outward': The 1936 Three-Year Plan
   for Industrial Development," *Illinois Papers in Asian Studies* 2 (1983) and *Germany and Republican China* (Stanford, 1984).
3. Donald G. Gillin, "China's First Five-Year Plan," *Journal of Asian Studies* 24,
   no. 2 (1965) and *Warlord: Yen Hsi-shan in Shansi Province, 1911–1949* (Princeton, 1967), chaps. 9 and 10.

ley has found, for example, that one-sixth of the adult population of eighteenth-century England had personal experience of life in London.[4] The percentage of adults with direct knowledge of some aspect of new economic methods was perhaps even higher in Meiji Japan, with its substantial personal mobility and thick population clusters surrounding a few large cities. China's population, by contrast, was widely dispersed, with hundreds of millions living far from the centers of economic innovation. Rozman's estimates suggest that less than 3 percent of China's mid-nineteenth century population lived in cities of 30,000 or more; Skinner's figures for 1893 indicate a comparable figure of only 4 percent.[5] The population of the treaty ports, as the cities open to foreign residence and business were termed, amounted to only a fraction of the urban total.[6] In Japan, by contrast, data for 1898 show 13.2 percent of the population located in cities of over 20,000 persons.[7] Even today, large segments of China's far-flung population have hardly begun to participate in the modern economy. In the decades preceding the Pacific War, China's physical and demographic size constituted a significant barrier to the spread of economic growth.

If ignorance limited potential opportunities to raise productivity by transferring resources into new activities, it is equally true that the competitive strength of China's inherited economy frequently slowed the advance of new products and methods even when they were well understood. Once novel methods gained an initial foothold, however, it often turned out that innovative arrangements complemented and strengthened existing forms of enterprise. Extensive complementarity between old and new forms of production, finance, transport, and trade meant that, in the absence of rapid demand expansion, new activities could flourish in the mar-

4. E. A. Wrigley, "A Simple Model of London's Importance in Changing English Society and Economy, 1650–1750," *Past and Present* 37 (1967).
5. Gilbert Rozman, *Urban Networks in Ch'ing China and Tokugawa Japan* (Princeton, 1973), 60, 272 and G. William Skinner, "Regional Urbanization in Nineteenth-Century China," and "Cities in the Hierarchy of Local Systems," in *The City in Late Imperial China*, ed. G. William Skinner (Stanford, 1977), 229, 287. The approximate date for Rozman's figures is inferred from Ping-ti Ho, *Studies on the Population of China, 1368–1953* (Cambridge, 1959), 282.
6. Figures for twenty-two major cities show a combined 1930 population of 14.3 million, or less than 3 percent of China's total population of 500–550 million (Murphey, *Shanghai*, 55 and Table 6.3).
7. *Hundred-Year Statistics of the Japanese Economy* (Tokyo, 1966), 14.

ketplace only by diverting customers from existing sellers. This often proved surprisingly difficult.

Both contemporary and retrospective accounts make much of the innate Chinese resistance to adopting foreign ways. Although this viewpoint is not without its kernel of truth, there is abundant evidence that in China, as elsewhere, the income-seeking behavior postulated by conventional theory dominates human response to economic opportunity. Following periods of debate in which rational and irrational arguments commingled in ways that hold no surprises for the student of nuclear power or other contemporary novelties, the Chinese soon began to patronize, and then to invest in steamships, telegraphs, railroads, banks, factories, and other innovations encompassing a wide range of foreign-style engineering and organizational techniques.

Some innovations, such as the telegraph, department stores, and north-south railroad lines, offered services that traditional agents could not provide. Other innovations faced stubborn competition from established enterprises that proved extremely hard to dislodge. Traditional agents actively sought official support, but the lobbying efforts of their modern-sector rivals, including both foreigners, with their potent diplomatic and military backing, and well-connected Chinese businessmen, were no less energetic. Although political intervention may at times have been decisive, the broader competition between new and old was fought in the marketplace, where the hardy persistence of traditional modes left little doubt of the continuing strength of inherited economic patterns.

There are endless examples of this vitality. Motor trucks and railways faced strong price competition from unmechanized carriers equipped with sailboats, wheelbarrows, and horse-drawn carts. Early mechanical presses extracted less oil from soybeans than existing handicraft operations. Foreign merchants complained of the seemingly limitless ability of Chinese rivals to reduce trading margins. The cooperation of indigenous financial institutions remained an indispensable link in China's external trade despite the presence of powerful foreign banking houses. The following chapters will focus in some detail on three instances of this competition involving handicraft cotton production, the *ch'ien-chuang* or "native banks," and unmechanized water transport. In each case, traditional operations managed to survive and even expand in the face of unrestricted competition from modern-sector rivals right up to the outbreak of World War II.

Why were major segments of China's inherited economy so conspicuously successful in defending themselves against competition from foreign and domestic substitutes embodying modern technology? Why is China seemingly different from Japan or India in this regard? Although a thorough investigation of these issues would necessitate a separate book, several factors may have predisposed Chinese economic agents to resist the incursion of new economic patterns.

I begin with China's substantial degree of premodern integration. If the economy had consisted of isolated and largely self-supplying households or villages with only rudimentary specialization and division of labor, traditional organizations could never have matched the cost advantages of modern technologies. As I will show, however, the intensity of domestic trade, as measured by the volume of freight traffic per unit of output, was quite large, especially in commercial regions well-served by water transport. Large-scale commodity flows were supported by sophisticated mercantile and banking institutions that were fully prepared for a competition in which ability to cut costs and profit margins would determine the outcome.

The impact of foreign trade expansion on the partially closed economies of nineteenth-century China and Japan was radically different. In Japan, the advent of foreign trade brought major changes in the domestic price structure. Imports of cotton goods, iron, and other products were vastly cheaper than domestic substitutes, which were quickly forced from the marketplace. At the same time, producers benefited from large increases in the price of new export staples like tea and silk. This "terms of trade" effect produced a large rise in real income.[8] It also encouraged the wholesale reallocation of resources as the production of importables plummeted while high profits lured resources into the newly dynamic export sector. At the same time, the quick triumph of imports over traditional domestic crafts created targets for future

8. J. Richard Huber, "Effect on Prices of Japan's Entry into World Commerce After 1858," *Journal of Political Economy* 79, no. 3 (1971).

waves of import substitution, first in textiles and later in other industries.

Despite the paucity of detailed studies on China's nineteenth-century foreign trade, it appears that the overall economic impact of expanded foreign commerce was modest. There seems to have been no dramatic shift in the terms of trade or in the patterns of resource allocation, even in the regions most affected by the growth of imports and exports. Both the initial disruption and the subsequent opportunity to raise output through international specialization seem smaller for China than for Japan. As a result, it appears that the expansion of foreign trade did not bring about a large-scale inter-industry migration of resources in China as occurred in Japan.[9]

This discussion of foreign trade leads to a more general issue involving the rate of traditional economic change. Recent work in Japanese economic history stresses the dynamism of the Tokugawa (1600–1868) economy, pointing to the expansion of population, output, internal commerce, financial institutions, and per capita incomes.[10] Many developments attributed to the seventeenth and eighteenth centuries, including the creation of rural markets and the development of rural-urban trade links, parallel changes that occurred much earlier in China. Tokugawa Japan is portrayed as moving toward levels of commercialization that seem typical of China during the Ming (1368–1644) or possibly even Sung (980–1260) as well as the Ch'ing (1644–1911) periods.

If the level, as opposed to the growth rate, of Tokugawa devel-

---

9. One exception to this statement concerns the regional impact of the migration of foreign trade from Canton to Shanghai in the wake of the 1842 treaty settlement. In addition to the obvious effects on the immediate hinterlands of the two cities, research by William T. Rowe shows that important shifts in the economic geography of Hunan province can be attributed to changes in the location of foreign trade.

10. E. S. Crawcour, "The Tokugawa Heritage," in *The State and Economic Enterprise in Japan*, ed. William W. Lockwood (Princeton, 1965); E. S. Crawcour and Kozo Yamamura, "The Tokugawa Monetary System: 1767–1868," *Economic Development and Cultural Change* 18, no. 4 (1970), part 1; Susan B. Hanley and Kozo Yamamura, "A Quiet Transformation in Tokugawa Economic History," *Journal of Asian Studies* 30, no. 2 (1971) and *Economic and Demographic Change in Preindustrial Japan, 1600–1868* (Princeton, 1977); and William B. Hauser, *Economic Institutional Change in Tokugawa Japan: Osaka and the Kinai Cotton Trade* (Cambridge, 1974).

opment resembled that of Ch'ing China, different pretrade rates of domestic change in the two countries may account for differing responses to new conditions. Although historians often point to the Japanese tradition of borrowing from abroad, it was perhaps the accumulation of recent experience in coping with relatively rapid change rather than the historic legacy of cultural borrowing that predisposed the Japanese to embrace new economic patterns while their Chinese counterparts chose to maintain existing operations, often reinforced with infusions of foreign methods, against the inroads of novel economic forms.

The weakness of the Chinese state constrained the spread of economic growth in many ways. Some observers identify official resistance as a central obstacle to modernization, but this exaggerates the power of Chinese governments. Official action often delayed individual innovations, as when China's first railway was purchased and then dismantled by the state, but such interference was episodic and temporary. No potentially profitable industries failed to appear in nineteenth- or early twentieth-century China because of official opposition.[11]

It is sometimes argued that new ventures were constrained not by official resistance, but by an excess of official participation, which burdened fledgling enterprises with bureaucracy, nepotism, and graft. Although these difficulties certainly existed, there is no convincing evidence that corruption in China was more virulent or debilitating than in Japan, the United States, or other places in which progress and peculation happily coexisted.

This study supports Perkins's view that the economic consequences of government inaction were far more significant than the effects of actual policy choices.[12] Government revenues were, as is shown in Chapter 1, consistently small, and expenditures were

11. Dwight H. Perkins, "Government as an Obstacle to Industrialization: The Case of Nineteenth-Century China," *Journal of Economic History* 27, no. 4 (1967).
12. Perkins, "Government as an Obstacle." An important exception concerns the 1875 decision to concentrate military resources on maintaining the security of land borders in central Asia rather than strengthening maritime defenses against Europe and Japan. But for this strategic error, the disastrous Sino-Japanese conflict of 1894–95 might never have arisen or, if it had, might have produced a different outcome. See Immanuel C. Y. Hsü, "The Great Debate in China, 1874: Maritime Defense vs. Frontier Defense," *Harvard Journal of Asiatic Studies* 25 (1964–65).

concentrated on security, administration, and debt service, areas with limited direct impact on economic growth. With significant exceptions, including semicolonial Japanese efforts in Manchuria, the industrial undertakings of the National Resource Commission, Yen Hsi-shan's projects in Shansi, and the state railway network operated by the Chinese government but built mainly with the proceeds of foreign bond sales, public investment had little impact on most sectors of China's economy until after 1949.

If governments lacked the resources to participate directly in economic growth, their ability to build an environment suitable for private-sector expansion was equally limited. Monetary unification, central banking, stable and predictable taxation, the development of social overhead facilities, the provision of subsidies to promising but initially unprofitable enterprises, and the manipulation of tariffs or subsidies to support a national development policy were among the possible indirect benefits of governmental action that were strikingly absent from the Chinese economic scene until the 1930s, when the Kuomintang administration began to introduce measures that echoed Japanese reforms of a half-century earlier.

Even law and order, the most basic contribution of the public sector to a nation's economic health, was denied to China's economy in the tumultuous decades following the collapse of the Manchu regime in 1911. Although I shall argue in Chapter 1 that historians often exaggerate the negative economic consequences of political turmoil during the so-called warlord era, there can be no doubt that shifting political alliances and the attendant military skirmishes, monetary irregularities, and transport disruptions piled large new uncertainties on the already tenuous prospects of new ventures and led directly to the collapse of some.

The pervasiveness of uncertainty can be seen merely by listing the major shocks that affected China's economy between the Sino-Japanese War of 1894–95 and the Japanese invasion of 1937. These include the Boxer Uprising of 1900, in which a foreign relief expedition sacked Peking; the Russo-Japanese conflict of 1904–5 fought largely on Chinese soil; the rubber panic of 1910; the ouster of the Manchu or Ch'ing dynasty in 1911 followed by the creation of a Chinese republic; the ensuing warlord years during which rival military factions struggled for domestic control and international recognition; World War I, which brought both opportunity and disruption to sectors linked with foreign trade; the North China famine of 1920–21; the Northern Expedition of 1926–27 leading to the formation of a new national government at Nanking; the Yangtze flood of 1931; Japan's creation of the colonial state of Manchoukuo in the northeast, with consequent disruptions of trade, revenue, and the balance of payments; the Japanese attack on Shanghai in 1932; and the world depression, which disrupted external markets and brought sharp fluctuations in the international value of China's currency.

This extraordinary list of shocks, to which must be added the normal fluctuations characteristic of any agrarian economy, produced truly remarkable levels of uncertainty. Under these circumstances, the sustained economic growth that forms the subject of this book represents a remarkable triumph of enterprise in the face of adversity.

The following chapters address the task of demonstrating that substantial and sustained expansion actually occurred in China's prewar economy, so much so that real aggregate output rose at an annual rate of approximately 2 percent between World War I and 1937, implying that China's national product was 40 percent larger during the early 1930s than during the years of World War I. Real output per head rose more than one-fifth during the same period. Even though the rapid growth of investment, which absorbed as much as one-fourth of incremental output, and government spending caused personal consumption to lag behind output growth, the average level of individual consumption increased by nearly one-tenth between World War I and the 1930s.

These conclusions are far from obvious. Historians often portray the prewar decades as a period of stagnation or decline during which growth and technological change proceeded in only a few isolated enterprises and localities and offered scant benefit to the economy at large. Some economists argue that social rigidities obstructed private investment. My research has convinced me that such judgments not only understate the scale and pace of growth in the modern sectors, but fundamentally misconstrue the nature of China's prewar economy by overlooking the extensive and, for the most part, mutually reinforcing linkages between new and inherited enterprise. Chapter 1 prepares the way for exploring these issues by focusing on four areas in which existing studies often misapprehend the basic features of China's prewar economy: the role of foreign influence, the nature of state involvement, the impact of military activity, and the organization of markets.

Chapters 2, 3, and 4 investigate the dimensions of prewar economic growth in the three major clusters of innovative activity: manufacturing, money and banking, and transport and communication. Chapter 2 describes the overall growth of manufacturing, which proceeded more rapidly than in contemporary Japan. Case studies of cotton textiles and matches illustrate the strong momentum of import substitution, the rapid influx of new technology, and the extensive linkages through which industrialization in one region or trade stimulated expansion elsewhere. China's monetary arrangements and banking institutions are the subject of Chapter 3. Here we see the most thoroughgoing prewar transformation of any economic sector, with banknotes and deposits replacing silver coin, ingots, and bullion as the chief components of the national money stock well in advance of the government's monetary reform of 1935. This monetary restructuring was carried out primarily by new Chinese commercial banks, which maintained close ties with both foreign financial institutions and older *ch'ien-chuang* or "native banks." Extensive links between different types of financial intermediaries strengthened the entire financial system, promoted economic integration, and enabled the *ch'ien-chuang* to prosper and expand. Rapid expansion of the banking system and the resulting monetary transformation also spared China from the worst effects of the world depression of the 1930s. Chapter 4 shows how the growth of new modes of transport and communication sharply reduced transactions costs across broad areas of China's economy. This led to large increases in domestic and international trade that benefited every sector of the economy, although political and military instability prevented the economy from reaping the full potential of these innovations in transport and communications.

Chapters 5 and 6 approach the growth of China's economy from broader perspectives. Chapter 5 focuses on investment, which, according to some authors, scarcely occurred in prewar China. A measure of the overall scale of modern-sector development is obtained by constructing and analyzing a time series of "modern-oriented" fixed investment covering the period 1903–36. The data reveal the existence of an investment spurt comparable in size and acceleration to the contemporaneous Japanese experience. More speculative estimates of other types of investment contribute to the finding that capital formation proportions rose during the prewar decades and that gross fixed capital formation exceeded 10 percent of total output during 1931–36.

Chapter 6 evaluates both the extent and the limits of China's prewar economic growth. A wide range of evidence points to the conclusion that China's prewar economy experienced a rising trend in per capita output and consumption. These changes were not confined to the cities. Data showing substantial long-term growth of real wages paid to farm laborers and to unskilled workers in nonfarm occupations that attracted rural workers indicate that incomes increased in the farm sector as well as in occupations more directly influenced by technological change and organizational innovation. The conclusion that real output per head increased nationally, and not just in a few sectors and localities, attests to the powerful spread effects of modern-sector development and to the flexibility and growth potential of older institutions and arrangements that dominated prewar economic activity.

It is not yet possible to determine when per capita output began to rise. Perhaps this transition to what Reynolds terms "intensive" growth occurred during the 1890s, when the impact of new technologies first attained quantitatively significant dimensions, or during the final decade of the Ch'ing dynasty (1644–1911). Alternatively, output per head may have begun to rise only after the Republican revolution of 1912, in which case this important transition occurred during a period of international depression so severe that "only a few countries" enjoying "special circumstances" managed comparable feats.[13] Either conclusion can only enhance the impression of powerful economic momentum that emerges from the chapters in this book.

Comparison with Japan points in the same direction. No one can doubt Japan's economic progress during the first four decades of the present century. The present analysis repeatedly shows that the dimensions of China's achievements were not markedly different from Japan's. Taking the period 1914/18 as a base, the index of

---

13. Lloyd G. Reynolds, *Economic Growth in the Third World, 1850–1980* (New Haven, 1985), 36.

1952 per capita output in the two economies is virtually identical. Although Japan's economy suffered extensive physical destruction from American bombing, it is quite possible that the political, military, and monetary instability that plagued China's economy between 1895 and 1950 was even more damaging.

Had China's political leaders provided private agents with a framework of stable property rights, monetary standards, and social overhead facilities of the sort created by Japan's Meiji oligarchs, China's prewar economy might have advanced far beyond the considerable achievements recorded in the absence of these favorable circumstances. In the event, a relatively stable institutional framework appeared only with the creation of the People's Republic in 1949. The subsequent rapid growth of China's economy can be seen as the second phase of a longer-term growth process dating back to the late nineteenth century. Rapid expansion of production during the 1950s followed the restoration of monetary stability and the resumption of normal transport and communication services, which permitted China to realize the untapped potential of prewar facilities and technologies. The growth of China's economy since the mid-1950s, with its reliance on a massive infusion of Soviet technology and equipment, seems far removed from the market economy of the prewar decades, but important continuities persist. The long-term consequences of prewar economic achievements will be considered in the final chapter.

This book is written in the conviction that a quantitative approach offers the most promising avenue for constructing an overall framework that can deepen our knowledge and understanding of issues relating to economic growth and stagnation in prewar China. In a large economy like China's, national or regional trends in output, incomes, investment, prices, taxes, wages, and the like are statistical phenomena whose dimensions cannot be inferred from individual testimony or other anecdotal evidence. Reliable generalizations require the statistical foundation that this volume seeks to establish. Some may argue that the quantitative materials available for studying prewar China are far from ideal. No one is better qualified than the present author to agree. Yet the volume of useful material is far larger than one might expect, and its coverage and quality, while leaving much to be desired, are not unusually poor when compared with materials routinely applied to similar studies of antebellum America, eighteenth- and nineteenth-century Europe, prewar Japan, or contemporary third-world nations. Until the historical materials are thoroughly explored, we cannot know how far the quantitative approach will lead.

In preparing the chapters that follow, the author has sought to apply Kelvin's famous observation that "where you cannot measure, your knowledge is meagre and unsatisfactory" without running afoul of Frank Knight's complaint that in the social sciences, "the Kelvin dictum very largely means in practice 'if you cannot measure, measure anyhow!'"[14] Whether the result would be more likely to satisfy Kelvin or outrage Knight is left for the reader to judge.

14. Melvin W. Reder, "Chicago and Economics: Permanence and Change," *Journal of Economic Literature* 20, no. 1 (1982):7 and Frank H. Knight, *On the History and Method of Economics* (Chicago, 1956), 166. Professor Reder kindly supplied the source for the Knight quotation.

Chapter One

China's Prewar Economy: An Overview

This book focuses on the modern sector of China's prewar economy. One's understanding of the interaction between modern and traditional sectors and the significance of modern-sector developments, however, is conditioned by perceptions of basic features of the economy as a whole. Here, there is little common ground in the historical literature on prewar China. Some authors view the prewar decades as the first phase of a long-term process of economic growth. In comparing 1936 with 1911, K. C. Yeh explains that:[1]

There had been discernible growth in total output. More significantly, distinct changes in the internal economic structure had taken place, indicating marked shifts from low to high productivity sectors, spread of modern technology in the manufacturing and transportation sectors, and increasing urbanization. Clearly economic modernization had begun, albeit slowly and restricted to a few sectors and regions.

The view that "economic modernization had begun" prior to the Pacific War, with the implied corollary that postwar growth under Communist leadership is an extension of earlier trends rather than a new departure, is not universally shared. Some writers stress the geographic limits of new change, arguing that modern-sector growth in the urban treaty ports had little impact on the traditional

1. K. C. Yeh, "China's National Income, 1931–36," in *Modern Chinese Economic History*, ed. Chi-ming Hou and Tzong-shian Yu (Taipei, 1979), 120.

economy. R. H. Tawney captured the view of many others when he wrote that "a modern fringe was stitched along the hem of the ancient garment. . . . The economic frontier between the West and China was moved inland."[2]

Despite mounting evidence of vigorous development in some regions and sectors, some authors continue to present the prewar decades as a period of economic stagnation or even decline. Chinese accounts often stress the inability of the prewar economy to escape the constraints of "semi-colonial and semi-feudal" conditions.[3] Western studies present similar views, noting the "shamefully meagre" results of economic modernization and asserting that "China's economic indexes registered no sign of progressive growth" prior to the Pacific War.[4]

In part, this clash of interpretations results from the paucity of systematic information, a difficulty that the present volume may help to overcome. Differing views also reflect diverse perceptions of how China's prewar economy actually functioned. Some authors, including a number of economic historians, see China's prewar economy as a market system with a high degree of competition and only slight governmental participation or interference. This view identifies low incomes, the high man-land ratio, governmental weakness, and pervasive insecurity as the chief obstacles to economic progress. Others perceive a system in which progressive initiative was stifled by a combination of state power, foreign influence, and monopolistic restrictions.

These disagreements about the nature of China's prewar economy, which are readily visible in contemporary as well as retrospective accounts, have not received the attention they deserve. The purpose of this chapter is to present an overview that will prepare the ground for the more detailed results of subsequent chapters. The focus is on the central features of China's prewar economy that are seen from widely differing perspectives by various authors: the extent and impact of foreign influence; the size

2. R. H. Tawney, *Land and Labor in China* (Boston, 1966), 13.
3. See, for example, K'ung Ching-wei, *Chung-kuo chin pai nien ching chi shih kang* (Changchun, 1980), 228.
4. Jerome Ch'en, *China and the West* (Bloomington, 1979), 379 and Wellington K. K. Chan, *Merchants, Mandarins and Modern Enterprise in Late Ch'ing China* (Cambridge, 1979), 1.

and scale of state participation in economic life; the impact of military activity; and the structure of markets.

My research on these issues indicates that *domestic* rather than external economic forces were mainly responsible for the state and evolution of the economy and that foreign economic influence flowed mainly through market channels. The economy was predominantly *private*, and the role of the state sector, though increasing over time, remained small. Despite the prominence of military figures among the political elite, the economy was basically *civilian* and the impact of the military correspondingly limited. Resources and products were allocated primarily through the market and most markets appear to have been highly *competitive*.

The key concepts included in these hypotheses—domestic, private, civilian, and competitive—suggest a somewhat novel view of China's prewar economy. From this viewpoint, the historical literature, seemingly influenced by Kuomintang and communist attacks on imperialism, landlords, monopoly, usury, and other forms of economic exploitation, places inordinate emphasis on the size and deleterious effects of foreign economic activity, on governmental economic strength, on the economic impact of militarism, banditry, and warfare, and on the extent of market power that might enable landed and mercantile elites to increase their share of income and wealth at the expense of their fellow Chinese.

Internal and External Economic Forces

The coming of the Europeans ranks among the major forces shaping China's modern history. Not only steamships, factories, and machine guns, but Christianity, democracy, pragmatism, socialism, and communism figure in the long list of outside influences on China's development. In the broadest sense, no one can deny the significance of foreign, specifically European, influence on any major aspect of modern Chinese life. The question at issue here is much narrower. Within the framework of a world in which the influence of Europe spread outward to encompass the globe, the problem is whether or not the special circumstances attending foreign-linked economic activity exercised a strong and decisive influence over the timing, pace, and pattern of long-term economic change in prewar China. To answer this question in the negative is not to deny the importance of foreign contacts in the larger sense noted above. One can argue, however, that within a broad framework that includes European influence, the course of China's economic evolution was shaped mainly by market forces and was not decisively affected by the special conditions attached to the foreign economic presence in China. I share the view of other economists that on balance foreign participation stimulated rather than retarded economic growth and structural change in the domestic economy.[5] But the fundamental point—one that makes it unnecessary to attach great weight to this possibly controversial position— is that the direct and specific influence of foreign activity on the size and composition of farm output, the money supply, the level of capital formation, the rate and pattern of modern-sector growth, interest rates, the size of government budgets, and other significant economic indicators was generally small.

The structure of China's economy makes it difficult to avoid the view that key economic forces originate in the domestic rather than the international sphere. The combined share of imports and exports in aggregate product often exceeds 50 percent in small trading nations. In China, as in other large countries, this ratio has always been low. The combined 1933 total of imports and exports amounted to no more than 8.5 percent of gross domestic product.[6] Furthermore, China's exports were more diversified than in most other low-income economies.[7] Even in regions that specialized in producing tea, mulberry, cotton handicrafts, and other exports or import substitutes, the growth of foreign trade represented more an extension of historic economic patterns than an intrusion of totally new forces.

5. Chi-ming Hou, *Foreign Investment and Economic Development in China, 1840–1937* (Cambridge, 1965), 216–22; Dwight H. Perkins, *Agricultural Development in China, 1368–1968* (Chicago, 1969), 133; and Robert F. Dernberger, "The Role of the Foreigner in China's Economic Development, 1840–1949," in *China's Modern Economy in Historical Perspective*, ed. Dwight H. Perkins (Stanford, 1975), 46.
6. The total trade of China proper and Manchuria with third countries is from Thomas G. Rawski, "Economic Growth and Integration in Prewar China" (Toronto, 1982), appendix G. The estimated output is from Ta-chung Liu and Kung-chia Yeh, *The Economy of the Chinese Mainland* (Princeton, 1965), 66.
7. Heywood Fleisig, "The United States and the Non-European Periphery During the Early Years of the Great Depression," in *The Great Depression Revisited*, ed. Herman van der Wee (The Hague, 1972), 171.

Given the small share of exports, imports, and other foreign-linked activities in China's economic aggregates, it is not surprising to find that the indirect consequences of the open economy policy forced on China's unwilling government by western arms far out-weighed the direct impact of internationalization. The limited scale of foreign trade meant that only a small fraction of China's production and consumption of foodgrains, textiles, and other major commodities crossed international boundaries. Nonetheless, the expansion of foreign commerce stimulated a gradual integration of Chinese markets for grain, cotton, cloth, and other major products into the world market system.[8] This development, which injected international market forces into the economic circumstances of hundreds of millions of Chinese farmers, including many who neither bought nor sold in foreign markets, was the most far-reaching economic consequence of the nineteenth-century treaty system. Expanded foreign contacts introduced new opportunities, resources, and technologies into China's economy, some of which, particularly in industry, transport, and finance, had a catalytic effect on the level of activity on the part of domestic agents and organizations. Finally, foreign communities offered resources of information and physical security that contributed significantly to the growth and stability of certain sectors of the domestic economy, particularly in times of warfare and extreme political uncertainty.

If the direct impact of foreign trade on overall agricultural and commercial activity remained modest, what of the effect of the foreign presence on China's nascent modern sector, in which the foreign share of ownership and control was often quite substantial? Many writers claim that the easy access allowed to foreign goods (which were subject only to nominal tariffs until the 1930s) and to foreign capital (which was free to enter into mining and manufacturing ventures under the 1895 treaty provisions) stunted the growth of China's modern sector and left industry with a legacy of structural and regional imbalance. The argument that free trade necessarily inhibits industrialization is difficult to reconcile with the successful experience of Victorian England, Meiji Japan, and modern Hong Kong, among others. China's prewar industrial sec-

8. Loren Brandt, "Chinese Agriculture and the International Economy, 1870s–1930s: A Reassessment," *Explorations in Economic History* 22 (1985).

tor was nearly as large as Japan's, and its growth rate, if anything, faster. Because the share of Chinese-owned establishments in factory activity remained relatively stable during the prewar decades, it is evident that Chinese participants made substantial contributions to industrial growth, including entrepreneurship and capital investments as well as labor and materials.

To compete with the products of foreign firms located overseas and in China's treaty ports, Chinese firms concentrated on textiles and other products that did not require complex technology or massive fixed investment. Within each industry, indigenous products clustered at the bottom end of the price-quality spectrum. As these industries developed, their requirements for repairs, machinery, chemicals, etc., spawned new generations of Chinese enterprises that soon began to compete with foreign suppliers in additional product lines, again concentrating on items that were simple, cheap, and usually of inferior quality. That Chinese industry turned out flour and yarn rather than steel and machine tools and that its products were shoddy rather than fine can hardly be blamed on the unequal treaties imposed on China by the European powers and Japan. The same progression of industries and the same neglect of quality are outstanding features of early industrial growth in other countries, of which the United States and Japan may be offered as particularly clear-cut instances.

Foreign enterprise often played a catalytic role in the genesis of new Chinese industries, whose managers learned of profitable sales opportunities by observing foreign business operations. As D. K. Lieu put it, "Foreign factories . . . were often the precursors of Chinese industrial development."[9] Accounts of innovative Chinese enterprises in industries ranging from condensed milk and processed eggs to cigarettes, chemicals, and machinery acknowledge the importance of imports or local foreign production in guiding Chinese ventures toward new markets. To cite a typical example: "Canvas was first imported into China from the United States, and having seen what profits were being made, Japanese manufacturers came into the Chinese market. . . . With the demand . . . becoming keener, the pioneer Chinese factory . . .

---

9. D. K. Lieu, *The Growth and Industrialization of Shanghai* (Shanghai, 1936), 60.

made its appearance."[10] Chinese businessmen often studied foreign operations from the inside:[11]

Supplies for making enamelware came originally from Japan, and in order to develop the industry in China a number of Japanese . . . organized the Wada Enamel Factory. . . . Subsequently a Chinese named Lo, after resigning from this Japanese company, opened his own establishment . . . and not long afterwards the Wada factory came under the control of the [Chinese-owned] Chu Feng concern.

In Manchuria, as elsewhere, "Chinese entrepreneurs followed the lead of foreigners in such fields as flour milling, soy-bean oil extraction, beet-sugar refining, tobacco products, and cotton textiles.[12]

Chinese firms successfully competed with foreign rivals in textiles, food processing, light engineering, acid and soda products, along with a wide range of additional items whose manufacture did not require massive block investments or sophisticated technology. Which new industries might have flourished in the absence of foreign competition? Would restrictions on foreign investment have brought forth new Chinese investments in excess of the amounts that foreigners actually supplied? Given the realities of Chinese transport, which regions might have developed into important centers of prewar industry in the absence of the quasi-independence that attracted industry to Shanghai and Tientsin? Without answers to these questions, it is difficult to attach much weight to assertions that China's modern sector was stifled and distorted by the foreign presence.

Competition between Chinese factories and foreign enterprises operating on Chinese soil created political as well as economic issues. Exemption from Chinese business taxes and other special privileges available to foreign firms infuriated all Chinese patriots, not just the business community. Foreign firms were seen as enjoying great advantages over Chinese rivals. They were said to use superior financial resources to equip their plants with modern ma-

10. *China Industrial Handbooks: Kiangsu* (Shanghai, 1933), 463.
11. Ibid., 811.
12. Edwin P. Reubens, "Opportunities, Governments and Economic Development in Manchuria, 1860–1940," in *The State and Economic Growth*, ed. Hugh G. J. Aitken (New York, 1959), 167.

chinery while the Chinese, burdened with higher taxes and interest costs, had to make do with equipment that was often worn out
or obsolescent. The foreigners, immune from taxation beyond the
paltry import levies, could market their products freely, unlike
Chinese firms that suffered from arbitrary taxation. The outcome
of the ensuing business competition is perceived as unfairly slanted
toward foreign firms, which are said to have overpowered indigenous enterprise. In the words of one writer: "With its superior
technology, managerial efficiency, and financial backing, foreign
enterprises in China waged an easy competition with native industries which before the 1930s never had a chance to establish
themselves."[13]

These popular arguments suffer from the fault of proving too
much. Historical accounts often exaggerate the size, cost advantages, and profitability of the foreign business establishment in prewar China. Even the definition of "foreign" enterprise must remain
imprecise, as Chinese capitalists regularly purchased shares in
nominally foreign concerns and used foreign flags of convenience
to shield their assets from domestic taxation.[14] The modest dimensions of foreign-owned industry in terms of scale, profitability, market share, and productivity advantage, discussed in detail in Chapter 2, raise doubts about assertions that high costs and taxes
hindered Chinese competition with foreign manufacturers. China's
manufacturing industries, most of which were owned and managed
by Chinese, grew rapidly and in directions parallel to those observed elsewhere. Since foreign enterprise failed to dominate even
the modern sectors, including manufacturing, which grew up primarily in Shanghai and other coastal treaty port cities, it is not
surprising that foreign business did not, as claimed by some ob-

13. Yu-kwei Cheng, *Foreign Trade and Industrial Development of China* (Wash-
    ington, D.C., 1956), 41.
14. On Chinese shareholding in foreign firms see Wang Ching-yü, "Sharehold-
    ings of Chinese Merchants in Nineteenth-Century Foreign Enterprise in
    China," *Li shih yen chiu* 4 (1965):68–69; Ellsworth C. Carlson, *The Kaiping
    Mines, 1877–1912* (Cambridge, 1971), 36; Kang Chao, *The Development of
    Cotton Textile Production in China* (Cambridge, 1977), 137–40; and Reubens,
    "Economic Development in Manchuria," 159. On flags of convenience, see
    Ting Jih-ch'u and Tu Hsün-ch'eng, "A Brief Account of Yü Hsia-ch'ing," *Li
    shih yen chiu* 3 (1981):162 and William T. Rowe, "Urban Society in Late Im-
    perial China: Hankow, 1796–1889" (Ph.D. diss., Columbia University, 1980),
    161–62.

servers, drain the wealth of China's economy. Indeed, China's long-standing pattern of merchandise trade deficit (commodity imports larger than commodity exports) and the inflow of precious metals (mainly silver) was maintained only because of a continuing *inflow* of investment funds from foreigners and overseas Chinese.[15]

Despite the rapid growth of modern-sector activity, its limits must not be forgotten. Even after several decades of expansion, the share of modern industry in estimated gross domestic product for 1933 was no more than 3 percent and that of the entire modern sector only 13 percent.[16] The modern sector remained small because its impressive Republican growth began from a tiny base. To answer the question of why China's modern sector was so small in 1911, and also to understand why it was so much smaller in relative terms than Japan's modern sector, requires analysis not of foreign influence, where nineteenth-century conditions were quite similar in the two countries, but of the weakness of the Chinese state.[17]

The unequal treaties prevented the governments of both China and Japan from using tariff policy to encourage domestic industry. But as economic theorists have long recognized and as the industrial history of Meiji Japan copiously illustrates, subsidies can offer domestic firms the same advantages as tariffs. Through most of the century following the Opium War, Chinese governments lacked both the revenue and the determination that enabled Japan's Meiji regime to circumvent the unequal treaties and help the private sector to build a viable industrial base.

The growth of weapons production in Republican China demonstrates that tariff protection was not required to support new industries whose products were ardently desired by the state. The collapse of central authority after the death of Yuan Shih-k'ai in

15. The logic of this argument, which is based on the structure of balance of payments accounts, is laid out in Cheng, *Foreign Trade and Industrial Development*, 14, 216 and Thomas G. Rawski, "China's Republican Economy: An Introduction" (Toronto, 1978), 10–13.

16. Liu and Yeh, *Economy of the Chinese Mainland*, 66, 89.

17. Frances V. Moulder's claim that China, unlike Japan, was "incorporated" into the nineteenth-century world economy ignores the much larger scale of international economic links, relative to domestic economic activity, on the Japanese side. Moulder eventually retreats from her initial assertions by noting the broad similarity of foreign-oriented economic activity in the two nations (*Japan, China and the Modern World Economy: Toward a Reinterpretation of East Asian Development ca. 1600 to ca. 1918* [Cambridge, 1977], 149–50).

1916 spurred competitive military buildups by regional, provincial, and local governments. Even though foreign arms salesmen, backed by their respective diplomatic establishments, competed vigorously for sales, the intense demand for arms spread a new industry across China's map: [18]

All the arsenals with productive capabilities were located in six provinces. When the central government collapsed in 1916, the arsenals became the private property of the militarists in control of these areas; a large number of armies were left with no assured sources of supply. Many militarists responded either by expanding the facilities of existing arsenals or by creating new ones. By the early 1920's almost every provincial capital had an arsenal equipped to manufacture small quantities of pistols, rifles, machine guns, and some artillery pieces. Furthermore, lesser militarists also resorted to every possible means of self-help, such as using local blacksmiths to make weapons.

Here, as in other areas, the militarists or "warlords" foreshadow future policies of the Chinese Communist Party and the People's Republic, in this instance by using self-reliance to create a far-flung network of rural small-scale industries. In a remote place like Pingliang (Kansu), a town with a 1953 population of 60,000, a foreign visitor reported in 1920 that the local commander had "put up a small machine shop which is run by water power . . . [with] four large lathes and two drill-presses. . . . He also has an arsenal where he makes his own ammunition cheaper than what it would cost at the Hanyang Arsenal. Guns and rifles are also repaired here." [19] At Kunming (Yunnan), the "obsolete and inadequate" arsenal managed to produce smokeless and black powder as well as ammunition for rifles, machine guns, and mountain guns. A 1929 Hankow press report placed the number of arsenals at "over 100" in Szechwan province alone, although most were small units that could manufacture only ammunition. [20]

A considerable armaments industry grew from these unlikely

18. Hsi-sheng Ch'i, *Warlord Politics in China, 1916–1928* (Stanford, 1976), 118–19.
19. U.S. Department of State, *Records of the Department of State Relating to Internal Affairs of China, 1910–29* (Washington, D.C., 1975), 893.20/41. The population data are from Nai-ruenn Chen, *Chinese Economic Statistics: A Handbook for Mainland China* (Chicago, 1967), 129.
20. U.S. Department of State, *Internal Affairs*, 893.20/58 and 893.20/159.

beginnings. By the 1930s, the larger arsenals could manufacture "light arms of good quality and by 1937 the supply of light weapons was said to be sufficient to equip practically all of the Chinese infantry divisions."[21] The better-equipped arsenals turned out modest quantities of more complex equipment, including artillery, armored trains, and even aircraft. They also manufactured machinery for their own use and for sale to other plants.[22] After Japanese invaders forced the Nationalist government to retreat from Nanking to Szechwan, the combined efforts of government arsenals, private machine shops, and village industrial cooperatives supplied light weapons that Japanese intelligence reports rated as "medium" in quality.[23]

The conclusion to be drawn from this history is that in China, as elsewhere, determined governments can create, subsidize, and patronize new industries without recourse to tariffs or trade controls of any kind. If newly created industries outgrow initial economic and technical weaknesses, they may contribute to subsequent development. Yamamura's illuminating study of Meiji militarism shows that war and preparation for war sparked the expansion of arsenals and other state-supported plants that "acted as highly effective centers for the absorption and dissemination of Western technologies and skills" in Japan. Surely it is equally true that China's high level of military activity encouraged "the rapid dissemination of modern technology . . . and a suddenly accelerated growth in the fledgling and often struggling private machine and machine-tool makers who received increased . . . military demand."[24]

The frequency with which Japan's government served as a patron of new economic activities and the rarity with which the Chinese

21. F. F. Liu, *A Military History of Modern China* (Princeton, 1956), 155.

22. Ch'i, *Warlord Politics*, 119; *The China Year Book, 1923* (Tientsin, 1923), 579; Donald G. Gillin, *Warlord: Yen Hsi-shan in Shansi Province, 1911–1949* (Princeton, 1967), 28–29, 192; G. E. Hubbard, *Eastern Industrialization and Its Effect on the West* (London, 1935), 193; and James E. Sheridan, *China in Disintegration: The Republican Era in Chinese History, 1912–1949* (New York, 1975), 196.

23. Liu, *Military History*, 160.

24. Kozo Yamamura, "Success Illgotten? The Role of Meiji Militarism in Japan's Technological Progress," *Journal of Economic History* 37, no. 1 (1977): 113, 121.

state intervened in a similarly supportive fashion provides a key to Japan's relative success in economic modernization before World War II. Behind this contrast lies the fiscal weakness of the Chinese state, a topic to which I now turn.

Private Sector and Public Sector

There is no definitive study of the role of government in China's prewar economy. Focusing on the Nanking decade (1927–37), Eastman notes "the Nationalist government's tendency to dominate the economy at the expense of private capital" and also "a growing tendency for the government to participate in the economy and, in some kinds of private enterprise, to replace private with state ownership," but cautions that the extent of state domination "ought not be exaggerated."[25] Students of provincial developments are less restrained in their assessments. Jerome Ch'en writes of "extortionate taxes on agriculture" and "crushingly heavy taxes" in Szechwan. Kapp offers this description of conditions in the same province:

The principal function of militarist government in Szechwan was the extraction of the wealth and resources of local society for military use. . . . The modest welfare and service functions which had once accompanied tax collection were neglected. Though official corruption and "squeeze" were prevalent in provincial and local government before 1911, the ascendancy of the extractive process had profound effects on Chinese society in the Republican period.

Gillin asserts that Yen Hsi-shan "taxed his subjects unmercifully," with the result that "by 1936 the inhabitants of Shansi were among the most heavily taxed people in China." Sheridan offers a broader summary: "The warlords tapped almost every conceivable source of revenue, and in the process worked tremendous hardships on the people. The land tax, which was completely in the hands of

25. Lloyd E. Eastman, *The Abortive Revolution: China Under Nationalist Rule, 1927–1937* (Cambridge, 1974), 237–38. Parks M. Coble, *The Shanghai Capitalists and the Nationalist Government, 1927–1937* (Cambridge, 1980) and Richard C. Bush, "Industry and Politics in Kuomintang China" (Ph.D. diss., Columbia University, 1978) reach opposite conclusions about the extent of the Nanking government's control over Shanghai's industrialists, with Coble emphasizing the importance of state power and Bush stressing the success of Shanghai textile magnates in pursuing their own interests.

provincial military leaders after 1919, became an instrument of terrible exploitation."[26]

The implied picture of an economy in which the role of the state is large, particularly in terms of channeling resources from the private sector to the military, is echoed by many others. Unfortunately, these authors rarely attempt to measure the size of the resource flows involved or to relate them to total output. This is the task of the following pages, which focus on the relatively abundant data available for the Nanking decade.

The Central Government During the Nanking Decade

There are ample data regarding the revenue and expenditure of the central government during the Nanking period (1927–37). The Nanking regime employed modest numbers of financial and statistical specialists, and assigned considerable priority to improving the volume and quality of statistical data: "By the mid-1930s most ministries had assigned personnel to take charge of statistical and accounting matters."[27] Keeping track of revenue and outlay was especially important. The similarity of data presented in published and internal reports enhances one's confidence that fiscal data relating to the central government were accepted and used within official circles. There is little risk in assuming that the fiscal aggregates for the central government are reasonably accurate.

Table 1.1 presents official data on the size and structure of central government revenue and outlay along with estimates of China's gross domestic product (GDP) for fiscal 1931–36.[28] Both revenue and expenditure rose substantially under the Nationalist administration, although continuing deficits demonstrate the failure of tax receipts to keep pace with public spending. On the revenue side,

26. Jerome Ch'en, "Historical Background," in *Modern China's Search for a Political Form*, ed. Jack Gray (London, 1969), 30–32; Robert A. Kapp, *Szechwan and the Chinese Republic* (New Haven, 1973), 40; Gillin, *Warlord: Yen Hsi-shan in Shansi Province*, 138; and James E. Sheridan, *Chinese Warlord: The Career of Feng Yü-hsiang* (Stanford, 1966), 24.

27. Hung-mao Tien, *Government and Politics in Kuomintang China, 1927–1937* (Stanford, 1972), 24–25.

28. Between 1927 and 1938, the Chinese fiscal year ran from July 1 to June 30. I refer to the year ending June 30, 1932, as fiscal 1932, and so on. See Arthur N. Young, *China's Wartime Finance and Inflation, 1937–1945* (Cambridge, 1965), 11.

there were only modest changes in the sources of taxation: customs duties (higher tariffs on a slowly rising volume of trade) and salt taxes (now remitted to the center with greater regularity than before 1927) remained dominant. New revenues came from the "consolidated taxes" or excise levies applied to products of Chinese-owned modern enterprise: cigarettes, cigars, cotton yarn, wheat flour, matches, cement, beer, and foreign-style wine and liquor.[29] Military outlays aimed at strengthening Nanking's domestic authority and, to a lesser extent, preserving China's territorial integrity, were the leading item of expenditure, followed by loan and indemnity service required to maintain the confidence of foreign and domestic lenders and preserve the regime's borrowing capabilities.

Comparing these revenue and outlay totals with K. C. Yeh's estimates of gross domestic product shows that despite a considerable expansion of the central government's budget, expenditures never surpassed 4 percent of total output and revenues remained under 3 percent.[30] Leaving aside the regional impact and progressivity of taxation, to be discussed below, the major economic effects of Nanking's modest fiscal activities should emerge in the military sphere, the capital markets, and the industries producing the most heavily taxed commodities, namely salt and the modern-sector products subject to the consolidated tax. None of these effects appears large. The influence of military spending is discussed at length in the following section. Government borrowing probably raised interest rates and may have diverted funds from more productive uses in the private sector. But an annual flow of 100–300 million yuan is hardly decisive even when compared with the low investment totals estimated by Liu and Yeh for 1933.[31]

This drain of funds into the public sector was partially or perhaps

29. Tien, *Government and Politics*, 79.
30. Subtracting regional GDP from the totals shown in Line 4 of Table 1.1 to reflect the removal of Manchuria from Chinese control would slightly increase the share of Nanking's revenue and expenditure in GDP for China proper. The estimates of Manchurian regional product appear in Alexander Eckstein, Kang Chao, and John K. Chang, "The Economic Development of Manchuria: The Rise of a Frontier Economy," *Journal of Economic History* 34, no. 1 (1974):254.
31. The estimates are 1.6 billion yuan for gross and 0.5 billion for net investment (Liu and Yeh, *Economy of the Chinese Mainland*, 228). As Chapter 5 will show, these figures substantially understate the level of investment activity in prewar China.

Table 1.1
Central Government Fiscal Aggregates and GDP, Fiscal 1932-36

	Fiscal Year Ending June 30				
	1932	1933	1934	1935	1936
1. Revenue					
Million yuan	619	614	689	745	817
Percentage share					
a. Customs	59.8	53.1	51.1	47.4	33.3
b. Salt tax	23.2	25.7	25.7	22.4	22.5
c. Consolidated taxes	14.4	13.0	15.4	14.1	16.5
d. Other (excl. borrowing)	2.6	8.1	7.8	16.1	27.7
2. Borrowing (million yuan)	130	112	179	225	276
3. Expenditure					
Million yuan	749	726	896	1031	1182
Percentage share					
a. Military	40.6	44.2	41.6	37.6	33.0
b. Indemnity/debt service	36.0	28.9	27.3	23.1	24.9
c. Other	23.4	26.9	31.1	39.3	42.1
4. Gross domestic product (million yuan)					
a. GDP, 1933 prices	29020	29465	28180	27995	30015
b. Price index (1933=100)	115.2	104.1	96.8	93.2	98.7
c. GDP, current prices	33431	30673	27278	26091	29625
5. GDP share (percentage)					
a. Revenue	1.8	2.0	2.5	2.8	2.8
b. Expenditure	2.2	2.4	3.3	2.0	4.0

Sources: Lines 1-3: Young, China's Nation-Building Effort (Stanford, 1971), 443-40.

Line 4a: K. C. Yeh, "National Income," p. 98. The entry for 1932 is the average of Yeh's figures for 1931 and 1932, etc.

Line 4b: calculated from Shanghai wholesale price data shown in Young, Nation-Building, 170-71. The figure for fiscal 1932 is the average of annual indexes for 1931 and 1932, etc.

Line 4c: Calculated from Lines 4a and 4b.

Line 5a: Calculated from Lines 1 and 4c.

Line 5b: Calculated from Lines 3 and 4c.

Note: Column totals may not add to 100 percent because of rounding error.

wholly offset by other governmental actions that improved the economic climate and stimulated private investment. Monetary, banking, and tariff reforms are examples of Nanking policies that benefited the private sector. Taxes on modern-sector products may have dampened demand in some instances or encouraged imports in others, but the same industries were most likely to benefit from other government policies. In any event, commodity taxes did not prevent China's small industrial sector from increasing its share of total output, capital, and employment during the Nanking period.

Provincial Governments

If the revenues and outlays of the Nanking government are generally recognized as small in proportion to national output and income, the same cannot be said of provincial taxation and spending. How large were provincial taxes? Data on provincial expenditures compiled by Nanking sources for the fiscal years 1932–36 appear in Table 1.2. For fiscal 1932 (beginning July 1, 1931), the data for nineteen provinces indicate combined outlays of 348.2 million yuan. C. M. Chang argues that "on the basis of estimates for former years, the total expenditure" of the omitted regions, including Manchuria, Szechwan, Kiangsi, and several small units, "would amount to more than $50,000,000. Thus the cost of all provinces would *in toto* amount to some $400,000,000 approximately."[32] Since this calculation assigns only 13 percent of total outlays to areas that contained about one-fourth of China's population, it probably understates total spending.[33] A more reasonable figure may be derived by adding a figure of 100 million yuan for Szechwan and assuming that per capita outlays in the remaining regions resembled those in provinces for which data exist. Total provincial expenditures for fiscal 1932 (in million yuan) would then become:

A.	From Table 1.2	348.2
B.	Szechwan	100.0
C.	Subtotal of above	448.2
D.	Population share of regions included in subtotal	0.866
E.	Estimated total for provincial outlays (C/D)	517.6

Comparing this total of roughly 500 million yuan with the figures for central government expenditure shown in Table 1.1 produces a

32. C. M. Chang, "Local Government Expenditure in China," *Monthly Bulletin on Economic China* 7, no. 6 (1934):235. Note that Chang uses the symbol "$" to denote Chinese yuan.
33. Population data are from Liu and Yeh, *Economy of the Chinese Mainland*, 178.

Table 1.2
Provincial Expenditures, Fiscal 1932-36
(million yuan)

	Fiscal Year Ending June 30				
Province	1932	1933	1934	1935	1936
A. Kuomintang Influence[a]					
Anhwei	15.6	9.9	11.1	11.1	11.2
Chekiang	25.2	24.7	23.1	...	21.1
Fukien	30.8	26.2	16.9	...	19.3
Honan	17.8	10.1	11.3	...	...
Hunan	17.1	15.4	14.3	14.1	16.6
Hupeh	28.0	17.0	17.6	18.7	24.6
Kansu	...	12.1	...	4.6	4.7
Kiangsi	...	17.7	17.1	21.9	19.0
Kiangsu	26.2	25.6	21.8	26.9	31.6
Shensi	20.8	...	...	...	18.2
B. Unaffiliated with Nanking					
Chahar	2.3	3.0	3.9	3.5	3.1
Hopei	40.5[b]	25.3[b]	25.8	14.5[c]	...
Kwangsi	11.0	13.2	...	...	...
Kwangtung	43.1	...	...	...	...
Kweichow	8.9	6.0	6.1	6.0	...
Ninghsia	3.3	2.2	1.4	1.5	4.0
Shansi	17.8	13.7	...	...	...
Shantung	24.6	24.5	23.6	23.6	25.0
Sinkiang	8.9	...	...	...	...
Tsinghai	0.9[d]	0.9	0.9	...	1.0
Yünnan	5.4	4.3	3.6	13.6	15.4

[a]These provinces were included in Nanking's "Bandit Suppression Zones" (Tien, Government and Politics, p. 192).

[b]Including Jehol.

[c]Prasenjit Duara, "State Involution: A Study of Local Finances in North China, 1911-1935," (Berkeley, 1986), table 1.

[d]Excludes amounts tabulated in terms of grain.

Source: Except as noted, Chang Sen, "Land Taxes and Regional Finance," Ti-cheng yüeh-k'an 4, no. 2-3 (1936):172-203.

sum of reported and estimated provincial expenditures well below both the revenue and the outlay totals for the central government in that year. In addition, Table 1.2 shows that reported expenditures did not grow significantly after 1931. Stagnation or even decline of reported outlays is especially notable in the provinces under strong Kuomintang influence (which are also the provinces most likely to have reported reasonably accurate fiscal totals to

Nanking). Among these provinces, only Kiangsu shows a substantial rise in expenditure and this is more than offset by a reported decline of 12.5 million yuan in annual outlays for the municipality of Nanking between fiscal 1932 and 1936.[34] Among the larger unaffiliated provinces, only Yunnan reported significant growth in public outlays after 1932.

This picture of provincial outlays (and also revenues, for which similar data appear in the source cited in Table 1.2) as relatively small and fixed, conflicts so violently with the historical literature that further investigation seems essential. Fragmentary data for Szechwan, widely recognized as the "most notorious example" of high taxation, can illustrate the size of revenues in relation to output for China's most populous province.[35] Jerome Ch'en presents the following revenue information (in million yuan) for Liu Hsiang's Twenty-first Army in Szechwan:[36]

	1930	*1931*
"Cruel taxes" (*k'o-tsa*)	11.0	8.5
Opium	13.6	10.6
Salt	4.8	3.9
Stamp, tobacco, and wine taxes	. . .	3.4
Other	. . .	0.1
Total	31.3	33.4

Following Kapp's statement that taxes were used mainly for military purposes, tax collections and military strength (measured by manpower) should be closely related in Szechwan's various military regions. Kapp's data indicate that the Twenty-first Army accounted for 32 percent of the total troop strength of Szechwan's major warlords; a Japanese account credits Liu with 37 percent of the total.[37] Ignoring Liu Hsiang's control of Chungking's rich commerce, which made him the best financed of the Szechwan militarists, and

34. Chang Sen, "Land Taxes and Regional Finance," *Ti cheng yüeh k'an* 4, no. 2–3 (1936):172–203.
35. Tien, *Government and Politics*, 161.
36. Ch'en, "Historical Background," 30–31. The original source is Feng Ho-fa, *Chung-kuo nung ts'un ching chi tzu liao* (Shanghai, 1933), 1:829. Column totals may not check because of rounding error.
37. Kapp, *Szechwan*, 37.

also the activities of minor military figures leads to an estimate of
the combined revenue of the major military groups that controlled
most of the province. This estimate amounts to triple the total for
Liu Hsiang's Twenty-first Army or in the neighborhood of 94 million yuan for 1930 and 100 million yuan for 1931.

The general validity of this result is supported by Ch'en's fiscal
data showing peak provincial spending of 91 million yuan in 1934
and a prewar study that gives the following figures for annual provincial revenue and outlay (in million yuan): [38]

Year	Revenue	Military Outlay	Adminis- trative Outlay	Total Outlay
1921–22	26.6	23.5	2.1	. . .
1925	. . .	30–31	. . .	. . .
1928	. . .	. . .	. . .	100+

These approximate totals for provincial government activity in
Szechwan are compared with available indicators of the province's
output in Table 1.3. The results show that provincial taxes and expenditures in Szechwan during the early 1930s were equivalent to
approximately 12 percent of the annual rice crop, 3 percent of total
farm output, and only two percent of provincial product. Even
with a generous allowance for error, these comparisons undercut
extravagant claims about the scale of provincial taxation in Szechwan. The data show that Szechwan was a high-tax area. Provincial
revenue of 100 million yuan for 1931 implies a per capita taxation
of roughly 1.80 yuan for Szechwan or more than double the figure
of 0.83 yuan per person derived from revenue reports and population estimates for eight provinces under Kuomintang influence in
fiscal 1932. [39] Szechwan was also an area where taxes seem to have
risen with exceptional rapidity prior to 1930. This is suggested by
Jerome Ch'en's compilation of fiscal data, Lo Chieh-fu's figures reported above, and J. L. Buck's "index numbers of taxes paid by

38. Jerome Ch'en, "Local Government Finances in Republican China," *Republican China* 10, no. 2 (1985):51; Lo Chieh-fu, *Chung-kuo ts'ai cheng wen t'i*
   (Shanghai, 1933), 101–2.
39. The provinces are those shown in panel A of Table 1.2. The population figures
   are from Liu and Yeh, *Economy of the Chinese Mainland*, 178.

Table 1.3
Tax Revenue and Economic Activity in Szechwan Province, Early 1930s

Szechwan indicators	1933 Estimate (million yuan) (1)	1931 Tax Revenue as Percentage of 1933 Indicator (2)
A. Total value of rice crop	838.6	11.9%
B. Total value of agricultural output	3,553	2.8
C. Gross provincial product	5,010	2.0

Sources and methods of calculation:

Column (1):

    Line A: The value of the 1933 rice crop is the product of the 1933 paddy rice output and the 1933 Szechwan farm price of paddy rice. The data are from Liu and Yeh, Economy of the Chinese Mainland, 290, 330.

    Line B: The value of 1933 agricultural output is obtained by assuming that the share of rice in total output is the same in 1933 as it is in 1957. For 1957, the output value for rice is obtained by multiplying rice output by the 1952 Szechwan price (Chen, Chinese Economic Statistics, 361 and Liu and Yeh, Economy of the Chinese Mainland, 375). The resulting figure accounts for 23.6 percent of the province's 1957 agricultural output total of 6,040 million yuan (at 1952 prices; see Nicholas R. Lardy, Economic Growth and Distribution in China [New York, 1978], p. 198). The estimated agricultural output value for 1933 then becomes 838.62 million yuan divided by 0.236 or 3,553 million yuan (at 1933 prices).

    Line C: The gross provincial product for 1933 is estimated as follows: national GDP for 1933 is 29.88 billion yuan or 1.41 times the gross value of agricultural output (Liu and Yeh, Economy of the Chinese Mainland, 66, 140). Assuming identical structures of farm costs and total output at the national and provincial levels, a crude estimate of Szechwan's 1933 provincial product can be obtained by multiplying agricultural output value (derived in Line B above) by 1.41.

Column (2): Based on 1931 revenue of 100 million yuan (see text).

farmers to the hsien [county] government."[40] This only adds to the significance of the present results, which suggest that even in Szechwan, and even after what Sheridan calls "the long years of incredible tax exploitation," warlords proved incapable of wresting more than a small fraction of economic output from producers and consumers.[41]

40. Ch'en, "Local Government Finances," 51 and John L. Buck, *Land Utilization in China, Statistics* (New York, 1982), 167. Ch'en's data show that provincial expenditure tripled between 1925 and 1934.
41. Sheridan, *China in Disintegration*, 199.

Local Governments

Information on local finances is not easy to obtain. Table 1.4 presents data on average expenditures for counties in Hopei and Chekiang in 1931 or 1933 and average revenues for counties in Kiangsu, Anhwei, and Honan in 1935 as well as figures for 1933 or 1935 administrative outlays at the county level in Anhwei, Honan, Hupeh, and Kiangsi. By assuming that the 1935 share of administrative expenses in county outlay was the same for Hupeh, Anhwei, and Kiangsi as for Honan, the number of provinces for which average county revenue or expenditure can be approximated rises to eight. Under this assumption, average county revenue or spending for 578 (of about 2,000) counties may be estimated at 125,000 yuan for

Table 1.4
Annual Revenue and Expenditure for County Governments, 1931-35
(yuan)

Province	Year	Number of counties	Average administrative expenditure	Reported (R) or Derived (D) Revenue or Expenditure
Chekiang	1933[a]	66	...	67,661
Hopei	1931	130	...	63,956
Kiangsu	1936[a]	60	...	513,945(R)
Anhwei	1936[a]	61	15,688[b]	109,707(R)
Honan	1936[a]	110	9,829[b]	71,120(R)
Hupeh	1933	70	12,571[b]	89,792(D)[c]
Kiangsi	1933	81	13,975[b]	99,821(D)[c]
Average county Revenue/Outlay		578	...	125,437[d]

[a]Denotes fiscal year ending June 30 of year shown.

[b]Tien, Government and Politics, p. 105.

[c]The total expenditure is derived from administrative outlay by assuming the latter to occupy 14 percent of the former; this figure is based on the ratio of 1933 administrative outlay to total 1936 expenditure for Anhwei (14.3 percent) and Honan (13.8 percent).

[d]A weighted average of provincial figures using the number of counties as weights.

Sources: Except as noted, the data for Chekiang and Hopei are from Chang, "Local Government Expenditure," 235-36; data for Kiangsu, Anhwei, and Honan are from Chang, "Land Taxes and Regional Finance," 209-25.

the mid-1930s, implying total spending at the county level of approximately 250 million yuan.[42]

C. M. Chang presents expenditure data for fiscal 1931 covering the municipalities of Nanking, Shanghai, Peking, Tientsin, and Tsingtao. With outlays for these cities amounting to 44.6 million yuan, Chang concludes that "the total expenditure of the principal cities would amount, therefore, to about" 70 million yuan for fiscal 1932.[43]

Total Spending by All Levels of Government

The data and estimates compiled in the previous pages are combined into a single estimate of total government spending in Table 1.5. These results are subject to both major and minor qualifications. The latter include various assumptions used to derive expenditure totals for provincial and county governments and the exaggeration of total spending arising from double counting of subsidies paid by Nanking and the provinces to lower administrative levels. The major qualifications arise from the exclusion from published totals of revenues collected and spent by garrison administrations and the activities financed by semi-autonomous government agencies; concealed expenditure is another potentially large category of unrecorded outlay.[44]

To deal with the existence of unrecorded expenditures at the provincial level and below, I calculate total outlays in two ways. Version A is simply the sum of reported and estimated outlays for various levels of government. But C. M. Chang notes that because "there are many items of expenditures which are invisible in the budgets and . . . [because] these items often amount to stupendous sums, we may safely conclude that the actual expenditures of all units of local government, including wastes and leakages,

42. The calculations in Table 1.4 assume equality of annual revenue and outlay; any surplus or borrowing by county governments is ignored.
43. Chang, "Local Government," 235.
44. The importance of garrison administrations is noted in Ch'en, "Local Government Finances," 44–45. Outlays financed outside county budgets are mentioned in Philip A. Kuhn, "Local Taxation and Finance in Republican China," in *Select Papers for the Center for Far Eastern Studies*, ed. Susan Mann Jones (Chicago, 1979), 128.

Table 1.5
Government Spending in China for 1931

Level of Government	Spending (million yuan)
Central	749
Provincial	518
County	250
Municipal	70
Total government spending	
A. Sum of above	1,587
B. Adjusted	2,425[a]
Gross domestic product	33,431
Government outlay as percentage of GDP	
Version A	4.7%
Version B	7.2%

[a]Calculated by assuming that junior governments spend two yuan for each yuan of reported outlay.

Sources: Table 1.1 and text.

would be no less than twice [the sums indicated by published accounts]."[45]

Chang's belief that the "leakage" of provincial and local revenues may have reached amounts comparable to recorded fiscal totals is echoed in other contemporary accounts. Discussions of likin taxes on domestic trade often claimed that only half of the amount collected was remitted to the proper authorities.[46] During a 1935 campaign to raise the rate at which locally collected taxes were remitted to Shansi's provincial government, a supporter of provincial leader Yen Hsi-shan "accused members of the gentry and village officials of stealing or misappropriating public funds to the extent

45. Chang, "Local Government," 236.
46. D. K. Lieu, *China's Industries and Finance* (Peking, 1927), 143. Similar claims appear in Stanley F. Wright, *Kiangsi Native Trade and Its Taxation* (New York, 1980), 101–2 and "Finance Minister's Second Annual Report," *Chinese Economic Journal* 8, no. 4 (1931):334–35.

of Ch$10 million a year."[47] If each of Shansi's approximately one hundred counties spent in the neighborhood of 125,000 yuan annually, peculation of 10 million yuan would attain the same order of magnitude as actual spending.

Peculation, irregular fiscal impositions, and unrecorded outlays are inevitably difficult to verify. To avoid the danger of understating both revenue and expenditure, Table 1.5 includes a separate calculation of the financial scale of prewar government activity, Version B, which is derived by assuming that actual outlays of China's provinces, counties and municipalities were exactly double the figures obtained in Version A. The objective here is to make allowance for both unrecorded spending and embezzlement of tax funds to produce a total that reflects the actual magnitude of fiscal flows from the viewpoint of citizens and taxpayers. The results show a ratio of government outlay to total output of 4.7 or 7.2 percent for 1931/32. Although the expenditures of the central government outpaced Yeh's estimate of total output growth between 1931 and 1936 (Table 1.1) and outlays in some provinces (for example, Yunnan) rose between 1931 and 1936 (Table 1.2), outlays declined elsewhere, particularly in provinces closely tied to the Nanking government (Table 1.2). With output rising (Table 1.1), it is by no means certain that the share of government spending in total output rose significantly during the 1930s.

These calculations leave little doubt of the fiscal weakness of prewar Chinese governments. This outcome is not affected even by the possibility of large errors in available fiscal data. Consider the figures for spending by county governments, perhaps the most tenuous of the expenditure figures. Jerome Ch'en reports financial returns for seven counties showing average budgets of 709,513 yuan, far above the average of 125,437 yuan for 578 counties derived in Table 1.4.[48]

Suppose that the higher average pertains not to seven counties, but to 578—the identical number included in Table 1.4. Average county expenditure (for 1,156 counties) would then rise to 417,475 yuan, implying total county spending of 2,000 times this figure or

47. Gillin, *Yen Hsi-shan,* 154–55.
48. Ch'en, "Local Government Finances," 43–44, including one figure that Ch'en describes as "too high."

835 million yuan, more than triple the amount shown in Table 1.5. Compounding this large upward revision with the further assumption (Version B) that actual spending was double the new figure of reported and estimated spending, the ratio of total government outlay to gross domestic product (GDP) rises only to 9 percent.

The conclusion that taxes and public spending remained below 10 percent of total output draws further support from computations of tax burdens. With an aggregate product of roughly 30 billion yuan (Table 1.1) and a population of approximately 500 million, per capita product in the 1930s was roughly 60 yuan; Liu and Yeh estimate personal consumption at 56 yuan per person for 1933.[49] A tax burden of 5–6 yuan per head would thus correspond roughly to a 10 percent governmental share of total output. Fragmentary data fall well short of this range. Jerome Ch'en's figures for overall tax burden in six counties produce an average of 2.71 yuan per head.[50] In Ting county (Hopei), Sidney Gamble concluded that "the recorded and estimated amounts received in 1929 by national, provincial and hsien [county] governmental agencies" amounted to 1.25 yuan per person; "a rough estimate of the unreported village assessments and a guess as to the profit of non-governmental tax collectors [tax farmers] would make the total . . . perhaps" 2.25 yuan per capita, still only 5.1 percent of local incomes, which averaged 43.7 yuan each year.[51] Philip Huang cites 1937 data for a Hopei village showing tax payments amounting to 0.3–5.9 percent of household income.[52]

Comparative data for thirty low-income nations during 1957–60 include only two cases, Afghanistan and Ethiopia, in which state revenues fall below 10 percent of aggregate output.[53] Governments not only in India, Pakistan, and Indonesia, but even in Liberia, Paraguay, and the Sudan controlled substantially larger shares of

49. Liu and Yeh, *Economy of the Chinese Mainland*, 68.
50. Ch'en, "Local Government Finances," 44, omitting one figure that the author describes as "too high."
51. Sidney D. Gamble, *Ting Hsien: A North China Rural Community* (Reprint, Stanford, 1968), 167, 117.
52. Philip C. C. Huang, *The Peasant Economy and Social Change in North China* (Stanford, 1985), 282.
53. Harley H. Hinrichs, "Determinants of Government Revenue Shares Among Less-Developed Countries," *Economic Journal* 75 (1965):552.

national output than the political leaders of prewar China did.[54] Unless one assumes that more than three yuan of taxes or payments in kind were collected and/or expended for each yuan of reported spending by junior governments, China's ratio of government spending (and tax collections) to total output prior to the outbreak of the Sino-Japanese War in 1937 almost certainly fell short of the 10 percent figure recorded for Japan in 1880 (when the Meiji regime was so pressed for funds that it felt obliged to curb its small program of developmental outlays), not to mention the ratios of 13 and 29 percent achieved by the People's Republic of China in 1952 and 1957 respectively.[55]

These results make it abundantly clear that the extent and impact of Chinese taxation remained modest throughout the prewar decades. Even at low levels of per capita income, such terms as "crushing," "cruel," "extortionate," and "oppressive" cannot accurately describe the general impact of a tax system that barely managed to garner *one-twentieth* of total output. Residents of particular villages, towns, counties, and even whole provinces paid taxes in excess of the overall average of 5 to 7 percent of current output. At times, taxes certainly caused distress. But unless the data compiled in the preceding pages are utterly divorced from reality, tax-imposed economic hardship can only have been episodic. Despite the existence of a voluminous literature of tax protest, a long-standing Chinese tradition, the prewar decades witnessed no major departure from the equally venerable Chinese tradition of low taxes.

The small size of government relative to the national economy and the large share of military outlays and loan repayments in public spending together imply that the private sector dominated China's civilian economy, with the forces of the market outweighing administrative measures by a wide margin. Even in the Lower Yangtze area where the Nanking government was strongest, the

---

54. Prewar China conforms to Hinrichs's rule of thumb for poor nations: the ratio of state revenue to total output "is likely to equal 5% plus one half" the ratio of imports to output, the latter being about 4 percent for China in the early 1930s (ibid., 554).

55. Koichi Emi, *Government Fiscal Outlays and Economic Growth in Japan 1868–1960* (Tokyo, 1963), chap. 2; Thomas C. Smith, *Political Change and Industrial Development in Japan: Government Enterprise, 1868–1880* (Stanford, 1955), chaps. 7–8; and Liu and Yeh, *Economy of the Chinese Mainland*, 66–67, 109.

composition of output, relative prices, technology, income distribution, fluctuations in the money supply, and the ebb and flow of the business cycle were all determined by market forces that remained essentially impervious to state policy. Aside from regions affected by the construction of new transport and communication links, civilian government actions had little impact in rural areas prior to the great inflation of the 1940s.

These findings point to new directions for research. Voluminous historical materials show the efforts of officials at every level to increase revenues. Why did these initiatives reap so little success? After all, central government revenues alone amounted to 1 or 2 percent of total output in 1900.[56] There is abundant evidence of governmental weakness. Military leaders found themselves obliged to negotiate tax rates with merchants or with mobs of irate farmers who publicized their opinions with violent riots.[57] Endless struggles among localities, provinces, and the center over the proceeds of the salt tax signify a general inability to expand the tax base: Why battle over crumbs if the fiscal pie could be readily enlarged? Why do provincial expenditures stagnate or decline in the regions that formed Nanking's tax base? Why could Nanking increase county-level expenditure only by reducing provincial spending?[58] Historians have neglected the question of how the civilian public managed to resist widespread official efforts to raise taxes.

The Regional Distribution and Progressivity of Taxation

Provincial taxation and spending were much larger in per capita terms in some regions than in others. The same appears true of central government taxes, most of which came from a small group of provinces. Did the uneven regional pattern of tax incidence increase or reduce the burden of taxation on the Chinese public? Were taxes progressive, with the ratio of tax to income rising with income level or, as is often asserted, regressive, with poor house-

56. Perkins, "Government as an Obstacle," 487.
57. Earl Swisher, *Canton in Revolution: The Collected Papers of Earl Swisher, 1925–1928*, ed. Kenneth W. Rea (Boulder, 1977), 80 and Kapp, *Szechwan*, 51–52.
58. Tien, *Government and Politics*, 105–6.

holds paying above-average shares of their incomes to the tax collector? Although these complex matters cannot be resolved, there is considerable evidence that casts doubt on the common and largely unverified claim that taxes were usually paid by those least able to afford them.

In considering the regional impact of taxation, it is essential to recognize wide variations in the level of per capita income both among and within China's provinces. The extent of interregional income differences is apparent from Table 1.6, which reports average levels of per capita agricultural output (excluding handicrafts and sidelines) for three income classes in each of six groups of counties classified according to the level of average income. These data, which are expressed in grain equivalents rather than monetary units, show that class labels based on the relative position of individual households in local village economies conceal vast differences in absolute income levels.[59] "Poor peasants" in prosperous Region 1 earn incomes that amount to less than half those enjoyed by their wealthy neighbors, but these same "poor peasants" produce more than "middle peasants" in all other regions and six times as much as "poor peasants" in the impoverished localities grouped in Region 6. The presence of such wide income disparities makes it difficult to gauge the progressivity of taxation. Since the poorer inhabitants of Regions 1 and 2 are among the upper third of all rural income recipients, taxes imposed on them may be both locally regressive and nationally progressive. Wide income differences between segments of individual provinces (Chekiang, Hunan, Yunnan, and Sinkiang all have areas in both Regions 1 and 6) mean that regional tax inequity within single provinces may appear progressive when viewed from a wider perspective.

Wealthy regions tend to cluster around navigable waterways. Their inhabitants, both rich and poor (the latter often occupying advantageous positions in the national income distribution), participate more extensively in trade than residents of less prosperous regions because superior (water) transport facilities create more trading opportunities and because access to water generates higher farm yields that provide a surplus to exchange for merchandise

59. Although the data in Table 1.6 pertain to the early 1950s, there is no reason
    to expect interregional income variations to have changed markedly between
    the 1920s or 1930s and 1952.

Table 1.6
Per Capita Agricultural Output by Region and Class in
Rural China, 1951-52

Region	Number of Counties[a]	Regional Percentage[b] of Agricultural Population	Output	Average Agricultural Output Per Capita[c] (standard catties of grain)			
				Overall	Rich	Middle	Poor
1	107	3.0	8.5	1800	3300	2000	1500
2	145	5.7	10.8	1250	2300	1400	1000
3	257	11.1	14.8	900	1600	1000	760
4	523	24.4	25.4	700	1250	770	600
5	824	41.4	32.6	500	900	550	420
6	343	14.3	7.9	300	540	330	250
Total	2209	100.0	100.0	641	...	...	...

Note: Figures exclude sideline income.

[a]Counties and municipalities.

[b]Totals may not check because of rounding error.

[c]One catty equals 0.5 kilogram.

Source: Li Ch'eng-jui, <u>Chung-hua jen-min kung-ho-kuo nung yeh shui shih kao</u> (Peking, 1959), 134-36. These data are discussed in detail by Charles R. Roll, <u>The Distribution of Rural Incomes in China</u> (New York, 1980), chap. 4.

from other regions. For this reason, taxes on trade, including customs duties, consolidated taxes, and various likin imposts on goods in transit all tended to be paid by high income groups.[60]

With the notable exception of the salt tax, which "was primarily a tax on salt carried long distance by water" that rich localities frequently avoided, levies collected by the Nanking government seem to have fallen mainly on well-to-do groups and regions.[61]

60. The discussion focuses on who paid the taxes. To ascertain the distribution of ultimate tax burden is a complex and often impossible task. The common assumption that merchants and landlords could readily "pass along" tax burdens to less advantaged groups has little basis either in economic theory, which concludes that tax shifting depends on the relative price-responsiveness of supply and demand, or in historical circumstance, which shows wealthy Chinese strenuously resisting all forms of tax payments.

61. S. A. M. Adshead, *The Modernization of the Chinese Salt Administration, 1900–1920* (Cambridge, 1970), 21.

Most of Nanking's revenues came from the provinces listed in the upper panel of Table 1.2 (except Kansu and Shensi), but "within these provinces . . . Nanking's ability to tax was largely limited to the urban areas—the industrial, commercial and administrative centers," in other words, the most prosperous and developed areas, including some of the richest localities in all China.[62]

What of provincial and local revenues, which, as noted above, may have exceeded central government income? Here, observations by J. B. Whitney appear relevant: "As the distance from the center increases, variable costs [of collecting taxes] are liable to rise since communications will be less good and the people, probably receiving few administrative favors, will be less amenable to paying taxes than those nearer the center."[63] Whitney's hypothesis that taxes bore most heavily on urban areas and well-traveled trade routes probably applies to provincial and local levies as well. The importance of commercial taxes, which, as argued above, were likely to be paid by high-income households, is also visible at the provincial level. In Szechwan, Chungking's commerce was the key to Liu Hsiang's primacy among provincial military groups, giving him "a strong advantage over other Szechwanese militarists in his efforts to maintain a well-equipped, large, and, by provincial standards, effective army . . . [that] even managed to purchase a small number of French biplanes."[64] Liu's rivals suffered from the need to depend on the slim pickings offered by agricultural taxation. Shansi was another province in which commercial taxes were the key to raising total revenue. Gillin presents data implying that despite a 25 percent increase in land tax collections, the share of land taxes in total revenue declined from 80 percent to less than 55 percent as revenues rose during the 1920s and 1930s.[65] New revenues came mainly from nonagricultural taxes on industry, transport, and commerce.

Militarists often sought to expand trade by urging or forcing farmers to grow cash crops. Yen Hsi-shan promoted cotton cultivation in Shansi, as did the communist leaders of the Shen-Kan-Ning border region. Kwangsi officials promoted exports of t'ung

62. Tien, *Government and Politics*, 82.
63. Cited in ibid.
64. Kapp, *Szechwan*, 42.
65. Gillin, *Yen Hsi-shan*, 138.

oil. Opium was the preferred export in several provinces.[66] Rural commercialization seems closely linked with revenue prospects, again suggesting the limited scope of direct agricultural taxation and the leading role of commerce as a vehicle for enlarging the tax base at every level.

This brief account cannot pretend to be definitive, but there is enough evidence to suggest that taxation was frequently progressive in the sense that wealthy commercial and urban regions and their rural hinterlands paid considerably more taxes per head than poorer areas. The extent of progressivity in the local sense—that is, whether rich or poor households in a county or standard marketing area pay larger shares of their incomes in taxes—is very difficult to judge. Philip Huang's data for two Hopei villages suggest local progressivity, with households identified as tenants or as "poor peasants" subject to the lowest rates of taxation.[67] Prosperous households often paid substantial taxes. Wealthy citizens consumed a disproportionate share of more heavily taxed manufactures and trade goods. They also suffered most from forced loans, ransom demands, impromptu levies on travelers, and other irregular impositions. Small transactions might escape the taxman's notice. At festival time in Ting county (Hopei), tax collectors "were so busy with the larger sales that they made no effort to collect on the smaller ones. Sales of fruit and vegetables under 50 catties [55 pounds] were exempt, as were sales to peddlers."[68] Whether, on balance, taxes were progressive or regressive must remain an open question.

Summary

Chinese governments remained fiscally weak during the entire period preceding the Pacific War. The inability of China's politi-

66. Gillin, *Yen Hsi-shan*, 93–94; Peter Schran, *Guerrilla Economy* (Albany, 1976), 92–93; Diana Lary, *Region and Nation* (Cambridge, 1974), 189–90. The widely repeated claim that "the percentage of cultivated land devoted to opium increased from 3 in 1914–19 to 20 in 1929–33" (Ch'en, "Historical Background," 32–33) is highly improbable. The decline in grain output implied by these statements is not reflected in available estimates. Furthermore, the underlying data imply improbably high indexes of multiple cropping.
67. Huang, *Peasant Economy*, 282–83.
68. Gamble, *Ting Hsien*, 166–67.

cal authorities to gain control over substantial financial resources meant that important economic magnitudes were determined mainly within the private sector. While the consequences of official inaction—pervasive insecurity, limited expansion of social overhead facilities, etc.—certainly retarded the growth of China's prewar economy, the impact of official actions on the private sector, favorable or otherwise, surely remained small.

If this is so, it would appear that historians have lavished disproportionate attention on fiscal matters and have at times exaggerated the consequences of taxation. Without denying the existence of local excesses, corrupt practices, and regressive elements in the tax structure, there is no escaping the conclusion that taxes and associated surcharges took only a small share of output. If taxes surpassed the overall 1930s average of roughly 5 to 7 percent of total product in some regions, collections must have been that much lower elsewhere. Even if taxes created occasional economic hardship, the small size of the overall tax burden meant that fiscal pressure could not begin to displace population growth, flood, drought, and business fluctuations as the leading sources of economic distress for China's farmers, traders, and workers.

Whatever its magnitude, the burden of taxation must be weighed against the benefits derived from the expenditure of public monies. The primacy of military spending in government budgets raises the possibility, widely echoed in the historical literature, that government spending actually caused large welfare losses among a population harassed by unruly soldiers and overrun by warring armies. If the burden of taxes was light, might not the burden of government military expenditures have been far greater?

Militarism and the Chinese Economy

Most observers agree that militarism was a major and disruptive influence on economic life in prewar China. Sheridan's view is perhaps representative:[69]

Warlordism had a damaging and inhibiting effect on the Chinese economy. Chronic warfare and the disorderly conditions associated with war-

69. Sheridan, *China in Disintegration*, 102–3.

lordism devastated crops and farming facilities. Orderly and productive agriculture was constantly disrupted by the threat of hostilities, the conscription of peasants as soldiers or carriers, the seizure of farm vehicles and animals, the omnipresent danger of bandit raids, and the ruthless exploitation of the peasantry. . . . Trade was also restricted . . . by multifarious and arbitrary taxes. . . . The seizure of goods by troops or bandits, the frequent manipulation of currency, the military control of transport systems, all damaged trade. Long-range economic projects were not feasible where the future was so uncertain.

These phenomena persisted after 1927. Many provinces remained under the rule of military leaders with varying degrees of independence from Nanking, which allocated a large portion of its own modest revenues to the army.

The negative features of militarism were very real. Warfare and banditry did disrupt farming, transport, and commerce; manpower and resources were commandeered for military use; governments did spend most of their income on the military. At the same time, Sheridan's uncompromisingly negative summary distorts the complex reality of the period. Militarists also introduced progressive innovations whose positive contribution was far from trivial. The same lust for power that spawned disruptive warfare stimulated the development of industry, agriculture, transport, and education. Militarism encouraged the spread of productive skills as well as looting, public health as well as conscription. In short, one cannot assess the economic impact of militarism without attempting to balance its positive and negative features.

Whatever the balance, the size of the military impact on the economy requires investigation. Did the warfare and military maneuvering that dominated elite politics in Republican times exert a controlling influence on economic life? Or was the military situation itself shaped by economic realities, more a consequence than a determinant of economic patterns? The discussion begins by considering the size of China's military establishment.

The Size of China's Military Establishment

The inflated rhetoric that dominates both contemporary and retrospective accounts of prewar China gives the impression of a highly militarized society. One reads of "swollen armies," a "spiral of militarization," "chronic warfare," and so on. But how large was China's military? There is no exact information on the size of China's armies or their budgets, but rough approximations can be made: they show a military establishment of modest dimensions.

Table 1.7 contains crude estimates of the size of China's armed forces and of military spending prior to World War II. Military expenditure rose rapidly after 1912, and may have reached 4 percent of total output by the early 1930s.[70] Since it is not certain that military outlays rose during the 1930s—as Tien observes, Nanking's rising outlays may have been offset by declining provincial spending—I take the 4 percent figure as representative of the outcome of several decades of rising military activity.[71] This is by no means a large figure. Nations spending 3 to 4 percent of GDP on military activity during 1957–59 included Pakistan, Malaya, Australia, Switzerland, Belgium, Thailand, Norway, and West Germany, none of which can be described as being highly militarized.[72]

When compared with her enormous population, China's armies were of modest size even in terms of manpower. Rough 1933 figures on age and sex distributions compiled by Liu and Yeh indicate that there were about 116 million Chinese males between the ages of fifteen and forty-four. The military occupied slightly over two million or less than 2 percent of males in this age group.[73] Further evidence of the small impact of soldiering comes from Buck's finding that less than one farm household in one hundred reported income from military service; Buck's informants were more likely to obtain subsidiary income as scholars or even officials than from military activity.[74]

Once again, there is a conflict between the literature emphasizing the extent of militarism and the data suggesting that the military commanded only a small fraction of China's human as well as financial resources. A review of the economic impact of warfare and

70. Calculated from the spending estimates for 1931 in Table 1.7 and the GDP estimate for fiscal 1932 in Table 1.1.
71. Tien, *Government and Politics*, 172.
72. Based on United Nations figures cited in Lorne J. Kavic, *India's Quest for Security* (Berkeley, 1967), 222. The corresponding figures for India, the People's Republic of China, the Soviet Union, and the United States were 2.4, 4.4, 6.9, and 9.8 percent.
73. Table 1.7 and Liu and Yeh, *Economy of the Chinese Mainland*, 180–81.
74. Buck, *Statistics*, 309–10.

Table 1.7
Size of Armies and Military Spending, ca. 1900-1935

Year	Number of Soldiers (thousands)	Annual Military Spending (million yuan)
Late Ch'ing	500	100
1913	1,500	...
1915	750	...
1916	500	142
1918	1,000	...
1919	750-1,400[a]	...
1924	1,500	...
1925	1,500[b]	...
1928	2,000	800
1929	1,620[c]	...
1931	...	1,335[d]
1935	2,233[e]	...

[a]U.S. Department of State, Internal Affairs, 893.22/6.

[b]Ibid., 893.20/68, from the North China Standard of February 19, 1925.

[c]Sheridan, Chinese Warlord, 243; this total includes 340,000 "miscellaneous" troops. U.S. Department of State, Internal Affairs includes six different estimates of 1929 troop strength ranging from 1,500 to 2,225 thousand men (see 893.20/104; 893.20/120; 893.20/122; 893.20/132).

[d]This is a high estimate based on Version B of estimated government spending (Table 1.5). The central government military outlay for fiscal 1931 is from Albert Feuerwerker, The Chinese Economy, 1912-1949 (Ann Arbor, 1968), 53. The recorded military (including police) outlay of junior governments is calculated from the unadjusted spending totals shown in Table 1.5 and the following shares of military outlays in total spending: provinces, 14.66 percent; municipalities, 16.45 percent; counties, 38.92 percent (Chang, "Local Government Expenditure," 236, 243). All unrecorded outlays (assumed equal to the reported total of junior government expenditures) are assigned to the military category.

[e]China Year Book, 1935 (Tientsin, 1935), 432, including the "fighting strength" of national and provincial forces.

Source: Except as noted, Ch'i, Warlord Politics, 78, 169.

military regimes in prewar China may illuminate the reality behind these disagreements.

Warfare in Republican China

Recent studies have upset the view that warfare between Chinese militarists was a comic-opera phenomenon in which opposing armies exchanged threats rather than bullets. H. S. Ch'i, for example, shows that the conflicts of the 1918–27 decade produced growing casualty levels. His evidence of high mortality among Kuomintang officers in the Northern Expedition offers convincing proof that intense fighting did occur.[75] From the present perspective, what matters is not that battles were fierce and deadly, but that they were few and far between. Financial and geographic limitations made it impossible for military leaders to keep large armies in the field. Shortages of ammunition meant that "few could afford extensive weapons training"; many troops had no firearms at all.[76] Sustained positional warfare as practiced in Europe was unknown in China "primarily for economic reasons," because China's poorly financed generals could not "afford to provision and maintain the large armies required for trench warfare."[77]

The same financial limitations that constrained the size of armies and the quantity and sophistication of weaponry also curtailed the duration of military mobilization and the extent of troop deployments. As a result, major wars were brief and casualties correspondingly small in number. This is evident from Table 1.8, which reproduces Ch'i's information on major wars between 1917 and 1930. These figures, which incorporate the higher of alternative casualty estimates in all cases, yield a cumulative total of about 400,000 casualties during a fourteen-year period. Although this is a large number, it is trivial in a demographic aggregate of China's size. Assuming a population of 500 million and annual mortality of 27 per thousand, the number of annual deaths from all causes becomes 13.5 million.[78] Even if each of the 415,700 estimated casualties shown in Table 1.8 received fatal injuries, the resulting total of battle deaths would amount to an annual average of less than 30,000. Under these assumptions, scarcely one death in 500 occurred on the battlefields of major wars between 1917 and 1930.

Warfare and casualties were not limited to the major conflicts listed in Table 1.8. Local clashes occurred in many places, often

75. Ch'i, *Warlord Politics*, chap 6.
76. Quotation from Diana Lary, *Warlord Soldiers: Chinese Common Soldiers* (Cambridge, 1985), 37. Kapp, *Szechwan*, 37; Ch'i, *Warlord Politics*, 200; and many others report the scarcity of weapons.
77. Ch'i, *Warlord Politics*, 127.
78. Mortality estimates are from Liu and Yeh, *Economy of the Chinese Mainland*, 175.

Table 1.8
Major Wars, 1917-30

Year	War	Provinces Involved		Troops Mobilized (thousands)	Casualties[a] (thousands)
		In War Zone	Total		
1917	Anti-Restoration	1	1	55	0.1
1918	Honan Campaign	1	5	100	2
1920	Chihli-Anhwei	3	6	120	3.6
1922	Chihli-Fengtien	4	10	225	30
1924	Chihli-Fengtien	5	14	450	26
1926	Feng Yü-hsiang vs. Kuo-min chün	8	13	600	...
1926/28	Northern Expedition	12	20	1,100	54
1929/30	Chiang K'ai-shek vs. Feng Yü-hsiang and Yen Hsi-shan	...	...	...	300[b]

[a]The higher of alternative casualty figures is used in all cases.

[b]Sheridan, China in Disintegration, 89 (no source is provided for this figure).

Source: Except as noted, Ch'i, Warlord Politics, 32, 137-38, 168, 217.

with dire results for noncombatants: "After one brief conflict between Yunnanese and Szechwanese troops in Chengtu in 1917, an estimated 3,000 civilians lost their lives from rifle and shell fire and more than 600 houses were burned, though casualties among the troops did not exceed 50 on either side."[79] Many of these incidents had little connection with warlordism, representing rather a continuation of the episodic feuds, plundering, and banditry that had become a normal feature of rural life since the mid-nineteenth cen-

79. Sheridan, *China in Disintegration*, 89; see also Lary, *Warlord Soldiers*, chap. 6.

tury, if not earlier.[80] The frequency of local violence does not alter the main point that military action was not a statistically important cause of death in prewar China. One percent appears to be a high estimate of the share of mortality resulting from military action during the years known as the "warlord era."

As with taxation, the incidence of warfare was geographically uneven. Ch'i divides China into mountainous and littoral zones. In the mountainous zones, communication was so primitive that major battles were almost impossible:[81]

In provinces like Shensi, Szechwan, Yunnan, Kweichow, Kwangsi, western Kwangtung, and Fukien, where modern communications were grossly inadequate, we find small armies fighting each other in a highly concentrated area. . . . Most battles involved only a few hundred men, or at most a few thousand. . . . The warring parties probably spent more time in maneuvering for position than in joining battle. . . . When militarists actually did fight, the wars were usually of low intensity. Most of the time wars *affected only the immediate vicinity* of the battlefield and thus the direct participants, and there were few casualties. Thus "skirmishes" described the situation more accurately than "wars."

On the plains, communications were better developed, but the locus of fighting was equally restricted:[82]

Defense of the main communication arteries became a paramount concern as the militarists recognized that without them their territories would be vulnerable. Furthermore the widespread use of artillery and concentration of large numbers of troops during later campaigns *made it almost impossible to fight battles except on relatively flat land along railway lines and main highways.* . . . In some cases much of the fighting was actually done *within a few miles of the railway tracks.* The restricted area of fighting helped make armored trains . . . an extremely potent instrument of war.

Statements about the large number of "wars" in Republican China must be understood in light of these observations.

80. See C. K. Yang, "Some Preliminary Statistical Patterns of Mass Actions in Nineteenth-Century China," in *Conflict and Control in Late Imperial China,* ed. Frederic Wakeman and Carolyn Grant (Berkeley, 1975), 174–210 and Philip Kuhn, who writes of the "continuous state of militarization" of the South China countryside in *Rebellion and Its Enemies in Late Imperial China* (Cambridge, 1970), 78.
81. Ch'i, *Warlord Politics,* 132–34, with emphasis added.
82. Ibid., 128, with emphasis added.

The limited extent and restricted geographic scope of warfare upsets the sweeping generalizations that dot the historical literature. Large armies did not march and countermarch across China's rural landscape. Sheridan's claim that "chronic warfare and disorderly conditions associated with warlordism devastated agriculture" can only be true of what Ch'i terms "the areas hardest hit by militarism."[83] And Ch'i's own research goes a long way toward showing these areas to be limited both in size and population. The local economies of the areas adjacent to the railways of North China showed no cumulative decline. On the contrary, Liang's detailed investigation shows that in spite of the negative impact of military disruptions, railway construction led to substantial increases in farm output and land values and encouraged migration into villages adjacent to the railway lines.[84]

Even though the disruptions and uncertainty associated with militarism stunted the growth of railway traffic (as will be shown in Chapter 4), the industrial and mining enterprises that depended most on the very communication arteries over which the militarists struggled managed to prosper and expand despite periodic disruptions of service, commandeering of equipment, irregular surcharges, and other upsets. If the modern sector expanded rapidly in the face of military disruption, the impact of warfare on agriculture can hardly have extended far beyond those few localities unfortunate enough to fall in the path of major campaigns. This conclusion draws support from the evidence of growing domestic trade and rising per capita farm output discussed in Chapters 4 and 6. These results lead me to view anecdotal reports of local violence, destruction of farm capital, and rural depopulation as isolated rather than common occurrences.

I conclude that existing accounts tend to overstate the impact of warfare on China's economy during the years 1912–37. Major wars did gain intensity as armies acquired greater mobility and firepower, but these conflicts were few in number, of brief duration, and confined to small areas. The frequency and consequences of minor local conflicts may not have differed substantially from events of the half-century preceding the fall of the Manchu dynasty. To argue that this level of military activity was sufficient to

83. Sheridan, *China in Disintegration*, 102; Ch'i, *Warlord Politics*, 171.
84. Ernest P. Liang, *China: Railways and Agricultural Development, 1875–1935* (Chicago, 1982), 141–44.

cause a general social and economic crisis runs far beyond existing evidence. This view was certainly not shared by Buck's respondents in 146 widely scattered counties who provided the following opinions on the causes of famine during the period 1850–1932 (the figures represent the number of counties reporting each cause of famine):[85]

Drought	266
Flood	127
Insects	54
War	18
Frost	11
Wind	10

Similar results emerge from Philip Huang's information on six villages in Hopei and Shantung, provinces that suffered more than their share of militarism and warfare. Of thirty-two reported disasters during 1917–41, only six were man-made, an average of one per quarter-century in each village.[86] Even though Buck's data include the Taiping period and Huang's cover the initial years of the Pacific War, periods that saw sustained warfare on a scale unknown in Republican civil strife, rural informants identify nature rather than man as the chief architect of agrarian distress.

Military Government in Regions of Territorial Stability

In addition to mobilizing armies and fighting wars, military men occupied leading positions among China's prewar political elite. The performance of military governments is thus an important aspect of the relationship between the military and the economy in China. A number of provinces and regions were controlled by military figures whose territorial bases remained stable for many years. These regimes, several of which have been studied in great detail,

---

85. Buck, *Statistics*, 19. In these data, one county may report multiple causes for a single famine.
86. Huang, *Peasant Economy*, 213. I assume six floods during 1917–41 in a village described as experiencing an average of one major flood every four years.

display common features that differentiate them from unstable military rule.

In the absence of large-scale foreign aid, the military, and hence political, strength of a territorially based regime such as Yen Hsi-shan's in Shansi or Liu Hsiang's in Szechwan flowed from the prosperity and more particularly from the commercial prosperity of the warlord's home region. In Liaoning, "the promotion of business became a regular item of discussion at the meetings of civil and military leaders that [regional warlord] Chang [Tso-lin] used to call from time to time."[87] Prosperity meant greater revenue and commercial prosperity enriched the sectors that governments were best able to tax. Commercial strength rested on the activities of merchants whose power arose not from military prowess but from local knowledge, business acumen, and commercial contacts, areas in which military leaders possessed little competence. Military governments typically held the physical means to expropriate mercantile wealth, but stripping merchants of their current stocks of wealth threatened to interrupt future flows of resources and products on which military finances remained crucially dependent.

This explains why strong and avaricious militarists not only refrained from imposing "extortionate" taxes on commerce, but took care to maintain good relations with the business community:[88]

Liu Hsiang's Twenty-first Army taxed the internal and external trade of [Chungking] and especially in the 1930s raised additional funds from the city's powerful merchant community through bond issues and "voluntary" contributions. Despite occasional disputes with Chungking's mercantile associations over taxation policies, Liu Hsiang carefully and successfully cultivated his ties with the city's businessmen and financiers through his policies and through close personal contacts.

Why does a potent general of Liu's caliber take care to seek cordial relations with defenseless merchants? In this case, it appears that Liu's financial dependence on Chungking's trade flows obliged him to limit taxation to levels established in personal negotiations with the "powerful merchant community." Despite his access to physical force, the militarist whose time horizon encompassed tomorrow

87. Gavan McCormack, *Chang Tso-lin in Northeast China, 1911–1928* (Stanford, 1977), 94.
88. Kapp, *Szechwan*, 42.

as well as today was obliged to exercise moderation in his role as
tax collector. For, "as Szechwanese merchants had been quick to
point out . . . the armies' quest for revenue could become self-
defeating if taxes drove . . . commodity prices so high that exports
could not be sold."[89] One large trading firm moved its operations
from Chungking to Hankow in the early 1920s to escape the financial demands of competing military factions.[90] Others could do
the same.

Earl Swisher's observations at Canton in 1927 illustrate another
aspect of mercantile strength:[91]

August 21: Yesterday there was a general panic over the paper money
which has been issued by the Nanking government. . . . There was a run
on the Central Bank to redeem the paper for silver. . . . Even here in the
village yesterday, they would not accept paper money.

August 29: There has been continued refusal to accept paper money. . . .
The banks are still redeeming it for silver and it looks like confidence
should be restored before long.

August 31: The lack of confidence in paper . . . *was interpreted as a protest of the merchants against the heavy luxury tax on goods.* . . . General
Li Chi-shen came back to Canton Saturday and promised to remove the
luxury tax if the merchants would agree to the abolition of likin and the
new surtax of 12% on imports. I think that confidence will be soon
restored.

Soon thereafter, the Chamber of Commerce and the Bankers'
Guild, having forced the military to rescind tax increases by threatening to destroy the paper currency, advised their members to accept paper money at par.[92]

Military commanders were forced to recognize the distinction
between military and economic control in rural as well as in urban
areas. Many observers have noted that strong governmental control over village China comes only after 1949. The frequency and
success with which localities resist the directives and policies of
China's present government points to the likelihood that prewar
governments were even more dependent on the consent of the

89. Ibid., 94.
90. U.S. Department of State, *Internal Affairs*, 893.20/62.
91. Swisher, *Canton in Revolution*, 77–80, with emphasis added. Likin refers to
    transit taxes on interregional commodity flows.
92. Ibid., 121–22.

governed in seeking to collect taxes and implement programs. As in many developing countries, military leaders in China were too few and too inexperienced to administer the territories they controlled. The administration of warlord areas rested in civilian hands. Tien's statistics show that military men predominated only at the level of the provincial governors. Among high-level provincial and municipal administrators in 1936, 58.3 percent were college educated and only 25.5 percent had studied at military schools. Of nearly 4,000 county magistrates in 1931–32, only 12–16 percent had received military education, while over half had attended colleges and legal or administrative academies. Tien concludes that "if one is to make a tentative generalization, it appears that provincial political power was largely controlled by military men, who recruited college-educated elites to assist them."[93]

The background of these civilian officials is not known in detail, but fragmentary evidence suggests that traditional local elites continued to function in their accustomed role as intermediaries between the provincial or county governments and the local communities of which they were influential members. Tien reports that 59.7 percent of magistrates in 1931–32 were natives of the provinces in which they served; only 36.7 percent were outsiders.[94] Other sources specifically mention the continuing role of prominent local families:[95]

Upper-level bureaucratic posts [in all regions] were held by chief lieutenants of the warlords, and most of the remaining posts by members of powerful local elites.

[Shansi governor Yen Hsi-shan] enjoyed much support among the younger members of the gentry, especially those having a modern education. Two-thirds of the bureaucrats . . . in T'aiyuan were less than forty years old and virtually all had attended colleges or middle schools, generally in Shansi.

These materials begin to convey a sense of the limited administrative power of military governments. In Szechwan, Robert Kapp finds that tax collection was assigned either to traditional tax specialists, who were historically incapable of collecting large agricultural taxes, or to the local militia—presumably including some of

93. Tien, *Government and Politics*, chap. 8; the quotation is from p. 143.
94. Ibid., 137; 16.4 percent were not classified.
95. Tien, *Government and Politics*, 20; Gillin, *Yen Hsi-shan*, 173.

the taxpayers themselves—who were unlikely to take extraordinary pains to damage their neighbors (and their own standing in the community) for the sake of distant outsiders.[96]

In short, the military leaders may have possessed most of the guns, but unless their interest was focused exclusively on immediate goals, they could anticipate only limited success in translating coercive power into economic control. As a result, when military regimes aspired to build territorial bases for future expansion, the economic evils attributed to warlord regimes were often muted.

The same militarists supported a surprising variety of progressive activities. Provincial governments sought to increase production of both weapons and commercial crops. Militarily inspired construction of roads and railways improved transport for both commodities and passengers.[97] Benefits were particularly large in years of harvest failure.[98] Commerce flourished in some areas of military rule. Contrary to Robert Kapp's assertion that "uncontrolled taxation . . . stifled Szechwan's internal and export-import trade," customs figures show that the current value of direct foreign trade at the river ports of Chungking, Wan-hsien, and I-ch'ang *increased* by 75 percent between 1921/24 and 1929/32; the Minsheng Company, a large business involved with transport, trade, and manufacturing in Szechwan, expanded steadily between 1925 and 1935.[99] Military figures were also prominent in the development of China's coal industry; commercial investors welcomed partners whose military connections promised funds and physical security, the latter being especially important for enterprises located far from the protective umbrella of the foreign concessions in major treaty ports.[100]

All of these reforms had definite limits. Some were never more

96. Kapp, *Szechwan*, 45.
97. See, among others, Gillin, *Yen Hsi-shan*, 91 and Li Hsiao-yung, "Development of Highway Transport in Republican Fukien," *Chung-kuo she hui ching chi shih yen chiu* 2 (1986):93.
98. On the contribution of roads and railways to famine relief, see Gillin, *Yen Hsi-shan*, 91; *The North China Famine of 1920–1921 with Special Reference to the West Chihli Area* (Peking, 1922), 10; and Walter H. Mallory, *China: Land of Famine* (New York, 1926), 136–39.
99. Kapp, *Szechwan*, 56; *The China Year Book*, various issues; and *Min-sheng shih-yeh kung-ssu shih i chou nien chi nien k'an* (Chungking, 1937), 123, 171.
100. Tim Wright, "Entrepreneurs, Politicians and the Chinese Coal Industry, 1895–1937," *Modern Asian Studies* 14, no. 4 (1980).

than paper programs. Others affected only small areas or foundered for lack of funds or expertise. Even so, the results were not insignificant. Initial modernizing efforts are feeble and problematic in all societies and failure is common everywhere. Some of the militarists' economic ventures produced notable long-term consequences. Following Yen Hsi-shan's industrialization efforts, for example, Shansi's 1957 level of per capita industrial output surpassed all regions but Shanghai, Tientsin, and the three northeastern provinces.[101]

This discussion suggests that stable military regimes provided significant benefits that partly, and perhaps entirely, offset the negative economic effects of military control.

The Military Impact on the Economy in Periods of Instability

If stable military governments may have contributed positively to regional development, unstable military regimes certainly failed to do so. From the viewpoint of long-range economic improvements, instability encouraged the worst features of military rule. Individual soldiers practiced simple robbery, as did roving bands of demobilized troops and outlaws. Larger military units extracted tribute from villages and towns by threatening death or devastation to any who failed to pay. When faced with defeat, even progressive militarists turned to ruthless conscription. In Shansi, Yen Hsi-shan "refused to punish an army commander who executed prominent members of the local gentry because they failed to meet his demands for money" in an emergency.[102] Such demands affected urban as well as rural areas. In preparing for the second Chihli-Fengtien War, Wu P'ei-fu requisitioned automobiles from Peking as well as carts and donkeys from rural communities; even foreign property was not exempt.[103] Currency manipulation was another disruptive crisis phenomenon: "Militarists inundated the market with new paper currency when they suddenly needed . . . to prepare for or to conduct civil wars."[104]

101. Nicholas R. Lardy, *Economic Growth and Distribution in China* (New York, 1979), 104.
102. Gillin, *Yen Hsi-shan*, 155.
103. Sheridan, *Warlord*, 26, 132, 309 n. 83.
104. Ch'i, *Warlord Politics*, 162.

These depredations had severe, though often temporary, effects on local and regional economies. In some areas, farmers could carry on only by incurring onerous costs for self-defense: [105]

At dawn, the night watchman of the village opened up the heavy wooden gates of the village. We . . . saw the farmers going out to the fields, each group accompanied by armed guards. All day long as the farmers work, these guards sit on little mounds among the paddy fields to protect them. The village had three high watchtowers, which are also used as forts against invading bands of robbers. . . . The farmers would be very prosperous if they were not continually the prey of robbers. Three [nearby] villages . . . are still occupied by robbers who levy tribute on all the farmers around.

These farmers might well have preferred a stable warlord regime to the anarchy described here. The importance of stability is also evident in a contemporary assertion that "Szechwan seems to have enjoyed greater tranquility than many downriver provinces despite the absence of centralized provincial control and . . . national authority." [106]

The overall impact of commercial disruption can be seen in the wild gyrations of foreign trade for a port like Changsha, which felt the impact of the Northern Expedition and subsequent political disruptions between 1926 and 1929. The current value of the port's direct foreign trade for the years 1927–29 fell substantially below the total for 1921–24; annual trade did not surpass the 1924 peak until 1931. [107] Such instability upset the plans, incomes, and supplies of producers and consumers as well as merchant intermediaries. Sometimes the results were not serious: goods prevented from reaching their destination along one route could be switched to another and the output of one supplier could be replaced elsewhere. [108] In other cases, however, the disruptions produced serious and lasting effects. The thriving handloom weaving industry of Pao-ti, a Hopei county north of Tientsin, was ruined by disruptions

105. Kwangtung report of 1927 cited in Swisher, *Canton in Revolution*, 83.
106. Kapp, *Szechwan*, 57.
107. Based on data from various issues of *The China Year Book*.
108. Tim Wright, "Growth of the Modern Chinese Coal Industry: An Analysis of Supply and Demand," *Modern China* 7, no. 3 (1981):344 and Arthur Rosenbaum, "Railway Enterprise and Economic Development: The Case of the Imperial Railways of North China, 1900–1911," *Modern China* 2, no. 2 (1976):249, 255–256.

associated with warlord rivalries and Japanese aggression. Civil war, unpredictable taxation, currency manipulation, transport interruptions, and outside invasion "affected very closely the very areas where the merchants of Paoti were wont to do business, weakened the stability of the money market, and created that general atmosphere of apprehension . . . in which . . . confidence in the normal processes of business disappears."[109] Mining also suffered frequent disruptions from military operations. Although Wright observes that "output recovered quite rapidly" with the restoration of peace, some mines suffered irreversible financial damage and were forced to close.[110] Chapter 4 will show that military-linked fluctuations limited the economic benefit of railway development to a fraction of its potential. After the start of the Pacific War, these disruptions attained major dimensions. By 1942, transport problems and peasant retreat from the market had reduced the output of Shanghai's Chinese-owned cotton mills to less than 6 percent of the 1936 figure.[111]

The overall impact of uncertainty, a key negative aspect of the prewar economic climate and one for which the military was chiefly responsible, is well expressed by Ch'i's observation that "political unrest and civil wars made any *long-range investment extremely precarious.*"[112] This was most unfortunate in a capital-scarce economy for it discouraged productive fixed investment by both well-to-do members of the gentry, whose warehouses, factories, or bank balances might disappear, and ambitious farmers, who could lose their hard-earned animals or carts. Pervasive uncertainty also hampered efforts to improve agricultural methods and techniques. Instability in North China ended attempts by Chinese textile interests to establish rural bases for collecting and processing cotton.[113]

109. H. D. Fong and H. H. Pi, "The Growth and Decline of Rural Industrial Enterprise in North China," *Nankai Social and Economic Quarterly* 8, no. 3 (1936):751.
110. Wright, "Growth of the Coal Industry," 344; Kung Chün, *Chung-kuo hsin kung yeh fa chan shih ta kang* (Shanghai, 1933), 209; and Ch'i, *Warlord Politics*, 172 describe the closure of the large Chung-hsing (Shantung) mine, which had formerly produced over 700,000 tons of coal annually, following military disruptions in 1926–28.
111. Wang Chi-shen, ed., *Chan shih Shang-hai ching chi* (Shanghai, 1945), 194.
112. Ch'i, *Warlord Politics*, 171–72, with emphasis added.
113. Howard L. Boorman, ed., *Biographical Dictionary of Republican China* (New York, 1967), 1:409–13.

In Kwangtung, government support of programs to develop scientific methods of silkworm rearing came too late: by 1927, it was reported that "the silk industry has collapsed in the last year because of inferior methods of production and the losses . . . due to bandits."[114]

Summary

This survey shows that the important subject of twentieth-century militarism and its effect on China's economy deserves further scholarly attention. Existing studies often overstate the economic significance of military activities by failing to recognize the modest resources available to military commanders. Tight budgets restricted manpower, weaponry, and mobility. The resulting shortages in turn constrained the scope, duration, and geographic extent of warfare and its attendant disruptions. The secondary literature also exaggerates the economic cost of military regimes by overlooking their limited power, overemphasizing their negative features, and neglecting their progressive dimensions. China's military sometimes lived up to its reputation as a drain on the economy, especially because of its effects on business uncertainty, but these negative effects were felt for the most part in regions plagued with shifting military administrations and in actual war zones.

Further research may achieve a balanced assessment of these positive and negative features and also elucidate the impact of military activity in different economic regions. Additional inquiry will perhaps confirm Donald Gillin's suggestion that: "the 'warlord period' of China's history was not merely an era of fruitless strife but rather a period of transition which witnessed changes so significant that without them the unification and modernization of China currently being undertaken would be impossible."[115]

Chinese Market Structures

National, provincial, and local governments controlled only a small share of the economic resources in prewar China. This means that

114. Swisher, *Canton in Revolution*, 46.
115. Gillin, *Yen Hsi-shan*, 296.

resource allocation occurred primarily within the private sector and that most economic processes were strongly tied to the marketplace. Market structure thus assumes great importance in analyzing China's prewar economy. Existing accounts often stress the importance of noncompetitive elements in private markets. Sheridan's description of China's peasantry as "unchanged in its poverty, ignorance, and hardship, the helpless prey of local officials, warlords, and the conservative local gentry" implies that the majority of Chinese households were easy marks for economic exploitation.[116] Robert Ash indicates that Kiangsu landlords could set rents on a take-it-or-leave-it basis without regard for tenant reactions.[117] At the local level, Feuerwerker offers the following summary:[118]

The local market tended to be monopsonistic for what the peasant sold and monopolistic for what he bought. He was subject to considerable price manipulation, which was intensified by the fact that supply would naturally be larger at harvest time when he wanted to sell and smaller in the spring when he wanted to buy. Moreover, in those areas near the major cities in eastern and south coastal China where the commercialization of agriculture had made some headway, exploitative collection systems . . . put the farmer at the mercy of the buyer. In general, the marketing process aggravated an already skewed distribution of the agricultural product between the producer and others.

With the exception of the reference to seasonal price variations, a feature common to all premodern agrarian economies, these statements appear extremely improbable. In a more recent study, Feuerwerker presents a very different view of prewar market conditions:[119]

While as a small individual buyer and seller the peasant was unable to influence the markets in which he had to trade . . . to suggest that increased commercialization of agriculture . . . had a negative effect on rural production and income is absurd. In the atomistic rural sector—where there were no barriers to entry (other than the often exaggerated information barrier), virtually no government intervention, and low capital

116. Sheridan, *China in Disintegration*, 23.
117. Robert Ash, *Land Tenure in Pre-Revolutionary China* (London, 1976), 39.
118. Albert Feuerwerker, *The Chinese Economy, 1912–1949* (Ann Arbor, 1968), 39.
119. Albert Feuerwerker, *Economic Trends in the Republic of China, 1912–1949* (Ann Arbor, 1977), 65–66.

requirements for all businesses—most types of commerce were quite competitive. . . . The local market has frequently been described as tending to monopsony for what the peasant sold and to monopoly for what he bought, but . . . few studies . . . document this assertion.

Before discussing the relative importance of competition and monopoly-monopsony in China's prewar economy, a brief review of the underlying economic analysis can illustrate the significance of these distinctions. A competitive market is one in which buyers and sellers are both numerous and well-informed. A competitive industry is one with many producers, none of which is large enough to influence the price of any input or product, and that has easy entry or exit. A monopolistic market is one with only one seller. A monopsonistic market has only one buyer. These terms are also applied loosely to situations in which small groups of sellers or buyers have sufficient "market power" to exercise partial control over prices. The main feature of competitive as opposed to monopolistic/monopsonistic markets is the presence of large numbers of well-informed and economically mobile producers, buyers, and sellers.

Why are competitive markets desirable? Economists have long understood that if all industries and markets are competitive (and assuming certain technical conditions), the following results should arise:

1. The allocation of resources will be efficient in the sense that the output of any commodity or service cannot rise unless the output of some other item falls. There is no slack that could permit output to rise simply by reshuffling resources. Only improved technology or increased resource supplies can permit a general increase in production.

2. The allocation of satisfaction will be efficient in the sense that it is not possible to increase the well-being of any individual without reducing the welfare of another. Again, there is no slack that could allow an all-round rise in satisfaction without access to extra resources or improved technology.

3. Productive resources will be priced so that each unit of land, labor, or capital earns an income equal to the amount by which total output would decline if that resource unit were withdrawn

from production. In this sense, resources can be said to earn what they contribute to total output.

None of these generally desirable consequences can be expected from an economy that contains significant deviations from the competitive ideal in the form of ignorance, immobility, monopoly, or monopsony.

It is essential to recognize the limited virtues of a competitive regime. Particularly significant is the absence of any claim to distributive justice. Personal incomes in a competitive economy depend on the distribution of resource ownership. Except in slave or serf societies, ownership of labor power is distributed in a relatively equal fashion. The degree of distributive inequality in a competitive economy thus depends largely on the distribution of ownership rights to land and capital. If these are evenly shared, income differentials will be narrow. If a small segment of the populace controls a large portion of society's wealth, a competitive economy will generate large income variations between propertied and laborer households.

This analysis can explain the desire of generations of economists to let the competitive or "free" market do its work, thus promoting "efficient" allocation and marginal-product pricing of resources. If society wishes to alter the resulting distribution of income, let the government redistribute property rights without disrupting the market mechanism. The appeal of competitive markets arises because departures from competition permit some resource owners (who possess market power) to earn more than they contribute while other resource units earn less than they contribute to total output (in the marginal product sense described above). Furthermore, departures from competition may reduce the aggregate total of output and satisfaction, causing the victims of market power to suffer doubly by receiving smaller shares of a shrunken economic pie.

This abstract view of the economic process is often too simple to apply to questions of policy and welfare in a modern industrial economy in which governments and technological change play important roles. But in prewar China, with its small government sector and moderate pace of technical and economic change, this elementary approach captures a large portion of economic reality and the simple issue of competition versus market power can be discussed in a straightforward manner. What, then, was the nature of markets in prewar China? To what extent were markets populated by the large numbers of well-informed buyers and sellers and the fluid resources postulated by the economist's competitive model? I begin with the question of numbers.

The huge population of China's provinces and even counties, the typically low income level, and the resulting standardization of commodities produced and traded guarantee that participants on one side of every important market were sufficiently numerous to prevent any individual from influencing price. No one will doubt that the sellers' side of autumn grain markets or the buyers' side of markets for grain in springtime, for salt, cotton cloth, land rentals, personal loans, etc. included sufficient numbers to meet the requirements of atomistic competition. What of the other side of these markets?

Here there is considerable evidence of large numbers of participants. Consider the following eloquent and explicit summary by Ramon Myers: [120]

Most households were within a half-day's travel of some periodic market, where a legion of merchants, brokers and peddlers circulated at prescribed times during the lunar month. The large numbers of buyers and sellers that haggled over prices suggests that price competition was intense. One foreign observer remarked that "in no other country are the free play of competition and the law of supply and demand still so completely relied upon for the regulation of prices." Powerful merchant guilds might exercise some restraint of trade in some markets, but "to avoid uncertainty and reduce risk, most merchants delegated their buying and selling to brokers" who had to compete with each other in the market. Equally important, there were so many merchants competing within each county that no single buyer could corner the market.

Myers goes on to cite an account of Hankow's rice market in 1913–14:

Rice exchange in Hankow is no different than in Shanghai, where it is handled through rice brokerage firms. . . . There are 20 rice brokerage firms. . . . However, there is no case where these firms buy large quantities of rice at a fixed time, or send agents to the rice producing areas to

120. Ramon H. Myers, "The Agrarian System," *The Cambridge History of China* (Cambridge, 1986), vol. 13:233–34.

corner the rice supply. Nor are there any examples where they resort to cunning means to collude with various shops which buy rice. We can say that these practices simply do not exist on a yearly basis, and for Chinese merchants this is one of their noteworthy characteristics.

The theme of numerous merchants engaged in intense price competition occurs again and again. Wusih (Kiangsu) had more than eighty rice dealers in the late nineteenth century; after the start of rail traffic along the Shanghai-Ningpo line in 1908, the number swelled to more than 140.[121] Donald Gillin writes that "private enterprises in Shansi during the 1930's were virtually all small, undercapitalized, and inefficient, while at the same time engaged in savage and mutually ruinous competition."[122] Wright refers to "the abundance of small-time entrepreneurs" in prewar China.[123] Ambitious men with no capital of their own could start out as commodity brokers, earning commissions by arranging transactions between sellers and buyers whose need to turn over their own small capital made them willing to pay intermediaries to search out trading partners.

The small size and limited financial resources typical of Chinese firms meant that entry and exit were easy in most branches of production and trade. Capital and skill migrated swiftly from unprofitable to profitable localities and lines of business. Evidence of diversification emerges not only from the behavior of great tycoons, whose fortunes rested on a judicious mix of investments spanning a wide range of industries, but also from the conduct of petty businessmen who moved from grain to weaving to money exchange with the ebb and flow of opportunity for profit.[124] This mobility of

121. *Chiang-su ch'eng shih li shih ti li* (Huai-yin, 1982), 39.
122. Gillin, *Yen Hsi-shan*, 133.
123. Wright, "Growth of Modern Coal Industry," 325.
124. Examples of diversification by business magnates appear in Bush, "Industry and Politics," 47–66; Wright, "Entrepreneurs"; Ting and Tu, "Yü Hsia-ch'ing"; and *Liu Hung-sheng ch'i yeh shih liao* (Shanghai, 1981) 1:1, which notes that Liu, who began his career as the Shanghai compradore for the Kaiping coal mines, gradually acquired interests in the match, cement, woolen, and coal industries and in wharves, warehousing, banking, and insurance. Fong and Pi, "Growth and Decline of Rural Enterprise," 716–17, offer a typical instance of diversification by small-scale merchants, noting that most cloth merchants in Pao-ti (Hopei) "remained in the cereal business" and that "probably all of the 93 firms" in the local cloth trade "had one subsidiary line or another," as did many of their workmen.

resources implies that lucrative nodes of market power would normally be dissolved by an influx of competitors eager to share in unusually high profits. As Kang Chao puts it: "Most cloth merchants were also money-changers or grain dealers, or both; they were thus in a position to close up shop without much hardship anytime they felt the profits were too low or the risks to high in the textile market. Furthermore, their high mobility permitted them to shift operations from one site to another with comparative ease."[125] D. K. Lieu notes that Chinese businesses aimed to earn quick profits from new activities, after which their owners remained poised to jump into more promising ventures should difficulties arise: "When they have made some money, they are ready to clear out at any time."[126] Ease of entry and exit is also evident in the frequency with which commercial firms closed during business crises and reappeared afterwards. Most of the seventy-odd Chinese tea firms in southern Anhwei closed during World War I, but fifty-four enterprises were back in business by 1922.[127]

At the local level, mercantile ranks were swelled by large numbers of itinerant peddlers, estimated by postwar writers to number 4.24 million in rural areas alone. Even without considering the migration of peddlers from one market to another, this figure implies a total of ninety-four peddlers for each of Skinner's 45,000 standard markets.[128] C. K. Yang's study of periodic markets in Tsou-p'ing (Shantung) corroborates Myers's picture of local markets as scenes of haggling among large numbers of sellers as well as buyers. Yang's findings are summarized in Table 1.9. They indicate that transactions in village-level markets were very small. With no more than a handful of potential customers for each seller, the

125. Kang Chao, "The Growth of a Modern Cotton Textile Industry and the Competition with Handicrafts," in *China's Modern Economy in Historical Perspective*, ed. Dwight H. Perkins (Stanford, 1975), 192.
126. Lieu, *Growth and Industrialization*, 103–4.
127. U.S. Dept. of State, *Internal Affairs*, 893.61332/11.
128. The number of peddlers is a 1952 figure cited by Liu and Yeh, *Economy of the Chinese Mainland*, 200, which apparently excludes sideline peddling by farmers. Since Liu and Yeh estimate that the total number of peddlers was about the same in 1933 as it was in 1952 (7.39 vs. 7.00 million, p. 69), the figure in the text can serve as a rough indicator of the number of rural peddlers in the 1930s. The number of standard markets is from G. William Skinner, "Chinese Peasants and the Closed Community: An Open and Shut Case," *Comparative Studies in Society and History* 13, no. 3 (1971):272.

income generated by the small volume of available business was minute. It is most unlikely that villagers stood in awe of local merchants whose incomes hardly surpassed their own meager earnings. In Tsou-p'ing, the profits amassed by petty traders with daily sales of less than 2.2 yuan (Table 1.9) can hardly have exceeded the incomes of farm laborers, who received cash wages of 0.33 or 0.75 yuan per day plus meals in nearby Hui-min and Lin-tzu counties.[129] Other instances of petty merchants with incomes similar to those of ordinary residents come from Hopei and the New Territories.[130]

The scale of commerce was not much larger at Tsou-p'ing's intermediate and central markets than at the village level, but competition was very much in evidence. Yang counted sixty-eight sellers of grain and beans, fifty-two stalls offering machine and handloom cloth, and fourteen money changers at Tsou-p'ing's intermediate market; at central markets, the number of competitors was even larger.[131]

A more general picture of market conditions may be drawn from the case of cotton and cotton goods, the circulation of which linked the mills of Shanghai and other urban centers to cotton-growing villages as far away as Shensi, handicraft weaving centers in Kiangsu and Hopei, and cloth buyers in towns and villages throughout China. The cotton trade, which spanned the largest and the smallest markets in China, illustrates the variety of organizational forms and the multiplicity of commercial channels that maintained price competition and thwarted efforts to accumulate market power. The competitive nature of national markets for cotton and cotton goods was recognized by foreign as well as Chinese observers. British diplomats advised their constituents "to remember that there is

129. Wage data are from Buck, *Statistics*, 328. Note that the figures in Table 1.9 exaggerate the sales of specialized merchants, who participated in only a fraction of total sales, the rest being transacted by farmers (Ching-kun Yang, *A North China Local Market Economy* [New York, 1944], 10).

130. Merchants in Hsü-shui county, Hopei, reportedly earned 100 yuan per year in the mid-1930s; in nearby An-kuo county, farm laborers earned 40 yuan plus board, and "workers" commanded annual salaries of about 60 yuan (*Chi Ch'a tiao ch'a t'ung chi ts'ung k'an* 1, no. 1 [1936]:99, 113). In the 1960s, village stores in the New Territories yielded daily profits as low as HK$5–9 while laborers earned HK$6–7 for casual work in farming or construction (Jack M. Potter, *Capitalism and the Chinese Peasant* [Berkeley, 1968], 76–77, 127–29).

131. Yang, *Local Market Economy*, 8–9.

Table 1.9
Market Conditions in Tsou-p'ing, Shantung, 1933

Market Participants	Basic Normal	Basic Peak[a]	Intermediate Normal	Intermediate Peak[a]	Central[b] A	Central[b] B[a]
Number of traders	18	126	324	994	1433	791
Number of buyers	200	500	800	4000	10000	8000
Buyers per trader	11	4	2	4	7	10
Daily sales volume (yuan)	39	880	1825	3765	5777	11465
Daily sales per trader (yuan)	2.2	7.0	5.6	3.8	4.0	14.5
Daily sales per buyer (yuan)	0.2	1.8	2.3	0.9	0.6	1.4

[a]Peak figures are for late fall markets when "poorer farmers sold their animals to avoid the expense of feeding them over the winter and early spring."

[b]A indicates the county seat; B refers to a central market in another town. Yang indicates that the majority of vendors were farmers and craftsmen rather than specialized merchants.

Source: Ch'ing-k'un Yang, A North China Local Market Economy (New York, 1944) 7, 10.

competition of the keenest kind in this market."[132] Major markets for cotton, yarn, and cloth attracted large and small merchants, including many with no funds of their own who operated as intermediaries, competing for commissions as small as five parts per thousand for arranging deals between traders whose need to turn over their capital encouraged them to pay for assistance in searching out business partners. The large numbers of merchants and the correspondingly rapid exchange of commercial intelligence created conditions in which even the largest firms were said to be unable to control or even anticipate market developments.[133]

132. Great Britain, Department of Overseas Trade, *The Commercial, Industrial and Economic Situation in China to September 1st, 1928* (London, 1928) 62.
133. See the series of studies prepared by the survey department of the Shanghai Commercial Savings Bank: *Mien?* (Shanghai, 1931), esp. 74–77; *Sha? Shanghai chih mien shao yü sha yeh* (Shanghai, 1931), esp. 120–23; and *Pu? Shanghai chih mien pu yü mien pu yeh* (Shanghai, 1932). Richard Bush directed me to these materials.

Detailed studies of rural cotton marketing reveal the strength of competitive forces at the village level.[134] Farmers could sell their cotton before or after the harvest, in seed or lint form, to petty farmer-merchants or larger, more specialized traders, and in local or outside markets.[135] Active competition pervaded the entire marketing process from farmgate sales to ginning, pressing, shipping, storage, finance, and brokerage. Buyers and sellers dealt with whomever offered attractive terms. They moved from market to market as price conditions changed. There were no significant entry barriers. Many farmers could afford to buy a ginning machine or set themselves up as petty traders. The ranks of brokers included villagers with no capital whatsoever. Even in the largest urban markets, "no license or special qualifications are required for a cotton broker. . . . Any one who is familiar with the market conditions and well known by the dealers and buyers is eligible to enter the business" and charge a commission of 0.25 percent for arranging transactions.[136] The efficiency of this marketing system and the absence of market power can be inferred from the willingness of commercially oriented rural elites to sell their cotton crops in local markets and from the gradual withdrawal of urban manufacturers and retailers from rural cotton markets, apparently because these well-informed commercial operators could economize by relying on middlemen rather than participating directly in cotton markets located far from their usual places of business.[137]

The cotton trade was not the only one in which the farmers' penchant for jumping into the sellers' side of the market blurred the distinction between producers and merchants. Buck's survey

134. The following discussion is based on T. S. Chu and T. Chin, *Marketing of Cotton in Hopei Province* (Peiping, 1929); Yeh Ch'ien-chi, "Production, Transport, and Marketing of Hsi-ho Cotton," in *Chung-kuo ching chi yen chiu*, ed. Fang Hsien-t'ing (Changsha, 1938); Ch'u Yü-ju, "Survey Report on the Yen-fu Cotton District [in North Kiangsu]," *Nung hang yüeh k'an* 1, no. 4 (1934): 35–42; *Mien?*; and Yoshida Kōichi, "Cotton Marketing in One Locality in China During the First Half of the Twentieth Century," *Shirin* 60, no. 2 (1977).

135. In Kiangsu, pawnshops provided warehouses in which farmers could store cotton and other crops which became security against loans; growers who anticipated rapid price increases could use these facilities to avoid the need to sell at low harvest-time prices ("Cotton Production at Taitsang, Kiangsu," *Chinese Economic Bulletin* 10, no. 325 [May 14, 1927], 256).

136. Chu and Chin, *Marketing of Cotton*, 20–21.

137. Huang, *Peasant Economy*, 72 and Chu and Chin, *Marketing of Cotton*, 20.

of some 15,000 farms in 1929–33 found that 15.8 percent or nearly one-sixth of farm households earned income as "merchants." [138] Even in a remote Yunnan village, Fei and Chang found villagers selling their own rice in dear markets and buying cheaper rice elsewhere for home consumption. [139]

Successful market activity requires access to commercial information. The presence of large numbers of buyers and sellers even at the village level ensured a considerable flow of information through personal communication. The growth of transport and communication facilities, to be discussed in Chapter 4, added to the flow of market information, especially in communities whose members participated in interregional trade or migration. In addition, widespread basic literacy helped ordinary Chinese, including farmers, to inform themselves about matters affecting their economic welfare. J. L. Buck found that in the 1930s, "45 percent of all males over seven years of age had received some schooling (an average of four years) and 30 percent were literate." [140] Evelyn Rawski describes the wide dispersion of written materials among China's populace, including farm households, and shows that on average, each household included one person who had received some formal education, however limited. [141]

Farmers used their education to acquire useful information. A diplomatic report lists detailed breakdowns of production costs per crop *mou* in Tsinan (Shantung) for 1924, noting that the figures were "compiled by the Pu Yi Sugar factory to show the cost and profits of sugar beet cultivation." [142] The Pu Yi firm's proprietors evidently believed that publishing detailed cost and profit data was a useful method of convincing local tenant farmers (the figures include rent but not taxes) to grow sugar beets rather than grain or vegetables. American tobacco specialists working for the British-American Tobacco Company (BAT) were surprised to find that Chinese farmers mastered new techniques "even quicker than the

138. Buck, *Statistics*, 309.
139. Hsiao-tung Fei and Chih-i Chang, *Earthbound China: A Study of Rural Economy in Yunnan* (Reprint, Chicago, 1975), 152.
140. Cited in Dwight H. Perkins, "Introduction," in *China's Modern Economy in Historical Perspective*, ed. Dwight H. Perkins (Stanford, 1975), 4.
141. Evelyn S. Rawski, *Education and Popular Literacy in Ch'ing China* (Ann Arbor, 1979).
142. U.S. Department of State, *Internal Affairs*, 893.61/29.

average farmer at home." When the Chinese-owned Nanyang Brothers Company challenged BAT's dominance of China's tobacco industry, "they distributed American seed, lent fertilizer, *published and circulated a manual* on the techniques of growing bright tobacco, and installed re-drying machinery."[143]

The written word enabled American scientists at Canton's Lingnan University to overcome initial opposition to the introduction of inspected (disease-free) eggs into the Kwangtung silk industry:[144]

At first it was necessary to give the inspected eggs to farmers. . . . Finally . . . the sale of a lot of egg sheets . . . which produced . . . unusually strong worms and cocoons broke down the opposition and men who had formerly opposed the work put themselves on record *in the village newspapers* urging people to buy Canton Christian College silk worm egg sheets. Since then, the demand has been so great that it has been impossible to meet it, and men have come from the remotest corners of the silk district begging the college to sell on their markets.

A final illustration of literacy among villagers comes from accounts of famine relief efforts during the drought of 1920–21 in North China. After identifying families eligible for food distribution, relief agencies at the county seat[145]

write a poster which the [village] chief takes back [to the village] with him. This poster tells who is to receive [grain] tickets and the date of grain distribution. The chief is also given a sheet of regulations to post with the list.

The headman is told to come to a certain place in a day or so for his tickets. The day before he receives them a notice is posted on the main street under the seal of the Relief Committee. This notice tells who has been chosen [to receive grain tickets]. This serves as a check upon the headman so that he is forced to distribute tickets as they have been written,

evidently because villagers could be expected to read simple documents that affected their well-being.

Peasants displayed sophistication of another sort by avoiding

---

143. Sherman Cochran, *Big Business in China: Sino-Foreign Rivalry in the Cigarette Industry, 1890–1930* (Cambridge, 1980), 26, 75, with emphasis added.
144. C. W. Howard, *The Sericulture Industry of South China* (Canton, 1923), 30–31, with emphasis added.
145. *North China Famine*, 125, 129

markets in which ignorance might expose them to great risk. A survey of Shansi province during the 1930s reports that paper money was not accepted beyond the immediate hinterland of the leading commercial centers.[146] This negative illustration underscores a significant point: with important exceptions (land rental, casual employment, personal credit), participation in the marketplace was most common among households best equipped to hold their own against the wiles of merchants, brokers, and other intermediaries.

Mobility—of resources, people, and ideas—is another essential component of a competitive economy that was often present in prewar China. The Chinese enjoyed substantial freedom of personal movement. There was no system of internal passports as in Tokugawa Japan. Permanent or temporary migration and military service exposed local youths to new communities, activities, and ideas and generated return flows of funds and information to their native places. New roads and railways catered to the strong demand for civilian travel and carried increased flows of information as well as commodities both to and from local markets.

These new developments built upon the considerable mobility inherent in the economy of imperial China. In many regions, the participation of outsiders strengthened competitive forces in local markets for land, labor, and credit. Farmers often left their home villages in search of short-term employment or better land. Merchants tended to ply their trade away from their home base. Mobility also extended to humbler levels of society. Flotillas of small craft manned by millions of boatmen plied China's navigable waters in search of passengers, freight, and bargains. Wu Pao-san placed the number of traditional sailing vessels at 988,000 in 1933.[147] A Japanese study reported that the total probably surpassed one million vessels.[148] On the North River near Canton an observer noted that "there are boats passing all the time." At Shanghai, traffic was still heavier: "[A] traffic count in 1919 on Soochow Creek near its mouth . . . found a 24-hour average of 1858 cargo boats between 10 and 90 tons capacity and 807 freight sampans passing the point

146. *Shan-hsi k'ao ch'a pao kao shu* (Shanghai, 1936), 307.
147. Wu Pao-san, *Chung-kuo kuo min so te, 1933 nien* (Shanghai, 1947), 2:181.
148. *Shina no kōun* (Tokyo, 1944), 52.

of count."[149] Liu and Yeh estimate that traditional transport occupied nearly eleven million persons in 1933.[150]

The abundant evidence of numerous merchants engaged in vigorous competition, the easy transfer of commercial capital from region to region and trade to trade, the widespread basic literacy and personal mobility even at the village level, and the extensive circulation of economic information within the peasant world lends strong support to the view that markets in China's prewar economy tended to be highly competitive.

But competition was not universal. There were regions in which landlords imposed conditions of partial servitude on tenants. Monopoly or monopsony power may have existed in some important markets. In localities with dense marketing networks, cheap transport, and multiple employment opportunities, grasping merchants, oppressive landlords, and harsh employers will lose their customers, tenants, and workers. This fundamental correlation between competition and choice points to a spatial resolution of the conflict between writers who emphasize competition and those who focus on the noncompetitive aspects of Chinese markets. Skinner's system of core and periphery provides an obvious point of departure for dividing China into regions of many and few economic alternatives.[151]

Core areas have well-developed networks of traditional transport, communication, and marketing. High yields from well-watered bottom lands and the advanced development of handicrafts, industrial crops, and sideline occupations enable core residents to earn relatively high incomes. They are both well-educated and commercially experienced. They use and understand paper money.

149. Swisher, *Canton in Revolution*, 27 and Rhoads Murphey, *Shanghai: Key to Modern China* (Cambridge, 1953), 91.
150. Liu and Yeh, *Economy of the Chinese Mainland*, 69.
151. The concept of regional cores and peripheries is widely used in studies of regional economics; see Harry W. Richardson, *Regional Economics* (Urbana, 1978), 50ff. Skinner presents his framework, which divides China into several macroregions, each of which is separated into a core and a periphery and further split into finer subdivisions, in "Cities and the Hierarchy of Local Systems," in *The City in Late Imperial China*, ed. G. William Skinner (Stanford, 1977). Barbara N. Sands and Ramon H. Myers, "The Spatial Approach to Chinese History: A Test," *Journal of Asian Studies* 45, no. 4 (1986) report empirical tests that fail to confirm the distinctions between core and periphery hypothesized by Skinner.

Their commercial and bureaucratic sophistication (for example, the "wily" Shanghainese) are feared and respected. These traits are shared by peasants as well as elites. All classes in rich regions enjoy incomes far above the national norm; surely their educational and commercial skills are equally distinctive.

If potential victims of exploitation among the core populace are able to sustain their own interests in the marketplace, potential exploiters are often too busy enlarging the scope of their business operations to devote great attention to rent gouging, usurious lending, short-weighting in trade, cornering local markets, or other avenues of market power that offer petty and ineffectual methods of raising profits in a flourishing economy. It is in the commercially oriented core regions that landlords become so preoccupied with urban business that they hire bursaries to collect rents and, in the process, find their rental income eroded by management fees, rent delinquency, and inflation.[152]

This is not to deny the presence of shady individuals and commercial fraud in core regions. What is asserted, however, is that the multifaceted core economy presents broad productive and commercial opportunities that induce the typical gentry-merchant-landlord-businessman-entrepreneur to direct his effort toward earning an income in return for service rendered rather than from sharp practice, a tendency further encouraged by the relative sophistication of both peasantry and city dwellers. The following description of Kiangnan silk growers illustrates the commercial and political skills of farmers in core regions:[153]

The farmers in particular were difficult to handle. They were not only mercenary but also adept at bargaining and very insolent. If they were forced to sell cocoons unprofitably, they would abuse the buyers and . . . attack them or set fire to their houses. When the price of cocoons was not satisfactory, they arbitrarily reduced the supply . . . [and] hoarded the goods until better prices could be obtained.

In the isolated and poor areas that Skinner identifies as peripheries, limited economic opportunities, low incomes, and low levels

152. Evelyn S. Rawski, *Agricultural Change and the Peasant Economy of South China* (Cambridge, 1972), 144–46.
153. Tomoo Suzuki, "The Shanghai Silk-Reeling Industry During the Period of the 1911 Revolution," in *The 1911 Revolution in China: Interpretive Essays*, ed. Shinkichi Etō and Harold Z. Schiffrin (Tokyo, 1984), 54.

of education and commercial experience among the farm populace fostered a climate in which monopoly, monopsony, and the attendant abuses might flourish. In northern Kiangsu, for example, [154]

there is a much thicker atmosphere of pre-capitalism. In the northernmost districts of the province, those landlords owning 10,000 to 20,000 mou each usually live in mud castles with armed guards, and their tenants are scattered in small villages within a two-mile radius, the castle acting as a trading centre for the whole community. Some of these big landlords maintain a rather large armed force, with 30 to 50 riflemen in addition to those armed with old-fashioned weapons.

In this zero-sum situation, the landlord prospers only by wringing a larger share of the meager local output from the farmers in the form of rent, profit, or interest. In a stagnant economy, exploitation rather than productivity offers the key to wealth.

If this distinction between competitive core markets and less competitive marketing in peripheral areas is accepted, the conclusion that most marketing occurred under substantially competitive conditions follows automatically from the undeniable concentration of all forms of commerce in core areas, where large numbers of merchants, easy transfer of resources between industries and localities, and ready access to commercial information produced market conditions closely akin to atomistic competition.

The Nature of China's Prewar Economy

This survey has emphasized the importance of domestic, private, civilian, and competitive elements in China's prewar economy. The unusual privileges available to foreign enterprise did not prevent Chinese business from dominating most sectors of the economy. Private interests outweighed government economic influence not because governments had no interest in economic control, but because officials lacked the resources to implement effective economic policies. Fiscal weakness curtailed the scale, scope, and duration of military activity. Despite the perpetual shortage of funds, China's militarists often disrupted normal economic activity and heightened the risk factor attached to long-term investments. For the most part, however, farmers, traders, and other civilian pro-

154. Quoted in Ash, *Land Tenure*, 10.

ducers succeeded in coping with the consequences of periodic military eruptions. Even in industries and regions dependent on railways, the leading victim of military struggles, there is evidence of considerable, albeit irregular, growth. Energetic price competition permeated the economy, especially in what Skinner terms the regional core areas.

This focus on competitive private enterprise managed by civilian Chinese entrepreneurs does not exclude influences from other sources that sometimes stimulated and, at other times, obstructed economic expansion. Foreign trade and investment, the policy actions of central and local governments, and the activities of military leaders and their armed forces all contributed to shaping the nature and evolution of economic activity in prewar China.

The foregoing survey leads to the conclusion that, despite these special features, the structure and development of China's prewar economy are best understood in terms of the analytic categories regularly applied to the study of economic growth and stagnation in other nations and time periods. The task of the remaining chapters is to apply these analytic categories to China's prewar economy. I begin with chapters focusing on manufacturing, banking, and transport, sectors which experienced major innovation during the early decades of the present century.

Chapter Two

Manufacturing

This chapter begins a survey of major developments in the modern sector of China's prewar economy by focusing on the growth of manufacturing. Although the discussion emphasizes the rapid pace of prewar industrial growth, it is essential to recognize from the outset that manufacturing remained small relative to the economy as a whole. Liu and Yeh find that factories, defined as manufacturing establishments of all sizes using mechanical power, contributed only 2.2 percent of net domestic product (NDP) in 1933.[1] Yet, as Rostow and many others have argued, the size and significance of new sectors need not coincide. Rosovsky sees Japan's transition to modern economic growth as complete by the late 1880s, when the share of mechanized operations in the national economy was probably no larger than in China during the 1930s.[2] Consideration of

1. Ta-chung Liu and Kung-chia Yeh, *The Economy of the Chinese Mainland: National Income and Economic Development, 1933–1959* (Princeton, 1965), 66, 430. This figure is based on 1933 prices. Calculations in terms of 1952 prices show factories contributing 5.5 percent of NDP for 1933 (ibid.), but these prices artificially inflate the relative value of industrial goods. The Manchurian portion of the 1933 manufacturing total records output for enterprises using mechanical power and employing five or more workers.
2. Henry Rosovsky, "Japan's Transition to Modern Economic Growth," in *Economic Growth in Two Systems*, ed. Henry Rosovsky (New York, 1966). The share of mining and manufacturing in Japanese NDP was 10.9 percent in 1885 and 11.2 percent in 1890, but much of this came from mining and handicrafts, the latter producing twice as much as "factories" in 1890. Furthermore, the definition of factories as industrial establishments with more than five workers no doubt included some unmechanized craft operations. Japanese data are from Kazushi Ohkawa, "Production Structure," in *Patterns of Japanese Economic Development*, ed. Kazushi Ohkawa and Miyohei Shinohara (New Haven, 1979), 37 and appendix table A10.

the effect of modern-sector growth in prewar China must therefore go beyond mere size and examine the interaction of developments in manufacturing with other sectors of the economy. Following a survey that delineates the dimensions of prewar factory industry, case studies of cotton textiles and matches illustrate in further detail the immediate characteristics and longer-term consequences of prewar industrialization.

Sources of Industrial Entrepreneurship

The development of factory industry rested in the hands of three groups of entrepreneurs: foreign businessmen, government officials, and the Chinese mercantile community. Foreign merchants, backed by the imperial policies of their home governments, were the first to appreciate China's industrial potential. Foreigners initially saw China as a market for imported manufactures. On gaining familiarity with local conditions, they began to recognize that domestic labor and materials could provide a foundation for local factory production.

Foreign-owned industry appeared decades before the Treaty of Shimonoseki (1895) formally permitted expatriates to construct and operate factories in China's treaty ports. Records assembled by Chinese historians show that dozens of factories, most in British or American hands and located at Shanghai, appeared between 1843 and 1895. Ship repair and the processing of wheat, oilseeds, sugar, tea, cotton, silkworm cocoons, and other farm produce were the most common lines of business, but foreign firms also turned out soap, matches, cosmetics, books, cement, tiles, paper, medicines, acids, liquor, rope, ice, and precious metals before the signing of the 1895 treaty.[3] The treaty stimulated a considerable expansion of foreign industrial enterprise, initially in cotton textiles and cigarettes in China proper and later in metallurgy, engineering, and soybean processing in Manchuria.

Foreign factories offered both a stimulus and an obstacle to the development of Chinese enterprise. Many of China's early industrialists benefited from working in or dealing with foreign establishments in China or Southeast Asia. Contact with foreign business

3. Ch'en Chen, Yao Lo, and Feng Hsien-chih, comps., *Chung-kuo chin tai kung yeh shih tzu liao*, Collection 2 (Peking, 1958), 19–23, 273–74.

exposed potential entrepreneurs to new products and technologies; it also revealed the strengths and weaknesses of foreign firms, knowledge which was of growing value as the relations between foreign and native industry expanded to encompass rivalry as well as partnership. Close observation of foreign firms equipped ambitious Chinese with concrete price and cost targets for successful competition with foreign products. Since most foreign enterprises remained dependent on Chinese agents for market intelligence and business contacts, commercial relations with foreign business produced a steady accumulation of Chinese mercantile wealth that supported new ventures in manufacturing and other sectors.[4]

Modernizing officials within China's central and provincial governments provided a further boost to innovation in manufacturing. Official efforts focused on the textile industry, which was quickly identified as an avenue for import substitution and potential growth, and on strategic industries such as metallurgy, shipbuilding, and munitions. Historical studies of these ventures emphasize policy errors, cumbersome management, and peculation. These problems, however serious, were not unique to China. Englishmen built factories in bogs; Americans failed to insure mills against fire; Japanese constructed ironworks without considering the quality of local materials; nepotism and graft thrived in Japan and in the foreign treaty-port communities as well as on the Chinese side.[5]

Despite the blunders that bedevil all efforts to master radically new technologies, the outcome of officially sponsored industrializa-

4. The large literature on the "compradore" system, under which Chinese businessmen served as intermediaries between foreign enterprise and the domestic economy, can be approached through Negishi Tadashi, *Baiben seido no kenkyū* (Tokyo, 1948); Yen-p'ing Hao, *The Compradore in Nineteenth Century China* (Cambridge, 1970); and Nieh Pao-chang, *Chung-kuo mai pan tzu ch'an chieh chi ti fa sheng* (Peking, 1979).

5. Nathan Rosenberg, ed., *The American System of Manufactures* (Edinburgh, 1969), notes that the foundations of the famous Enfield Armory "were located on a peat bog" (p. 54). George S. Gibb, *The Saco-Lowell Shops: Textile Machinery Building in New England, 1813–1949* (Cambridge, 1950), 109, 162, gives examples of uninsured fire damage. M. Gardner Clark, *The Development of China's Steel Industry and Soviet Technical Aid* (Ithaca, 1973), 1–3, describes early technical problems at the Anshan ironworks. On Japanese corruption, see Morikawa Tetsurō, *Nihon gigokushi* (Tokyo, 1976). William T. Rowe, "Urban Society in Late Imperial China" (Ph.D. diss., Columbia University, 1980), chap. 4, contains several examples of financial malpractice by foreign businessmen in China.

tion projects appears modestly successful. State-supported textile ventures contributed to the genesis of what became a highly dynamic industry. The K'ai-luan coal mining and industrial complex is still among China's largest. The Han-yang ironworks began production several years ahead of Japan's Yawata plant. Official support of defense industries also attained positive results. By the end of the nineteenth century, the Shanghai and Tientsin arsenals could supply a broad range of ordnance, ammunition, and naval vessels.[6]

In the long run, however, the role of the Chinese government in industrialization remained small. By the 1930s, the public sector accounted for only 3 percent of total sales by large-scale Chinese firms outside Manchuria, most of which were concentrated in the repair works of the national railways, a small number of arsenals, and the engineering and cement industries. The 1932 survey of large Chinese-owned factories in China proper recorded only 66 government-operated plants of the 2,435 investigated and most of these were in the hands of provincial authorities.[7] The Nanking government prepared ambitious and detailed plans for the construction of state-owned factories in metallurgy, engineering, and other industries, but the outbreak of the Sino-Japanese War in 1937 disrupted implementation efforts.[8] Manchurian industrialization involved considerable participation of the Japanese state, which, through its controlling interest in the South Manchurian Railway Company, became a major investor in transport, metallurgy, engineering, and other activities. After 1932, the economy of Japanese-controlled Manchoukuo came increasingly under the influence of official planning and regulation. But with Manchuria contributing no more than one-seventh of total manufacturing output (Table 2.3), the situation in China proper, where state participation in industry remained small and fragmented, dominated the national scene.

6. Thomas L. Kennedy, *The Arms of Kiangnan* (Boulder, 1978).
7. Data on the number of government firms and their sales share are from the 1932 survey of firms using mechanical power and employing thirty or more workers reported in Liu Ta-chün, *Chung-kuo kung yeh tiao ch'a pao kao* (Shanghai, 1937), 2:33–64, 377–428 (excluding water works). Where separate data are not shown, output value for some state-run firms was derived by assuming them to be of the same size as other plants in the same branch and location.
8. William C. Kirby, *Germany and Republican China* (Stanford, 1984), chap. 7.

Dimensions of Prewar Industrialization

Even if, as the Japanese case suggests, the quantitative dimension does not exclusively delineate the significance of industrial growth, it is nonetheless important to assess the scale of China's prewar industrialization. In a detailed study based on a sample of fifteen commodities, John K. Chang finds that the average annual growth of industrial value added between 1912 and 1936 amounted to 9.4 percent, slightly higher than the growth rate of Japanese factory output during the same period.[9] Most of the commodities included in Chang's study, however, are the products of mining rather than manufacturing. Net value added for pig iron, steel, cotton yarn, cotton cloth, and cement, the five manufactured items incorporated into Chang's calculations, rose from 13.3 million yuan in 1912 to 190.3 million yuan in 1936 (both in 1933 prices), which indicates an average annual growth of 11.7 percent, well above Chang's overall result. Value added for these five commodities amounted to 169.3 million yuan in 1933 or 26 percent of the estimated factory total for that year.[10] Any conclusion about long-term trends in manufacturing, then, depends on the performance of the sectors not covered in Chang's analysis, which contributed nearly three-quarters of the 1933 output total.

The growth rate of manufacturing output is explored in Appendix A, which uses data on industries accounting for about four-fifths of 1933 manufacturing output to derive an average growth rate for the period 1912–36. If sectoral growth rates are combined using 1933 value-added weights, the annual growth rate, based on 1933 prices, is 8.1 percent. It thus appears that Chang's small sample of manufactures, with its annual growth rate of 11.7 percent, may indeed overstate overall factory performance between 1912 and 1936. Even so, these results confirm Chang's view of manufacturing as a dynamic sector in China's prewar economy.

The international comparison of industrial growth rates shown in Table 2.1 emphasizes the speed of Chinese development, which

9. John K. Chang, *Industrial Development in Pre-Communist China* (Chicago, 1969), 71.
10. Value added for five commodities is calculated from data in Chang, *Industrial Development*, 117–29. Net value added for factories in 1933 is taken from Liu and Yeh, *Economy of the Chinese Mainland*, 66.

Manufacturing

Table 2.1
Industrial Growth Rates for Selected Nations, 1912-36

Sector	Growth Rate (percentage)
A. Industry (mining and manufacturing)	
China	9.4
Japan	6.6
U.K.	4.4
Russia/USSR	7.9
B. Factory Production	
China	8.1
Japan	8.8[a]
U.S.A.	2.8[b]

[a]Covers the period 1914-37.

[b]Figure for 1912 is the arithmetic average of data for 1909 and 1914; the figure for 1936 is the arithmetic average of the data for 1935 and 1937.

Sources: China: Appendix A and Chang, Industrial Development, 71. Japan: The figure for mining and manufacturing is from Shinohara Miyohei, Kôkôgyô (Tokyo, 1972), 147, 265; the figure for factory output at 1934-36 prices) is from Kazushi Ohkawa and Henry Rosovsky, Japanese Economic Growth (Stanford, 1973), 81. U. K. and USSR: calculated from B. R. Mitchell, European Historical Statistics, 1750-1970 (abridged edition, New York, 1978), 181. U.S.A.: The Statistical History of the United States from Colonial Times to the Present (Stamford, 1965), 414.

approaches or surpasses the achievements of other advanced and industrializing economies, including Japan and the USSR. Chinese industrial growth was broadly based, encompassing many trades (Appendix A). Manufacturing was not an enclave sector catering to external markets or controlled by foreign interests. Nearly three-fourths of industrial activity rested in the hands of private Chinese entrepreneurs (Table 2.3), most of whom conducted related businesses in other sectors of the economy. The most successful industries, including cotton textiles, cigarettes, matches, and rubber goods, served the needs of the domestic market.

The present estimate of the manufacturing growth between 1912 and 1936 is based on output data for the initial and terminal years only. The procedure followed in Appendix A produces an average growth rate for the entire period, but cannot illuminate the pace of growth during the intervening years. Despite the absence of systematic data, there is considerable evidence that the growth of manufacturing, though by no means constant over time, proceeded steadily throughout the prewar decades. Chang's data, which, as noted above, include only five products, show consistently rapid growth interrupted only by pauses in 1921–22, when value added in ferrous metals and cotton textiles declined, and 1933–36, when cotton textiles stagnated.[11] In fact, 1920–22, an interlude of declining output for cotton yarn, flour, pig iron, and perhaps cigarettes, appears to represent the only instance of a contraction in output during the period 1912–36.[12] In other years, the waning fortunes of some industries were counterbalanced by the rise of others. The stagnation of flour production and declining silk output in the late 1920s, for example, coincided with the buoyant expansion of cotton cloth, rubber, matches, and a number of smaller industries.

Despite rapid growth, China's nascent industries never attained a substantial share of national economic activity. This can be seen from Table 2.2, which compares China with Japan, a country where industry did come to occupy a considerable position in prewar economic aggregates. The comparison is a crude one because the Japanese figures, especially those labeled A in Table 2.2, include large components of handicraft output and employment whereas the Chinese figures are based on surveys of factory industry. The labor productivity data calculated in terms of gross output (or sales; Column 5) are of particular interest. They suggest that significant technological differences between Japanese and Chinese factories may have begun to appear only in the late 1920s. In both countries, factory industry raised labor productivity above the levels prevailing in other sectors (Column 6); superior relative labor productivity in China arises not because of the greater achievements of Chinese factories, but because productivity was increasing more rapidly outside the factory sector in Japan than in China. Columns 2 and 4, which relate factory industry to other sectors of

11. Chang, *Industrial Development*, 78–79.
12. Data for cotton yarn and pig iron are from ibid., 117 and 119; for flour, see *Chiu Chung-kuo chi chih mien fen kung yeh t'ung chi tzu liao* (Peking, 1966), 53. Sherman Cochran, *Big Business in China: Sino-Foreign Rivalry in the Cigarette Industry, 1890–1930* (Cambridge, 1980), 229, shows a slight drop in employment and in the number of machines operated by Chinese cigarette plants for 1921–22.

Table 2.2
Growth of the Factory Sector in China and Japan, 1896-1936
(Chinese yuan, 1933 prices)

Year	Factory Output GVIO (million) (1)	GDP Share (%) (2)	Factory Employment (1000s) (3)	Share (%) (4)	Factory Labor Productivity In Yuan (5)	Relative (National=100)[a] (6)
China[b]						
1916	704	0.8	...	...	...	...
1933	2646	2.1	1076	0.4	2459	517
Japan[c]						
1896 A	1810	8.8	...	...	...	...
1906 A	2336	11.0	2709	10.8	862	103
1916 A	4500	16.5	3668	13.8	1227	123
1919 A	5896	15.8	4285	15.8	1373	97
1919 B	3758	10.1	2249	8.3	1671	118
1926 A	7423	17.9	4906	17.2	1513	115
1926 B	5475	13.2	2577	9.1	2125	157
1936 A	15307	25.9	5588	17.7	2739	138
1936 B	12552	21.2	3758	11.9	3340	166

[a]The index of value added per worker in manufacturing, taking GDP per gainfully occupied worker for the same year as 100.

[b]China: The figures for 1933 are taken or calculated from Liu and Yeh, Economy of the Chinese Mainland, 66, 69, 428, 517. The figures for 1916 are derived from the 1933 data by applying estimated annual growth rates of 8.1 percent for factory output and 1.9 percent for total output (Table 6.11).

[c]Japan: Col. 1: The figures marked A are based on gross output totals in 1934-36 prices shown in Ohkawa and Shinohara, Patterns of Japanese Economic Development, table A21, converted to 1933 prices using the ratio of output in current and constant prices for 1933 in ibid, tables A19 and A21. Figures marked B are compiled from gross output totals in current prices from Shinohara, Kôkôgyô, table 48, omitting output from establishments with fewer than five workers; the value totals, mislabeled in the source, are in thousands of yen. The conversion to 1933 prices is based on implicit deflators for manufacturing shown in ibid., table 3. Conversion to Chinese yuan is based on the 1933 exchange rate shown in Liang-lin Hsiao, China's Foreign Trade Statistics, 1864-1949 (Cambridge, 1974), 192.

continued...

the economy, show that factory output and employment in China during the 1930s failed to attain the relative shares reached by Japanese industry at the end of the Russo-Japanese War (1905). The differences are so large that this conclusion is not endangered by the possibility that even the Japanese B data, which exclude

Table 2.2, continued

Col. 2: The figures marked A are the share of mining and
manufacturing in GDP valued at 1934-36 prices multiplied by the
ratio of value added in manufacturing to value added in mining and
manufacturing, based on Ohkawa Kazushi, Takamatsu Nobukiyo, and
Yamamoto Yuzo, Kokumin shotoku (Tokyo, 1974), tables 11 and 25 (col.
7). The figures marked B are calculated by multiplying figures
marked A by the ratio of A to B output totals for each year.

Col. 3: The figures marked A are from Ohkawa and Shinohara,
Patterns of Japanese Economic Development, table A54. The figures
marked B are compiled from Shinohara, Kōkōgyō, table 48, omitting
establishments with fewer than five workers.

Col. 4: Based on employment data in Col. 3 and the national
total of gainfully occupied workers from Ohkawa and Shinohara,
Patterns of Japanese Economic Development, table A53.

Col. 5: calculated from Cols. 1 and 3.

Col. 6: The annual rates of value added are from Ohkawa,
Takamatsu, and Yamamoto, Kokumin shotoku, tables 11 and 17 (series
A); factory output in constant 1934-36 prices is based on the
sources underlying Col. 1. GDP per gainful worker in 1934-36 prices
is calculated from Ohkawa and Shinohara, Patterns of Japanese
Economic Development, Tables A9 and A53.

enterprises with fewer than five workers, contain a substantial
share of handicraft activity.

Chinese industrialization was primarily a regional phenomenon.
The data assembled in Table 2.3 show that Kiangsu province (including Shanghai) and the northeast or Manchurian region produced nearly two-thirds of China's 1933 industrial output. In these
regions, the share of output occupied by manufacturing did expand. Industry's contribution to Manchuria's regional output rose
during the late 1930s to 8 percent or, if small-scale manufacturing
is included, 12 percent of the total; a crude estimate places the
1933 share of factories in regional product for the area that G. W.
Skinner defines as the Lower Yangtze core (including Shanghai) at
10 percent, as opposed to the national figure of 2.2 percent.[13] The
impact of industrialization on economic structure in these regions
parallels the Japanese situation, but with a lag of ten or fifteen
years. The great gap between the two economies arises because
the population of Manchuria and Kiangsu, although larger than

13. Alexander Eckstein, Kang Chao, and John K. Chang, "The Economic Devel-
opment of Manchuria: The Rise of a Frontier Economy," *Journal of Economic
History* 34, no. 1 (1974):255 and Thomas G. Rawski, "The Economy of the
Lower Yangtze Region, 1850–1980," (Toronto, 1984), table 5.

Table 2.3
Distribution and Nationality of Manufacturing Output in 1933
(Million yuan)

Region	Chinese Firms	Foreign Firms	Total	Percentage Share of Total
China Proper	1771.4[a]	497.4[a]	2268.8	85.8
Shanghai	727.7[b]	323.3[c]	1051.0	39.7
Kiangsu	225.7[b]	5.2[d]	230.9	8.7
Other	818.0[e]	168.9[e]	986.9	37.3
Manchuria	154.8[f]	221.9[g]	376.7[a]	14.2
National Total	1926.2	719.3	2645.5	
Percentage Share	72.8	27.2		100.0

Note: Column totals may not check because of rounding error.

[a]Liu and Yeh, Economy of the Chinese Mainland, 426-28.

[b]Liu, Chung-kuo kung yeh, 3: 2, 11, 32-89.

[c]C. F. Remer, Foreign Investments in China (New York, 1968), 73, presents data showing that 64.4 percent of allocable foreign assets in China during 1933 were located in Shanghai. Onoe Etsuzô, Chûgoku no sangyô ritchi ni kansuru kenkyû (Tokyo, 1971), 301, shows that 65.9 percent of foreign-owned cotton spindles were situated in Shanghai. I assume that Shanghai accounted for 65 percent of foreign-controlled manufacturing output in China proper in 1933.

[d]Yen Hsüeh-hsi, Chiang-su chin hsien tai ching chi shih wen chi (Nanking, 1983), 22, estimates that 2.3 percent of Kiangsu's industrial capital was foreign-owned in 1932; foreign firms are assumed to have produced 2.3 percent of provincial industrial output.

[e]Residual.

[f]The figure shown is the 1933 output total for Manchuria multiplied by the share of 1934 manufacturing output (41.4 percent) produced by "Chinese" and "Manchurian" firms as given in Manshû kôjô tôkei B, 1934 (Dairen, 1937), 60, 396.

[g]The figure shown is the 1933 output total for Manchuria multiplied by the share of 1934 manufacturing output (58.9 percent) produced by "Japanese" and "other" (including foreign and jointly owned) firms given in ibid.

the Japanese total, amounted to only one-seventh of China's population.

Even though prewar industrialization failed to generate major changes in China's overall economic structure, certain industries attained a substantial scale of operation. This is shown in Table 2.4, which compares physical output of major industrial products for

Table 2.4
Industrial Output Indicators for China and Japan, 1933

| Product[a] | Physical Production | | |
	China (A)	Japan (B)	Chinese Production as Percentage of Japanese
Cotton yarn	0.449	0.568	79 %
Cotton cloth	1036	1639	63
Wheat flour	1.66	1.05	158
Pig iron	0.5	1.4	36
Steel	0.03	3.2	1
Cement	0.7	4.2	19
Sulfuric acid	0.05	1.6	3

[a]The data for cotton cloth are in millions of yards; other output figures are in millions of tons.

Sources: China: cotton yarn output from modern mills is 2.358 million bales of 420 pounds each and factory cloth output is 25.260 million bolts of 41 yards each (Kang Chao, The Development of Cotton Textile Production in China [Cambridge, 1977], 229, 308, 312, 315). The output of wheat flour is 74.8 million sacks of 22.23 kilograms (Wu Pao-san, Chung-kuo kuo min so te, 1933 nien [Shanghai, 1947], 2: 128). For pig iron, steel and cement, see Chang, Industrial Development, 117, 119. The output of sulfuric acid in China proper may have amounted to ten thousand tons (Thomas G. Rawski, China's Transition to Industrialism: Producer Goods and Economic Development in the Twentieth Century [Ann Arbor, 1980], 19); for Manchuria, production in 1934 was 38,258 tons (Manshû kôjô tôkei B, 1934, 16).

Japan: The data for cotton yarn and cement are from Hundred-Year Statistics of the Japanese Economy (Tokyo, 1966), 100, 104. For cotton cloth, see Fujino Shôzaburô, Fujino Shirô, and Ono Akira, Sen'igyô (Tokyo, 1979), 240. For flour and sulfuric acid see Shinohara, Kôgyô, 176, 214. For pig iron and steel, see G. C. Allen, "The Heavy Industries," in The Industrialization of Japan and Manchukuo, 1930-1940, ed. E. B. Schumpeter (New York, 1940), 597.

China and Japan in 1933, by which time Japan had become a major force in world markets for industrial consumer goods, especially cotton textiles. In these consumer industries, the scale of Chinese manufacturing was roughly comparable to Japan's. Chinese factory production of cotton textiles amounted to about three-fourths of the Japanese total. This represented a major achievement. China's 1933 cotton consumption, most of which went to the factory sector, matched the combined total for Great Britain and Germany.[14] Aside from Japan, only the United States and India surpassed the scale of Chinese cotton textile production. The output of China's flour mills exceeded Japanese results by a wide margin. In producer industries, however, the data in Table 2.4 show Chinese output lagging far behind Japan's. Whatever their significance for local development or as preparation for future growth, the prewar achievements of Chinese producers in metallurgy, chemicals, and other basic industries failed to attain significant quantitative dimensions in international terms.

In assessing the impact of industrialization, it is essential to consider the possibility that factory products merely replaced handicraft goods and may have contributed very little to overall output growth. Factory and homespun yarn, manufactured and handloom cloth, cigarettes and loose tobacco, kerosene and vegetable oil, industrial and home-ground flour, or iron and wooden looms are examples of commodity pairs in which expanded factory output could and often did directly replace handicraft products. Despite such rivalry, most craft occupations survived and many prospered along with the rapid expansion of factory activity. The idea that growing sales of manufactures, however detrimental to the interests of particular groups of craftsmen, destroyed large portions of China's handicraft sector is not substantiated by available evidence.

K. C. Yeh's rough estimates indicate that handicraft production increased by 13 percent between 1914/18 and 1931/36 and showed no significant decline during 1931–36, both periods of rapid growth in manufacturing.[15] Trends in handicraft output are notoriously difficult to determine because of the paucity of systematic data, the variety of trades, and the large numbers of widely dispersed producers, but information on individual occupations, including some that faced significant factory competition, tends to confirm Yeh's view of handicrafts as an expanding sector of China's prewar economy. Wu Ch'eng-ming cites unpublished research by a Chinese scholar showing that even though seven of thirty-two

14. The Chinese total is from Table 2.10 below. The European data are from B. R. Mitchell, *European Historical Statistics, 1750–1970* (New York, 1978), 254–55.
15. K. C. Yeh, "China's National Income 1931–36," in *Modern Chinese Economic History*, ed. Chi-ming Hou and Tzong-shian Yu (Taipei, 1979), 97, 126.

traditional handicraft trades declined and ten stagnated after the
Opium War of 1840–42, fifteen trades expanded and moved toward machine production and eleven others were newly established during the late nineteenth and early twentieth centuries.[16]
My own compilation (Table 2.10) shows that despite periods of decline in the late nineteenth century and again in the late 1920s,
value added in the handicraft segment of cotton spinning and weaving, the largest craft occupation, increased considerably between
1901/10 and 1934/36. Sherman Cochran's study of the tobacco industry confirms[17]

the staying power of China's traditional handicraft industries. . . . The
gross value of hand-made tobacco products . . . rose from Y[uan] 38.5
million in 1914 to Y115.6 million in 1916; declined to about Y70 million
per year in 1917–18; fell to less than Y30 million per year in 1919–20;
but then recovered and surpassed previous levels, reaching between
Y128.9 and Y171.8 million by 1933.

China's flour mills had the capacity to process 3.1 million tons of
wheat during 1931–34, but because estimated wheat output rose
by 3.3 million tons between 1914/18 and 1931/37 the growth of
industrial milling could hardly have undercut handicraft processing, especially as imported wheat filled part of the mills' raw
material needs.[18]

Industrialization meant increased competition for some craftsmen, but the same transport networks that brought industrial
products to Chinese villages offered access to potential markets
that enabled some craft occupations to raise production for both
home and foreign consumption. Handloom cotton fabrics, knitwear, candles, soap, umbrellas, lace, embroidery, silks, rattan, and
bamboo goods were among the craft products that penetrated new
markets during the prewar decades. These expanding craft occupations often made use of factory-built machinery, tools, or materials. Other crafts appeared in response to the demands of growing

16. Wu Ch'eng-ming, *Chung-kuo tzu pen chu i yü kuo nei shih ch'ang* (Peking,
1985), 105.
17. Cochran, *Big Business*, 34 ("Y" indicates Chinese yuan).
18. Milling capacity and wheat imports are from *Chiu Chung-kuo mien fen*, 115,
135. Wheat output is from Dwight H. Perkins, *Agricultural Development in
China: 1368–1968* (Chicago, 1969), 276.

factory production, as when match factories employed household craftsmen to assemble matchboxes.[19] Hershatter observes that[20]

Manufacturing did not develop in a neat historical progression from household to workshop to modern mill. Instead, all three types of production emerged simultaneously, with each . . . sometimes helping to spur the other's growth. . . . Artisanal industries frequently developed in conjunction with the more "modern" factory sector. . . . [In many cases] it was the new [urban] economic activity . . . that created conditions for the development of handicraft industry.

In the absence of a comprehensive overview, these findings point to the tentative conclusion that China's growing output of manufactures did not lead to a broad decline of handicraft activity. Certain craft occupations in some localities suffered reverses because of factory competition, but available evidence confirms the view, implicit in Yeh's output estimates, that the combined market for factory and handicraft products grew with sufficient vigor to prevent a decline in overall demand for handicraft products.

If factory production contributed to increasing output rather than replacing craft activity, one may conclude that the scale of manufacturing growth in prewar China was indeed substantial. With annual real output growth reaching approximately 8 percent in the quarter-century preceding the outbreak of the Pacific War, and in all probability during the three decades preceding this period as well, descriptions of prewar Chinese industry as "stagnant" and "non-developing" are far removed from reality.[21]

Patterns of Dispersion, Structure, and Ownership

Industrial activity did not spread evenly across the Chinese landscape, but clustered in certain regions, notably Kiangsu province

19. David Faure, "The Rural Economy of Kiangsu Province, 1870–1911," *Journal of the Institute of Chinese Studies of the Chinese University of Hong Kong* 9, no. 2 (1978):413; Yokoyama Suguru, "Establishment of Match Manufacturing in China," *Hiroshima daigaku bungakubu kiyō* 25, no. 1 (1965):278.
20. Gail Hershatter, *The Workers of Tianjin, 1900–1949* (Stanford, 1986), 42, 47.
21. Shima Ichirō, *Chūgoku minzoku kōgyō no tenkai* (Tokyo, 1978), 41, states that his book seeks "to elucidate the reasons for stagnation and non-development of private industry" in prewar China.

(including Shanghai) and southeastern Manchuria, which together contributed nearly two-thirds of China's total manufacturing output in 1933 (Table 2.3). Such regional concentration of industry is by no means unique. In the United States, for example, the share of Massachusetts, New York, and Pennsylvania in national manufacturing output amounted to 52 percent in 1860 and 43 percent in 1900; adding Illinois and Ohio raises the total to 60 percent in both years.[22]

What economic forces determine the location of factories? Access to materials, product markets, and ancillary services are among the most important influences on location decisions. Shanghai's unique advantage in each of these areas made the great metropolis a natural industrial leader. Its location at the mouth of the Yangtze River offers access to a wide range of industrial materials and to vast markets for its products. As Murphey notes, "Shanghai's trade hinterland is the largest in the world. Nowhere else does a population or area of this size depend for its commercial intercourse on one master river system and one primate city."[23] Craig Dietrich's investigation of the sixteenth-century market for cotton textiles shows that Sung-chiang prefecture, in which Shanghai was located, commanded a sales potential well above that of whole provinces in other parts of China.[24] The Yangtze flows through the provinces of Kiangsu, Anhwei, Hupeh, and Szechwan; major tributaries reach into Kiangsi, Hunan, and Shensi as well. The combined 1850 population of these provinces exceeded 200 million persons, of whom a large percentage lived in regions linked to the Lower Yangtze area by well-traveled water routes. Coastal shipping provided easy access to another half dozen provinces populated by a further 100 million potential customers and suppliers.[25]

Chinese merchants recognized the locational advantages of the Lower Yangtze region centuries before the arrival of Western traders. It was the lure of access to existing trade routes and commodity flows that encouraged foreign interests to demand the

22. Albert W. Niemi, Jr., *State and Regional Patterns in American Manufacturing, 1860–1900* (Westport, 1974), 45–51.
23. Rhoads Murphey, *Shanghai: Key to Modern China* (Cambridge, 1953), 55.
24. Craig Dietrich, "Cotton Manufacture and Trade in China (ca. 1500–1800)" (Ph.D. diss., University of Chicago, 1970), appendix 3.
25. Population totals are from Perkins, *Agricultural Development*, 212.

opening of Shanghai to foreign trade and residence in the 1840s and to foreign manufacturing a half-century later. Traditional trade along the Yangtze was large. Murphey notes that Shanghai was perhaps "one of the leading ports of the world" in 1832; the scale of commerce along the Yangtze was so great that, a century earlier, shipments of several tens of thousands of tons of rice "over distances above a thousand miles could be planned, executed and completed in a matter of weeks without putting an appreciable strain on the existing transport facilities of even such comparatively backward . . . places as Hunan and Szechwan."[26]

When foreign trade, formerly confined to Canton, spread to Amoy, Foochow, Ningpo, and Shanghai in the wake of the Opium War of 1840–42, Shanghai, with its superior access to domestic products and markets, quickly emerged as the leading center of China's international commerce.[27] Despite the depredations of the Taiping uprising (1851–65), which ravaged much of the Lower Yangtze area, Shanghai's foreign trade in 1867 amounted to two-thirds of China's reported foreign trade.[28]

The growth of foreign trade added to Shanghai's natural advantages as an industrial center. Rising international commerce created demands for new types of services whose presence further reduced the local cost of producing and selling industrial goods. When the Treaty of Shimonoseki (1895) opened the door to the expansion of foreign-owned factories, Shanghai's high wages and land values failed to deter foreign and Chinese investors from concentrating their efforts in the great metropolis, which boasted unrivaled access to materials, markets, financial services, and skilled labor. Sources assembled by Chinese researchers show that one-half of foreign and one-third of Chinese industrial enterprises established before World War I were located in Shanghai.[29] Shang-

26. Murphey, *Shanghai*, 58–59; Han-sheng Chuan and Richard A. Kraus, *Mid-Ch'ing Rice Markets and Trade: An Essay in Price History* (Cambridge, 1975), 59.
27. The rapid growth of customs revenue at Shanghai relative to other ports began immediately after the treaty settlement; see John K. Fairbank, *Trade and Diplomacy on the China Coast* (Stanford, 1953), 262.
28. Liang-lin Hsiao, *China's Foreign Trade Statistics, 1864–1949* (Cambridge, 1974), 22, 175.
29. For Chinese firms (apparently excluding government-owned plants) established between 1863 and 1911, see Ch'en Chen and Yao Lo, comps., *Chung-kuo chin tai kung yeh shih tzu liao*, Collection 1 (Peking, 1957), 38–53. For

hai's position in prewar China closely resembled New York's status in the nineteenth-century American economy.[30] In both cases, superior access to information and transport routes attracted business and industry to a dominant city, which enlarged its initial advantage as scale effects stimulated the proliferation of a unique variety of ancillary services in finance, insurance, communication, repair, storage, and the like. Concentration of resources in a single center also brought cost increases that eventually encouraged the spread of industry to other locations.

This process occurred in China as well as in the United States. Shanghai became famous for its high land prices. Wages were also high. Table 2.5, which contains 1933 wage data for manufacturing enterprises with thirty or more workers in China proper, shows that Shanghai wages were 10 percent above the overall average and 18 percent higher than the average for all other areas. The full extent of the regional wage gap is masked by the concentration of low-wage industries in Shanghai. Data for individual industries typically show much larger wage gaps. In the largest sector, cotton textiles, Shanghai wages were 23–32 percent above the national average and 44–59 percent above average wages elsewhere. Shanghai's high costs stimulated industrial expansion in nearby Wusih (which earned the sobriquet of "little Shanghai"), Ch'angchou, Nanking, Chen-chiang, Nan-t'ung, Soochow, and other urban centers within the Lower Yangtze area. These cities were (and remain) natural candidates for industrial investment because they share Shanghai's locational advantages and offer additional benefits in the form of relatively low wages and land costs. The long-term consequences of these spread effects, which correspond to the "neighborhood effects" flowing from the development of regional economic centers in the United States, included a process of regional economic transformation that continues into the 1980s,

---

firms established between 1864 and 1913 by nationals of Great Britain, the U.S., Japan, France, and Germany, see Ch'en, Yao, and Feng, *Chung-kuo chin tai kung yeh*, Collection 2, 19–30, 269–76, 422–28, 719–21, and 757–60.

30. The centrality of New York is an important theme of Allan R. Pred, *Urban Growth and the Circulation of Information: The United States System of Cities, 1790–1840* (Cambridge, 1973). Diane Lindstrom, *Economic Development in the Philadelphia Region, 1810–1850* (New York, 1978), 30, shows the diversion of foreign trade activity to New York.

Table 2.5
Regional Differences in Factory Wages, 1933
(yuan)

Sector	Annual Factory Wages in China Proper (yuan)			
	Average	Shanghai	Other	Shanghai as Percentage of Other Areas
Matches	123	234	110	213
Cotton yarn	166	204	142	144
Cotton cloth	110	145	91	159
Silk yarn	45	48	44	109
Silk cloth	243	291	179	162
Flour milling	225	260	208	125
Cigarettes	176	181	57	318
All industry	163	178	151	118

Source: Wage figures are calculated from data on 1933
wage bill and year-end employment given in tables 8 and 11
of Liu, Chung-kuo kung-yeh, 2:243-91 and 377-428. The
figures for water works and hydroelectric plants are
omitted.

when the "Yangtze delta region" is where "township and village-based rural industry has developed furthest and fastest."[31]

The extension of transport, communication, and banking facilities along with the demonstration effect provided by profitable operations in Shanghai encouraged manufacturing ventures in lesser urban centers throughout China. Not only Canton, Tientsin, Tsingtao, and other major seaports, but also interior cities like Wuhan, Peking, Changsha, Chungking, Kunming, and Sian experienced significant industrial development. Businessmen with interests in commerce, transport, and finance expanded their portfolios to include industrial ventures. In Chungking, for example, the Min-sheng Company, a joint-stock venture that had started as a shipping concern, soon expanded into textile dyeing, ship repair,

31. Quotation from Robert Delfs, "Lesson from Sunan," *Far Eastern Economic Review*, June 4, 1987, 78. See also Pred, *Urban Growth*, 246 and Rawski, "Economy of the Lower Yangtze Region."

coal mining, and machinery manufacture.[32] Elsewhere, local raw materials attracted would-be industrialists, as when cotton mills were established in Sian (Shensi) and in Honan to draw on local cotton supplies.[33] Mining centers also attracted manufacturing ventures to take advantage of modern transport facilities and, in the case of coal mines, cheap fuel. Carlson reports that the nineteenth-century expansion of the Kaiping coal mines near T'ang-shan (Hopei) "stimulated local industries," including "brick and lime kilns, pottery works, and distilleries," as well as "the revival of several industries which were languishing or extinct" because of the decline of native mining in the area.[34] Secondary industrial centers generated their own "neighborhood effects" in the same way as Shanghai, but on a much smaller scale.

In Manchuria, the development of railroads and ports opened the way to an industrialization process built upon the region's agricultural surplus, which supported a growing food processing industry. The region's mineral wealth stimulated the Japanese to develop China's first heavy industry complex, including the mining of coal, iron ore, and oil shale and the large-scale manufacture of iron, steel, industrial machinery, and transport equipment.

Economic motives propelled industrial growth in all regions. In China proper and in Manchuria's small consumer goods sector, the overwhelming share of private capital, both Chinese and foreign, ensured the primacy of the profit motive. Even Japan's industrial efforts in Manchuria, financed and directed by such semiofficial agencies as the South Manchurian Railway Company, combined financial with political objectives. Voluminous and detailed economic research conducted by Japanese organizations, particularly the South Manchurian Railway and the Tōa Dōbunkai, attest to the importance of efficiency and cost control among Japanese objectives. Japanese ventures in Manchuria "followed . . . the apparent pattern of comparative advantage"; they were expected to earn profits and usually did so.[35]

32. *Min-sheng shih yeh kung ssu shih i chou nien chi nien k'an* (Chungking, 1937).
33. "Cotton Cultivation in Shensi," *Chinese Economic Monthly* 3, no. 5 (1926): 200–201.
34. Ellsworth C. Carlson, *The Kaiping Mines, 1877–1912* (Cambridge, 1971), 27.
35. Edwin P. Reubens, "Opportunities, Governments and Economic Development in Manchuria, 1860–1940," in *The State and Economic Growth*, ed. Hugh G. J. Aitken (New York, 1959), 169.

Turning from regional dispersion to commodity structure, Table 2.6 surveys the sectoral composition of factory output in 1933, the only year for which a detailed analysis is possible. The data show that consumer manufactures predominated: almost three-fourths of gross output and two-thirds of value added came from food, beverages, tobacco, textiles, clothing, and footwear. Both supply and demand conditions contributed to this feature of China's industrial structure.

On the supply side, the importance of agriculture in overall commodity production ensured that processing of farm products was the main occupation of early generations of factories. With the exception of clay and monetary metals, supplies of inorganic materials were not available in sufficient quantities for industrial use. Mineral deposits remained undiscovered or, if known, awaited large transport investments to facilitate commercial development.

On the demand side, the low incomes of Chinese households left little room for new commodities in their budgets. Industrial goods aimed at a mass market could only succeed as substitutes for the simple items that dominated most consumer outlays, above all, food and clothing. Manufactures outside the narrow category of processed farm products found a market only if they could offer large improvements over traditional alternatives: matches, needles, iron looms, and kerosene, which replaced vegetable oil for lighting, were among the small number of widely distributed factory products that were not made from farm produce. Foreign as well as domestic markets demanded Chinese farm goods: prewar manufactured exports consisted almost exclusively of cottons, silks, soybean products, and other farm-based commodities.

If the structure of prewar manufacturing was linked with the predominantly agricultural character of the economy, the sectoral composition of prewar industry should resemble patterns observed in other economies with large farm sectors. This is verified in Table 2.6, which compares the 1933 structure of Chinese manufacturing with similar data for low-income countries in the late 1950s, the United States in 1880, and prewar Japan. Although the categories used to classify industries are not fully consistent, it is evident that China's prewar industrial structure closely paralleled that of other farm-based economies. The data for nine countries with 1958 per capita incomes below US$100 reveal a sectoral structure close to China's 1933 pattern except for the low share of chemicals in the

Table 2.6
Sectoral Composition of Manufacturing, 1933, With Comparative Data
(in percentages)

Sector	Total Output		Value Added		
	China 1933 (1)	Japan 1922/31 (2)	China 1933 (3)	LDCs 1958 (4)	U.S. 1880 (5)
Food-beverage-tobacco	34.2	25.5	24.2	34.8	28
Textiles	36.0	35.7	37.5	17.6	18
Clothing and Footwear	4.1		5.3	2.5	
Wood products	0.9	3.1	0.4	5.3	18
Paper and printing	3.7	2.4	5.2	5.0	3.5
Leather and rubber	3.2	...	3.0	3.5	12
Chemicals	4.7	11.0	7.3	12.8	3.5
Nonmetallic minerals	2.4	3.0	4.1	4.5	2
Basic metals	1.3	7.1	2.4	1.9	13
Metal products	7.0	8.9	8.5	9.5	
Other	2.4	3.4	2.2	2.6	2
Total	100.0	100.0	100.0	100.0	100.0

Note: Column totals may not check because of rounding error.

Sources: Cols. 1 and 3 are from Appendix B.

Col. 2: Miyohei Shinohara, "Manufacturing," in *Patterns of Japanese Economic Development*, 105.

Col. 4: Based on data for nine less developed countries with per capita incomes under US$100 shown in Simon Kuznets, *Modern Economic Growth: Rate, Structure, and Spread* (New Haven, 1966), 403.

Col. 5: Based on data in 1929 prices shown in ibid., 137.

Chinese figures and the reversed role of textiles and food process-
ing, the two largest industries, with the former predominating in
China and the latter in other low-income economies.[36] The United
States data for 1880 are even closer to the Chinese figures, with

36. Chinese gross domestic product for 1933 is estimated at 66.47 billion yuan
(1957 prices). With a population of roughly 500 million and an official 1957
yuan value of US$0.38, the value of 1933 per capita product at 1957 prices may
be crudely estimated at US$53 (based on Liu and Yeh, *Economy of the Chinese
Mainland*, xvi, 67, 171).

major differences limited to textiles, which occupy a relatively small share of American manufacturing, and wood products, leather, and rubber, in which abundant forest and pasture land support a relatively high U.S. output share. The Japanese data, which are available only in gross value terms, also resemble the Chinese figures except for the relatively large shares of basic metals and chemicals and the relatively small share of food processing in Japan.

Chinese and foreign observers have often claimed that the special privileges available to foreign businesses in China's treaty ports and the inability of China's government to restrict commodity imports or control foreign investment led to an artificial distortion of both the spatial and the sectoral dispersion of prewar industry. The available data provide little support for this view. On the contrary, it appears that both the geographic and the sectoral structure of prewar manufacturing arose from the same type of cost-price considerations that dominate business decisions in any market economy. It is true that over one-fourth of manufacturing rested in foreign hands (Table 2.3) and that Chinese as well as foreign firms sought the relative security of the treaty ports, but these open ports, which numbered nearly fifty by 1900 and over one hundred by 1930, were themselves chosen for their anticipated economic advantages.[37] With so many privileged locations available, the concentration of manufacturing in Manchuria, where Japanese pressure secured concessions across a whole band of territory, and Shanghai emphasizes the purely economic attraction of these locations, as does the continued prominence of Shanghai, Kiangsu, and Manchuria in industrial activity nearly four decades after the government of the People's Republic announced its determination to rectify what were seen as artificial restrictions on the spread of industrialization.[38]

37. The open ports are listed in Yen Chung-p'ing, comp., *Chung-kuo chin tai ching chi shih t'ung chi tzu liao hsüan chi* (Peking, 1955), 43–48.
38. The share of these regions in Chinese industrial output (mining, manufacturing, and utilities) fell from 48.4 percent in 1952 to 34.2 percent in 1986. This decline of about four percentage points per decade is virtually identical with the drop in New England's share of value added in U.S. manufacturing between 1860 and 1900. See Nicholas R. Lardy, "Regional Growth and Income Distribution in China," in *China's Development Experience in Comparative Perspective*, ed. Robert F. Dernberger (Cambridge, 1980), 182; *Chung-kuo t'ung chi chai yao*, 1987 (Peking, 1987), 11; and Niemi, *American Manufacturing*, 14–15.

In view of the extravagant claims about the ease with which foreign firms could defeat Chinese rivals in the marketplace, it is perhaps surprising to discover that foreign factories (including some with Chinese shareholders or silent partners) produced no more than 27 percent of overall factory output in 1933 (Table 2.3).[39] Further insight into the position of foreign enterprise in Chinese manufacturing emerges from Table 2.7, which contains 1933 data on the share of foreign firms and on comparative labor productivity for foreign and Chinese firms in industries employing over ten thousand workers; the fifteen sectors included in Table 2.7 account for 86 percent of estimated 1933 factory employment.[40] If foreign firms used their financial strength to deploy expensive new technologies that remained inaccessible to undercapitalized Chinese enterprises, there should be a strong association between superior labor productivity (arising from more and better equipment in foreign firms) and high shares of foreign firms in total output (reflecting their competitive strength). In fact, this combination of circumstances rarely appears. Only five of fifteen sectors—machinery, iron and steel, brick and shingle, transport equipment, and edible oils—display both a substantial foreign output share (20 percent or more) and a substantial productivity differential (over 20 percent) favoring foreign firms. These sectors are relatively small, accounting for only one-sixth of the 921,000 workers in the fifteen industries included in Table 2.7. Furthermore, the share of foreign firms in total output for these five sectors (28.6 percent) hardly differs from the foreign output share in all fifteen sectors (26.7 percent). There is no consistent productivity differential favoring foreign firms in cotton textiles and cigarettes, the sectors with the largest foreign establishments. Some sectors in which foreign firms do show strong productivity advantage, including silk, clothing and attire, and printing, were nonetheless dominated by Chinese-owned enterprises. This suggests that the main determinants of the success or failure of foreign industrial enterprise lay elsewhere.

39. Wu Ch'eng-ming has produced detailed estimates suggesting a much higher share of foreign enterprise in the prewar capital stock. His figures for 1936, for example, show foreign firms accounting for 68 percent of total capital in industry and mining (*Chung-kuo tzu pen chu i*, 130). Liu and Yeh compare alternative estimates of the foreign share of factory output (*Economy of the Chinese Mainland*, 436–38).

40. Liu and Yeh, *Economy of the Chinese Mainland*, 428.

Table 2.7
Employment and Labor Productivity in Chinese- and Foreign-owned
Factories, 1933

Sector	Total Employment (thousands)	Foreign Share in GVIO[a] (%)	Output Value per Worker (yuan) Chinese Firms		Foreign Firms
			China Proper	Manchuria	
Cotton textiles	317	35.3	2442	2066	2558
Silk textiles	108	3.8	386	718	739
Clothing and attire	98	5.7	845	750	2450
Silk piece goods	87	3.8	921	600	750
Machinery	49	31.5	1256	470	1826
Cigarettes	44	52.8	6292	3889	5892
Printing	42	12.7	1620	1000	2935
Matches	37	19.3	1033	562	1161
Tranport equipment	27	47.5	1408	562	2744
Brick and shingle	23	30.1	325	312	521
Iron and steel	22	32.0	1509	866	2488
Edible oils	19	20.8	5747	9800	14043
Rice milling	19	7.8	10730	4588	3941
Rubber products	16	5.5	2387	...	3000
Wheat flour	12	6.0	20238	3800	23200

[a]GVIO indicates output or sales value.

Sources: The data for total employment and for output per worker in
Chinese and foreign firms in China proper are from Liu and Yeh, Economy of
the Chinese Mainland, table F-1. Output and employment in Manchuria are
separated into foreign (including "Japanese," and "other," and "jointly
managed" firms) and Chinese (including "Manchurian") components using
separate data on output and employment from Manshû kôjô tôkei B, 1934, 56-
59, 388-395. The figures for machinery include small electrical
appliances. Transport equipment includes shipbuilding. Rice milling
includes other husked grains. I ignore minor differences between the
Chinese yuan and Manchurian currency (see Table C.7).

Information on cotton textiles, China's largest industry and an
industry in which foreign firms occupied a substantial position despite their failure to achieve significantly higher labor productivity
than Chinese-owned firms, points to scale as an important determinant of profitability. There is little comparative cost data. Partial

Table 2.8
Partial Cost Comparisons for Chinese and Japanese Mills, 1935
(yuan per bale of 20-count yarn)

Item	Chinese Mills	Japanese Mills
Wages	10.50	5.80
Power	5.50	4.80
Machine repairs	1.80	0.60
Other repairs	0.40	0.40
Materials	1.70	0.50
Packing	1.50	1.20
Salaries	1.20	0.60
Sanitation	0.20	0.50
Transport	0.20	0.20
Management expenses	2.50	2.00
Taxes and interest	15.00	2.70
Insurance	0.20	0.10
Miscellaneous	3.00	1.00
Total of above items	43.70	20.40

Source: Yen Chung-p'ing, Chung-kuo mien fang chih shih kao (Peking, 1963), 203.

estimates of the cost of producing 20-count cotton yarn in Chinese and Japanese mills appear in a number of sources; one such comparison is reproduced in Table 2.8.[41] These figures invariably show that production costs at Japanese mills, which supplanted British firms as the chief foreign textile producers, were far less than comparable Chinese cost totals. But if Japanese firms could produce 20-count yarn more cheaply than Chinese manufacturers, why did

41. Similar data appear in Kang Chao, *The Development of Cotton Textile Production in China* (Cambridge, 1977), 157; *Jung chia ch'i yeh shih liao* (Shanghai, 1980), 1:535; and Takemoto Akira, "Development of Japanese Textile Firms in China and Their Background, 1914–1937," *Rokkadai ronshū* 24, no. 2 (1977):66.

Chinese manufacturers turn out 62 percent of all yarn between 17 and 23 counts during 1935–36?[42] Resolution of this puzzle lies in the partial nature of the cost data, which omit outlays on cotton, the main expense incurred by yarn producers. The average monthly wholesale price of 20-count yarn at Shanghai in 1935 was 190.84 yuan per bale, but the costs shown in Table 2.8 amount to only 11–23 percent of this figure. If Japanese firms economized in some areas, Chinese producers apparently matched or surpassed this advantage with savings in cotton consumption or depreciation charges, two major items excluded from the comparison.[43]

If foreign firms had attained unusually low costs, they should have earned higher profits than their Chinese rivals. Here again, it is difficult to confirm the traditional view. Numerous instances of losses, bankruptcies, and forced sales involving foreign manufacturers signal their susceptibility to China's uncertain business environment. Unsuccessful foreign firms often passed into the hands of Chinese competitors, with the erstwhile proprietors sometimes staying on to work for the new owners.[44] Remer and Hou have studied the financial statements of foreign businesses without finding evidence of unusual profitability, especially in manufacturing.[45] Dernberger notes that scattered reports "do not support the view that the foreign firm was more profitable than the Chinese enterprise."[46] I have found systematic profit comparisons only for cotton textiles. The data appear in Table 2.9, which summarizes Takemoto's compilation of profit data for several size classes of Japanese firms in both China and Japan and for a number of Chinese producers during the period 1914–37. The Japanese reports are ratios of annual profit to paid-up capital; the basis of the Chinese figures is not clearly specified. Although Takemoto does not discuss the

42. Yen Chung-p'ing, *Chung-kuo mien fang chih shih kao* (Peking, 1963), 202, which shows no significant change in the share of Chinese firms in this category of output between 1932 and 1936.

43. Price data are from *Shang-hai chieh fang ch'ien hou wu chia tzu liao hui pien, 1921–1957* (Shanghai, 1958), 233.

44. Chao, *Cotton Textile Production*, 137.

45. C. F. Remer, *Foreign Investments in China* (New York, 1968), 294 and Chi-ming Hou, *Foreign Investment and Economic Development in China, 1840–1937* (Cambridge, 1965), 112–18.

46. Robert F. Dernberger, "The Role of the Foreigner in China's Economic Development, 1840–1949," in *China's Modern Economy in Historical Perspective*, ed. Dwight H. Perkins (Stanford, 1975), 46.

Table 2.9
Average Annual Profits for Chinese and Japanese Textile Firms, 1914-37
(profits as a percentage of paid-up capital)

Period	Japanese Firms Located In[a]							Chinese Firms
	China			Japan				
	I	II	III	I	II	III	IV	
1914-37	...	...	41.9	12.9	16.2	26.0	35.5	...
1919-37	...	3.7	41.7	9.4	12.9	22.0	31.7	8.1[b]
1925-37	1.9	(2.2)	18.4	5.3	8.4	10.6	21.6	5.5[b]

[a]Size classifications are based on paid-up capital as of mid-1937. Class I includes firms with less than 5 million yen; Classes II and III correspond to capitalizations of 5-9.9 and 10-24.9 million yen respectively and Class IV includes firms capitalized at over 25 million yen. Figures in parentheses denote losses.

[b]Excluding 1930.

Source: Calculated from Takemoto, "Japanese Textile Firms in China," 61.

scale of the Chinese firms, a separate compilation shows that most Chinese textile manufacturers would fall within Takemoto's class I, corresponding to the smallest levels of capitalization.[47] Even though contemporary accounts insist that "every effort is being made to hide the profits of the [Shanghai] mills" to avoid taxation, the data in Table 2.9 suggest that Chinese firms surpassed the profitability of comparably sized Japanese enterprises.[48]

Takemoto's data show a clear pattern in which scale rather than nationality determined enterprise profitability. Japanese firms in both locations show a fairly regular association of profitability and scale. Large Japanese firms located in China tended to be more profitable than comparably sized producers in the home islands, whereas small Japanese firms tended to fare better at home than

47. Ignoring minor differences between the value of Japanese yen and Chinese yuan, data for the mid-1930s place sixteen of twenty-one Chinese cotton textile firms in class I, with paid-up capital below five million yuan. One firm falls in class II, and two each in the larger categories corresponding to classes III and IV. See Ch'en and Yao, *Chung-kuo chin tai kung yeh*, Collection 1, 649–55.
48. Arno S. Pearse, *The Cotton Industry of Japan and China* (Manchester, 1929), 159. See also Chao, *Cotton Textile Production*, 137–39.

in China. Chinese firms earned higher returns than small- and medium-sized (classes I and II) Japanese producers located in China, but failed to match the profitability of the largest Japanese manufacturers.

This survey leads to the conclusion that the rapid prewar development of Chinese factory industry was very much a product of market forces. The initial concentration of manufacturing in regions favored by easy access to materials and markets and the dominance of food processing, textiles, and other agriculturally based industries seem typical of the initial phase of industrialization in agrarian economies and cannot be attributed to political circumstances. Foreign manufacturers derived scant long-term benefit from the special treaty provisions that exempted them from certain forms of Chinese taxation. For foreign as well as Chinese firms, success or failure depended primarily on responsiveness to changing market requirements. Limited data indicate that large-scale manufacturing operations may have enjoyed exceptional success, perhaps because financial strength enabled large firms to withstand the vagaries of an unstable environment.

The growth of manufacturing in prewar China is further explored in the following case studies of cotton textiles, the largest factory industry and one that processed agricultural materials in competition with handicraft and imported textiles, and matches, a new consumer product using new types of materials.

Cotton Textiles

China's largest industry was cotton textiles. The size of the textile market and its well deserved reputation as a battleground between products from overseas factories, domestic plants operated by Chinese and foreign businesses, and Chinese handicraft producers has attracted the attention of many writers.[49] Rather than attempting to summarize the voluminous literature on Chinese textiles, this discussion will seek to highlight the main features of prewar textile development.

In Table 2.10, I compile data produced by scholars of China's

---

49. References to the enormous prewar literature on textiles appear in *Shina kōkōgyō ni kansuru shuyō bunken mokuroku* (Kyoto, 1940).

Table 2.10
Production and Supply of Cotton and Cotton Goods, 1871-1936
(Annual Averages for Selected Periods)

	1871/ 1880	1901/ 1910	1923/ 1924	1925/ 1927	1928/ 1930	1931/ 1933	1934/ 1936
Physical quantities							
1. Cotton (Mill. piculs)							
A. Output	7	7	14.4	13.2	13.8	13.3	17.3
B. Net imports	0.1	-0.7	0.4	1.3	1.7	2.6	0.4
C. Domestic supply	7.1	6.3	14.8	14.5	15.5	15.9	17.7
2. Yarn (Mill. piculs)							
A. Factory output	0	1.0	4.7	7.1	7.7	8.7	9.0
B. Craft output	4.9	2.4	6.3	4.4	3.3	2.7	3.1
C. Net imports	0.1	2.4	0.6	0.3	-0.1	-0.4	0.2
D. Domestic supply	5.0	5.8	11.6	11.8	10.9	11.0	11.9
3. Cloth (Mill. sq. yds.)							
A. Factory output	0	24	310	440	700	960	1260
B. Craft output	1612	1850	2924	3630	3060	2890	2880
C. Net imports	376	654	600	630	630	360	300
D. Domestic Supply	1988	2528	3834	4700	4390	4210	4440
Value Added (Million 1933 yuan)							
4. Factory sector							
A. Yarn	0	13.0	61.3	92.6	100.5	113.5	117.4
B. Cloth	0	1.1	14.3	20.2	32.2	44.2	58.0
C. Total	0	14.1	75.6	112.8	132.7	157.7	175.4
5. Handicraft Sector							
A. Yarn	40.6	19.9	52.2	36.4	27.3	22.4	25.7
B. Cloth	64.5	74.0	117.0	145.2	122.4	115.6	115.2
C. Total	105.1	93.9	169.2	181.6	149.7	138.0	140.9
6. Combined Total							
A. Factory	0	14.1	75.6	112.8	132.7	157.7	175.4
B. Handicraft	105.1	93.9	169.2	181.6	149.7	138.0	140.9
C. Total Output	105.1	108.0	244.8	294.4	282.4	295.7	316.3

continued...

Table 2.10, continued

Sources: Line 1A: For 1871-1910, Albert Feuerwerker, "Handicraft
and Manufactured Cotton Textiles in China, 1871-1910." Journal of
Economic History 30, no. 2 (1970):371; for 1923-26, Richard A.
Kraus, "Cotton and Cotton Goods in China, 1918-1936: The Impact of
Modernization on the Traditional Sector," table II.9.

Line 1B. For 1871-1910, Feuerwerker, "Cotton Textiles," 350,
355; for 1923-30, Hsiao, Foreign Trade, 39, 86; for 1931-36, Kraus,
"Cotton Goods," table II-14, which, unlike Hsiao, includes the
foreign trade of Manchuria as well as China proper (see pp. 51-52).

Line 2A: For 1871-1910, Feuerwerker, "Cotton Textiles," 372;
for 1923-36, Kraus, "Cotton Goods," table III.9.

Line 2B: For 1871-1910, Feuerwerker, "Cotton Textiles," 372; for
1923-24, the author's calculations based on Kraus's cotton supply
and input-output data; for 1925-36, Kraus, "Cotton Goods," table
VI.1.

Line 2C: For 1871-1910, Feuerwerker, "Cotton Textiles," 350,
355; for 1923-30, Hsiao, Foreign Trade, 39, 86; for 1931-36, Kraus,
"Cotton Goods," table III.9, which includes trade for both Manchuria
and China proper.

Line 3A: For 1871-1910, Feuerwerker, "Cotton Textiles," 372;
for 1923-36, Kraus, "Cotton Goods," table V.2.

Line 3B: For 1871-1910, Feuerwerker, "Cotton Textiles," 372; for
1923-24, the author's estimate is based on Kraus's yarn supply and
input-output data; for 1925-36, Kraus, "Cotton Goods," table V.2,
which gives a figure of 3,130 million square yards for 1924.

Line 3C: For 1871-1910, Feuerwerker, "Cotton Textiles," 359,
with adjustments for the Russo-Japanese War years of 1905-6 as
described on p. 360; for 1923-36, Kraus, "Cotton Goods," table V.2,
which includes trade in craft as well as factory cloth.

Lines 4-6. The value-added totals are based on physical output
figures and unit values derived from the following data. Prices:
factory yarn, 50.2 yuan/picul; craft yarn, 41.4 yuan/picul; factory
cloth, 7.67 yuan per bolt of 40 square yards; craft cloth, 7 yuan
per bolt. Gross value added per yuan of output value: factory yarn,
0.26; craft yarn, 0.20; factory cloth, 0.22; craft cloth, 0.23.
These data come from Liu and Yeh, Economy of the Chinese Mainland,
448, 449, 480, 522 and from Chao, Cotton Textile Production, 234.

textile industry for the purpose of discerning long-term trends in
the growth of output and trade in this important industry. These
figures show that China's textile industry expanded rapidly during
the half century preceding World War II. Growth was particularly
swift in the factory sector, where output of yarn and cloth rose by
350 and 1,770 percent respectively between 1912 and 1936 and the
combined value added for yarn and cloth grew at an annual rate of
about 9 percent between 1901/10 and 1934/36.[50] Kraus emphasizes

50. The data are from Table 2.10 and Chao, *Cotton Textile Production*, 308, 312.

the scale of this achievement in international terms, noting that by the early 1930s, textile factories consumed more cotton in China than in either Britain or Japan; indeed, "China's factory yarn industry grew faster to higher levels of production than any . . . in the world."[51]

Many authors have noted the growth of factory output. What has not received adequate emphasis is the substantial expansion of the entire Chinese market for textiles after 1870. The estimates presented in Table 2.10 show that domestic consumption of both yarn and cloth increased by more than 100 percent between 1871/80 and the 1930s, with most of the increase coming after the turn of the century. The figures also show that the combined output value of factory and handicraft textiles nearly tripled between 1901/10 and 1934/36. Although these data are subject to considerable margins of error, they are, with the exception of the rough estimates of handicraft production for 1923–24, based on painstaking sifting of evidence and verification of assumptions by Feuerwerker and Kraus. Even though the results of their studies cannot claim precision, the implication of major growth in the scale of China's textile market as well as in the volume of overall textile output appears well established.

The data in Table 2.10 also illuminate the timing of textile expansion and the relative importance of import substitution, export growth, and the expansion of domestic demand in absorbing rising textile output. The data for 1871/80 and 1901/10, which rest on crude estimates of cotton production, show that handicraft spinning output declined by one-half in the face of steeply rising imports and the initial development of factory yarn production. Handicraft cloth, by contrast, expanded modestly despite the growth of both imports and factory production. In the aggregate, these changes enlarged China's supply of textile products despite the absence of a significant increase in the level of domestic output measured in terms of value added.

The period between 1901/10 and 1923/27 brought dramatic output growth in every segment of China's cotton textile industry. This resulted in large increases in domestic sales and consumption,

51. Richard A. Kraus, "Cotton and Cotton Goods in China, 1918–1936: The Impact of Modernization on the Traditional Sector" (Ph.D. diss., Harvard University, 1968), 151–52.

which have been overlooked by previous authors, who tend to
assume a constant per capita consumption of textile goods.[52] All
writers note the rapid growth of manufacturing, with factory yarn
output rising from one to seven million annual piculs and annual
cloth manufacture surging from 24 to 440 million square yards during this period of roughly twenty-five years. Surprisingly, handicrafts seem to have prospered as well. Homespun yarn output regained most of the ground lost during the late nineteenth century
and the production of handicraft cloth nearly doubled between
1901/10 and 1925/27.[53]

Most of this growth went to satisfy increased domestic demand.
In yarn, an import surplus of 2.4 million piculs in 1901/10 dwindled
to 0.3 million by 1925/27, but the resulting gain of 2.1 million
piculs absorbed little more than one-quarter of incremental output
of factory and handicraft yarn. In the cloth sector, the decline in
imports was hardly significant, amounting to only 1 percent of the
output increment of nearly 1,900 million square yards.

Textile performance during the decade following 1927 was
mixed. The switch from an import to an export surplus in cotton
yarn brought an output gain of one-half million annual piculs, but
with no growth in domestic consumption, rising sales of factory
goods came mainly at the expense of homespun yarn, which fell
back toward the low output levels of the 1901/10 decade. The demand for cloth dropped slightly. Factory production continued to
grow, but at a reduced pace. Roughly two-thirds of the increase in
sales of factory cloth came at the expense of handloom cloth; the
remaining gains in sales replaced imports.

By the end of the Nanking decade, textile output, calculated in
terms of 1933 prices, was about three times the level of 1871/80 or
1901/10. Most of the growth came from factories, but the average
output value from the craft sector in 1934/36 was 35 percent above

52. Albert Feuerwerker, "Handicraft and Manufactured Cotton Textiles in China,
   1871–1910," *Journal of Economic History* 30, no. 2 (1970):368, assumes "that
   per capita cloth consumption over the past century varied, if at all, only within
   a narrow range." Bruce L. Reynolds, "The Impact of Trade and Foreign Investment on Industrialization: Chinese Textiles, 1875–1931" (Ph.D. diss.,
   University of Michigan, 1975), 58, makes the same assumption.
53. Loren Brandt informs me that substitution of Kang Chao's estimates of factory
   textile output for Kraus's figures in Table 2.10 would increase the estimated
   growth of handicraft textile production.

Table 2.11
Per Capita Output of Textiles and Consumption of Cotton Cloth, 1871-1936

Period	Population (millions)	Indicators of Per Capita Output and Consumption			
		Value Added, Cotton Yarn and Cloth (1933 yuan)			Consumption of Cloth
		Total	Factory	Handicraft	(square yards)
1871/80	350	0.30	0	0.30	5.7
1901/10	435[a]	0.25	0.03	0.22	5.8
1923/27	476	0.57	0.20	0.37	9.0
1934/36	500	0.63	0.35	0.28	8.9

[a]Indicates midpoint of range.

Sources: Population estimates are from Feuerwerker, "Cotton Textiles," 370; the figure for 1923/27 is calculated from the estimate for 1934/36 by assuming annual population growth of 0.5 percent. Cloth supply and value added are from Table 2.10. Value-added and cloth supply figures for 1923/27 are averages of separate figures for 1923/24 and 1925/27.

the comparable figure for 1871/80 and 50 percent higher than the handicraft total for 1901/10. Within handicrafts, weaving gained substantially, although output began to fall after 1925/27, whereas yarn experienced great instability, with an initial decline followed by rapid revival in the decade of World War I and another period of decline in the 1920s and 1930s.

This tripling of textile output implies major increases in per capita consumption of textiles as may be seen from the results derived in Table 2.11. An increase in per capita cloth consumption from 5.8 to 9.0 square yards between 1901/10 and 1923/27, followed by a decline to 8.9 square yards in 1934/36, suggests a general increase in living standards during the prewar decades, especially since cloth consumption seems to have risen with no major decline in the relative price of cloth.[54] This issue will be considered in further

54. *Nan-k'ai chih shu tzu liao hui pien, 1913–1952* (Peking, 1958), 11, shows that between 1913, when the index begins, and 1922, the prices of manufactured textiles rose by 52 percent, more than any other commodity group and much more than the wholesale price level, which increased by 29 percent. Between 1927 and 1936, textile prices declined marginally while the overall index rose

detail in Chapter 6. The alternative combination of rising per capita cloth consumption and stable or falling per capita income is extremely implausible. Feuerwerker points out that although factory cloth was less durable than handicraft products, it embodied other characteristics, such as finish, fineness, and color, that handloom weavers could not provide. In any case, with two-thirds of cloth supplies coming from craft producers as late as 1934–36, the lesser durability of factory cloth cannot offset the clear welfare gains implied by the large rise in per capita cloth supplies deduced in Table 2.11.

Might this startling picture of increasing per capita textile consumption arise from errors in the data compiled in Table 2.10? The results appear insensitive to possible errors in the demographic totals shown in Table 2.11. Using the larger population totals proposed by Peter Schran lowers the estimates of per capita output and consumption without affecting the growth rate of per capita textile output or cloth consumption between 1901/10 and 1934/36.[55] The literature contains no serious dispute over output or trade in manufactured yarn or cloth, but what of handicraft production? An influential study by Bruce Reynolds concludes that handicraft cloth output rose from 1,637 to 1,815 million square yards between 1875 and 1931, while handicraft yarn production plunged from 4.7 million to only 1.3 million piculs during the same period. Reynolds's estimates of 1931 handicraft output are thus only 63 percent (for cloth) and 48 percent (for yarn) of the annual averages for 1931/33 shown in Table 2.10. With these low output figures, Reynolds's total for per capita cloth consumption in 1931 is only 5.9 square yards, far

---

by 7 percent. The data relate to Tientsin, a major center of textile production. Information on the retail prices of handicraft cloth produced in Ting county, Hopei, a major center of craft activity, shows prices lagging behind both the general price index and the figures for factory cloth during 1913–22. During 1922–31, however, the average price of handicraft cloth rose by 45 percent, outpacing both the overall price index and indicators of factory cloth prices for Tientsin. See Sidney D. Gamble, *Ting Hsien: A North China Rural Community* (Reprint, Stanford, 1968), 326.

55. See Peter Schran, "China's Demographic Evolution 1850–1953 Reconsidered," *China Quarterly* 75 (1978). Schran proposes the following population totals: for 1871/80, 420 million; for 1901/10, 480 million; for 1923/27, 530 million; for 1934/36, 560 million.

below the present result.[56] Where do these differences come from? Reynolds begins by *assuming* constant annual cloth consumption of 5.8 square yards per person throughout the entire period from 1875 to 1931.[57] Taken together with the estimated population, this assumption generates figures for total cloth consumption. Foreign trade data allow him to determine the domestic cloth output, from which factory production can be subtracted to yield estimates of handloom cloth production. Because output data for factory yarn are readily available, handicraft yarn output may be deduced as the difference between the total yarn requirements for the production of factory and handicraft cloth and the supply of factory yarn from domestic and foreign producers.

Reynolds does not consider the cotton requirements implied by the assumed cloth supply totals. Beginning with Kraus's estimates of unit cotton requirements for factory yarn production in 1934, one can derive the following cotton requirements for producing Reynolds's 1931 yarn totals (in million piculs):[58]

A. Factory sector	8.248
B. Handicraft sector	1.300
C. Cotton used for yarn: (A) + (B)	9.548
D. Cotton used for padding	2.955
E. Domestic cotton requirements: (C) + (D)	12.503
F. Net cotton imports (imports − exports)	3.863
G. Implied 1931 cotton harvest: (E) − (F)	8.640

56. Bruce L. Reynolds, "Weft: The Technological Sanctuary of Chinese Handspun Yarn," *Ch'ing-shih wen-t'i* 3, no. 2 (1974):6, with quantities converted at 133.33 pounds to the picul and an assumed 1931 population of 500 million.

57. Reynolds, "Trade and Foreign Investment," 58. This assumption is based on the results of budget studies conducted during the 1920s and 1930s (pp. 305–20) and on the presumed long-term constancy of per capita incomes (pp. 88–99). Reynolds states that his 1931 consumption figure of 5.8 square yards of cotton cloth per person carries a margin of error as small as 10 or even 5 percent (p. 99).

58. Factory cotton consumption is from Reynolds's output figure and Kraus's 1931 estimate of 1.137 piculs of cotton per picul of yarn ("Cotton Goods," 72, 74). The cotton requirements for craft spinning are assumed equal to Reynolds's output estimate plus Feuerwerker's 5 percent allowance for waste ("Cotton

But this implied cotton harvest of 8.6 million piculs is far below other estimates of cotton output in the early 1930s and the differences are far too large to attribute to changes in stocks (cotton output is given in million piculs):[59]

Author	Period	Cotton Output
Kraus	1931	12.9
Perkins	1931–37	15.6
Liu and Yeh	1933	15.7
Feuerwerker	1931–36	13.4
Hsü	1933	11.4–15.9
Chao	1923–36	11.0–19.9

Despite instances of incompleteness and inconsistency, cotton statistics were among the most carefully compiled and intensively scrutinized agricultural data for the 1930s. H. D. Fong, a well-informed economist who wrote extensively about cotton textiles during the 1930s, insisted that contemporary data, which form the basis for retrospective output estimates by Kraus, Perkins, and others *understated* actual cotton production in the late 1920s and early 1930s.[60] Without evidence to support Reynolds's implicit claim that 1931 cotton output was far below the range envisioned in other studies, particularly Kraus's detailed review of provincial output data, it would appear that Reynolds's figures for the 1931 output of

---

Textiles," 350, 353). Figures for cotton padding and net imports are from Kraus, "Cotton Goods," table III.11 and Hsiao, *Foreign Trade*, 39, 86.

59. Kraus's output estimates are from Table 2.10. Perkins's figures, converted from piculs of 110 pounds, are from his *Agricultural Development*, 293. The estimates by Liu and Yeh, similarly converted, are from their *Economy of the Chinese Mainland*, 300. Feuerwerker's figures are from his "Cotton Textiles," 364. The figures reported by Hsü Tao-fu are the sum of provincial reports given in terms of *shih piculs*, the lower figure covering eleven and the latter total eighteen provinces; see his *Chung-kuo chin tai nung yeh sheng ch'an chi mao i t'ung chi tzu liao* (Shanghai, 1983), 203–12. Chao's figures indicate the lowest (1931) and highest (1936) estimates of annual cotton output in his series, which covers 1923–36 (*Cotton Textile Production*, 224).

60. H. D. Fong, *Cotton Industry and Trade in China* (Tientsin, 1932), 1:chap. 2.

handicraft spinning and weaving require major upward adjustment to bring the associated cotton requirements into line with better-informed estimates of available supplies. Barring a highly improbable demonstration that Kraus and others have massively overestimated cotton production during the 1930s, Reynolds's conclusions regarding the level of handicraft textile output must be discarded.

Reynolds's view that handicraft output declined sharply between the 1870s and the 1930s may be correct even if his output estimates for the latter period are too low. Again, the problem centers on the estimated level of cotton production. If Reynolds's finding of low handicraft output for the 1930s is rejected because of the improbably low level of associated cotton output, his conclusion that craft output declined substantially between 1875 and 1931, instead of rising by one-third, as shown in Table 2.10, would be sustained if Feuerwerker's estimate of cotton output for the 1870s were substantially understated.

China's prewar cotton output was highly concentrated. In 1933, Kiangsu, Hupeh, Honan, Hopei, and Shantung provinces supplied about three-quarters of total output.[61] While there are no time series for provincial output extending back to the nineteenth century, cotton output in each of these provinces, and also in Shensi, responded positively to rising prices, improved transport and marketing facilities, and, especially in the case of Kiangsu, to the explosive growth of demand from nearby cotton mills. The importance of each of these factors is extensively documented.[62] If it could be shown that large declines in cotton output occurred simultaneously elsewhere, then the sort of handicraft decline hy-

61. Kraus, "Cotton Goods," table II.4, shows these provinces as contributing 83 percent of the combined 1933 output of a sample of provinces that, according to figures compiled by the National Agricultural Research Board, accounted for about 90 percent of national cotton output in 1933 (p. 24).

62. See, among others, "Cotton Cultivation in Shensi," 197–201; T. S. Chu and T. Chin, *Marketing of Cotton in Hopei Province* (Peiping, 1929); Yeh Ch'ien-chi, "Production, Transport, and Marketing of Hsi-ho Cotton," in *Chung-kuo ching chi yen chiu*, ed. Fang Hsien-t'ing (Changsha, 1938); Yen, *Chung-kuo mien fang chih*, 304–9; and Yoshida Kōichi, "Cotton Marketing in One Locality in China During the First Half of the Twentieth Century," *Shirin* 60, no. 2 (1977).

pothesized by Reynolds might become plausible.[63] Pending further
study of nineteenth-century cotton growing, however, it seems
reasonable to conclude that the picture of textile development
summarized in Tables 2.10 and 2.11, which includes the long-term
expansion of production in both the handicraft and the factory sectors as well as a major rise in per capita consumption of cotton cloth
in the decades following the 1911 Revolution, fits available evidence far better than more pessimistic interpretations offered by
other writers.

China's rapidly growing cotton textile industry was fiercely competitive. Commercial rivalries were somewhat relieved by market
segmentation. The superior durability of handloom cloth, for example, made it the fabric of choice for rural buyers who could
afford to invest in long-wearing fabrics. Urban residents often
dressed in handicraft cloth: in Tientsin, "clothing was made at
home from Gaoyang [Hopei] homespun. . . . Workers preferred
homespun clothing . . . because it was sturdy and did not show
dirt."[64] Factory cloth appealed to buyers who could not afford the
more expensive craft products or whose tastes emphasized appearance rather than durability. On the supply side, Chinese factories
tended to produce low-count yarns, while Japanese firms concentrated on finer yarns. Even with these divisions, however, textile
markets remained intensely competitive:[65]

There is no Chinese industry in which competition is as severe as in textiles. It is natural for goods from distant Lancashire and nearby Osaka to
compete against the products of Japanese firms in China. But there is
fierce rivalry between Chinese sellers from the interior and the treaty
ports, from north and south, unrelieved by cooperation or regulation.
Only those who succeed in cutting costs emerge victorious.

The combination of intense competition and fluctuations arising
from economic and political shocks made textiles a risky business.
Profits varied dramatically from year to year and failure was common among foreign as well as indigenous firms.[66] The uncertainty

63. Kraus, "Cotton Goods," 162, speculates that cotton output may have declined
   by 20 percent or more between 1870 and 1900.
64. Hershatter, *Workers of Tianjin*, 72.
65. Hotchi Zenjirō, "The Present Situation of China's Cotton Textile Industry,"
   Mantetsu chōsa geppō 15, no. 12 (1935):11.
66. Chao, *Cotton Textile Production*, 114–16, 121, 125.

prevalent in the Chinese market emerges from profit comparisons between Japanese textile firms in China and Japan: although profits on the Chinese side were higher in slightly more than half of the reporting periods, losses were much more common for firms doing business in China and the profits of these firms showed a much higher variance than the financial results for enterprises operating only in Japan.[67]

With foreign firms free to establish new domestic plants and with no effective restriction on imports before 1931, when tariffs began to rise above the long-standing 5 percent ad valorem rate, the survival and expansion of Chinese textile producers depended on aggressive entrepreneurship and adroit management. Burdened with weak financial reserves and high interest rates, Chinese managers drove their mills ruthlessly and succeeded in raising output per spindle above the level attained by their Japanese rivals.[68] Spindle speed and other technical indicators rose sharply during the 1920s.[69] The operations of Chinese factory managers in domestic cotton markets, often denounced as wasteful speculation, may have lowered raw material costs, which dominate production expenses in the textile business. Japanese observers praised the technical progressiveness of their Chinese competitors, citing rising labor productivity, renovation of equipment, and improved supervisory organization as factors responsible for falling costs.[70]

The overall performance of Chinese textile firms confirms this favorable view of Chinese management capabilities. Although the Chinese share of textile equipment (spindles and looms) declined from near 60 percent to about 50 percent between 1913 and 1936, the stock of Chinese-owned machinery rose by 467 percent (spindles) and 1,175 percent (looms) during the same period.[71]

67. Takemoto, "Japanese Textile Firms in China," 61. In both China and Japan, the variance of the profit series summarized in Table 2.9 declines with enterprise scale as measured by paid-up capital, but within each size class, the variance of the profit series is much higher for the firms operating in China than for those located in Japan.

68. Fong, *Cotton Industry and Trade*, 1:90–91. Hotchi, "Textile Industry," presents data showing that in 1934 Chinese firms possessed only 56 percent of all cotton spindles but produced 71 percent of overall yarn output by weight.

69. Hotchi, "Textile Industry," 13.

70. Hotchi, "Textile Industry," 11–13.

71. Yen, *Chung-kuo mien fang chih*, 354–55. The classification of equipment owned by Sino-foreign firms is not specified.

Sales by Chinese firms amounted to 61 percent of the estimated cotton textile production for 1933.[72] By this time, exports of Chinese textile products had begun to reach beyond the overseas Chinese communities into purely foreign markets, especially in the Middle East.[73]

The rapid growth of textile production and the success of Chinese firms in overcoming the difficulties posed by business fluctuations and strong competition from handicrafts, imports, and local foreign-owned factories created spread effects that stimulated the development of many regions and sectors of China's economy. In the 1930s, spinning equipment was divided in roughly equal shares between Chinese firms and foreign, mostly Japanese, enterprises. Foreign equipment was concentrated in Shanghai, Tientsin, Tsingtao, and Manchuria, with two-thirds of foreign-owned spindles clustered in Shanghai alone.[74] Chinese-owned equipment, however, was more widely dispersed. Shanghai accounted for only 39 percent of total spindlage, which amounted to over one million units in 1932. Improved transport and communications in the interior and rising land and labor costs in Shanghai and other major centers encouraged Chinese entrepreneurs to build textile plants in cotton-growing districts and commercial centers involved in the cotton trade. Wuhan and Wusih (Kiangsu) each reported about 200,000 spindles, Tientsin and Nan-t'ung (Kiangsu) each had about 100,000, and a number of localities, including Chengchow (Honan), Changsha (Hunan), Tsingtao, and Wu and Wu-chin counties (Kiangsu) reported totals of approximately 50,000 Chinese-owned spindles in 1932, with many other centers reporting smaller factory installations.[75] By 1936, textile mills existed in fourteen provinces of China proper as well as in Japanese-controlled Manchuria.[76] The spread of factory textile production from the coastal treaty ports contributed to the beginnings of regional industrialization in Hopei, Honan, Hupeh, and especially in Kiangsu. Textile factories

---

72. Liu and Yeh, *Economy of the Chinese Mainland*, 426–28.
73. Chao, *Cotton Textile Production*, 86.
74. 1936 data from Onoe Etsuzō, *Chūgoku no sangyō ritchi ni kansuru kenkyū* (Tokyo, 1971), 301.
75. Liu, *Chung-kuo kung yeh*, 3:40, 45, 174, 295 and Yen, *Chung-kuo chin tai ching chi t'ung chi*, 109.
76. Chao, *Cotton Textile Production*, 130.

appeared even in the remote southwestern province of Yunnan despite the absence of local cotton supplies.[77]

By the mid-1930s, China's cotton textile factories employed over 300,000 workers, consumed more cotton than the combined textile sectors of Britain and Germany, and operated commensurately large quantities of equipment. The rapid expansion of textile factories spawned large demands for a variety of products and services. In China, as in many other economies, the accumulation of mechanical and metalworking skills resulting from repair work in textile factories was a major contributor to the emergence of an engineering industry. The requirements of textile manufacturers for dyes, bleaching agents, and other chemicals provided an important stimulus to the expansion of domestic chemical production. Transport was another sector affected by the growth of textile production. By the 1930s, China's factories processed over one-half million tons of cotton and shipped out an equivalent weight of yarn and cloth; with one-fifth of national cloth output originating in Shanghai alone, the volume of freight traffic in cotton and cotton goods rose because of the increased concentration of production as well as the growing output volume. The fuel requirements of textile plants contributed additional demand to the transport sector. The industry's need for cotton stimulated the growth of cotton output noted in Table 2.10. Textile industrialists, recognizing their dependence on the volume and quality of local cotton, campaigned vigorously, although without lasting success, to improve the quality of domestic cotton.

In short, although neither the development of textile manufacturing nor the broader industrialization process produced a rapid overall transformation of China's prewar economy, textile development produced many of the same results in China as in other industrializing nations.

The Match Industry

Matches, along with kerosene, were the only completely new consumer goods to gain widespread popularity in prewar China. Un-

77. See *Yün-nan kung shang yeh kai k'uang* (Kunming, 1924), chart 4, and Donald S. Sutton, "Reflections on the Economic Effects of the Haiphong-Kunming Railway, 1910–1940" (Pittsburgh, 1978), 10.

like factory cotton goods, manufactured cigarettes, milled flour, and other industrial products that differ from traditional craft substitutes only because they result from applying machine rather than handicraft techniques to process agricultural materials, matches and kerosene use nontraditional materials to provide consumers with distinctively new products.

Match imports were first reported in the 1860s. The import totals, summarized in Table 2.12, show rapid and steady growth to a peak of 600,000 cases in 1912.[78] Europe was the initial source of imports, but Japan emerged as the leading supplier after 1895. Importers of matches included European and Japanese traders as well as Chinese firms based in Canton, Shanghai, and Yen-t'ai (Shantung) that sold rice and other Chinese products to Japan in exchange for matches.

The simple technology of match manufacture, which involves cutting wood into match sticks, coating the tips with a mixture of explosive, binding agents, and glue, and packing the matches into boxes, encouraged early experiments with domestic production. Wei Sheng-hsien, an overseas Chinese merchant, is credited with establishing the first Chinese match enterprise at Fo-shan (Kwangtung) in 1879. A foreign firm, Major Brothers, appeared in the following year. Chinese researchers have noted a total of seventeen Chinese and several foreign plants established before 1900.[79] The industry spread rapidly: available records show that fifty-two Chinese enterprises appeared in eleven provinces between 1905 and 1913. Another 113 firms sprang up between 1914 and 1927, with nearly every province now represented in the total. The industry also included a handful of foreign-owned plants, mostly under Japanese and Swedish control. Match factories ranged from large, automated operations employing several thousand workers to tiny workshops using only a bare minimum of equipment.[80]

The majority of these plants were financially successful. The

78. The most common measures of prewar match output were the case (*hsiang*) containing 50 gross (*lo*) of matchboxes (*lo*), each containing about 70 matches. One case thus contains approximately 50 × 144 × 70 or 504,000 matches. See *Chung-kuo min tsu huo ch'ai kung yeh* (Peking, 1963), 1.
79. Information on nineteenth-century importers and manufacturers is from ibid., chap. 1 and appendix 1.
80. Chinese and foreign-owned firms are listed in ibid., 284–99, 300–301.

Table 2.12
Matches in China: Imports, New Plants and Prices, 1891-1936

Year	Annual Imports (mill. cases) (1)	Number of New Plants (2)	Average Price (yuan/case) Shanghai (3)	Tientsin (4)	
				A	B
1891-1895	0.12	5	...	...	...
1896-1900	0.20	5	...	...	...
1901-1905	0.36	8	...	...	...
1906-1910	0.48	20	...	...	...
1911-1915	0.51	36	...	31.6[a]	...
1916-1920	0.26	48	...	40.7	...
1921-1925	0.06	34	33.7[b]	44.0	...
1926	0.07	7	36.3	45.0	29.0
1927	0.12	7	42.9	45.0	...
1928	0.13	15	46.0	46.6	...
1929	0.17	4	45.5	48.7	...
1930	0.17	11	47.0	...	30.1
1931	0.05	10	79.1	...	56.5
1932	0.01	18	77.4	...	64.0
1933	0.02	3	58.6	...	64.0
1934	0.01	4	51.8	...	...
1935	0.01	6	49.7	...	...
1936	0.01	2	60.5	...	...

[a]1914-1915 only.   [b]1925 only.

Sources: Col. 1: For 1891-1932, Chung-kuo huo ch'ai, 303-5, converted to cases of 50 gross; the data for 1932 probably exclude minor imports into Manchuria. The data for 1933-34 are from Chūka minkoku oyobi Manshūkoku bōeki tōkeihyō (Tokyo, 1939), 69, 136. The quantity of imports for 1934 is derived from the value data by assuming that unit values remained unchanged from 1933. The quantity of imports during 1935-36 is calculated from the 1934 figure using percentage changes in the value of imports into China proper shown in Hsiao, Foreign Trade, 68.

Col. 2: Compiled from Chung-kuo huo ch'ai, 6, 284-98, excluding numerous plants for which no initial date is given.

Col. 3: Shang-hai chieh fang ch'ien hou wu chia tzu liao hui pien, 1921-1957 (Shanghai, 1958), 285.

Col. 4: Nan-k'ai chih shu tzu liao, 82. Before 1926, figures shown in the table are averages of annual price data. Series A and B are for different brands of matches.

most comprehensive survey lists 255 Chinese firms established between 1879 and 1933, of which 185 were still in existence at the end of this period.[81] In view of normal attrition among new ven-

81. Ibid., 5-7, 20-21, 41, 284-98. The total of 255 firms includes 29 listed without initial dates (pp. 284-98) that appear to have been established prior to 1934.

tures and numerous references to the "oppression" of Chinese firms by foreign rivals, this is a high rate of survival.[82] Despite the gloomy tenor of historians' observations, the available data show that the match industry compiled an enviable record of growth and import replacement.

The trade figures in Table 2.12 show that match imports declined rapidly from their 1912 peak. A modest revival of import sales in the late 1920s aroused bitter accusations of dumping, but had little impact on the national match market. A new protective tariff enforced at the end of 1930 effectively removed foreign matches from the Chinese market. Data on the establishment of private Chinese producers, also shown in Table 2.12, and on the value of imported match-making materials, which rose rapidly after 1905, point to growing domestic production as the cause of declining imports.[83] Import replacement, which is conventionally attributed to China's economic isolation during World War I, actually began before the outbreak of war and gathered speed after the cessation of hostilities in Europe.

Estimates of domestic production, summarized in Table 2.13, confirm the impression of rapid growth. Even with due allowance for possible data errors, Table 2.13 shows that China's match industry enjoyed considerable growth between 1913 and the 1930s. Comparing the midpoint of the 1913 output range with national output for 1931–33 gives an average annual growth rate of 8.9 percent during the intervening two decades. Rapid output growth meant that domestic matches rapidly supplanted imports as the main source of supply. This is shown in Table 2.14. In 1913, imports occupied at least two-thirds of China's match market. By 1930, the last year before the imposition of a 40 percent tariff eliminated foreign suppliers, the share of imports in domestic match sales had plunged to only 13 percent. Furthermore, the figures in

82. Chang, *Industrial Development*, 45, comments that "the overall position of the Chinese-owned companies remained relatively weak and insignificant" in the match industry because of "waves of foreign competition." Typical complaints of dumping and competition from foreign producers in China appear in Ch'en Chen, comp., *Chung-kuo chin tai kung yeh shih tzu liao*, Collection 4, (Peking, 1961), 629, 651–52.

83. Data on imports of match materials are shown in Ch'en, *Chung-kuo chin tai kung yeh*, Collection 4, 630.

Table 2.13
Match Production in China, 1913-34
(Million Cases)

Year	China Proper			Manchuria			National Total		
	Ch (1)	F (2)	Total (3)	Ch (4)	F (5)	Total (6)	Ch (7)	F (8)	Total (9)
1913	...	...	...	...	...	...	...	...	.15-.28
1926	...	...	...	...	...	.19	...	...	...
1927	...	...	...	...	...	.31	...	...	...
1928	.76	...	...	...	...	.57	...	...	1.33+
1929	.73	...	...	...	...	.44	...	...	1.17+
1930	.68	.13	.81	.21	.15	.36	.89	.28	1.17
1931	.84	.13	.97	.28	.07	.35	1.12	.20	1.32
1932	.88	.13	1.01	...	...	.19[a]	...	...	1.20[a]
1933	.91	.12	1.03	.21	.15	.36	1.12	.27	1.39
1934	.85	.09	.94	...	...	...	...	...	...

Notes: Ch indicates output from Chinese-owned plants; F indicates output from foreign-owned plants.

[a]Probable underestimates.

Sources: Col. 1: For 1928-33, Chung-kuo huo ch'ai, 42-43, gives the total output for 1931-33 along with figures for Chinese-owned plants in seven provinces for 1928-33. These provinces contributed 84.5 percent of the recorded output for 1931-33. The estimates for 1928-30 assume that the seven provinces accounted for 84.5 percent of total output in these years as well. For 1934: Ch'en, Chung-kuo chin tai kung yeh, Collection 4, 642-43.

Col. 2: For 1931-33: Chung-kuo huo ch'ai, 42; for 1934, Ch'en, Chung-kuo chin tai kung yeh, Collection 4, 642-43; the figure for 1930 is assumed to be identical with 1931 and 1932.

Cols. 3, 6, 7-9: The sums of the components. The entry for 1913 in Col. 9 is from Appendix A.

Cols. 4-6: For 1926-30, Manshū kayakurui tōsei oyobi matchi kōgyō hōsaku (n.p., 1935), 34, 35, 41; for 1931, The Manchoukuo Yearbook, 1934 (Tokyo, 1934), 420; for 1932, Manshū sangyō tōkei 1932 (Dairen, 1933), 120; for 1933, Wu Pao-san, Chung-kuo kuo min so te, 1933 nien (Shanghai, 1947), 2:74.

Table 2.14 show that Chinese firms dominated domestic production, accounting for roughly four-fifths of output in 1933.[84]

Between 1913 and the early 1930s, Chinese match producers

84. *Chung-kuo huo ch'ai*, 42, gives the share of foreign firms as 24 percent of factory output and 20 percent of total output (including handicrafts).

Table 2.14
Sources of Match Supply, 1913 and 1930-33
(million cases)

	1913	1930	1931	1932	1933
Domestic output	.18-.29	1.17	1.32	1.20	1.39
Chinese plants	...	.89	...	...	1.12
Foreign plants	...	.28	...	...	0.29
Imports	0.57	0.17	0.05	0.01	0.02
Total	.75-.86	1.34	1.37	1.21	1.41
Percentage shares[a]					
Domestic output	23-34	87	96	99	98
Chinese plants	...	66	...	...	79
Foreign plants	...	21	...	...	20
Imports	76-66	13	4	1	1
Total	100	100	100	100	100

[a]Column totals may not check because of rounding error.

Sources: Tables 2.12 and 2.13 and Chung-kuo huo-ch'ai, 303.

achieved rapid output growth, rolled back the share of imports in total sales, and foiled the attempts of powerful foreign business combines, notably the Swedish match cartel, to dominate the domestic market through imports or local production. In addition, the industry experienced a gradual process of specialization and the development of backward linkages. By the 1930s, widely dispersed woodworking plants supplied the industry with matchsticks and matchboxes. There were also a few suppliers of paper wrappings, glue, and chemicals used in match heads, although most of these materials continued to be imported.[85] Producers often divided their facilities into separate plants for different processes. Wei Ling, a firm located in Shenyang, operated "three factories for packing and labelling, for applying chemicals to sticks, and for making sticks." This "efficiency scheme" enabled the firm to absorb

85. "Match Industry in China," *Chinese Economic Journal* 10, no. 3 (1932): 202–4; Z. T. Kyi, "Match-making Industry," *Chinese Economic Journal* 4 (1929):305; and *Chung-kuo huo ch'ai*, 66.

"the Mukden [Shenyang] Match Mfg. Co., a big Japanese financed concern."[86] Machinery producers began to supply equipment to the match industry. A 1935 survey reported that "although the earlier plants used Japanese machinery, those established in the past seven or eight years all use Chinese equipment," which sold for 30 percent less than Japanese equipment that was only slightly more productive.[87]

The substantial achievements of China's match producers raise interesting questions concerning the ability of this industry to survive and expand in an environment of free trade, rivalry with predatory foreign combines, and economic instability. Three separate characteristics—technology, transport, and demand—seem important in explaining the performance of China's match industry. Producers in prewar China used a wide spectrum of manufacturing techniques. Some firms operated on a large scale, using state-of-the-art machinery and sophisticated internal organization. Liu Hung-sheng, a Shanghai-born compradore-industrialist with interests in coal mining, shipping, cement, textiles, and banking, established a match plant at Soochow in 1920 and gradually expanded his interests to include match factories in Shanghai and Hankow, production of matchsticks, glue, and other materials, and a printing plant that made labels for matchboxes. Liu purchased new equipment embodying advanced technology, conducted research into match chemistry, subjected his operations to detailed cost and profit analysis, and maintained a large and complex sales organization that distributed over sixty brands of matches under carefully articulated pricing policies.[88] Other producers entered the industry with minute assets, relying on hand-labor and their own business acumen to eke out a profit.

The flexibility of match-making technology encouraged the proliferation of large and small plants using various combinations of mechanized and manual methods. In the West and in the largest Chinese plants, contemporary descriptions noted that "mechanical devices are everywhere in evidence in the manufacture of

86. Kyi, "Match-making Industry," 307.
87. *Matchi kōgyō hōkokusho* (Nanking, 1940), 24 and Liu, *Chung-kuo kung yeh,* 1:33–34.
88. *Chung-kuo huo ch'ai,* chap. 3 and *Liu Hung-sheng ch'i yeh shih liao* (Shanghai, 1981), 1:74–154, 2:146–251.

matches," but in smaller Chinese plants, the low cost of labor encouraged the use of manual techniques. Some tasks were assigned to workers who operated in their own homes. Inside the factories, "juvenile workers fill the boxes by hand with incredible speed," eliminating the need for packing machinery.[89] When machinery was used, the factory manager could choose between electric-powered equipment and cheaper hand-operated devices at nearly every stage of the production process.[90] This technological flexibility enabled primitive workshops to survive and compete with more sophisticated producers, including such international giants as the Swedish Match Corporation. Scale economies, if present, were not sufficiently pronounced to force small producers from the marketplace.

In their competition with large factories, small-scale match producers benefited from the high cost of domestic transport. Matches are bulky, with a low ratio of weight and value to volume, vulnerable to water damage, and explosive. It is much easier and cheaper to transport a ton of timber or chemicals than it is to move a ton of matches over the same distance. Since the market for matches extended throughout China, the friction of distance offered effective protection for local producers, even if their costs were considerably higher than those of larger and better-equipped, but distant rivals. High transport costs helped domestic producers to withstand international competition. Local manufacturers, especially those drawing on nearby forest resources to make matchsticks, benefited similarly in their competition with products shipped from plants in Shanghai, Tientsin, and other industrial centers.

Spatial dispersion was only one among several aspects of demand that helped shape the evolution of China's match industry. The use of matches gradually spread from the largest cities across the entire country. Assuming national consumption of 1.3 million cases and a population of 500 million for the early 1930s implies that the average Chinese used 3.6 matches per day.[91] Matches

89. Kyi, "Match-Making Industry," 309.
90. Yokoyama Suguru, "Establishment of Match Manufacturing in China," *Hiroshima daigaku bungakubu kiyō* 25, no. 1 (1965):272. Ch'en, *Chung-kuo chin tai kung yeh*, Collection 4, 638–39, confirms that small plants employed hand labor to perform many tasks for which larger establishments used machines.
91. Annual production of 1.3 million cases, each containing 50 gross of boxes, at 70 matches per box implies a yearly supply of 655.2 billion matches. With a population of 500 million, per capita use is 3.6 matches per day.

were most popular among urban consumers: a 1938 estimate placed daily consumption by Tientsin residents at 8.4 matches. Farm households also used matches to light tobacco, mosquito repellent, and fires for cooking and heating.[92] The distinctive seasonal pattern of match demand, with sales highest in the post-harvest months of October, November, and December, indicates that matches were bought by rural residents and not just by relatively wealthy urbanites (whose consumption of cigarettes presumably showed little seasonal fluctuation).[93] Seasonal demand fluctuations benefited small-scale producers whose low fixed costs permitted them to close down during slack periods. Large producers, burdened with costly machinery and high interest charges, faced the unpleasant choice of operating below capacity or of financing large inventories in anticipation of future sales.

The appeal of matches to all classes of Chinese, including many with very low incomes, ensured a ready demand for inferior goods by consumers willing to accept poor quality in return for low price. This demand for cheap matches provided ample marketing opportunities for small-scale producers who used inferior wood, chemicals, and equipment to turn out matches that, although less attractive than expensive factory products, appealed to poor customers whose alternative was flint and steel.

Anecdotal accounts of competition in the match industry suggest a highly segmented market. Individual producers viewed demand for their wares as inelastic, meaning that higher prices would raise sales revenues despite lower volume. There were frequent complaints that prices were too low, a condition invariably attributed to the dumping of low-cost Japanese or Swedish matches into the Chinese market. Available price data, summarized in Table 2.12, offer no support for these claims. Between 1913 and 1929, the price of *Pei-yang* brand matches sold in Tientsin rose by 62.4 percent compared with 60.8 percent for all consumer manufactures and only 36 percent for manufactured producer goods. In Shanghai, the price of Swedish *Feng-huang* matches, a high-priced vari-

---

92. *Chung-kuo huo ch'ai*, 46.
93. Tax records show that fourth-quarter shipments of matches accounted for 30.2, 27.4, and 29.0 percent of the annual totals for 1932, 1933, and 1934; see *Matchi kōgyō hōkokusho*, 91–92. Seasonal sales peaks were attributed to demand from traveling merchants who stocked up in the fourth quarter (Ch'en, *Chung-kuo chin tai kung yeh*, Collection 4, 644).

ety, rose by 35.0 percent between 1925 and 1929, while the index for manufactures rose by only 4.8 percent.[94] During 1927–29, years in which Swedish dumping is alleged to have reached its peak, the volume of imports failed to regain pre-1920 levels; available price data show no downward trend in either annual or monthly match prices reported for either Shanghai or Tientsin (Table 2.12).[95]

If imports failed to retain a large market share and also failed to depress prices, why did they attract widespread unfavorable notice? One plausible explanation is that the availability of foreign matches frustrated the efforts of major Chinese producers to organize regional cartels for the purpose of restricting output and raising prices in the face of inelastic demand.[96] In December 1930, the Nanking government responded to the industry's complaints by raising the import duty on foreign matches from 7.5 to 40 percent.[97] This effectively removed foreign matches from the Chinese market, as is evident from Table 2.12. But the new tariff did not bring an end to the industry's complaints, which now focused on the new consolidated tax applied to matches starting in February 1931 and idle capacity, which was attributed to excessive taxation and clandestine match imports into North China by the Japanese.

A more probable source of idle capacity is to be found in price data that show the Shanghai wholesale price of *Yü-ch'iao* safety matches leaping from 40.07 yuan per case in January 1931 to 50.32 yuan in the following month and 65.30 yuan in March. In Tientsin, the wholesale price of *Fan-wan* matches jumped from 30–31 yuan throughout 1930 to 33 yuan in March 1931, 43.4 yuan in April, 59 yuan in May, and 64 yuan in June, a price that was maintained until 1934.[98] Chinese producers, who had attempted to form car-

94. Price indexes for manufactures are annual averages from *Nan-k'ai chih shu tzu liao*, 13 and *Shang-hai wu chia tzu liao*, 135.
95. Annual data are shown in Table 2.12. Monthly data appear in *Nan-k'ai chih shu tzu liao*, 111 (for 1928–29 only) and *Shang-hai wu chia tzu liao*, 286–87. For allegations of Swedish dumping, see *Chung-kuo huo ch'ai*, 25–34; "Match Industry in China," 205–6; *Matchi kōgyō hōkokusho*, 3–4, 55; and Ch'en, Yao, and Feng, *Chung-kuo chin tai kung yeh*, Collection 2, 822–35.
96. With inelastic demand, higher prices produce greater revenues despite reduced sales volume. Lower volume means lower production costs, so that price increases contribute doubly to raising profit by both increasing total revenue and lowering total cost.
97. *Matchi kōgyō hōkokusho*, 5.
98. Ibid., 55 and *Nan-k'ai chih shu tzu liao*, 111–12.

tels on several previous occasions, evidently felt that the new tariff offered an opportunity to increase profits by restricting output and raising prices.[99]

A 1932 survey expatiated on the virtues of the China Match Company, a combine organized in 1930, in the following terms:[100]

> One of the most important moves on the part of the China manufacturers was the organization of the China Match Co. . . . an amalgamation of three well-known factories. . . . Competition . . . has been avoided, and the Company has been able to raise the price of matches from time to time when necessary. . . . Most important of all, costs of production have been very substantially reduced.

Following these huge increases in price and profit margins, the tax on matches, set first at 5–10 yuan and later at 10.8–21 yuan per case, should be seen as Nanking's attempt to share in the windfall resulting from the new tariff rather than as a sudden assault on the industry's prosperity. In any event, the tax was widely evaded, with actual collections falling considerably short of the posted rates.[101]

Unfortunately for the industry, deflation and domestic competition brought an early end to this bonanza. The combination of high profits, low capital cost, and simple technology attracted thirty-nine new firms into the match industry during 1930–32 (Table

99. *Chung-kuo huo ch'ai*, 13–15, mentions efforts to form cartels among producers in Canton and Szechwan as early as 1905. Chinese and Japanese manufacturers in Manchuria formed a joint industry association in 1923. The market-sharing arrangements proposed in 1929 failed only because Swedish interests refused to cooperate (*Manshū kayakurui tōsei oyobi matchi kōgyō hōsaku* [N.p., 1935], 50 and *The Manchoukuo Year Book, 1934* [Tokyo, 1934], 420). At times, cartel arrangements seemingly involved official participation. In March 1931, "a report from Mukden [Shenyang]" noted that "Chinese authorities had decided to proceed with the immediate establishment of a match monopoly in the North Eastern provinces" which would exclude imported goods (*China Weekly Review*, April 11, 1931, 204; May 9, 1931, 357; and May 16, 1931, 394).

100. "Match Industry in China," 207–8.

101. *Matchi kōgyō hōkokusho*, 36–37, includes government admissions that tax evasion could not be stopped; see also *Chung-kuo huo ch'ai*, 43, 53. In 1934, when the official rates were 10.80–21.00 yuan per case, the revenue from the match tax amounted to about 7 million yuan (the average for two fiscal years ending June 1934 and June 1935 from Arthur N. Young, *China's Nation-Building Effort, 1927–1937: The Financial and Economic Record* [Stanford, 1971], 433) and the output of matches in China proper was about one million cases, suggesting an actual tax burden of about seven yuan per case, or between one-third and two-thirds of the official rate.

2.12). Prices began to sag. By 1933, *Yü-ch'iao* safety matches had dropped from their 1931 peak of 65.53 yuan and the 1932 high of 59.65 yuan to a year-end low of only 43.50 yuan per case. A year later, the price had fallen to the January 1931 level of 40 yuan. There was no relief in 1935 or 1936, as the price remained below 40 yuan.[102] The government now refused to lower the tax rate and the industry found itself mired in a genuine cost squeeze in which weak demand, rising taxes, and idle capacity deprived many firms of their profitability and drove some into bankruptcy.

The prewar history of China's match industry thus closes with an ironic twist. Patriotic Chinese scholars, echoed by foreign historians, have transformed the self-seeking rhetoric of would-be monopolists into a story of unequal combat between predatory foreigners, a grasping government, and a group of weak but intrepid industrialists. In fact, it was the domestic producers who nearly succeeded in cornering China's match market. The actions of the Swedes, who eventually agreed to join a cartel arranged by Liu Hung-sheng, may have held match prices in check until Nanking intervened with prohibitively high tariffs.[103] Prior to 1936, Swedish sales efforts not only lowered Chinese living costs, but by encouraging the spread of match consumption spurred the growth of a market from which they were quickly excluded, first by Chinese competition and then by the government's new tariff.

The Process of Industrialization
in Prewar China

Abundant materials testify to the presence of a limited, but dynamic and robust process of industrialization in China during the first four decades of the present century. Manufacturing output grew rapidly from a tiny base. The geographic pattern and sectoral composition of industrial expansion largely reflected the dictates of market forces. Domestic entrepreneurs and managers achieved conspicuous success in the face of generally unrestricted competition from manufactured imports and China-based foreign enterprise. Although many accounts emphasize the significance of rivalry between Chinese and foreign producers, the most important

102. *Matchi kōgyō hōkokusho*, 55.
103. Sherman Cochran informs me that the Swedish match combine joined Liu's sales cartel in 1936–37.

function of foreign products and foreign firms was to point the way for Chinese imitators who rapidly attained strong, often commanding, positions in a long succession of markets initially dominated by foreign products. The history of wire nail manufacture at Shanghai is typical. This industry "began as so many others with a rapid increase in imports, followed by not very successful Chinese efforts to manufacture the article, then the organization of a larger plant . . . using foreign capital and foreign technical assistance; and finally the emergence of a Chinese modern industry."[104] Although the industries that sprang up in this fashion never occupied a large share of China's national product prior to the Pacific War, some segments of industry attained quite substantial size: China's production of manufactured cotton goods was among the world's largest; by 1927, electric power sales in Shanghai, a good indicator of industrial activity, had surpassed comparable figures for the British industrial centers of Manchester and Birmingham.[105]

Despite its limited scale, prewar industrialization influenced China's economy in numerous ways. Growing manufacture of textiles, wheat flour, cigarettes, edible oil, and other agriculturally based products generated massive new demands for the commercial cropping of farm products, especially cotton, silkworm cocoons, wheat, tobacco, and soybeans. These new forces encouraged farmers across wide regions of China to restructure their cropping arrangements, marketing behavior, and work schedules. New industries also required large quantities of coal, salt, paper, and other nonfarm products; the expansion of production in these areas absorbed village workers and added another dimension to the impact of industrialization on Chinese agriculture. Chinese farmers also gained access to small but growing supplies of domestically manufactured agricultural inputs, including diesel and electric pumps, rice milling machines, cotton gins, baling equipment, and chemical fertilizers.[106]

104. H. D. Fong, "Industrial Capital in China," *Nankai Social and Economic Quarterly* 9, no. 1 (1936):54.
105. Kung Chün, *Chung-kuo hsin kung yeh fa chan shih ta kang* (Shanghai, 1933), 238–41.
106. See, among many others, H. D. Lamson, "The Effect of Industrialization upon Village Livelihood," *Chinese Economic Journal* 9, no. 4 (1931):1063; *Shan-hsi k'ao ch'a pao kao shu* (Shanghai, 1936), 49; *China Weekly Review*, April 25, 1931, 275; *Chinese Economic Bulletin* 11, no. 336 (1927):63; and *Tung fang tsa chih* 28, no. 21 (1931):23–26.

Industrial growth increased the demand for a variety of services. Accumulation of metal-working skills from repair work for steamships, railways, mines, and textile plants spawned an engineering industry that quickly began to imitate a broad range of foreign machinery, tools, and metal products and gradually supplanted many varieties of equipment imports, especially at the low end of the price-quality spectrum. Available data show a steep increase in the ratio of domestic to imported equipment.[107]

Finally, industrial development offered new opportunities for China's handicraft sector. From the craft viewpoint, the growth of manufacturing was not an unmixed blessing. Many craftsmen, particularly in cotton spinning, suffered financial loss when former customers began purchasing manufactured substitutes. But industrialization opened new vistas to craft producers that were quickly explored by China's "abundance of small-time entrepreneurs."[108] New avenues for craft development emerged as a by-product of industrial growth because manufacturing operations typically encompassed only certain segments of the production process and because low labor costs, the willingness of Chinese customers to sacrifice quality to obtain low-priced goods, and the efficient operation of traditional economic networks enabled craft production to compete with modern factories in a surprising range of trades. Co-production arrangements were common, with factories and craft workshops executing different stages of fabrication; the popularity of manufactured yarn and iron looms among handicraft weavers, who continue to ply their trade in Shanghai's suburbs even in the 1980s, is only the most prominent example.[109] Craftsmen resorted increasingly to industrially supplied materials, tools, and hand- or electric-powered machines, using some products of indus-

107. For an extended analysis of the scale and significance of prewar engineering development, see Thomas G. Rawski, "Economic Growth and Integration in Prewar China" (Toronto, 1982), appendix C and *China's Transition to Industrialism: Producer Goods and Economic Development in the Twentieth Century* (Ann Arbor, 1980), chap. 2 and Shigeru Ishikawa, "The Development of Capital Goods Sector: Experience of Pre-PRC China" (Geneva, 1985).

108. Tim Wright, "Growth of the Modern Chinese Coal Industry: An Analysis of Supply and Demand," *Modern China* 7, no. 3 (1981):325.

109. Hsia Lin-ken, "On the Transformation of Cotton Textile Handicraft Industry in the Modern Shanghai Region," *Chung-kuo she hui ching chi shih yen chiu* 3 (1984):29.

try to enhance their power to compete against other industrial goods in domestic and foreign markets.

The immediate and long-term economic significance of initial manufacturing efforts in China, as in Japan and elsewhere, extends well beyond the modest share of total output occupied by factory production. The impact of manufacturing on Chinese economic patterns and structures was magnified by new developments in banking, finance, transport, and communication that eased the path toward commercialization, integration, and growth. These changes form the subject matter of the following chapters.

Chapter Three

Banking and the
Monetary System

In China, as in many nations, a limited supply of money, credit, transfer arrangements, and other financial services restricted the development of new industries and the expansion of older trades. The relaxation of financial constraints occupies an important position in the story of China's prewar economic development. Increases in the number and function of financial intermediaries, the quantity of money, the variety of banking and credit facilities, and the strength and stability of the whole monetary system brought unprecedented economic integration and encouraged potential buyers and sellers to increase their reliance on the market as a source of income and supply. Together with reductions in the cost of transport and communication, a topic to be considered in the following chapter, an expanded supply of money and credit provided an important stimulus to the growth of specialization, production, and trade.

The impact of new monetary and financial patterns on China's economy was broader and deeper than the effects of contemporaneous developments in industry and transportation. New monetary arrangements penetrated all but the most isolated regions and affected every sector of the economy. Even the daily transactions of the farm populace reflected the progress of monetary developments originating in Shanghai and other coastal centers. The first four decades of the twentieth century witnessed an unprecedented expansion of the money economy and a substantial increase in the degree of national economic integration. The money stock shifted from earlier arrangements based on copper cash and uncoined silver to a new structure in which bank liabilities—deposits and notes—occupied the central position. These changes occurred mainly within the private sector, with government policy occupying an important position only in the closing years of the Nanking decade.

Contemporary and historical accounts often overlook the magnitude and consequences of these changes. The objective of this chapter is to sketch the outlines of the inherited financial system, trace the evolution of new banking institutions, both foreign and Chinese, discuss the development of traditional intermediaries, and investigate the macroeconomic consequences of monetary and financial change. The quantitative backdrop to the discussion is contained in Appendix C, which provides annual estimates of the national money stock and its components—coined and uncoined silver, copper coin, and the notes and deposits of modern and old-style financial institutions—for the years 1910–36. Although the underlying data present numerous difficulties, the results make it possible to reconstruct the broad contours of monetary change in prewar China and to trace the impact of monetary developments on production and exchange.

Money, Finance, and the Economy

Money and credit occupy important positions whenever production and exchange outgrow the confines of specialization for local barter. Suppose that farmers in location A wish to produce cotton to be sold in a distant location X. Farmers desire to be paid for their crop on delivery at A, but consumers will not begin to advance funds until products made from the cotton are put on sale in retail outlets at X, which may be hundreds of miles distant from A. Exchange is impossible without a means of *financing* the cotton shipment during the interval between delivery at A and eventual sale at X. The longer the period of transit and the more complex the series of processing operations (ginning, packing, spinning, dyeing, weaving, etc.) separating original supplier and final purchaser, the greater the requirement for financing, both in terms of duration and amount.

Chinese sources attest to the centrality of credit in prewar commerce. In the cotton cloth trade, the need for credit was described
as brief, but crucial; without credit, merchants could not expand
their operations.[1] Efforts to increase exports of sesame seeds foundered on the high cost of finance. Top quality seeds from Po county
(Anhwei) could not be profitably moved to major markets because
the trip "entailed a loss of interest alone of at least 30 days on
capital outlay." Efforts to market seeds grown in Honan "did not
prove a financial success, chiefly owing to the heavy loss in interest
through the junks taking 30 days . . . to reach Pangpu."[2]

Figure 3.1 presents a schematic view of this situation. A(d) represents the cost of delivering a particular product (pottery, for
example) from point A to location d. B(d) indicates the cost of delivering identical pottery produced at B to various locations. Under
the hypothesized cost conditions, buyers located between A and C
will purchase their supplies from producers located at A. Consumers situated between C and B, however, will obtain their pottery from suppliers at location B even though production costs at
B (measured by the vertical distance Bb) are double those at A
(measured by Aa). If delivery costs fall from A(d) to A*(d), low-
cost pottery from A will now dominate the market at all points
between A and B, including B itself. Following this change, consumers located all along the route linking A and B will be able to
obtain their accustomed quantities of pottery at lower prices than
before. The reduced price will increase the quantity of pottery demanded. The associated increase in purchasing power (buyers can
purchase the same mix of products as before and retain extra cash
following the reduction in pottery price) will lead to increased demand for a variety of commodities and services. If pottery production involves scale economies, the concentration of production at
A will bring further reductions in production cost and selling
prices, leading to further increases in the real income of pottery
buyers. Higher purchasing power will encourage producers to increase the output of other goods and will also provide opportunities
for displaced potters at B to redeploy their resources in pursuit of
new markets.

1. *Pu? Shang-hai chih mien pu yü mien pu yeh* (Shanghai, 1932), 127.
2. China. The Maritime Customs. *Returns of Trade and Trade Reports, 1914*
(Shanghai, 1915), 2:648, 650.

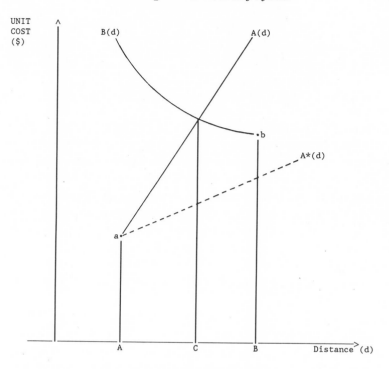

FIGURE 3.1. Impact of Improved Financial or Transport Arrangements on Patterns of Trade

Aa and Bb indicate unit cost for goods producted at Locations A or B.

A(d) and B(d) indicate the full cost of delivering one unit of goods made at Locations A or B to Location d.

A*(d) indicates the full cost of delivering one unit of goods made at A to Location d after a reduction in interest charges, transactions costs, or transport fees.

Even though Figure 3.1 omits a number of salient features, including product quality and the possibility of specialization along the lines of *comparative* rather than absolute advantage (that is, each location specializes in the production of goods for which its costs are *relatively*—not necessarily *absolutely*—lower than elsewhere), the diagram illustrates the important possibility that high delivery expenses may obstruct economic expansion. As a Customs officer observed of the trade in sesame seeds, without an improved delivery system "this important and, to the farmer, lucrative business must continue to be restricted."[3] The diagram also shows that transport costs and finance charges affect trade in an identical fashion. The benefits arising from reduced delivery costs [the shift from $A(d)$ to $A^*(d)$] are no different if the change arises from lower interest rates, reduced fuel charges, or quicker transit time.

The development of financial institutions can affect production and exchange by providing new forms of payment, improving the distribution of credit, and increasing the supply of funds. All three changes were much in evidence in prewar China. The substitution of banknotes, bank drafts, bills of exchange, or checks for cash payments facilitates trade by economizing on time, shipping costs, and risk. With 4,000 prewar silver dollars weighing approximately one ton, the cost of moving large sums of money, especially in rural areas where the risk of robbery called for employment of armed escorts, was far from trivial; the decline of currency escort services is a useful index of the spread of bank transfers as a substitute for shipments of hard cash.[4]

By promoting economic integration, financial development improves the efficiency of credit allocation. When financial opportunities are limited, potential lenders face a severely restricted choice of outlets for their funds. In the absence of interregional financial networks, the owners of funds accumulated in one region may have no channel to communicate with would-be borrowers offering high-yielding projects in other regions. As a result, inferior projects in capital-rich regions may obtain ample funding while more productive opportunities elsewhere languish. As new financial institutions begin to move funds from low- to high-yielding locations, the resulting increase in returns is likely to stimulate a general rise in the volume of available credit. Even in the absence of higher earnings for lenders (note that increasing efficiency in financial businesses creates the possibility of both higher returns to savers *and* lower costs for borrowers), an expanding variety of financial instruments can be expected to increase the volume of credit as lenders are increasingly able to assign funds to a range of

3. Ibid., 649.
4. See Eduard Kann, *The Currencies of China*, 2d ed. (Shanghai, 1926), 169 and Pi Hsiang-hui, "Forms of Financial Flows in Pao-ti County, Hopei," in *Chung-kuo ching chi yen chiu*, ed. Fang Hsien-t'ing (Changsha, 1938), 2:839–40.

financial assets (stocks, bonds, deposits, mortgages, etc.) and build portfolios reflecting their preferences regarding yield, risk, asset maturities, and the regional or sectoral direction of lending.

Monetary and financial deepening refers to a rising ratio of money and credit to current output as well as to society's stock of tangible capital, its growing variety of payment mechanisms, an increase in the ability of lenders and borrowers to obtain access to projects and funds in businesses and locations far removed from their own, and an expanding range of direct and indirect financial instruments available to borrowers and lenders. Monetary and financial deepening can contribute significantly to the development of production and exchange.

One further consequence of financial development requires attention. This concerns the link between monetary developments and economic stability. Modern governments regulate the monetary and financial system as part of a stabilization policy. Excessive monetary growth can generate inflation, while monetary contraction or inadequate expansion can retard growth or even force output to decline. Monetary policy hardly existed in prewar China. Yet the process of financial deepening described in the following pages was far enough advanced to enable China's economy to avoid the worst consequences of the world depression of the 1930s even in the absence of purposeful and effective official stabilization policy. Ironically, the very changes that allowed China to overcome destabilizing shocks in the early 1930s created the possibility for domestically induced instability in the form of hyperinflation a few years later.

The discussion of financial development and its consequences begins with a review of the monetary and financial institutions of the late imperial era.

The Monetary System in
Late Imperial China

Prior to the creation of foreign banking institutions in the mid-nineteenth century, China's indigenous financial system represented a complex and sophisticated adaptation to the requirements of an agrarian economy with substantial local and interregional trade.[5] A bimetallic currency system used minted copper cash to settle retail transactions, while silver provided the medium of exchange for large-scale trade and the unit of account for business and government. China's silver money included sycee, or silver ingots, cast in the form of "shoes" by private smelters that stamped the weight and fineness on each shoe, along with broken silver and, following the rise of European trade beginning in the seventeenth century, coined silver imported from Europe and the Americas. Banks and merchants also issued small quantities of paper notes.

The size of China's economy, the scale of commerce, and the multiplicity of monetary vehicles created vast opportunities for financial intermediation. Merchants, taxpayers, government offices, artisans, and consumers needed to convert funds from copper to silver or vice versa. Domestic commerce could benefit from interregional remittances to avoid expensive and risky shipments of silver. The state's administrative and military activities frequently required the transfer of funds from one location to another. With no unified medium of account or standard of value, even the counting of large sums became a highly specialized occupation.

China's financial system paralleled that of preindustrial Europe in its complexity and sophistication. There were numerous intermediaries, from local money changers and pawnshops to large institutions with far-flung networks of branches or correspondents. The variety of services available was similarly broad, ranging from deposits, exchange, currency transfer, and loans, available through small institutions, to large interregional transfers and the financing of long-distance trade, which was offered by larger firms. The larger institutions fell into two categories: the Shansi banks and the *ch'ien-chuang*, or native banks. The Shansi banks, named for their province of origin, specialized in interregional transfers. Much of their business involved government funds. Because of their deep involvement with Ch'ing finances and the inroads of government-sponsored banks into their remittance business, the Shansi banks

5. Among many descriptions of Ch'ing monetary and financial systems, I have benefited from two accounts by Yeh-chien Wang: "Evolution of the Chinese Monetary System, 1644–1850," in *Modern Chinese Economic History*, ed. Chi-ming Hou and Tzong-shian Yu (Taipei, 1979) and *Chung-kuo chin tai huo pi yü yin hang ti yen chin (1644–1937)* (Taipei, 1981).

failed to survive the Republican revolution of 1911 and quickly faded into obscurity.

The *ch'ien-chuang* were local institutions linked mainly by correspondent relationships with banks in other commercial centers, although some maintained small networks of branches. *Ch'ien-chuang* were owned by individuals, partnerships, or small groups of stockholders who bore unlimited liability for the discharge of bank obligations. The *ch'ien-chuang* accepted deposits, extended loans and undertook direct investments in business ventures, conducted interregional transfers, prepared and accepted bills of exchange, issued banknotes and orders (promises to pay specific sums on specified future dates), transferred funds among depositors, and performed other functions associated with these services. Personal reputation and credit, rather than tangible collateral, served as the cornerstone of native bank operations. Although free of government supervision, the *ch'ien-chuang* were subject to self-regulation through their own guilds, which also performed some central banking functions, including the provision of interbank clearing facilities in the largest commercial centers.

Ch'ing financial arrangements provided sufficient credit and transfer facilities to support a large volume of domestic trade, but the system remained severely flawed. The main difficulty was the absence of a convenient and inexpensive medium of exchange. Local wholesale transactions were settled smoothly and cheaply by transferring bank credits from buyer to seller. But with different units of *tael* account prevailing in different commercial centers and sometimes even in different trades within a single city, the settlement of interregional and intersectoral wholesale transactions required either the transfer and assay of silver ingots or what amounted to a foreign exchange transaction between different bookkeeping currencies.[6]

6. If a Shanghai merchant purchased goods in Hankow, the seller would expect payment in Hankow *taels*, the local unit of account. To obtain local bank credit in Hankow *taels*, the buyer would either import silver or sell bank credits denominated in Shanghai *taels*. The relative price of Shanghai and Hankow *taels* could fluctuate in response to shifts in supply and demand that were, in turn, linked to changes in trade flows involving the two centers. A surge in demand for Hankow products would push up the price of Hankow *taels* just as an increase in British (or world) demand for French goods might raise the franc relative to the pound.

Another serious problem was the lack of security in a banking system that was often only as strong as its weakest member. The bankruptcy of an owner or major customer of even a single bank could trigger a series of local business failures. The diversity of interests typical of Chinese businessmen and the importance of credit in financing commercial flows meant that difficulties in a single commercial center or a particular trade quickly spread to other localities or businesses. Larger disruptions resulting from natural disasters, political disturbances, or financial excesses, such as the speculative boom in rubber shares of 1908–10, created waves of bankruptcies that reverberated throughout China's financial centers.[7]

Major Banking Institutions
Foreign Banks

The limited ability of China's financial system to provide a flexible supply of secure and easily transferable monetary assets encouraged the development first of foreign and then of Chinese banks modeled on European and Japanese practice. Foreign penetration of China's financial system began with the introduction of European and American coined silver to China's coastal trading regions in the sixteenth century. Chinese traders welcomed the Carolus dollar and later the Mexican silver dollar because these coins fulfilled the long-standing need for convenient, easily negotiable, low-risk monetary instruments. Silver dollars allowed merchants to partially circumvent the costly and time-consuming process of weighing and assaying silver. The demand for silver dollars was so strong that they often commanded a premium over their actual silver content. In the 1850s, the Carolus dollar was worth up to

7. The collapse of rubber prices in 1910 led to the failure of a large Chinese bank in Manila and then to the collapse of the state bank of Chekiang, two large Shanghai banks, and smaller firms in Shanghai, Peking, Canton, Ningpo, Nanking, and Hankow. See Ray O. Hall, *Chapters and Documents on Chinese National Banking* (Shanghai, 1920), 23–26. The ties between finance and commerce are reflected in frequent statements linking tight credit with stagnant commodity sales. See, for example, "Selected Documents and Telegrams on the Commercial and Financial Crises at Ningpo and Shanghai During the Hsüan-t'ung Reign (1908–1911)," *Li shih tang an* 3 (1984):36–41.

80 percent more in the Shanghai market than its intrinsic silver value.[8]

The expansion of foreign trade in the wake of the treaties of 1842, 1858, and 1860 created fresh demands for credit and transfer facilities which encouraged the creation of foreign banking outlets in the treaty ports. The first foreign firm, the (British) Oriental Bank, which opened in 1848, was an offshoot of an institution operating in India. The Hong Kong and Shanghai Bank, formed in 1864, was the first bank established for the express purpose of entering Chinese finance. Other institutions followed. By the mid-1930s, the number of foreign banks, including subsidiaries of banks with overseas headquarters, had risen to fifty-three firms with over 150 offices.[9]

Historical writing about foreign bank activities is colored by patriotic outrage over the liberties granted to these institutions under the "unequal" treaties. The foreign banking establishment is pictured as a colossus that quickly came to dominate China's financial system, using its treaty privileges to amass easy profits. Chang Yu-lan presents a typically intemperate indictment alleging that foreign banks attained indirect control of the domestic economy and used it to disrupt domestic enterprises, wreck the rural economy, upset indigenous craft occupations, control raw material prices, and exploit farmers.[10] More concretely, Djang Siao-mei insists that foreign banks could "manipulate the rate of exchange at will, in order to profit at the expense of the Chinese. For example, the rate of exchange as declared by the Hong Kong and Shanghai Banking Corporation was invariably higher than usual at times when payments were made by the Chinese government to settle its foreign debts."[11] Djang's specific allegation, which is echoed by numerous

8. E[duard] Kann, "What Is a Shanghai Tael?" *Chinese Economic Journal* 1 (1927):769. The persistence of this premium for foreign coin can be seen from reports in William F. Spaulding, *Eastern Exchange, Currency and Finance*, 2d ed. (London, 1917), 330; Maurice Collis, *Wayfoong: The Hongkong and Shanghai Banking Corporation* (London, 1965), 25; and Yen-p'ing Hao, *The Commercial Revolution in Nineteenth-Century China: The Rise of Sino-Western Mercantile Capitalism* (Berkeley, 1986), 39–42.
9. Wu Ch'eng-hsi, *Chung-kuo ti yin hang* (Shanghai, 1934), 103.
10. Chang Yu-lan, *Chung-kuo yin hang fa chan shih* (Shanghai, 1957), 9.
11. "Banking, Currency and Credit," *The Chinese Year Book, 1935–36* (Shanghai, 1935), 1449.

writers, appears to lack substance and the broader view articulated by Chang and many others exaggerates the stability, unity, and profitability of the foreign banking establishment as well as its independence from the Chinese financial system.[12]

Foreign banks grew up with the expansion of international trade in China's treaty ports. They financed the activities of exporters and importers, dealt in foreign exchange, acted as bankers to the foreign-controlled customs system, accepted deposits, and issued banknotes. Involvement with foreign trade and government borrowing drew foreign banks into intimate contact with domestic finance. The impact of Chinese financial practices on foreign banking establishments is visible in their use of the *tael* as a unit of account for deposits, loans, and banknotes, the foreign banks' dependence on Chinese compradores to transact much of their business, the use of packing credits and other arrangements sanctioned by Eastern custom rather than Western law, and the intimate relations that grew up between foreign banks and domestic financial intermediaries, especially the *ch'ien-chuang.*[13]

Financial ties with European and American trading houses drew foreign bankers into credit arrangements involving Chinese merchants who collected goods for export and distributed products imported from abroad.[14] Foreign banks were relatively well supplied with liquid funds but lacked the information essential to differentiate among potential Chinese borrowers. This combination of

12. On the issue of exchange rate manipulation, see Ralph W. Huenemann, *The Dragon and the Iron Horse: The Economics of Railroads in China, 1876–1937* (Cambridge, 1984), 115–18. Proponents of the Bank of Communications argued that a new bank was needed to do away with the exorbitant profits earned by foreign banks from exchange transactions. The bank's subsequent inattention to the foreign exchange market suggests that the potential profits of exchange business were not large. See Hall, *Chinese National Banking*, 90.

13. On the use of *tael* rather than dollar units for banknotes and accounts and the continuation of the much maligned compradore system, see Hsien K'o, *Chin pai nien lai ti kuo chu i tsai Hua yin hang fa hsing chih pi kai k'uang* (Shanghai, 1958), 10, 40; "Foreign Banks in Shanghai," *Shang-hai shih t'ung-chih-kuan ch'i-k'an* 2, no. 2 (1934):591; "The Reminiscences of Ch'en Kuang-fu (K. P. Chen) (December 20, 1881–July 1, 1976) as told to Julie Lien-ying How" (Columbia University Oral History Project, 1960–61), 38; Parks M. Coble, *The Shanghai Capitalists and the Nationalist Government, 1927–1937* (Cambridge, 1980), 23; and Ting Jih-ch'u and Tu Hsün-ch'eng, "A Brief Account of Yü Hsia-ch'ing," *Li shih yen chiu* 3 (1981):149–50.

14. Hao, *The Commercial Revolution*, 77, 95–96, 152–53.

strength and ignorance made them natural business partners for the native banks, who possessed excellent commercial intelligence but lacked ready cash. Foreign banks provided short-term unsecured credits known as "chop loans" to native bankers, who used the funds to finance the flow of trade goods to and from the major port cities. This system broke down in the 1910 crisis when many *ch'ien-chuang* defaulted on their obligations. The foreign lenders retaliated by refusing to extend further unsecured credits.

After 1911, foreign banks relied increasingly on their own compradores to collect information about domestic merchants and to act as guarantors for loans to Chinese businesses. Because bank compradores were themselves often native bankers, this procedure continued the tradition of joint financing of foreign trade by foreign banks and *ch'ien-chuang*. The aftermath of the Japanese attack on Shanghai in January 1932 illustrated the undiminished role of native banks in the financing of foreign trade. Fearing a wholesale removal of silver to the relative security of foreign bank vaults, the *ch'ien-chuang* refused to pay out silver against their commercial obligations, "confining their business to 'paper' which is passed from one native bank to another and is not negotiable with any foreign bank." The foreign commercial press lamented the result: that "practically nothing has been removed from the Shanghai godowns [warehouses], since the end of January; nothing has been paid for or cleared. . . . And there it remains and probably must remain until the native banks are willing to pay out cash against the orders drawn on them."[15]

Foreign banks shared some of the weaknesses of the Chinese financial system. Bank failures were not uncommon.[16] Problems arose when bankers mixed personal interests with bank affairs or made unauthorized use of bank funds to finance speculative ventures.[17] Foreign banks also lacked the mutual support derived from

15. *Finance and Commerce*, February 17, 1932, 1, 3.
16. For details of numerous failures, see A. S. J. Baster, *The International Banks* (London, 1935), 38, 164, 166, 175–76, 232; "Foreign Banks in Shanghai," 597–99; and Hsien, *Ti kuo chu i tsai Hua yin hang*, 23, 40. Kia-ngau Chang [Chang Chia-ao] writes that foreign banks "suffered a rapid series of catastrophes" in the wake of the First World War ("Toward Modernization of China's Currency and Banking, 1927–1937," in *The Strenuous Decade: China's Nation-Building Efforts, 1927–1937*, ed. Paul K. T. Sih [New York, 1970], 139).
17. Collis, *Wayfoong*, 34–35, gives examples of both.

a central regulatory body. They competed fiercely among themselves, with alliances and rivalries often reflecting the vagaries of international politics, as when the British-dominated Hong Kong and Shanghai Bank financed the Chinese government's efforts to resist not only domestic rebellion, but also "French aggression," "Russian menace," and "Japanese danger."[18] Fellow nationals also engaged in divisive feuds, as when the important firm of Jardine, Matheson refused to deal with the Hong Kong and Shanghai Bank through the first thirteen years of the bank's existence. This situation continued. Writing in the 1940s, Tamagna noted that "foreign banks maintained a strictly individualistic attitude, and cooperation or common policy beyond syndicates for the issue of loans was almost unknown."[19]

Despite these difficulties, the deposit services and notes of foreign banks gained increasing acceptance among Chinese as well as foreign businesses because they served to ameliorate the weaknesses of the Ch'ing system. Deposits in foreign banks, if not entirely free of risk, offered security against Chinese government action. This appealed to many Chinese. Notes issued by foreign banks were welcomed for the same reasons as foreign coin. Transactions settled in banknotes dispensed with all costs of shroffage, or currency evaluation. Holding foreign banknotes involved some risk, but major foreign institutions were often seen as more stable than competing Chinese banks.

Chinese Commercial Banks

Chinese commercial banking began in the last five years of the nineteenth century. The accumulation of several decades of experience with foreign banks gave Chinese officials and financiers a good understanding of the functions and profitability of commercial banks. At the same time, growing numbers of Chinese industrial enterprises and rising interest in railway expansion raised the demand for financial services beyond the capabilities of existing domestic institutions. The first public proposal for a Chinese bank seems to have come in 1896 from Sheng Hsüan-huai, an entrepre-

18. Collis, *Wayfoong*, 65–67.
19. Frank M. Tamagna, *Banking and Finance in China* (New York, 1942), 116.

neur and bureaucrat whose varied career taught him the advantages of new methods and gave him a desire to compete with foreign enterprise. Even before this, native bankers established a commercial bank at Wuhan in 1891, displaying the entrepreneurial leadership of old-time financiers so typical of prewar China.[20] New financial institutions, including semiofficial customs banks and government mints at Chi-lin and Tientsin, already existed, but Sheng now urged the creation of a bank to facilitate the mobilization of capital for railway construction and government loans and to dispense with the expensive services of foreign banks.[21]

Sheng's bank, the *Chung-kuo t'ung-shang yin-hang* (The Imperial Bank of China), opened in 1897. Unlike the native banks, this was a joint stock company whose shareholders bore only a limited liability to the bank's creditors. Sheng's prospectus promised that "all business methods pursued by the Bank will be entirely on the foreign plan, as has been the case with the Hong Kong and Shanghai Bank, which is to be made the model of this Bank in everything."[22] Loans would be based on tangible collateral rather than the borrower's reputation. The Imperial Bank failed to achieve the stature and power to which Sheng aspired. Sheng's efforts to have his bank appointed as the custodian of government revenue or the initiator of a unified national currency never bore fruit and the Imperial Bank drifted into obscurity as a minor commercial intermediary.

During the first decade of the twentieth century, the idea of establishing banking institutions to control government revenues and to support a unified currency, an objective formally adopted in the Mackay Treaty of 1902, figured in the creation of two new institutions with national aspirations, the Hu-pu Bank (later to become the Bank of China) and the Bank of Communications.[23] An appreciation of the benefits to be derived from commercial banking was not limited to official circles in Peking. Mercantile groups and

20. William T. Rowe, *Hankow: Commerce and Society in a Chinese City, 1796–1889* (Stanford, 1984), 159.

21. Albert Feuerwerker, *China's Early Industrialization: Sheng Hsüan-huai (1844–1916) and Mandarin Enterprise* (Cambridge, 1958), 226–27. The returned student Yung Wing also proposed the creation of a bank in 1896 (p. 299); Sheng's bureaucratic allies may have quashed this initiative.

22. Feuerwerker, *China's Early Industrialization*, 228–29.

23. Hall, *Chinese National Banking*, chaps. 2–5.

regional governments actively promoted private as well as official institutions beginning around 1898. Government banks offered the prospect of income from transfer and exchange fees, an inexpensive means of borrowing funds, and the opportunity to use note issue to add to official resources. Mercantile groups saw similar advantages in organizing commercial banks.

Modern banking grew rapidly. Incomplete compilations show that a total of 17 banks had been founded by 1911; 109 new institutions appeared during the following decade, 138 between 1922 and 1931, and a further 76 between 1932 and 1937. An undoubtedly incomplete total of 390 new banks, including 50 whose inception cannot be dated, is recorded for the years 1903–36. Many new institutions failed to survive: of 390 new banks, only 164 were operating in 1936.[24] This high mortality rate was more a sign of the times than an indication of reckless operation by Chinese financiers. Foreign banks, which operated in a similarly unregulated environment, disappeared with equal rapidity.

As the Chinese banking system expanded, some of the initial objectives were gradually attained. The Bank of China and the Bank of Communications, rival semiofficial institutions that competed for official business, gained increasing control over central government revenues formerly handled by traditional intermediaries and foreign banks. Chinese banks established themselves as major forces in Shanghai and other financial centers. Their deposits and note issue, shown in Table 3.1, soon came to dominate the national totals.

The activities of Chinese commercial banks extended beyond the major cities to hundreds of smaller centers along major and secondary trade and transport arteries. Table 3.2, which gives the number of bank outlets, including branches and agencies (*fen-hang* and *chih-hang*) by province, shows that the number of bank offices had surpassed 1,700 by the mid-1930s. The Bank of China boasted more than 200 outlets and the Bank of Communications over 120.[25] The wide dispersion of branches and agencies can be seen from Table 3.2. In Kiangsu, the province with the most bank outlets, 248 offices outside the major cities of Shanghai and Nanking were

24. *Ch'üan kuo yin hang nien chien*, 1937 (Shanghai, 1937), 7–8.
25. Ibid., 75 and Bank of China, *Report of the Chairman to the Annual Meeting of Shareholders, April 3, 1937* (Shanghai, 1937), 9.

Table 3.1

Shares of Various Institutions in Deposits and Note Issue, 1912-36
(Year-end percentages)

Year	Deposits of All Banks			Banknotes Issued by		
	Modern Banks		Native Banks	Domestic Banks		Foreign
	Chinese	Foreign		China Proper	Manchuria	Banks
1912	64	29	8	34	20[a]	46
1915	56	34	11	40	20[a]	40
1920	43	32	24	46	28[a]	26
1925	42	25	33	50	28[a]	23
1930	51	26	22	56	20	24
1936	75	14	11	81	10[b]	9
Total Amount for 1936 (1912=100)	962	402	1120	3751	796	291

[a]Residual.

[b]Banknotes issued by the Central Bank of Manchoukuo are included in the 1936 total for domestic banks in Manchuria.

Sources: Tables C.9 and C.15.

scattered among 61 different centers. Banks operated in 52 localities in Chekiang, 51 in Hopei, and 32 in Szechwan.

The expansion of the financial network proceeded at a rapid pace during the 1930s, when more than three-fourths of the branches operating in 1937 were opened. Their rapid growth enabled the notes of Chinese banks to replace foreign banknotes as the common tender throughout the Yangtze Basin, including Shanghai. By 1937, there were over a thousand Chinese commercial bank outlets in the Yangtze provinces of Kiangsu, Chekiang, Anhwei, Kiangsi, Hupeh, Hunan, and Szechwan, including 849 located outside the major trade centers of Shanghai and Wuhan. Foreign banks, by contrast, operated exclusively in these two centers.[26] By the 1930s, the expansion of China's banking system had restricted large-scale

26. *Ch'üan kuo yin hang nien chien,* 1937, 546–50.

Table 3.2
Regional Distribution Offices of Chinese Banks in China Proper, 1936

Province (City)[a]	Number of Offices	Number of Locations
Kiangsu	487	63
(Shanghai)	(181)	
(Nanking)	(58)	
Hopei	199	51
(Tientsin)	(68)	
(Peking)	(57)	
Chekiang	175	52
(Hangchow)	(27)	
Szechwan	125	32
(Chungking)	(29)	
Kiangsi	82	36
Anhwei	80	37
Fukien	74	52
Honan	73	31
Hupeh	72	18
(Hankow)	(30)	
Shantung	62	17
(Tsingtao)	(23)	
Kwangtung	59	13
(Canton)	(35)	
Shensi	50	27
Kwangsi	44	32
Hunan	44	15
Shansi	23	17
Others	46	33
Total for China Proper	1,695	526

[a]Each province or city reporting twenty or more officies is enumerated separately.

Source: Ch'üan kuo yin hang nien chien, 1937 (Shanghai, 1937), 601-741.

circulation of foreign banknotes to border areas: Japanese notes in Manchuria and Fukien, notes of the Hong Kong and Shanghai Bank in Hong Kong and Kwangtung, notes of French banks in the southwest, and so on. The growth of deposits and note issue demonstrated growing public confidence in the domestic financial system.

The large network of bank branches formed during the 1930s represented a major step in the direction of an integrated national capital market. Intermediaries capable of responding quickly to financial changes in the major cities now existed in hundreds of communities dispersed across all of China's provinces. At the same time, the spread of banking outlets beyond major trading centers created new links between China's urban-based modern sector and the rural economy. Although commercial banks directed only a small fraction of their lending to agricultural borrowers, the indirect effects of bank expansion through the trading network for farm produce brought city and village into closer economic contact than ever before.

Despite these signs of development, Chinese commercial banks never turned into the vehicles for capital mobilization envisioned by Sheng Hsüan-huai. Caught between the long-standing expertise of foreign banks in financing international transactions and the entrenched interests of the *ch'ien-chuang* in domestic trade, the commercial banks were forced to depend on the government as their chief customer and as a major source of funds. With good returns available from government bonds, in contrast with the tough competition and considerable risk in private-sector loans and investments, commercial banks directed large flows of funds into government coffers. Loans to commerce and industry expanded with the growth of assets and expertise, but lagged behind government bonds in the investment portfolios of the major banks. Although this state of affairs has drawn considerable criticism, it is difficult to see how commercial banks could have altered their lending practices without adding greatly to the risk assumed by depositors and bankers alike. Industrial loans were particularly risky, as can be seen from the frequency with which both commercial and native banks found themselves obliged to step into the uncomfortable role of partnership with defaulting industrial borrowers.[27] As in the United States a century earlier, commercial bankers sensibly refrained from committing short-term deposits to long-term ventures.[28]

Business ethics was another sphere in which Chinese banks failed to meet expectations. In his proposals for the Imperial Bank of China, Sheng Hsüan-huai promised that "All mandarinic etiquette and custom will be unhesitatingly tabooed. . . . 'Integrity, Impartiality, and Strict Attention to Business' will be the motto of the Bank. No favouritism or nepotism will be permitted."[29] These lofty ambitions were attained only in part. The intimate involvement of commercial banks in government finance did not permit bankers to escape the intense maneuvering that was a constant feature of China's unstable polity. Politically inspired suspensions of convertibility and excessive note issue were not uncommon; a withdrawal of public confidence and the depreciation of inconvertible banknotes followed these episodes with predictable regularity.

The largest banks, however, resisted political interference with considerable success. As early as 1906, the leadership of the Ta Ch'ing Bank (subsequently to become the Bank of China) "favorably impressed the business community in China . . . by its firm refusal to lend to the Viceroy of the Liang-Kuang provinces during the famine" of 1906–7 without security.[30] A decade later, the Bank of China refused to supply funds to support the imperial ambitions of Yüan Shih-k'ai. When the Peking government ordered a suspension of convertibility, the bankers rebelled: "Following the lead of the great Shanghai branch, numerous branches of the Bank of China refused to obey the Moratorium Order" of 1916.[31] This demonstration of independence attracted immediate financial support from the foreign banking community and symbolized the efforts of Chinese bankers to remain aloof from political conflicts.

27. D. K. Lieu, *The Growth and Industrialization of Shanghai* (Shanghai, 1936), 95 and H. D. Fong, "Industrial Capital in China," *Nankai Social and Economic Quarterly* 9, no. 1 (1936):85.
28. Allan R. Pred, *The Spatial Dynamics of U.S. Urban-Industrial Growth, 1800–1914* (Cambridge, 1966), 152–56, describes the unwillingness of bankers to finance fixed industrial investments during the early nineteenth century. The resulting undercapitalization of manufacturing enterprises is exactly what one encounters in prewar China.
29. Feuerwerker, *China's Early Industrialization*, 228–29.
30. Hall, *Chinese National Banking*, 21.
31. Ibid., 74.

Currency unification was a final objective that was only partially attained in prewar China. The monetary system included a confusing jumble of silver ingots, coins, notes, and *tael* units of account, each with a plethora of local variations; there was also a subsidiary copper currency, again with a multiplicity of unstandardized coins and notes. Until 1928, governments did little to promote unification; indeed, they were perhaps the leading beneficiaries of the multiple currency system, profiting regularly from the issue of debased coins and unbacked paper currency. Some progress occurred in the private sector, where the large commercial banks began to issue notes on behalf of smaller institutions in return for reserve-like deposits.

The pace of reform quickened under the Nanking government of 1927–37. The Central Bank of China, a government-controlled commercial bank with some central banking features, was established in 1928. At the same time, Shanghai bankers in both the modern and the *ch'ien-chuang* sectors initiated joint reserve funds to enhance liquidity and security. In 1932, the government decreed the abolition of the *tael* as a unit of account, eliminating the complication and expense of maintaining separate dollar and *tael* accounts. In 1933, Shanghai bankers established an interbank clearing facility, ending their traditional reliance on the native bankers' guild for clearing services. Following a period of extreme instability resulting from the world depression and the United States silver purchase program of 1934, the Nanking government acted quickly and decisively to nationalize silver stocks and install a fiduciary currency in the monetary reform of November 1935.

Native Banks

How did the *ch'ien-chuang* or native banks respond to the rise of foreign and Chinese-operated commercial banks? Although some authors describe the prewar decades of the present century as a period of decline for old-style financial intermediaries, the evidence pertaining to Shanghai and Tientsin, cities which experienced the most extensive development of new banking and financial arrangements, show the *ch'ien-chuang* continuing to prosper and expand until the 1930s. If inherited banking institutions could thrive in the modernizing economies of the large treaty ports where domestic and foreign rivals offered strong competition for deposit and loan business, their continued vitality in the interior cannot be doubted, for in domestic trade, the native banks "held the ganglions of the financial lines of the country."[32] The present survey focuses on the largest cities, where the operations of the *ch'ien-chuang* were best documented and faced the strongest challenge from new intermediaries. In banking, as in other sectors of the economy, significant complementarities between new and old forms of enterprise permitted traditional operators to adapt successfully to a changing economic environment. In addition to the receipt of chop loans and the joint financing of foreign trade described above, *ch'ien-chuang* were deeply involved in the development of industry and commercial banking. These sectors in turn provided opportunities for the native banks to prosper and expand.

Table 3.3 summarizes the available quantitative information about the development of native banks in Shanghai. New institutions continued to appear until 1935 and again after 1940, but established firms disappeared more rapidly, leading to a gradual decline in the number of firms from a peak of eighty-nine in 1924 to forty-six, or barely half as many, on the eve of the Sino-Japanese War. This numerical decline concealed a process of consolidation. Shanghai native bank capital grew rapidly, increasing at an annual rate of 10.2 percent between 1912 and 1936. The volume of clearing house transactions, reflecting the scale of native bank business, grew at an average rate of 3.2 percent between 1925 and 1936 (Table 3.3) despite the creation of rival clearing facilities by Shanghai's commercial banks in 1933. The continued success of native banks rested on their ability to provide flexible and convenient service to business clients. Native bankers were quick to adapt their operations to the changing requirements of the marketplace, offering such novelties as passbook and accounting systems adopted from the practice of commercial banks, telephonic communication, and even pick-up and delivery banking service for busy clients.[33]

Native banks, like other financial institutions, experienced great difficulties during the depression years of the 1930s, but profits

32. Tamagna, *Banking*, 47.
33. George H. Chang, "A Brief Survey of Chinese Native Banks," *Central Bank of China Bulletin* 4, no. 1 (1938):25–32 and "The Practice of Shanghai Native Banks," *Central Bank of China Bulletin* 4, no. 4 (1938) and 5, no. 2 (1939).

Table 3.3
Shanghai Native Banks, 1912-36

Year	Number of Units			Capital (Thousand yuan)		Volume of Clearings (Thousand yuan)
	New	Failed	Total	Total	Per Unit	
1912	4	27	28	1488	53	...
1913	3	0	31	1684	54	...
1914	9	0	40	2049	51	...
1915	2	0	42	2161	52	...
1916	10	3	49	2829	58	...
1917	0	0	49	2829	58	...
1918	19	6	62	4390	71	...
1919	7	2	67	5295	79	...
1920	4	0	71	7768	109	...
1921	4	6	69	8431	122	...
1922	10	5	74	10797	146	...
1923	15	5	84	14502	173	...
1924	7	2	89	16625	187	6459[a]
1925	5	11	83	16659	201	11255
1926	6	2	87	18757	216	15274
1927	2	4	85	19007	224	12365
1928	0	5	80	17989	225	14776
1929	1	3	78	18527	238	16858
1930	3	4	77	19378	252	21457
1931	4	5	76	20245	266	26982
1932	1	5	72	21385	297	18018
1933	3	7	68	21798	321	13990[b]
1934	2	5	65	20702	318	14561
1935	0	10	55	19382	352	13581
1936	0	7	48	18000	375	16482

[a]Figure is for April-December only.

[b]Modern bankers' clearing house opened in this year.

Source: Shang-hai ch'ien chuang shih liao (Shanghai, 1960), 188, 191, 203, 260, 262, 313.

remained positive and available data indicate that *ch'ien-chuang* owners maintained or even enlarged their financial commitments to these intermediaries throughout the prewar period. There is scant support for the view that the native bank sector was in a state of "collapse," "dying a natural death," or even suffering a "gradual decline."[34] With the paid-up capital and deposits of the Shanghai

34. Quotations are from Tamagna, *Banking*, 94; Andrea L. McElderry, *Shanghai Old-Style Banks (Ch'ien-Chuang), 1800–1935* (Ann Arbor, 1976), 191; and F. Y. Chang, "Banking and Currency," in *The Chinese Year Book, 1936–37* (Shanghai, 1936), 794.

ch'ien-chuang growing at rates comparable to commercial bank capital, industrial output, and modern-sector capital formation, it is essential to inquire how these old-style banking enterprises successfully adjusted to the rapidly changing economic environment of China's treaty ports.

Detailed information about the operations of the native banks shows how these institutions responded to new opportunities and new forms of competition. Data on the business affairs of several Shanghai *ch'ien-chuang*, apparently selected because of the completeness of their records, confirm the overall picture of capital and deposit growth shown in Table 3.3. They also show that the native banks were quick to associate themselves with the most dynamic sectors of China's prewar economy. For each of the several Shanghai firms for which there are data, industrial loans formed a substantial segment of total assets during the 1930s; the consideration of personal loans to industrialists, which seem to be excluded from the industrial loan category, would raise the share of *ch'ien-chuang* loans devoted to industrial finance. The industrial borrowers included many firms in the cotton, silk, and woolen textile industry along with smaller numbers of iron works, flour mills, chemical plants, and cement producers. There are many examples of long-term financial ties between native bankers and industrialists. In some cases, business failures obliged the *ch'ien-chuang* to assume control of industrial ventures.[35]

Evidence of close links between the native banks and the most dynamic sectors of China's prewar economy comes from many other regions. Leading industrialists themselves were often involved with *ch'ien-chuang*, as with the Jung family, whose textile and flour holdings placed them among the ranks of China's wealthiest businessmen. Liu Hung-sheng, another prominent industrialist, and Chin Jung-ch'ing, described as "the 'founding father' of modern Shanghai finance," are examples of men whose business activities included ownership or management of native banks.[36] *Ch'ien-chuang* also maintained close financial ties with other native banks and commercial banking institutions, both Chinese and foreign. I have already noted the long-standing cooperation be-

35. *Shang-hai ch'ien chuang shih liao* (Shanghai, 1960), 772–854.
36. Ibid., 267 and Susan Mann Jones, "The Ningpo Pang and Financial Power at Shanghai," in *The Chinese City Between Two Worlds*, ed. Mark Elvin and G. William Skinner (Stanford, 1974), 94.

tween the *ch'ien-chuang* and the foreign banks. This cooperation remained essential to the smooth flow of China's international trade throughout the prewar decades. The native banks also maintained close ties with domestic financial intermediaries. The Shanghai firms mentioned above were enmeshed in a system of mutual deposits with domestic financial institutions.[37] A broader data set for Tientsin shows the same pattern of large mutual deposits among commercial and native banks. Information on 195 native banks shows the following relations for year-end 1940 (in million yuan; figures in parentheses indicate percentages of total deposits or loans):[38]

	Native Bank Deposits from		Native Bank Loans to	
Modern banks	16.1	(10.8%)	28.9	(18.1%)
Native banks	28.9	(19.4%)	31.7	(19.8%)

In the absence of a central bank, prudent operation of the *ch'ien-chuang*, whose shareholders bore unlimited liability to their creditors, necessitated a web of interlocking deposits with cooperating institutions, both locally and in distant financial centers, as a means of ensuring liquidity in the event of business setbacks for the firm, its owners, or important clients.

Ties between the native banks and the modern sector of China's prewar economy did not end with the exchange of deposits and the granting of loans; they also encompassed many personal connections as well. Bankers and industrialists frequently held shares in native banks and native bankers often supported new ventures in the modern sector. A list of the shareholders in Tientsin native banks includes manufacturers of flour, cement, iron, and textiles as well as participants in commercial banking, trucking, and foreign trade and many others identified as merchants, landlords, or shareholders in other native banks.[39]

The connections between the native banks and the modern sector extended to labor as well as capital. Interviews with *ch'ien-chuang* personnel in Peking and Tientsin found "some of the native

37. *Shang-hai ch'ien chuang shih liao*, 788–91, 806–7, 824–25, 836–37, 844–45.
38. *Tenshin no gingō* (Dairen, 1942), part II, table 4.
39. Ibid., part III, statistics, 264–78.

banks employing former employees of modern banks as chief accountants."[40] Tamagna found that native banks employed people whose special task was to maintain "relations with modern banks."[41] New financial institutions found it equally helpful to employ men with special knowledge of the *ch'ien-chuang*. Foreign bank compradores were often drawn from the ranks of the native banking community. Chinese commercial banks also hired experienced workers from the *ch'ien-chuang*. The circulation of personnel not only distributed expertise, but also cemented personal ties between the various types of intermediaries. Sometimes the objective of distributing expertise predominated. In other cases, as when many graduates of schools established for the sons of Shanghai *ch'ien-chuang* employees became employees of commercial banks, the exchange of personnel served to promote a community of interest within the financial sector as a whole.[42]

The managers of banks and *ch'ien-chuang* worked together to finance private-sector projects and participated in the same mercantile associations. Cooperation between old and new financial intermediaries also involved the performance of various agency functions. Banks issued banknotes on behalf of *ch'ien-chuang*. Native banks acted as conduits channeling foreign funds into the domestic economy through the financing of commercial dealing in import and export goods. Foreign banks also offered short-term call loans to *ch'ien-chuang* that faced liquidity shortages.[43] Following an erosion of confidence in this system after native bankers' guilds refused to guarantee repayment of orders issued by bankrupt institutions, modern Chinese banks "took over some of the business formerly transacted through foreign institutions," pointing once again to the difficulty of maintaining foreign trade ties without the commercial expertise of the *ch'ien-chuang*.[44]

---

40. Chien-ming Li, *The Accounting System of Native Banks in Peking and Tientsin* (Tientsin, 1941), vi.
41. Tamagna, *Banking*, 59.
42. *Shang-hai shih ssu li ch'ien yeh ch'u chi chung hsüeh, hsiao hsüeh shih chou nien chi nien k'an* (n.p., 1935). Note the parallel with Gary C. Hamilton's observation that young men apprenticed in one trade might "enter a different but related business by exploiting the expertise and contacts established in the former business" ("Nineteenth Century Chinese Merchant Associations: Conspiracy or Combination?" *Ch'ing-shih wen-t'i* 3, no. 8 [1977]:64).
43. Tamagna, *Banking*, 110–11.
44. Quotation from Tamagna, *Banking*, 111–12.

Clearing arrangements also involved extensive cooperation among different financial groups. The Shanghai *ch'ien-chuang* established a clearing house in 1890. Until the commercial banks opened a rival clearing operation in 1933, nonmembers, including Chinese and foreign commercial banks as well as secondary native banks, "were obliged to maintain a deposit with a member native bank in order to have the privilege of cashing their credits."[45] In the 1930s, the situation was reversed by the creation of new clearing houses first in Shanghai (1933) and then in Hangchow, Tientsin, and Nanking. Now reserves formerly held in native banks flowed into the Bank of China and the Bank of Communications as "native banks found it convenient to keep current accounts with modern banks in order to avail themselves . . . of the modern clearing house for their collection from other modern banks."[46]

Financial Change and the Economy

Each of the three major groups of banking institutions experienced a separate pattern of growth and development during the prewar decades and each carved out its own area of specialization and expertise. Complementarity and cooperation between the various financial groups provided a sufficient degree of integration, even in the absence of purposive governmental policy or regulatory authority, to support the growth of production and domestic and international trade in prewar China. Rather than add further details about cooperation among different segments of the financial community, the remainder of this chapter focuses on the broader impact of financial development in the areas of economic integration, growth, and stability.

Financial Development and Economic Integration

Economic integration is a significant aspect of modernization. Backward economies typically suffer from extreme market segmentation, which is visible in the wide differentials, unrelated to transport costs, separating the prices of similar commodities or services

45. Tamagna, *Banking*, 64, 77.
46. Tamagna, *Banking*, 64.

in different sectors and regions. The development process gradually erodes barriers to the circulation of goods, leading to the emergence first of regional and eventually of national markets for such items as foodstuffs, labor, and funds.

Integration is not a new theme in Chinese economic history. National markets for luxury goods and interregional financial links between major commercial centers existed for centuries before the Opium Wars. Yeh-chien Wang's research on grain prices suggests the presence of national markets linking even remote regions to the central grain marts of the Lower Yangtze region as early as the eighteenth century.[47] Even so, the twentieth century brings a significant extension of market integration stemming from the growth of the banking system, improvements in transport and communication, and the determination of financial elites to expand their business horizons to include the rural sector.

Integration within the urban sector is a familiar story. Bank branches spread rapidly across China's urban landscape. Nonfinancial enterprises, including the British-American Tobacco Company and the industrial-commercial conglomerates led by T. C. Jung, Liu Hung-sheng, and others, built similarly far-flung commercial networks. By the late 1920s, the headquarters of these firms and business groups, typically located at Shanghai, received systematic intelligence on commercial conditions in dozens of localities. Firms located outside the great metropolis found it advantageous to maintain listening posts at Shanghai.[48] Sherman Cochran's account of T. C. Jung's management methods illustrates both the significance of these new information flows and their effect on economic integration. Jung overruled his brother's choice of a site for their Shanghai business office, insisting on a location with the best possible telephone service. Once installed in the new location, Jung's firm "was sensitive to wholesalers' reports on fluctuations in local demand" and "regularly transferred cotton textiles from branch to branch and city to city to capitalize on shifts in demand." To ensure the implementation of policies based on centralized accumulation of market intelligence, "Jung insisted that prices be set at [the

47. Yeh-chien Wang, "Spatial and Temporal Patterns of Grain Prices in China, 1740–1910" (Kent, 1984).

48. Chin Chi-shuo, "Shanghai's Changing Economic Position and Role Before and After Liberation," *She hui k'o hsüeh* 10 (1984):16.

company's] headquarters in Shanghai . . . [and] appointed only [fellow] Wusih natives to positions as managers and assistant managers . . . and he required that these managers take instructions from him at noon every single day." [49]

The expansion of bank operations led to similar results. Chang Chia-ao recalls that the offices of the Shanghai and Commercial Savings Bank [50]

> were established near the railway depots in Shanghai and Nanking in 1917 to attend to mortgage of goods in transit. In the course of time, these operations were extended to other railway centers in China. In the meantime, godowns [warehouses] were set up to facilitate the mortgages of merchandise. . . . Godowns . . . or agencies were set up in interior points where large quantities of native produce were marketed. This was clearly a departure from the practice of . . . [other] banks which sought security in the foreign concessions.

These operations, which channeled the funds collected in Shanghai and other coastal cities into the financing of trade in interior areas, "definitely helped reduce interest rates in the interior," thus promoting national integration of capital markets. [51] Another account of early operations by the same bank resembles a textbook description of economic integration: "The very first thing I did was to send money to Wusih and Changchow where there was a demand for loans . . . and . . . interest rates were higher than those in Shanghai. Our first business transaction provided the bank with an interest rate of 1.2% per month . . . [whereas] the bank only paid six percent interest [per annum]." [52]

The interregional transfer of commodities or funds from low- to high-price markets was not limited to the internal operations of multibranch firms. Even before 1911, interprovincial consortia of *ch'ien-chuang* raised considerable sums to support new ventures in the cement and oil milling industries. [53] It now became common

49. Sherman Cochran, "Controlling a National Market in China: Interregional Trade in Tobacco Products and Cotton Textiles, 1850–1984" (Ithaca, 1984), 18–19.
50. "Chang Chia-ao" (Columbia University Oral History Project, n.d.), 22.
51. Ibid.
52. "The Reminiscences of Ch'en Kuang-fu," 38.
53. Yokoyama Suguru, "On the Relation Between Private Chinese Industrial Capital and the Native Banks," *Shakai keizai shigaku* 27, no. 3 (1961):226.

for businessmen to invest directly in enterprises far removed from their home bases. Coal mine operators raised funds from distant regions "either through personal connections or by telegraphed appeals."[54] The Hua-chang Antimony Refining Company, a Hunan enterprise with shareholders in at least five provinces, found that "holders of idle funds throughout the land eagerly lent their fluid resources to the company for short terms."[55]

In addition to supporting local business development, bankers were quick to grasp profitable lending opportunities in distant places. The Tientsin-based Kincheng (Chin-ch'eng) Bank began lending funds to Min-sheng, a dynamic transport and industrial conglomerate based in distant Chungking, in 1928. By 1935, the bank, having noted the scarcity of capital and lack of commercially oriented intermediaries in Szechwan, opened an office in Chungking.[56] Kincheng's lending in Szechwan is not an isolated case. The same bank joined with other intermediaries to finance the construction of highways linking Chekiang and Kiangsi and consortia of Shanghai banks financed industrial projects in Hunan, highway construction in Chekiang, and transport and communication investments in Hunan.[57]

The effects of integration were not limited to large-scale enterprise. Accounts of trade and finance in Pao-ti (Hopei), for example, an area north of Tientsin that straddled a venerable trade route linking North China with territory beyond the Great Wall, illustrate the impact of urban financial development on money markets in local trading centers. During the first two decades of the twentieth century, local and interregional trade in this region shifted from a cash basis to arrangements under which most mercantile obligations were settled by exchanging drafts on Tientsin accounts. This reduced transactions costs, increased liquidity, and closely in-

54. Tim Wright, "Growth of the Modern Chinese Coal Industry: An Analysis of Supply and Demand," *Modern China* 7, no. 3 (1981):322. See also Wright, "Entrepreneurs, Politicians and the Chinese Coal Industry, 1895–1937," *Modern Asian Studies* 14, no. 4 (1980):600, for the involvement of Shanghai merchants in coal mining.

55. Angus McDonald, Jr., *The Urban Origins of Rural Revolution: Elites and the Masses in Hunan Province, China, 1911–1927* (Berkeley, 1978), 72, 74.

56. *Chin-ch'eng yin hang shih liao* (Shanghai, 1983), 252, 438.

57. *Finance and Commerce*, June 6, 1934, 657; May 31, 1933, 619; June 28, 1933, 740; and July 26, 1933, 98.

tegrated local money markets with financial networks in Tientsin.[58] Similar changes occurred in localities adjacent to major commercial centers and important trade routes in many regions of China.[59]

Perhaps the most significant aspect of the banks' contribution to economic integration concerns their involvement with the rural economy. All types of banking institutions had long participated indirectly in agricultural finance through their support of trade in agricultural commodities. Loans to brokers, shippers, traders, and exporters of tea, silk, grain, cotton, soybeans, beancakes, and other farm products swelled the overall supply of loanable funds in rural areas by increasing the liquidity of merchants who in turn frequently loaned cash or farm inputs (seed, fertilizer) to cultivators or invested in pawnshops that served a rural clientele.[60] The growing involvement of China's largest financial institutions in the rural economy signified an unprecedented move toward national economic integration.

Banknotes circulated widely in rural China. As early as 1917, a survey of Hopei province reported the use of paper money in thirty-seven of fifty-five counties.[61] Surveys conducted during the 1930s commonly reported the circulation of banknotes in rural areas. Hsü-shui county, for example, located on the Peking-Hankow railway but "with no important cities or market towns," reported the use of notes issued by seven national and provincial banks.[62] In areas removed from major transport routes, Shansi villagers were said to favor metal currency, but survey data nonetheless show a considerable variety of notes issued by national, pro-

58. See Pi, "Financial Flows in Pao-ti," 2:839–43 and H. D. Fong and H. H. Pi, "The Growth and Decline of Rural Industrial Enterprise in North China: A Case Study of the Cotton Handloom Weaving Industry in Paoti," *Nankai Social and Economic Quarterly* 8, no. 3 (1936).

59. See *China Industrial Handbooks: Kiangsu* (Shanghai, 1933), 911–13, on the emergence of unified native bank interest rates in southern Kiangsu.

60. Loans to farmers from produce and freight brokers are noted in *China Industrial Handbooks: Chekiang* (Shanghai, 1935), 52–57 and *China Industrial Handbooks: Kiangsu*, 38–40.

61. *Chih-li sheng ti i tz'u shih yeh tiao ch'a* (Tientsin, 1917). In thirteen of thirty-seven counties noting the presence of banknotes, their use was described as "slight" (*shao*). The source provides no report on the use of banknotes in eighty-eight additional counties.

62. *Chi Ch'a tiao ch'a t'ung chi ts'ung k'an* 1, no. 1 (1936):99. For a Kiangsu example, see *Su nung* 2, no. 5 (1931):12–13.

vincial, and even county banks as well as by village and town cooperatives and private money shops, *ch'ien-chuang*, and pawnshops.[63]

Remarkable evidence of the penetration of banknotes into the
rural economy comes from accounts of communist base areas established precisely because of their isolation from major transport (and
hence trade) routes. Before the local soviet regimes could introduce their own paper money, they found themselves obliged to
deal with notes issued by individual merchants and industrialists,
local merchant groups, commercial banks, and the Nanking government, all of which already circulated even in remote rural locations. In 1928, the *Hai-Lu-Feng* soviet government added its
own overmarks to notes issued by a local textile plant. In Kiangsi
and Fukien, authorities of local soviets "redeemed for limited
periods the paper notes issued by the Bank of China, Chung-nan
Bank, Yü-min Bank, and various merchant associations" before restricting note circulation to their own currency.[64]

The circulation of banknotes in the countryside, although expanding the lending power of urban banks, did not of necessity
draw bankers into direct ties with the farm economy. It was the
growing impact of farm conditions on the supply of cotton, wheat,
tobacco, cocoons, and other materials essential to urban industry
along with the potential significance of farmers as a source of loan
demand that turned the attention of China's bankers toward direct
rural involvement. Shortly before 1930, the banking community
seems to have concluded that its own development, as well as the
nation's, required a major expansion of organized financial intermediation in the countryside. Although this redefinition of objectives brought no dramatic realignment in bank portfolios, the 1930s
witnessed a steady increase in the banks' involvement with agriculture. This strengthened financial ties between city and village
and injected substantial quantities of new funds into the farm
sector.

One result of this growing concern with the farm economy was
the appearance of specialized banking institutions intended to
serve agriculture. In 1915, the Peking government established the
Nung-kung yin-hang (The Agro-Industrial Bank) with branches in

63. *Shan-hsi k'ao ch'a pao kao shu* (Shanghai, 1936), 307–9.
64. Yü T'ao, "Currency Circulation in Base Areas During the Period of the Land
Revolution," *Chung-kuo ch'ien pi* 1 (1983):41.

urban centers and county seats. New provincial institutions included the Kiangsu Farmers' Bank (established 1927), the Farmers'
Bank of Chekiang (1927), and the Kwangtung Provincial Bank of
Agriculture and Industry (1933). Farm-oriented banks also appeared at the county level in Hopei, Kwangtung, Szechwan, Shantung, and Kiangsu.[65]

Anxious to stabilize the supply of agricultural materials to the
urban economy, banks expanded their storage facilities and increased loans against commodity security deposited in their warehouses. These were not new policies. Some banks had, as noted
above, begun to lend against commodity deposits before 1920.
Pawnshops located in small towns had long engaged in the business
of advancing funds against deposits of grain and other crops, an
arrangement that enabled farmers to withhold their products in
anticipation of higher prices even if they lacked the cash to finance
essential purchases during the interim. Banks loaned funds directly to pawnshops that advanced funds against deposits of grain
and other crops as well as clothing, furniture, and property
deeds.[66] Banks also advanced funds to urban industrial and commercial firms against stocks of cotton, yarn, and other materials.

The scale of bank warehousing operations, however, now entered a period of swift expansion. By 1933, the Bank of China
operated more than thirty warehouses. The Bank viewed its large
stocks of cotton, cocoons, rice, grains, tobacco, and tea, which
amounted to as much as one-fifth of nationwide commercial inventories of these crops, as a prelude to a program of commodity price
stabilization.[67] Other banks followed suit on a smaller scale, opening warehouses for their own use and for the storage of commodity
stocks owned by other businesses.[68]

Concern with the quality as well as the volume of supplies
shipped from rural areas encouraged the banks to intervene directly in agricultural production. The Tientsin-based Kincheng
Bank exemplifies the growing links between major banks and farm-

---

65. *Chung-kuo nung yeh chin jung kai yao* (Shanghai, 1936), 68, 85–86, 121,
176, 186, 215, 229.
66. Ibid., 24–25, 93–94, 121, 150, 153; *China Industrial Handbooks: Chekiang*, 811.
67. *Chung-kuo nung yeh chin jung kai yao*, 244.
68. Ibid., 245.

ing. The category of "agricultural loans" first entered the bank's accounts in 1928. By 1937, these loans, which included tiny advances of less than ten yuan to individual farmers as well as loans to cooperatives and mutual aid teams in Hopei and Chahar, amounted to two million yuan, a sum that represented only one facet of the bank's rapidly growing participation in agricultural finance.[69] The bank also financed investments in dairying and other urban farming ventures, supported land reclamation projects, and established branches in seven Hopei counties to purchase local cotton for shipment to the cities either as agent for individual farmers or on the bank's own account.[70]

In addition to its own operations, the Kincheng Bank joined with other organizations in a variety of agriculture-related projects. The bank took an active part in financing cotton marketing cooperatives across North China. It joined with four other banks to establish the "China Agricultural Cooperative Loan Consortium," which, according to contemporary sources, supported cotton cooperatives in Shensi, Shansi, and Honan, helped to start a cotton improvement institute in Shensi, and lent funds to encourage the production, sale, and use of cotton, activities that reportedly had an "extremely large impact" in the cotton districts.[71] This consortium, which quickly grew to include ten banks, soon extended its operations into Hopei and Anhwei provinces, began to build a network of cotton improvement stations, expanded its cotton loans to encompass ginning and grading as well as production, transport, and storage, and began to finance local wheat crops and to issue loans against deposits of rice or wheat.[72] The Kincheng Bank also participated in the government-sponsored Agricultural Capital Bureau, the Hopei Cotton Improvement Society, and ancillary arrangements linked to the Nanking government's Central Agricultural Experiment Station.[73] The bank joined with Nankai University, the North China Reform Institute, and local reform groups to upgrade

69. *Chin-ch'eng yin hang shih liao*, 460–61, 470.
70. Ibid., 460–61, 465.
71. Ibid., 460. The quotation is from *Chung-kuo nung yeh chin jung kai yao*, 134, which identifies this financial group under a slightly different name.
72. *Chung-kuo nung yeh chin jung kai yao*, 143 and *Chin-ch'eng yin hang shih liao*, 468.
73. Ibid., 460, 470–71.

cotton growing in Ting county, Hopei, and also contributed to a broader program of research, training, and development designed to increase cotton acreage and production and develop Hopei into a significant cotton exporter.[74]

Other banks followed similar policies. The Agricultural Capital Bureau enrolled thirty commercial banks, each bank promising to devote an initial minimum of 1 percent of savings deposits to agricultural lending.[75] Major Shanghai banks pursued new business in rural districts that supplied cotton and other commercial crops to urban processing industries; loan recipients included cooperatives, rural pawnshops, commercial brokers, and even individual farmers.[76] Even foreign banks lent funds secured by mortgaged land to small farmers in Kiangsu.[77] Small regional banks, some of which may have obtained funds from large urban-based financial institutions, added a new source of finance to the rural economy in regions as diverse as Hunan, Szechwan, Kwangsi, Kwangtung, Shantung, Hopei, Kiangsu, and Chekiang.[78]

Starting from an estimated 3.6 million yuan in 1931, bank lending to agriculture rose quickly to a total of 126 million yuan in 1934 and, after falling in 1935, increased further to 151 million yuan or 4.4 percent of total bank lending in 1936.[79] This outcome may be compared with recent figures which give the share of "agricultural" loans, most of which probably support rural industry, as no more than 7 percent of the national total of bank lending in the People's Republic of China during 1979–83.[80]

Although the annual volume of rural bank lending never ex-

74. Ibid., 461, 465–67.
75. Ibid., 470–71.
76. *Chung-kuo nung yeh chin jung kai yao*, 38, 112, 134–39, 150, 244–60; *China Industrial Handbooks: Kiangsu*, 38–40.
77. Ibid.
78. *Chung-kuo nung yeh chin jung kai yao*, 64, 68, 80–81, 85–86, 121, 176, 186, 215, 222–23, 229, 245.
79. Data on agricultural lending is from Yen Mu-yu, "Amount of Bank Lending to Agriculture in China, 1931–37," *Yen-ching ta-hsüeh ching chi hsüeh pao* 2 (1941):table 5. Total bank lending is from *Ch'üan kuo yin hang nien chien, 1937*, 52–53.
80. The share of bank loans directed to rural communes, production brigades, and state farms varied between 6.4 and 7.0 percent of loans issued by state credit agencies between 1979 and 1983; see *Chung-kuo t'ung chi nien chien, 1984* (Peking, 1984), 422.

ceeded one-twentieth of total bank deposits, the resulting extension of credit added a quantitatively significant dimension to the
pool of rural financial resources. Improved access to credit brought
significant benefits to both the farm sector, which, for reasons laid
out in the earlier discussion concerning Figure 3.1, enjoyed higher
sales volumes and product prices and lower interest rates than before, and the bankers, who found their agricultural clients desper-
ately anxious to preserve access to credit by fulfilling all repayment
obligations.[81]

Another way to appreciate the extent as well as the benefits of
financial integration is to examine the negative consequences that
followed an unexpected severance of financial links between city
and farm. A striking example arose in the aftermath of the Japanese
attack on the Chinese section of Shanghai in January 1932. The
cessation of business in China's financial center at the lunar new
year, the traditional season for settling business debts, reverberated throughout the Yangtze region:[82]

The custom . . . of closing . . . accounts at the end of the Chinese year
was, as a result of the Shanghai crisis, completely upset. The farmers
refused to settle their accounts with the business men in the villages and
towns, and they in turn were unable to complete their transactions with
business firms in the cities. . . . The unavoidable result was that loans
made in the interior by native banks in Shanghai became almost irrecov-
erable. The system of financing the interior was thus brought to a standstill, and credit was entirely shaken. . . . With credit facilities no longer
available, and no local storage accommodation, the farmers were forced
to sell their crops for what they would fetch and regardless of price. The
credit conditions which were the immediate outcome of the Shanghai crisis thus directly affected the agricultural situation, producing a serious fall
in agricultural prices.

This episode illustrates the presence of large flows of funds from
urban financial intermediaries into rural areas and indicates that,

81. On rising prices, see *Chung-kuo nung yeh chin jung kai yao*, 134. Interest
    rates in rural Kwangsi were from 3.0 to 5.3 percent per month vs. 1 percent
    or less charged by banks on farm loans in Chekiang and Hopei (*China Indus-
    trial Handbooks: Chekiang*, 52–57 and *Chin-ch'eng yin hang shih liao*, 464).
    A 1935 report on cotton loans in Hopei noted a delinquency rate of one-
    sixteenth of one percent (ibid., 466).
82. Bank of China, *Report of the General Manager to the Annual Meeting of
    Shareholders, April 8, 1933* (Shanghai, 1933), 22–23.

despite high nominal interest charges, rural borrowers obtained considerable amounts of credit that brought them important benefits.

Close economic ties between the cities of the Yangtze delta and the surrounding countryside were, of course, not a creation of the twentieth century. What is new, however, is the intensification of economic integration across broad regions of the Chinese landscape. More than ever before, markets for industrial and handicraft products, funds, and even agricultural inputs and outputs can be described as national in scope. Together with the development of transport and communication networks, it was the growth and spread of new financial institutions and monetary arrangements that propelled China's economy in the direction of national integration during the first four decades of the twentieth century.

Financial Development
and Economic Growth

The shortage of financial capital tightly constrained the expansion of production and trade in all sectors of the Ch'ing economy. Its consequences are visible in many areas of economic life. The scarcity of capital made it difficult for farmers to finance the extra costs involved in shifting from subsistence crops to commercial production. The lack of funds also restricted the size and scope of mercantile activity. During the imperial era, China's economy spawned a variety of institutions that alleviated the effects of the shortage of capital. Farmers formed revolving credit societies. Merchants employed brokers who performed a variety of services, but whose essential function was to hasten the rate at which commodity stocks could be turned over, thus expanding the volume of trade that could be conducted with a fixed financial base. The urgency of saving time allowed men with no financial assets to begin brokerage careers on the strength of their personal integrity and willingness to spend long hours in search of potential trading partners for merchants who willingly paid fees for successful introductions.

The poverty of China's economy was a fundamental cause of the scarcity of capital. Equally important, however, was the poverty of financial institutions and the consequent failure to mobilize existing savings into pools that could be tapped by individuals and organizations that required financial support to increase current flows of production and trade. The success of China's banking community in collecting and redistributing available funds can be seen in the extent to which new ventures in industry, mining, transport, trade, and even agriculture depended on loans from financial intermediaries and in the remarkable changes in the size and structure of China's money supply that occurred during the prewar decades.

This discussion of prewar monetary growth is based on Appendix C, which lays out detailed annual estimates of China's money stock for the years 1910–36. The figures come from a variety of sources, including some of questionable reliability and others that are mutually inconsistent. The gaps in available sources are of necessity filled by means of plausible, but unverifiable, assumptions. The resulting figures giving the size, growth, and composition of China's prewar money supply suffer from a variety of errors and omissions, which are discussed at some length in the appendix. Given that no official or private agency attempted to compile national monetary aggregates at any time prior to World War II, the existence of such difficulties is hardly surprising. Despite these problems, the results obtained in Appendix C seem sufficiently accurate to indicate broad trends in the size, structure, and growth of the money supply between 1910 and 1936. Great care has been taken to avoid assumptions that might exaggerate the growth rate of the monetary aggregates.

Rapid monetary growth brought dramatic changes in the composition of China's money stock. This is shown in Table 3.4, which gives the shares of the money stock occupied by silver and copper coin and banknotes and bank deposits for benchmark years between 1910 and 1936.[83] Focusing on the more reliable data for M2, the data show that metal coins, silver "shoes," and bullion initially dominated the money stock. Silver and copper amounted to 58 (Version A) or 72 (Version B) percent of the 1910 money supply—perhaps more, because of the possibility that the early totals

---

83. The standard definition of a nation's money stock includes currency (monetary metals, coin, and banknotes) circulating outside the banking system and bank deposits. The money stock can be defined narrowly (M1) or broadly (M2) depending on whether only demand deposits or both demand and savings or time deposits are included in the total.

Table 3.4
Composition of Chinese Monetary Aggregates, 1910-36
(Percentage shares)

Year	Silver[a]	Copper	Notes	Deposits[b]	Total[c]
M1, Version A					
1910	43.3	22.1	6.1	28.5	100.0
1915	45.2	19.0	10.4	25.5	100.0
1920	42.8	14.2	11.4	31.6	100.0
1925	37.7	9.5	15.4	37.4	100.0
1930	32.3	5.6	18.1	44.0	100.0
1936	-1.1[d]	3.8	36.9	60.4	100.0
M1, Version B					
1910	63.4	14.3	3.9	18.4	100.0
1915	63.7	12.6	6.9	16.9	100.0
1920	59.6	10.0	8.0	22.3	100.0
1925	52.3	7.3	11.8	28.6	100.0
1930	43.6	4.7	15.0	36.6	100.0
1936	12.5	3.3	31.9	52.3	100.0
M2, Version A					
1910	38.6	19.7	5.4	36.3	100.0
1915	40.7	17.1	9.4	32.8	100.0
1920	37.7	12.5	10.0	39.8	100.0
1925	33.0	8.3	13.5	45.2	100.0
1930	27.8	4.9	15.6	51.7	100.0
1936	-0.8[d]	2.9	28.4	69.5	100.0
M2, Version B					
1910	58.7	13.2	3.7	24.4	100.0
1915	59.4	11.7	6.4	22.5	100.0
1920	54.4	9.2	7.3	29.1	100.0
1925	47.1	6.6	10.7	35.7	100.0
1930	38.5	4.1	13.3	44.1	100.0
1936	9.9	2.6	25.4	62.1	100.0

[a]Net of reserve against banknotes assumed equal to 60 percent of issue.

[b]Net of interbank deposits assumed equal to 30 percent of native bank deposits and 4 percent of deposits in Chinese and foreign modern banks; the figures for M1 are also net of estimated time deposits.

[c]Totals may not check because of rounding error.

[d]The negative figure indicates that estimated silver stocks are less than 60 percent of total note issue.

Source: Calculated from Tables C.16 and C.17.

for bank deposits are too large. Deposits and banknotes occupied only 28 (Version B) or 42 (Version A) percent of the initial money stock. The figures for M1 (a narrower monetary aggregate that differs from M2 in that time or savings deposits are excluded) indicate a still larger role for hard currency in the initial money stock. By 1936, the monetary structure had experienced a major transformation. Money now meant primarily bank liabilities (notes and deposits) rather than metallic currency, which accounted for less than one-sixth of the money stock and was reduced to a distinctly secondary position.

The rapid growth of the ratio of money to the nominal value of current output (Table 3.6) indicates a substantial spread of the money economy. More and more Chinese were regularly involved in markets where commodities and services were exchanged for money. As noted above, banknotes circulated widely, even in remote areas. The banker Chang Chia-ao observed that "the habit of using banknotes had been fully developed during the . . . twenty years" before the Pacific War. Wright's description of customs procedures during the 1920s noted that "the use of sycee [silver 'shoes'] is fast disappearing, giving place first to the silver dollar or kindred coinage and latterly to the bank-note."[84] Detailed reports on customs payments confirm this assessment: although metal currency remained popular in some localities, including Chungking and Foochow, notes and checks figured prominently in the accounts at most major centers, at many minor ports, and even at some of the native customs posts that levied fees on domestic junk traffic. By 1926, the share of native customs revenues paid in hard currency amounted to only 2 percent at Canton, 5 percent at Tientsin, 27 percent at Chiu-chiang, 33 percent at Ningpo, 38 percent at Wenchow, and 50 percent at Amoy.[85]

Although it is difficult to document the economic impact of monetization with precision, it appears that in China, as elsewhere, the expansion of the money economy stimulated the development of production and trade both by lowering interest charges and transactions costs and by relaxing long-standing constraints on

84. Chang, "Toward Modernization," 158; Stanley F. Wright, *The Collection and Disposal of the Maritime and Native Customs Revenue Since the Revolution of 1911* (Shanghai, 1927), 20.
85. Ibid., 8–19.

the supply of capital. The role of commercial and native banks in the financing of modern sector ventures is well-known. Railways, mines, factories, power plants, and even agricultural ventures such as land reclamation, dairy production, and cotton cooperatives relied extensively on bank loans to finance their operations.[86]

By the late 1920s, if not before, banks, mines, major factories, and other large-scale enterprises could tap national capital markets to obtain funds. Major banks, operating far-flung branch networks, could attract deposits from all regions and recycle them to the areas of greatest demand. Even medium-sized enterprises such as the Szechwan-based Min-sheng Company, which employed 3,900 workers in 1936, or Shanghai's Ta-lung Machinery Works, with 1,300 workers in 1933, enjoyed ready access to funds from commercial banks as well as *ch'ien-chuang*.[87] Information on corporate shareholding supports this notion of progress toward a national capital market. As mentioned above, major enterprises in mining and metallurgy telegraphed nationwide appeals for share capital. Shareholders of the Kincheng Bank were spread across all of north, northeast, and central China.[88] These opportunities for tapping capital originating in distant places represent a significant departure that surely increased the domestic capacity to finance investment projects in all sectors of the economy.

The expansion of banking facilities often followed the development of new transport routes. The completion of the Peking-Hankow rail line in 1906 stimulated an expansion of mining and commercial farming in adjacent areas of the North China plain. Clients of the Tientsin-based Kincheng Bank located along the rail line, including the Chiao-tso Coal Mine and the Tao-ch'ing Railway, pressed the Bank's Peking office to commence banking opera-

86. *Shang-hai ch'ien chuang shih liao*, 784–87, 802–5, 820–22, 842–45; *Chin-ch'eng yin hang shih liao*, 460–61; *Chung-kuo nung yeh chin jung kai yao*, 135–37; Leonard G. Ting, "Chinese Modern Banks and the Finance of Government and Industry," *Nankai Social and Economic Quarterly* 8, no. 3 (1935):602–4; and Fong, "Industrial Capital in China," 79–89. Lieu, *Growth and Industrialization of Shanghai*, chap. 4, repeatedly notes the joint participation of native and commercial banks in industrial finance.

87. *Min-sheng shih-yeh kung-ssu shih i chou nien chi nien k'an* (Chungking, 1937), 83 and Thomas G. Rawski, *China's Transition to Industrialism: Producer Goods and Economic Development in the Twentieth Century* (Ann Arbor, 1980), 9.

88. *Chin-ch'eng yin hang shih liao*, 23–33.

tions in their localities. Following these requests, the Bank opened new offices in Chiao-tso, in nearby Hsin-hsiang (both in Honan), and also at Pao-ting (Hopei), which was favored because of its political role as a provincial government seat and by its location on the rail line. By the 1930s, the Bank had begun to anticipate the economic impact of rail development by opening branches along the western end of the Lung-hai railway as construction progressed. Once the line was completed, the Bank quickly moved to establish an office at the eastern terminus, Lien-yün-kang (Kiangsu), where "commerce visibly develops every day."[89]

The increased supplies of money and credit arising from the expansion of private banking played a key role in the growth of commercial cropping in many regions of prewar China. The commercialization of agriculture requires increased cash payments to growers as well as extra financing for an extended period between the harvest of crops and the delivery of finished products to the ultimate consumer. The substitution of banknotes, drafts, and bills of exchange for the costly and risky alternative of delivering large quantities of silver to the countryside at harvest time sharply reduced the expense of moving farm produce to distant markets and presented agricultural communities with new opportunities to improve their incomes.

Han-seng Chen vividly describes the consequences of injecting cash into the village economies of Shantung, Honan, and Anhwei:[90]

Perhaps the most significant fact . . . is that the tobacco companies . . . have always given cash payments for the [American tobacco] leaves. This has given a tremendous stimulus to the peasants. Here, as everywhere else in China, the peasants have found themselves in urgent need of ready cash which is hard to obtain. Since the completion of the Kiao-tsi [Tsingtao-Chinan] Railway in 1904, of the Ping-han [Peking-Hankow] in 1906, and of the Tsin-pu [Tientsin-P'u-k'ou] in 1912, money economy has gone forward with rapid strides. . . . When the poverty-stricken peasants saw the attractive price offered for tobacco grown from American seed and the immediate cash payment made at the time of sale, they naturally abandoned the native seed. . . . Even those who had never planted any

89. Ibid., 250–51.
90. Han-seng Chen, *Industrial Capital and Chinese Peasants* (Reprint, New York, 1980), 7.

tobacco were tempted to reduce their grain fields in order to go in for tobacco farming.

Chen's account emphasizes the contribution of the commercial banks and other sources of urban funds in the growth of tobacco production.[91] Myers gives a broader picture of how native banks contributed to the commercialization of farming in North China:[92]

Native banks, located principally in Tientsin, Chinan, Peking, Shihmen and Tsingtao, had branch banks in the county seats of districts specializing in wheat, cotton, and peanuts. Their loans to merchants played an important role in financing the growth of these staple trades. With native bank credit merchants were able to send their brokers to various market towns to purchase industrial crops and grain. This bank credit made for a large share of their working capital to make purchases, hold stocks, and then sell to factories, exporters, and other merchants.

In the south, accounts of the silk trade show that the banking system supported the expansion of both primary production and processing activities in a similar fashion.[93]

Can monetary data help to determine whether these stimuli produced important changes in national economic aggregates? Estimates of the annual growth rate of China's money stock over various periods between 1910 and 1936 appear in Table 3.5. Two sets of growth rates are given, corresponding to the separate monetary totals (based on two different estimates of China's stock of monetary silver) built up in Appendix C. Both sets show rapid monetary growth, ranging from 4.6 to 6.6 percent per year over the whole period. Both series point to a considerable acceleration of monetary growth during the 1920s and 1930s.

These findings raise the possibility, to be explored more fully in Chapter 6, that China's economy grew considerably faster between World War I and the 1930s than the 1 percent annual rate derived

91. Ibid., 9–15.
92. Ramon H. Myers, *The Chinese Peasant Economy: Agricultural Development in Hopei and Shantung, 1890–1949* (Cambridge, 1970), 244.
93. Robert Y. Eng, "Chinese Entrepreneurs, the Government and the Foreign Sector: The Canton and Shanghai Silk-Reeling Enterprises, 1861–1932," *Modern Asian Studies* 18, no. 3 (1984):361–65; David Faure, "The Plight of the Farmers: A Study of the Rural Economy of Jiangnan and the Pearl River Delta, 1870–1937," *Modern China* 11, no. 1 (1985):10.

Table 3.5
Annual Growth Rate of Chinese Money Supply, 1910-36

Period	M1 Version		M2 Version	
	A	B	A	B
1910-20	1.8%	1.2%	2.0%	1.4%
1910-25	3.8	2.6	4.0	2.9
1910-30	5.0	3.6	5.2	3.9
1910-36	5.3	4.0	5.8	4.6
1914-36	6.0	4.6	6.6	5.3

Source: Log-linear regressions calculated from data in Tables
C.16 and C.17.

in previous studies. Available data show that, between 1910 and
1936, the annual rate of price increase was approximately 2 percent.[94] Monetary growth in the range of 5–6 percent and price
increases in the range of 2 percent imply that the real value of the
money stock grew at an annual rate of 3 or 4 percent between 1910
and 1936. Existing estimates of output growth, by contrast, indicate annual growth of roughly 1 percent in gross domestic product
between 1914/18 and 1933 or 1936 (Table 6.1). Together, these
estimates of monetary and output growth imply that Chinese
households and businesses experienced major increases in the ratio
of money holdings to current output and income during the decades prior to the Sino-Japanese War. An alternate way of expressing this is to note that the velocity of monetary circulation, which
measures the frequency with which money changes hands, declined substantially. Since the monetary totals, if anything, err by

94. The Nankai index of Tientsin wholesale prices shows an increase of 65.4 percent between 1913 and 1936. To obtain a figure for 1910, I use the annual
average of separate price indexes for import and export products; these figures
show a very small price increase of 2.8 percent between 1910 and 1913. With
1910 taken as the base, the resulting linked index reaches a figure of 169.4 in
1936, indicating an annual inflation rate of 2.0 percent between 1910 and 1936.
See *Nan-k'ai chih shu tzu liao hui pien, 1913–1952* (Peking, 1958), 11 and
Franklin L. Ho, *Index Numbers of the Quantities and Prices of Imports and
Exports and of the Barter Terms of Trade in China, 1867–1928* (Tientsin,
1930), 24.

Table 3.6
Velocity Implications of Chinese National Product Estimates

Year	Real GDP (1)	Price Index (2)	Nominal GDP (3)	Money Stock (M2) (4)		Velocity (5)	
				A	B	A	B
1914/18	24.25	0.737	17.87	2.22	3.24	8.05	5.52
1931	28.57	1.213	34.66	6.14	7.16	5.64	4.84
1932	29.47	1.118	32.95	6.43	7.45	5.12	4.42
1933	29.46	1.000	29.46	6.82	7.84	4.32	3.76
1934	26.90	0.914	24.59	6.92	7.95	3.55	3.09
1935	29.09	0.946	27.52	7.57	8.59	3.64	3.20
1936	30.94	1.095	33.88	8.57	9.10	3.95	3.53
1931-36 average	29.07	1.048	30.46	7.08	8.10	4.30	3.76

Sources: Col. 1: Gross domestic product (billion 1933 yuan) is
from K. C. Yeh, "China's National Income, 1931-36," in Modern
Chinese Economic History, ed. Chi-ming Hou and Tzong-shian Yu
(Taipei, 1979), 98, 110.

Col. 2: Tientsin wholesale price index with 1933 base is
calculated from Nan-k'ai chih shu tzu liao, 11.

Col. 3: Gross domestic product (billion current yuan) is derived
by multiplying annual entries in Cols. 1 and 2.

Col. 4: Annual year-end money stock (M2) (billion yuan), Versions
A and B, is from Table C.16.

Col. 5: The estimated income velocity of circulation is the
quotient of nominal GDP (Col. 3) and year-end money stock
(Col. 4A or 4B).

understating the growth of the money supply, the growth of money
balances and concomitant reduction in velocity may exceed the
amounts that can be inferred from the new estimates for China's
monetary aggregates and the output estimates compiled by Yeh
and Perkins.

These calculations are performed in Table 3.6 using Yeh's output
estimates and the M2 money supply series derived in Table C.16.
They indicate that the velocity of circulation declined by 32–46
percent between 1914/18 and 1934. Alternatively, the figures show

that the economy-wide ratio of money balances to output increased by 47–87 percent between 1914/18 and 1931/36.[95]

There are reasons to anticipate an increase in the ratio of money balances to the money value of output as an economy undergoes a process of commercialization as occurred in prewar China. Farmers who rarely attend markets may have little need to hold cash balances, but farmers with similar income levels who visit markets at weekly or monthly intervals may find it convenient to hold larger amounts of money. At the same time, however, the expansion of the banking system and the growth of transport and communication facilities characteristic of prewar China might have reduced the necessary ratio of money balances to output and caused velocity to rise. The spread of banking and the growing use of telegraphic and telephone transfers of funds eliminated the need to move large quantities of cash in order to facilitate commodity transfers. Furthermore, the absence of bank regulation or deposit insurance made money a highly risky asset. Except for silver and (often debased) copper coins, which accounted for an ever-shrinking share of the monetary totals, holders of money exposed themselves to very real risks of total loss through bank failure or currency depreciation.

What can international comparisons tell about changes in velocity? Bordo and Jonung have found that a declining velocity of circulation (the ratio of nominal output to M2 money supply) is typical of nations in the early phases of economic growth in both the nineteenth and the twentieth centuries.[96] Table 3.7 presents comparative data on the annual rates of velocity decline for twenty-year periods in the United States and Japan. These comparisons, while not directly applicable to the Chinese case, suggest that the reductions derived in Table 3.6 are large, but not impossibly so. Were it not for the greater risk attached to money-holding in prewar China, one might conclude that the Japanese figures for 1890–1920 confirm the plausibility of the results shown in Table 3.6.

95. Perkins's estimate of 27.5 percent real output growth between 1914–18 and 1933 (Table 6.1), together with the price and monetary data shown in Table 3.6, implies that the 1933 velocity was 56 (Version A) or 72 (Version B) percent of the initial level, essentially the same outcome derived in Table 3.6 from Yeh's output figures.

96. Michael D. Bordo and Lars Jonung, *The Long-run Behavior of the Velocity of Circulation: The international evidence* (Cambridge, 1987), chaps. 2 and 6.

Table 3.7
International Data on Annual Rates of Velocity Decline

Country and Period	Annual Rate of Velocity Decline	
United States		
1869-1889	2.0%	
1880-1900	2.6	
1890-1910	1.2	
Japan		
1890-1910	4.1	
1900-1920	2.9	
1910-1930	2.3	
1916-1936	1.1	
China	Version A	Version B
1916-1934	4.4%	2.4%
1916-1936	3.5	2.2
1914/18-1931/36	3.5	2.2

Sources: The U.S. data are from Milton Friedman and Anna Jacobson Schwartz, A Monetary History of the United States, 1867-1960 (Princeton, 1963), 774. The Japanese data are based on national product estimates (current prices) in Patterns of Japanese Economic Development, ed. Kazushi Ohkawa and Miyohei Shinohara (New Haven, 1979), 266-68 and money supply totals (currency in circulation plus total deposits) calculated from Hundred-Year Statistics, 166-67, 194. The Chinese data are calculated from Table 3.6 using K. C. Yeh's estimates of gross domestic product and money supply data (M2) from Table C.16. The calculations using 1916 as an endpoint assume that aggregate output for 1916 was equal to the average figure for 1914/18.

A more relevant comparison is with Manchuria, for which there are detailed monetary data beginning in 1932 as well as reasonably sound output figures for selected years. The velocity implications of these estimates are calculated in Table 3.8. The results are surprising. They show that the velocity in the Manchurian region was somewhat higher than the national totals derived in Table 3.6. Even after several years of very rapid inflation, the relatively developed and geographically compact Manchurian region shows stable velocity figures similar to the national figures for 1934–36 derived in Table 3.6.

This review of evidence regarding the velocity of monetary circulation points to the possibility that the national velocity results derived in Table 3.6 decline with improbable speed. Or, what

Table 3.8
Regional Product, Money Supply and Velocity in Manchuria,
1934-41

Year	Real GDP (1)	Price Index (2)	Nominal GDP (3)	Money Stock (4)	Velocity (5)
1934	2.677	1.000	2.677	0.667	3.95
1936	3.289	1.146	3.769	0.967	3.90
1939	4.175	1.958	8.175	2.161	3.78
1941	4.733	2.680	12.684	3.529	3.59

Sources: Col. 1: Gross domestic product, billion Manchoukuo yuan (or yen), 1934 prices, from Alexander Eckstein, Kang Chao, and John K. Chang, "The Economic Development of Manchuria: The Rise of a Frontier Economy," *Journal of Economic History* 34, no. 1 (1974):254.

Col. 2: The price is index calculated from the index of retail prices in Hsinking (Changchun) shown in *Manshū kaihatsu yonjū nenshi* 2:882.

Col. 3: Gross domestic product in current prices, billions of Manchoukuo yuan (or yen); for each year, the figure is obtained by multiplying entries in Cols. 1 and 2.

Col. 4: The regional money stock, year-end total, is calculated as the sum of currency in circulation and bank deposits from the data in *Manshū chūō ginkō jūnenshi*, appendix, 1, 8.

Col. 5: The income velocity of circulation for each year is the quotient of nominal GDP (Col. 3) and money stock (Col. 4).

amounts to the same thing, one may suspect that the figures in Table 3.6 imply improbably large increases in the national ratio of money holdings per yuan of output. The suggestion that velocity declines at an unacceptably rapid pace is not definitive. The rate of decline is not impossibly high. But why, in a highly risky economy undergoing rapid expansion of financial services, should average money balances per yuan of output rise, perhaps by as much as 87 percent, between 1914/18 and 1931/36? If, as suggested by international data, velocity declines with economic and financial development, why does Manchuria, an advanced region for which there are excellent monetary and good output data, show substantially higher velocity than the nation as a whole? These questions raise the possibility that my calculations substantially overstate the decline in velocity of circulation between 1914/18 and 1931/36, especially since the money supply figures may understate monetary growth, implying a still faster decline of velocity.

The measurement of velocity is based on the accounting identity

$$Mv = PT \text{ or } v = PT/M$$

where M, v, P, and T denote money supply, velocity, price level, and real output. If the decline in v is overstated, there are three possible explanations. Prices may have risen faster than is indicated by the figures in Tables 3.6 and 3.8, but major underestimation of inflation is most unlikely. Loren Brandt's research demonstrates close interregional price correlations along major trade routes in the period under review.[97] The use of a price index for Tientsin, a major commercial center with extensive trade ties to China's coastal and Yangtze provinces as well as to the interior provinces of the north, northeast, and northwest, leaves little chance of underestimating the rate of inflation. A second possible cause of an artificially rapid reduction in the measured velocity is an overestimate of monetary growth. This possibility is carefully avoided throughout Appendix C. This leaves as the final possibility a substantial underestimate of real output growth between 1914/18 and 1936.

This is perhaps the most important consequence of the money supply estimates summarized in Table 3.6. These new monetary totals, together with existing estimates of real output growth, generate surprisingly rapid reductions in velocity. The substantial gap between the measured velocity for all China and the considerably higher figures for Manchuria add substance to the suspicion that the results of Table 3.6 overstate the decline in velocity. If velocity decline is indeed overestimated, the most probable explanation is that *real output grew considerably faster between World War I and the Sino-Japanese War than the 1 percent annual rate obtained by Yeh and by Perkins.* The possibility that existing estimates of prewar Chinese economic growth require drastic upward revision will receive detailed consideration in Chapter 6.

For the present, it will suffice to conclude only that, by providing farmers as well as traders and manufacturers with opportunities

97. Loren L. Brandt, Jr., "Population Growth, Agricultural Change and Economic Integration in Central and Eastern China: 1890's–1930's" (Ph.D. diss., University of Illinois, 1983), chap. 4.

to finance new forms of production and exchange, the development of financial institutions and the spread of new monetary arrangements, together with contemporaneous improvements in transport and communication, raised the level of production and consumption substantially above what would otherwise have prevailed. The expanded specialization and division of labor permitted by monetary expansion and financial deepening stimulated considerable increases in the overall volume of production and exchange. This in itself is a highly significant achievement in a financial milieu characterized by a near-total absence of state-imposed uniformity and regulation.

Financial Development and Economic Stability

In the wake of the 1935 reform, China's monetary system was well along the path toward a managed currency of the sort familiar in the industrial world. For the first time there was a uniform monetary accounting unit. The creation of a uniform paper currency convertible into foreign exchange eliminated the notes of provincial, native, and foreign banks from circulation at least within the regions controlled by the Nanking government. New issues of subsidiary coinage were beginning to supplant the nonstandard and often debased tokens issued by various provincial and national agencies. There were plans to transform the Central Bank of China into a reserve institution designed to protect the security of the commercial banking system. Pending such changes, other mechanisms, including reserve funds accumulated on the joint initiative of leading private banks, provided an increasing degree of protection for depositors.

These impressive and productive reforms suffered from the weakness inherent in any fiduciary currency system. Without a concrete link between the currency and an external standard of value (gold, silver, foreign exchange), only custom and discipline prevent the government from depreciating the value of the currency through excessive borrowing or uncontrolled note issue. Japan's invasion of China in 1937 forced the Nanking administration to flee to the interior, stripping the government of its coastal revenue base while simultaneously generating strong demands for higher wartime spending. Soon thereafter, the government did resort to excessive note issue and the ensuing hyperinflation became a key factor in its eventual defeat by forces loyal to China's communist party.

The ultimate outcome of China's shift to a fiduciary currency system should not obscure the real and significant accomplishments of the financial sector during the prewar decades. The expansion of commercial banking promoted economic integration and permanently transformed the economy from primary dependence on metallic currency (silver and copper) into a new pattern in which bank money formed the principal medium of exchange. The resulting expansion of loanable funds and reduction in transactions costs stimulated the entire economy. A further achievement, largely a consequence of the others, was China's success in avoiding severe deflation and economic dislocation during the world depression of the 1930s.

With banking operations confined almost entirely to the private sector throughout most of the prewar period, the rapid expansion of commercial banking and the gradual emergence of banknotes and deposits as the chief components of the national money stock could occur only in response to voluntary increases in the private demand for bank money. The estimates of the interwar growth of real output, prices, and money supply assembled in Table 3.9 make it possible to quantify the appetite of the Chinese public for bank money. Whatever estimate of real output growth is selected, there is a substantial increase in monetization, with the ratio of money stock to the nominal value of aggregate output rising by a minimum of two-thirds between 1914/18 and 1933. With the composition of the money stock shifting rapidly away from hard currency toward banknotes and deposits, the ratio of bank money to nominal output rose to about three times its initial level between World War I and the mid-1930s. The growing popularity of bank money reflects the benefits of replacing hard currency even in the absence of official supervision of banking and despite the dangers of periodic bank runs and excessive note issue.

The success of private bankers in selling new monetary instruments to the Chinese public paved the way for the Nanking government's monetary reform of 1935. Without the prior expansion of bank money and the attendant penetration of banknotes and

Table 3.9
Estimated Growth of Money and Aggregate Output, 1914/18 to
1933/36
(1914/18 average = 100)

	Real Gross Domestic Product Estimate Prepared By	
	K. C. Yeh (1933)	Dwight H. Perkins (1933)
1. Real output index	120.1	127.5
2. Wholesale price index	140.0	140.0
3. Index of nominal output	168.1	178.5
4. Index of money stock		
Version A	307.7	307.7
Version B	295.5	295.5
5. Index for stock of bank money	505.9	505.9
6. Ratio: Money stock to nominal GDP (1914/18=100)		
Version A	183	172
Version B	176	166
7 Ratio: Bank Money to Nominal GDP (1914/18=100)	301	283

Sources: Line 1: The index of gross domestic product in real terms is from Yeh, "National Income," 97, 126 and Dwight H. Perkins, "Growth and Changing Structure of China's Twentieth-Century Economy," in China's Modern Economy in Historical Perspective, ed. Dwight H. Perkins (Stanford, 1975), 126.

Line 2: The index of Tientsin wholesale prices is from Nan-k'ai chih shu tzu liao, 11.

Line 3: Calculated from Lines 1 and 2.

Line 4: Calculated from the estimated money stock (M2) in Table C.16.

Line 5: The index of bank money (banknotes and deposits) is calculated from Table C.16.

Line 6: Calculated from Lines 3 and 4.

Line 7: Calculated from Lines 3 and 5.

bank credit into the rural trading network, the sudden nationalization of silver and the ensuing shift to a wholly fiduciary currency system would have created massive disruption. The same public acceptance of new forms of money provided the key to stabilizing China's economy during the 1930s, a period of extraordinary domestic and external shocks.

The sequence of shocks inflicted on China's economy beginning in 1929 was indeed remarkable. The immediate impact of the New York stock market collapse and the ensuing depression of production and trade in the industrial nations was muted in China by the declining price of silver. Since China, alone among the major nations of the world, used silver as the basis for her currency, falling silver prices meant the devaluation of the Chinese currency, which in turn raised the domestic price of imports and lowered the overseas price of China's exports. These tendencies acted to reinforce demand for Chinese products both at home and abroad.

Despite the short-term benefits of falling silver, the negative impact of the world economic decline quickly made itself felt in China. Exports of silk, a luxury product that was already suffering from Japanese competition and the development of synthetic substitutes, crashed. Overseas sales of raw silk, China's largest foreign exchange earner, dropped by one-third in 1929–30 and fell a further 50 percent in 1931–32; with prices plunging, revenues declined even faster. Exports of tea, another major trade item, dropped by 23 percent during 1929–30. Remittances from overseas Chinese fell sharply and investment outlays by foreign firms in China proper probably declined as well. These negative factors may have roughly balanced the initial advantages of falling silver prices. The volume of exports fell by 4.4 percent in 1928–29 and a further 12.1 percent in 1929–30, but a slight recovery in 1930–31 left 1931 exports at 87.4 percent of the 1928 total. With world imports falling by 42 percent between 1929 and 1931, China clearly escaped the brunt of the international depression in these years.[98]

Beginning in 1931, however, China's economy was rocked by a succession of domestic problems. The summer of 1931 brought massive flooding to the Yangtze valley, "the most disastrous for

98. Trade data are from Liang-lin Hsiao, *China's Foreign Trade Statistics, 1864–1949* (Cambridge, 1974) and Charles P. Kindleberger, *The World in Depression, 1929–1939* (Berkeley, 1973), 172.

sixty years," according to one source. Estimates of the central government, confirmed by private bankers, suggested that 24–36 percent of China's normal production of rice, cotton, millet, and kaoliang (sorghum) were washed away.[99] In September of the same year, Japanese troops based in the South Manchurian Railway concession launched their conquest of Manchuria by occupying Shenyang (also known as Fengtien or Mukden), the political center of the northeast. Military action and the resulting uncertainty disrupted commerce, transportation, and credit throughout Manchuria and across much of North China. The Chinese public responded by boycotting Japanese products and firms. Japan retaliated in January 1932 by attacking the Chinese section of Shanghai. Fighting was brief but intense, with the Japanese resorting to naval and aerial bombardment and the Chinese offering tenacious resistance. Along with physical damage to factories, utilities, railways, businesses, and residential buildings, the cessation of business in China's financial center at the lunar new year, the season for settling business debts, disrupted trade throughout the Yangtze region.

In March 1932, the Japanese, having completed their military occupation of the northeast, proclaimed the region as the independent state of Manchoukuo. The alienation of Manchuria, which became a puppet state controlled by Japan, deprived China of a rich and dynamic region that had contributed one-third of the nation's total exports, produced a regular trade surplus, furnished considerable revenues to the Nanking government, and provided a market for large flows of goods and labor from China's northern provinces.

At the end of 1932, the international price of silver began to rise. This increase, which resulted from the abandonment of the gold standard by Great Britain, Japan, and the United States, meant an upward revaluation of China's monetary unit in world currency markets. With rising silver, both Chinese and foreign buyers now found the prices of Chinese goods increasing relative to the cost of foreign products; the substitution of foreign for Chinese goods at home and abroad began to reduce the demand for Chinese output.

99. Bank of China, *Report of the General Manager to the Annual Meeting of Shareholders, March 19, 1932* (Shanghai, 1932), 22.

China faced not only the danger of falling demand but also, because silver appreciation threatened to enlarge a trade deficit already swollen by the loss of Manchuria, a new risk of monetary contraction resulting from the export of silver to bridge the trade gap. China's long-standing silver inflow was reversed after 1931 and small silver exports were recorded in both 1932 and 1933.

In the meantime, the elected representatives of American mining states began to press the U.S. government for a large increase in silver prices to stimulate production in their home districts. Despite considerable opposition from American and British economists as well as the Chinese and Mexican governments, to whom higher silver prices promised further unwanted currency appreciation, President Roosevelt agreed to enlarge America's silver purchase program beginning in 1934. As silver prices rose in New York, silver coin and bullion began to leave China to be sold at high prices to the U.S. Treasury. The Nanking government attempted to halt the silver drain by imposing an export tax in October 1934, but this merely encouraged smuggling.

This situation continued until late 1935. While the Nanking government struggled to escape the consequences of high silver prices and desultory international negotiations dragged on, the outflow of silver continued. Foreign banks smuggled large amounts of silver out of the country, sometimes using military protection to evade customs inquiries. The Japanese, anxious to destabilize China's economy as a prelude to further military encroachment, were particularly active exporters of silver. Finally, in late 1935, China's monetary reform, together with a belated American reevaluation of the silver purchase program, put an end to China's silver crisis.

Between 1931 and 1936, however, the data in Table C.1 indicate that China's stock of silver, including ingots as well as coined metal, declined by nearly half. Because the figures in Table C.1 incorporate estimates of smuggling as well as an uncertain initial figure, there can be no claim of precision. Whatever the exact amount, a very large percentage of China's silver stock disappeared within a few years. By 1936, it is quite likely that the quantity of silver in China had fallen to a level as low as before World War I.

What was the effect of these shocks on China's economy? One might expect to observe a large decline in output, especially because of the potentially deflationary impact of the huge outflow of silver on a system in which the national government could not control the size of the overall money stock. In fact, there was no large economic contraction in China during the depression years. Comparative data assembled in Table 3.10 show that China avoided the steep decline suffered by America's economy during the depression years of the 1930s.

The real output performance of the two economies is compared in Panel 1 of Table 3.10. United States output, measured in terms of constant prices, began to decline in 1929–30; at the bottom of the slide, real GNP in 1933 was more than 30 percent below the 1929 level. In China, as noted above, the impact of the world depression was initially muted by the falling value of silver; it was only when silver began to rise in 1932 that China faced the danger of domestic deflation. When the decline in output arrived, however, it was both brief and relatively mild. K. C. Yeh's estimates of gross domestic product in Line B of Panel 1 show that aggregate output stagnated in 1932–33 and dropped by 8.7 percent in 1933–34. The latter was essentially an agricultural phenomenon: farm output fell by 11.9 percent, while output in the rest of the economy declined by 3.0 percent. Yeh's sectoral output estimates show a similar pattern of a general upward movement interrupted by episodic reversals. Yeh's thirteen economic sectors show eleven instances of annual output reduction during 1931–36 as opposed to forty-four instances of annual increase. Only handicrafts and unmechanized transport and communications have a lower output in 1936 than in 1931 and even then the decline is less than 5 percent.

Yeh's estimates include Manchuria, where economic trends diverged sharply from conditions in China proper under the large-scale investment programs that followed Japan's military takeover of 1931. Although there is no separate series of aggregate output for China proper, information about manufacturing, investment, and railway traffic indicates that conclusions derived from aggregate output data apply to China proper as well as to the entire nation. The Chinese figures for manufacturing output (Panel 2) show that, although lagging behind the growth of industry in Manchuria, manufacturing in China proper continued to expand its real output throughout the depression years. The contrast with the United States, where the Federal Reserve index of industrial production plunged by 36 percent between 1929 and 1933, is striking.

Table 3.10
Economic Fluctuations in China and the United States, 1928-36
(annual percentage change from previous year)

	1929	1930	1931	1932	1933	1934	1935	1936
1. Real GNP								
A. U.S.	+6.3	-13.7	-5.9	-14.6	-2.9	+8.9	+13.1	+10.4
B. China	...	...	...	+3.2	0.0	-8.7	+8.1	+6.4
2. Manufacturing Output								
A. U.S.	+11.5	-17.2	-19.8	-23.1	+20.0	+8.3	+17.9	+19.6
B. China								
National	...	...	...	+9.1	+1.8	+5.4	+8.1	+15.3
China Proper	...	...	...	+6.2	-1.0	+5.1	+7.7	+9.2
3. Railway Activity								
A. U.S.	+3.2	-14.3	-19.4	-24.4	+6.5	+7.8	+4.9	+20.3
B. China	+7.0	...	...	0.0	+7.0	+31.4	+3.5	0.0
4. Investment Volume								
A. U.S.	...	-32.6	-36.4	-74.0	+2.6	+85.0	+118.0	+30.4
B. China[a]								
National	+19.7	-5.0	-0.6	+2.6	+19.5	+22.9	+1.2	+8.6
China Proper	+22.4	-0.8	+11.1	+3.4	+5.2	0.0	+2.7	+14.7
5. Money Wages								
A. U.S.	+0.2	-7.1	-10.2	-18.3	-1.9	+10.0	+9.4	+8.2
B. China	...	+16.8	-3.5	-0.7	+0.4	-4.2	-1.7	-2.0
6. Urban Retail Prices								
A. U.S.	0.0	-2.6	-9.0	-10.2	-5.3	+3.4	+2.6	+1.0
B. China	...	+14.0	+0.7	+0.2	-13.1	-6.6	+7.5	+5.6
7. Urban Wholesale Prices								
A. U.S.	-1.6	-9.4	-15.5	-11.2	+1.7	+13.8	+6.8	+1.0
B. China	+3.9	+7.8	+7.2	-11.8	-8.5	+0.6	+4.4	+15.0

continued...

Railway traffic (Panel 3), which provides a good indicator of activity in industry and mining, shows a similar picture. The Chinese data are based on the volume of freight traffic on China's state-owned railway network, located almost entirely in China proper. The data are incomplete, but there is no sign of declining traffic.

Table 3.10, continued

	1929	1930	1931	1932	1933	1934	1935	1936
8. Prices Received by Farmers								
A. U.S.	0.0	-15.6	-30.4	-25.3	+7.7	+28.6	+21.1	+4.6
B. China	+15.9	+11.9	-18.0	-7.0	-23.7	+21.1	+12.8	+4.1
9. Money Stock								
A. U.S.	+0.7	-1.3	-3.0	-14.2	-9.3	+8.3	+10.9	+9.9
B. China	+11.5	+12.6	+3.8	+4.7	+6.0	+1.6	+9.3	+13.3
10. Bank Deposits								
A. U.S.	+0.2	+3.6	-5.3	-20.3	-8.5	+11.5	+10.3	+13.2
B. China	+14.4	+20.2	+5.9	+8.0	+10.6	+7.7	+18.2	+17.1

^aModern-oriented investment only.

Sources: U.S. data are from The Statistical History of the United States from Colonial Times to the Present (Stamford, 1965), 139 (line 1A), 409 (line 2A), 431 (line 3A), 143 (line 4A), 92 (line 5A), 125-26 (line 6A), 117 (line 7A), 283 (line 8A), 646 (line 9A), and 625 (line 10A).

Chinese data: Line 1B from Yeh, "China's National Income, 1931-36," 97.

Line 2B: Calculated from K. C. Yeh, "Capital Formation in Mainland China: 1931-36 and 1952-57" (Ph.D. diss., Columbia University, 1964), 225, omitting electrical appliances, for which Yeh provides no regional breakdown.

Line 3B: Ton-kilometers of freight carriage on China's national railway system only, from Yen Chung-p'ing, comp., Chung-kuo chin tai ching chi shih t'ung chi tzu liao hsüan chi (Peking, 1955), 207-8.

Line 4B: Table 5.2.

Line 5B: Data for 1930/34 are average hourly wages in Shanghai industries from T. Y. Tsha, "A Study of Wage Rates in Shanghai, 1930-34," Nankai Social and Economic Quarterly 8, no. 3 (1935):503. For 1929/30 and 1934/36 I use monthly wages for Shanghai cotton textile workers shown in Table 6.6; for 1936, I use the average of alternate figures from Table 6.6.

continued...

In the United States, by contrast, railway freight traffic, a standard business-cycle indicator, dropped precipitously after 1929; even after four years of recovery, 1936 freight traffic on U.S. railways had barely regained three-fourths of the 1929 level.

Investment data, reported in Panel 4 of Table 3.10, offer an even

Table 3.10, continued

Line 6B: Shanghai cost-of-living figures for the month of June given in Arthur N. Young, China's Nation-Building Effort, 1927-1937 (Stanford, 1971), 475-78.

Line 7B: The Shanghai index of wholesale prices is from Shanghai chieh fang ch'ien hou wu chia tzu liao hui pien, 1921-1957 (Shanghai, 1958), 47.

Line 8B: The prices received by farmers in Wuchin, Kiangsu are from Young, Nation-Building, 479 and for 1928/29 from John L. Buck, Land Utilization in China, Statistics (Reprint, New York, 1982), 149.

Line 9B: Table C.16, Version A of the estimated money stock (M2).

Line 10B: Table C.15.

greater contrast. Investment collapsed in the United States, with gross private domestic investment in 1933 amounting, in real terms, to only 11 percent of the 1929 total. For China, my measure of modern-oriented fixed investment, to be discussed in Chapter 5, shows rapid growth, despite periodic setbacks, in both China proper and Manchuria. In China proper, rising investment, nearly all in the private sector, coincided with a reduction in new foreign investment and a drop in remittances from overseas Chinese. This means that Chinese businessmen saw growing opportunities for new or expanded economic ventures and managed to obtain sufficient funds to finance a growing volume of modern-oriented investment during the depression years.

These data leave little doubt that contemporary and retrospective accounts of the early 1930s as years of desperate crisis for China's economy contain large elements of exaggeration, particularly with regard to the modern and urban sectors.[100] The general strength of the urban economy is reflected in the stability of urban money wages, represented here by the Shanghai figures shown in Panel 5 of Table 3.10. The moderate decline in Shanghai wages is far smaller than the steep drop in U.S. manufacturing wages. A comparison of wage trends with the retail price indicators displayed in Panel 6 of Table 3.10 shows that real wages (adjusted for

100. Lieu, *Growth and Industrialization of Shanghai*, notes the continued development of cotton textiles "even during the very recent period of general depression" (p. 31) as well as rising Shanghai land prices until 1933 (p. 140).

price change) paid to Shanghai factory workers experienced no significant decline during the depression years.

Even though China avoided the large drop in production, investment, and prices experienced in the United States and most of Europe, the economic environment of the 1930s produced grave trials for Chinese households and businesses. The principal cause of these difficulties was the decline of prices summarized in Panels 6, 7, and 8 of Table 3.10. Panels 6 and 7 contain retail and wholesale price indexes for the United States and several Chinese cities. These data show that Chinese deflation began later, was less severe, and ended more rapidly than in the U.S. Despite the relative mildness of deflation in China, two or three years of falling prices were more than enough to create severe difficulties for many urban enterprises. Chinese businesses often borrowed heavily. Large debts expose borrowers to high risks of insolvency in times of deflation because it obliges them to sell an increasing volume of goods to service a fixed amount of debt. Rising interest rates (reflecting the increased risk of default) and falling values for real estate and other illiquid assets mean higher finance costs and lower collateral values for many borrowers, adding to the credit squeeze. Faced with these difficult conditions, many enterprises, including such prominent ventures as the textile and flour empire of the wealthy Jung family, teetered at the edge of bankruptcy and some failed to meet their obligations.

In any market economy, low elasticities of supply and demand cause the prices of farm products to display higher volatility than general price indexes. Deflation brings large downswings in the prices received by farmers. The data in Panel 8 of Table 3.10 show exactly this trend in both the U.S. and China. Although the Chinese data indicate a somewhat shorter and milder fall than in the United States, the deflation of farm prices was severe and protracted in both countries, with harsh effects on debtor households. The relatively low incomes and scant financial reserves of Chinese farmers magnified the impact of deflation, while the relatively low share of marketed goods in total farm output acted in the opposite direction. The impact of deflation on Chinese agriculture varied with the degree of market exposure and was therefore greatest in the relatively prosperous commercial regions whose inhabitants were best prepared to cope with hard times. Even so, the degree of dislocation was undoubtedly severe, particularly where farmers' reserves were already depleted by the 1931 Yangtze floods. It is in highly commercial farming regions, and only in these areas, that the effect of the depression in China may be compared with the hardships experienced by both urban and rural residents in the major industrial nations.

Why, with the single exception of commercial farming regions hit hardest by falling farm prices, did China escape the downward spiral that engulfed much of the world economy during the early 1930s? The information in Panels 9 and 10 of Table 3.10 directs attention to the monetary sector of China's economy. While the American money stock plunged by one-fourth between 1929 and 1933 and did not regain its 1929 level until 1937, China's money stock rose steadily throughout the depression years. America's banking crisis brought large reductions in deposits and loans which were not reversed until the late 1930s, but Chinese banks enjoyed uninterrupted growth, with estimated deposits rising by no less than 126 percent between 1929 and 1936 (Table C.15).

The continued expansion of China's money stock staved off deep and prolonged deflation and the associated reductions in output, employment, and real income despite the drain of metallic currency associated with the rising world price of silver.[101] Monetary growth hinged on the willingness of the Chinese public, developed gradually over the preceding decades, to hold a growing fraction of their liquid assets in the form of bank money, including paper notes and bank deposits, in place of silver bullion and coin. Even in 1934 and 1935, when large amounts of silver were shipped abroad, the public absorbed still larger quantities of bank money, allowing the money stock to rise and avoiding the lengthy deflation that affected the industrial nations.

Conclusion

Money and finance occupy a unique position in China's prewar economy. Only this sector experienced a thorough transformation of structure and function down to the village and household level

---

101. For further analysis of this point, see Loren Brandt and Thomas Sargent, "Interpreting New Evidence About China and U.S. Silver Purchases" (Stanford, 1987).

prior to the Pacific War. The monetary system of the 1930s, in which even farmers made regular use of banknotes and borrowed money from sources directly involved in organized financial markets, differed radically from the arrangements prevalent in the late nineteenth century, when banks and banknotes touched the economic lives of only a small minority of China's populace.

New figures describing the growth of China's money supply and its constituent elements, summarized in Tables 3.4 and 3.5, present a picture of rapid monetary growth and confirm the substitution of bank money for hard currency that is reported in documentary accounts. The swift expansion of the money stock and the unprecedented multiplication of financial intermediaries brought important and largely beneficial changes to the entire economy. There was a significant increase in economic integration among regions, between city and village, and within different segments of the financial community. Financial development contributed to economic growth as the increased circulation of funds and the reduced costs of financing production and exchange brought new opportunities to many participants in China's prewar economy. The widely remarked commercialization of prewar agriculture was highly dependent on new sources of finance. Calculations involving the velocity of monetary circulation, which measures the ratio of output value to money supply, raise the possibility, to be fully explored in Chapter 6, that China's prewar economy grew considerably faster than indicated in previous studies. Finally, the development of banking and finance enlarged the capacity of China's market economy to withstand economic shocks, even in the absence of an official stabilization policy.

Chapter Four

Transport and Communication

Beginning in the 1890s, new forms of transport and communication transformed commerce and accelerated the growth of commercial production in every sector of China's economy. Motorized water and rail traffic permanently altered China's economic landscape. At the same time, the spread of telegraphic and telephonic communication expanded information networks. New modes of transport and communication contributed to a rapid growth of domestic trade and caused a dramatic contraction of economic space. Both the expansion of commerce and the breaching of impediments to communication promoted a deepening of regional and national economic integration.

Innovations in transport and communication that speed the circulation of information, open new trade routes, or reduce the cost of moving commodities along existing networks encourage specialization, the division of labor, and increased productivity in the same way as the reductions in the cost of finance and exchange previously discussed in connection with Figure 3.1. The construction of north-south railways connecting the major cities of Manchuria with Peking in the north, Hankow in Central China, and, eventually, Canton in the south, along with the north-south line linking Tientsin, P'u-k'ou, and, with a ferry transfer across the Yangtze River, Nanking and Shanghai, brought a major reorientation of domestic commodity flows that had formerly moved mainly along the east-west axes of the major river systems: the Amur, Sungari, and Liao in Manchuria, the Yangtze in Central China, and the West River in South China.

New opportunities for large-scale north-south trade and falling costs along older trade routes opened new markets to many commodity-producing sectors of China's prewar economy. Grain farmers in Manchuria, cotton growers in Hopei, Shansi, and Shensi, miners in Hopei and Shantung, and craftsmen in Kiangsu, Chekiang, Shantung, and Hopei were among the numerous producers who found that transport improvements brought access to expanded markets. Changing relative costs created additional opportunities, as when falling prices for coal and kerosene stimulated the expansion of energy-using industries, including tobacco farming as well as the manufacture of electricity, cement, ceramics, and glass; cheap mineral fuels also freed farmers from exclusive reliance on the land to obtain energy for cooking, lighting, and heating.

The reduced costs arising from improved finance, transport, and communication benefited unmechanized carriers as well as the operators of new transport modes. Although competition between new and old forms of transport deprived some traditional carriers of their livelihood, the limited growth of motorized rail and water networks increased overall demand for the services of wooden sailing vessels (junks) and other unmechanized carriers who moved commodities and passengers to and from the railway stations and new-style wharves and supplied expanding numbers of specialized producers with a growing variety of goods obtained through the market rather than from household production. With their greater flexibility, low costs, and convenient service, old-style carriers managed to survive and expand even where, as at Shanghai and Tientsin, they encountered head-on competition with rail and shipping lines that enjoyed the patronage of foreign governments as well as that of Chinese officials.

The Economic Effects of Improved
Transport and Communication

Trade among individuals and between town and country, region and region, or nation and nation arises from differences in production costs between potential trading partners. If such cost differences exist, mutually advantageous exchange is possible, but only if information flows, financial arrangements, and transport facilities are sufficiently developed to keep the costs of exchange well below the prospective gains from trade. These costs include the expense of obtaining information about distant markets, shipping trade goods to and from these markets, financing goods in transit, and collecting, converting, and remitting the payments arising from trade. Some of these costs depend on the nature of the banking and financial system; the previous chapter has shown how the growth of banking stimulated China's foreign and domestic trade by lowering the cost of financing interregional commodity exchange. Other costs depend on the nature of transport and communications systems.

China's premodern transport and communications facilities were slow. Large-scale trade flowed mainly on rivers, most running from west to east, and along the coast. Aside from coastal shipping and the Grand Canal, which provided an inland water route linking the Lower Yangtze area with Peking, north-south traffic was limited to light, valuable products that could bear the high cost of land transfer by means of carts, animals, or human carriers. Rapid transmission of information via government horse relays or private homing pigeons existed, but most information flows followed the same slow channels as commercial freight and passenger traffic: riverine or ocean-going sailing vessels (junks) and land traffic via cart, animal train, or human carrier.[1] Although these technologies supported a large volume of commercial traffic, high transport costs often prevented producers from entering lucrative markets, as when "extremely heavy expense for freight" prevented low-cost egg producers of northern Anhwei from supplying large quantities to exporters headquartered at Shanghai.[2] Under these conditions, new means of moving commodities and information held the promise of major reductions in exchange costs and hence large increases in the flow of internal trade.

The development of transport and communication can reduce exchange or transaction costs and stimulate both trade and economic growth. Comparative figures for the 1930s show that mecha-

1. Government couriers could travel 600 *li* or roughly 200 miles per day (Liang-jen Chang, "Post Office," *The Chinese Year Book, 1935–36* [Shanghai, 1935; reprint, Nendeln, 1968], 700). Evelyn S. Rawski reports the use of carrier pigeons; see *Education and Popular Literacy in Ch'ing China* (Ann Arbor, 1979), 11.
2. *China Industrial Handbooks: Kiangsu* (Shanghai, 1933), 567–68.

nized carriers often lowered freight rates in China, especially when they replaced unmechanized overland carriage (the figures represent freight cost per ton-kilometer):[3]

Railway	0.02 yuan
Steamship	0.02−0.24
Sailboat	0.02−0.13
Cart	0.05−0.17
Wheelbarrow	0.10−0.14
Pack animal	0.10−0.35
Human porter	0.20−0.35

Reduced transport costs expand marketing opportunities for all producers. A new railway, for example, might permit urban textile manufacturers to reach larger numbers of potential customers and suppliers without lowering selling prices or raising the unit cost of raw materials. If transport improvements raise the speed of traffic, additional savings become possible as the time elapsed, and hence the interest charges accumulated between the acquisition of materials and the receipt of sales revenues, shrinks. Scale economies offer another possible source of cost reduction. Rural households located along new or improved transport lines will benefit from similar changes. Liang illustrates the increase in farmgate crop prices that accompanied improved freight service in many localities.[4] Other studies show how transport development lowered the price of externally supplied goods and allowed more sellers to compete in local markets.[5] The result may be a simultaneous increase in the terms of trade (the unit price of goods sold divided by the

3. Ralph W. Huenemann, *The Dragon and the Iron Horse: The Economics of Railroads in China, 1876–1937* (Cambridge, 1984), 222–23 and Ernest P. Liang, *China: Railways and Agricultural Development, 1875–1935* (Chicago, 1982), 20.

4. Liang, *Railways*, chap. 5.

5. David D. Buck reports an immediate drop of 60 percent in coal prices along the railway linking Tsingtao and Tsinan (Shantung) following its completion in 1904 (*Urban Change in China: Politics and Development in Tsinan, Shantung, 1890–1949* [Madison, 1978], 45). S. A. M. Adshead shows how transport improvements permitted northern salt to "invade the markets of the Yangtze valley" as "a real competitor . . . against the traditional sources of supply" (*The Modernization of the Chinese Salt Administration, 1900–1920* [Cambridge, 1970], 50–51).

unit price of goods purchased) facing many participants in the market. Writing in the late 1920s, Ming-ju Cheng observed that:[6]

Good communications make possible the growth of a "money crop." . . . An excellent illustration of this is seen in the countryside to the north of Tientsin, which is a great fruit-growing area. Before the coming of the railway, one copper would buy ten large and juicy peaches, but they would rot before they could be conveyed as far as Tientsin. Now . . . the traveller must pay 10 coppers for a single peach. The whole countryside around Ch'angli has become covered with orchards and vineyards, which exist to satisfy the great demand for fruit in Tientsin and Peiping [Peking].

This was no isolated case: some contemporary observers expressed concern over the speed at which rising prices acted to suck foodstuffs out of rural producing areas.[7]

Improved access to distant markets benefits the sellers of labor as well as goods. According to Ming-ju Cheng:[8]

The construction of roads and railways will also improve the position of agricultural laborers by enabling them to seek employment in the towns when their services are not required on the farms. . . . During the winter season . . . about 2,500,000 country people migrate to the cities in search of employment, and the sum of their annual remittance home amounts to twenty million dollars.

The actual numbers of migrants and remittances were probably much larger: recorded annual two-way population movement into and out of Manchuria alone surpassed 1.5 million persons in the late 1920s.[9]

Not everyone, however, benefits immediately from improved transport and communication. Suppose a new rail line links a textile manufacturing center with a rural community that, because of

6. Ming-ju Cheng, *The Influence of Communications Internal and External upon the Economic Future of China* (London, 1930), 147.
7. Charles F. Hancock, "Introduction and Influence of Modern Machinery in China" (M.A. thesis, University of Texas, 1926), 92ff.
8. Cheng, *Influence of Communications*, 147–48, citing *Chinese Economic Journal* for an estimate of remittances.
9. Shu-hwai Wang, "The Effect of Railroad Transportation in China, 1912–1927," *Chung-yang yen-chiu-yuan chin tai shih yen chiu so chi k'an* 12 (1983):336 and Thomas R. Gottschang, "Migration from North China to Manchuria: An Economic History, 1891–1942" (Ph.D. diss., University of Michigan, 1982), 94–100.

poor transport facilities, has concentrated on subsistence farming even though its climate and soil are well suited to cotton culture. With the rail line in place, farmers will soon discover the profitability of growing cotton for the urban market. At the same time, however, local grain growers may suffer reduced incomes because of unexpected competition from outside. These farmers may recover and even surpass their former incomes by switching to cotton or other products in demand along the rail line, but rural specialists in grain milling, for example, may find the required adjustment more difficult, as will local craftsmen whose wares may suddenly face intensified competition from urban or even foreign manufactures that now arrive cheaply and quickly from distant places. Similar adjustments may occur in and around the cities. Suburban farmers who had grown cotton for the textile mills may find their products driven from the market by cheaper and more suitable supplies from the new cotton region. But the expansion of textile manufacture permitted by a wider market may enlarge the urban demand for vegetables and factory workers, thus creating new outlets for both the labor and the products of urban and suburban workers.

Transport improvements may therefore be expected to provide immediate increases in real income for many, but not all, of those affected. Some households or businesses will require painful adjustments in order to benefit from the new situation. Individuals or groups with special skills or investments appropriate to the old, but not to the new state of affairs may be unable to maintain their original income levels. This is not inconsistent with trade theory, which predicts only that, by encouraging increased specialization and division of labor along the lines of comparative cost advantage, the reduction of barriers to trade will benefit whole communities to such an extent that, under normal conditions, all participants *could* (but in reality need not) be made better off as a result of the change.

This analysis ignores the issue of risk. Accelerated information flows, which typically accompany the development of transport networks, reduce the risk of increased participation in trade. Specialization, which follows the expansion of transport links, increases risk. How does better communication reduce risk? A merchant contemplating a shipment of goods to a distant outlet must base his decision on the most recent market information. Once he decides to ship his goods, the financial implications may not be determined until the goods actually reach their destination and these consequences will remain unknown to the merchant until a message travels back to the point of origin. Thus the planning and execution of business decisions involving interregional trade requires a total of three one-way voyages, two for information and one for commodities. To take a concrete example, the travel time from Peking to Hankow was approximately fifty days in 1880.[10] Thus the financial ramifications of a decision to ship goods from Hankow to the capital might take up to five months to work themselves out. Hankow merchants might avoid the risks associated with such long delays by selling Peking-bound goods to long-distance traders at Hankow, but then the price received would reflect the risk of fluctuations in the prices of goods or exchange during the extended course of the transaction. Although individuals can avoid risks (at a price), the conduct of long-distance trade requires *someone* to absorb these risks, which impose costs entirely separate from more routine outlays on freight, insurance, storage, packing, taxes, and currency exchange associated with interregional commerce.

By the 1930s and 1940s, the growth of mechanized transport and communication had reduced trade risk by slashing the time required to move goods and messages between major commercial centers. Shipments from Hankow to Peking, for example, required two rather than fifty days following the completion of the Peking-Hankow railway in 1905. Steamships and railways reduced travel time between Chengtu and Peking from eighty days in the late Ch'ing to 10.3 days. The completion of the southern extension of the Peking-Hankow line lowered transit time between Canton and Peking from ninety days before 1900 to 3.3 days after 1936.[11] These changes affected even remote areas that lacked direct ties to railways and steamship lines. C. K. Yang found that the transit time between Peking and various points on China's outer perime-

10. J. B. R. Whitney, *China: Area, Administration, and Nation Building* (Chicago, 1970), 46.
11. Ibid.

ter declined by a minimum of 84 percent between the nineteenth century and the late 1940s.[12] With telegraph and telephone networks eliminating delays in transmitting important messages, a Hankow merchant could ascertain market conditions in Peking, pack and deliver his goods to market, and receive payment within a few days. Progress of this magnitude encouraged internal as well as international trade, especially in regions fortunate enough to have easy access to improved transport and communication networks.

The beneficial effects of improved transport and communication on trade, specialization, productivity, and incomes depend crucially on the reliability of the new modes of transferring goods and information. This is because specialization creates interdependence. Once the railway linked them to the textile mills of Tientsin and Shanghai, farmers in Hopei's Hsi-ho district increased their incomes by shifting from subsistence cropping to specialized cotton growing.[13] But with food supplies increasingly shipped in from external markets and financed by earnings from cotton sales, cotton growers in the Hsi-ho area might find themselves worse off than before if floods or warfare caused lengthy disruptions of railway service. Without reliable transport, the local price of cotton would plunge dramatically, leading to a steep decline in money incomes; food prices could also shoot up as a result of the specialization-induced reduction of local supplies and the absence of shipments from grain-growing areas linked to the railway. Unless the gains from specialization are very great, the introduction of unreliable transport improvements will encourage wary farmers to hedge their bets by growing a mixture of cash and subsistence crops. This is perhaps part of the reason why Barbara Sands finds that Shansi farmers "pursued conservative cropping strategies, devoting the bulk of their lands to foodgrains," even though an expansion of cotton cultivation might have "brought higher returns."[14]

12. Yang Ch'ing-k'un, "The Contraction of Space in Modern China," *Ling-nan hsüeh pao* 12, no. 1 (1949):155–56.
13. Yeh Ch'ien-chi, "Production, Transport, and Marketing for Hsi-ho Cotton," in *Chung-kuo ching chi yen chiu*, ed. Fang Hsien-t'ing (Changsha, 1938), 1:196.
14. Barbara N. Sands, "Agricultural Decisionmaking Under Uncertainty: The Case of the Shanxi Farmers, 1931–1936" (Tucson, 1987), 14.

Water Carriage

Water carriage represented the principal means of long-distance transport in imperial China. Even local traffic followed water routes whenever possible. In the words of Julean Arnold, "Every stream in China, no matter how shallow, carries craft engaged in some sort of cargo transportation."[15] This reflected the immense cost advantage of water over land carriage for all but the shortest journeys and the most precious cargoes. Steam and motor vessels enhanced this advantage by adding new types of services along the coast, on major rivers, and some smaller waterways. Motor vessels charged higher fees for passengers and freight than sailing craft, but offered superior speed, reliability, and safety from military or political interference. Although sailing craft and mechanized shippers often competed for the same cargoes, with new technology displacing the old along some routes, the traffic borne by mechanized ships represented a net gain to the economy because sailboat traffic, far from withering away, actually increased even around major ports served by the largest numbers of steam and motor vessels. As a result, the prewar history of water carriage is one of growth rather than displacement, with the use of inherited modes expanding along with the rise of new technology.

Mechanized Coastal and Inland Shipping

Steamships first appeared in Chinese waters in the 1850s and were quickly introduced on the Yangtze as well as along coastal routes. Chinese businessmen showed immediate interest in steamers: the first commercial steamer to navigate the Yangtze was partly owned by Chinese.[16] The commercial use of steam and motor vessels developed along the coast, on major rivers, and along their larger tributaries. The available data on the size of China's fleet of commercial motor vessels appear in Table 4.1, which shows steady

15. Julean Arnold, "How Low Silver Affects China's Trade," *China Weekly Review* 55, no. 1 (1930):16.
16. Thomas G. Rawski, "Chinese Dominance of Treaty Port Commerce and Its Implications, 1860–1875," *Explorations in Economic History* 7, no. 4 (1970):458.

Table 4.1
Motorized Ships and Shipping in China, 1882-1935
(tonnage data in thousands of tons)

Year	Motorized Vessels Number	Tonnage	Tonnage Cleared for Interport Trade
1872	...	...	3295
1882	30	...	6746
1885	27	25	6873
1890	101	30	9471
1895	145	33	10669
1900	517	18[a]	15003
1905	542	46	25813
1910	317[b]	101[b]	31845
1915	1559	193	33195
1920	2280	304	37871
1924	2734	446	47992
1930	2792	415	53213
1935	3895[c]	675[c]	52418

[a]Indicates data that appear to be unrealistically low.

[b]Yen Chung-p'ing also reports alternative figures of 885 vessels amounting to 89 thousand tons (cited Yen, Chung-kuo chin tai ching chi shih, 227).

[c]Excludes Manchuria.

Source: For numbers and tonnage of vessels, Yen, Chung-kuo chin tai ching chi shih, 227-229. For tonnage cleared, Liang-lin Hsiao, China's Foreign Trade Statistics, 1864-1949 (Cambridge, 1974), 250-51. Hsiao's figures for 1935, which exclude Manchuria, are increased by adding tonnage entered and cleared in Manchurian ports from or to Chinese ports as noted in Annual Returns of the Foreign Trade of Manchoukuo, 1936 (Dairen, 1937) 1:8-9. This modified total excludes interport ship movements within Manchuria. Note that the figures for number and tonnage of vessels are compiled from three different sources covering 1882-1905, 1910-24, and 1930-35.

growth between 1882 and 1924, stagnation during the period surrounding the Northern Expedition (1926–27) when military leaders forcibly commandeered many civilian vessels, and renewed growth during the 1930s. Although these data come from a variety of possibly incomplete sources and must therefore be treated with reserve, there does appear to be a trend toward smaller vessels: ships of less than 100 tons increased from 4 percent of the tonnage estimate in 1910 to 12 percent in 1924 and 14 percent in 1935 while the tonnage share occupied by the largest vessels of over 1,000 tons declined from 80 percent to 68 percent of the total between 1910 and 1935.[17] This appears to reflect the spread of motorized shipping services to a growing number of smaller ports: Kiangsu, Chekiang, Hupeh, Hunan, Szechwan, and Kiangsi were among the interior provinces where growing numbers of small motor vessels appeared during the 1930s.[18]

Another measure of the growth of steamship traffic comes from Maritime Customs data on tonnage entered and cleared for interport trade; data for benchmark years during 1872–1931 are compiled in Tables 4.1 and 4.2. Long-term trend lines calculated from annual figures of tonnage entered and cleared for interport trade produce the following rates of annual traffic growth:[19]

1872–1895	5.6 percent
1872–1911	5.8
1872–1921	5.2
1872–1931	4.8

17. Calculated from Yen Chung-p'ing, *Chung-kuo chin tai ching chi shih t'ung chi tzu liao hsüan chi* (Peking, 1955), 227–28.
18. Note the exclusion of Manchurian ports beginning in 1932. On the regional spread of steamship traffic, see Ting Jih-ch'u and Tu Hsün-ch'eng, "A Brief Account of Yü Hsia-ch'ing," *Li shih yen chiu* 3 (1981):162; *China Industrial Handbooks: Chekiang* (Shanghai, 1935), 857–900; Cheng, *Influence of Communications*, 29–30; and Stanley F. Wright, *Kiangsi Native Trade and Its Taxation* (Shanghai, 1920), 7, 106
19. Annual data are reported in Liang-lin Hsiao, *China's Foreign Trade Statistics, 1864–1949* (Cambridge, 1974), 250–51. The calculations terminate in 1931 to avoid bias resulting from the exclusion of Manchurian data beginning in 1932. The data may include small amounts of junk tonnage; they exclude steamer traffic between centers other than treaty ports. Rhoads Murphey's claim that the Maritime Customs data are "grossly misleading" because most of the reported increases in traffic and trade represent "a shift from traditional to steam carriage and from unrecorded to recorded" shipments (*The Outsiders: The Western Experience in India and China* [Ann Arbor, 1977], 197, 203) is overstated. The stability of Shanghai's share of overall foreign trade after 1885 (calculated from Hsiao, *Foreign Trade Statistics*, 22–24, 175–76) suggests that the growth rate of recorded trade is not seriously altered by the gradual increase in the number of reporting stations. Although the recorded growth of steamship traffic was perhaps inflated by the gradual addition of new Maritime

These results indicate stable expansion at an annual rate slightly above 5.5 percent between 1872 and 1911; for these years, there is little variance from the trend line of steady growth. After 1911, growth is slower than before, with a considerable increase in variability. Even so, stability remained high. In the sixty years between 1872 and 1931, recorded traffic declined only eighteen times; eight of the annual declines are less than 5 percent, and only one—the 1926–27 disruption caused by the Northern Expedition—exceeds 10 percent of the previous year's traffic.

Steam and motor vessels moved considerable quantities of passengers and freight. During the postwar recovery years of 1949–52, motor vessels amounting to perhaps 200,000 deadweight tons hauled an annual maximum of 14 million tons of goods for a total of 10.6 billion ton-kilometers.[20] Prewar steam tonnage reached a peak of roughly three times the early post-1949 figure (Table 4.1). Since the level of commercial activity during 1949–52 may not have regained the prewar peak, it is possible that freight volume per ton of capacity was similar in 1930 or 1935 to 1949 or 1952, in which case motor vessels may have carried 35–40 million annual tons of freight for a total haulage of 25–30 billion ton-kilometers in China proper (excluding Manchuria) during the 1930s. The plausible assumption that cargo turnover expanded in rough proportion to the shipping clearance patterns reported in the right-hand column of Table 4.1 implies that the largest advances in motorized domestic water traffic occurred between 1895 and 1910, when clearances perhaps tripled from ten to thirty million tons, and between the end of World War I and the late 1920s, when a similar increase

---

Customs stations, another bias arising from the spread of motor vessels to ports outside the customs network is also present, and acts in the opposite direction. The issue of trade diversion from traditional to mechanized carriage is discussed below.

20. Nai-ruenn Chen, *Chinese Economic Statistics: A Handbook for Mainland China* (Chicago, 1967), 373, gives the volume and turnover of freight. Yuan-li Wu, *The Spatial Economy of Communist China* (New York, 1967), 112, reports 200,000 gross tons of shipping available at the end of 1949. *Chung-kuo ching chi nien chien, 1981* (Peking, 1981), 4–111 gives the "early post-liberation" stock as 34,000 tons of coastal and less than 200,000 tons of Yangtze shipping. Ch'iu Ch'i-hua, *Wo kuo fa chan yün shu ho yu tien ti ti i ko wu nien chi hua* (Peking, 1956), 6–8, gives larger tonnage figures but lower data for freight haulage than the other sources.

Table 4.2
Volume and Value of Foreign and Domestic Trade Via Maritime Customs,
Selected Years, 1891-1931

Year	Foreign Trade			Domestic Interport Trade		
	Tonnage[a]	Value Data[b]		Tonnage	Value Data[b]	
		Import	Export		Inbound	Outbound
1891	3.4	136	103	10.5	210	186
1901	6.5	277	178	17.7	367	509
1911	13.1	482	388	29.8	512	492
1921	15.9	933	628	41.4	861	867
1931	25.6	1448	924	54.4	1272	1258

Note: These data are restricted to shipments controlled by the
Maritime Customs; with minor exceptions, they include only motorized
shipping passing through the centers designated as "treaty ports," a
category that encompassed all major ocean and river ports. The
series stops in 1931 to avoid complications arising from the loss of
Manchuria and abolition of the tael.

[a]Tonnage figures indicate thousands of tons of shipping entered
and cleared through Maritime Customs in foreign and domestic
interport trade.

[b]Value data are in millions of Hai-kuan taels (a Hai-kuan tael is
a silver-based accounting unit equivalent to 1.55 Chinese silver
dollars or yuan).

Source: Hsiao, Foreign Trade Statistics, 202-3, 208-9, 216-17,
222-23, 236-37, 250-51.

raised the annual total of domestic clearances to more than 50 million tons. As will be seen below, this growing traffic represented a net increase in commercial activity rather than a substitution of steam for sailboat carriage.

Available shipping statistics suggest that much of the freight carried on motor vessels consisted of goods involved in international trade. This can be seen from Table 4.2, which presents data on the tonnage and also the value of freight cleared through the Maritime Customs in foreign and interport trade. The tonnage figures are consistently higher for domestic than they are for international movements. However, the domestic figures contain an element of double counting: a vessel calling at several ports on a journey along the Yangtze, for example, may be entered and cleared more than once. Thus the value figures, which appear free of this bias, give a more accurate picture of the relative size of foreign and domestic trade supervised by the Maritime Customs (which did not compile statistics on the junk trade or land traffic).

Following the late nineteenth-century period in which the value of steamship freight is considerably larger for domestic than it is for international traffic, the twentieth-century figures for the two categories fall very close together. This suggests that domestic steamship freight consisted largely of goods imported from or bound for international destinations. The correspondence is by no means exact. Considerable quantities of internationally traded commodities were assembled and distributed by rail in North China, by junk in Central and South China, and by rail, junk, and horse-drawn cart in Manchuria. Many trade goods, however, were shipped by motor vessels, especially in the Yangtze area, an area which accounted for half of China's international commerce.[21] Even without a detailed breakdown, it is evident that the share of internationally traded goods in the cargoes hauled by domestic motor vessels was large. In 1931, for example, assuming that half of all foreign trade goods were collected and distributed by rail, junk, or cart produces a 47 percent share of foreign trade goods in the value of interport steamship cargoes. The proportion of domestic steamship cargoes linked to foreign trade may have been larger or smaller than this figure, but it was clearly very substantial.

Agricultural products and manufactured goods were the largest categories of water-borne freight in the modern sector. Goods destined for export came mainly from agriculture: t'ung oil from Szechwan, tea from Fukien, soybeans from Manchuria, and silk from the Lower Yangtze area. Domestic shipments also included large quantities of farm products: cotton from North and Central China, grain from the surplus provinces in the Yangtze basin, beans and bean products from the northeast. Foreign and domestic manufactures figured prominently in steamship cargoes: textiles, matches, flour, and cigarettes were among the industrial goods that flowed in steadily rising volumes from the coastal cities to the in-

21. The share of Shanghai and the Yangtze ports in the national total of exports plus net imports (i.e., total imports less re-exports) was 50.1 percent in 1911, 47.7 percent in 1921, and 51.3 percent in 1931; calculated from Hsiao, *Foreign Trade Statistics*, 23–24, 176–78.

terior, often by means of mechanized vessels. There was also some traffic in minerals and mineral products: coal, iron ore, cement, kerosene, and antimony, among others, but minerals did not play as large a role in shipping as in railroad traffic.

Passenger carriage, although not easily quantified, was also significant. Ships plying coastal and river routes carried large numbers of passengers; poor and thrifty travelers were packed onto or between decks. Motor vessels carried a large two-way flow of long-term and seasonal migrants between North China and Manchuria: in the peak years of 1927 and 1928, the Maritime Customs recorded nearly one million annual trips by passengers traveling on ships between ports in Manchuria and North China.[22]

Despite this considerable scale of operations, motor vessels traversed only a fraction of China's inland waterways. A Japanese survey published in 1936 reported 3,219 kilometers of waterways open to traffic by large motor vessels, including 1,848 kilometers on the Yangtze (between Shanghai and Hankow) and 1,014 on the Amur in the northeast. Shallow draft vessels and smaller motor ships could reach an additional 12,217 kilometers, leaving 22,512 kilometers or nearly 60 percent of all water routes accessible only to sailing vessels.[23]

Much of the maritime and riverine traffic involving steam or motor vessels was controlled by foreigners. Meaningful estimates of foreign ownership are difficult to obtain because many Chinese vessels operated under foreign flags to evade internal taxes; Chinese also held shares in foreign shipping ventures.[24] Remer, writing in the 1930s, stated that "over half the steam shipping in Chinese waters is owned by foreigners and under foreign flags."[25] Data for 1935 show that sixteen Japanese and British firms operated

22. See the data for two-way traffic tabulated in Gottschang, "Migration from North China," 91–92.
23. Baba Kuwatarō, *Shina suiun ron* (Shanghai, 1936), 12 (including Manchuria). Figures for 1949 give larger totals for navigable waterways and sections passable to motor vessels, with the latter amounting to only one-third of the total; see Chen, *Chinese Economic Statistics*, 372.
24. Ting and Tu, "Yü Hsia-ch'ing," 162; Paul King, *In the Chinese Customs Service: A Personal Record of Forty-seven Years* (London, 1924), 194–97; Rawski, "Treaty Port Commerce," 458–59; and Angus McDonald, Jr., *The Urban Origins of Rural Revolution: Elites and the Masses in Hunan Province, China, 1911–1927* (Berkeley, 1978), 65.
25. C. F. Remer, *Foreign Investments in China* (New York, 1968), 87.

446,000 tons of shipping, or two-thirds of the estimated stock of motor vessels.[26] The large share of foreign-flag vessels offended Chinese patriots, but reduced the disruptive impact of military and political conflict on internal trade flows, a topic to be discussed below.

Unmechanized Water Carriage

Despite the rapid development of mechanized land and water transport, inherited technologies continued to play an important role in the movement of commodities and passengers throughout the prewar decades and well into the postwar era. Whole provinces, including some of China's largest, remained untouched by railways until the 1950s and many waterways were too small or shallow to accommodate motorized shipping. As a result, vehicles powered by wind, animals, and humans continued to occupy a large share of transport activity in prewar China. Liu and Yeh estimate that traditional modes accounted for 73.6 percent of overall value added in transport and communications in 1933 and 49.0 percent of the comparable total for 1953.[27] Any assessment of the impact of technological change on prewar transportation must therefore encompass inherited forms of unmechanized carriage, of which sailing craft, or junks, were by far the most important component.

The growth of steamship and rail traffic can be measured with reasonable accuracy. Rail freight volume grew from 1.9 to 12.8 billion ton-kilometers between 1907 and 1933, indicating average growth of 7.7 percent per year.[28] The value of interport water trade compiled by China's Maritime Customs inspectorate, which supervised traffic by steam- and motor-powered vessels, grew at annual rates of 8.65 percent during 1913–30 and 7.6 percent during 1913–36.[29] With domestic prices increasing at somewhat more

26. Yen, *Chung-kuo chin tai ching chi shih*, 234.
27. Ta-chung Liu and Kung-chia Yeh, *The Economy of the Chinese Mainland: National Income and Economic Development, 1933–1959* (Princeton, 1965), 66.
28. Huenemann, *The Dragon and the Iron Horse*, 222. These data include Manchuria.
29. Growth rate for 1913–30 is from Ramon H. Myers, "The World Depression and the Chinese Economy" (Stanford, 1986), 19. I have recalculated Myers's figures for 1936 by adding trade between China and Manchoukuo to his 1936 total, which appears to come directly from the Maritime Customs figures, and therefore excludes the northeast beginning in 1932.

than 2 percent per year during 1913–36, the volume of water-borne trade carried by steam and motor vessels grew at an annual rate of perhaps 6 percent.[30] But do these figures indicate *trade creation*, reflecting the considerable expansion of China's domestic economy, or *trade diversion*, with mechanized land and water carriage representing a mere transfer of activity from unmechanized carriers with little or no change in overall traffic volume? Available data show that junk traffic increased substantially at the very time that rail and steamship traffic were growing at rapid rates.

The continuing importance of sailboat traffic in the overall transport picture is beyond doubt. Japanese observers at Hankow reported between fourteen and fifteen thousand junks at anchor at any given time around 1920 in the Han River alone, half again as many as are mentioned in nineteenth-century accounts.[31] Another Japanese source comments that "after the port was opened [to foreigners] and steamship traffic began, the use of junks did not decline; now, a yearly total of 24 or 25 to 30,000 junks is said to enter the port."[32] Japanese studies of the Yangtze delta, an area well served by railways and motor vessels, estimated that 45 percent of annual prewar freight shipments of nine million tons traveled on sailing craft as opposed to 32 percent by motor vessel and 23 percent by rail. Even in the delta, with its highly developed steamship traffic, routing charts show that junks continued to haul many important products to and from Shanghai and its rapidly modernizing hinterland.[33] As late as 1959, a survey of Kiangsu province noted that "the largest share of transport volume in this province is occupied by wooden sailing vessels"; junks reportedly carried 79 percent of all freight transported along China's inland waterways in 1949 and 84 percent in 1956.[34]

Junk traffic was not only large, but also stable or rising. There

30. Inflation information is based on the Tientsin wholesale price index shown in *Nan-k'ai chih shu tzu liao hui pien, 1913–1952* (Peking, 1958), 11.
31. *Shina shōbetsu zenshi* (Tokyo, 1918), 9:48; and William T. Rowe, *Hankow: Commerce and Society in a Chinese City, 1796–1889* (Stanford, 1984), 26.
32. *Shina kaikōjōshi* (Tokyo, 1922–24), 2:525.
33. "Survey Report on Routes and Quantities of Raw Material Shipments in Central China," *Chōsa geppō* 2, no. 6 (1941):133–61 (routing charts) and 244–45 (freight volume).
34. *Chiang-su shih nien, 1949–1959* (Nanking, 1959), 191; *Chung-kuo ching-chi nien-chien, 1981*, 4–111; and Willy Kraus, *Economic Development and Social Change in the People's Republic of China* (New York, 1979), 79.

are few reports of riots directed at the modern shipping sector even though Chinese boatmen held a well deserved reputation for violence. In the 1880s, officials opposed to railway construction found ready allies in "the junk people, who were glad enough to seize the chance of a dispute" by claiming that railway bridges would obstruct sailboat traffic.[35] In 1900, railway vandals reportedly included "people who used to make a living at Tungchow [Hopei] by boat and are starving because of the railway."[36] "Violence" and "intimidation" were standard practice for Kiangsi watermen, who avoided taxes "by open display of force."[37] In 1926, junkmen rioted to protest against steamship competition.[38] But such incidents were quite exceptional: one writer comments that: "The record shows . . . that, as in the case of the competition between the railway and the cart, the new machine has not . . . by any means crowded the old handicraft device out altogether. The only place where there has been friction as a result of junk versus steamer competition is in the Yangtze Gorges."[39] Despite occasional reference to unemployment among boatmen, studies of collective violence by C. K. Yang and David Faure reveal no evidence of the large-scale disorders that might be expected if large numbers of watermen had been displaced by new modes of transportation.[40]

A variety of data confirm the impression that sailboat traffic in-

35. Ellsworth C. Carlson, *The Kaiping Mines, 1877–1912* (Cambridge, 1971), 25.
36. Ralph W. Huenemann, "The Dragon and the Iron Horse: The Economics of Railroads in China, 1876–1937" (Ph.D. diss., Harvard University, 1981), 86.
37. Wright, *Kiangsi Native Trade*, 133.
38. Cheng, *Influence of Communications*, 29–30
39. Grover Clark, *Economic Rivalries in China* (New Haven, 1932), 38.
40. For mention of unemployment among boatmen, see Huenemann, *The Dragon and the Iron Horse*, 55–56, 86; Arthur Rosenbaum, "Railway Enterprise and Economic Development: The Case of the Imperial Railways of North China, 1900–1911," *Modern China* 2, no. 2 (1976):249; and *Finance and Commerce*, September 5, 1934, 259. C. K. Yang, "Some Preliminary Statistical Patterns of Mass Actions in Nineteenth-Century China," in *Conflict and Control in Late Imperial China*, ed. Frederic Wakeman and Carolyn Grant (Berkeley, 1975), 199, attributes only 5 (or 1.5 percent) of 327 incidents to craftsmen, miners, and sailors during 1896–1911; for 1796–1895, the comparable figure is 41 (or 1.4 percent) of 3,182 incidents. David W. Faure's compilation of violent incidents during 1870–1911 includes only occasional reference to incidents involving "boatmen" (p. 480) or "former transport workers" (p. 492); an attack on steam vessels (p. 486) followed damage to dykes ("Local Political Disturbances in Kiangsu Province, China, 1870–1911" [Ph.D. diss., Princeton University, 1976]).

creased along with the rise of mechanized water transport. The continued prosperity of the boat-building industry demonstrates that junk traffic did not decline. Quantitative reports show significant increases in the volume of junk traffic during the 1920s and 1930s at Hankow, Tsingtao, Dairen, and Ying-k'ou, all of which were major ports served by steam and rail carriers, as well as growing junk-borne shipments of wheat to Shanghai and cotton to Tientsin. Since wheat and cotton could reach Shanghai and Tientsin by rail from North China or Manchuria and by steamship from Dairen, Lien-yün-kang, Vancouver, Sydney, Seattle, or Bombay, the success of junk operators in capturing a growing volume of Shanghai's wheat traffic and Tientsin's cotton trade and in maintaining or increasing the volume of traffic at major port cities despite intense and unrestricted competition from all forms of mechanized transportation indicates a general pattern of growth in the junk sector.

Boat Building.   Wooden sailing vessels have long service lives. A 1941 survey of forty Soochow-based junks noted that older vessels remained in use even though their cargo capacity declined; the survey vessels included four craft over forty-five years old.[41] Under these circumstances, a decline in the volume of junk traffic creates a surplus of equipment. Since idle junks can easily be kept in readiness in or alongside local waterways, a backlog of idle vessels should quickly erode the demand for new ships. This is exactly what occurred along the Liao River, where the diversion of water-borne traffic to the railways caused observers to note that "there are no new ships built for the river and [the] majority of the ships now being used are those constructed more than ten years ago."[42] One might expect these tendencies to be especially pronounced in areas like the Yangtze delta where the competition from new transport modes was most intense.

   The information about boat building in the Yangtze delta, however, shows that the industry continued to thrive throughout the prewar period. The 1941 survey data for Soochow reveal an average age of nineteen and a median of sixteen years for the ships studied; fourteen of thirty-six ships were less than ten years old.[43]

41. *Chūshi no minsengyō* (Tokyo, 1943), 25–27.
42. *The Manchuria Year Book, 1932–33* (Tokyo, 1932), 284.
43. *Chūshi no minsengyō*, 26–27. No age is given for four of the craft surveyed.

Junks enumerated in this survey were built at shipyards throughout the delta area, including Shanghai, Wusih, Hangchow, Shao-
hsing, Soochow, Chia-ting, Ch'ung-ming Island, and Ch'ang-chou,
all centers of motorized water traffic.[44] A 1934 survey found that
two-thirds of forty junk-producing shipyards in the Shanghai area
had been established since 1920.[45] Another study listed over
twenty places near Shanghai and along both banks of the Yangtze
in the delta region where junkyards continued to operate after
1940 despite a precipitous decline in junk traffic following Japan's
occupation of the Lower Yangtze region.[46] In addition to small
firms run by single shipwrights with a few helpers, there were
larger shipyards employing over one hundred workers, one of
which turned out 120 new vessels and overhauled 320 older craft
each year.[47] Other reports from the 1930s and early 1940s refer to
the continued operation of native shipyards in many locations outside the Yangtze delta, including Tientsin, Hupeh, Wan-hsien
(Szechwan), Wu-chou (Kwangsi), Ho-k'ou (Yunnan), and Swatow
(Kwangtung).[48] The continued vigor of the junk construction industry, which prompted Stanley Wright to comment on the "never-
ceasing demand of the native shipwrights" for the produce of
Kiangsi's timber districts, confirms the view that transport activity
by sailing craft did not decline prior to the Pacific War.[49]

Cotton Shipments into Tientsin, 1921–30.   Tientsin's cotton textile industry was second only to Shanghai's. Some 85 to 90 percent
of Tientsin's cotton supplies arrived from Hopei province, with
Shansi and Shensi providing the remainder.[50] Within Hopei, the
bulk of Tientsin's cotton originated in the Hsi-ho (West River) district, which is roughly bisected from north to south by the Peking-
Hankow railway. As a major seaport, Tientsin could easily obtain

44. Ibid., 4.
45. *Chiao t'ung nien chien, 1935* (Shanghai, 1935), 181–83.
46. *Shina no kōun* (Tokyo, 1944), 83–84. Japanese observers reported that junk
    carriage of freight in the delta region dropped from 4.1 to 0.5 million annual
    tons after the occupation ("Survey Report on Material Shipments," 245).
47. *Shina no kōun*, 84–86.
48. *Shina no kōun*, 83; *Chiao t'ung tsa chih* 3, no. 3–4 (1935):101; and *China
    Proper* (Cambridge, 1945), 3:246, 248, 372.
49. Wright, *Kiangsi Native Trade*, 32.
50. T. S. Chu and T. Chin, *Marketing of Cotton in Hopei Province* (Peiping,
    1929), 16–17.

domestic or foreign cotton by coastal or ocean freighters arriving from Chinese or overseas ports. How did sailing craft fare in the competition to supply cotton to Tientsin's mills?

Data presented in Table 4.3 show that the junk carriage of cotton into Tientsin expanded rapidly at the expense of rail traffic, which was hampered by frequent military disruptions. These figures illustrate the flexibility of unmechanized carriers, including carts as well as sailing craft, which more than tripled their cotton deliveries to Tientsin between 1922 and 1928, increasing their combined annual shipments by over forty thousand tons.

Wheat Shipments into Shanghai, 1914–34.   The volume of wheat shipped into Shanghai by sailing craft can be estimated as follows:

Wheat arriving by junk =   [1] wheat required by Shanghai flour mills
                              − [2] import of wheat from abroad
                              − [3] Maritime Customs inflow of domestic wheat carried by steamships
                              + [4] Maritime Customs exports of wheat (to foreign or Chinese ports)
                              − [5] inflow of domestic wheat by rail

This approach may understate the volume of wheat carried by junk (but not necessarily its rate of growth) through the omission of junk-borne shipments out of Shanghai and the neglect of the wheat requirements of users other than mechanized flour mills. Arrivals by cart or pack animal are ignored. The results, presented in Table 4.4, show that the estimated arrival of wheat by junk increased from a maximum (assuming no rail shipment of wheat into Shanghai) of 139,000 tons in 1914 to 227,000 tons in 1932, 163,000 tons in 1933, and 337,000 tons in 1934. These figures understate the growth of junk shipments because there is no figure for railway shipments of wheat in 1914.

Sailing craft delivered much larger quantities of wheat to Shanghai in the 1930s than they had two decades earlier. The average of 242,000 tons for 1932–34, derived from Table 4.4, is 74 percent above the (excessive) figure of 139,000 tons obtained for 1914. Any rail shipments of wheat to Shanghai in 1914 would increase this difference. Chinese Native Customs figures show junk-borne wheat imports into Shanghai of only 24,000 tons in 1914, suggest-

Table 4.3
Cotton Shipments to Tientsin by Various Carriers, 1920-31
(thousand tan)

Year	Quantity Arriving by Means of					Percentage Arriving Via			
	Rail	Junk	Steamer	Cart	Total	Rail	Junk	Steam	Cart
1920	496	126	18	13	653	76	19	3	2
1921	724	215	145	4	1088	66	20	13	--
1922	716	230	179	14	1139	63	20	16	1
1923	382	159	50	14	605	63	26	8	2
1924	464	575	4	18	1061	44	54	--	2
1925	73	842	36	30	981	7	86	4	3
1926	227	957	170	49	1403	16	68	12	4
1927	304	846	94	62	1306	23	65	7	5
1928	65	422	40	30	557	12	76	7	5
1929	167	683	266	38	1154	14	59	23	3

Note: -- indicates less than 0.5 percent.

Source: The data for rail, junk, and cart during 1920-29 are
from T'ien-chin mien hua yün hsiao kai k'uang (Peking, 1934), 10.
The data for steamship arrivals are from the Maritime Customs
records of cotton arrivals from foreign and Chinese ports: for 1920-
22, The Foreign Trade of China 1922 (Shanghai, 1923), part 2, 1:277
and 2:665; for 1923, The Foreign Trade of China, 1923 (Shanghai,
1924), part 2, 1:279 and 2:681; for 1924-26, The Foreign Trade of
China 1926 (Shanghai, 1927), part 2, 1: 105 and 2: 171; for 1927-29,
The Foreign Trade of China, 1929 (Shanghai, 1930), part 2, 1:104 and
2:161.

ing that average junk-borne wheat imports into Shanghai during
1932–34 were ten times the amount observed in 1914.[51]
    Whether the volume of wheat shipped by junk into Shanghai
increased by 74 percent or by 900 percent between 1914 and 1932/
34 is not clear. What is clear is that even with assumptions that
produce high figures for junk carriage in 1914 and low figures for
later years, the results show an increasing volume of junk traffic
into the port of Shanghai during the prewar decades.

Junk Traffic at Coastal Ports.   Contemporary accounts, including the normally well-informed reports included in the annual and
decennial Maritime Customs reports, often remarked on the decline of junk traffic, as when the author of the Tientsin report for
1914 observed the following:[52]

51. *Returns of Trade and Trade Reports, 1914* (Shanghai, 1915), part 1, 3:768.
52. *Returns of Trade and Trade Reports, 1914*, part 2, 1:274, with emphasis
added.

the junk trade seems doomed to dwindle to insignificance, owing to the gradual preponderance of steam. 480 northern junks entered during the year, against 1,137 in 1908, when the junk trade may be said to have reached its zenith. . . . The decadence is also shown in the gradually diminishing number of southern junks *coming under our cognizance*, only

Table 4.4
Sources of Wheat Supply for Shanghai Flour Mills, 1914-34

	1914	1932	1933	1934
Shanghai flour output (10,000 bags)	496	2896	3368	3067
[1] Wheat required by mills (1000 metric tons)	161	938	1091	994
[2] Net import from abroad (1000 metric tons)	0	666	858	465
[3] Customs inflow from Chinese ports (1000 metric tons)	23	3	19	59
[4] Maritime Customs exports to all ports (1000 metric tons)	1	16	25	0
[5] Wheat arrival by railway (1000 metric tons)	?	58	76	133
Residual: junk shipments (1000 metric tons) [1]-[2]-[3]+[4]-[5]	≤139	227	163	337

Sources: Line 1: Wheat requirements are based on reported flour sales (assumed identical with flour production) by Shanghai mills. Annual data for 1914-36 appear in Chiu Chung-kuo chi chih mien fen kung yeh t'ung chi tzu liao (Peking, 1966), 52. The missing figure for 1934 is filled in by linear interpolation. These data are in bags of 49-50 pounds (ibid.). Each bag of flour required 53.57 catties of wheat (ibid., 137). This information is used to convert flour sales (assumed to equal output) into the wheat requirements shown in Line 1 (neglecting differences in the conversion rate of Chinese and foreign wheat). I ignore possible differences between wheat requirements and wheat arrivals caused by changes in Shanghai wheat inventories.

Line 2: Shanghai imports of wheat from abroad are reported in Chiu Chung-kuo chi chih mien fen kung yeh, 116-17, but with major unexplained differences from the Maritime Customs figures from 1933 on. There are no imports in 1914. For 1932-34 I use the largest available import figures (producing smaller residual estimates of junk traffic); for 1932 and 1933, The Trade of China, 1933 (Shanghai, 1934) 3:229; for 1934, Ch'en Po-chuang, Hsiao mai chi mien fen (Shanghai, 1936),30 (note that Ch'en gives a smaller import total of 408 thousand tons in his table 8).

continued...

Table 4.4, continued

Line 3: Wheat inflow by steam or motor vessel: Maritime Customs
imports from domestic ports reported by the Customs: for 1914, see
Returns of Trade and Trade Reports, 1914 (Shanghai, 1915), 3:752;
for 1932-34, see Shang-hai mai fen shih ch'ang tiao ch'a (Shanghai,
1935), 14.

Line 4: Original exports to Chinese or foreign ports as reported
by the Maritime Customs: for 1914, Returns of Trade and Trade
Reports, 1914, 3:772; for 1932-34, Shang-hai mai fen shih ch'ang
tiao ch'a, 14.

Line 5: Wheat arriving by rail: for 1932-34, based on Shang-hai
mai fen shih ch'ang tiao ch'a, 19. The figure for 1932 excludes the
four months of February through May; I therefore multiply the amount
given in the source by 1.5; the figure for 1934 is double the amount
shown in the source, which covers only the first six months of the
year.

six having entered and seven cleared, as against 22 and 17 respectively in
1908. The volume of trade shows even more strikingly the fate of sailing
craft.

The difficulty here arises from the phrase "coming under our cognizance," which raises the possibility that such accounts were
based on trends in the small fraction of sail-borne trade that was
enumerated and taxed through Maritime Customs offices. Since
Ying-k'ou reported an annual average of 1,484 junks arriving from
or departing for Tientsin during 1920–25, while Dairen reported a
comparable average of 215 junks for 1916–25, it is impossible to
believe that only 480 "northern junks" arrived at Tientsin in 1914.
Indeed, it appears that this and many other reports massively
understate the importance of junk traffic.[53]

Many authors explicitly recognize that responsibility for the
junk trade rested primarily in the hands of the so-called Native
Customs (*Ch'ang-kuan*) rather than the Maritime Customs (*Hai-
kuan*). A 1933 report concerning Nanking, for example, noted that
"since Customs statistics cover shipments by steamer only, they
are of little value for gauging year-to-year variations in the local
trade of Nanking [where] . . . the Tientsin-Pukow Railway brings
down a wide variety of cargo for shipment by steamer, while . . .
much of the local produce goes out of the port by rail, road, or
junk."[54] Maritime Customs shipping statistics routinely excluded

53. For Ying-k'ou, see *Namboku Manshū no shuyō kaikō kakō* (Dairen, 1927),
    210; for Dairen, see *Shina no janku to Nanman no sankō* (Dairen, 1927), 20.
54. *The Trade of China, 1933* (Shanghai, 1934), 1:16.

large numbers of sailing craft and, it would appear, small motor vessels as well. In 1933, when shipping tables showed 18,115 vessels entered and cleared in foreign and domestic trade through the Maritime Customs office at Shanghai, "The number of vessels entering and clearing under General Regulations at the port of Shanghai was 18,115, aggregating to 35.2 million tons; and the number entering and clearing under Inland Waters Steam Navigation Regulations was 28,270, aggregating 4.1 million tons. . . . These statistics are *exclusive of the 61,401 junks entered and cleared.*"[55]

The problem here is to avoid misleading observations based on the Maritime Customs figures alone. Tables 4.5 and 4.6 present information from the Native Customs records showing time trends in the volume of junk shipping and the value of junk-borne trade in several coastal ports. These figures reveal no sign of a general decline in junk traffic in ports served by steamships and, in most cases, by rail as well. On the contrary, average annual growth rates, calculated from Tables 4.5 and 4.6, indicate increases in both the volume and the value of junk traffic:

	Tonnage	Value	Period Covered
Dairen	6.9%	9.8%	1911–26; 1912–26
Ying-k'ou	2.5	1.5	1920–25; 1912–26
Tientsin	. . .	9.6	1912–25
Tsingtao	4.9	5.4	1903–16; 1912–26
Chefoo (Yen-t'ai)	. . .	3.4	1912–25
Above 5 ports	. . .	4.5	1912–25
Wenchow	2.4	. . .	1911–31

With the exception of the Wenchow data for 1924–31, which yield negative growth because of the sharp drop in 1930–31, the trend of available tonnage figures is uniformly upward. The value of junk-borne trade at five North China ports grew at 4.5 percent annually in nominal terms or, using the Tientsin index of wholesale prices as a deflator, by roughly 1.4 percent per year after allowing for inflation.[56] With shipping tonnage rising at annual rates of 2.4–6.9 percent in several major ports, I adopt 2 percent as a rough esti-

55. For shipping reports, see ibid., 1:80–81; quotation from 1:19, with emphasis added.
56. The exponential growth rate of Tientsin wholesale prices was 3.1 percent during 1913–25. See *Nan-k'ai chih shu tzu liao hui pien, 1913–1952,* 13.

Transport and Communication

Table 4.5
Growth of Junk Traffic at Several Ports, 1903-31
(Vessels entered or cleared; thousands of tons)

Year	Dairen		Tsingtao		Ying-k'ou		Wenchow	
	No.	Tons	No.	Tons	No.	Tons	No.	Tons
1903	...	...	6333	...	...	...	...	...
1904	...	...	8507	...	...	...	...	...
1905	...	...	8925	...	...	...	...	...
1906	...	...	8663	181	...	...	...	...
1907	...	...	7654	175	...	...	...	...
1908	8318	...	11564	200	...	...	...	...
1909	9812	...	12083	212	...	...	...	...
1910	7152	...	11300	212	...	...	...	...
1911	8721	80	8876	236	...	...	6006	77
1912	7700	76	10490	206	...	...	4472	58
1913	11782	83	10030	200	...	...	12485	117
1914	12763	120	...	...	...	...	14680	140
1915	14653	127	...	...	...	...	13502	198
1916	18459	162	36051	333	...	...	14724	162
1917	22984	216	...	...	...	...	7950	142
1918	24720	301	...	...	...	...	8419	186
1919	17578	178	...	...	...	...	8507	218
1920	19138	194	...	...	6480	390	7827	178
1921	17935	219	...	...	8525	480	...	...
1922	19552	248	...	...	8594	530	...	...
1923	17884	198	...	...	8541	510	...	...
1924	15375	154	...	...	6990	380	6162	181
1925	19580	221	...	...	9612	540	6962	206
1926	...	240	...	...	...	...	5845	194
1927	...	...	...	...	...	...	5608	181
1928	...	...	...	...	...	...	5645	169
1929	...	...	...	...	...	...	7343	169
1930	...	...	...	...	...	...	7044	175
1931	...	...	...	...	...	...	4153	127

Note: The figures include the number and tonnage of vessels entered and cleared. Original data converted to tons at the rate of 10 shih or 16.54 tan (piculs) per ton. Tsingtao figures for 1916 may not be comparable with earlier data; Tsingtao data shown for 1916 include shipping both inside and outside the port; the figures for the former category alone include 26,752 vessels entered/cleared with capacity 169,000 tons. For Ying-k'ou, smaller totals appear on p. 105 of the indicated source.

Sources: For Dairen, Shina no janku, 18 (numbers and 1914 tonnage), and 31. For Tsingtao, Santô kenkyû shiryô (Tsingtao, 1920) 2:83-84, 90-91; for Ying-k'ou, Namboku Manshû, 210. For Wenchow, Shina kaikôjôshi (Tokyo, 1922-24) 1:1108-9 (for 1911-20) and Liu Yen-nung, "Shipping Conditions in the Port of Wenchow," Chiao t'ung tsa chih 3, no. 3 (1935):59-60.

Table 4.6
Annual Value of Junk-Borne Trade by Port
(Million Hai-kuan taels)

Year	Dairen	Ying-k'ou	Tientsin	Chih-fu[a]	Tsingtao	Total of 5 Ports
1912	2.6	11.3	0.6	5.3	6.3	26.1
1913	2.8	9.6	0.6	5.6	5.7	24.3
1914	2.2	9.8	0.8	5.4	3.1	21.3
1915	4.2	10.9	0.7	5.8	1.1	22.7
1916	4.2	8.9	0.5	5.0	4.3	22.9
1917	5.7	11.3	1.0	4.9	4.7	27.6
1918	8.2	14.6	1.3	5.2	5.9	35.2
1919	5.2	12.3	1.1	6.9	7.3	32.8
1920	7.1	13.5	1.0	6.2	8.2	36.0
1921	8.3	12.1	1.7	6.7	8.9	37.7
1922	9.2	13.0	2.0	7.8	5.3	37.3
1923	7.7	14.7	1.9	9.6	7.8	41.7
1924	6.2	8.6	1.5	6.9	8.6	30.8
1925	9.8	13.4	1.6	7.0	7.3	39.1
1926	9.8	12.0	...	...	11.5	...
1927	...	...	...	...	10.6	...
1928	...	...	...	...	10.6	...
1929	...	...	...	...	13.5	...
1930	...	...	...	...	20.0	...

[a]Chih-fu refers to the north Shantung port also known as Chefoo.

Source: Shina no janku, 29-30; Tsingtao figures for 1926-30 are from Horiuchi Sumiyo, "Conditions of the Junk Trade Around Tsingtao," Mantetsu chôsa geppô 22, no. 9 (1942):126.

mate of the annual growth in the value of services provided by sailboat transportation between 1895 and 1936.

Summary. This survey shows that there was no general decline in junk traffic despite the transfer of important cargoes from sailing craft to steam vessels along some major routes. Indeed, available data relating to such major centers of mechanized transport development as Hankow, Tientsin, Shanghai, Dairen, and Tsingtao show unmechanized water carriage expanding alongside the steadily growing traffic by steam and motor vessels. With the business lost to steamships and railways outweighed by new demands arising from expanding domestic trade and the collection and distribution services required by mechanized carriers, the predominant impact of new modes of water carriage was to increase traffic rather than displace unmechanized carriers.

Railroads

Chinese railroad development began inauspiciously with foreigners constructing a short line from Shanghai to Wu-sung in 1876. The line was soon purchased by the Chinese government, torn up, and shipped to Taiwan. Railroads continued to generate controversy between reformers who recognized their military and commercial value and conservatives suspicious of foreign influence and concerned about possible economic and social disruptions. As a result, the active encouragement of railway construction appeared only after 1895.

The subsequent progress of railway expansion is summarized in Table 4.7. Three periods may be distinguished: an initial growth spurt between 1895 and 1913 with a high rate of expansion from a tiny base; a second period from 1914 to 1927 in which growth slowed because of World War I, which interrupted access to European financing and equipment, and the civil wars of the 1920s; and a decade of renewed growth after 1927 during which both the Kuomintang government in Nanking and the Japanese authorities in Manchuria vigorously promoted railway construction.

China's prewar rail network, although large enough to have a significant economic impact on some regions of the country, was much smaller than India's. In 1936, China's rail lines amounted to slightly over 20,000 kilometers, with about 40 percent of this total concentrated in Manchuria; at that time, India's rail system included about 72,000 kilometers of track. In 1936, freight traffic on China's railways amounted to 14.6 billion ton-kilometers as opposed to 33.5 billion ton-kilometers in India.[57]

As of 1936, China's rail network, shown in Map 2, included three major elements: the Manchurian rail system; north-south lines from Peking to Canton and from Tientsin through Nanking and into Anhwei; and a series of east-west lines running roughly parallel to the Yangtze River. In Manchuria, railway development was spurred

---

57. Indian data are from Murphey, *The Outsiders*, 110.

Table 4.7
Growth of Chinese Railways, 1895-1937

Year	Length of Track (kilometers)	Freight Traffic (million Ton-km)		Passenger Traffic (million Passenger-km)
		Total	Per Route-km	
1895	410	150	0.36	100
1907	6494	1850	0.28	1130
1915	10506	5850	0.56	3340
1919	11199	7300	0.65	4080
1924	12691	10000	0.79	5280
1933	15807	12800	0.81	7110
1936	20746	14600[a]	0.70	...
1949	21800	18400	0.84	13000
1952	22900	60160	2.63	20060
1957	26700	134590	5.04	36130
1983	51600	664600	12.88	309500

Period	New Lines per Year (km)	Annual Growth of Track Length
1895-1913	512	20.0 %
1913-1927	298	2.5
1928-1937	763	4.6

[a]Calculated from the 1933 figure by assuming the same percentage increase as indicated by the combined totals for China's National Railway system and the South Manchurian Railway (SMR), which together contributed 88.3 percent of the 1933 total. 1933-36 increases for the national railways and the SMR are from Yen Chung-p'ing, Chung-kuo chin tai ching chi shih, 207-8 and Manshū kaihatsu yonjū nenshi (Tokyo, 1964-65) 1:301.

Sources: Huenemann, The Dragon and the Iron Horse, 76-77, 222; Chen, Chinese Economic Statistics, 374 and Chung-kuo t'ung chi nien chien, 1984 (Peking, 1984), 273, 279, 283.

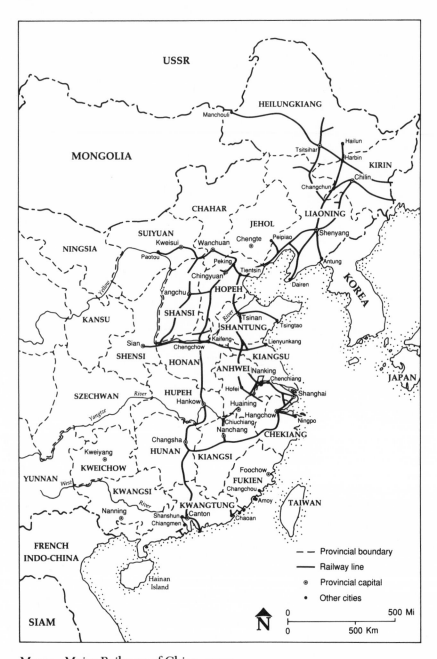

Map 2. Major Railways of China, 1937.
Source: Based on Chi-Keung Leung, *China: Railway Patterns and National Goals* (Chicago, 1960), 61.

by political rivalry among Russia, Japan, and China. By 1936, the Japanese controlled an extensive rail system built around a T-shaped core of trunk lines running from Dairen in the south to Hei-ho on the Soviet border and from Man-chou-li on Manchuria's northwestern border with the USSR southeastwards through Harbin to Sui-fen-ho, with links to Vladivostok and Korea.[58] Railroads acted as a leading sector in the development of Manchuria's economy. The level of railway development paralleled Japan's: Manchurian freight traffic in 1936 amounted to 160 ton-kilometers per capita, only slightly below the Japanese figure of 179 ton-kilometers for 1930.[59] Railways opened up the interior of Manchuria to commercial farming and supported the mining and metallurgy sectors in Liaoning. Regional income estimates show modern transport and communications following factory industry and construction as the fastest-growing sectors of Manchuria's economy between 1924 and 1941.[60]

The main north-south line, the longest of the prewar Chinese lines, was the Peking-Hankow route completed in 1905. The southward extension of the line to Canton began at the same time, but was completed only in 1936. The Peking-Hankow line began the process of opening the North China plain, a region ill-served by water routes, to the expansion of commerce and industry. The railway offered vast new markets to the manufactures of Shanghai, which could move by water to Hankow or Tientsin and then by rail into Honan and Hopei, and the grain surpluses of Manchuria, which could now forestall the periodic famines that had struck the northern plains over the centuries.

The second north-south route ran from Tientsin in the north to P'u-k'ou, on the north bank of the Yangtze opposite Nanking, and

58. Shun-hsin Chou, "Railway Development and Economic Growth in Manchuria," *China Quarterly* 45 (1971).
59. Manchurian freight traffic (for the South Manchurian Railway only) of 6.4 billion ton-kilometers is from *Manshū kaihatsu yonjū nenshi* (Tokyo, 1964–65), 1:301; a population of 40 million persons is assumed. Japanese figures are from *Hundred-Year Statistics of the Japanese Economy* (Tokyo, 1966), 12, 115.
60. Alexander Eckstein, Kang Chao, and John K. Chang, "The Economic Development of Manchuria: The Rise of a Frontier Economy," *Journal of Economic History* 34, no. 1 (1974):255.

then southward into Anhwei and eastward from Nanking to Shanghai, Hangchow, and Ningpo (Chekiang). This route supplemented
existing north-south water routes along the coast and natural and
artificial waterways in the interior.

The prewar rail system included four substantial east-west lines
in China proper. The northernmost of these routes extended from
Paotow (Inner Mongolia) in the west to Tientsin, where it linked
with the coastal line to Manchuria. Another route extended north
from the southwestern corner of Shansi to the provincial capital of
Taiyuan, then eastward, crossing the Peking-Hankow line and the
Tientsin-P'u-k'ou line, continuing to the major port of Tsingtao. A
third line began west of Sian (Shensi) and stretched eastward to the
port of Lien-yün-kang (Kiangsu), crossing the Peking-Hankow line
at Chengchow (Honan) and the Tientsin-P'u-k'ou route at Hsü-
chou (Kiangsu). The southernmost route extended from central
Kwangsi province to Heng-yang (Hunan), where it met the southern extension of the Peking-Hankow-Canton route, continuing
across Kiangsi to Nan-ch'ang and then to Hangchow, where it met
lines leading to Shanghai and Ningpo.

Although some provinces, including Szechwan, China's most
populous, acquired no railways before the Pacific War, railway construction raised the proportion of China's population and output
with easy access to inexpensive long-distance transport. This expansion of transport facilities and the resulting stimulus to specialization and trade created a great potential for economic change,
including urbanization, cropping patterns, industrialization, energy use, and long-distance trade. This potential was only partially
realized during the prewar era.

Cargo traffic hauled by railways represents trade creation on a
massive scale. Since man- and animal-powered land carriage was
incapable of delivering more than several billion ton-kilometers of
annual cargo turnover (Table 4.10 and Appendix D), the growing
volume of railway traffic, which reached ten billion ton-kilometers
in 1924 and nearly fifteen billion ton-kilometers in 1936, must be
seen as a net addition to overall freight traffic. The large share of
new products in railway cargoes, especially coal, which never
moved in large quantities prior to the advent of railways, confirms
this assessment.

Other Forms of Transport and Communication

Roads

Land traffic in Ch'ing China meant carriage by animal-drawn cart, pack animal, or porter. Transport costs for these carriers were high and traffic correspondingly small. Huenemann concludes that a "reasonable estimate of the average" cost for overland transport "might well be 0.20 yuan per ton-km," ten times the charge for water or rail transport.[61] Routes used for land carriage consisted mainly of cart tracks, often impassable in wet weather, or mere paths.

Interest in motor roads dates from the 1920s. During the North China famine of 1920–21, public and private relief agencies employed famine victims to construct roads. In Shansi, for example, over 1,000 kilometers of roads were built in this way.[62] Regional military rivalries spurred road construction by local commanders who were anxious to improve troop mobility and, by encouraging commerce, increase tax revenues. Railway expansion stimulated the construction of feeder roads: surveys of the 1930s show that many Hopei counties were served by small trucking firms that moved goods and passengers to and from stations along the Peking-Hankow line.[63] Private business firms also entered this field. A 1922 report noted that: "We are now witnessing . . . the picture of the Chinese authorities being moved from below, the initiative coming from the merchants rather than from the Government. . . . Companies are being organized in all parts of the country to build roads and operate autobus services."[64] Merchant groups constructed toll roads in parts of Chekiang and Kiangsu.[65]

61. Huenemann, *The Dragon and the Iron Horse*, 223–25.
62. *Shan-hsi k'ao ch'a pao kao shu* (Shanghai, 1936), 276–79 and Donald G. Gillin, *Warlord: Yen Hsi-shan in Shansi Province, 1911–1949* (Princeton, 1967), 91.
63. See the materials published in various issues of *Chi Ch'a tiao ch'a t'ung chi ts'ung k'an* 1–2 (1936–37).
64. *Far Eastern Review* of January 1922, quoted in Milton T. Stauffer, *The Christian Occupation of China* (Shanghai, 1922), 18.
65. Cheng, *Influence of Communications*, 66 and Ting and Tu, "Yü Hsia-ch'ing," 163.

Table 4.8
Length of Motor Roads in China, 1927-79
(thousand kilometers)

Year	Length
1927	29
1928	30
1929	35
1930	47
1931	66
1932	71
1933	72
1934	85
1935	96
1936	111
1949	81
1952	127
1957	255
1965	514
1975	784
1979	876

Period	Exponential Growth Rate
1927-36	15.8 percent per year
1949-79	7.7

Sources: Arthur N. Young, China's Nation-Building Effort, 1927-1937 (Stanford, 1971), 396-97; Chung-kuo ching chi nien chien 1981 (Peking, 1981), vi-18.

Road building jumped ahead during the Nanking decade when, as shown in Table 4.8, the growth of motor roads proceeded at an annual rate of nearly 16 percent or more than double the rate recorded during the first three decades of the People's Republic. The primary motive for construction remained military, but there is abundant evidence of a growing economic impact as well. A series of British reports emphasized both the scale of construction and the extensive commercial use of roads:[66]

Reports from all parts of China tell of the construction of new roads. . . . Some are well constructed . . . more are bad or at least indifferent. . . .

66. Quotations are from Great Britain, Department of Overseas Trade, *Economic Conditions in China to September 1st, 1929* (London, 1930), 26 and *The Commercial, Industrial and Economic Situation In China to September 1st, 1928* (London, 1928), 31.

But . . . even now they form a network of communication between Chinese towns and villages which enables the Chinese merchant and farmer to make journeys unheard of a few years ago. . . . Omnibusses, locally constructed on chassis imported from abroad, are making their appearance all over the country. . . . With passengers packed like sardines inside and luggage piled dangerously high on top they bump noisily along the highways.

Perhaps the most interesting feature of this road building activity is that the new roads are being freely used for motor 'bus and motor lorry services often . . . covering considerable distances.

Both contemporary and retrospective accounts complain that roads were built with conscripted (and often uncompensated) rural labor, that repairs were neglected, that toll stations and transport monopolies restricted access to new roads, that civilian traffic was excluded, and that the new roads were not laid out with due regard for economic efficiency.[67] Despite these difficulties, numerous reports document the use of civil and even "military roads . . . for commercial and industrial purposes."[68] A balanced assessment of prewar road building must emphasize the stimulus not only to the flow of commodities but also to the circulation of people and information, the transmission of news, and the opening of new horizons to millions of rural Chinese whose knowledge was bounded by the friction of distance, an impediment that new roads began to dissolve in many parts of China during the prewar decades.[69]

Civil Aviation

Chinese interest in aviation dates from the beginning of the Republican era, when "a school of aeronautics and a repair shop" were established near Peking. "A number of airplanes were built at the school shop and a few foreign motors were copied with the cooperation of the arsenals." The school closed for lack of funds,

67. See Lloyd E. Eastman, *The Abortive Revolution: China Under Nationalist Rule, 1927–1937* (Cambridge, 1974), 209–12.
68. Cheng, *Influence of Communications*, 63.
69. H. D. Lamson, "The Effect of Industrialization upon Village Livelihood," *Chinese Economic Journal* 9, no. 4 (1931) includes several concrete instances (e.g., pp. 1061, 1075) illustrating the effect of communication along roadways on the spread of knowledge, information, and rumor among villagers.

but was revived after World War I when the Chinese government acquired over 100 airplanes.[70] Similar efforts were made at Foochow and in Shansi.[71] Although military considerations dominated the growth of aviation in prewar China, civil air traffic expanded as well. By the mid-1930s, passenger flights linked nearly forty major cities.[72]

Telecommunications

The development of telecommunications in China dates from the success of a Danish firm, acting in secrecy, in completing a telegraph cable linking Shanghai and the nearby port of Wu-sung.[73] By the 1930s, China possessed a system of telecommunications which, though rudimentary by Western standards, was large enough to have a considerable effect on the economy.

The telegraph was the chief vehicle for rapid long-distance communication in prewar China. Both private entrepreneurs and provincial governments built telegraph lines in the late nineteenth century. The private lines were nationalized in 1902, the provincial government lines in 1911.[74] Basic data on the subsequent development of the telegraph system under government control appear in Table 4.9. In the mid-1930s, the telegraph network included over one thousand stations and one hundred thousand kilometers of lines connecting all important centers of population and trade.

The history of telephonic communication parallels that of the telegraph.[75] The first exchanges were installed in Shanghai, Hankow, and other treaty ports by foreign businesses; Chinese entrepreneurs and local governments followed suit. By 1912 there were

70. S. K. Yao, "Aviation," in *The Chinese Year Book, 1935–36* (Reprint, Nendeln, 1968), 1:594.
71. Cheng, *Influence of Communications*, 113.
72. Yao, "Aviation," 1:595.
73. Shu-hwai Wang, "China's Modernization in Communications, 1860–1916: A Regional Comparison," in *Modern Chinese Economic History*, ed. Chi-ming Hou and Tzong-shian Yu (Taipei, 1979), 336.
74. Wang, "China's Modernization," 337. Jen-kuang Yen, "Telecommunications," in *The Chinese Year Book, 1935–36* (Reprint, Nendeln, 1968), 1:673, places the takeover of private lines in 1908.
75. This summary is based on Wang, "China's Modernization"; Yu-ching Wen, "Electrical Communications," in *The Chinese Year Book, 1936–37* (Reprint, Nendeln, 1968); and Yen, "Telecommunications."

Table 4.9
Development of China's Telegraph System, 1912-1935

Year	Number of Offices	Length of Lines (thousand km)	Telegraph Instruments	Inland Telegrams (millions)
1912	565	62	787	1.9
1922	928	90	2244	2.5
1932[a]	1094	100	1914	4.0
1935[a]	1346	99	2443	4.0[b]

[a]Data for Manchuria are presumably excluded from the figures for 1932 and 1935.

[b]Indicates data for 1934.

Source: Yu-ching Wen, "Electrical Communications," in The Chinese Year Book, 1936-37 (Shanghai, 1936), 1086, 1109.

perhaps 20,000 telephone subscribers in China who obtained services from various Chinese and foreign exchanges. After 1900, the Chinese Telegraph Administration, which later became subordinate to the Ministry of Communications, began to take control of telephone service. By the mid-1930s, the ministry operated local networks in twenty-five cities and provided a modest long-distance network.

These communication systems enjoyed wide commercial use. In the first half of 1935, for example, less than one-fifth of 2.1 million telegrams were official; the remainder were private and consisted mainly of business information, which could be transmitted in private code. The data for 1912 show that shops and companies formed the largest group of subscribers to Chinese-owned telephone systems, accounting for 42 percent of the total as compared with 26 percent for government offices and 20 percent for private residences.[76] Anecdotal evidence confirms the commercial significance of telecommunications. In Manchuria, the telephone system was "of the greatest advantage for the grain trade. . . . Russian as well as Chinese merchants avail themselves to a great extent of this installation."[77] Even in the sleepy market town of Tsou-p'ing

76. Wang, "China's Modernization," 343.
77. *North Manchuria and the Chinese Eastern Railway* (Reprint, New York, 1982), 99.

(Shantung), C. K. Yang found that the telephone was accessible to citizens with urgent messages.[78] In the Hsi-ho district of southwest Hopei, cotton merchants obtained market information from Tientsin by telegram and letter.[79]

The Post Office

In 1896, following initial experimentation by the Maritime Customs, China's government established a national post office modeled on foreign systems. Although the postal statistics show a considerable growth of traffic and revenue, the new post office offered no new services, merely providing an inadequate replacement for the long-established private letter-carriers, or *min-hsin-chü*. These private firms, "with their close relations with the public, together with cheap rates and safe deliveries, rendered it practically impossible for the newly-established Post Office to compete." The government, acting in classic bureaucratic fashion, responded by suppressing the private carriers.[80] Postal services, whether offered by official or private agencies, provided a means to transmit commercial information over long distances. The post was also used to ship bulky commodities like handicraft cloth and as a remittance agency.[81]

Transport Intensity
in China's Prewar Economy

Table 4.10 presents a quantitative picture of the evolution of transportation in China's prewar economy. The assumptions used to construct these results are described in Appendix D. As might be

78. Ching-kun Yang, *A North China Local Market Economy: A Summary of a Study of Periodic Markets in Chowping Hsien, Shantung* (New York, 1944), 29.
79. Yeh, "Hsi-ho Cotton," 1:220.
80. Chang, "Post Office," 1:700–702. On private carriers, see Ying-wen Cheng, *Postal Communication in China and Its Modernization, 1860–1896* (Cambridge, 1970), chap. 3.
81. Kang Chao, *The Development of Cotton Textile Production in China* (Cambridge, 1977), 196, reports that handicraft cloth produced in Wei county (Shantung), where handicraft textile production employed up to 150,000 persons, "was shipped through railway freight and post offices to major cities in Honan, Anhwei and Shensi." On postal remittances, see Chang, "Post Office," 1:711–12.

anticipated, the figures for modern conveyances, particularly railways, are more firmly based than those for unmechanized carriers.
The tonnage figures in Tables 4.5 and 4.6 raise the possibility that
the assumed 2 percent annual growth rate for junk traffic is too low.
But unless the 1936 total for junk traffic is too small, raising the
long-term growth rate for this sector would lower the estimated
volume of junk traffic in 1895 and 1907 and lead to improbable
increases in the share of mechanized conveyances in overall transport volume for the early years. Despite the use of crude assumptions, the results in Table 4.10 do indicate the general trend of
prewar transport growth and the rough breakdown of total freight
carriage among the various transport modes.

The figures in Table 4.10 sketch a history of continuous, but
irregular, growth and structural change, with the share of mechanized conveyances in overall transport activity gradually rising to
about 40 percent. Despite the impact of military disruption on
their operations, especially during the 1920s, railroads grew faster
than all other sectors of the transport industry, rising from a tiny
base at a high, but declining, rate that averages out to over 11
percent annually between 1895 and 1936. Steamship traffic expanded more slowly, at an average annual rate of 4 percent. The
overall rate of growth, derived from the performance of rail and
steam and the (assumed) annual growth rates of 2 and 1 percent for
sailboat and land traffic respectively, fluctuates around a gently declining trend. In contrast to the conventional view of World War I
as a "golden age" for the modern sector, these figures suggest a
distinct sag in growth during 1915–19, indicating that the temporary slackening of foreign participation was by no means an unmixed blessing for the domestic economy; this theme will recur in
Chapter 5.

This compilation of transport data can also provide a fresh approach to the perennial question of how far commercialization had
proceeded in China's prewar economy. This is addressed in Table
4.11, which contains comparative measures of transport intensity
for China in 1933 and the United States in 1859/60 and 1869/70.
Although geographic variations may lead to wide intercountry
variations in the level of transport activity per dollar or per physical
unit of output, these measures of transport intensity should rise
steadily as an economy industrializes and its citizens attain higher

Table 4.10
Estimated Volume of Freight Transport, 1895-1936
(billion ton-kilometers)

Year	Rail	Steam Ships	Junk	Land	Total Freight Volume		
					Volume	Index	Modern Share
	(1)	(2)	(3)	(4)	(5)	(6)	(7)
1895	0.2	5.2	24.1	2.7	32.2	100.0	16.8%
1907	1.8	13.7	30.6	3.0	49.1	152.5	31.6
1915	5.8	16.3	35.8	3.2	61.1	189.8	36.2
1919	7.3	17.3	38.8	3.4	66.8	207.4	36.8
1924	10.0	23.5	42.8	3.5	79.8	247.8	42.0
1933	12.8	25.9[a]	51.2	3.9	93.8[a]	291.3[a]	41.2
1936	14.6	26.6[a]	54.3	4.0	99.5[a]	309.0[a]	41.4

Average Annual Growth Rate of Estimated Volume of Freight Transport

Period	All Sectors	Excluding Land Carriage
1895-1907	3.6%	4.1%
1907-1915	2.8	2.9
1915-1919	2.2	2.3
1919-1924	3.6	3.8
1924-1933	1.8[a]	1.8[a]
1933-1936	2.0	2.0
1895-1924	3.1	3.3
1895-1936	2.8[a]	2.9[a]
1915-1936	2.3[a]	2.4[a]

[a]Underestimate due to omission of interport steamship traffic among Manchurian ports.

Notes: The figures for junk traffic are derived from the estimated 1936 total by assuming annual growth of 2 percent. Estimate for land carriage (including freight moved by trucks and busses) for 1936 is a crude guess; I assume 1 percent annual growth during 1895-1936. Col. 7 reports the share of railways and steamships in estimated annual freight volume.

Sources: Table 4.7 and Appendix D.

living standards. This is because both industrialization and rising personal incomes involve rapid increases in the intensity of commodity exchange as producers and consumers come to depend on ever larger volumes of commodity purchases to satisfy their personal and business needs. From this viewpoint, transport intensity

Table 4.11
Comparative Transport Intensity: China (1933) and U.S. (1860-70)

	China 1933	United States 1859/60	United States 1869/70
1. Aggregate output, (current prices, in billions of local currency)	29.13	4.17	6.71
2. Commodity output, (current prices, in billions of local currency)	22.19	2.57	4.82
3. Base year price of wheat (local currency per metric ton)	92.0	33.5	43.7
4. Price index for 1933 (base year equals 1.000)	1.000	1.153	0.748
5. Aggregate output (billion U.S. dollars, 1933 prices)	7.68	4.81	5.02
6. Commodity output (billion U.S. dollars, 1933 prices)	5.85	2.96	3.60
7. Aggregate output (wheat equivalent million metric tons)	316.5	124.5	153.5
8. Transport turnover (billion metric ton-km)	96.5	49.3	64.5
9. Transport intensity A. Ton-km per dollar of aggregate product at 1933 prices	12.2	10.2	12.8
B. Ton-km per dollar of commodity output at 1933 prices	16.0	16.6	17.9
C. Ton-km per ton of wheat-equivalent produced	296.4	396.0	420.2
D. Ton-km per capita	187.6	1565.1	1616.5

continued...

may provide a good index of commercialization. Indeed, several measures of transport intensity for the United States are uniformly higher in 1869/70 than a decade earlier (Table 4.11). Despite the absence of firm estimates for Chinese output growth (to be discussed in Chapter 6), the long-term growth of Chinese freight traffic (Table 4.10) indicates that transport volume per unit of Chinese output also increased considerably, especially between 1895 and 1924.

Direct comparison between the measures of transport intensity

Table 4.11, continued

Sources: Line 1: China: K. C. Yeh, "China's National Income,
1931-36," in Modern Chinese Economic History, ed. Chi-ming Hou and
Tzong-shian Yu (Taipei, 1979), 97. U.S.: Gordon O. Holmes, "U.S.
Transport Intensity, ca. 1860-1870" (Toronto, 1981), table 8.

Line 2: China: The sum of value added for agriculture,
manufacturing (including handicrafts), mining, utilities, and
construction from Yeh, "China's National Income, 1931-36," 97.
U.S.: Holmes, "U.S. Transport," table 7.

Line 3: China: The 1933 price of 4.6 yuan per picul or, at 20
piculs per metric ton, 92 yuan per ton (Ta-chung Liu and Kung-chia
Yeh, The Economy of the Chinese Mainland: National Income and
Economic Development, 1933-1959 [Princeton, 1965] xvi, 325). U.S.:
The average of prices for No. 2 winter and No. 2 spring wheat for
1858-62 and 1868-72 shown in Holmes, "U.S. Transport," table 9,
converted at 37.04 bushels per metric ton.

Line 4: U.S.: Based on price indexes for commodity production
shown in Holmes, "U.S. Transport," table 7. I use the same index to
deflate both aggregate output and commodity production.

Line 5: U.S.: Line 1 x Line 4. China: The product of Line 1
converted to U.S. dollars at the 1933 rate of US$0.2635 per Chinese
yuan, shown in Hsiao, Trade Statistics, 192, and Line 4.

Line 6: Line 2 x Line 4.

Line 7: Line 1 divided by Line 3. This calculation indicates
the quantity of wheat that could be purchased for a sum equal to the
base-year value of aggregate output if the unit price were equal to
the base-year domestic price of wheat. Its purpose is to create a
means of comparing national outputs across time and space by
expressing them in common commodity units.

Line 8: China: Table 4.10. U.S.: Holmes, "U.S. Transport,"
table 6.

Line 9: Calculated from Lines 5-8. Population figures: for
China, 500 million (Table 6.3); for the U.S., 31.5 million (1860)
and 39.9 million (1870) (See The Statistical History of the United
States from Colonial Times to the Present [Stamford, 1965]), 7).

for the two countries produces the surprising result that the level
of transport intensity in prewar China was little different from
American conditions of the 1860s. On a per capita basis, transport
services were far more abundant in mid-nineteenth century America than in prewar China (Line 9D); this reflects higher American
income levels. But the measures of freight carriage per dollar of
aggregate output (including services) or commodity production
(Lines 9A and 9B) are nearly identical in the two economies. If the
aggregate outputs are converted to wheat-equivalent using the respective national wheat prices (Line 9C), the American economy

displays higher transport intensity, but this may arise from the un-usually low level of Chinese farm prices in 1933 (Table 3.10).

On the premise that transport intensity and commercialization are intimately related, these results permit a view of Chinese mar-ket orientation that is more general than previous attempts to specify the percentage of crops marketed by farmers in various re-gions. These new data indicate that the degree of transport inten-sity and hence the extent of commercialization in China during the 1930s roughly paralleled the conditions prevailing seventy years earlier in the United States just prior to the great surge of post–Civil War railway construction. Both nations included great trading regions as well as isolated communities with only tenuous eco-nomic links to the outside world. But the overall similarity of re-sults for the two economies indicates that the notion of China's prewar economy as dominated by largely self-sufficient rural com-munities with only marginal links with external markets is not ten-able. With farming contributing almost two-thirds of China's 1933 national product and with perhaps 80 percent of households resi-dent in farming communities, the finding that the volume of freight carriage per dollar of output was similar in China and the post-bellum United States must apply to the farm sector. The query "How commercialized were China's farmers in the 1930s?" re-quires an answer couched in terms of China's similarity with the highly market-oriented American economy of 1860 or 1870.

Transport, Communications, and the Economy

China experienced a partial revolution in transport and communi-cation during the half century preceding the Pacific War. The im-pact of new opportunities arising from transport innovation is no-where more visible than in the development of China's mining industry. The rapid prewar expansion of mining was closely linked with the growth of railways, which provided an important source of new demand for coal as well as the only feasible method of mov-ing large quantities of mineral products from interior locations in Shansi, Hopei, and the northeast to distant markets. In 1934, for example, a year in which China's output of minerals and mineral products amounted to perhaps 30–35 million tons, railways hauled at least 27 million tons of mineral freight. Thus the bulk of all mineral ores and products were transported by the railroads, which themselves consumed 4–5 million annual tons of coal in the mid-1930s.

Mechanized coal mining arose in response to new demand from steamships in the mid-nineteenth century, which "stimulated British interest in Chinese coal . . . as early as 1864."[82] Prior to the advent of railways, access to coal was restricted to the coal districts themselves, coastal ports open to sea-borne imports, and consumers with direct water connections to domestic mines. All this changed after railway construction expanded the market for coal extracted from large mines in the north and the northeast. Even in Peking, "situated almost astride a coalfield," railways brought steep reductions in fuel costs: between 1900 and 1917, a local cost-of-living index rose by 26 percent, but the price of coal briquettes plunged by 32 percent.[83]

Falling energy costs stimulated new activity in a wide range of industries. Cheap coal spurred the expansion of thermal power-generating facilities throughout urban areas of North and Central China. Lower prices and greater supplies of electricity in turn encouraged mechanization in all sectors. Wherever power lines could be tapped, the advantages of machine power became available without constructing large power plants or installing heavy engines.[84] Many industrial plants used coal to generate both heat and motive power; railway development and the consequent drop in coal prices reduced their fuel costs as well as the expense of shipping their products to distant markets. This double benefit enhanced the capacity of Chinese producers to compete with imports and, by facilitating access to new markets (see Figure 3.1), offered new opportunities to take advantage of scale economies. The link between railway development, cheap fuel, and industrialization

82. Tim Wright, *Coal Mining in China's Economy and Society, 1895–1937* (Cambridge, 1984), 52.
83. Wright, *Coal Mining*, 46–47.
84. Ryoshin Minami, "The Introduction of Electric Power and Its Impact on the Manufacturing Industries: With Special Reference to Smaller Scale Plants," in *Japanese Industrialization and Its Social Consequences*, ed. Hugh T. Patrick (Berkeley, 1976), 299–325, vividly describes the benefits of greater availability of electricity in prewar Japan.

was well understood by contemporary observers. D. K. Lieu (Liu Ta-chün) identified railways as "one of the most important" factors "that promote industrial development."[85] British observers recalled the 1920s as a period remarkable for "the number of mills and factories of all kinds which were springing up all along the principal railway lines."[86] Not the least of the industrial ventures stimulated by railway expansion were the factories and workshops maintained by the railways themselves, which performed repairs and also manufactured bridgework, rolling stock, and even locomotives. In addition to railway workshops, manufacturers of cement, textiles, flour, cigarettes, matches, chemicals, and many other goods set up factories along major rail lines and at important junctions, including Harbin, Shenyang (Mukden), Peking, Shih-chia-chuang, Chengchow, Sian, Te-chou, Hsü-chou, Chu-chou, and Heng-yang.

Handicraft industries also benefited from improved transport networks. Although the expansion of international trade and domestic factory production reduced the demand for some handicraft products, notably homespun cotton yarn, the general trend of demand for handicraft products was upward. The beneficial impact of new transport facilities on handicrafts is evident from the location of new centers of craft activity. The proximity of dynamic craft producers like the textile centers of Kaoyang (Hopei) and Weihsien (Shantung) and the lace, knitwear, and hair-net makers of Shantung, Kiangsu, and Chekiang to railways and coastal ports shows that the advantage of access to cheap transport for collection of materials and distribution of output to domestic and overseas customers outweighed the disadvantage of locating in places that were readily accessible to competing factory products. Transport improvements were particularly beneficial to energy-intensive craft operations producing brick, lime, ceramics, silk, and liquor. Lower fuel prices "led to the revival of native industries which had earlier languished because of the high cost of fuel."[87]

China's farm sector experienced a major increase in commercialization during the late nineteenth and early twentieth centuries. The expansion of production for the market was encouraged and

85. D. K. Lieu, *China's Industries and Finance* (Peking, 1927), 19.
86. Great Britain, Department of Overseas Trade, *Commercial Situation*, 34.
87. Wright, *Coal Mining*, 46 and Carlson, *Kaiping*, 27.

226   Transport and Communication

often initiated by the appearance of new forms of transportation
and, as noted in Chapter 3, by monetary and financial developments, both of which acted in similar fashion to increase farm-gate
prices of agricultural goods and reduce the cost of delivering agricultural produce to distant buyers. The improvement in farmers'
terms of trade was considerable. Buck's data show that prices received by farmers rose by more than 200 percent between 1900
and 1930, while prices paid by farmers rose only 117 percent between 1907 and 1930.[88] Brandt shows that farmers' terms of trade
began to improve as early as 1880.[89] These price changes were not
evenly distributed across space, but offered special advantages to
farmers located near major transit routes. Liang presents examples
of increases in farm-gate prices far above Buck's national averages
in Ching county (Hopei), located on the Tientsin-P'u-k'ou rail line
and in Chang-li county (Hopei) on the line linking Peking with
Shenyang.[90]

Although inadequate data prevent the achievement of a scholarly consensus on the actual ratio of off-farm sales to total output
in various years, the upward trend in this important indicator of
market orientation is beyond question.[91] The output of industrial
crops, including cotton, tobacco, soybeans, oilseeds, peanuts, and
groundnuts, all with high ratios of commercial sales to production,
expanded rapidly. The market-oriented production of fruits, vegetables, and animal products (eggs, wool, hides, meat) also increased considerably in prewar China. Farmers who devoted their
efforts to commercial production of plant and animal products of
necessity relied on outside sources for a rising share of their food
supplies. In the absence of large-scale food imports, growing specialization in nonfood products necessitated a concomitant increase
in market-oriented production of grain and other foodstuffs. Wu
Ch'eng-ming finds that the share of commercial grain production

88. Liang, Railways, 100–101.
89. Loren Brandt, Commercialization and Agricultural Development: Central
    and Eastern China, 1870s–1930s (New York, forthcoming), chap. 3.
90. Liang, Railways, 102–3.
91. Ramon H. Myers, "The Commercialization of Agriculture in Modern China,"
    in Economic Organization in Chinese Society, ed. W. E. Willmott (Stanford,
    1972), 173–91 and "The Agrarian System," in The Cambridge History of
    China, vol. 13, Republican China, 1912–1949, part 2 (Cambridge, 1986) and
    Brandt, Commercialization and Agricultural Development, chap. 4.

(excluding rent or loan payments in kind and sales within local farming communities) rose from 10 to 16 and then to 22 percent in 1840, 1894, and 1919.[92] Transport improvements may have brought additional expansion of local trade by facilitating exchange based on local variation in tastes, climate, and growing conditions. In Chekiang, for example, large interregional rice flows allowed farmers to produce the varieties best suited to local growing conditions and sell their output to consumers elsewhere in the province, using the proceeds to finance purchases of (domestic) imports more suited to their own taste.[93]

A rising share of commercial production and a corresponding decline in household and local self-sufficiency was most visible in North China, where high transport costs had impeded commercialization prior to the construction of railways. The key role of railways in the commercialization process emerges from a variety of sources. Cotton from the Hsi-ho district of western Hopei first appeared in the Tientsin market in 1908, soon after the completion of the Peking-Hankow rail line that cuts through the Hsi-ho area.[94] Using information from gazetteers and from J. L. Buck's farm surveys, Ernest Liang finds that population density, land productivity, and commercial cropping all rose in counties located along new rail lines relative to nearby counties without rail connections.[95] Han-seng Chen is most specific on the link between railway development and the spread of commercial cropping:[96]

As the area in American seed tobacco expanded along the Tsingtao-Tsinan Railway, the B.A.T. [British-American Tobacco Company] network of leaf collection spread with it. Near the railway stations leaf-collecting establishments were set up.

Since the completion of the Kiao-tsi [Tsingtao-Tsinan] Railway in 1904, of the Ping-han [Peking-Hankow] in 1906, and of the Tsin-pu [Tientsin–P'u-k'ou] in 1912, money economy has gone forward with rapid strides.

92. Wu Ch'eng-ming, *Chung-kuo tzu pen chu i yü kuo nei shih ch'ang* (Peking, 1985), 110.
93. Chang P'ei-kang and Chang Chih-i, *Che-chiang sheng shih liang chih yün hsiao* (Changsha, 1940), 18–20.
94. Chu and Chin, *Marketing of Cotton*, 5.
95. Liang, *Railways*, chap. 5.
96. Han-seng Chen, *Industrial Capital and Chinese Peasants* (New York, 1980), 7, 25.

Purchasing agents for cotton as well as tobacco clustered at railway stations. Studies of local economic patterns in Hopei during the 1930s show a strong orientation of land and water traffic toward the rail lines.

Even where railways did not bring about factory expansion or major shifts in cropping patterns, the influence of expanded trading opportunities is visible in the composition and orientation of commercial activity.[97] C. K. Yang's study of marketing in Tsou-p'ing county (Shantung), conducted during 1932–33, showed that this commercial backwater, where trade was dominated by exchange among local farmers, received one-fourth of its market supplies from more than 100 miles away, with 22 percent being shipped by railway or steamer.[98]

The impact of improvements in transportation and monetary arrangements on rural life extended far beyond the gradual increase in market involvement reported in contemporary accounts and confirmed by subsequent researchers. Commercialization brought new choices to villagers that offered higher incomes and living standards than would otherwise have been attainable. Farmers in many areas of China, especially in the north, experienced lengthy periods of seasonal idleness that sharply limited their annual earnings. In addition to stimulating handicraft production, which drew on seasonal household workers in rural villages, improved transport facilities brought new outlets for previously idle manpower by facilitating migration and permitting new labor-intensive cropping patterns.

Seasonal and permanent migration from North China farming communities to urban areas and the booming frontier provinces of the northeast improved the fortunes of millions of rural households. Thomas Gottschang's study of labor flows between North China and Manchuria reveals the economic nature of this massive human tide. His materials show that the volume of migration increased when wage differentials between North China and Manchuria expanded (and contracted when wage differences declined), increased during periods of natural or man-made disaster in North China (and declined during years of disaster in Manchuria), increased with the expansion of Manchuria's rail network (which

97. See the local studies published in volumes 1 and 2 of *Chi Ch'a tiao ch'a t'ung chi ts'ung k'an.*
98. Yang, *A North China Local Market Economy,* 35–37.

allowed migrants easier access to job opportunities), and declined with the expansion of railway lines in North China. This last result is particularly noteworthy. Although one might expect that, by reducing travel costs and transit time, railway expansion in the migrants' home regions would stimulate an exodus of labor, Gottschang's findings suggest that the beneficial impact of railway construction on local economic opportunities was so strong that local railway development was negatively associated with out-migration despite its tendency to lower the cost of travel to distant places.[99]

Improved transport arrangements offered opportunities to raise incomes in regions that could adopt new cropping patterns and make fuller use of available resources, especially human and animal labor. Traditional cultivation routines generated enormous labor demands in the peak farming seasons, normally in early summer and at the autumn harvest, but required far less labor at other seasons, and almost none for four or five months beginning in mid- or late October.[100] With their large labor requirements, cash crops like cotton and tobacco offered promising alternatives, but only if the seasonal distribution of labor use was different from the normal pattern for food crops.

Tobacco illustrates the potential impact of new crops on the farming cycle. Transport improvement played a key role in the spread of tobacco cultivation. Railways offered a means of shipping tobacco leaves to urban cigarette factories and also lowered the cost of coal in the growing districts. Cheap coal was essential for processing tobacco leaves; it also allowed farmers to replace the sorghum stalks traditionally used as household fuel, thus reducing the cost of diverting farmland from grain growing to tobacco culture, expanding the potential supply of green manure or animal fodder, and reducing the destructive practice of stripping branches from trees.[101]

Tobacco requires prodigious quantities of labor, more than any

99. Thomas R. Gottschang, "Structural Change, Disasters, and Migration: The Historical Case of Manchuria," *Economic Development and Cultural Change* 35, no. 3 (1987):478–79.
100. See John L. Buck, *Chinese Farm Economy* (Chicago, 1930), chap. 8.
101. On the benefits of increased rural consumption of coal, see W. Y. Swen, "Types of Farming, Costs of Production and Annual Labor Distribution in Weihsien County, Shantung, China," *Chinese Economic Journal* 3, no. 2 (1928):650.

other commercial crop grown in China.[102] Furthermore, at least in Wei county, Shantung (located in one of the principal tobacco regions), the distribution of labor requirements had the effect of extending the seasonal demand for farm labor without significantly increasing peak labor requirements. A 1924 survey of twenty-four farms in this locality showed that tobacco, which accounted for 5.2 percent of cultivated area, contributed no less than 79 percent of the total demand for labor from October 15 to November 30. Eliminating all labor requirements for tobacco would reduce peak labor requirements (in late June) by only 3.8 percent.[103] Even without considering the possible labor requirements of drying, bundling, carrying, and processing locally grown tobacco leaves, these survey data show that adding tobacco to the local cropping pattern significantly reduced the agricultural slack season, which otherwise would extend from mid-October to late March. Since peak labor requirements were increased only slightly, the opportunity cost attached to the labor absorbed in tobacco growing was small. Even if, as reported in some accounts, the hourly or daily earnings of tobacco growers fell below the year-round average, the resulting incomes represented a significant gain to local farmers, whose best alternative might have involved unremunerative idleness.[104] These benefits, and the consequent competition for resources needed to grow tobacco, explain the high and steeply rising price of tobacco land, its high rental value, and the willingness of farmers not only to provide land and labor, but also to build and maintain costly drying houses.[105]

The Complementarity Between Old and New Transport Modes

New forms of water and overland transportation brought significant change in both the volume and the pattern of production and trade.

102. Chen, *Industrial Capital*, 55.
103. Swen, "Types of Farming," 657.
104. Chen, *Industrial Capital*, chap. 7, and others argue that average returns to labor supplied by owner-cultivators fell below the implicit wages associated with other crops, but fail to consider the implications of seasonal variations in demand for, and hence the opportunity cost or value of, farm labor.
105. Swen, "Types of Farming," 645, notes that tobacco land commanded top prices in Wei county in 1924, and that "land values . . . have risen . . . some

These shifts cannot be attributed solely to the impact of new technologies. It was not the steamship and the railroad alone, but a new configuration of transport technologies based on fruitful combinations of old and new equipment that supported higher levels of specialization and commercialization in prewar China.

Competition between new and old forms of transportation was overshadowed by the general expansion of demand for transport services resulting from falling transactions costs and economic growth. Railways took over some haulage formerly performed by carts and porters, but the scale of railway freight turnover quickly eclipsed the national total of freight moved by nonmechanized land carriers (Table 4.10). Since carts, barrows, porters, and pack animals continued to serve customers in many regions that lacked railroads and convenient water carriage, new opportunities to haul goods to and from railroad terminals probably resulted in a net increase in demand for their services. Sailing craft, which served hundreds of small ports where steamships and railways had yet to penetrate, benefited in similar fashion from opportunities to collect and distribute produce carried by modern conveyances even though they lost business to mechanized shipping on long-distance ocean and river routes.

Contemporary accounts amply document the sharing of transport business among multiple transport modes. Transshipment between mechanized and old-fashioned vehicles was commonplace, as when alum rock mined in Chekiang was shipped to major domestic ports along a route that required the successive use of porters, junks, and steamships.[106] The products of China's new factories and mines as well as goods shipped to or from major cities and foreign countries often moved by junks, which carried not only

219 percent in the last five years." Chen, *Industrial Capital*, reports wide ownership of drying houses costing $160 to build, each sufficient to process the tobacco leaves harvested from 2–3 *mou* of land (pp. 58, 76); he reckons the cost of fuel, equipment, and repairs for these drying houses (excluding interest on capital cost) at $3 per *mou* (p. 58) and shows that tobacco land commanded rents more than double the level for other fields (p. 83). During the period covered by Chen's study, John L. Buck reports that the annual wages of long-term farm workers in Wei county amounted to 38.3 yuan (cash) or 85.3 yuan (including room and board). See *Land Utilization in China, Statistics* (New York, 1982), 318.

106. *China Industrial Handbooks: Chekiang,* 459.

grain, salt, fruits, vegetables, and timber, but also coal, cotton textiles, petroleum, kerosene, potable water, ceramics, and fertilizers.[107] Some owners even equipped their craft with diesel-powered
pumps that allowed them to supplement their income by offering
irrigation services to local farmers.[108]

Junk operators continued to perform well even in the face of
direct competition from railways and steamships. Although rail and
steam carriage displaced sailing craft on some routes, abundant
evidence documents the competitive strength of sail transport.
Huenemann finds that although railways dominated passenger carriage and the shipment of perishable goods, they failed to displace
general cargo traffic from junk operators traversing nearby waterways. The tendency for general cargo to move along water routes
was "so strong . . . that the proportion of passenger revenues to
total revenues turns out to be a nearly perfect indicator of the degree of water competition a railway faced."[109] In addition to low
rates, flexibility, and convenience, junk transport offered quali-
tative advantages for cargoes in danger of breakage, crushing, or
drying out.[110]

The existence of alternative transport modes was a boon to shippers faced with high transport costs and possible disruption of service. Strong competition from water carriage encouraged railways
to slash freight charges.[111] Shippers also used the existence of alternative routes to force reductions in taxes. In Kiangsi, the arrival
of steamships offered "a wholesome deterrent to likin rapacity"
that had previously inflated the cost of shipments by junk.[112] In
Kiangsu, small motor vessels facilitated tax avoidance by cotton
shippers.[113]

Multiple transport opportunities helped to preserve long-
distance trade in a highly unstable political environment. When
banditry and high taxation threatened commodity shipments along

---

107. *China Industrial Handbooks: Chekiang*, 857–900 and *China Industrial
      Handbooks: Kiangsu*, 995-1026 are filled with examples of products trans-
      ported by sailing craft.
108. *Ta-lung chi ch'i ch'ang ti fa sheng fa chan yü kai tsao* (Shanghai, 1959), 20.
109. Huenemann, *The Dragon and the Iron Horse*, 197.
110. *Shina no janku*, 48–49.
111. Wang, "The Effect of Railroad Transportation," 314.
112. Wright, *Kiangsi Native Trade*, 106.
113. Ting and Tu, "Yü Hsia-ch'ing," 149.

the upper reaches of the Yangtze River, Shanghai merchants diverted yarn shipments to Canton "for forwarding via the West River, Kwangtung and Kwangsi to" destinations in Yunnan and Kweichow.[114] A more significant illustration concerns the disruptions that wracked China's railroads during the mid- and late-1920s, reducing "the once flourishing railway system . . . to a deplorable state of disorganization and bankruptcy."[115] Even though the carriage of agricultural goods on China's system of state-owned railways declined sharply after 1920, there is no sign of retreat from the trend toward increasing commercialization of agriculture.[116] As noted earlier, the decline of rail services did not slow the shipment of west Hopei cotton into Tientsin because "the new mills . . . drew on a combination of old and new cotton-producing centers, linked with the city through a combination of old and new transportation networks. . . . Cotton-growing areas . . . came to rely on a combination of river and rail transport to supply Tianjin [Tientsin]."[117] In other regions as well, traditional transport modes evidently experienced little difficulty in taking up the slack resulting from disruptions of rail or steamship services that accompanied frequent interludes of civil strife, especially during the 1920s.

Summary

This survey of transport and communications has revealed a number of important conclusions. This sector experienced substantial expansion and technological transformation in prewar China. The total haulage of goods, as estimated in Table 4.10, tripled between 1895 and 1936, implying annual growth of roughly 3 percent, a figure which is well ahead of population increase. Both the old and

114. Great Britain, Department of Overseas Trade, *Economic Conditions in China to August 20th, 1930* (London, 1930), 32.
115. Great Britain, Department of Overseas Trade, *Commercial Situation*, 25–26.
116. Data compiled in Yen, *Chung-kuo chin tai ching chi shih*, show that tonnage and turnover of agricultural freight on the national railways reached their highest prewar levels in 1921 and 1920 respectively, with maximum figures for the 1930s amounting to only 88 and 80 percent of the previous peak levels (pp. 211–12). An examination of scattered information for constituent rail lines confirms the validity of these trends.
117. Philip C. C. Huang, *The Peasant Economy and Social Change in North China* (Stanford, 1985), 131.

the new segments of the transport sector participated in prewar expansion. The new segments grew from small beginnings in the late nineteenth century to account for an estimated 40 percent of freight carriage in 1936.

In transport and communication, as with banking, the most dramatic changes occurred in major cities, where the contraction of space could be seen everywhere in the form of railways, trucks, buses, steamships, telegraph and telephone lines, and even aircraft. But in transport, as with finance, the impact of partial modernization spread far beyond the port cities where innovation commenced and progressed furthest. The contrast between urban and rural technology in transport, communication, and other sectors has led some observers to offer the view that the port cities "remained largely separate from . . . the rest of the Chinese economy" and that urban innovations failed to "stimulate new economic activity elsewhere in the country."[118] But in transport, as in finance, detailed investigation shows that the impact of innovation spread far beyond the cities that anchored China's prewar networks for the transfer of commodities, passengers, and information. As Skinner puts it: "Agrarian modernization begins with successive waves of commercialization whose advancing rim is always well ahead of the area served by modern transport."[119] The accumulating evidence about financial integration and interregional price correlations confirms the impact of urban innovations on China's national economy. A 1924 survey of Manchuria illustrates the deepening economic integration characteristic of China's prewar economy, noting that "cereal prices at various points . . . cannot have a separate existence, but must conform to those in the largest grain trade centers, such as Harbin, Changchun and Dairen," which were in turn linked by rail, water, and telegraph lines to grain markets in Central China, the Yangtze valley, and around the Pacific rim.[120]

In the twentieth century, if not earlier, rural-urban transactions and even local village exchange in many regions bear the stamp of forces originating in Shanghai or even in the international market-

---

118. Murphey, *The Outsiders*, 127.
119. G. William Skinner, "Marketing and Social Structure in Rural China," part 2, *Journal of Asian Studies* 24, no. 2 (1965):214.
120. *North Manchuria and the Chinese Eastern Railway*, 121.

place. The price of foodgrains across wide areas of China followed world trends. The prices of cotton, tobacco, oilseeds, mulberry leaves, silkworm eggs, cocoons, tea, soybeans, wool, and many other village products, along with the relative prices of the farmland and village labor that produced these goods, were in part determined by demands emanating from urban factories and trading houses, most of which were located at Shanghai, or international demands mediated through Shanghai-based traders. The prices of kerosene, cotton yarn, cigarettes, matches, and other widely circulated consumer manufactures responded similarly. The prices formed in the Lower Yangtze core set the terms of trade for farmers' transactions in commodity markets throughout the steadily expanding commercially developed regions of China.

Improved transport and communication stimulated a considerable redirection of production toward the market. Here again, simultaneous improvements in exchange facilities resulting from the growth of banking and the spread of fiduciary currency contributed prominently to encouraging economic change. An international comparison of transport intensity shows that the ratio of transport volume to overall production in China during the 1930s closely paralleled conditions in the highly commercialized and substantially integrated American economy of the 1860s.

As in the United States and elsewhere, the reduction of transactions costs arising from innovations in transport, communication, and finance improved the economic circumstances of most citizens by broadening their choices—of occupation, of cropping regime, of location, of trading partners. The large size and wide distribution of benefits arising from these innovations is visible most compellingly in matters of life and death. In the summer of 1921, twenty million residents of drought-stricken North China found themselves "without food or other resources to avoid hunger." In 1876–79, a drought-induced famine covering "practically the same area" had killed 9–13 million people. This tragedy was not repeated:[121]

That the famine of 1920 to 1921 did not result in the death rate such as the earlier one did, is in a large measure due to the railroads which belted

121. *The North China Famine of 1920–1921 with Special Reference to the West Chihli Area* (Peking, 1922), 10, 21; earlier quotations from vii and 7.

almost all sections of the famine area, and made possible the transmission of grain from other sections of China. . . . As a result of this, there was a very large shipment from the markets of Manchuria and Kalgan [Chang-chia-k'ou] to the famine areas. This . . . kept prices of grain down. . . . People who had money to buy grain could do so at fair prices. In the famine of forty years ago this was impossible. This experience offers a great testimony to the value of proper communications.

As Perkins has emphasized, the same transport improvements that increased China's ability to resist regional famines also removed historical constraints on urbanization, which proceeded at an accelerated pace during the first four decades of the present century.[122]

Examining the fortunes of communities that failed to benefit from transport innovation offers another perspective on the significance of these developments. In many regions, towns located on new railway lines prospered while nearby nonrailway communities suffered relative, if not absolute, economic decline.[123] Even in regions blessed with vibrant commercial systems, isolation could restrict incomes to dismally low levels: "Farms in the Kiangning hsien [county], Kiangsu, area, are near the market town of Chun-hwa, about fifteen kilometers southeast of Nanking. Transportation is by donkey chiefly and is so uneconomical that prices of farm products are necessarily low compared with the market price in Nanking."[124] High transport costs prevented farmers from Hsü-chou (Kiangsu) and Pang-pu (Anhwei) from underselling imported wheat in the nearby Shanghai market; as a result, wheat prices and incomes of wheat farmers in these districts remained low.[125]

The blessing of efficient transport is also reflected in comments on the high economic cost associated with the severing of transport links. Whether caused by nature or man, a reversal of transport innovation sharply curtailed economic welfare:[126]

122. Dwight H. Perkins, *Agricultural Development in China, 1368–1968* (Chicago, 1969), chap. 7.
123. Lieu, *China's Industries and Finance*, 19–20.
124. Quoted in David Faure, "The Rural Economy of Kiangsu Province, 1870–1911," *Journal of the Institute of Chinese Studies of the Chinese University of Hong Kong* 9, no. 2 (1978):405.
125. *Finance and Commerce*, March 4, 1931, 5.
126. Buck, *Chinese Farm Economy*, 16; Huang, *Peasant Economy and Social Change*, 78.

At Laian Hsien [Anhwei] low water in the canal often prevents shipment of the rice crop and when such a condition prevails the price is very low.

As far back as anyone could remember, the villagers [of a northeast Hopei community] had grown fruit, especially pears, for the Manchurian market. Profit-oriented managerial farming had been quite highly developed here until the Japanese closed the Manchurian frontier to trade with China proper in 1931. After that, the village economy . . . declined steadily.

When train service was halted, the prices of goods supplied from outside soared at Paoting.[127]

The benefits of modern transport development were real and important. But it is abundantly clear that prewar China realized only a fraction of the potential for economic advance created by innovations in transport and communication. Political instability, particularly as it affected the operation of railways, was the major reason for the large gap between the actual and the potential impact of transport improvements on China's prewar economy. The shifting currents of Chinese politics meant that traffic along railway lines was interrupted at boundaries separating the control of one military faction from another. Satisfactory arrangements for through traffic were never concluded, largely because militarists refused to permit rolling stock to pass under the control of potential rivals. Even in peacetime, political disunity stunted the growth of domestic trade. As a result, the intensity of railroad utilization in prewar China consistently fell below levels attained even in 1949 and never reached one-third of the figure for 1952 (Table 4.7). In wartime, China's rail lines often became the focus of military activity, with locomotives and rolling stock confiscated or destroyed and normal traffic disrupted. Everywhere in China, the process of specialization and the division of labor, with its attendant increases in productivity, was inhibited by the fear of war or banditry, both of which often deprived farmers, merchants, and craftsmen of the gains from trade.

The full realization of the opportunities arising from prewar reductions in transactions costs awaited the imposition of national unity under a new political order. Whether the significant, but limited, array of new opportunities created by innovations in trans-

127. "Retail Prices in Paoting," *Chinese Economic Bulletin* 11, no. 352 (1927):271.

port, communications, and finance permitted higher levels of per capita output and income in prewar China or merely enabled the teeming populace to hold its own in the face of political turbulence and declining farm size, will be considered in Chapter 6. In any case, the development of transport and communication networks created new economic opportunities the consequences of which are reflected in the rising levels of monetization and commercialization discerned in this and the previous chapter.

Chapter Five

Investment

Having completed a survey of industry, finance, and transport, the three sectors that experienced the broadest development of innovative activity during the prewar decades, I turn to macroeconomic questions. To what extent did the entire Chinese economy feel the impact of the new departures analyzed in the previous chapters? I begin with an analysis of investment.

In the past, economists often argued that a rise in the ratio of saving and investment to total output held the key to accelerated growth of low-income economies. W. Arthur Lewis stated that "the central problem in the theory of economic growth is to understand the process by which a community is converted from being a 5 per cent to a 12 per cent saver"; Walt Rostow identified "a rise in the rate of productive investment from, say, 5% or less to over 10% of national income" as a primary component of economic "take-off," or self-sustaining growth.[1] Although economists now view large increases in saving and investment as neither necessary nor sufficient to initiate a long-term growth process, few would question the assertion that a low-income nation cannot generate sustained expansion of total and per capita production if saving and investment do not surpass the Lewis-Rostow benchmark of 5 percent of total output.

Students of prewar China have relied on the investment esti-

1. W. Arthur Lewis, *The Theory of Economic Growth* (Homewood, 1955), 225–26 and W. W. Rostow, *The Stages of Economic Growth: A Non-Communist Manifesto* (Cambridge, 1965), 39.

mates constructed by K. C. Yeh to assess this important aspect of economic performance. Yeh's figures for the years 1931–36, summarized in Table 5.1, fit closely with the Lewis-Rostow conception of a stagnant economy. The ratio of investment to total output averages just under 5 percent of total output. The figures in Table 5.1 pertain to fixed investment (structures, equipment, and other productive assets with useful lifetimes exceeding one year), but Yeh's figures for total investment (including changes in inventories) yield identical results.[2] With depreciation—the amount needed to offset wear and tear on previously installed fixed assets—occupying 3–4 percent of total output, net fixed investment (excluding depreciation), as measured by Yeh, consistently fell below 2 percent of total output. Low as they are, Yeh's figures indicate higher investment levels than earlier studies, which in many instances show negative totals for annual net investment during 1931–36.[3]

Reference to extremely low capital formation proportions plays a prominent part in interpretations of Chinese economic experience that emphasize the centrality of sweeping social transformation as a prerequisite to economic growth. Slow prewar growth is attributed to low saving and investment, which, in turn, are linked with prewar social formations. Lippit asserts that low rates of return, social instability, and elite consumption patterns all "tended to minimize the actual saving or investment share" of prewar output and insists that "what investment did take place tended to be of an 'unproductive' kind—e.g., investment in luxury housing or in inventories."[4] Further statements by Lippit and Riskin expand on the theme of social obstacles to development:[5]

The class interests opposed to development, although less monolithic than in the imperial era, continued to predominate throughout the Re-

2. K. C. Yeh, "Capital Formation," in *Economic Trends in Communist China*, ed. Alexander Eckstein, Walter Galenson, and Ta-chung Liu (Chicago, 1968), 510.
3. Kung-chia Yeh, "Capital Formation in Mainland China: 1931–36 and 1952–57" (Ph.D. diss., Columbia University, 1964), 109. Negative net investment can occur if total investment falls short of annual depreciation.
4. Victor D. Lippit, *Land Reform and Economic Development in China: A Study of Institutional Change and Development Finance* (White Plains, 1974), 27.
5. Victor D. Lippit, *The Economic Development of China* (Armonk, 1987), 104 and Carl Riskin, *China's Political Economy: The Quest for Development Since 1949* (Oxford, 1987), 32–33.

Table 5.1
K. C. Yeh's Estimates of Fixed Investment, 1931-36
(billion 1933 yuan)

Category	1931	1932	1933	1934	1935	1936
Absolute amounts (billion 1933 yuan)						
1. Gross domestic fixed capital formation (GDFCF)	1.273	1.288	1.417	1.461	1.525	1.688
2. Depreciation	0.980	1.020	1.020	0.970	1.050	1.100
3. Net domestic fixed capital formation (NDFCF)	0.293	0.268	0.397	0.491	0.475	0.588
4. Gross domestic product (GDP)	28.89	29.92	29.83	27.34	29.56	31.39
5. Net domestic product (NDP)	28.60	29.65	29.43	26.85	29.08	30.80
Capital formation proportions (percent)						
6. 100 x GDFCF / GDP	4.4	4.3	4.8	5.3	5.2	5.4
7. 100 x NDFCF / NDP	1.0	0.9	1.3	1.8	1.6	1.9

Source: Kung-chia Yeh, "Capital Formation in Mainland China:
1931-36 and 1952-57" (Ph.D. diss., Columbia University, 1964), 183,
302.

publican period [1912–49]; economic development—or the social change needed to assure it—was not in the objective interest of those who wielded power in society.

Socioeconomic conditions in the villages . . . did hinder investment, innovation, and growth. High rents and increasingly insecure tenancy discouraged investment by tenants, while fragmentation of holdings discouraged technical improvements. . . . Few peasants . . . were willing to trust their fate to an unpredictable market. . . . The clue to this disparity [between potential and actual investment] . . . must be sought in the nature of the traditional rural society.

Chinese authors take the same approach. Wang Hai-po, for example, argues that evidence of low prewar investment "profoundly displays in its economic aspect the extreme rottenness of imperialism, feudalism and bureaucratic capitalism."[6]

These authors, who rely heavily on studies showing low capital formation proportions, deny that the prewar decades witnessed significant gains in output and living standards. There is ample reason to doubt the severity of social constraints on prewar economic expansion. The previous chapters show that Chinese businesses responded quickly to opportunities for productive investment, that conservative obstruction failed to prevent the spread of innovation, and that falling transactions costs encouraged farm households to expand their participation in the marketplace. If these observations are typical of China's entire economy, and not restricted to a few localities, it should be possible to demonstrate that prewar investment was substantially above the small figures reported in Table 5.1. This is the objective of the present chapter, which begins with an analysis of the use of industrial manufactures for investment purposes and proceeds to a more speculative discussion of overall capital formation and savings behavior.

Modern-Oriented Fixed Investment
Method

Quantitative analysis of trends in what I call "modern-oriented" fixed capital formation for prewar China is based on methods adapted from Ingvar Svennilson's study of the interwar European economy. Desirous of making international investment comparisons involving national accounting systems that were both incomplete and methodologically diverse, Svennilson used the geometric mean of separate quantity indexes measuring the apparent consumption of cement and steel as his index of investment activity. The resulting measures fit closely with more elaborate estimates for the United States and Germany.[7]

The present study applies Svennilson's insights about the close

6. Wang Hai-po, "Proportional Relations Between Accumulation and Consumption," in *Chung-kuo ching chi chieh kou wen t'i yen chiu*, ed. Ma Hung and Sun Hsiang-ch'ing (Peking, 1981), 2:565.

7. Ingvar Svennilson, *Growth and Stagnation in the European Economy* (Geneva, 1954), 227–30. Apparent consumption or domestic disappearance, calculated by subtracting exports from the sum of domestic production and im-

association between aggregate investment and physical consumption of investment goods to prewar China. My index of modern-oriented gross domestic fixed capital formation (GDFCF) is the geometric mean of separate indexes showing the apparent consumption of cement, iron and steel products, and machinery. Machinery is included as a separate component because of the predominance of imports in apparent consumption and the relative ease of measuring the value of additions to the stock of machinery rather than following Svennilson's method of estimating the steel content of machinery supplies.[8] As with Svennilson's European data, the available measures of Chinese fixed investment, in this case for 1952–57, correspond well to the patterns shown by the less complex index derived from the apparent consumption of a small number of investment goods.[9]

Annual estimates for the value of modern-oriented GDFCF are constructed from time series for the apparent consumption of cement, iron and steel products, and machinery. In each case, the apparent consumption for the nation is calculated as the sum of domestic production and net imports (Equation 5.1). Separate regional estimates for China proper and Manchuria are developed from data on regional production, net imports, and, where possible, interregional commodity shipments (Equations 5.2a and 5.2b). Inventory changes and time lags between production (or importation) and disposition are ignored.

To calculate an annual index of fixed investment, each series of apparent commodity consumption is converted to index-number form with 1933 as the base year. The national (Equation 5.3) or regional (Equations 5.4a and 5.4b) index of modern-oriented gross domestic fixed capital formation, with 1933 = 100, is then calculated as the geometric mean of the three indexes of commodity consumption for each year. The following equations summarize the procedure:

---

ports, refers to the quantity of a commodity absorbed by an economy during a specified period.
8. Including machinery as a separate component introduces an element of double counting in instances when imported iron and steel products are fabricated into machinery. The resulting error, however, is small. See Thomas G. Rawski, "Economic Growth and Integration in Prewar China" (Toronto, 1982), 124.
9. Rawski, "Economic Growth and Integration," appendix D.

(5.1) $A_{int} = Q_{int} + M_{int} - E_{int} = A_{ict} + A_{imt}$

(5.2a) $A_{ict} = Q_{ict} + M_{ict} - E_{ict} + H_{imct} - H_{icmt}$

(5.2b) $A_{imt} = Q_{imt} + M_{imt} - E_{imt} - H_{imct} + H_{icmt}$

(5.3) $J_{nt} = (I_{1nt} I_{2nt} I_{3nt})^{1/3}$

(5.4a) $J_{ct} = (I_{1ct} I_{2ct} I_{3ct})^{1/3}$

(5.4b) $J_{mt} = (I_{1mt} I_{2mt} I_{3mt})^{1/3}$

where $i = 1,2,3$, represent the three commodities; n, c, and m indicate geographic entities: national, China proper, and Manchuria; t is a time subscript; A, Q, E, and M represent apparent consumption, domestic production, exports to foreign countries and imports from foreign countries; H represents domestic interregional trade flows from China to Manchuria (H_{cm}) or from Manchuria to China (H_{mc}); I_{ijt} is an index of apparent consumption of commodity i in region j during year t ($1933 = 100$) and J_{jt} is an index of modern-oriented gross domestic fixed capital formation in region j during year t ($1933 = 100$).

The conversion of these index number measures of national and regional investment to monetary totals in 1933 prices begins by extending the index of modern-oriented fixed capital formation, J_{nt}, to the years 1952–57. If all recorded investment during 1952–57 is assumed to be "modern-oriented" in the sense described above, K. C. Yeh's annual estimates of aggregate fixed capital for 1931–36 and 1952–57 can be used to attach monetary values to the entire series of national totals for modern-oriented GDFCF. The near identity of the 1922 shares for China proper in apparent consumption of cement, iron and steel products, and machinery makes it possible to monetize the regional indexes of modern-oriented GDFCF for China proper and Manchuria.[10] The results are summarized in Table 5.2.

The statistical base for these calculations is good. Foreign trade data, which relate mainly to imports, are taken from the published records of the foreign-administered Chinese Maritime Customs. Given the long prior experience of the Maritime Customs in compiling trade statistics, the concentration of trade in investment goods at the largest ports with the best developed recording sys-

---

10. For details, see Rawski, "Economic Growth and Integration," appendix D. Yeh's investment figures appear in his "Capital Formation in Mainland China," 76a.

Table 5.2
National and Regional Estimates of Modern-Oriented GDFCF, 1903-36

Year	National Index of Apparent Consumption (1933 = 100)				Modern Oriented GDFCF (million 1933 yuan)		
	Cement	Iron-Steel	Machinery	J_{nt}	National	China Proper	Manchuria
1903	1.9	19.5	12.8	7.8	81	76	5
1904	1.4	19.0	12.8	7.0	72	71	1
1905	3.0	21.7	18.3	10.6	110	105	5
1906	4.9	23.6	26.6	14.5	150	145	5
1907	8.6	21.9	27.9	17.4	180	152	28
1908	7.6	23.4	18.6	14.9	154	112	42
1909	9.8	34.1	15.2	17.2	178	142	36
1910	14.1	35.5	20.0	21.6	223	158	65
1911	11.2	25.0	14.9	16.9	166	125	41
1912	13.6	17.9	16.2	15.8	163	120	43
1913	12.2	33.3	19.7	20.0	207	161	46
1914	17.3	34.4	28.9	25.8	267	214	53
1915	16.2	23.0	14.8	17.7	183	139	44
1916	17.4	23.2	32.3	23.5	243	158	85
1917	18.5	18.0	25.0	20.3	210	137	73
1918	19.8	17.5	29.2	21.6	223	134	89
1919	26.7	53.1	55.3	42.8	442	282	160
1920	27.7	52.3	67.4	46.0	476	352	124
1921	34.9	41.9	108.9	54.2	560	442	118
1922	44.5	46.3	114.7	61.8	639	532	107
1923	44.1	32.8	71.6	47.0	486	353	133
1924	39.4	46.8	70.1	50.6	523	358	165
1925	39.9	49.1	62.8	49.7	514	376	138
1926	54.9	59.9	70.2	61.3	634	444	190
1927	52.2	50.8	70.1	57.1	590	388	202
1928	61.1	80.3	76.4	72.1	746	505	241
1929	77.0	89.7	93.3	86.4	893	618	275
1930	72.7	80.6	94.1	82.0	848	613	235
1931	74.9	80.8	89.4	81.5	843	681	162
1932	83.6	84.8	82.7	83.7	865	704	161
1933	100.0	100.0	100.0	100.0	1034	741	293
1934	105.9	137.4	127.5	122.9	1271	741	530
1935	102.0	148.4	127.6	124.5	1287	761	526
1936	133.1	140.1	132.6	135.2	1398	873	525

Source: Rawski, "Economic Growth and Integration," Appendixes A, B, C, and D.

tems, the homogeneous nature of two of the commodity categories used in this study (tons of cement and iron and steel products), and the absence of incentives for smuggling investment goods either to or from China, there can be little doubt that the Maritime Customs figures provide reasonably accurate data on international commodity flows.[11] The manufacture of cement and iron and steel was limited to a small number of plants whose records have been studied in considerable detail. Again, it is difficult to doubt the broad accuracy of available data. The weak links in the estimates of apparent consumption of investment goods lie in the area of domestic machinery manufacture, for which the figures for 1903–30 are little more than conjecture, and interregional trade flows, for which information is often unavailable. But because machinery supplies are dominated by imports throughout the period of analysis and trade in investment goods between China and Manchuria was minuscule, these difficulties do not seriously hamper the application of Svennilson's approach to the problem of estimating a time series of modern-oriented fixed investment in prewar China.[12]

What are the characteristics of the resulting time series estimates of national and regional fixed investment in modern-oriented activities? In principle, all modern-oriented investment effort is included in the calculation, with "modern" defined in terms of the presence of manufactured investment goods, namely cement, iron and steel products, and machinery. Projects that absorb these commodities are included in the estimates no matter what sector of the economy they inhabit and without regard to the nationality of the entrepreneurs involved. Investments in partially

11. Liang-lin Hsiao, *China's Foreign Trade Statistics, 1864–1949* (Cambridge, 1974), 3–16, provides a brief survey of prewar trade data along with references to more detailed evaluations. Rhoads Murphey's argument that the trade figures exaggerate the growth of commodity flows because of expanding geographic coverage and the diversion of goods from unrecorded carriers does not apply to the time period and commodities used in the present study; see *The Outsiders* (Ann Arbor, 1977), chap. 11.
12. The share of domestic production in apparent consumption of machinery at the national level is: for 1905, zero; for 1915, 26.7 percent; for 1925, 35.8 percent; and for 1935, 38.0 percent. Interregional flows of machinery and equipment can be measured only for 1932–36. Shipments of machinery and equipment from China proper reach a peak of 1.6 percent of Manchurian imports of these goods in 1936. See Rawski, "Economic Growth and Integration," appendix C.

mechanized handicrafts, water control projects using concrete structures, or farm purchases of diesel pumps are included to the extent that they absorb the key investment goods used in this study. With close correspondence between the index of modern-oriented gross fixed investment J_{nt} and K. C. Yeh's estimate of fixed investment for 1952–57—with the exception of 1956, an unusual year of "high tide" in investment, J_{nt} differs from an index of Yeh's estimates by 3–11 percent—the new time series appears to provide a reasonable estimate of the annual level and time trend of national and regional modern-oriented GDFCF in China between 1903 and 1936.[13]

This new measure does not include all investment. Modern-oriented GDFCF excludes new fixed assets created without using the key commodities of cement, iron and steel, or machinery. There is also a leakage of investment goods into civilian or military consumption to the extent that motor vehicles, bicycles, or other commodities included in the measure as investment goods were actually used as consumer durables. Although arms and ammunition are not included in machinery imports, the diversion of bicycles, trucks, airplanes, or other machinery to military use would lead to a similar overstatement of investment. In addition, the figures in Table 5.2 incorporate rough and ready adjustments required to bridge gaps in available data, particularly in the estimation of domestic machinery production before 1931. The conversion of the investment index into monetary terms depends on estimates by Liu and Yeh of price shifts between 1933 and 1952; in the case of machinery prices, the empirical foundation of these estimates is weak.

A final problem concerns the identification of modern-oriented fixed investment with the modern sector of China's economy, which is normally taken to include the output of factories, mines, utilities, construction, modern transport and communications,

13. The index J_{nt} amounts to only 78.9 percent of Yeh's estimated index of aggregate fixed investment for 1956 (1952 = 100). However, 1956 was a year of economic "high tide" that foreshadowed the excesses of the "Great Leap" of 1958–60. With great pressure to raise investment achievements, the high 1956 ratio of reported investment outlays to physical consumption of investment goods may reflect weaknesses in the expenditure data underlying Yeh's estimate rather than in my calculations. See Rawski, "Economic Growth and Integration," appendix D.

and a portion of the services sector.[14] The comparison between modern-oriented fixed investment and modern sector output ignores the divergences between the two concepts that arise from the presence of farm tractors, mechanized handicraft equipment, and other instances of modern-oriented investment in traditional sectors of the economy or the continuation of investment activity outside the scope of modern-oriented GDFCF in mining or other areas classified as part of the modern sector.

Although none of these issues appears quantitatively significant, the results in Table 5.2 must be taken as approximations rather than as precise measures of actual investment levels. Even so, the broad agreement between J_{nt} and Yeh's estimates for 1952–57, the general consistency among the commodity indexes, the quality of both the underlying trade statistics for all three investment goods and the domestic output estimates for cement and iron and steel, and the successful outcome of Svennilson's European application of his method all suggest that the estimates summarized in Table 5.2 provide a substantially accurate representation of historic trends in the level and growth of modern-oriented GDFCF in China's prewar economy.

New Estimates of Modern-Oriented
Fixed Investment

New estimates of modern-oriented gross domestic fixed capital formation during the years 1903–36 for China and two geographic components, China proper and Manchuria, are compiled in Table 5.2. These data show that modern-oriented GDFCF experienced a strong upward trend in China proper, Manchuria, and the nation as a whole throughout the period of analysis. In addition, there is a distinct upward break both in the level and, for China proper, in the growth rate of modern-oriented fixed investment beginning immediately after World War I.

The upward trend of modern-oriented fixed investment is a strong one. If annual fluctuations are smoothed by constructing five-year moving averages, the resulting series of smoothed national investment totals declines only twice between 1907 and 1934;

14. Ta-chung Liu and Kung-chia Yeh, *The Economy of the Chinese Mainland* (Princeton, 1965), 87–90.

a similarly smoothed series of private nonagricultural GDFCF in Japan shows eight annual declines during the same years.[15] The increased volume of investment and, for China proper, the acceleration of growth after World War I, are clearly visible in the data. The results in Table 5.2 show that the *average* annual level of fixed investment for the entire nation and each region during 1919–36 was more than 150 percent above the *maximum* level achieved during 1903–18. In each case, the *lowest* annual investment figure for the later period is at least 20 percent above the pre-1919 *peak*. The underlying estimates of national and regional apparent consumption of cement, iron and steel, and machinery tell the same story. Despite considerable annual fluctuations, the post-1918 commodity totals remain above the maximum levels recorded during 1903–18 with few exceptions.

These findings contradict the common interpretation of 1914–18 as a "golden age" for Chinese industrial development. Although the temporary withdrawal of European competition may have enabled fledgling Chinese industrial firms to earn large profits, the accelerated expansion of capacity coincided with the return of normal foreign competition starting in 1919. For sectors that required cement, steel, and machinery to expand their capacity, World War I emerges as a period of unusually low investment. If we create a "dummy variable" D which takes on the value one during the years 1914–18 and zero for other years, its consistently negative coefficient in regression equations of the following form (with t-statistics in parentheses):

$$ln(J_{ct}) = -132.42 + 0.071t - 0.365D \quad (R^2 = 0.94)$$
$$(-19.5) \quad (20.1) \quad (-3.7)$$

indicates that the war years dragged modern-oriented GDFCF, in this case for China proper during 1903–36, below its long-term trend line.

The measures of investment growth displayed in Table 5.3 confirm both the rapid growth of modern-oriented GDFCF and its post–World War I acceleration in China proper. Although the high prewar growth rate for Manchurian investment, which began from

15. See Rawski, "Economic Growth and Integration," table 2 and Kazushi Oh-kawa and Henry Rosovsky, *Japanese Economic Growth: Trend Acceleration in the Twentieth Century* (Stanford, 1973), 294.

a tiny initial base and reflected the active development of major projects in railway construction and ferrous metallurgy, was not maintained during 1919–36, the upward break in the level of investment was so large that the growth rate for modern-oriented GDFCF over the entire period 1903–36 is considerably higher for the nation and for China proper than during either the pre- or post–World War I subperiods.

Table 5.3 compares growth rates for modern-oriented fixed investment in China and its two major regions with data for several Japanese investment aggregates. The results form a fairly consistent pattern: during the early portion of the period up to and including World War I, investment growth tended to be more rapid in Japan than in China. After 1918, however, the relation is reversed. Chinese investment outgrew the Japanese aggregates by a large margin. If the entire period 1903–36 is examined, the Chinese measures retain a substantial advantage. The Manchurian data form an exception to this pattern, with the rate of investment growth falling sharply after World War I. This is not surprising since modern-oriented fixed investment in Manchuria was dominated by Japanese projects and in part represents an extension of Japan's domestic economy.

These comparisons overstate Chinese investment performance because the Chinese data are restricted to modern-oriented fixed investment whereas aggregate fixed investment on the Japanese side includes investment outlays associated with agriculture and other slow-growing industries. This bias may be reduced by focusing on the Japanese figures for private nonagricultural investment (Line B3) and fixed investment in what economists refer to as the M+ sector (mining, manufacturing, construction, utilities, transport, and communication; Line B4). These aggregates contain some slow-growing elements like residential construction and handicraft investments that would fall outside the scope of modern-oriented fixed investment on the Chinese side, but the share of these activities is small. To further sharpen the comparison, it is perhaps appropriate to focus on investment activity in China proper on the grounds that Manchurian investment behavior is linked as much to Japanese as to Chinese economic trends.

Restricting the comparison to Japanese performance in increasing private, nonagricultural fixed investment or fixed investment

Table 5.3
Average Annual Growth Rate for Fixed Investment, China and Japan, 1903-36
(percent)

Fixed Investment Region or Category	1903-18	1919-36	1903-36
A. China: Modern-oriented GDFCF			
1. National total	6.4	6.5	8.1
2. China proper	3.6	5.7	7.3
3. Manchuria	22.7	8.0	12.7
B. Japan: GDFCF			
1. Aggregate	5.8	1.8	4.4
2. Private sector	5.0	2.5	3.7
3. Private nonagricultural	9.9[a]	2.0	4.6[a]
4. Mining, manufacturing, construction & facilitating industries	8.8[a]	2.6[a]	5.0[a]

Note: Calculated from linear regressions of the form $\ln Y_t = a + bt$, where the Y variables are listed in the rows of the table and t represents time.

[a]Series begins in 1905.

Sources: The values of Y for Lines A1-A3 are from Table 5.2. For Lines B1-B2, see Kazushi Ohkawa and Miyohei Shinohara, eds., Patterns of Japanese Economic Development (New Haven, 1979), 355-56, 359-61. For Lines B3-B4, see Ohkawa and Rosovsky, Japanese Economic Growth, 294. All Japanese data are in constant 1934-36 prices.

in the M+ sector and China's achievements in raising modern-oriented fixed investment in China proper eliminates much of the bias enhancing the relative growth of fixed investment in China. The results of this more balanced comparison, however, are essentially the same as before. Again, investment grows more rapidly in Japan before 1919 and in China thereafter. Over the whole period, the Chinese aggregate substantially outperforms the Japanese series.

These comparisons indicate that, at least with regard to the "modern-oriented" activities associated with the use of cement, iron and steel products, and modern machinery, China experienced a significant investment spurt during the prewar decades. Modern-oriented fixed investment grew more rapidly than comparable Japanese aggregates, especially after World War I. By the 1930s, the scale of modern-oriented fixed investment in China proper matched Japanese investment in the roughly comparable category of mining, manufacturing, construction, and facilitating industries.[16] What can be said of the level and trend of overall investment in prewar China? To answer this question requires consideration of investments conducted without the use of cement, steel, and machinery.

Nonmodern Fixed Investment: Speculative Estimates

The preceding discussion of modern-oriented fixed investment draws on solidly based quantitative indicators of production and trade. Extending these results requires an excursion into areas lacking suitably detailed quantitative material to seek out indications of the order of magnitude of investment activity in agriculture, residential housing, unmechanized transport, and other areas in which capital formation involved little or no use of factory-produced investment goods.

Investment in Agriculture

Despite reports that some farmers, particularly in the prosperous south Kiangsu regions near Shanghai, used diesel-powered pumps, electric rice mills, and even imported tractors, the vast majority of agricultural investment remains outside the estimates of modern-oriented fixed capital formation.[17] I divide farm investment into separate categories of depreciation and new or net investment.

Agricultural Depreciation. The sole estimate of depreciation in farming appears to be that of Liu and Yeh, who assign 2 percent of

16. Rawski, "Economic Growth and Integration," table 7.
17. The use of tractors and mechanical pumps is described in *Andersen, Meyer & Company Limited of China. Its History: Its Organization Today* (Shanghai, 1931) and *Shanhai tokubetsushi Kateiku nōson jittai chōsa hōkokusho* (Shanghai, 1940), 64, 69, 76–77.

1933 farm output value to this category.[18] The 2 percent figure comes from J. L. Buck's farm surveys of the early 1920s, which reported a "decrease of capital" amounting to an average of 2 percent of "total farm receipts."[19] Unfortunately, changes in the value of "capital" as defined in Buck's survey bear no relation to the economic concept of depreciation. Buck's "capital" category includes land, rent deposits, feed, seeds, other supplies, trees, farm buildings, tools, and livestock, of which only the portion of land value derived from man-made improvements (fencing, irrigation channels, etc.) represents a depreciable asset. With land occupying three-fourths of Buck's "capital" figures, increases or decreases in this category (which may reflect changes in rent deposits, mortgage arrangements, the purchase or sale of feed, seed, fertilizer, or tools, the planting or felling of trees, and the purchase, sale, or construction of farm buildings), cannot be expected to yield even the most approximate measure of depreciation.[20]

Having rejected the figure proposed by Liu and Yeh, I turn for an alternative to data for Meiji Japan, where crop mix, farm technology, and income levels roughly paralleled conditions in prewar China. Japanese scholars have derived annual depreciation estimates from farm surveys that show the value and average lifetime of livestock, trees, tools, and farm buildings.[21] The results, summarized in Table 5.4, show that the ratio of depreciation to total output value varied from 9.5 to 11.7 percent between 1895 and 1935. In the absence of similar results based on Chinese farm surveys, these Japanese data offer a guide for estimating depreciation in China's farm sector.[22] Because the Japanese data exclude additions to the agricultural capital stock resulting from land improvement and water control projects carried out under government auspices as well as by individual households, the figures in Table 5.4 undoubtedly understate the ratio of depreciation to total farm

18. Liu and Yeh, *Economy of the Chinese Mainland*, 419.
19. John L. Buck, *Chinese Farm Economy: A Study of 2,866 Farms in Seventeen Localities and Seven Provinces in China* (Chicago, 1930), 65, 75.
20. Buck, *Chinese Farm Economy*, 57–66.
21. Umemura Mataji et al., *Nōringyō* (Tokyo, 1966), 214, 252–53.
22. Chinese data similar to those employed in Japanese studies of agricultural depreciation exist in numerous sources, including Buck, *Chinese Farm Economy*, 57–67; *Kita Shina ni okeru mensakuchi nōson jijō (Kahokushō Tsūken Kokaison)* (Tientsin, 1936), 74–82; and *Kōsōshō Sōkōken nōson jittai chōsa hōkokusho* (Shanghai, 1940), appendix table 7.

Investment

Table 5.4

Cost and Input Structure for Japanese Agriculture, 1895-1935

	1895	1905	1915	1925	1935	Growth, 1915-35 Cumulative (%)	Annual Rate (%)
1. Depr/GVAO[a]	.111	.117	.095	.095	.105	10.5	0.5
2. Net Capital/ Gross VA[b]	1.58	1.40	1.24	1.22	1.20	-(3.2)	-(0.2)
Per farm worker amount of[c]							
3. Land (tan)[d]	3.57	3.81	4.19	4.30	4.47	6.7	0.3
4. Current inputs[e] A. Total	20.2	23.6	32.0	40.2	49.3	54.1	2.2
B. Agric. origin	12.8	13.2	14.2	13.4	13.6	-(4.2)	-(0.2)
C. Nonagric. origin	7.4	10.4	17.8	26.8	35.7	100.6	3.5
5. Net capital[f]	175	185	203	213	230	13.3	0.6
6. Gross value added[g]	111	132	164	174	192	17.1	0.8

Source: Umemura Mataji, Nōringyō, 152-53, 214, 228-29.

Notes: All monetary totals are in constant prices of 1934-36. The figures in parentheses indicate negative percentage changes and growth rates.

[a]Line 1: The ratio of depreciation to total value of farm output (GVAO).

[b]Line 2: The ratio of net capital to gross value added.

[c]Seven-year moving averages. Except as noted, the figures show yen per worker.

[d]Line 3: Arable land per worker gainfully occupied in farming. 1 tan = 0.245 acre.

[e]Line 4: The value of current farm inputs: total (4A) or agriculturally-based (4B) per worker gainfully occupied in farming.

[f]Line 5: The net capital per worker gainfully occupied in farming.

[g]Line 6: The gross value added per worker gainfully occupied in farming.

output.[23] Even so, to avoid possible overstatement of Chinese investment levels, I shall assume that depreciation amounted to 7 percent of the total value of prewar Chinese farm output.

Net Investment in Agriculture.   The expansion of output normally requires new fixed investments beyond the depreciation expenses that offset the declining productivity of aging tools, buildings, trees, and animals. The literature on prewar Chinese agriculture offers many examples of net agricultural investment. The spread of tobacco cultivation required farmers to construct drying houses at a cost of 53–80 yuan per *mou* of tobacco land.[24] The growing labor intensity associated with the cultivation of cotton, tobacco, and other cash crops required greater use of both draft animals and hand tools. An increasing market orientation necessitated the expansion of storage and transport capability, including that maintained by farmers themselves.

How can one trace the aggregate consequences of these changes? In Chapter 6, I conclude that agricultural labor productivity, as measured by competitively determined farm wages, increased at an annual rate of approximately 0.8 percent between 1914/18 and 1931/36 (Table 6.11). This implies substantial net agricultural investment during the prewar decades. For suggestions of how much net investment might have occurred, I turn again to comparison with Japan.

Farm output reflects the combined use of land, current inputs (fertilizer, water, seed), fixed capital, technology, and labor. Table 5.5 compares available data on farm input and output per man-year for interwar agriculture in China and Japan. Arable land per farm worker rose in Japan and declined in China. Current inputs per farm worker rose steeply in Japan. Although there are no comparable data for China, I anticipate that, with farm-based inputs predominating (as in nineteenth-century Japan), the growth of current input per worker must be lower in China than in Japan. Assuming equal growth of current input per worker surely exaggerates the

23. Kazushi Ohkawa, "Phases of Agricultural Development and Economic Growth," in *Agriculture and Economic Growth: Japan's Experience*, ed. Kazushi Ohkawa, Bruce F. Johnston, and Hiromitsu Kaneda (Princeton, 1970), 23–24.
24. Han-seng Chen, *Industrial Capital and Chinese Peasants* (New York, 1980), 58.

Table 5.5
Farm Input and Output Per Worker in Prewar China and Japan
ca. 1914/18 - 1931/36

	China	Japan
Land per worker	decline of 2-7% (-0.1 to -0.4% per year)	increase of 6.7% (+0.3% per year)
Current inputs per worker Farm origin organic fertilizer, etc.	?	decline of 4% (-0.2% per year)
Nonfarm origin chemical fertilizer, machinery, etc.	?	increase of 101% (+3.5% per year)
Total	assume identical with Japan	increase of 54% (+2.2% per year)
Net capital per worker	with relatively slow technical change, should exceed Japanese figure; assume 0.6% annual growth	increase of 13.3% (+0.6% per year)
Gross value added per worker	increase of 15% (+0.8% per year)	increase of 17% (+0.8% per year)

Sources: Japanese data: Based on seven-year moving averages, centered on 1915 and 1935, from Table 5.4. Chinese data: Land per worker is based on the cultivated area for 1913 and 1933 shown in Dwight H. Perkins, Agricultural Development in China, 1368-1968 (Chicago, 1969), 236 and the alternative population totals for 1914/18 and 1931/36 shown in Table 6.3. Current input and net capital per worker: see text. Gross value added per worker is from Chapter 6.

availability of resources to Chinese farmers. The rate of technical progress in Japanese farming, with its extensive network of agricultural experimentation and farm extension services, surely surpassed comparable developments in China, where political unrest, weak industry associations, and the impotence of the state inhibited the spread of long-staple cotton, disease-free silkworm eggs, and other productivity-enhancing innovations.[25]

25. Limited diffusion of new agricultural methods is evident in T. S. Chu and T. Chin, *Marketing of Cotton in Hopei Province* (Peiping, 1929), 29, who note "few tangible results" in cotton improvement. Lillian M. Li, *China's Silk Trade: Traditional Industry in the Modern World, 1842–1937* (Cambridge, 1981), 198–206, contrasts the superior performance of Japan's silk industry with slow progress in China. Ramon H. Myers, "Wheat in China—Past, Pres-

Reproducible capital (excluding land) is the remaining category. In Japan, rising labor productivity in farming was supported by improved technology and increases in the amounts of all inputs—land, current inputs, and capital—available to the average farm worker. In China, where the growth of farm labor productivity matched the Japanese results shown in Table 5.5, arable land per farm worker declined, technical progress was relatively slow, and increases in current inputs at best equalled and more probably lagged well behind Japan's. Under these circumstances, it is most likely that net capital per farm worker rose more rapidly in China than in Japan. At a minimum, I assume that net capital per Chinese farm worker rose at the same 0.6 percent rate shown for Japan in Table 5.5.

The ratio between net capital and gross value added in Japanese agriculture clustered around 1.2 between 1915 and 1935 (Table 5.4); the same figure emerges from Buck's Chinese survey data for the early 1920s.[26] To avoid possible overestimate of capital requirements, I assign a value of 1.0 to the agricultural capital-output ratio.

These results permit an estimate of net annual agricultural investment for 1931–36 and 1914–18. With a capital-output ratio of 1.0, the stock of farm capital is identical with the annual total of gross value added, which is taken from K. C. Yeh's estimates for 1931–36 and derived for 1914–18 by applying the rate of output growth obtained in Table 6.11. Annual net investment is the amount required to raise capital per farm worker by 0.6 percent each year. Observing no evidence of substantial change in the ratio of labor force to population or farm workers to overall employment, I assume that the farm labor force grew at the same rate as the

---

ent and Future," *China Quarterly* 74 (1978):318, observes that pre-1949 efforts failed to create a workable extension system that could deliver the results of "scientific research on wheat to [Chinese] farmers."

26. Buck, *Chinese Farm Economy*, 57, 65. Buck's 2,866 farms reported an average capital (buildings, livestock, trees, and farm equipment) of 400.02 yuan; average farm receipts (including off-farm sales and self-consumed farm produce but excluding "increase of capital") amounted to 368.62 yuan, which is converted to gross value added by applying the 1933 coefficient of 0.906 derived in Liu and Yeh, *Economy of the Chinese Mainland*, 140.

entire population, 0.6 percent per year.[27] The results appear in Line 2A-2 of Table 5.6.

Nonmodern Investment Outside Agriculture

What can be said of nonagricultural investment that used no cement, iron and steel, or manufactured machinery? This category includes the construction and renovation of housing, the fabrication of sailboats, carts, and other unmechanized transport equipment, the manufacture of wooden tools for craft use, and the application of nonmanufactured materials and manual techniques to build roads, bridges, canals, and nonagricultural water management projects. The work of K. C. Yeh provides data on handicraft capital goods as well as partial coverage of residential construction.

Yeh estimates the annual production of handicraft capital goods during 1931/36 at 0.12 billion yuan.[28] I add transport equipment (sailboats, barrows, carts), the largest component, to the fixed investment total together with one-third of the value included in Yeh's nontransport categories; the results appear in Line 2B of Table 5.6. The remaining amounts are excluded because I have already considered net investment in agriculture, which contributed roughly two-thirds of total output during the prewar decades.

Turning to the housing sector, Yeh finds that repairs amounted to roughly 10 percent of the value of actual and imputed rentals, of which half represents major alterations that should be included in fixed capital formation. Yeh also assumes that depreciation of residential buildings is equivalent to 10 percent of actual and imputed rental.[29] I follow Yeh in assigning 5 percent of residential rents, which Yeh estimates at an annual average of 1.04 billion yuan during 1931–36, to major alterations and 10 percent to depreciation (Lines 2C-1 and 2C-2 of Table 5.6).[30]

27. I use the lower of the alternative growth rates shown in Table 6.11 for both agricultural output growth (preferred variant) and population (Version B). Use of higher growth rates for population and farm output produces slightly higher investment totals.

28. Yeh, "Capital Formation in Mainland China," 312. Data are in 1933 prices.

29. Yeh, "Capital Formation in Mainland China," 262, 314.

30. Average rental total, in 1933 prices, is from K. C. Yeh, "China's National Income, 1931–36," in Modern Chinese Economic History, ed. Chi-ming Hou and Tzong-shian Yu (Taipei, 1979), 97.

Lack of information necessitates the omission of additional fixed investment categories, of which the construction of roads and housing is perhaps most significant.

Investment and Saving in China's Prewar Economy: Overall Results

The limited information about overall capital formation is summarized in Table 5.6. With the objective of demonstrating that the level of capital formation was well above the range considered in previous studies, it is important to ensure that the numerous assumptions required to obtain the speculative figures for agriculture, crafts, and housing reported in Line 2 of Table 5.6 do not exaggerate the scale of investment. At every turn, my assumptions force estimated investment *below* what would appear reasonable. Agricultural depreciation is taken as 7 percent of the gross value of agricultural output vs. 9–12 percent (or higher) in Japan; net capital per farm worker is assumed to grow at the same rate as in Japan, even though, with land per worker falling, slow technical change, and the probable slow growth of current inputs, faster capital deepening was probably required to achieve comparable growth of farm labor productivity. I use the lower of alternative figures for population growth; this reduces calculated net farm investment by lowering the estimated growth of the farm labor force. Because of these assumptions and also because there are no figures for certain segments of investment, notably residential construction and road building, both of which used neither cement nor steel, the results should, if anything, understate the actual level of fixed investment during 1931–36.

The outcome of this analysis, summarized in Table 5.6, shows that gross domestic capital formation during the period 1931–36 surpassed 10 percent of gross domestic product, more than double the 4.9 percent ratio reported in K. C. Yeh's study (Table 5.1). Omissions and restrictive assumptions impart a downward bias to this ratio. One plausible revision of these calculations, raising the rate of agricultural depreciation from 7 to 9 percent of farm output, would raise the fixed investment-GDP ratio to 11.7 percent. The inclusion of omitted items could easily raise fixed investment to 12 or 13 percent of gross domestic product during 1931–36.

Table 5.6
Gross Domestic Fixed Capital Formation, 1914/18 and 1931/36
(annual averages, billion yuan, 1933 prices)

	1914/18	1931/36	Average Annual Growth Rate
1. Modern-oriented	0.225	1.116	9.6%
2. Nonmodern	...	1.887	...
A. Agriculture	1.282	1.636	1.4
1. Depreciation	1.110	1.416	1.4
2. Net investment	0.172	0.220	1.4
B. Craft Capital Goods	...	0.095	...
C. Residential	...	0.156	...
1. Depreciation	...	0.104	...
2. Major repairs	...	0.052	...
3. Total GDFCF	...	3.003+	...
4. GDP, 1933 PRICES	22.84	29.13	1.4
5. GDFCF/GDP (percent) A. Aggregate	...	10.3+	...
B. Partial: Items 1 and 2A only	6.6	9.4	...

Sources and notes: Line 1: Table 5.2. Lines 2, 2A, 2C, 3: the sum of
the components. Line 2A-1: 7 percent of the gross value of agricultural
output or, using the 90.6 percent rate of value added in Liu and Yeh,
Economy of the Chinese Mainland, 140, 7.73 percent of gross value added,
for which the 1931/36 average is taken from K. C. Yeh, "China's National
Income, 1931-36," in Modern Chinese Economic History, ed. Chi-ming Hou and
Tzong-shian Yu (Taipei, 1979), 97, and the 1914/18 average is calculated
by applying the average agricultural growth rate of 1.4 percent (low
population variant) from Table 6.11 over a period of 17.5 years. Line 2A-
2: the initial capital stock is assumed equal to the annual gross value
added for agriculture, with net investment equal to 1.2 percent of the
initial stock (see text). Line 2B: 1931/36 average for full amount of
handicraft transport equipment plus one-third of other craft capital goods
tabulated in Yeh, "Capital Formation in Mainland China," 312. Line 2C-1:
assumed equal to 10 percent of actual and imputed residential rentals as
estimated in ibid., 262, 314. Line 2C-2: major repairs are assumed equal
to 5 percent of actual and imputed residential rents (ibid.). Line 4:
Table 6.14 (based on population 2).

Whatever the precise figures, I conclude that China's prewar
economy generated substantial investment flows, with capital formation proportions attaining levels far above the low figures presented in earlier studies. Despite the inhibiting effect of extreme
uncertainty, the ratio of gross fixed investment to gross domestic

Table 5.7
Chinese and Japanese Capital Formation Proportions
(ratio of gross domestic fixed capital formation to gross domestic product)

Year	China	Japan
1885	...	0.090
1895	...	0.105
1905	...	0.132
1914/18	...	0.150
1925	...	0.168
1931/36	0.104+	0.171

Source: for China, Table 5.6. For Japan, Ohkawa and
Shinohara, eds., _Patterns of Japanese Economic Development_,
279-80 and 357-61.

product during 1931–36 surpassed the 10 percent mark. Political stability might well have raised prewar capital formation proportions above the levels recorded during the 1950s.[31] The comparison of partial results for 1914–18 with corresponding figures for 1931–36 (Line 5B of Table 5.6) suggests a rising trend for prewar capital formation proportions. Because, as noted above, the war years 1914–18 appear to represent an interlude of abnormally low investment, at least in the modern sector, one must be wary of assuming a steady increase in the ratio of fixed investment to total output. The comparison of these estimates for Chinese fixed investment ratios with the Japanese data presented in Table 5.7 indicates that the Chinese figures for the 1930s, while falling short of contemporaneous Japanese investment ratios, are roughly comparable with Japanese achievements of two or three decades earlier.

How was this investment financed? In the 1930s, the contribution of foreign savings was small. The balance of payments data compiled by Yu-kuei Cheng make it possible to estimate the net inflows of investable funds for 1931–36. The calculations, summarized in Table 5.8, yield an annual average of 121.8 million yuan. Because Cheng's data exclude Manchuria beginning with 1932, I

31. Using 1933 prices, K. C. Yeh finds that gross domestic capital formation amounted to 18.2 percent of China's gross domestic product during 1952–57 ("Capital Formation," 510).

Table 5.8
Sources of Investable Funds, Annual Average, 1931-36

| | Amount | | Share[a] |
	(million Hai-kuan taels)	(million yuan)	(percent)
1. Annual fixed investment, 1931-36		3003	100.0
2. Foreign sources of funds		488	16.2
A. China Proper[b]			
1. Overseas Chinese remittances	HKT163.8		
2. New foreign business investment	33.8[c]		
3. Outward remittances by foreigners	-(0.6)[d]		
4. Profit remitted by foreign business	-(24.3)[e]		
5. Capital flight	-(93.6)[f]		
Total: 1 + 2 - (3 + 4 + 5) (million Hai-kuan taels)	79.1		
Total: (million Chinese yuan)		121.8[g]	
B. Manchuria: modern-oriented GDFCF		366.2	
3. Domestic sources of funds		2515	83.7

Sources: Line 1: Table 5.6. Lines 2A-1 to 2A-5: Yu-kwei Cheng, Foreign Trade and Industrial Development of China (Washington, D.C., 1956), 260. Line 2B: Table 5.2. Line 3 is a residual.

[a]Column totals may not check because of rounding error.

[b]These figures include Manchurian totals for 1931 only.

[c]The average for five years only; the source presents no data for 1935. Data for 1933 and 1934 include foreign loans to the Chinese government.

[d]Data are available only for 1932.

[e]An average based on 1931-35 only; 1936 data include freight and insurance fees.

[f]The data cover 1934-36 only; I assume no capital flight during 1931-33.

[g]Converted at 1.55 Chinese yuan (dollars) per tael.

supplement his results (Line 2A) by assuming that all modern-oriented fixed investment in Manchuria during 1931–36 was financed from abroad. Even though this exaggerates the contribution of external funds, the resulting total of 488 million yuan amounts to only one-sixth of the estimated annual fixed investment of 3.041 billion yuan for the years 1931–36.

These crude results may not accurately reflect the impact of external funds on domestic investment. On the one hand, overseas Chinese remittances, the largest category of funds flowing into China proper, sometimes supported relatives' consumption in the migrants' home communities rather than financing investments. On the other hand, foreign-controlled funds available for investment included the retained earnings of businesses conducted in China as well as the amounts listed in Table 5.8. Nonetheless, the findings summarized in Table 5.8 show conclusively that domestic savings provided the major source of funding for Chinese investment during 1931–36. This is true not only of overall investment, but even for modern-oriented fixed investment in China proper, where a crude measure of investable funds from abroad for 1931–36 (Line 2A in Table 5.8) amounts to only one-sixth of average modern-oriented fixed investment in the same period (Table 5.2). The commanding position of domestic savings is perhaps not surprising in view of the large share of agriculture in overall investment (Line 2A, Table 5.6) and the limited involvement of foreign investment in farming.

Although there is less information for earlier years, the small size of modern-oriented investment and the correspondingly larger share of agricultural projects in the (unknown) investment total suggest a relatively modest role for overseas funds in financing domestic investment during earlier periods as well as the 1930s. The same data can be used to show that the marginal propensity to save, which describes the fraction of each increment to income that is withheld from consumption, was high, contradicting assertions that poverty and the maldistribution of wealth rendered the Chinese public unable or, in the case of rich households, unwilling to accumulate savings.

Following Table 5.6, I assume that fixed investment rose from 7 to 11 percent of total output between 1914/18 and 1931/36. Investment is necessarily equal to total savings, which can come from domestic or foreign sources. Domestic savings may be derived, as in Table 5.8, by subtracting foreign savings from estimated investment. For 1914/18, I assume the supply of foreign savings to be equal to the average for 1912 and 1913. An annual figure of $82.5 million (1933 prices) is derived as the difference between inflows and outflows of international remittances, foreign borrowing by China's government, and new foreign business investment.[32] This result, together with the GDP estimates in Tables 6.13 and 6.14, implies that the average propensity to save (the ratio of domestic saving to total output) increased from 6.6 to 10.7 percent between 1914/18 and 1931/36 and that the marginal propensity to save (the ratio of extra saving to extra output) was 20.9 percent.

Even though these calculations, like many studies of savings in low-income nations, are crude approximations, the general picture is clear. Despite low living standards, Chinese households and businesses saved a modest fraction of their current income. When income increased, savings rose much faster, resulting in a significant increase in the average propensity to save even in the absence of political stability and public policies intended to promote domestic savings, factors that development specialists regard as important determinants of savings behavior.[33] Given the small size of the modern sector and the large fraction of investment directed toward farming, it is difficult to doubt that farmers, landlords, and craftsmen contributed substantially to the rapidly expanding pool of domestic savings.

A final point concerns the regional distribution of investment. The tendency for innovative activities to cluster in a few locations, particularly Shanghai and southern Liaoning province, is widely remarked, and for good reason. Nearly 55 percent of 1933 factory

32. Nai-ruenn Chen, "China's Balance of Payments: The Experience of Financing a Long-term Trade Deficit in the Twentieth Century," in *Modern Chinese Economic History*, ed. Chi-ming Hou and Tzong-shian Yu (Taipei, 1979), 411–13. Figures in U.S. dollars are converted to Chinese yuan using the *tael* exchange rates shown in Hsiao, *Foreign Trade Statistics*, 191–92 and the conversion of 1.55 Haikuan *taels* per standard dollar. The resulting annual average of $130.2 million was converted to 1933 prices using the Nan-k'ai index of wholesale price change between 1913 and 1933 shown in *Shang-hai chieh fang ch'ien hou wu chia tzu liao hui pien, 1921–1957* (Shanghai, 1958), 175.

33. Malcolm Gillis et al., *Economics of Development* (New York, 1983), chap. 11.

output originated in Shanghai and Manchuria; Shanghai alone claimed over half of China's stock of cotton spindles and annual production of rubber, silk cloth, castings, and glass.[34] The prominence and rapid growth of manufacturing and the accumulations of wealth in major cities, especially Shanghai, has led to the belief that interior agrarian regions derived little or no benefit from urban development. Rather than recount the many instances in which innovations in urban-based manufacturing, banking, transport, or communications benefited localities far removed from coastal urban centers, information about internal trade patterns can serve to document the existence of important financial flows from the cities to finance economic expansion in the interior.[35]

With manufacturing output in and around major cities growing much faster than agricultural or handicraft production in nonindustrial regions that purchased ever larger quantities of manufactures, the domestic balance of trade turned emphatically against nonindustrial regions during the early decades of the twentieth century. This result is visible from a survey of trade in Kwangsi province which records (largely domestic) "imports" and "exports" at the county level, revealing a combined annual import surplus of 5.2 million yuan for the eighty-nine counties investigated.[36]

In domestic, as in international, trade, such a deficit can be offset or "financed" by currency transfers from deficit to surplus regions or by capital flows from surplus to deficit regions in the form of loans or investments. Did Shanghai "drain the wealth" of nonindustrial regions by extracting large flows of currency in return for growing shipments of manufactures? Despite the extensive publicity given to statistics of silver flows into the great metropolis, this seems most improbable. By reducing the money stock in deficit regions, large annual currency drains (five million yuan in the case of Kwangsi) would have induced regional deflation and led to higher interest rates and lower commodity prices, output, incomes, and interregional imports in deficit regions. The simultaneous influx of funds into surplus areas would lead to lower interest

34. Rawski, "Economic Growth and Integration," table 8.
35. The following passage draws on Thomas G. Rawski, "The Economy of the Lower Yangtze Region, 1850–1980" (Toronto, 1984).
36. *Kuang-hsi sheng ko hsien ch'u ju ching ta tsung huo wu kai k'uang* (n.p., 1934).

---

rates and rising commodity prices that would further impede sales of manufactures into the deficit regions. Since many accounts point to an interregional convergence rather than divergence of prices and interest rates in prewar China, one must conclude that domestic interregional trade imbalances were financed not by currency drain from the deficit regions, but by return flows of capital from the surplus regions in the form of loans and direct investments in such areas as Kwangsi province.[37] Thus the benefits of modern-sector growth were spread widely (although by no means evenly) across China's landscape despite the concentration of factories and other modern innovations in a few coastal cities. Here again, the large share of agriculture in the investment totals (Table 5.6) fits well with the view of a regionally dispersed investment effort and poorly with alternative approaches.

Conclusion

Previous studies have identified extremely low levels of domestic saving and investment as fundamental obstacles to the prewar development of China's economy. This chapter demonstrates that, even in the face of extreme uncertainty, China's prewar economy generated considerable flows of investments, most of which were financed from domestic savings. A new measure of modern-oriented fixed investment, based on methods initially applied to interwar Europe, reveals strong upward investment momentum beginning as early as 1903, with sharp acceleration evident in China proper after World War I. Also, World War I emerges as a period of abnormally low investment rather than a "golden age" for new enterprise.

Lacking detailed data, more speculative procedures are needed to obtain crude estimates for major investment categories that did not employ the key goods—cement, steel, and machinery—used to measure modern-oriented fixed investment. My results, which probably understate the level of investment effort, show that the

37. On the convergence of prices and interest rates, see Loren Brandt, "Chinese Agriculture and the International Economy, 1870s-1930s: A Reassessment," *Explorations in Economic History* 22 (1985); *North Manchuria and the Chinese Eastern Railway* (Harbin, 1924), 121; and the materials cited in the section on "Financial Development and Economic Integration" in Chapter 3.

gross fixed investment of all types surpassed one-tenth and perhaps reached one-seventh of total output during 1931–36. Incomplete figures indicate that even for 1914–18, the ratio of fixed investment to total output was considerably above the 5 percent level envisioned by earlier studies of the 1930s. Reference to comparable Japanese figures shows that China's prewar ratio of investment to output had reached levels that, several decades previously, had enabled Japan to embark on a notably successful path of economic modernization.

Together with information on the inflow of foreign savings, estimates of investment spending can be used to calculate crude measures of domestic savings. The results indicate that a rapid increase in the ratio of savings to output, an important feature of explosive postwar growth in Korea and Taiwan, was also prominent in China's prewar economy.

These findings undercut the view that substantial saving and investment awaited sweeping social transformation. Despite massive uncertainty, China's prewar economy managed to produce a large and growing volume of investment, mostly financed by domestic savings. Although severe data limitations make it impossible to compile a detailed record of prewar saving and investment, the consequences of prewar capital formation are reflected in the rate and pattern of economic growth, which is the focus of the next chapter.

Chapter Six

Economic Growth
in Prewar China

The foregoing chapters have investigated several dimensions of economic change in China from 1895 to the outbreak of the Pacific War in 1937. During this period of approximately four decades, China experienced rapid industrialization, a considerable expansion of modern networks of transport and communication, a sweeping transformation of the monetary and financial system, and a rapid and accelerating growth of modern-oriented fixed investment. These innovations appear complementary with older forms of economic activity. In certain regions, notably Manchuria and the Lower Yangtze, the combination of rapid growth in the small modern sector and continued expansion of inherited activities resulted in a cumulative development process involving widespread application of new technologies to economic activity, important changes in economic structure, increasing openness to external economic forces, and gradual increases in average levels of per capita output and income for regional populations of tens of millions of people.

What can be said of trends in economic growth and welfare at the national level? The evidence of rapid increases in investment, growing per capita consumption of cotton textiles, and the sustained expansion of the real (that is, inflation-adjusted) money stock points toward a widespread process of rising output and income per head. Do these findings nullify the familiar view that prewar China experienced no substantial change in per capita output or income at the national level? The objective of this chapter is to demonstrate that China's economic growth between 1914/18 and the 1930s was sufficiently widespread and sustained to produce substantial increases in per capita output of commodities and services as well as a modest rise in per capita consumption at the national level, not just in particular advanced regions. The implications of these findings are pursued in the concluding chapter.

This analysis of prewar trends in aggregate output and consumption makes use of the concepts of national income accounting. The gross domestic product is a measure of society's annual output of final commodities and services.[1] The total product can be measured as the sum of value added (annual sales value minus purchases of fertilizer, electricity, and other produced inputs) across all sectors of the economy. The percentage growth of total product, which forms the focus of this chapter, can be calculated from estimates of the percentage growth in various sectors of the economy and the shares or relative significance of each sector in a particular base year. In the case of prewar China, the availability of extensive data resulting from detailed studies by Wu Pao-san, Ta-chung Liu, and Kung-chia Yeh dictates the choice of 1933 as the base year for the calculations.

Another approach to measuring national product is to study expenditure rather than production. Each unit of output is allocated to private consumption, government consumption, private or government domestic investment (including changes in inventories, which become the repository for unsold goods), or to purchasers in foreign countries. Information on the proportion of total expenditure occupied by domestic investment, government spending, and net exports (exports minus imports of commodities and services) can be used to calculate the share of consumption in total output or expenditure for initial and terminal years. Together with an estimated growth rate of total output, knowledge about expenditure

---

1. "Gross" means that there is no deduction for depreciation of long-lived productive assets (housing, machines, cattle). "Domestic" indicates the inclusion of all activities within society's borders (in this case, China proper plus Manchuria) without considering the nationality of the agents involved (i.e., there is no distinction between Chinese- and foreign-owned firms). In statistical practice, the differences between China's gross and net (of depreciation) product or between domestic and national product (the latter including only output from agencies controlled by Chinese nationals) are too small to affect the conclusions.

shares makes it possible to determine the time trend of private consumption.

Before analyzing changes in aggregate output, expenditure shares, and consumption between 1914/18 and 1931/36, it is essential to emphasize the limited scope of this investigation. The goal is to demonstrate that the *national average level* of per capita production and private consumption rose during the two prewar decades. This follows the traditional approach of economists who define "modern economic growth" as a substantial and sustained increase in the average level of per capita output.[2] I compare two periods: 1914/18 and 1931/36. The finding that average per capita output and consumption were higher in the latter period than in the former need not imply a unilinear or steady growth process for the intervening years. Indeed, the method used here ignores the short-term economic fluctuations associated with domestic turmoil in the 1920s and international political and economic instability during the 1930s.

Even though I argue that the period from 1914/18 to 1931/36 was one of substantial growth, it is important to avoid exaggeration that could arise from measurements linking early years of cyclical depression with final years of cyclical prosperity. In the present case, I link 1914/18, which is often identified as an interlude of relative prosperity because the temporary cessation of European overseas business activity offered unusually favorable opportunities to Chinese producers, with 1931/36, which brought economic disruption first from the Japanese attack on Shanghai and the occupation of Manchuria and later from the impact of the world depression.[3] If anything, this approach measures from "peak to trough," perhaps understating the underlying trend of growth. As a result, neglecting the details of annual output fluctuations should not lead

2. Lewis defines economic growth as rising "output per head of population." Kuznets observes that "the distinctive characteristic of modern economic growth is the combination of high rates of increase in population with high rates of increase in per capita product." Reynolds defines "intensive growth" as a "sustained rise in per capita output." See W. Arthur Lewis, *The Theory of Economic Growth* (Homewood, 1955), 9; Simon Kuznets, *Modern Economic Growth: Rate, Structure, and Spread* (New Haven, 1966), 63; and Lloyd G. Reynolds, *Economic Growth in the Third World, 1850–1980* (New Haven, 1985), 8.

3. Many authors identify the years 1914–21 as a "golden age" for domestic industry; see Chou Hsiu-luan, *Ti i tzu shih chieh ta chan shih ch'i Chung-kuo min tsu kung yeh ti fa chan* (Shanghai, 1958).

to any exaggeration of the overall pace of prewar economic growth.
Another limitation concerns distribution. To conclude that Chinese per capita output rose by 1.2–1.3 percent per year and that per capita consumption rose by approximately 0.5 percent annually between 1914/18 and 1931/36 carries no implications for changes in the *distribution* of income. A finding of rising per capita output or consumption does not establish that all or even most Chinese citizens enjoyed improved economic circumstances. Some individuals or groups suffer declining fortunes even in the most buoyantly expansive economies. Regional growth in Manchuria, where recent estimates suggest annual growth rates of 4.1 and 1.7 percent for aggregate and per capita output respectively during 1924–41, and probably in the Lower Yangtze areas of China may have progressed more rapidly than the national average, thus ensuring that other regions experienced below average, and possibly negative, growth.[4] The large literature on the relation between growth and distribution includes analyses and case studies showing that large segments of the domestic populace (for example, households in the poorest 20 or 40 percent of the income distribution) may suffer a relative or even an absolute decline in income despite substantial growth of the national average level of per capita production and income.[5] Further study will be required to determine the possible relevance of these models to prewar China. In the meantime, I conclude only that the higher the overall growth of average output and consumption, the greater the likelihood that most Chinese enjoyed improved economic circumstances. Although my findings imply a more sanguine view of the fortunes of the average Chinese household than the view that emerges from earlier studies reporting no significant prewar change in per capita production, the present results are consistent with a variety of distributive outcomes.

Whatever one's views about economic fluctuations or the distribution of income and wealth in prewar China, information about trends in average per capita product, income, and consumption provides essential background information with which to assess economic performance as well as the impact of economic change

4. Manchurian figures calculated from Kang Chao, *The Economic Development of Manchuria: The Rise of a Frontier Economy* (Ann Arbor, 1983), 34.
5. Hollis Chenery et al., *Redistribution with Growth* (London, 1974), xiii, begin with the assertion that rapid output growth in low-income nations during the 1960s provided "little or no benefit to perhaps a third of their population."

Table 6.1
Prior Estimates of Aggregate Real Output Growth, 1914-36

Sector	Terminal Year Weight	Output Index Terminal Year (Base period=100)	Average Annual Growth Rate
A. Yeh estimates, 1914/18 to 1931/36, 1933 prices			
Agriculture	0.629	114.5	0.8%
Modern Industry	0.042	366.7	7.7
Handicrafts	0.075	113.0	0.7
Construction	0.016	184.6	3.5
Transp. and Comm. Modern	0.017	200.0	4.0
Traditional	0.039	104.5	0.3
Trade	0.093	121.5	1.1
Finance	0.010	164.7	2.9
Govt. services	0.031	119.7	1.0
Personal services	0.012	116.7	0.9
Residential rent	0.036	114.3	0.8
Gross domestic product	1.000	120.1	1.1
B. Perkins estimates, 1914/18 to 1933, 1957 prices			
Agriculture	0.571	117.0	1.0
Industry and Transport Modern	0.074	419.2	8.8
Other	0.117	100.4	0.0
Services	0.203	125.2	1.3
Depreciation	0.035	...[a]	...[a]
Gross domestic product	1.000	126.4	1.4

[a]No figure given in source.

Sources: K. C. Yeh, "China's National Income, 1931-36," in
Modern Chinese Economic History, ed. Chi-ming Hou and Tzong-shian Yu
(Taipei, 1979), 126 and Dwight H. Perkins, "Growth and Changing
Structure of China's Twentieth-Century Economy," in China's Modern
Economy in Historical Perspective, ed. Dwight H. Perkins (Stanford,
1975), 117. The annual growth rates for Yeh's estimates are
computed over a period of 17.5 years (mid-1916 to the end of 1933).
The annual growth rates for Perkins's estimates are computed over a
period of 17 years (1916 to 1933).

on broader social processes. Two scholars, K. C. Yeh and Dwight Perkins, have produced quantitative estimates of the trends in China's gross domestic product between World War I and the 1930s. Table 6.1 summarizes their conclusions. Both authors necessarily employ flimsy data and crude approximations. Although the weak underpinnings of their results admit the possibility of revisions in either direction, both Yeh and Perkins find that national economic growth proceeded at an annual rate somewhat above 1 percent between 1914/18 and the 1930s, a figure only slightly above the crude estimates of population growth available for the prewar years. Allowing for a considerable margin of error in the figures for both production and population, the general implication of these studies is that "there is little evidence of significant improvement in living standards; and estimates of national income for the 1930s reveal an economic structure little different from that in earlier centuries."[6] The preceding analysis of the trends in industry, finance, transport, and communication reveals important shifts in economic structure. What remains is to show that these developments produced quantitatively significant changes in the national indicators of total and per capita output and consumption.

It is my contention that many of the sectoral growth rates proposed by Yeh and Perkins require substantial revision. The intent of the following discussion is to provide a firm quantitative foundation for the conclusion that China's turbulent society experienced a substantial increase in average levels of per capita production and consumption during the interwar decades of the present century. I now turn to evidence supporting this viewpoint, first with regard to nonfarm sectors of the economy and then with respect to agriculture.

The Growth of Production Outside Agriculture, 1914/18 to 1931/36

Previous chapters have produced evidence of more rapid growth in several nonagricultural sectors of China's economy than is credited by either Yeh or Perkins. Table 6.2 presents calculations intended to show the effect of revisions in sectoral growth rates on

6. Reynolds, *Economic Growth*, 273.

Table 6.2
Initial Revision of Aggregate Output Data, 1914/18 to 1931/36
(based on Yeh's estimates in 1933 prices)

Sector	Weight	Output Index for 1931/36 (1914/18 = 100)		Average Annual Growth Rate (%) 1914/18 to 1931/36	
		1A	1B	2A	2B
Agriculture	0.629	115.0	129.8[a]	0.8	1.5[a]
Modern Industry	0.042	390.8[a]		8.1[a]	
Handicrafts	0.075	127.5[a]		1.4[a]	
Construction	0.016	219.7		4.6	
Transp. and Comm. Modern	0.017	167.7		3.0[a]	
Traditional	0.039	139.0		1.9[a]	
Trade	0.093	154.0		2.5[a]	
Finance	0.010	234.9[a]		5.0[a]	
Govt. Services	0.031	179.5		3.4[a]	
Personal Services	0.012	117.0		0.9	
Residential Rent	0.036	115.0		0.8	
Gross Domestic Product	1.000	127.3	138.3	1.4	1.9

Note: The usual formulations for calculating the global growth rate from sectoral rates are invalid here because the weights refer to the terminal rather than the initial structure of output. In this table and also in Table 6.11, r, the growth rate of total output Y is derived from the sectoral growth rates (r_i) using the following relationship:

$$(1+r)^t = Y(t)/Y(o) = 1/[\sum_i a_i/(1+r_i)^t]$$

where Y(o) and Y(t) refer to total output in the initial and terminal years, t indicates the number of years elapsed between the initial and terminal dates, and the subscript i denotes the various sectors (agriculture, handicrafts etc.) of the economy, and a_i are sectoral weights in 1933 GDP given in the first column.

[a]Indicates sectoral data different from those shown in Panel A of Table 6.1.

Source: Table 6.1 and text.

the behavior of aggregate output. The table is based on Yeh's figures, which offer greater sectoral detail than Perkins's results.

Mining, Manufacturing, and Utilities

Yeh assigns an annual growth rate of 7.7 percent to "modern industry," which apparently includes factories, modern mines, and utilities. My calculations, based on a considerably larger product sample than was available to earlier studies, show that manufacturing output (with value-added weights) grew at an annual rate of 8.1 percent between 1912 and 1936 (Table A.1). Even though John K. Chang's output estimates for cotton textiles, electricity, pig iron, and steel grow rapidly during 1912–14, shifting the initial year by two years should cause no important variation in the results.[7] For mining, Chang's data for nine products indicate annual value-added growth of 4.5 percent between 1914 and 1936.[8] Tim Wright's estimates of electricity output, which I take as representative of the utility category, grow at an annual rate of 14.1 percent between 1914 and 1936.[9] If these components are weighted by their shares in 1933 value added, the growth rate for the products of modern industry between 1914 and 1936 becomes 8.1 percent; I apply this rate to the period 1914/18 to 1931/36.[10]

Handicrafts

Yeh assigns an annual growth rate of 0.7 percent to the handicraft sector. Table 2.10, however, shows that the value added in cotton textile handicrafts grew at exactly double this rate between 1901/

7. John K. Chang, *Industrial Development in Pre-Communist China* (Chicago, 1969), 117–22.
8. Log-linear regression results calculated from data on output and 1933 unit value added for coal, iron ore, antimony, copper, gold, mercury, tin, tungsten, and crude oil in ibid., 117–23, 128.
9. The log-linear regression result is calculated from output totals in Tim Wright, "A New Series for Electric Power Production in Pre-1937 China" (Murdoch, n.d.), 9.
10. Estimated net value added by factories, mines, and utilities for 1933 (billion yuan at 1933 prices) is 0.64, 0.13, and 0.21; see Ta-chung Liu and Kung-chia Yeh, *The Economy of the Chinese Mainland: National Income and Economic Development, 1933–1959* (Princeton, 1965), 66. The percentage growth rate for modern industry is calculated from the formula given in Table 6.2.

10 and 1934/36 despite severe competition from the products of cotton factories in China and abroad. Because cotton textiles were the largest craft sector and faced stronger competition from domestic and foreign manufactures than most craft occupations, I take 1.4 percent, the growth rate for textile handicrafts, as an estimated growth rate for the entire handicraft sector.

Construction

The data and estimates assembled in Chapter 5, while not complete, suggest that the ratio of gross domestic fixed capital formation to gross domestic product may have risen from .07 to .11 between 1914/18 and 1931/36. Taking 1.9 percent, the midpoint of preferred rates derived in Table 6.11, as the annual growth rate of total output during the same period, the annual growth rate for fixed investment becomes 4.6 percent. I take this as a rough estimate for the growth of construction activity between 1914/18 and 1931/36.[11]

Transport and Communication

Here, Yeh assigns growth rates of 4.0 and 0.3 percent to modern and traditional activity respectively. The detailed compilation of information in Table 4.10 yields annual growth of 3.0 percent for combined freight carriage by rail and steamship between 1915 and 1936. This figure is too low, however, because the 1936 data on steamship traffic do not include interport traffic within Manchuria. I ignore this minor deficiency and apply the 3.0 percent rate to all of modern transport and communication, neglecting possible differences between the growth of freight traffic and the volume of passenger carriage and communications.

Following Table 4.10, I assume annual growth of 2 percent for junk trade and 1 percent for nonmechanized land traffic. Of these the first is far more important. In view of the figures reported in Tables 4.3–4.6, the 2 percent figure probably understates the

---

11. The use of the 4.6 percent figure in deriving the results shown in Table 6.11 introduces an element of circularity into this procedure, but the impact of possible variation in the growth of construction on the estimated growth rate for total output is minute.

growth rate of sailboat traffic volume in prewar China.[12] None-theless, to avoid a possible exaggeration of upward momentum, the estimate of traditional transport and communication activity uses the growth rate of 1.9 percent per year derived from the data on traditional land and water traffic during 1915–36 (Table 4.10).

Trade

Yeh assigns a growth rate of 1.1 percent for the combined output of wholesale and retail trade, implying that the volume of trade and commercial services expanded only slightly ahead of population. This ignores the rapid spread of trade and commerce visible throughout the economy. The yearly volume of foreign trade rose by 98 percent between 1914/18 and 1931/36, indicating an average annual growth of 2.9 percent.[13] The best available figures for the much larger volume of internal trade are the estimates of freight carriage reported in Table 4.10, which show average annual growth of 2.5 percent between 1915 and 1936. I adopt this figure as an estimate of the growth of wholesale and retail trade between 1914/18 and 1931/36.

Finance

Yeh adopts a growth rate of 2.9 percent for the finance sector. The results of my compilation of monetary figures, which, for example, show the combined deposits of traditional and modern (including foreign) banks increasing at an annual rate of 10.6 percent between 1914/18 and 1931/36 (Table C.15), indicate a rapid and continuous expansion of financial intermediation throughout the prewar decades. Even though a considerable portion of this growth may represent a substitution of institutional for informal intermediation, it

12. As noted in Chapter 4, information compiled in Table 4.6 suggests a lower growth rate for the value, in real terms, of junk cargoes. The growth of traffic volume, however, appears to provide a better indicator of the value of transport services than the trend in the value of cargo shipped.

13. Calculated from Thomas G. Rawski, "Economic Growth and Integration in Prewar China" (Toronto, 1982), 49. These data reflect the international maritime commerce of China proper and Manchuria. Most compendia of Chinese foreign trade data omit Manchuria's overseas trade, which represents a significant fraction of the national total, beginning with Japan's occupation of Manchuria in 1932.

seems reasonable to use 5 percent, the average long-term growth
rate of money supply reported in Table 3.5, to estimate the rate of
of output growth in finance.

Government

Yeh assigns a growth rate of 1.0 percent to the government sector,
for which expenditure is the economist's traditional measure of the
quantity of services produced. Despite my argument (Chapter 1)
that many observers overstate the scale of government fiscal activity, it is clear that taxes and government spending grew faster
than population in prewar China. Although Yeh's figure is too low,
it is not easy to specify a replacement. Yeh-chien Wang finds that
total tax revenue in 1908 was approximately 292 million *taels* or, at
1.55 silver dollars to the *tael*, $450 million at current prices or
roughly $859 million in terms of 1931 prices.[14] Government spend-
ing in 1931 was approximately $1.587–2.425 billion (Table 1.5).
After subtracting central government borrowing of $0.1 billion for
the fiscal year beginning in July 1931 (Table 1.1), these two figures
yield an average annual growth rate for revenue during 1908–31 of
2.4–4.4 percent. I assume an annual growth of 3.4 percent for
1914/18 to 1931/36.

Other Nonagricultural Sectors

I retain Yeh's figures for the growth of personal services and residential rent, both of which imply no growth in per capita output.

The Impact of Revised
Nonfarm Production Estimates
on Aggregate Output Growth

The impact of these changes on the estimated growth of aggregate
output between 1914/18 and 1931/36 is examined in the columns

14. Yeh-chien Wang, *Land Taxation in Imperial China, 1750–1911* (Cambridge,
1973), 74. The conversion to dollars follows Eduard Kann, *The Currencies of
China*, 2d ed. (Shanghai, 1927), 84, 171. The conversion to 1931 prices is based
on index numbers of silver prices paid to agricultural producers in Wuchin
county, Kiangsu (for 1908–13), and the Nan-k'ai index of North China whole-

marked A in Table 6.2. These calculations, which retain Yeh's estimated 0.8 percent annual rate of output growth for agriculture, imply a considerable revision of Yeh's findings concerning prewar growth trends in China's economy. These initial results raise the estimated growth rate of aggregate output at constant prices from 1.1 to a higher figure of 1.4 percent per year. They imply that total output during 1931/36 was approximately 27 percent above the 1914/18 base, just above the range of increases (20–26 percent) reported by Yeh and Perkins (Table 6.1).

The implications of these modifications can be seen in Table 6.3, which compares the changes in per capita output derived from the Perkins-Yeh output figures with results based on the present revisions to nonagricultural output estimates (Column A). Alternative population totals are used to reflect uncertainty about both the size and the growth rate of China's prewar population. Schran's population figures (version 2) incorporate a larger total and a smaller growth rate than Perkins's demographic totals (version 1). With either population series, the modifications to the nonagricultural output estimates described in Columns 1A and 2A of Table 6.2 lead to changes in the time trend of per capita real output. These revisions indicate a considerably higher cumulative growth of per capita gross domestic product than Yeh's figures. They suggest a cumulative rise in output per head of 9–15 percent during the two prewar decades, considerably above the comparable figures of 3–8 percent resulting from Yeh's study (Table 6.3) and slightly above Perkins's results. Given the considerable error margins that must be attached to estimates of both product and population, Yeh's calculations essentially indicate no significant change in per capita output between 1914/18 and 1931/36. The revisions shown in Column A of Tables 6.2 and 6.3, however, portray the same period as one of some growth, with per capita product rising by up to one-seventh during the last two prewar decades.

Even with generous allowance for possible error, the results in Table 6.3 demonstrate the possibility that prewar China experienced substantial economic growth, both in terms of aggregate and

---

sale prices (for 1913–31); see L. L. Chang, "Farm Prices in Wuchin, Kiangsu, China," *Chinese Economic Journal* 10, no. 6 (1932):464 and *Shang-hai chieh fang ch'ien hou wu chia tzu liao hui pien, 1921–1957* (Shanghai, 1958), 175.

Table 6.3
Initial Revision of Prewar Trends in Real Product Per Capita
(Based on Yeh's estimates, 1933 prices)

	Index for 1931/36 (1914/18 = 100)			Average Annual Growth 1914/18 to 1931/36		
	Original	Revised A	B	Original	Revised A	B
Gross domestic product	120.1	127.3	138.3	1.1	1.4	1.9
Population						
1. Perkins	117.0	117.0	117.0	0.9	0.9	0.9
2. Schran	111.0	111.0	111.0	0.6	0.6	0.6
Per capita product						
1. Perkins population	102.6	108.8	118.2	0.1	0.5	1.0
2. Schran population	108.2	114.7	124.6	0.4	0.8	1.3

Sources: Output data are from Tables 6.1 and 6.2. Population 1
is from Perkins, "Growth and Changing Structure," who gives totals
of 430 and 500 million for 1914/18 and 1933 (p. 122). Population 2
is based on Peter Schran, "China's Demographic Evolution 1850-1953
Reconsidered," China Quarterly 75 (1978), who gives totals of 490
million for 1913 (which I amend to 500 million for 1914/18) and 550
million for 1933 (p. 644). The average annual growth rates for
population are based on a seventeen-year interval (1916 to 1933).
The indexes of population size are based on cumulation of these
growth rates over a period of 17.5 years (1914/18 to 1931/36).

in terms of per capita output. The confirmation of this view requires careful attention to the complex and controversial subject of
measuring agricultural output growth.

Agricultural Production Trends, 1914/18 to 1931/36: A Survey of the Evidence

Agriculture, which contributed more than 60 percent of prewar
aggregate output (Table 6.2) must constitute an important focus of
any effort to determine the direction and magnitude of trends in
China's prewar economy. Unfortunately, the verification of trends
in prewar farm output is extremely difficult, partly because of the
limited quantity and quality of statistical data, but also because

of the extraordinary geographic and biological diversity within China's farm economy. It is therefore hardly surprising that scholars have failed to agree on a consistent interpretation of prewar developments in China's rural economy.

Two observations should preface the study of agricultural production trends. First, the predominant share of agriculture in Chinese economic life means that alternate views of agricultural performance exert an important influence on the outcome of any quantitative analysis of prewar economic trends. Revising the estimated rate of prewar agricultural growth from the Yeh-Perkins range of 0.8–1.0 percent (Table 6.1) to 1.5 percent (Column B in Tables 6.2 and 6.3) would signify a major reinterpretation of China's prewar economic history. A higher growth rate of farm output, if substantiated, would indicate an economy in which agricultural output runs ahead of population growth rather than, as suggested by earlier research, barely keeps pace with demographic expansion. The literature of development economics places great emphasis on increased per capita production of farm products as a vehicle for facilitating urbanization, industrialization, accumulation, export growth, and other important processes that contribute to overall economic growth.

Along with its interpretive significance, the quantitative impact of raising the estimated rate of prewar agricultural growth from 0.8 to 1.5 percent is highly significant. A comparison of Columns A and B in Tables 6.2 and 6.3 shows that the higher growth rate for agriculture adds about 10 percentage points to the 1931/36 index of total and per capita product (with 1914/18 = 100). The average growth rate of total and per capita product jumps by 0.5 percent and the increase in per capita real product over two decades rises from 9–15 percent (Column A, Table 6.3) to 18–25 percent (Column B, Table 6.3). The latter result, if confirmed, would establish the hypothesis of a rising national average of output per head in prewar China beyond all reasonable doubt.

Second, severe data limitations, to be discussed below, make it impossible to rely on crop statistics to construct dependable estimates of agricultural production growth. Instead, I assemble evidence relating to changes in economic variables that are closely linked to per capita farm output. These include survey data on changes in farm incomes, trends in consumption of cotton cloth, and changes in wages earned by agricultural laborers and unskilled workers in cotton textile mills and coal mines, both of which recruited most of their work force from rural villages. The goal of this analysis is to amass a sufficient variety of evidence to evaluate the hypothesis of rising real incomes in the countryside, which I interpret as roughly equivalent to rising per capita farm output. Because no single piece of evidence is free of qualification or potential weakness, the confirmation of rising per capita farm income and output depends on consistent support from a variety of statistical indicators. The development of separate strands of analysis, all pointing in the same direction, may encourage potential critics to search for quantitative evidence relating to large segments of the rural populace that contradicts the present argument. In the absence of such evidence, I offer the materials in the following pages to support the view that increasing per capita output of farm products further enhanced the trend of rising output per head, which was suggested by my analysis of output growth in the nonfarm segment of China's prewar economy.

The Inadequacy of Existing Output Statistics for Major Farm Crops

Several scholars have used compendia of agricultural statistics published during the Republican decades to estimate trends in prewar agricultural production. Their results, based on a variety of estimating procedures, are similar. Dwight Perkins finds that the average yearly grain output increased by a cumulative total of 7.8 percent between 1914/18 and 1931/37. K. C. Yeh reports an estimated increase of 7.2 percent over the same interval. Hsü Tao-fu concludes that grain production rose by 18.0 percent during the same years.[15] With grain output rising by a cumulative total of perhaps 8–18 percent during a period of approximately 18 years and the population rising by 11–17 percent over the same time span (Table 6.3), how reliable is the conclusion that the maximum

15. Dwight H. Perkins, *Agricultural Development in China, 1368–1968* (Chicago, 1969), 289; K. C. Yeh, "China's National Income, 1931–36," in *Modern Chinese Economic History*, ed. Chi-ming Hou and Tzong-shian Yu (Taipei, 1979), 127; and Hsü Tao-fu, *Chung-kuo chin tai nung yeh sheng ch'an chi mao yi t'ung chi tzu liao* (Shanghai, 1983), 339.

increase in per capita grain production during this period was extremely small? Unfortunately, the underlying data are so problematic that, pending further detailed research, no confidence whatever should be attached to this result, nor can the studies by Perkins, Hsü, and Yeh be used to reject the hypothesis that per capita grain output may have increased during the prewar decades.

A close examination of alternative estimates for the output of rice, the leading Chinese grain crop, shows why the results of published studies are not acceptable even as rough approximations to actual trends. Table 6.4 presents data on the regional distribution of rice production during 1914/18 and 1931/37 and the estimated growth of provincial output between 1914/18 and 1931/37 for eight major rice-growing provinces. A comparison of the results calculated from Perkins's estimates and Hsü's data (Yeh's study gives no provincial detail) reveals wide disparities in every direction.

The first two columns of Table 6.4 compare the relative size of average provincial rice output for 1914/18 shown in the two studies using the estimated production in Kiangsu as a base. Perkins finds average Chekiang output to be 53 percent higher than Kiangsu's, but Hsü's data portray Chekiang's output as only 16 percent above Kiangsu's. The variation for other provinces is equally large, ranging from Hunan, where Perkins's relative output figure is 18 percent higher than Hsü's, to Kiangsi, where Perkins's estimate of relative output is only half of Hsü's.

The second pair of columns, which compares the relative size of the average provincial rice output for 1931/37 in the two studies, reveals still wider discrepancies, even though the rapid development of national capacity for collecting economic statistics during the 1920s and 1930s leads one to anticipate a considerable improvement in data quality. Only Kiangsi and Kwangtung display figures that are remotely similar in the two studies. The figures for the other provinces are completely different. Was Szechwan's average rice harvest during 1931/37 more than double (Perkins) or only one-third larger (Hsü) than Kiangsu's? Was Anhwei's harvest similar to (Perkins) or only a small fraction of (Hsü) Kiangsu's?

The right-hand pair of columns compares the estimated growth of rice output for various provinces between 1914/18 and 1931/37 as derived in the two studies. The figures for Hupeh and Kiangsi are very close, but for the other provinces, there is no agreement

Table 6.4
Alternative Estimates of Provincial Rice Output
1914/18 and 1931/37

Province	1914/18 Output (Kiangsu = 100)		1931/37 Rice Output (Kiangsu = 100)		(1914/18 = 100)	
	Perkins	Hsü[a]	Perkins	Hsü[a]	Perkins	Hsü[a]
1. Kiangsu	100.0	100.0	100.0	100.0	98.6	267.4
2. Chekiang	152.7	115.5	123.0	84.6	79.6	196.1
3. Anhwei	104.4	85.5	93.5	38.9	88.4	121.7
4. Hupeh	119.5	170.2	120.9	65.6	100.0	103.1
5. Hunan	165.3	140.4	154.3	98.0	92.3	186.8
6. Kiangsi	119.2	239.0	87.0	69.4	72.2	77.7
7. Kwangtung	179.3	...	181.4	154.4	100.0	...
8. Szechwan	215.6	...	218.1	134.0	100.0	...

	Perkins	Hsü
Growth of average annual rice output in provinces 1-6, 1914/18 to 1931/37	-12%	+22%
Output from provinces 1-6 as share of estimated national total		
1914/18	54%	34%
1931/37	50	49

[a]Rice output from the Hsü compendium is the sum of separate figures for ordinary and glutinous rice. In calculating average output from Hsü's data, I have omitted all years for which production figures for either or both varieties are missing as well as data that Hsü identifies as incomplete or dubious.

Sources: Perkins, *Agricultural Development*, 276; Hsü Tao-fu, *Chung-kuo chin tai nung yeh*, 23-54, 339.

about even the direction, let alone the magnitude, of change. Did Kiangsu's rice crop zoom upward with an increase of 167 percent (Hsü) or drift marginally downward (Perkins)? Did Chekiang nearly double its harvest (Hsü) or experience a substantial decline (Perkins)?

Finally, I combine the results for six major producers (excluding Kwangtung and Szechwan, for which Hsü's data are inadequate for making long-term comparisons). Perkins finds that rice output in these provinces slipped by 12 percent between 1914/18 and 1931/ 37. Hsü's data indicate an increase of 22 percent in average rice production for the same provinces. Dropping Kiangsi magnifies the disparity: with only five provinces, Perkins's figures show a drop of 9 percent, Hsü's an increase of 69 percent. Perkins's data indicate that the share of the six provinces in national rice production fell from 54 to 50 percent between 1914/18 and 1931/37; Hsü's show the share of the same provinces jumping from 34 to 49 percent of the national total in the same period.

The only reasonable conclusion to be drawn from Table 6.4 is that, in the absence of detailed analysis of the statistical compendia underlying the studies by Perkins, Hsü, and others, any estimate of rice production must be qualified by very large margins of error. An inspection of Hsü's compilation of provincial acreage, output, and yield data for rice and other crops during 1914–37 offers little hope that the confusion evident in Table 6.4 can easily be overcome for any major agricultural product. With this dubious empirical base, the view, shared by Hsü, Perkins, and Yeh, that there was little or no change in per capita farm output between 1914/18 and the 1930s, cannot be regarded as firmly established. Pending a thorough reworking of existing agricultural statistics, there is no alternative to relying on indirect evidence to reach conclusions about the controversial issue of prewar trends in Chinese farm output. As I will show, available materials contain important evidence of rising per capita income and output in China's rural economy during the first four decades of the present century.

Agricultural Output Trends, 1914/18 to 1931/36: A Survey of the Indirect Evidence

Previous chapters have shown that China's farm sector enjoyed new opportunities arising from the expansion of foreign trade, which opened new markets to China's tea, silk, soybeans, and other agricultural produce, from the development of the domestic financial system, which made it easier and cheaper to finance rural commerce, and from expanded networks of transport and communication, which lowered the cost of obtaining market information and moving products across space. Large reductions in transport and transactions costs create the possibility of rapid commercialization and output growth in any farm economy. In light of the explosive growth of Chinese farm output and income that followed the reforms of the late 1970s, which also represent a sharp reduction in transactions costs, it is natural to look for evidence of rising output, income, and productivity in response to new marketing opportunities during the prewar decades.

If the limited quantity and quality of available data make it difficult to measure trends in farm output during the early decades of the present century, how can one investigate the possibility of sustained increases in per capita output? One approach is to look for evidence of significant changes in farm incomes, which are closely linked with agricultural productivity. Income originating in agricultural production takes the form of labor income accruing to self-employed owner- and tenant-farmers and agricultural laborers, rental income received by landlords, interest payments earned by moneylenders, and profit received by employers of agricultural workers. Rough calculations by Victor Lippit indicate that land rents, rural interest payments, and farm business profits amounted respectively to 16.4, 5.2, and 4.4 percent of 1933 agricultural output, leaving 74 percent as labor income.[16]

Myers and Feuerwerker find no evidence of significant shifts in the rate of tenancy between the 1880s and the 1930s; Lippit anticipates that "nineteenth-century figures" for the functional distribution of agricultural incomes "would not have been very different" from his 1933 results.[17] This apparent stability in the division of agricultural incomes among the owners of land, labor, and capital means that trends in the labor earnings of farmers will accurately reflect trends in agricultural output. Under these circumstances, wages of farm laborers and workers in nonagricultural occupations

16. Victor D. Lippit, *Land Reform and Economic Development in China: A Study of Institutional Change and Development Finance* (White Plains, 1974), 65–71.
17. Ramon H. Myers, *The Chinese Peasant Economy: Agricultural Development in Hopei and Shantung, 1940–1949* (Cambridge, 1970), 235; Albert Feuerwerker, *Economic Trends in the Republic of China, 1912–1949* (Ann Arbor, 1977), 60; and Victor D. Lippit, *The Economic Development of China* (Armonk, 1987), 89.

open to unskilled village recruits emerge as potentially important indicators of trends in agricultural output. Before turning to wage trends, I begin with information on farmers' perceptions of trends in living standards and on the consumption of cotton textiles.

Survey Evidence of Rising Rural Living Standards

Between 1929 and 1933, John L. Buck, an American economist teaching at the University of Nanking, collected large quantities of data on China's farm economy by sending his students to study the local economies of their native areas. The result was a large sample of economic conditions that covered substantial regions of rural China. One of the questions asked by Buck's interviewers concerned recent changes in living standards. The answers obtained during 1929–33 (expressed here as percentages) were as follows: [18]

Region	Number of Localities	Improved	Deterio- rated	No Change
China proper	216	82%	11%	7%
Shensi province	18	17	83	0
Other areas	198	88	4	8

Many Chinese farmers consulted during the years 1929–33, a period often described as one of agrarian crisis, viewed the recent past as a period of rising living standards. Only one area, the winter wheat and millet region of northern Shensi, produced consistently negative reports. If Shensi, which provided China's fledgling communist party with a secure base before and during the Sino-Japanese War, is excluded from the total, nearly nine of ten localities reported improved living standards. Even with Shensi included, more than 80 percent of reporting localities noted rising standards of living.

Do Buck's informants constitute a representative sample of Chi-

18. John L. Buck, *Land Utilization in China, Statistics* (Reprint, New York, 1982), 400–401. Buck's survey covered 216 localities in 142 counties and 21 provinces. There are no citations for Kwangtung, Kwangsi, or Fukien and only one for the three northeastern provinces.

nese farm families? Perhaps not. Buck's investigators focused on commercialized areas that may have enjoyed unusual economic opportunities. Their analysis of individual localities was far from systematic. In each locality surveyed, information was gathered from three farms. The average size of the farms sampled with regard to living standards, 7.5 acres, is much larger than the average size (4.18 acres) of farms studied in Buck's much larger surveys or other large-scale investigations.[19] Furthermore, the number of farms involved in Buck's investigation of changes in living standards was very small (442 farms vs. 16,786 in his larger farm survey).[20] Since farm families with a recent history of upward socioeconomic mobility tend to operate large farms and those suffering downward mobility tend to have small landholdings, a sample of large farms may include a much higher proportion of families reporting recent economic gains than would be found in the overall population. Although Buck's information about living standards supports the view that farm incomes were rising in prewar China, the small size and skewed nature of the underlying sample severely limits its significance.

Buck's investigators recorded not only the direction of change in reported living standards, but also the reasons for these movements. Most informants reported rising living standards, and the reason most frequently given was "improved clothing."[21] If the majority of communities throughout China, and not just in Buck's reporting areas, experienced rising living standards during the prewar decades and if improved clothing was the most prominent indicator of this change, it should be possible to verify this trend with reference to production and consumption of cotton cloth, the main item of clothing, at the national level.[22]

19. *Ch'üan kuo t'u ti tiao ch'a pao kao kang yao* (Nanking, 1937), 23–28, a much larger study involving more than 30 million households, includes data indicating an average farm size of 2.3–4.2 acres.
20. John L. Buck, *Land Utilization in China* (Chicago, 1937), 438. I am indebted to Barry Naughton for drawing my attention to the limitations of Buck's information on living standards.
21. Buck, *Statistics*, 400.
22. Buck notes that 90 percent of work garments and 69 percent of dress garments owned by proprietors of large farms were made of cotton. Comparable figures for garments owned by proprietors of small farms were 90 percent and 86 percent (*Statistics*, 351–53).

The Rising Consumption of Cotton Cloth

Data compiled in Chapter 2 show that China's domestic production of factory and handicraft cotton textiles more than doubled between 1901/10 and 1934/36 (Table 2.10, Line 6A) and that per capita consumption of cotton cloth during the 1920s and 1930s was approximately 50 percent higher than during 1871/80 or 1901/10 (Table 2.11).

If these figures are accurate, the hypothesis of rising rural living standards must be regarded as firmly established. Studies of consumption patterns in many countries show that the income elasticity of demand for clothing, defined as the ratio of percentage change in expenditure on clothing to percentage change in income, is significantly above unity.[23] This means that when incomes rise (or fall), expenditures on clothing typically rise (or fall) by a greater percentage than income. Rising (or falling) income is linked with an increased (or reduced) share of clothing in total expenditures. Unless there is a large reduction in the price of textiles relative to other important consumer goods, which did not occur in prewar China, the application of international evidence concerning the income elasticity of demand for textiles suggests that an increase of over 20 percent in per capita cloth consumption provides strong evidence of rising per capita incomes. If the national average figure for per capita consumption of cotton cloth rose by anything approaching 50 percent between 1901/10 and 1923/25 or 1934/36 (Table 2.11), the inference of rising living standards in the rural communities that housed the vast majority of China's prewar populace is inescapable.

But are these results correct? I have already shown in Chapter 2 that these estimates of cloth production are consistent with available information about cotton supplies. What of the possible inconsistency between my finding of annual per capita consumption of

23. H. S. Houthakker observes that in the absence of detailed information, "one would not be very far astray by putting the partial elasticity [of demand] with respect to total expenditure at . . . 1.2 for clothing," i.e., expecting a 10 percent rise in income to result in an increase of 12 percent in outlays on clothing ("An International Comparison of Household Expenditure Patterns, Commemorating the Centenary of Engel's Law," *Econometrica* 25, no. 4 [1957]:550).

7.9 to 9.2 square yards of cotton cloth during the 1920s and 1930s and Bruce Reynolds's much lower figure of 5.8 square yards per person derived from budget studies conducted during the same period?[24] These budget studies were difficult to conduct and remain difficult to interpret because of the great variety of textile products purchased by Chinese households. A 1927–28 study of 305 laborer households in Shanghai illustrates these problems.[25] Households in this sample purchased forty-six types of piece goods, thirty-three varieties of ready-made clothes, eight types of bedding, and thirty-eight other clothing items. How much cotton cloth was purchased? For piece goods, I simply add up purchases of cotton fabrics.[26] The cloth content of ready-made clothes can be calculated from figures on the amount of material contained in shirts, trousers, coats, etc.[27] I use Reynolds's figures for the cloth content of bedding, and follow his lead in ignoring possible cotton content in "other" clothing articles, a category that includes towels, handkerchieves, and scarves, some of which were no doubt made of cotton cloth. The estimated annual per capita cotton consumption (in square yards per person) for the 305 families covered in the Shanghai study then becomes:[28]

---

24. Bruce L. Reynolds, "The Impact of Trade and Foreign Investment on Industrialization: Chinese Textiles, 1875–1931" (Ph.D. diss., University of Michigan, 1975), appendix H, 305–20, draws on forty-three separate budget studies to derive an annual consumption figure of 5.8 square yards per person, which he regards as within 5 or 10 percent of the actual figure for 1931 (p. 99).

25. *Standard of Living of Shanghai Laborers* (Shanghai, 1934), 149–51.

26. I rely on the tariff schedule reproduced in Julean Arnold, *Commercial Handbook of China* (Washington, D.C., 1920) 2:89–90, to determine which fabrics were made of cotton. Fabrics identified as mixtures of cotton and other fabrics were assumed to be half cotton. I follow Reynolds in adding 3.465 *ch'ih* (one *ch'ih* equals 0.3861 square yards) of "native sheetings" to the total; these are listed in another summary of the same Shanghai budget study.

27. Reynolds, "Trade and Foreign Investment," 319. These data come from L. K. Tao, *Livelihood in Peking: An Analysis of the Budgets of Sixty Families* (Peking, 1928). Cloth content was doubled or tripled for garments described as "double" or both "lined" and "double," e.g., "lined double trousers" are assumed to require three times the fabric content of "trousers." Children's garments were assumed to require one-fourth the fabric used for adult clothing.

28. Reynolds's data from ibid., 318. I use Reynolds's conversion factor of 0.3861 square yards per *ch'ih* of cloth. Alternative figures for piece goods depend on the treatment of "imitation serges" and "piece goods not otherwise recorded," categories for which cotton content cannot be determined.

	Reynolds	Present Study
Piece goods	6.57	7.9–8.2
Ready-made clothing	0.17	0.69
Bedding	0.11	0.11
Total	6.85	8.7–9.0

These calculations illustrate the wide margin of error that must surround conclusions derived from prewar budget studies. The Shanghai study, which Reynolds uses to support a national average consumption figure of 5.8 square yards per capita, is entirely consistent with my radically different findings. Pending a thorough review of the numerous prewar budget studies, I conclude that the evidence concerning textile consumption offers strong, but not fully conclusive, support for the contention that real incomes were rising, hence per capita output in the Chinese countryside prior to the Pacific War was also rising.

Rising Agricultural Wages

Impressive evidence of rising living standards comes from information about trends in wages paid to agricultural laborers. Buck's data for 144 counties show that 14.1 percent of farm households earned income from working on other farms and that 15 percent of farm work was performed by hired workers.[29] Other reports indicating that hired farm laborers accounted for about 10 percent of the entire rural population confirm Buck's data.[30] With a substantial minority of the rural populace directly involved in the rural labor markets as buyers, sellers, or (at different seasons of the farm cycle) both—in some regions, one-third of all farms hired short- or long-term workers—farm wages should move in tandem with the earnings associated with the labor of the more numerous self-employed operators of family farms or rented plots.[31] Many hired laborers were themselves independent farmers, working on their

---

29. Buck, *Statistics*, 305, 309.
30. Ch'en Cheng-mo, *Ko sheng nung kung ku yung hsi kuan chi hsü kung chuang k'uang* (Nanking, 1935), 58.
31. Ch'en T'ing-hsüan, "The Feudal Nature of Farm Employment Relations in Modern China," *Chung-kuo ching chi shih yen chiu* 3 (1987):122.

own or rented land. If the wages of hired labor, negotiated among millions of farmers and laborers in markets replete with every characteristic of the economist's notion of "perfect competition," deviate substantially from the value of the extra harvest obtained by hiring extra labor, this gap should gradually disappear as farmer-workers and farmer-employers adjust their behavior in response to the disparity between wages and labor productivity.

If wages rise above the returns to self-employed farm labor, smallholders and tenant farmers will attempt to sell more days of their labor and devote less attention to their own plots; this will force wages to decline toward the level of earnings from self-employment. If wages drop below the returns from self-employment, farm workers, many of whom own or rent small plots, will partially withdraw from agricultural labor markets, forcing farm wages to rise toward equality with the return to self-employed farm work. Similar adjustments on the part of employers will help close any gap between earnings available to self-employed and hired farm workers.

Reduced transport costs and improved access to market information characteristic of the prewar decades should accelerate the pace of adjustment and reduce the possibility of protracted divergence between the earnings of hired and self-employed farm workers. Indeed, since hired workers could be found on both small and large farms and with little evidence of systematic differences in crop selection or farming practice between larger and smaller farms, the productivity and labor earnings of hired and self-employed farm workers in nearby localities would tend toward the same level as well as displaying a common trend.[32]

32. Huang's argument that labor income of self-employed farmers fell short of the earnings of farm workers in prewar North China rests on data for a single village in a single year. Brandt has shown that similar data for other villages, and even for the same village in other years, do not support Huang's position. Huang fails to consider possible differences in the age and sex structure of self-employed and hired workers and in the work schedules of the two groups. The actual hourly or daily productivity of hired and self-employed workers performing comparable tasks may be identical, but if hired workers are able-bodied males who concentrate their efforts on fieldwork, their average yearly productivity in crop-growing should exceed that of family workers because the latter include women, children, and older persons and because the tasks of family workers include cooking, washing, childcare, and handicraft production as well as farming. Huang's interview material portraying self-employed workers as more diligent than hired hands supports the expectation that his pro-

This analysis leads to the expectation that the wage incomes of the minority of farm employees and the labor earnings of the self-employed majority of tenants and owner-farmers should rise and fall together. The overwhelming share of labor earnings (as opposed to income from land rental, moneylending, mercantile activity, etc.) in the total livelihood of each of these groups permits the use of relatively abundant data on trends in farm wages as a proxy (or substitute) for information on long-term income growth for self-employed farmers. In choosing among daily, monthly, and annual farm wages, I place greatest confidence in annual figures, which are not subject to the large seasonal fluctuations that complicate comparisons involving daily or monthly farm wages.

The largest body of information on trends in farm wages comes from the study by John Buck, whose students collected time series data on farm wages in the one hundred counties shown in Map 3. These data appear in the form of index numbers of wages in each county and cover varying time spans. All of the series end in 1929–33; some begin as early as 1901, others as late as 1926. Most of the series cover the period 1908–13 to 1929–31. Criticism of Buck's survey of living standards on the grounds that the farms involved were atypically large seems irrelevant to the present circumstances. There is no reason to expect the proprietors of large farms to recollect different historic wage costs than other informants. The weakness of the wage series lies in its unavoidable dependence on the memory (and possibly written records) of village informants to reconstruct wage trends stretching back two or even three decades. Other problems involve possible distortions in converting wages into a common currency base or changes in the ratio of cash income to total (including room, board, etc.) compensation for farm workers.

Despite these qualifications and obvious deficiencies with certain figures attributed to particular localities, Buck's data do represent a substantial source of information about trends in money incomes for a significant rural group. Buck himself used these data

---

ductivity calculations may produce misleading results. See Philip C. C. Huang, *The Peasant Economy and Social Change in North China* (Stanford, 1985), esp. 70, 156–61, 166, 188–89, 196, 254 and Loren Brandt's review in *Economic Development and Cultural Change* 35, no. 3 (1987).

Map 3. Localities Providing Long-Term Farm Wage Data Analyzed in Table 6.5.

Source: John L. Buck, *Land Utilization in China, Atlas* (Nanking, 1937).

to investigate long-term trends in the earnings of farm workers. For each year between 1901 and 1933, Buck averaged all available county-level wage indexes; the number of localities covered ranged from only eight in 1901 to ninety in 1926–29. The growth rate of the resulting national index of wages for yearly contract workers in agriculture is 4.0 percent per annum, which compares favorably with the growth rates of Buck's series for retail prices paid (2.8 percent annual growth) and received (3.7 percent annual growth) by farmers and with the price of rice in Shanghai, China's largest market for farm products (2.8 percent annual growth).[33]

The results of a more comprehensive analysis of Buck's farm wage data are summarized in Table 6.5. They show a broadly rising trend for the real wages of farm workers, supporting the hypothesis of a general increase in productivity and living standards. The annual changes and long-term growth rates described in this table relate to real (that is, inflation-adjusted) wages and refer exclusively to China proper. To convert Buck's index of money wages into real terms, I have used L. L. Chang's indexes of prices received (for 1901–10) and paid (for 1910–33) by farmers in Wuchin county, Kiangsu. Chang's study appears to contain the only price index materials that both cover the entire period involved and relate to rural rather than urban price conditions. I prefer the index of prices paid by farmers, which reflects the purchasing power of rural incomes, but this series does not begin until 1910. Although price trends in Wuchin undoubtedly differed from those that farm workers encountered elsewhere in China, Brandt's finding of strong interregional links between prices of major food and fiber crops suggests that the magnitude of error introduced by the use of a single price series to deflate wage indexes from different regions is likely to be small.[34]

33. The growth rates are calculated from regression equations of the form

$$ln\ p(t) = a + bt$$

where $ln\ p$ is the natural logarithm of an index or series of wages or prices, a and b are statistically derived parameters of the regression equation, and t represents time. Data for Shanghai rice prices are from the sources cited in Table 6.6. Other data are from Buck, *Statistics*, 351–55. The regressions for prices paid and received by farmers span the years 1906–33.

34. Loren Brandt, "Chinese Agriculture and the International Economy, 1870s–1930s: A Reassessment," *Explorations in Economic History* 22 (1985) and supplemented by Brandt's unpublished work on wheat and cotton. Lien Wang,

Table 6.5
Analysis of Buck Data on Agricultural Wages, 1901-33

A. Provincial Breakdown

Province	Number of Counties				Provincial Average of County		
	Total	With Rising Real Wages			Real Wage Growth Rates		
		1901-1933	1914-1933	1925-1933	1901-1933	1914-1933	1925-1933
Kansu	5	3	4	2	-0.4%	0.0%	0.9%
Ninghsia	1	1	1	0	1.8	1.8	-1.2
Shansi	10	7	7	4	0.0	1.2	0.4
Shensi	8	6	6	6	1.0	1.5	3.9
Suiyuan	1	0	0	1	-1.6	-1.6	0.9
Tsinghai	2	0	0	0	-3.6	-4.2	-0.6
Honan	8	4	6	7	0.4	2.0	3.2
Hopei	6	6	6	6	2.2	4.0	6.2
Shantung	13	6	7	10	0.7	0.8	4.9
Anhwei	4	3	3	2	1.8	2.7	2.2
Chekiang	11	7	7	8	0.2	0.6	1.9
Hupeh	4	0	0	1	-4.3	-4.0	-2.8
Kiangsi	5	4	3	2	0.8	1.1	1.3
Kiangsu	3	2	2	1	1.2	1.0	-1.8
Hunan	2	1	1	1	0.1	1.2	0.0
Szechwan	2	0	0	1	-3.0	-4.8	5.1
Fukien	1	1	1	1	3.3	6.2	12.5
Kwangsi	4	1	1	0	-1.2	1.7	-2.9
Kwangtung	2	2	2	1	1.0	1.2	1.0
Kweichow	5	3	4	5	1.5	2.7	3.7
Yunnan	3	3	3	3	5.0	5.8	4.6
Totals	100	60	64	62	0.5	1.2	2.1

continued...

The analysis of Buck's farm wage data is based on the calculation of separate long-term growth rates for real wages in one hundred counties; the results appear in Table 6.5. Even though the county-level growth rates cover different time periods and include some extreme values that suggest defective observations, their distribution clearly supports the hypothesis of rising wages, productivity, and living standards in prewar China. Over the period 1901–33, sixty of one hundred growth rates are positive, only forty are zero

---

"Farm Prices in Szechwan 1910–1934," *Economic Facts* 9 (1938):416–17, illustrates the similarity of farm price trends in coastal Kiangsu and interior Szechwan provinces.

Table 6.5, continued

B. Statistical Distribution of County-Level Annual Growth Rates for Real Wages

	1901-1933	1914-1933	1925-1933
Negative growth			
Below -4.0%	10	8	7
-3.1 to -4.0%	3	3	3
-2.1 to -3.0	3	2	6
-1.1 to -2.0	4	8	10
0.0 to -1.0	20	15	12
Positive growth			
0.1 to 1.0%	20	13	10
1.1 to 2.0%	19	16	6
2.1 to 3.0%	8	9	7
3.1 to 4.0%	7	9	9
Above 4.0%	6	17	30
Median rate of growth	0.4	1.2	1.6

Notes: The growth rates for deflated real wages are calculated for each county using the county wage index and the indexes from Wuchin county, Kiangsu, for prices received (1901-9) and paid (1910-33) by farmers. All these data are given in Buck Statistics, 149-52. The columns marked 1901-33 include all years for which wage data are available; some of the series begin after 1901 and/or terminate before 1933. The columns marked 1914-33 exclude all data from 1901-13 and the columns marked 1925-33 exclude all data from 1901-24. I have attempted no correction for data based on nonstandard currencies or for entries showing improbably large annual changes.

or negative. The average of one hundred county growth rates is 0.5 percent per annum during 1901–33; the median, perhaps more significant due to the presence of extreme values, is 0.4 percent, indicating that half the counties surveyed experienced real wage growth above this annual rate. The preponderance of rising wages is evident if one omits counties in which wages changed at an average yearly rate of less than 0.5 percent in either direction; of the counties in which real wages changed more rapidly, forty-eight, or nearly two-thirds, increased, while only twenty-nine, or 38 percent, declined.

The data also reveal a distinct acceleration of wage growth. Separate tabulations for 1914–33 and 1925–33 show sharp increases for both the average and the median figures calculated from one hundred county-level wage series. The median annual growth rate for real farm wages increases from 0.4 percent for 1901–33 to

1.2 percent for 1914–33 and 1.6 percent for 1925–33. Except for six provinces containing only eighteen of one hundred cases, the average of county growth rates within each province is higher for 1925–33 than for 1901–33, often by a wide margin. The provincial average of county-level growth rates rises steadily between the periods shown in the right-hand columns of Table 6.5 for eleven provinces including sixty-seven of one hundred county figures.

These materials offer evidence of widespread and substantial, although by no means uniform, increases in real incomes for rural wage laborers and, by extension, for self-employed owner and tenant farmers in a large number of widely dispersed areas stretching across China proper. Scattered data for other areas in China proper, including Shansi, Ting county (Hopei), and parts of Kiangsu and Chekiang, offer further evidence of rising farm wages.[35]

Even though Buck's figures offer strong support for the hypothesis of a rising national average level of per capita farm output and income, they cannot be taken as definitive. Buck's survey methods were not systematic. The data analyzed in Table 6.5 cover only 5 percent of China's approximately two thousand counties. The home communities of Buck's students, however far-flung, do not constitute a random sample of China's farm economy, nor do his students' local informants necessarily constitute a suitable cross section of the population in individual localities. Furthermore, there is no information on how Buck's assistants obtained retrospective wage and price data covering periods of up to three decades; how, for example, were wage figures for 1901 (presumably paid in copper coins or traditional copper cash) converted to silver units? Because these questions cannot be answered, further evidence is needed to support the hypothesis of rising per capita output, income, and living standards in rural China prior to the Pacific War.

35. For Ting county, see n. 66; for Kiangsu, see Table 6.7. Walter H. Mallory reported a doubling of Shansi farm wages in the decade ending in the mid-1920s (*China: Land of Famine* [New York, 1926], 12). Terry M. Weidner, "Rural Economy and Local Government in Nationalist China: Chekiang Province, 1927–1937" (Ph.D. diss., University of California, Davis, 1980), 83–84, writes that "the wages paid hired farm labor in Chekiang during the [late 1920s] . . . were . . . sharply higher than the average wages paid in preceding years," especially for long-term labor; in one county, farm wages in 1927 were "more than double the standard farm wage in 1907."

Rising Rural Incomes:
Wages in Cotton Textile Factories

Wage trends in nonfarm occupations that employed large numbers of villagers can provide indirect evidence of changes in rural income levels. The logic of this approach is simple. Profit-seeking employers have no incentive to pay more than the minimum wage required to attract unskilled workers, especially if their products enter competitive markets that offer little opportunity to "pass along" higher wage costs in the form of increased product prices. In prewar China, the number of available recruits for unskilled occupations was essentially limitless. The large scale of internal migration demonstrates that employers could attract labor into new regions or occupations by offering wages above those available to potential migrants in their home districts. Thomas Gottschang's study of labor flows from North China to Manchuria, which saw an annual average of about one-half million people moving in both directions between 1891 and 1942, finds that "the majority of migrants were not blindly fleeing the ravages of war and famine, but were pursuing carefully calculated economic opportunities." The responsiveness of North China farmers to economic opportunity in distant regions is reflected in Gottschang's finding that the rate of migration rose and fell with the gap between the wages in the migrants' home districts of Hopei and Shantung and the wages in Manchuria.[36]

In the absence of government intervention or effective trade union pressure, there was no economic reason for nonfarm employers to raise the wages of unskilled workers unless rising village incomes threatened to dry up the flow of new recruits from the countryside. As long as nonagricultural employment amounted to only a small fraction of the potential labor pool, the operators of factories and mines could expand their unskilled work force without substantially increasing the gap between nonfarm wages and agricultural incomes in the surrounding countryside. Under these conditions, entry-level wages for unskilled workers outside the farm

36. Thomas R. Gottschang, "Economic Development in Northeast China" (Worcester, 1984), 24, and "Structural Change, Disasters, and Migration: The Historical Case of Manchuria," *Economic Development and Cultural Change* 35, no. 3 (1987):480–81.

sector need not rise unless higher productivity in farming leads to a general increase in incomes and living standards in regions that supply factory labor. In the case of prewar China, research by Thomas Wiens verifies that the "national industrial wage structure" of the 1930s "was related to the regional structure of agricultural wages," and that farm wages were "market determined" and not controlled by subsistence requirements, living costs, or local custom.[37] Further information on the relation between agricultural incomes and nonfarm wages emerges from wage trends in cotton spinning and coal mining, two industries that employed large numbers of village migrants.

China's largest prewar industry was cotton textiles. Textile markets were fiercely competitive. Precarious finances gave manufacturers the utmost incentive to exercise stringent control over all costs, including wages. In the words of D. K. Lieu: "The psychology of . . . people who promote industries . . . is quite obvious. They prefer low costs in order to enable them to compete with other factories. . . . Anything that will lower the cost of production and make it unnecessary to invest large sums of money is always welcome to them."[38] Shanghai's textile mills, which dominated the industry, employed large numbers of young women, many of whom were recruited from rural areas by labor contractors. Emily Honig notes that recruiters supplied young village girls with "high-heeled shoes to wear so that they would appear tall enough to reach the bar at the gate that was used to measure the minimum height requirement" of the Shanghai cotton mills.[39] The low skill levels of entering workers and their close ties with the rural economy of the surrounding countryside make textile wages a good test of possible interactions between urban wage rates and rural income levels.

Table 6.6 presents time series data on the wages of workers in Shanghai textile plants. Nominal payments are converted into real wages using the Shanghai wholesale rice price, a technique applied

37. Thomas B. Wiens, *The Microeconomics of Peasant Economy in China, 1912–1940* (New York, 1982), 169–81.
38. D. K. Lieu, *The Growth and Industrialization of Shanghai* (Shanghai, 1936), 103.
39. Emily Honig, "The Contract Labor System and Women Workers: Pre-Liberation Cotton Mills of Shanghai," *Modern China* 9, no. 4 (1983):429.

Table 6.6
Nominal and Real Wages for Shanghai Textile Workers, 1915-40

Year	Nominal Wage (yuan)		Rice Price (yuan per shih)	Real Wage (shih of rice)	
	Daily	Monthly (includes subsidy)		Daily	Monthly
	(1)	(2)	(3)	(4)	(5)
1910	0.26[a]	...	7.13	.036	...
1911	0.26[a]	...	7.98	.032	...
1912	0.27[a]	...	7.94	.034	...
1913	0.27[a]	...	7.21	.037	...
1914	0.27[a]	...	6.42	.042	...
1915	0.27[a]	5.00-6.50[a]	7.40	.036	0.68-0.88
1916	0.27[a]	...	7.12	.038	...
1917	0.27[a]	...	6.52	.041	...
1918	0.27[a]	...	6.62	.041	...
1919	0.29[a]	...	6.94	.042	...
1920	...	6.75-8.78[a]	9.61	...	0.70-0.91
1924	...	9.44	10.29	...	...
1925	...	11.42	10.20	...	...
1927	...	11.89	13.94	...	0.85
1929	...	10.70	12.44	...	0.86
1930	0.42[a]	12.50	15.86	.026	0.79
1931	0.42[a]	...	12.03	.035	...
1932	0.46[a]	13.99	11.62	.040	1.20
1933	0.45[a]	13.98	8.38	.054	1.67
1934	0.46[a]	12.25	10.26	.045	1.19
1935	...	12.04	12.18	...	0.99
1936	...	12.82 10.73[b]	10.43	...	1.23 (1.03)[b]
1937	...	11.09	12.20	...	0.91
1938	...	13.56	13.75	...	0.99
1939	...	17.51	23.72	...	0.74
1940	...	28.08	63.27	...	0.44

[a]Source specifies that wage figures apply to female workers.

[b]The data pertain to Shen-hsin no. 9 mill. The data for 1924-27 are from the same firm's no. 1 mill. Other data for 1932-36 are from Shen-hsin's no. 1 and no. 8 mills.

continued...

in several recent studies by Chinese economic historians. In the absence of broad indexes of price movements or living costs spanning the entire period of analysis, this approach offers a reasonable method of deflating nominal wages for a low income economy in which staple foodgrains occupy a large share of household budgets.

Table 6.6, continued

    Source: Daily wages during 1910-19 for female workers in cotton
    spinning plants are from "Explanation of Table Showing Trends in
    Major Wages and Prices for Shanghai in the Past Ten Years," Chiao yü
    yü chih yeh 22 (1920). Daily wages for 1930-34 are derived from
    hourly wages and hours worked by female cotton spinning operatives
    recorded in Wage Rates in Shanghai (Shanghai, 1935), 98-99. Monthly
    wage data are from Huang Han-min, "Brief Analysis of Annual
    Fluctuations in Nominal Wage Income of Shanghai Workers, 1927-1936,"
    Shang-hai ching chi k'o hsüeh 1 (1985):43 (for 1929 and 1930) and
    "Analysis of Pre-Liberation Wage Level for Shanghai Workers," Shang-
    hai ching chi k'o hsüeh 3 (1984):51-58 (for other years). Annual
    average prices for "keng" rice are from Feng Liu-t'ang, ed., Shang-
    hai min shih wen t'i (Shanghai, 1931), 147-48 (for 1910-24) and from
    Shang-hai chieh fang ch'ien hou wu chia tzu liao hui pien, 1927-1957
    (Shanghai, 1958), 213 (for 1925-40).

The real wage figures in Columns 4 and 5 indicate the rice equivalent of the corresponding nominal wage payments recorded in Columns 1 and 2.

The daily wage figures in Column 1 refer to the earnings of female operatives in cotton spinning plants. The wage figures for 1910–19 confirm that large increases in factory output and employment did not require higher wages. The output of factory yarn, most of which was made in Shanghai, jumped from 472 to 918 thousand bales between 1910 and 1919.[40] Although this no doubt entailed a corresponding increase in demand for mill workers, the figures in Table 6.6 show no significant rise in money wages between 1910 and 1919; the variations in real wages reflect the impact of price fluctuations on static wage payments.

The monthly wage figures shown in Column 2 are the result of recent archival research by a Chinese scholar, Huang Han-min, who has adjusted the wage totals to include bonuses, fines, and supplements to basic compensation. The monthly data are therefore more complete than the daily wage figures. Huang's figures for 1915 and 1920 are for female workers. Huang does not identify the sex of workers whose wages are recorded in later years, but the figures appear to refer to female workers who dominated Shanghai's textile work force.

The data collected in Table 6.6 show that real wages paid to Shanghai cotton textile workers increased during the two decades

40. Kang Chao, *The Development of Cotton Textile Production in China* (Cambridge, 1977), 308.

prior to the outbreak of the Pacific War in 1937. The daily wage totals show a small rise of 0.4 percent per year in real wages. The average purchasing power of daily wages for female workers in 1930–34 is 10 percent above the comparable figure for 1910–14. Comparing 1931–34 with 1911–14 increases the difference to 20 percent. The monthly wage figures, which provide a fuller picture of both compensation and employment, show much larger increases, apparently because of rapidly growing wage supplements. The average of monthly real wages (Column 5) in 1932–36 is 39–85 percent above the figure for 1915 and 35–80 percent above the wage levels reported for 1920. Real wages appear to have risen sharply between 1927 and 1932. Regression analysis shows daily real wages rising at an annual rate of 0.4 percent during 1910–36; monthly real wages, which better reflect total compensation, rise at annual rates of 1.4–3.0 percent depending on the treatment of years for which alternative figures appear in Table 6.6.[41] This clear upward trend in real wages for cotton textile workers was not confined to Shanghai. Information for 1920 on wages paid to female workers in cotton spinning plants shows that Shanghai workers received somewhat higher compensation than mill hands elsewhere in Kiangsu or in other provinces.[42] The data for 1930 show no increase in this gap between wages in Shanghai and other textile centers.[43] With living costs in major industrial centers following

41. Calculated by regressing the logarithm of real wages (dependent variable) against a constant term and time trend (independent variables). The regression involving daily wages offers a poor fit. Similar log-linear regression equations establishing trend lines for monthly real wages produce substantial correlation coefficients and (in most cases) satisfy the usual significance tests. Using the higher of alternative monthly wage figures for 1915 and 1920 and the lower alternative for 1936, choices that reduce the estimated growth rate, puts monthly real wage growth at 1.4 percent per year. Using midpoints for 1915, 1920, and 1936 raises the growth rate to 2.1 percent; substituting the higher figure for 1936 and the lower alternatives for 1915 and 1920 yields a maximum growth rate of 3.0 percent.

42. The average of the minimum and maximum daily wage reported for thirteen Shanghai mills in 1920 was 0.24 and 0.54 yuan. The average for nine Kiangsu mills was 0.16 and 0.50 yuan. For seven mills in other provinces, the average minimum and maximum wage was 0.15 and 0.50 yuan. See (*Ti chiu tz'u*) *nung shang t'ung chi piao* (Peking, 1924), 272–75.

43. Average monthly wages in 1930 for female employees of six Kiangsu cotton textile mills (spinning and weaving) were 13.54 yuan; for ten mills in other provinces, the average was 12.44 yuan. Daily wages for female workers in Shanghai spinning and weaving mills during 1930 are reported as 0.425 and

similar trends, I conclude that real wage increases in Shanghai's textile mills were matched or perhaps surpassed elsewhere.

Huang Han-min attributes prewar wage behavior to a number of factors, especially the pressure exerted by the Shanghai labor movement and shifts in business conditions. But the timing of the wage increases shown in Table 6.6 is inconsistent with the view that union pressures forced wages up, for the largest wage increases came after the Kuomintang's suppression of the Shanghai labor movement in 1927. High wages persisted into the 1930s when the adverse consequences of the world depression, natural disasters, and military disturbances in China placed factory workers "on the defensive against mass dismissals, factory closures, wage reductions, and reduced working hours."[44] Why should profit-seeking businessmen have paid higher real wages to a work force that was largely female, transient, unskilled, and unorganized unless market conditions compelled employers to offer higher pay in order to secure an adequate flow of prospective employees from the villages surrounding major textile centers? And why should prospective textile workers have required rising real wage payments to attract them into urban occupations unless alternative income opportunities in their home communities had improved markedly during the decades following the collapse of the Ch'ing dynasty in 1911?

Mark Rebick has confirmed the link between textile wages and farm wages in Japan, where "both the annual and daily agricultural wages for females are well correlated with the cotton textile wage" in this female-dominated industry during 1909–30.[45] In the case of Kiangsu province, the source for the majority of textile workers in Shanghai and, because of the leading position of Shanghai and Kiangsu in the industry, for all China, information on wages paid

---

0.475 yuan respectively; assuming thirty workdays, monthly wages could be no more than 12.75–14.25 yuan. Shanghai data are from *Wage Rates in Shanghai* (Shanghai, 1935), 99, 107. Other data are from *Ch'üan kuo kung jen sheng huo chi kung yeh sheng ch'an tiao ch'a t'ung chi pao kao shu* (Nanking, 1930), 2:1–67.

44. Jürgen Osterhammel, "Imperialism in Transition: British Business and the Chinese Authorities, 1931–37," *China Quarterly* 98 (1984):277.

45. Mark Rebick, "Labour-Tying in Japanese Agriculture, 1894–1940" (Toronto, 1984), 8.

to farm laborers provides ample evidence of a general rise in rural wage levels. Buck's data provide long-term real growth rates for farm wages deflated as described above for three counties: there are substantial increases for Wusih (1.4 percent per year during 1908–33), a textile center in the Yangtze delta region, and for Yench'eng (3.1 percent per year during 1909–33), a region that supplied labor to the Shanghai mills, and a substantial decrease in Wuchin (− 1.0 percent per year for 1918–30), another county in the delta region.[46] To supplement these inconclusive results, Table 6.7 presents data on annual wages paid to male and female farm workers in forty-four Kiangsu counties between 1923/25 and 1932. The sources present information on daily and monthly wages as well, but I use annual figures to avoid possible distortion arising from the wide seasonal variation of daily and monthly farm wages. Even though ignorance of the procedures used to obtain wage figures necessitates ample allowance for data errors, the figures show an unmistakable and nearly uniform upward trend in rural wages throughout the province between 1923/25 and 1932. If data showing local real wage shifts of less than 10 percent in either direction are taken as indicating wage stability, the data may be decomposed as follows (the figures represent the number of counties in each category):

	Rising Wages	*Falling Wages*	*Stable Wages*
Females	15	3	1
Males	34	1	9

With 49 of 53 significant changes in the upward direction and the real wage index rising by an average of 46 percent for female farm workers and 45 percent for male farm workers on yearly contracts even using the lower of alternative wage figures for 1932 and excluding cases with suspiciously high percentage increases (see note *a* in Table 6.7), it is evident that real wages paid to Kiangsu farm laborers rose sharply between the mid-1920s and the early 1930s.

I anticipate that wage trends for unorganized and unskilled textile workers are closely linked to changes in productivity and earnings in rural occupations available to potential textile employees. The real earnings of cotton textile workers moved upward between

---

46. These results are taken from the calculations underlying Table 6.5.

Table 6.7
Trends in Annual Wages for Farm Workers in Kiangsu, 1923-1932

| County | Annual Farm Wages | | | | Price Deflator | 1932 Real Wage Index (1923/25 = 100) | |
| | Males | | Females | | | | |
	1923/25	1932	1923/25	1932		Male	Female
Nan-hui	32.33	36	16.50	24	1.218	91.4	119.4
Feng-hsien	31.2	40	...	30	1.218	105.3	...
Sung-chiang	28.71	108	12.00	72	1.218	308.9	492.6[a]
Ch'uan-sha	36.00	85	...	45	1.218	193.9	...
Shang-hai	37.33	50	27.00	...	1.218	110.0	...
Ch'ing-p'u	23.60	40[b]	...	...	1.218	139.2	...
Chin-shan	32.80	36	16.00	...	1.218	90.1	...
Wu-chiang	28.14	50[b]	...	...	1.218	145.9	...
K'un-shan	23.25	30	25.00	...	1.218	105.9	...
Chia-ting	26.13	50	12.00	...	1.218	157.1	...
Pao-shan	36.33	70	16.00	50	1.218	158.2	256.6
Ch'ung-ming	21.78	36	9.50	18	1.218	135.7	155.6
T'ai-tsang	27.33	40	24.00	40	1.218	120.2	136.8
Ch'ang-shu	28.13	60[b]	25.20	...	1.218	175.1	...
Wusih	35.83	60	18.33	...	1.218	137.5	...
Chiang-yin	27.3	40	21.10	20	1.218	120.3	77.8
Wu-chin	25.88	55	12.00	25	1.218	174.5	171.0
I-hsing	32.88	70	...	50	1.218	174.8	...
Li-yang	22.88	40[b]	6.00	10[b]	1.218	143.5	136.8
Li-shui	33.27	40	10.00	30	1.218	98.7	246.3
Chu-jung	23.78	50	11.80	30	1.218	172.6	208.8
Liu-ho	54.78	100	40.00	70	1.218	149.9	143.7
I-ch'eng	27.25	140	16.00	100	1.243	413.3[a]	502.8[a]
Chin-t'an	19.8	40[b]	10.67	20[b]	1.218	165.9	153.9
Tan-yang	22.82	50	11.00	70	1.218	179.9	522.5[a]
Yang-chung	15.63	30	...	15	1.218	157.6	...
T'ai-hsing	16.88	20[b]	8.13	10[b]	1.218	97.3	101.0
Chiang-tu	29.15	50	19.20	...	1.243	138.0	...
Kao-yü	31.85	50	26.92	30	1.243	126.3	89.6
Pao-ying	28.38	20	16.69	10	1.243	56.7	50.3
Huai-an	28.33	40	11.25	...	1.243	113.6	...
Huai-yin	20.40	40	...	...	1.243	157.8	...
Ssu-yang	19.91	36	...	26	1.243	145.5	...
Wu	32.22	50	20.22	...	1.218	127.4	...
Lien-shui	18.73	25	...	15	1.243	107.4	...
Fou-ning	22.25	40[b]	...	20	1.243	144.6	...
Yen-ch'eng	23.13	50	...	20	1.243	173.9	...
Hsing-hua	23.90	100	16.14	...	1.243	336.6[a]	...
Tung-t'ai	21.36	90	...	70	1.243	339.0[a]	...
T'ai	16.20	60	6.50	...	1.243	298.0	...
Ju-kao	10.46	18[b]	7.00	12[b]	1.218	141.3	140.7
Ch'ing-chiang	19.00	80	10.14	...	1.218	345.7[a]	...
Nan-t'ung	15.27	20[b]	...	10[b]	1.218	107.5	...
Hai-men	19.67	120	11.00	74	1.218	500.9[a]	552.3[a]
Average of all figures						172.4	197.8
Average of all figures excluding items marked [a]						144.9	145.9

Table 6.7, continued

[a]Indicates data showing improbably large wage increases.

[b]Lower of alternative wage figures used for 1932.

Sources: The wage data for 1923/25 are from Ch'en Ta, Chung-kuo lao kung wen t'i (Shanghai, 1929), 356-64; for 1932, from China Industrial Handbooks, Kiangsu (Shanghai, 1933), 36-37. The price deflator is the index of retail prices paid by farmers in Wuchin county, Kiangsu, as reported in A. B. Lewis and Lien Wang, "Farm Prices in Wuchin, Kiangsu," Economic Facts 2 (1936):87. Since the price index is the same for 1923 and 1925, nominal wage changes between these years and 1932 were deflated by the same figure, 1.218; nominal wage changes between 1924 and 1932 were deflated by a factor of 1.243.

1910 and the mid-1930s, with most of the rise concentrated in the final prewar decade. This suggests a concomitant rise in productivity and income in the agricultural regions that supplied labor to the textile industry. In the case of Kiangsu, the province that housed the largest concentration of textile mills and supplied the largest cohort of prewar textile employees, large increases in the real value of rural wages occur during the same period that the real earnings of textile workers rise substantially. This evidence is fully consistent with the hypothesis of rising rural productivity, incomes, and living standards and the view that wage trends in unskilled nonfarm occupations can be taken as indicators of changes in agricultural productivity.

Rising Rural Incomes: Wages in Coal Mining

Coal mining offers an opportunity to investigate the hypothesis of rising rural incomes from a different perspective. In contrast to cotton textiles, in which a primarily female labor force worked in urban locations concentrated in the Yangtze delta area of Kiangsu province, coal mines employed male workers in rural locations, including many in the northern provinces of Hopei, Shantung, and Shansi. The rural character of the unskilled work force in mining is readily apparent from contemporary accounts. Small mines employed seasonal workers who returned to their villages during periods of peak farm activity. Mine operators either curtailed production during the summer months or raised wages to encourage

workers to remain on the job.[47] Price competition between products from domestic and foreign mines was a regular feature of
China's prewar coal markets. Although Wright finds that "politics
played a central role both in the general development of the [coal]
industry and in the relations between individual mines," selling
prices were determined by market forces that remained outside
the control of the mine operators.[48] In the major port cities,
domestic coal from different regions faced competition from Japanese imports. In the countryside, traditional small-scale mines
were capable of "spoiling the market" for coal from large-scale
operations.[49]

In this environment, control of production and transport costs
was essential to profitability. The regular publication of comparative cost data reflected the mining community's keen interest in
the competitive position of various enterprises. Despite the low
wages paid to Chinese employees, labor costs contributed significantly to financial results. Between 1920 and 1936, total wage payments at the K'ai-luan mines, a major coal complex in North China,
amounted to 55 percent of cumulative profits for the whole enterprise, of which coal mining formed only one segment; in some
years, wage payments exceeded annual profits.[50] Under these circumstances, mine operators had every incentive to resist wage increases. My analysis of real wage trends in coal mining focuses on
two major enterprises for which time series data could be located:
the K'ai-luan complex in Hopei province and the Chung-hsing
mine in neighboring Shantung.

The K'ai-luan colliery, located east of Peking near the city of
T'ang-shan, was among the most technically progressive enterprises in prewar China. The Kaiping mines, originally established
by Chinese capital in an area that had long supported unmechanized small-scale mining, fell into foreign hands in 1900 and

47. Tezuka Masao and Maeda Takahisa, Shina shotankō jittai chōsa hōkoku:
Santōsho Hakuzan dohō tankō o chūshin toshite (Tokyo, 1943), 47 and Tim
Wright, "Growth of the Modern Chinese Coal Industry: An Analysis of Supply
and Demand," Modern China 7, no. 3 (1981):324.
48. Tim Wright, "Entrepreneurs, Politicians and the Chinese Coal Industry,
1895–1937," Modern Asian Studies 14, no. 4 (1980):596.
49. Ibid., 595–96.
50. Chiu Chung-kuo K'ai-luan mei k'uang ti kung tzu chih tu ho pao kung chih
tu (Tientsin, 1983), 144–45.

merged in 1912 with a rival Chinese firm to create K'ai-luan.[51] Historians at Nan-k'ai University have recently published time series data for K'ai-luan wages based on detailed archival research.[52] The Nan-k'ai authors compile separate wage series for different groups of workers and try to reduce a complex wage system that included bonuses and payments in kind to equivalent cash payments. At K'ai-luan, as at other mines, employees were divided into two groups: "inside workers" (*li kung*) employed directly by the mine's management and "outside workers" (*wai kung*), who were hired, supervised, and paid by labor contractors and had no direct dealings with management.[53] The Nan-k'ai study tabulates wage data for three groups of workers: machine operators, underground coal workers, and underground laborers, of which the last two were outside workers and the first were hired directly. I focus on the underground laborers who, unlike the others, are specifically described as "unskilled." Their ties to the farm economy should be much closer than those of the technically trained machine operators and coal workers.[54]

Table 6.8 reproduces the Nan-k'ai data on nominal and real wages of "miscellaneous underground laborers" at K'ai-luan. Real wages are obtained by deflating money wages by the price of flour, the principal foodstuff consumed by miners and their families. The real wage data measure the amount of flour that workers could purchase with their monthly wages at various dates. The only difficulty with these figures is the apparent exaggeration of the rise in flour prices during 1935–36; I have supplemented the original figure with what appears to be a more reasonable estimate.

What do these data show? The Nan-k'ai authors emphasize the low level of wages and note the inability of mine workers to achieve

51. On the history of K'ai-luan, see Ellsworth C. Carlson, *The Kaiping Mines, 1877–1912* (Cambridge, 1971).
52. I have used two studies: Yen Kuang-hua and Ting Ch'ang-ch'ing, "The Level of Workers' Wages at the Old K'ai-luan Coal Mines," *Nan-k'ai ching-chi yen-chiu-so chi k'an* 2 (1982) and *Chiu Chung-kuo K'ai-luan mei k'uang*. Where the data presented in the two sources differ, I assume that the latter publication takes precedence.
53. Information about labor contractors offers further insight into the agrarian nature of the work force in coal mines. A 1920 survey listed farming as the father's occupation for twenty of twenty-two labor contractors. See *Kairan tankō rōdō chōsa hōkoku* (Peking, 1943), 1:39–41.
54. On the three groups, see Yen and Ting, "Wages," 37.

Table 6.8
Nominal and Real Wages of Underground Laborers at K'ai-luan Mines,
1887-1944

Year	Average Monthly Wage (total compensation)		Real Wage Index Based on Nominal Wage and Flour Prices (1920 = 100)
	Yuan	Flour Equivalent (bags)	
1887	3.47	3.61	176.1
1905	5.34	3.28	160.0
1920	6.41	2.05	100.0
1922	6.94	2.16	105.4
1924	7.74	2.46	120.0
1927	8.54	2.18	106.3
1929	10.68	2.87	140.0
1931	14.40	4.29	209.3
1935	14.40	4.91	239.5
1936	14.52	2.91	142.0
		(3.81)[a]	(185.8)[a]
1938	18.39	3.41	166.3
1939	27.50	3.20	156.1
1941	80.28	3.58	174.6
1942	91.87	3.48	169.8
1943	439.40	3.38	164.9
1944	1985.60	2.92	142.4

Log-linear regression results: (Standard errors in parentheses)	Constant	Time Trend	R^2
1920-1936			
A. Original price data:	-82.080 (27.541)	0.043 (0.143)	0.60
B. Revised price data:	-102.490 (19.814)	0.054 (0.010)	0.82
1920-1944			
A. Original price data:	-37 415 (13.589)	0.020 (0.007)	0.40
B. Revised price data:	-39.076 (14.068)	0.021 (0.007)	0.40

[a]Derived from an assumed 30 percent increase in flour prices during 1935/36 based on the behavior of Tientsin flour prices shown in Nan-k'ai chih shu tzu liao, 70.

Source: Except as noted, the data on wages and flour prices are from Chiu Chung-kuo K'ai-luan mei k'uang, 126.

what contemporary accounts regarded as a respectable standard of living.[55] The figures show a decline in real wages between 1887 and 1920, but this outcome depends on an unspecified conversion from copper cash to silver and on flimsy estimates of flour prices for 1887 and 1905.[56] The figures beginning in 1920 are solidly based on archival materials and can be checked against published sources of wage and price data. They show an unmistakable rise in real wages that accelerates after 1927. Real wages rise steadily from 1927 to a 1935 peak. Although worker incomes declined in real terms after 1935, real wages remained distinctly above the levels reported for the 1920s. The purchasing power of monthly wages in any year between 1929 and 1945 surpassed the comparable figure for any year between 1920 and 1927 by a minimum of 17 percent. The average of real wages in 1935/36 surpassed the average for 1924/27 by 68–88 percent, depending on which figure is used for 1936.

Regression analysis of real wage growth summarized in the lower segment of Table 6.8 confirms the impression of substantial wage increase, with the annual growth rate of real wages for "miscellaneous underground laborers" amounting to 4.3–5.4 percent between 1920 and 1936, depending on which price figure is used for 1936. The upward trend of real wages is also evident if the analysis is extended to 1944. Information about average wages for the entire K'ai-luan work force shows a similar pattern of rising real wages.[57]

Why did real wages rise? The Nan-k'ai authors cite two reasons: union pressure and market forces. Union pressure certainly existed. Strikes occurred in 1920 and 1922 and another was threatened in 1929.[58] Labor unrest was reported between 1934 and 1936.[59] Agreements between workers and management had a last-

55. Yen and Ting, "Wages," 40.
56. Yen and Ting, "Wages," 41, where daily wages for 1887 and 1905 are given in "yuan" even though payment in silver is highly improbable, especially for 1887.
57. If the method of Table 6.8 is applied to average wage data for all K'ai-luan mine workers (shown in *Chiu Chung-kuo K'ai-luan mei k'uang*, 142), average real wage growth during 1920–36 amounts to 4.4–5.0 percent per year.
58. Yen and Ting, "Wages," 41.
59. Osterhammel notes that "miners were killed [during confrontations between labor and management] in January and March 1934. . . . Discontent among the miners was ruthlessly put down in July 1935 and in May/June 1936" ("Imperialism in Transition," 278).

ing impact: a contract executed in 1941 refers to union agreements of ten and twelve years earlier.[60] Yet union efforts seem to have slackened just as real wages began to rise. The Nan-k'ai authors make no mention of union pressure for higher wages after 1924, arguing instead that higher real wages during the 1930s were a sham because the gains were not permanent.[61]

A surprising feature of wage behavior is that skilled workers received the lowest pay increases. Between 1927 and 1935 the real wages of skilled machine operators and coal workers rose by 54 and 107 percent respectively, while the purchasing power commanded by unskilled general laborers jumped by no less than 125 percent. This occurred even though company records from the mid-1920s indicate the need to raise wages of skilled workers to prevent them from completing the mine's training program and then departing for more lucrative opportunities with the railways or in Tientsin.[62] With no record of vigorous union agitation for wage increases after 1924, it appears that differential pay increases favoring unskilled workers also represent a managerial response to market pressures.

This view draws support from Buck's long-term farm wage data for six Hopei counties, all of which show a rising real wage trend (Table 6.5). Farm wages in Ch'ang-li county, which borders the county in which K'ai-luan is located, rose at an average annual rate of 5.0 percent (after adjustment for inflation) between 1905 and 1929.[63] Further evidence of rising wages comes from data for the mid-1920s indicating that yearly contracts for male farm laborers paid as little as 11 yuan in some localities, 30–40 yuan in others, and 60–70 yuan in Ch'in-huang-tao and T'ang-shan (near K'ai-luan).[64] Although both samples are very small, Buck's Hopei wage figures for 1929–33 are considerably higher. The lowest cash payment recorded by Buck is 33.3 yuan, or nearly triple the figure of

60. *Kairan tankō rōdō chōsa hōkoku*, 1:93.
61. Yen and Ting, "Wages," 41–42.
62. *Chiu Chung-kuo K'ai-luan mei k'uang*, 123, 126, 127 and Yen and Ting, "Wages," 42.
63. Based on the calculations underlying Table 6.5.
64. The data are from *(Ti i tz'u) Chung-kuo lao tung nien chien* (Peking, 1928), 539–42, citing sources published in 1926 and 1927. Excluding exceptional figures and payments reported in strings of copper cash, two localities report annual wages below 20 yuan, one reports a range of 20–30 yuan, four fall within the range of 30–40 yuan, two report 60–70 yuan, and one indicates a range of 40–80 yuan. All figures refer to cash payments only.

11.3 yuan reported for Pao-fu-shih (near Peking) a few years earlier. Both the median and the mean of Buck's data exceed comparable statistics derived from earlier reports by slightly over 10 yuan.[65] Ting county also reported steep increases in farm wages, with annual payments rising by 50–100 percent during 1910–20 and another 100 percent or more during 1920–30, while monthly and daily wages increased even faster.[66] With the cost-of-living index for Tientsin workers rising by only 6 percent between 1926/27 and 1929/33 and the Tientsin price level increasing by 72 percent between 1913 and 1930, these pay increases seem to reflect substantial rises in real incomes for farm laborers.[67]

Additional support for a market-linked explanation of rising wages at K'ai-luan comes from data on the level of farm wages during the early 1930s in Hopei, home of 90 percent of K'ai-luan's workers.[68] A 1932 national survey reported average cash payments of 43.89 yuan (plus room and board) to male farm workers under annual contract in ninety-two Hopei counties.[69] Buck's figures for nine counties during 1929–33 indicate a similar average cash payment of 45.74 yuan for annual labor contracts. Total employment costs (in yuan) in localities covered by Buck's survey, including the cash value of room and board, amounted to:[70]

	Number of Localities	Average	Median	Range
Daily wages	9	0.52	0.50	0.38–0.72
Monthly wages	9	9.42	9.00	6.8–13.5
Annual wages	9	88.36	81.33	68.7–125

65. The median and mean of the Buck data (cash payments only) are 44.0 and 45.7 yuan (*Statistics*, 328). The median and mean of the earlier data (using mid-points whenever wages were expressed as ranges of figures) are 33.1 and 35.0 yuan.
66. Sidney D. Gamble, *Ting Hsien: A North China Rural Community* (Reprint, Stanford, 1968), 229.
67. The cost-of-living index is from *Kahoku ni okeru kōtsū unyu rōdōsha chōsa* (Peking, 1942), 146. The price index is from *Nan-k'ai chih shu tzu liao hui pien, 1913–1952* (Peking, 1958), 11.
68. Data (for 1935) on miners' origins are from *Kairan tankō rōdō chōsa hōkoku*, 2:23–24.
69. "Wages of Farm Labor in Different Provinces," *T'ung chi yüeh pao* 13 (1933):100.
70. Buck, *Statistics*, 328. Monthly wages are for periods during the growing season.

Daily and monthly wages paid to K'ai-luan's unskilled workers during 1924–27 fell well short of the average or median earnings reported for Hopei farm workers during 1929–33. Buck's sample of farm wages is a small one, but its results closely resemble data produced by the much larger study cited previously (see note 69). In Ch'ang-li county farmers reported monthly farm labor costs (including room and board) of 8.2 yuan during 1929–33, well above monthly wages at nearby K'ai-luan during 1920–24.[71]

Comparing the K'ai-luan wage figures with the earnings of Hopei farm laborers suggests a market-oriented explanation of rising wages for unskilled miners. If Buck's data are representative of rural wage conditions in the regions from which K'ai-luan drew its unskilled workers, the upward trend in rural wages seemingly necessitated substantial increases in entry-level mining wages to induce even landless laborers to leave their villages and take up the dangerous occupation of mining. Even with large wage increases, the daily wage of 0.48 yuan paid to K'ai-luan's general laborers between 1931 and 1935 barely matched the average farm wage reported by Buck's Hopei informants; in Ch'ang-li, the cost of daily farm labor during the growing season was given as 0.50 yuan.[72] Although union pressures may have contributed to raising the earnings of workers at K'ai-luan, this analysis of trends in Hopei farm wages points to an upward trend in rural labor productivity—reflected in rising farm wages—as the underlying cause. Higher wages at K'ai-luan were required to keep pace with rising farm wages in nearby rural communities.

The Chung-hsing coal mine, located on the border between I and Teng counties in southwestern Shantung, is another coal enterprise for which there is detailed information on wage trends. Wage data are available for two groups of workers: Group A, which included men with technical skills, and Group C, which accounted for the largest number of mine employees. I focus on the latter, who are described as "mostly unskilled but including a small segment of semi-skilled workers," and especially on data for the 25 percent of workers in the C category who received the lowest wages, a group undoubtedly dominated by unskilled men who

71. Buck, *Statistics*, 328.
72. *Chiu Chung-kuo K'ai-luan mei k'uang*, 126 and Buck, *Statistics*, 328.

maintained close links to the regional agrarian economy.[73] Information about wage payments to this subset of Group C workers at Chung-hsing appears in Table 6.9. I have followed the Nan-k'ai study of the K'ai-luan mine in deflating money wages by the price of flour to obtain a series of real wage estimates that measure the purchasing power of miners' wages in terms of bags of flour. Real wages for the lowest-paid 25 percent of Group C workers at Chung-hsing increased briefly during 1917–19, dropped sharply during 1919–21, fluctuated around the low 1921 figure for the next five years, and then rose steeply to a 1931 level that surpassed the previous 1919 peak by nearly 25 percent. Wage data from another source indicate that real wage gains were maintained or increased between 1931 and 1933. Log-linear regression analysis yields a growth rate of 1.5 percent for real wages of the lowest-paid 25 percent of Chung-hsing miners between 1917 and 1933. The timing of real wage increases at Chung-hsing fits closely with the parallel increase for K'ai-luan described above. I cannot determine whether real wages remained at high levels after 1933 at Chung-hsing as occurred at K'ai-luan.

The authors of a survey of Chung-hsing's labor force noted the rapid wage increases of the late 1920s and did not hesitate to attribute improved pay scales to the efforts of the workers' trade union.[74] Their description of the union's organization, activities, and financing, however, leaves little doubt that the union was too weak to influence the company's wage policies. The labor survey refers to three rounds of union-management negotiations in February and August of 1929 and in March 1931. The first two rounds of bargaining led to published agreements, but many provisions were not implemented, perhaps because the union was not formally established until the end of 1930, after which implementation of earlier agreements became one of its chief objectives. Union efforts may have contributed to wage increases obtained in 1930–31, but it is unlikely that informal worker groups forced the much larger increases recorded between 1926 and 1930, especially since their main efforts were directed toward improvements in "education,

---

73. Shih Yü-shou and Liu Hsin-ch'üan, "Survey of Workers at the Chung-hsing Coal Mine in Shantung," *She hui k'o hsüeh tsa chih* 3, no. 1 (1932):62.
74. The following paragraph draws on Shih and Liu, "Survey of Workers," 77–79.

Table 6.9
Nominal and Real Wages at Chung-hsing Coal Mine, Shantung, 1917-31
(July wages for lowest-paid quarter of Group C workers)

Year	Average Monthly Wage (basic wage only) Yuan	Flour Equivalent (bags)a	Real Wage Index Based On Nominal Wage and Flour Prices (1920 = 100)
1917	6.58	2.67	120.8
1918	6.72	2.74	124.0
1919	6.67	3.15	142.5
1920	5.96	2.24	100.0
1921	5.96	2.06	93.2
1922	5.99	2.12	95.9
1923	6.54	2.31	104.6
1924	6.53	2.43	110.0
1925	6.59	2.05	92.8
1926	6.28	1.97	89.1
1927	7.19	2.12	95.9
1928	7.44	2.39	108.1
1929	9.02	2.81	127.1
1930	10.00	2.88	130.2
1931	11.07	3.82	170.5
1932	...	...	...
1933	8.54a	3.57a	159.4

aIn 1931, the average basic wage of workers in the lowest quartile of Group C was 67 percent of the average earnings of 1036 workers in Groups A and C (Shih and Liu, "Survey of Workers," 41, 65; total 1931 employment was 1040). In 1933, the daily wage of all workers averaged 0.51 yuan. Taking 67 percent of this as the norm for the lowest quartile of Group C workers and multiplying by an assumed monthly work schedule of 25 days gives the 1933 wage figures shown above.

Source: The daily wage average for 1933 is from Tezuka Masao, Shina jūkōgyō hattatsushi (Kyoto, 1944), 350; monthly wages for other years are from Shih and Liu, "Survey of Workers," 63. The conversion to flour equivalent is based on annual prices of "Red Gunboat" brand flour shown in Nan-k'ai chih shu tzu liao, 70.

health, entertainment and other welfare measures" for the miners.[75] The absence of higher wages from the list of union objectives is hardly surprising when one examines the union's financial base, which consisted mainly of grants from the company. Monthly dues of workers in groups A and C, accounting for 95 percent of the

75. Ibid., 78.

work force, amounted to approximately 40 yuan, only a small fraction of the company's monthly subsidy of 500 yuan to the union.[76]

As at K'ai-luan, a comparison of miners' incomes with agricultural wages points to rising supply price as a plausible explanation of pay increases for unskilled miners. Buck gives the following data on farm wages (including payments in kind) in Shantung during 1929–33 (in yuan):[77]

	Number of Localities	Average	Median	Range
Daily wages	14	0.54	0.52	0.27–0.90
Monthly wages	13	9.50	9.49	4.7–13.9
Annual wages	14	83.66	84.83	51–126.3

July wages paid to Chung-hsing's unskilled workers during 1929–31 averaged 10.03 yuan, slightly above the average and median remuneration for farm workers during the growing season. But the 1920–26 average mining wage of 6.0–6.6 yuan per month or (assuming twelve months' work) 70–80 yuan per year does not compare favorably with the rural wage data shown above, which include monthly outlays of 7.21 yuan for farm workers in I county itself. If farm wages in Buck's reporting areas provide a good sample of rural labor market conditions in areas from which Chung-hsing recruited unskilled workers, it is difficult to see how the mine could have recruited workers before 1929 unless farm wages were substantially lower than the figures reported for 1929–33.[78]

The number of Group C workers dropped from 1,145 in 1924 to a low of 712 in 1928 and then recovered gradually to 822 in 1930–31. The biggest drop came in 1927–28, when employment

76. Ibid., 77–78. Dues are calculated from the fee scale shown on p. 78. There were also initiation fees of 0.10 yuan per member and "small" temporary fees.
77. Buck, *Statistics*, 328. Monthly wages are for periods during the growing season. All wage data include the cash value of meals and other payments in kind.
78. Buck's data may understate rural wage rates, which would strengthen the argument made in the text. "Wages of Farm Labor in Different Provinces," 100, gives 45.81 yuan as the average cash wage payment for yearly farm workers in seventy-six Shantung counties. Buck's average cash payment in fourteen localities is only 36.75 yuan (*Statistics*, 328).

fell by nearly 350 men. In the same year, however, the number of former employees registered with the company as job seekers fell from 96 to only 17. Although disruptions associated with the Northern Expedition affected this enterprise, the combination of rising wages, falling employment, and a reduced number of job-seekers is entirely consistent with the view that unskilled workers were departing in search of better job opportunities, which forced the company to offer higher wages to maintain even a reduced complement of unskilled workers at this mine.

Unlike Hopei, where farm wages (Table 6.5) and mine wages (Table 6.8) increase together, there is no consistent pattern of wage change in Shantung, where rising mine wages (Table 6.9) are accompanied by a mixture of rising and falling farm wages (Table 6.5). Farm wages show a declining trend in four of five counties in the vicinity of Chung-hsing's location in southwest Shantung. For adjacent I county, real farm wages show an average annual decline of 0.8 percent between 1906 and 1930; for 1925–30, however, real wages rise by 4.4 percent per year.[79]

A closer inspection reveals an underlying relationship between farm wages in I county and the earnings of unskilled miners at the nearby Chung-hsing colliery. Thomas Gottschang has compiled information on natural and man-made disasters in western Shantung. Inserting a dummy variable indicating the presence of major disasters reveals a clear association between current mine wages and the previous year's farm wages:[80]

$$MINEWAGE(t) = 3.00 + 4.51AGWAGE(t-1) - 1.66DISASTER(t) \qquad R^2 = 0.55$$
$$(2.39) \quad (2.23) (0.48)$$

On average, this result indicates that an increase of one percentage point in the index of local farm wages was associated with a 4.5

79. Based on the calculations underlying Table 6.5.
80. *MINEWAGE* indicates money wages at Chung-hsing (Table 6.9); *AGWAGE* is an index of money wages paid to yearly farm laborers in I county (based on materials underlying Table 6.5); *DISASTER* is a dummy variable whose value is unity in years for which Gottschang identifies minor disasters in western Shantung and zero otherwise; and *t* represents time. The figures in parentheses are standard error terms. See Thomas R. Gottschang, "Migration from North China to Manchuria: An Economic History, 1891–1942" (Ph.D. diss., University of Michigan, 1982), 214–15; minor disasters are those coded 1 or 2 in Gottschang's tables.

Table 6.10
Wages of Unskilled Workers at Modern Coal Mines, ca. 1920
(yuan)

Location (Province)	Year	Wage Payment		Source
		Daily	Monthly	
K'ai-luan (Hopei)				
Underground workers	1920	.25-.35	...	(1) p. 278
All workers	1920	0.31	8.33	(2) p. 128
Chung-hsing (Shantung)				
All Group C workers	1920	...	7.64	(3) p. 63
Pao-chin (Shansi)				
Coal extraction	1918	0.27	...	(1) p. 282
	1919	0.32	...	
	1920	0.17	...	
	1921	0.43	...	
	1922	0.42	...	
Liu-chiang (Hopei)				
Coal extraction	1921	0.32	...	(1) p. 283
Coal worker	1921	...	5.00[a]	(1) p. 283
Tzu-ch'üan (Shantung)				
Coal extraction	1920	.22-.55	...	(1) p. 285
Men-t'ou-kou (Hopei)				
Laborer	1922	.25-.50	...	(1) p. 290

[a]Indicates compensation in kind paid in addition to money wages.

Sources: (1) (Ti yi tzu) Chung-kuo lao tung nien chien.

(2) Chiu Chung-kuo K'ai-luan mei k'uang.

(3) Shih and Liu, "Survey of Workers."

yuan rise in monthly mine wages in the next year. The presence of (mostly natural) disasters was associated with a reduced gap between wages of farm and mine laborers, presumably because of disaster-induced increases in the supply of laborers seeking nonagricultural work. This evidence of close association between the wages of miners and the wages of farm laborers suggests that in Shantung, as in Hopei, rising real wages for coal miners may be attributable to productivity-linked increases in real wages paid to farm laborers.

Wage levels at K'ai-luan and Chung-hsing during the 1930s were similar to those at other mines. One survey of twenty-seven mines in ten provinces showed daily wages at the two mines somewhat above the average, but with higher productivity, the ratio of daily output per miner to daily wages differed only fractionally from the overall average.[81] As is evident from Table 6.10, wages at K'ai-luan and Chung-hsing were not abnormally low during the 1910s and early 1920s. Therefore, I conclude that in coal mining, as in cotton textiles, the evidence of rising real wages at particular enterprises and localities is indicative of industry-wide trends spanning several provinces. In both textiles and coal mining, close links between farm and nonfarm wages support the hypothesis that rising wages in nonfarm occupations employing unskilled workers from rural communities reflected rising labor productivity and rising labor income for agricultural workers as well as for self-employed owner and tenant farmers.

New Estimates of Agricultural Output Growth Between 1914/18 and 1931/36

This study has produced a variety of direct and indirect evidence of increasing per capita output, income, and living standards in large areas of rural China prior to the outbreak of the Pacific War in 1937. Historical materials show rising real wages for agricultural laborers in many provinces of China proper during the first three decades of the present century. Interview materials from 1929–33 show that a large majority of rural respondents in many provinces viewed the recent past as a period of rising living standards. The most common explanation of this change, the increased consumption of textiles, is reflected in national totals showing that per capita consumption of cotton cloth rose by 50 percent or more between 1901/10 and the 1920s and that the new, higher standard of dress was maintained during the 1930s. Information on wages earned by unskilled workers in cotton textiles and coal mining, industries that

81. Tezuka Masao, *Shina jūkōgyō hattatsushi* (Kyoto, 1944), 350–51. The data are for 1933 and 1934. They show daily wages of 0.58 yuan for K'ai-luan, 0.51 yuan for Chung-hsing, and an average of 0.47 yuan for twenty-seven mines. Another survey by Ch'en Wen-lu, "Minimum Wages and the Living Standards of Chinese Workers," *Lao tung chi pao* 3 (1934):81–82, showed average daily wages of 0.52 yuan for K'ai-luan, an improbably high figure of 1.53 yuan for Chung-hsing, and a mean figure of 0.62 yuan for twenty-eight mines.

employed large numbers of villagers from a number of provinces in North and Central China, reveals substantial increases in real earnings that seem to reflect an increasing supply price of rural labor resulting from rising productivity and incomes in the farm sector.

These results lead me to conclude that earlier studies by Perkins and Yeh, which show farm output rising at 0.8 to 1.0 percent per annum in the aggregate and changing between −0.1 and +0.3 percent annually in per capita terms, significantly underestimate the growth of agricultural output during the period 1914/18 to 1931/36.[82] The maximum growth of per capita farm output allowed by the Perkins-Yeh estimates is 0.3 percent per year. This figure, which cumulates to an increase of only 5.4 percent between 1914/ 18 and 1936, is not consistent with findings arising from Buck's study of agricultural wages, trends in cloth consumption, or the behavior of nonfarm wages, each of which stands on a firmer empirical base than Perkins's or Yeh's estimates of trends in farm output.

If previous estimates of agricultural output growth for the years 1914/18 to 1931/36 are too low, how fast did agricultural production expand? Pending a careful reconstruction of prewar trends in agricultural production, the unsatisfactory nature of existing output data necessitates recourse to indirect evidence that provides no obvious numerical alternative to the figures offered by Yeh and Perkins. With a variety of quantitative evidence that is consistent with the hypothesis of rising prewar real income and output per person in China's farm sector and inconsistent with the alternative views, I begin with the conclusion that agricultural production clearly outpaced population growth.

Is it possible to use information on wage trends to generate plausible estimates of agricultural output growth? Agricultural output is the product of agricultural employment and output per farm worker; its growth rate is the sum of the growth rates of the agricultural work force and farm labor productivity. Since the share of farm workers in the national labor force apparently remained stable until well into the post-1949 era, this ratio can hardly have de-

82. Based on agricultural output estimates by Perkins and Yeh (Table 6.1) and alternative estimates of population growth (Table 6.3).

clined during the early decades of the present century.[83] With a
constant proportion of farm workers in the national labor force, the
growth rate of agricultural employment must be the same as the
growth rate of the entire labor force. Ignoring possible changes in
the age structure of the population, this means that the rate of
population growth and the growth rate of agricultural employment
must be identical.

Can wage data be used to measure trends in output per farm
worker? There are three distinct difficulties. The first concerns the
relation between wage data and *marginal* labor productivity (the
effect on output of removing one worker from the production process). Second, can trends in marginal labor productivity illuminate
changes in *average* output per farmer? And third, can wage information from a modest sample of counties provide adequate information for gauging nationwide economic trends?

Under competitive market conditions, trends in real farm wages
can be expected to reflect changes in marginal farm labor productivity in the absence of significant changes in the farmer-employers'
terms of trade with other sectors of the economy. If the ratio of
crop prices received by farmers to prices paid by farmers increases,
farm wages may outgrow marginal productivity. In the Chinese
case, available evidence shows that although the farmer-employers'
terms of trade rose during the half-century prior to the Pacific War,
they declined slightly between 1901/10 or 1914/18 and 1931/36.[84]
For this reason, there is no reason to expect real wages to outgrow
marginal labor productivity in the farm sector.

Whether marginal and average labor productivity move together depends on the nature of agricultural production tech-

83. Liu and Yeh, *Economy of the Chinese Mainland*, 69, show agricultural employment declining from 79.0 percent of the national total in 1933 to 77.1
percent in 1957. Chinese estimates of the post-1949 decline in agriculture's
share of total employment, which surely exceeded any prewar changes in the
sectoral structure of employment, show the share of agriculture declining from
83.5 to 80.8 percent between 1952 and 1970 (*China: Socialist Economic Development* [Washington, D.C., 1983], 1:395). I ignore the possible impact of
changes in the age structure of China's prewar population.

84. This result is based on indexes of prices paid and received by farmers for
Wuchin (Kiangsu) during 1910–33 and on more comprehensive price series
compiled by Loren Brandt. See Buck, *Statistics*, 149–50 and Brandt, *Commercialization and Agricultural Development: Central and Eastern China,
1870s–1930s* (New York, forthcoming), table 4.13.

nology. Previous empirical work by Dittrich and Myers, Wiens, and Brandt assumes that the Cobb-Douglas production function, a mathematical relationship between inputs and outputs that economists have successfully applied to a wide range of statistical analyses, adequately describes agricultural technology in prewar China.[85] The Cobb-Douglas relationship implies identical time trends for marginal and average labor productivity. To conclude that rising real wages in farming signify an identical upward trend in the average productivity of farm labor thus requires an assumption, but this very assumption undergirds all prior studies of production relationships in prewar Chinese farming.

How large a sample is required to support the inference that wage advance in localities included in the sample can be taken as representative of conditions in China generally? Evidence of rising real wages in rural China begins with Buck's figures for one hundred counties (Table 6.5), along with data for an additional forty-one Kiangsu counties (Table 6.7), and scattered wage information for a few other areas. Information on particular enterprises in cotton textiles and coal mining reveals a consistent pattern of rising nonfarm wages for unskilled village migrants and rising farm wages in nearby rural communities that supplied labor to the mills or the mines. These results are not limited to the enterprises described in Tables 6.6, 6.8, and 6.9, but appear generally valid for mines and mills throughout China and, one must presume, for the rural communities that offered alternative employment opportunities for mine and mill employees. The precise specification of areas where developments in nearby coal mines and textile mills lead to the expectation of rising farm wages is not possible. In general, however, the patterns of industrial location indicate the regions involved: the North China provinces of Hopei, Shantung, Shansi, and Honan and the three northeastern provinces, where large-scale coal mining was concentrated; the major textile centers located at Shanghai and Wusih in the Yangtze delta area, Tientsin,

85. Scott R. Dittrich and Ramon H. Myers, "Resource Allocation in Traditional Agriculture: Republican China, 1937–1940," *Journal of Political Economy* 79, no. 4 (1971):891; Wiens, *Microeconomics of Peasant Economy*, 212–15; and Loren Brandt, "Farm Household Behavior, Factor Markets, and the Distributive Consequences of Commercialization in Early Twentieth-Century China," *Journal of Economic History* 47, no. 3 (1987):726.

and Tsingtao (Shantung) in the north and, on a smaller scale, Canton, Wuhan, and several other urban centers.

If, in addition to the localities covered in Tables 6.5 and 6.7, it were possible to enumerate all regions that regularly supplied labor to the cotton mills or coal mines, the resulting tabulation would probably include 200–300 counties. Buck's investigators "were instructed to make the farm studies in counties which were typical of larger areas" and his maps indicate that for each county surveyed, an average of 1.85 adjacent counties were specifically identified as having "similar conditions."[86] Applying this ratio to all of the localities for which wage information can be obtained or inferred raises the total from 200–300 to 570–855 counties. Whether evidence of rising wages from 10–15 percent (or, using Buck's total of 2.85 counties for every survey location, 28–43 percent) of China's approximately 2,000 counties is sufficient to establish national labor market trends depends critically on the nature of the market mechanism in prewar China. If one believes that markets functioned smoothly and efficiently so that rising wages in one location quickly encouraged an influx of labor from nearby communities, which would themselves then experience wage increases followed by secondary inmigration from more remote areas, it is difficult to resist the conclusion that the consequences of wage increases in several hundred widely scattered localities would have rippled across the entire economy, leaving only the most isolated areas unaffected. If, however, one is impressed with the obstacles to transferring information and manpower from place to place within China's prewar market structure, a different view is possible. This view holds that wages in a few localities could rise and remain considerably above the levels prevalent in nearby communities without attracting a significant labor influx that would tend to whittle away the newly emergent wage differential.

Because the pages of this book are filled with indications that changing commercial conditions elicited swift responses from income-seeking participants from every socioeconomic grouping, in all types of markets, and in every region of China during the decades prior to World War II, the author's commitment to the

86. Both the quotation and the tabulation of adjacent counties (excluding double counting of areas linked to two or more survey locations) are from John L. Buck, *Land Utilization in China, Atlas* (Nanking, 1937), 7.

former viewpoint will come as no surprise. Peter Schran's study of price behavior for a variety of commodities and services, including farm labor, draft animals, and even rural land values, finds that price changes "were passed along to numerous minor markets" across the country with the result that price movements parallel to changes in national price averages occurred "in most of the localities at most times."[87] Work by Loren Brandt and Barbara Sands on the dissemination of price information across far-flung trade networks, Gottschang's research on the economics of peasant migration, and the Dittrich-Myers finding that "in spite of increasing market uncertainty," North China peasants "were allocating their labor and land very efficiently" all confirm that changes in commodity prices spread rapidly across space and elicited quick reactions both at the original location and elsewhere in China's prewar economy.[88]

To cite a concrete example, the labor market in the county seat of Shuang-ch'eng (Heilungkiang) reportedly drew its labor supply from a radius of 10–15 miles, with would-be farm workers arriving from further away during peak farming seasons.[89] If workers who traveled fifteen miles to reach Shuang-ch'eng were willing to travel the same distance in another direction to obtain higher wages, wage changes at Shuang-ch'eng would influence conditions of supply and demand over an area of nearly 3,000 square miles (the area of a circle with a radius of thirty miles centered at Shuang-ch'eng). But the influence of economic opportunities in Manchuria extended far beyond the orbit of local pedestrians. Heilungkiang attracted migrants not only from the North China provinces of Hopei and Shantung, but even from distant Hupei, where a recent survey reports that "from the mid-nineteenth century, people from T'ienmen [county] emigrated [to the northeast and then] from Heilungkiang to Russia."[90] With responsiveness to price change evident in

87. Peter Schran, "What Can Prices Tell Us About China's Modern Economic History?" (Urbana, 1988), 14.
88. Brandt, "Agriculture and the International Economy"; Barbara N. Sands, "Agricultural Decisionmaking Under Uncertainty: The Case of the Shanxi Farmers, 1931–36" (Tucson, 1987), 12–13; Gottschang, "Structural Change, Disasters, and Migration"; and Dittrich and Myers, "Resource Allocation," 887.
89. *Rōdōsha o chūshin to shite mitaru Hokuman nōson no nōgyō keiei jijō* (Harbin, 1939), 2:40.
90. *Hu-pei shih hsien kai k'uang* (Wuhan, 1984), 415.

materials ranging from local anecdotes to large-scale statistical compendia reflecting the economic decisions of millions of households, it is difficult to reject the view that wage increases for unskilled workers in a widely dispersed group of localities would have attracted a sufficiently large inflow of would-be laborers to have prevented a continued rise in wages *unless wages were increasing at similar rates in surrounding regions for which we have no long-term wage data.*

If one is convinced of the responsiveness of Chinese market behavior and therefore prepared to believe that rising wages or other market changes observed in some localities quickly affected commercial affairs elsewhere, and with the further assumption that prewar agricultural production technology fit the requirements of the Cobb-Douglas functional form, it is possible to use Buck's long-term data on farm wages to suggest specific numerical alternatives to the improbably low figures for agricultural output growth offered by Dwight Perkins and K. C. Yeh. Buck's wage data, summarized in Table 6.5, indicate the following percentage rates of annual real wage growth in one hundred counties spanning twenty-one provinces (each set of growth rates includes figures derived from shorter intervals within the indicated time period):

	1901–33	1915–33	1925–33
Average of county figures	0.5	1.2	2.1
Median of county figures	0.4	1.2	1.6

I take the prewar rate of population growth plus 0.4 percent, the median of long-term growth rates for real farm wages during 1901–33, as a minimum estimate of the annual growth rate of agricultural output between 1914/18 and 1931/36. This is a very conservative procedure because the 0.4 percent figure is well below the 1.2 percent median growth rate for farm wages during 1914–33 obtained in Table 6.5. With population growing at estimated annual rates of 0.6 or 0.9 percent (Table 6.3), the minimum estimated rate of agricultural output growth becomes 1.0–1.3 percent, a modest increase over the annual rates of 0.8–1.0 proposed by Perkins and Yeh (Table 6.1).

The range of 1.0–1.3 percent, while not implausible, probably understates the growth of agricultural production between 1914/18 and 1931/36. This seems particularly likely in light of the much higher growth rates of transport and trade. Even though commercialization no doubt raised the growth rate of off-farm crop sales above the rate of farm output growth, it is difficult to imagine that the volume of traditional freight traffic could have risen at double the growth rate of farm output. Yet this is the improbable implication of a 1 percent growth rate for farm output and the 1.9 percent growth rate for traditional transport activity shown in Table 6.2.

Nor does annual agricultural growth of 1.0–1.3 percent mesh well with the finding, based on far better statistical evidence, that overall transport volume increased at 2.3 percent annually during 1915–36 (Table 4.10). Mineral products and manufactures dominated prewar rail freight, but railways accounted for less than one-seventh of total freight volume in 1936 (Table 4.10). The share of farm products in freight haulage was considerably higher for steamship traffic, which occupied one-fourth of total freight carriage in 1936. The carriage of farm products was the chief business of sailing vessels, which hauled 38 percent more freight in 1936 than the combined total for modern conveyances (Table 4.10). Could freight carriage have risen by two-thirds nationally and by one-half in the sailboat sector if farm output had risen by only 19–25 percent between 1914/18 and 1936? This is another unlikely implication of these minimum estimates of farm output growth.

With the output of cotton and other nonfood crops running well ahead of the agricultural total, these minimum growth rates leave only thin margins for a rising per capita supply of food. Although the finding that the available data and estimates point to a 50 percent increase in per capita consumption of cotton textiles (Table 2.11) depends on questionable estimates of cotton harvests, even a 20 percent increase in per capita textile consumption would indicate that the minimum figures for agricultural growth, which show farm output per head rising by only 7 percent between 1914/18 and 1931/36, with food output growing even slower, are suspiciously low.[91]

91. Houthakker's international comparisons suggest that "one would not be very far astray" by assuming that low-income populations that experience rising real incomes will raise their expenditure on clothing twice as rapidly as on food ("International Comparison," 550). A rise of 20 percent in per capita supply of textiles together with a rise of 4–6 percent in per capita food supplies would thus represent an unusual behavior pattern. This discussion overlooks China's small foreign trade balance in foodstuffs.

These considerations lead me to consider a higher growth rate for farm output between 1914/18 and 1931/36. The logic of market integration, coupled with impressive evidence of flexibility and responsiveness to changes in the price of many commodities and services in China's prewar economy, suggest the sum of estimated population growth and 1.2 percent, the median growth rate of county-level farm wages derived for 1914–33 in Table 6.5, as a sensible estimate for Chinese agricultural output growth between 1914/18 and 1931/36. But this rate could be too high. If the localities included in Buck's study, with their generally favorable location with respect to transport routes and marketing opportunities, enjoyed unusual opportunities to raise productivity (and hence, wages) and if market imperfections, geographic barriers, and political forces combined to limit the impact of productivity and wage increases that would normally arise in a competitive market system, then the 1.2 percent figure could exaggerate the growth of farm labor productivity. Although there is no shortage of examples illustrating the potential of market power, physical barriers, social rigidities, or political action to attenuate the transmission of relative price changes between markets, the abundant evidence documenting the free play of market forces convinces me that such examples are episodic rather than endemic features of China's prewar economy.[92] Nevertheless, to ignore the possible obstacles to the ripple effects of wage changes risks serious overstatement of agricultural output growth. Furthermore, the assumption of Cobb-Douglas production technology may be incorrect. If Chinese agricultural technology conforms to Japanese farm production relations derived by Archibald and Brandt, wages and marginal labor productivity might grow faster than average output per farm worker.[93]

I therefore adopt the sum of population growth and 1.2 percent, the median annual growth rate of farm wages for 1914–33 (Table 6.5), as a maximal estimate of prewar agricultural growth. I take

92. Kenneth Pomeranz's discovery that local governments in Shantung managed to enforce anachronistic exchange rates during the 1920s and early 1930s offers a particularly vivid case of political truncation of market imperatives ("Local Interest Story: Political Conflict and Regional Differences in the Shandong Capital Market, 1900–1937" [New Haven, 1988], 17–30).

93. Sandra O. Archibald and Loren Brandt, "A Flexible Model of Factor Biased Technological Change: An Application to Japanese Agriculture" (Stanford, 1987).

the sum of population growth and 0.8 percent, the latter being equidistant from the possibly excessive 1.2 percent figure and the seemingly inadequate 0.4 percent figure discussed above, as my central or preferred estimate of annual growth in Chinese agricultural output between 1914/18 and 1931/36.

Under this approach, the central or preferred annual growth rate for farm output ranges from 1.4 to 1.7 percent per year (depending on the rate of population growth), implying that total farm output rose by 28–34 percent between 1914/18 and 1931/36 (as opposed to 15 percent with Yeh's 0.8 percent growth rate or 19–25 percent under my minimum growth rate assumptions) and that per capita farm production increased by 15–16 percent (rather than 7 percent under the minimum growth assumptions). These results seem more consistent with available information about transport, trade, and consumption than the minimum figures discussed earlier.[94] It should be emphasized that these estimates, as well as the still higher annual rate of population increase plus 1.2 percent adopted as a maximum estimate for the rate of prewar agricultural output growth, remain subject to revision on the basis of future studies of farm output trends.

Trends in Aggregate and Per Capita
Output Growth: A Revised View

It is now possible to combine the analysis of individual sectors into summary measures of Chinese economic growth during the period 1914/18 to 1931/36. The results, based on 1933 prices, appear in Table 6.11. In view of the considerable error margins that must be attached to any reconstruction of prewar economic trends, I propose three separate growth rates for each sector, corresponding to low, preferred, and high estimates of long-term growth trends. Sectoral figures based on relatively firm empirical foundations are *underlined* in Table 6.11. Except for agriculture, discussed above, and personal services and residential rent, two small sectors for which no significant data are presently available, the preferred sectoral growth rates represent the outcome of empirical investigations reported in this study. Low and high sectoral growth rates are

94. The calculations in this paragraph are based on a period of 17.5 years.

Table 6.11
Revised Estimates for Growth of Chinese GDP, 1914/18 to 1931/36

	Weights	Yeh Estimate (%)	Estimates Based on Present Study		
			Low Estimate (%)	Preferred Estimate (%)	High Estimate (%)

A. Average annual growth rates, 1914/18 - 1931/36

	Weights	Yeh Estimate	Low Estimate	Preferred Estimate	High Estimate
Agriculture	0.629	0.8	1.0-1.3[a]	1.4-1.7[a]	1.8-2.1[a]
Industry	0.042	7.7	4.9	8.1	9.5
Handicrafts	0.075	0.7	1.0	1.4	2.0
Construction	0.016	3.5	4.0	4.6	5.5
Transp. and Comm. Modern	0.017	4.0	2.8	3.0	3.5
Traditional	0.039	0.3	1.5	1.9	2.5
Trade	0.093	1.1	2.0	2.5	3.0
Finance	0.010	2.9	3.0	5.0	6.0
Government services	0.031	1.0	2.4	3.4	4.4
Personal services	0.012	0.8	0.8	1.5	2.0
Residential rent	0.036	0.9	0.9	1.5	2.0
Gross domestic product	1.000	1.1	1.3-1.5[b]	1.8-2.0[b]	2.3-2.5[b]
Population 1. Perkins variant		0.9	0.9	0.9	0.9
2. Schran variant		0.6	0.6	0.6	0.6
GDP per capita Population 1		0.1	0.6[a]	1.1[a]	1.6[a]
Population 2		0.4	0.7[a]	1.2[a]	1.7[a]

continued...

intended to provide lower and upper bounds for reasonable estimates of sectoral performance. They reflect the author's judgment
and, except for a few figures, are not based on firm quantitative
foundations.

My assessment of changes in per capita output rests on alternative sets of population data; this reflects the current lack of reliable

Table 6.11, continued

	Yeh Estimate (1914/18=100)	Estimates Based on Present Study (1914/18=100)		
		Low Estimate	Preferred Estimate	High Estimate
B. Indexes for 1931/36				
Gross domestic product (GDP)	120.1	126.3-130.7	137.5-142.4	149.2-154.5
Population 1. Perkins variant	117.0	117.0	117.0	117.0
2. Schran variant	111.0	111.0	111.0	111.0
GDP per capita Population 1	102.6	111.7[a]	121.7[a]	132.0[a]
Population 2	108.2	113.8[a]	123.9[a]	134.4[a]

Note: sectoral growth rates with relatively firm empirical foundations are underlined in this table.

[a]The rate of agricultural growth is assumed to equal the rate of population growth plus 0.4 (low estimate), 0.8 percent (preferred estimate), or 1.2 percent (high estimate) per annum. Output performance derived from the lower figure for agricultural growth in each column is related to the Schran population variant; output totals derived from the higher alternative for agricultural growth are combined with the Perkins population variant.

[b]The calculation of the overall growth rate from sectoral rates is discussed in the notes to Table 6.2.

Source: Text and Tables 6.1 and 6.3.

demographic figures for prewar China. Although the rate of population growth, which is incorporated into my agricultural output figures, influences the estimated growth rates for total output derived in Table 6.11, the use of population totals other than those included in Table 6.11 would have little impact on the resulting trends in per capita output. If the rate of population growth were lowered to 0.4 or even 0.3 percent per annum, the growth rate of per capita output (preferred variant) would rise to 1.3 percent, not far above the 1.2 percent level associated with Population 2 in

Table 6.11; raising the rate of population growth to 1.4 percent does not push the growth rate of per capita output between 1914/ 18 and 1931/36 below the 1.1 percent figure derived from Population 1 in Table 6.11.

The results summarized in Table 6.11 represent a major revision of previous efforts to establish the quantitative dimensions of China's prewar economic performance. These findings show that, despite political and economic instability, natural catastrophes, civil strife, and foreign aggression, China's prewar economy achieved substantial growth of total and per capita output during the decades between the outbreak of World War I and the Japanese invasion of China proper. Dwight Perkins's estimated growth rate of 1.4 percent per year, the highest figure derived from previous studies (Table 6.1), represents a lower boundary for a range of possible aggregate growth rates that includes figures as high as 2.5 percent per year. The preferred figures indicate annual output growth of 1.8–2.0 percent between 1914/18 and 1931/36, with total output rising during this interval by 38–42 percent, substantially above the 20–26 percent range derived from earlier research (Table 6.1).

The results in Table 6.11 represent a striking reversal of earlier findings concerning trends in per capita output. As noted above, Yeh and Perkins find that output per head rose by less than 10 percent during the interwar decades. My results indicate a much higher growth of per capita product. The minimum figures show a rise of 12–14 percent between 1914/18 and 1931/36, while the preferred measure indicates that real output per person increased by 22–24 percent during the same period. The preferred measures indicate that China's annual rate of per capita output growth surpassed 1 percent during the interwar decades, a rate that approached comparable Japanese figures for the period 1897–1931.[95] With substantial increases in per capita output cumulating over

95. The average annual growth of Japanese per capita GNP (smoothed series, 1934/36 prices) for several intervals during 1897–1931 ranges from 0.86 to 1.66 percent (Kazushi Ohkawa and Henry Rosovsky, *Japanese Economic Growth: Trend Acceleration in the Twentieth Century* [Stanford, 1973], 25). For 1917–31, the growth of Japanese per capita real product averaged 1.33 percent.

two and, given the long-term behavior of agricultural wages, probably three or even four decades, these findings lead to the conclusion that China's economy, displaying both real per capita growth and modest structural change, embarked upon a substantial process of economic expansion during the decades prior to World War II.

Does the output growth summarized in Table 6.11 represent a sustained upward trend in production and output per head even though the period spanned by our data covers only two decades? Kuznets observes that "a substantial rise [in total or per capita product] over . . . fifteen to twenty years . . . may be treated as evidence of a rising secular trend." Firm identification of sustained growth also requires forward momentum strong enough to "transcend . . . short-term fluctuations."[96] Since the present study links 1914/18, a period of cyclical economic upswing, with 1931/36, an interval in which major floods and external economic and military pressures retarded economic performance, the measurements summarized in Table 6.11 already demonstrate the capacity of China's prewar economy to expand in the face of short-term downswings.

China's economic position in 1949, following twelve years of large-scale warfare and unprecedented hyperinflation, provides additional evidence of the sustained nature of economic change. In Table 6.12, I derive a rough estimate of total output in 1949 following the method of Ta-chung Liu, who used economic data from the period 1952–57 to construct statistical relationships that could be combined with the limited information then available to derive estimates of overall economic performance for 1958–65. Liu's procedures can be used to estimate total product for 1949, another year for which only a few statistical indicators exist. The output in what Liu calls the "traditional" sectors, designated by the symbol V_o, is derived in Lines 4–8 of Table 6.12 by inserting estimated 1949 output of grain and cotton into Liu's formulas. I obtain estimates for modern-sector output by exploiting the near-perfect correlation between Liu's figures for this variable (designated V_m) and national production of electricity during 1952–57 (Line 9). The fig-

96. Kuznets, *Modern Economic Growth*, 27.

Table 6.12
Estimated Level of Aggregate and Per Capita Output in 1949

	1933 A	1933 B	1949	1952
Physical Output				
1. Grain (MMT)	195.7[a]	164.4[b]	134.2[c]	232.8[a]
2. Cotton (MMT)	0.95[a]	0.95[a]	0.44[d]	1.30[a]
3. Electricity (BKWH)	2.85[e]	2.85[e]	4.31[d]	7.26[d]
Values (billion 1952 yuan)				
4. Grain	20.98[f]	17.62[b]	12.47[g]	21.63[f]
5. Cotton	1.61[f]	1.61[f]	0.75[g]	2.22[f]
6. SGC = Sum of 4 & 5	22.59	19.23	13.22	23.85
7. Liu's A = 1.452 x SGC	32.80	27.92	19.20	34.63
8. Liu's V_o=8.65 + 1.1A	44.73	39.36	29.77	46.49[h]
9. Liu's V_m	. . .	. . .	17.18[i]	21.65[h]
10. Liu's G	1.43[j]	1.43[j]	1.31[k]	3.27[h]
11. Net domestic product $V_o + V_m + G$	59.49[j]	54.12[m]	48.26	71.41[h]
12. Population (mill.)	500[n]	500[n]	536[n]	569[n]
13. Per capita NDP (yuan)	119.0	108.3	90.0	125.5
14. Index				
1933A = 100	100.0	91.0	75.6	105.5
1933B = 100	109.9	100.0	83.1	115.9
1952 = 100	94.8	86.3	71.7	100.0

Note: MMT indicates million metric tons
BKWH indicates billion kilowatt-hours

[a]Liu and Yeh, *Economy of the Chinese Mainland*, p. 135, converted at 20 piculs per metric ton (p. xvi); potatoes are included at one-fourth their actual weight.

[b]Dwight H. Perkins, *Agricultural Development in China, 1368-1968*, (Chicago, 1969), 30, estimates the average value of 1931/37 grain output in terms of a range whose midpoint is 84 percent of the Liu-Yeh figure for 1933. My alternative figure for 1933 grain output and value (Version B) is 84 percent of the comparable Liu-Yeh totals (Version A).

continued...

Table 6.12, continued

[c]Kang Chao, Agricultural Production in Communist China, 1949-1965 (Madison, 1970), 227.

[d]Chen, Chinese Economic Statistics, 186, 338.

[e]Wright, "A New Series for Electric Power Production in Pre-1937 China," 9.

[f]The estimates of Liu and Yeh are reported in Economy of the Chinese Mainland, 397.

[g]The price for cotton is from ibid., 381; for grain, I assume that the 1949 product mix resembled the 1952 situation, for which an average price of 92.9 yuan per ton may be derived from ibid., 135 and 397. The data for 1933 in the same source yield an average price of 107.2 yuan. In both cases, I convert piculs to tons at 20:1.

[h]Ta-chung Liu, "Quantitative Trends in the Economy," 162-63.

[i]Calculated from 1949 electricity output and the regression equation $V_m = 10.059 + 1.605E$ ($R^2 = 0.99$) for 1952-57, where V_m is from ibid., 162-63 and E is the annual electricity output in BKWH from Chen, Chinese Economic Statistics, 186-87. A similar projection based on the prewar relationship (for 1931-36) between annual electricity output and the sum of the annual value added by factories, mines, utilities, construction, modern transport and communication, trade, and finance produces nearly identical results.

[j]Liu and Yeh, Economy of the Chinese Mainland, 66.

[k]Government revenue and expenditure in 1950 were 37 and 40 percent of the 1952 totals (Chen, Chinese Economic Statistics, 441, 446); I assume that 1949 value added by government was two-fifths of the 1952 figure provided by Liu and Yeh.

[m]The figure shown is based on the Liu-Yeh estimate (Version A) less the difference between the Liu-Yeh and Perkins figures for V_o shown in Line 8 above.

[n]The population totals for 1933 are from Liu and Yeh, Economy of the Chinese Mainland, 102; for 1949 and 1952, mid-year estimates are calculated or extrapolated from year-end figures shown in Chung-kuo t'ung chi nien chien, 1984 (Peking, 1984), 81.

ure for value added by government G is based on information about state revenues (Line 10). Aggregate output (net domestic product) is obtained as the sum of V_o, V_m, and G (Line 11). Total and per capita output can then be compared with figures for 1933 and 1952.

Disregarding minor differences involving the concept (net or gross domestic product), the price base (1933 or 1952), and the period (1933 or 1931/36) used to measure output, the results in

Tables 6.11 and 6.12 show the following long-term trends in aggregate and per capita product (1914/18 = 100):[97]

	1931/36	*1946*	*1949*	*1952*
China: total output	140.0	132.0	119.0	166.0
China: per capita output	122.8	110.6	97.4	145.3
Japan: total output	175.2	114.9	152.9	215.1
Japan: per capita output	139.8	81.5	100.6	136.1

Even at the economic nadir following long years of war-related destruction and inflation, China's aggregate output remained well above the level attained under the cyclical prosperity of 1914/18. Even per capita output seems to have remained at or near the 1914/18 level. The relatively high level of per capita output recorded for 1952, long before investment programs implemented by the People's Republic began to influence the level of production, demonstrates the lasting impact of economic growth in prewar China.

Comparison with long-term trends in aggregate and per capita Japanese output strengthens the impression that China's performance represents a sustained economic uptrend. There is universal agreement that Japan's prewar economy was engaged in an ongoing process of what Kuznets terms "modern economic growth" and that Japan's rapid recovery from wartime devastation reflects the continuing momentum of prewar and wartime expansion. Close parallels in the long-term trend of per capita output for the two nations suggest that the same conclusions must apply to China. For China, as for Japan, the sustained upward movement of per capita output, achieved in spite of economic shocks arising from

97. The figures for China are based on preferred output series linking 1914/18 with 1931/36 (Table 6.11). I ignore any difference between 1933 and 1931/36 in linking 1931/36 with 1949. Midpoints are used to bridge ranges of total or per capita output. The percent change in total output (at 1933 prices) between 1933 and 1946 is from Pao-san Ou, *National Income of China, 1933, 1936 and 1946* (Nanking, 1947), 12–13. The figures for 1949 and 1952 are based on percentage changes in output and population for 1933–49 and 1949–52 derived in Table 6.12. I assume a 1914/18 population of 465 million, the midpoint of alternative figures shown in Table 6.3. The Japanese figures are from estimates of gross national expenditure (1934–36 prices) and population totals shown in Ohkawa and Rosovsky, *Japanese Economic Growth*, 288–89, 310–11.

domestic upheaval and international instability and maintained in the face of staggering wartime destruction, reflects a decisive upward break from historic patterns of economic evolution.

Trends in Aggregate and Per Capita Personal Consumption

China experienced a rising trend of total and per capita product. The real (that is, inflation-adjusted) value of output per head in 1931/36 was substantially higher than during 1914/18; the most probable estimate places the increase in per capita product at approximately 23 percent during the interwar decades (Table 6.11). Appraising the impact of rising output on economic welfare calls for measures of the changes in the level of personal consumption to supplement the estimates of output growth. This is necessary because consumption, although linked to production, need not change at the same rate or even in the same direction as overall output.[98]

As noted at the beginning of this chapter, all final outputs are allocated to private consumption, investment (which includes changes in stocks of unsold goods), government consumption, or net exports. Information about trends in the output shares absorbed by investment, public consumption, and net exports in 1914/18 and 1931/36 permits estimation of the share, and hence the volume, of output devoted to personal consumption in each period.

Investment

On the basis of incomplete materials compiled in Chapter 5, I assume that gross domestic fixed capital formation increased from approximately 7 to 11 percent of gross domestic product between 1914/18 and 1931/36. I incorporate these results into the present

98. Large increases in investment, public spending, or net exports could create a situation in which average consumption per head declines despite a rising trend of output per person. Nicholas R. Lardy finds that consumption lagged far behind output growth between 1957 and the late 1970s ("Consumption and Living Standards in China, 1978–83," *China Quarterly* 100 [1984]).

analysis, making no allowance for possible inventory accumulation, for which there are no data.

Government Spending

Ideally, this analysis requires estimates of government spending on currently consumed commodities and services (for example, office supplies, the wages of civil servants, etc.). Expenditures on road building and other types of construction, already included in investment, should be excluded from the figures for public-sector consumption, as should transfer payments (pensions, subsidies) to civilian individuals or organizations. Lacking a detailed breakdown of government spending into separate categories of current commodities or services, investment, and transfer payments, I ignore these distinctions and assume that public spending was entirely devoted to acquiring current commodities and services. Given the overwhelming share of debt service, military spending, and administrative costs in total spending of prewar governments at all levels, the error introduced by this assumption cannot be large.[99]

Previous chapters have shown that the combined total of government spending for 1931 amounted to 4.7–7.2 percent of that year's gross domestic product (Table 1.5), that the share of government spending in total output probably changed little during the 1930s (Chapter 1), and that the long-term real growth rate of government spending was approximately 3.4 percent (Table 6.11). Taking 6.0 percent as a representative figure for the ratio of public spending to total output during the 1930s and combining earlier results with the preferred estimate of 1.9 percent per year (Table 6.11) for the growth rate of aggregate output between 1914/18 and 1931/36, I conclude that the share of government spending in total output increased from approximately 4.6 to 6.0 percent between 1914/18 and 1931/36.[100]

99. Information on the expenditures by the Nanking government during 1928–37, for example, shows that annual outlays on debt service and the military alone occupied almost 75 percent of total spending (Feuerwerker, *Economic Trends in the Republic of China, 1912–1949*, 82–83).
100. The calculation is $0.049 = 0.06 \times (1.022/1.034)^{17.5}$. Any error in estimating the growth rate of public spending has no effect on the estimated growth of personal consumption. If the true growth rate of prewar public spending is higher than the present figure, a correction would raise the estimated growth

Net Exports

The ratio of net exports to national product is calculated from data for 1912/13 and 1930/31 presented in Table 6.13. Net exports of commodities and services are equivalent to the annual current account balance in China's balance of payments accounts. This amount is the difference (positive or negative) between *inpayments* arising from exports of Chinese merchandise, outlays by foreign tourists, diplomats, etc. in China, foreign payments for interest, dividends, freight, insurance, etc. to Chinese sellers or lenders, and remittances from overseas Chinese, and *outpayments* to foreigners arising from Chinese imports of foreign merchandise, overseas expenditures by Chinese diplomats or tourists, Chinese payments for interest, dividends, etc. to foreign sellers or lenders, and transfers by Chinese to foreign recipients. The results show negative net exports amounting to 0.3 percent of estimated total output in both 1912/13 and 1930/31. The stability and minute size of this ratio makes it possible to disregard any minor inaccuracies in data or calculations. I assume that net exports were negative and that their total was equivalent to 0.3 percent of gross domestic product in both 1914/18 and 1931/36.

Personal Consumption

There is now sufficient information to investigate long-term changes in aggregate and per capita personal consumption. The results appear in Table 6.14. The increases in the share of total expenditure occupied by government outlays and especially by fixed investment reduced the expenditure share of personal consumption from 88.7 to 83.3 percent between 1914/18 and 1931/36. A falling share of personal consumption means that aggregate and per capita consumption must grow more slowly than aggregate and per capita output. This is reflected in my estimates, which are de-

---

of output (Table 6.11) and simultaneously lower the estimate of personal consumption by an identical amount. An overestimate of public expenditure growth would also produce no error in the estimate of consumption trends. This arises from the arithmetic identity that allows personal consumption to be calculated by subtracting investment, government consumption, and net exports from total output.

Table 6.13
China's Ratio of Net Exports to Aggregate Output, 1912/13 and 1930/31

Category	1912/1913		1930/1931	
	Inpayments	Outpayments	Inpayments	Outpayments

A. Current account balance, million Hai-kuan taels, current prices

1. Merchandise trade	287.2	384.4	414.8	550.0
2. Foreign expenditure	55.8	10.9	63.1	15.4
3. Interest and amortization		40.0		32.1
4. Remittances	42.9	14.7	88.0	0.2
5. Business profits				40.0
6. Total	385.9	450.0	565.9	637.7
7. Net exports a. Current prices		-64.1		-71.8
b. 1933 prices		-37.0		-64.5

B. Ratio of net exports to GDP, 1933 prices, million yuan

1. Net exports, 1933 prices		-57.0		-99.3
2. Gross domestic product		20360		28570
3. Ratio: net exports/GDP		-0.003		-0.003

Sources and Notes: The balance of trade data in Part A are from Nai-ruenn Chen, "China's Balance of Payments: The Experience of Financing a Long-term Trade Deficit in the Twentieth Century," in Modern Chinese Economic History, ed. Chi-ming Hou and Tzong-shian Yu (Taipei, 1979), 411-14. Outpayments in Line A2 include freight, insurance, and motion picture royalties. Conversion to 1933 prices in Line A7-b is based on the index of import prices in Liang-lin Hsiao, China's Foreign Trade Statistics, 1864-1949 (Cambridge, 1974), 275; with 1912/13 as 100, the price index reaches 192.9 in 1931 and declines to 173.2 in 1933. Line B1 converted at 1 Hai-kuan tael = $1.55. The gross domestic product figures in Line B2 for 1931 are from Yeh, "China's National Income, 1931-36," 97; for 1912/13 calculated on the basis of average annual growth of 1.9 percent (Table 6.11) over an eighteen-year period.

rived separately for the alternate demographic profiles introduced earlier. The results show that total consumption rose by 20–26 percent between 1914/18 and 1931/36 (Line 3), considerably less than the 38–42 percent growth of total output (preferred version) obtained in Table 6.11. Real levels of consumption per head rose by

Table 6.14
Trends in Personal Consumption, 1914/18 to 1931/36

	1914/18 Population 1	1914/18 Population 2	1931/36 Population 1	1931/36 Population 2
1. Expenditure shares A. Total	100.0	100.0	100.0	100.0
B. Investment	7.0	7.0	11.0	11.0
C. Government	4.6	4.6	6.0	6.0
D. Net exports	-0.3	-0.3	-0.3	-0.3
E. Consumption	88.7	88.7	83.3	83.3
2. Gross domestic product (billion yuan, 1933 prices)	21.69	22.84	29.13	29.13
3. Total consumption (billion yuan, 1933 prices)	19.24	20.26	24.26	24.26
4. Population (mill.)	430	500	500	550
5. Per capita consumption A. 1933 yuan	44.7	40.5	48.5	44.1
B. Index, 1914/18=100	100.0	100.0	108.5	108.9
C. Annual rate of growth 1914/18 to 1931/36 Population 1: Population 2:		0.9% 0.6%		

Sources and Notes: Line 1: Text; Line 1E equals Line 1A minus the sum of Lines 1B through 1D; Line 2: The figure for 1931/36 is from Yeh, "China's National Income, 1931/36", 97; the figures for 1914/18 are derived from the population-linked rates of output growth (preferred variant) shown in Table 6.11; with 1914/18 as 100, the total output for 1931/36 is 149.3 (Population 1) or 144.3 (Population 2). Line 3: Calculated from Lines 1E and 2. Line 4: Data shown in Table 6.3. Line 5: Calculated from Lines 3 and 4.

nearly 10 percent between 1914/18 and 1931/36, implying that per capita consumption rose by 0.5 percent annually. The declining share of output destined for consumption reduced the growth rate of per capita consumption to less than half of the comparable figures for total product.

Summary

I conclude this chapter with a brief summary of the principal quantitative findings concerning the growth of China's economy between 1914/18 and 1931/36. These results are based on an extensive review of the materials bearing on the performance of most sectors of the economy. I find that the period between 1914/18 and 1931/36 witnessed significant and sustained increases in aggregate and per capita output and consumption at the national level. These new results represent a considerable upward revision of previous studies by Perkins and Yeh, which reported aggregate output growth cumulating to 20–26 percent and increases in per capita product amounting to 3–14 percent during this period. Their results are roughly comparable to my lower-bound estimates of overall economic performance. My preferred estimates, supported by a quantitative analysis of the main sectors of China's prewar economy, indicate much higher cumulative growth of 38–42 percent for total product and 22–24 percent for output per head. These results are not sensitive to possible changes in the assumed growth rate of the population, a variable that I have not considered in detail. My analysis includes upper-bound estimates of output growth that further increase the range of possible outcomes.

The crude indicators of aggregate economic performance for 1946 and 1949 show that the consequences of prewar growth were strong enough to avoid reversal in the chaos and destruction of large-scale warfare and the unprecedented hyperinflation between 1937 and 1949. Even at the nadir of national economic fortunes in 1949, aggregate output surpassed the 1914/18 baseline by a considerable margin; per capita output may have fallen slightly below the 1914/18 figure during the thirteen years of war- and inflation-induced disruption, but quickly regained and surpassed the higher levels achieved during the early 1930s. These results strongly reinforce the notion that China's prewar growth represents a firmly established long-term trend, as does the close parallel between the long-term performance of Chinese and Japanese per capita output between 1914 and 1952.

Finally, I provide estimates of the growth of private consumption between 1914/18 and 1931/36. The results show that, although lagging behind output growth due to expenditure shifts favoring investment and government spending, private consumption spending increased in both aggregate and per capita terms. Based on the preferred growth rates for total output, I find that China's national average level of private consumption spending per person, a fundamental indicator of trends in economic welfare, increased in real terms by nearly 10 percent between 1914/18 and 1931/36.

Chapter Seven

Conclusion

The sustained expansion of output per head became a regular feature of Chinese economic life in the early decades of the present century. This fact, with its momentous economic and social implications, represents the principal finding of my study. Although it is not possible to assign a precise date to the origins of modern economic growth, the mechanism of prewar development can be specified in considerable detail. Economic growth was rooted in the expansion of foreign trade. New overseas demands for agricultural exports contributed to the acceleration of a trend toward commercial farming that predated the breaching of China's trade barriers in the mid-nineteenth century. The penetration of foreign goods created opportunities for introducing new products, materials, and processes into China's economy. Innovations in money and finance and in transport and communication magnified the impact of external trade on domestic economic life. Measures initially intended to smooth the path of foreign trade gradually came to affect large segments of China's economy. The impact of reduced transport costs, improved access to credit, popularization of banknotes, and expanded information flows was not limited to localities with long histories of active involvement in long-distance trade, but extended to communities that had formerly remained outside the ambit of regional and national markets.

The quantitative results of this study map the approximate dimensions of economic growth in prewar China. Between 1914/18 and 1931/36, total output, as measured by gross domestic product, rose by two-fifths, implying an increase of 20–25 percent in inflation-

344

adjusted output per head. With a rising share of output devoted to investment and government spending, average private consumption spending per person rose more slowly, increasing by approximately one-tenth. Investment activity expanded rapidly, with fixed capital formation surpassing 10 percent of total output during the years 1931–36. The growing volume of investment was financed primarily from domestic savings, which occupied an increasing share of total income during the prewar decades. Prewar economic growth, while falling short of contemporaneous Japanese achievements, produced sufficiently large advances so that the economic decline brought about by war and hyperinflation failed to reduce per capita output significantly below the level of 1914/18.

The impulse for growth radiated outward from advanced regions, notably the Lower Yangtze area and the northeastern provinces, which enjoyed unusually rapid development. Factories, wharves, banks, and other visible manifestations of economic change clustered in these regions, especially in Shanghai. And yet, the process of economic growth that originated and reached its greatest intensity in the environs of the coastal cities achieved national dimensions. Not just manufacturing, banking, and railways, but every significant sector of China's economy advanced well ahead of population growth during the decades covered by my quantitative materials.

The complementarity, or mutual reinforcement, of forward momentum across economic sectors was a prominent feature of Chinese development. China's prewar economic growth bears little relation to the process of "creative destruction" envisioned by Joseph Schumpeter, in which new industries emerge from the financial wreckage of their predecessors. Traditional economic agents, strengthened by the benefits arising from the growth of new forms of economic activity, managed to prosper and expand even in and around the dynamic urban centers where they faced unrestricted competition from modern enterprise. The history of native banking, sailboat transport, and handicraft production illustrates and confirms this general harmony of economic interest between new and inherited enterprise in prewar China. The virtual absence of state encouragement enhanced the significance of supportive interdependence among various segments of the private sector.

The same complementarity is visible in agriculture, the largest segment of China's prewar economy. The prominence of farm products among exports and industrial raw materials placed agriculture in a central position from the start of China's modern development process. Farmers received few direct benefits from urban-based innovation and the rate of technological progress in agriculture remained low, but the indirect consequences of new patterns of trade, manufacturing, transport, and finance brought new opportunities for Chinese villagers to improve their economic circumstances through a classic process of specialization and division of labor of the sort associated with the name of Adam Smith. Expanded information flows, reduced transactions costs, and the increasing commercial availability of items formerly produced for home consumption encouraged growing numbers of farm households to accept the risk of producing more crops and handicrafts for the market. Specialization raised productivity because land was increasingly deployed to grow the crops best suited to its physical features and also because farmers and craftsmen gained expertise by concentrating on a reduced variety of products. The cumulative effects of growing farm productivity are reflected in a widespread rise in farm wages dating from the early years of the present century, and perhaps earlier.

These conclusions, like those of any quantitative study, must rest on an evaluation of the underlying data. The need to balance the limitations of existing statistical materials against the data required to complete this study has been a constant preoccupation in the preparation of this book. Despite all efforts to assemble reliable quantitative materials, the data used in this study suffer from many limitations. But my conclusions rest on a wide range of statistics, each embodying its own particular strengths and defects. The consistent support for the view of prewar China as a growing economy that emerges from unrelated statistics about money, transport, wages, consumption, investment, saving, and other aspects of economic life represents the strongest underpinning for my findings.

Perhaps the most controversial aspect of this study concerns the role assigned to the market itself. Many aspects of my analysis, especially the indirect estimation of agricultural output growth, rest on the belief that prewar China illustrates the market economy par excellence. This viewpoint is rejected by authors who assert that labor markets in the T'ang-shan region of Hopei province, home of the K'ai-luan coal fields discussed in Chapter 6, appeared only in the 1930s, and, more generally, that as late as the closing decades of the nineteenth century, "China's labor market was still in the process of formation, so that wage levels did not determine whether or not the supply of labor would be adequate."[1] The present study, together with research by many others, offers ample evidence that Chinese buyers and sellers responded promptly to price signals throughout the period under review. Nevertheless, further inquiry into market functioning, particularly for labor markets, which stand at the center of many disputes in the field of modern Chinese economic history, may extend our insight into the structure and operation of China's prewar economy.

Rampant instability posed formidable obstacles to economic development throughout the period of study. In addition to domestic political fragmentation, the international economy, which in the late nineteenth century had supplied an "engine of growth" for low income nations, entered after 1913 what W. A. Lewis has termed "the greatest depression." Although this led to "a period of disaster" for Third World economies generally, with development coming "to a standstill" in the 1930s, China's economic momentum was strong enough to produce a substantial growth spurt even in the face of impotent governments, internal disorder, and external threats.[2] Evidently the seed of economic opportunity fell on extraordinarily fertile soil in China. While many authors seem preoccupied with the notion that economic progress in China necessarily awaited the completion of sweeping social reforms, my results raise the opposite question: what social conditions contributed to the economic gains achieved in prewar China despite seemingly intractable political and economic obstacles?

Recent discussion of East Asia's remarkable economic gains has focused primarily on the postwar experience of Japan and the smaller "new industrial countries." The discovery that, with the

---

1. Ting Ch'ang-ch'ing, Yen Kuang-hua, and Liu Fo-ting, "Views on the Problem of Working Class Impoverishment in Old China: Analysis of the Level and Trend of K'ai-luan Coal Miners' Wages," *Nan-kai ching-chi yen-chiu-so nien k'an* (1984), 307–8.

2. W. Arthur Lewis, *Growth and Fluctuations, 1870–1913* (London, 1978), 225, 227.

exception of the war period 1937–49, China's economy has now
experienced seven decades of rising aggregate and per capita output stretching back to 1914, if not earlier, points to the necessity
of integrating China into the discussion of East Asian economic
achievements and extending the analysis backward in time. In view
of the geopolitical diversity of the East Asian region, one may
speculate that Chinese cultural traditions, which permeate the historical background of each of the East Asian economies, may hold
essential clues to the sources of their extraordinary economic progress. Many aspects of imperial Chinese society, ranging from the
prevalence of marketing and market-related institutions to widespread participation in complex organizations and harsh social competition in which family strategies often resemble the behavior of
competitive business firms, cast China's inherited economic culture as a promising training ground for participation in the contemporary world market economy.

Distribution, which is largely excluded from this analysis, provides another dimension of East Asian comparisons. The substantial growth of wages paid to agricultural laborers, who surely
occupied a low position on the ladder of income and wealth, suggests that China may fit the pattern observed in Japan, Korea, and
Taiwan, under which economic expansion does not widen the disparity between the incomes of rich and poor. Here again, there is
ample opportunity for further study.

China's prewar economic advance stopped well short of its potential. There is evidence of neglected economic opportunity in
the low utilization of railways, the stunted growth or collapse of
viable businesses constrained by lack of credit, and the truncation
of productivity-enhancing specialization resulting from the disruption of interregional trade by domestic and international military
struggles. The communist victory in China's protracted civil wars
led to the creation of the People's Republic in 1949. The return of
domestic peace and political integration for the first time in forty
years produced a growth spurt in the 1950s that largely reflected
the unfulfilled potential of China's prewar economy. As in Japan,
a new political system and a new leadership group directed the
economy along new paths that soon outstripped the prewar pace of
economic change. And in China, as in Japan, the structure and
operation of the postwar economy retains central features that en-

dure across the political divide separating the 1930s from the 1950s and beyond.

Continuity is most evident in the countryside, where the recent revival of a market economy based on household enterprise offers startling proof of both the survival of presocialist economic patterns and the dynamic potential of a market system in rural China. Recent economic advances in rural China arise from precisely the same causes—the reduction of transactions costs and new opportunities for specialization and the division of labor—that appear as sources of rural growth during the prewar decades. In the 1980s, as in the 1920s and 1930s, improvements in rural productivity arise primarily from the more effective allocation of existing resources rather than from new investment or the introduction of new technologies.

High and rapidly growing investment levels are often cited as a hallmark of Chinese economic policy since 1949. But a simple projection of the time series for modern-oriented gross domestic fixed capital formation reveals that, despite the modest capital formation proportions of the 1930s, the powerful and effective intervention of China's post-1949 central planning apparatus has failed to push investment performance beyond the trend lines established during the prewar decades.[3] This outcome does not overshadow the achievements of China's present regime in raising investment rates and promoting industrialization on a national scale. It does, however, reveal China's post-1949 economic expansion as one phase of a long-term process whose origins lie in the economy of the prewar decades.

The mechanism of development finance embodies equally significant links with the past. The prewar expansion of modern industry was financed by profits from the sale of agriculturally based consumer manufactures, principally cotton textiles, produced in Shanghai and other Lower Yangtze cities. The same mechanism still operates, with national and regional government budgets replacing private industrialists and financiers as the conduit through which profits are channeled into the hands of investors. The Lower Yangtze provinces of Kiangsu (including Shanghai), Chekiang, and

3. Thomas G. Rawski, "Economic Growth and Integration in Prewar China" (Toronto, 1982), 70–71.

Anhwei retain their key fiscal role, providing nearly two-fifths of national revenue—far more than their share in population, output, or profit.[4] Shanghai's net contribution to the national budget virtually matches the combined fiscal effort of the fourteen next largest major cities.[5]

Prewar economic patterns survive even in sectors, like industry, that have experienced enormous increases in scale since 1949 under policies that have assigned consistently low investment allocations to the old centers of coastal industry, particularly Shanghai. Today, as sixty years ago, the greatest concentration of industry, the finest quality and broadest variety of manufactured goods, the highest industrial productivity, the lowest costs, and the cutting edge of technological innovation all cluster around Shanghai. In education, science, finance, and many other fields, intellectual leadership has, until very recently, rested in the hands of men and women trained in the prewar era.

Where the policies of the People's Republic have undercut the market-based economic patterns of the past, Chinese economists now recommend a return to traditional structures for the sake of efficiency, confirming the view that the geographic dispersion and commodity composition of industry and other prewar economic arrangements arose primarily in response to market forces rather than political circumstances. The retreat from collective agriculture and state procurement of farm produce is the most prominent example, but there are many others. China now welcomes foreign business investment under special provisions that often parallel features of the prewar treaty port system. The influential economist Hsüeh Mu-ch'iao [Xue Muqiao] calls for the revival of "the old business activities of banks" and cites the British-American Tobacco Company, long excoriated as an imperialist exploiter, as a model for Chinese managers to follow.[6] Other authors call for the

4. Thomas G. Rawski, "The Economy of the Lower Yangtze Region, 1850–1980" (Toronto, 1984), table 6.
5. Based on industrial tax and profit less state sector investment outlay; see *Chung-kuo t'ung chi nien chien, 1981* (Peking, 1982), 27–86.
6. Hsüeh Mu-ch'iao, "Some Opinions on Reforming the Economic System," in U.S. Foreign Broadcast Information Service, *Daily Report: China,* June 25, 1980, L18 and Sherman Cochran, "Controlling a National Market in China: Interregional Trade in Tobacco Products and Cotton Textiles, 1850–1984" (Ithaca, 1984), 56–57.

renewed use of "the traditional economic connections formed in history" to improve the efficiency of China's foreign and domestic commerce.[7] There is widespread advocacy of financial reforms that would allow would-be entrepreneurs to obtain funds from bank loans or share subscriptions without seeking approval or budget allocations from plan authorities.

Having experienced both the benefits and the shortcomings of development under a system of bureaucratic resource allocation, China's leaders have embarked on a series of ambitious experiments intended to combine the advantages of planned and market economies into a single package. Although the outcome of their effort remains uncertain, this study of China's prewar economy, in which profit-seeking individual response to market forces formed the main component of economic life, illustrates the expansive potential of a private economy in a Chinese setting. Despite the heavy burden of domestic political strife, periodic warfare, and chronic instability, China's prewar economy mustered enough entrepreneurship and flexibility to attain a significant increase in average living standards, placing China within the ranks of the economically progressive low-income nations long before the advent of land reform, socialization of industry, or state-led development planning. Dramatic improvements in Chinese economic performance may be expected if China's current regime succeeds in harnessing the energies responsible for these achievements.

7. "Role of Major Ports in Foreign Trade Viewed," in U.S. Foreign Broadcast Information Service, *Daily Report: China*, August 2, 1982, K14 and "Consignment Trading," in British Broadcasting Corporation, *Summary of World Broadcasts: Part 3, The Far East, Weekly Economic Report*, W1098 (1980):A2.

Appendix A

The Growth of Output
in Chinese Manufacturing,
1912–36

The only estimate of long-term industrial output growth in prewar China is John K. Chang's series which, as noted in Chapter 2, consists mainly of mining products.[1] The purpose of this appendix is to construct an estimate of output growth for manufacturing alone between 1912 and 1936. The results, summarized in Table A.1, are more comprehensive than Chang's. The share of 1933 value added and employment contributed by manufacturing sectors included in the present estimate is 73 and 88 percent respectively, whereas the manufacturing sectors included in Chang's sample account for only one-quarter of factory output and one-third of factory employment in 1933.[2] To gain broader coverage, however, it is necessary to focus exclusively on the initial and terminal years. The present analysis is limited to a point estimate of average annual output growth between 1912 and 1936. There are not enough data to obtain time series estimates of manufacturing output for a sample significantly larger than Chang's. The distortion introduced by using point estimates may not be large. For cotton yarn, the growth rate calculated from 1912 and 1936 data is 9.1 percent. If the 1912/36 growth rate is calculated from a log-linear regression applied to Chang's annual output figures, the growth rate becomes 7.8 percent, a change that alters the estimated growth rate of the entire

1. John K. Chang, *Industrial Development in Pre-Communist China: A Quantitative Analysis* (Chicago, 1969).
2. Calculated from Ta-chung Liu and Kung-chia Yeh, *The Economy of the Chinese Mainland: National Income and Economic Development, 1933–1959* (Princeton, 1965), 426–28.

Table A.1
Estimated Growth Rate of Manufacturing Output, 1912-36

Sector	Average Annual Growth Rate 1912/36 (%)	1933 Estimate of Sectoral	
		Gross Value Added (Million Yuan)	Employment (Thousands)
Pig iron	20	18	21[a]
Steel	23	1	1[a]
Cotton yarn	9.1	134	198
Cotton cloth	17.5	62	118
Cement	11.6	14	10
Cigarettes	20	126	45
Rubber	30	9[b]	16
Matches	8	20	37
Machinery and transp. equip.	10	39	75[c]
Brick and shingle	10	4[d]	22
Silk and silk piece goods	0	43	195
Edible oil	3	16	19
Rice milling	1	1	19
Flour	6.7	19	12
Sample total		506	788
Overall total		577	1076
Sample share (%)		87.7	73.2

Sample growth rate: Weighted average of sectoral figures using the formula shown in the notes to Table 6.2: value-added weights, 8.1%; employment weights, 4.9%.

[a]Combined total of 22 thousand allocated in proportion to value-added totals.

[b]Footwear only.

[c]Includes machinery, electrical appliances, transport equipment, shipbuilding, and repair.

[d]Based on gross output and rate of value added given in Liu and Yeh, *Economy of the Chinese Mainland*, 426, 442.

Source: Except as noted, 1933 data are from ibid., 146, 426-28. The derivation of sectoral growth rates is described in the text of this appendix.

sample by less than half of one percentage point. For cotton cloth, the two growth rates are nearly identical.[3]

My calculation includes all manufacturing industries employing more than 10,000 workers in 1933 except for "printing and publishing" and "clothing and apparel," which are omitted because there are no plausible output figures for 1912. The cement industry, which employed just under

3. Regressions based on data in Chang, *Industrial Development*, 119, 122.

10,000 workers in 1933, is included. The overall growth rate of manufacturing output is derived from estimates of sectoral output growth during 1912–36 and 1933 figures for sectoral value added and employment. The 1933 data come from the national income study by Liu and Yeh and require no explanation. The output growth for the first five industries in Table A.1 is calculated from Chang's physical output estimates.[4] The estimated growth rates for the remaining industries are based on the following considerations:

Cigarettes. The British-American Tobacco Company (BAT), the largest firm in this industry, increased its Chinese sales volume at an average yearly rate of 14.1 percent between 1912 and 1928.[5] Since its business shifted from importing toward increased concentration on local manufacturing during this time, BAT's Chinese factory output presumably rose by at least 15 percent per year during this period. The numbers of cigarette machines and workers in Chinese-owned cigarette factories increased at annual rates of 26 and 30 percent between 1912 and 1936.[6] Given the dominant role of BAT in China's cigarette industry, I conclude that cigarette production probably expanded at an annual rate of about 20 percent between 1912 and 1936.

Rubber. The growth of domestic rubber manufacturing may be inferred from data on imports of natural rubber, which rose from an annual average of nine tons during 1911–19 to several hundred tons during the mid-1920s, surpassed 1,000 tons in 1929, 3,000 tons in 1931, and then leaped to a yearly average of at least 14,000 tons during 1932–36.[7] After 1931, annual imports exceeded the combined total for all previous years by large margins. This explosion of raw material imports followed a swift expansion of domestic production facilities: 94 percent of nearly 13,000 workers employed in Shanghai's rubber industry in 1931 were attached to firms established in 1928 or later.[8] The average annual growth of rubber

4. Chang, *Industrial Development*, 117–23.
5. Sherman Cochran, *Big Business in China: Sino-Foreign Rivalry in the Cigarette Industry, 1890–1930* (Cambridge, 1980), 225.
6. Ibid., 229.
7. Import data for 1911–31 are from *Shang-hai min tsu hsiang chiao kung yeh* (Peking, 1979), 4, 5, 20, 33, 34, converted at 1 quintal = 1.67548 piculs and 1 picul = 60.453 kg. For 1932–36, the same source shows average annual imports of 13,111 tons for China proper only. Manchurian imports amounted to an average of 1,350 tons in 1933 and 1934 (*Chūka minkoku oyobi Manshū-koku bōeki tōkei hyō, 1934* [Tokyo, 1939], 135).
8. *Shang-hai min tsu hsiang chiao kung yeh,* 15–19.

imports between 1912 and 1936 is at least 36 percent.[9] I assume annual output growth averaging 30 percent between 1912 and 1936.

Matches. Data for this important industry are both scarce and confusing, but the following rough estimate of output growth can be offered. A Japanese survey conducted in 1913 reported a monthly output of 11,270 cases of matches from seven plants.[10] In addition to an eighth plant for which output was not specified, this report lists twenty other plants that were not inspected. Since the reported capital of the seven plants amounted to 91 percent of the total for the 21 plants for which there are no output data, one may guess that total match output in 1913 was in the neighborhood of 23,000 boxes per month or, assuming year-round production, 276,000 boxes per year.[11]

A rough confirmation of this result can be obtained from data on imports of match-making materials, which amounted to 1.6 million *Hai-kuan taels* in 1913.[12] Since all materials were imported in this period and materials costs probably amounted to about 55 percent of total cost (based on data for 1929 and 1933), domestic production in 1913 should be about 2.9 million *Hai-kuan taels*, or 4.5 million yuan. The Tientsin wholesale price of matches in 1913 was 30 yuan per case, implying domestic production in that year of about 150,000 cases.[13]

I conclude that match output in 1913 amounted to something like 150,000–276,000 cases. I have found no output figures for 1936, but the 1933 total of 1.39 million cases (Table 2.13) seems fairly well established. With these figures, the average annual growth rate for 1913–33 falls in the range of 8.4–11.8 percent. Since output may not have grown between 1933 and 1936, the lower segment of this range offers the most reasonable estimate of annual output growth for the entire period ending in 1936.[14]

9. Calculated by assuming 1912 imports of nine tons, which is the annual average reported for 1911–14 in ibid., 4.

10. *Shina matchi kōgyō jōtai shisatsu hōkoku* (Osaka, 1913), frontmatter. Mikio Kuwayama kindly found me a copy of this unique source.

11. Ibid. In calculating the total capital figures, I equated 72 *taels* to 100 yuan following Eduard Kann, *The Currencies of China*, 2d ed. (Shanghai, 1927), 171.

12. Ch'en Chen, comp., *Chung-kuo chin tai kung yeh shih tzu liao*, Collection 4 (Peking, 1961), 1:656.

13. On imported materials, see Yokoyama Suguru, "Establishment of Match Manufacturing in China," *Hiroshima daigaku bungakubu kiyō* 25, no. 1 (1965):267–70. Cost figures are from *Chung-kuo min tsu huo ch'ai kung yeh* (Peking, 1963), 29 and Liu Ta-chün, *Chung-kuo kung yeh tiao ch'a pao kao* (Shanghai, 1937), 2:397. Conversion of 1.55 yuan per Hai-kuan *tael* follows Kann, *Currencies of China*, 84, 171. Tientsin price data are from *Nan-k'ai chih shu tzu liao hui pien, 1913–1952* (Peking, 1958), 82.

14. *Hokushi shōhin sōran* (Tokyo, 1943), 163, shows declining match output in North China between 1933 and 1935.

I assume average growth of 8 percent for match output between 1912 and 1936.

Machinery and Transport Equipment. Output in this sector for 1936 amounted to 134 million yuan (at 1933 prices).[15] In constructing the estimates of machinery absorption reported in Table 5.2 it is assumed that factory output in this sector was negligible before 1913, but this may be erroneous.[16] If output had expanded at an annual rate of 10 percent between 1912 and 1936, the 1912 output would be 13.6 million yuan (at 1933 prices). Since this figure may easily be too high, the 10 percent figure used in my calculations may represent a modest estimate of the growth of factory output for machinery and transport equipment between 1912 and 1936.

Brick and Shingles. There are no detailed output figures for this industry in the early period. In addition to widely scattered local manufacture, commercial production developed in association with cement manufacture in Hopei and Kwangtung.[17] With output linked to the growth of the cement industry and domestic demand also related to the growth of domestic requirements for cement, it is reasonable to assume that production in this branch moved together with cement output, which grew at an estimated average rate of 11.6 percent between 1912 and 1936 (Table A.1). I assume a 10 percent annual growth rate for the brick and shingle industry during the same period.

Silk and Silk Piece Goods. This large sector suffered a major decline beginning in the late 1920s on account of Japanese competition and falling foreign demand. Despite a confusing variety of evidence, it is reasonably clear that after rising for about fifteen years after the 1911 revolution silk production fell substantially, leaving 1936 output no larger than the level of 1912. Perkins's data show a rise of only 3.2 percent in cocoon output between 1914/18 and the early 1930s.[18] Li's figures on the size of Shanghai's steam filature industry show an identical number of firms for 1912 and 1936, although the number of basins declined by 17 percent.[19] Ex-

---

15. Kung-chia Yeh, "Capital Formation in Mainland China: 1931–36 and 1952– 57" (Ph.D. diss., Columbia University, 1964), 305.

16. Thomas G. Rawski, "Economic Growth and Integration in Prewar China" (Toronto, 1982), appendix C.

17. Baba Kuwatarō, *Shina no mengyō* (Shanghai, 1924), 847.

18. Dwight H. Perkins, *Agricultural Development in China, 1368–1968* (Chicago, 1969), 286.

19. Lillian M. Li, *China's Silk Trade: Traditional Industry in the Modern World, 1842–1937* (Cambridge, 1981), 166.

ports of raw silk and silk fabrics took 74 percent of the estimated cocoon output in 1925–26, with the quantity of exports almost exactly matching the totals for 1912. Ten years later, export volume had dropped by about 60 percent.[20] Although these figures point to a possible decline in output between 1912 and 1936, the data are far from satisfactory. I assume a zero growth rate for silk and silk products between 1912 and 1936.

Flour. The figure for this branch is based on output growth at Shanghai, which accounted for about 45 percent of total flour output in the mid-1930s.[21] Time series data for flour sales by Shanghai mills during 1914–36 and wheat consumption by Shanghai mills during 1912–36 show identical average growth rates of 6.7 percent per year.[22] I assume that total flour output during 1912–36 grew at an average annual rate of 6.7 percent between 1912 and 1936.

Edible Oils. The production of oil-bearing crops, including soybeans, peanuts, rape, and sesame, rose by 45 percent between 1914/18 and 1931/37, implying an annual growth of about 2 percent.[23] Since factory milling probably grew faster than oilseed production, I assume annual growth of 3 percent for the oil-pressing industry between 1912 and 1936.

Rice Milling. Perkins finds that China's output of rice declined by 6 percent between 1914/18 and 1931/37, with most of the drop attributed to the Yangtze provinces of Chekiang, Hunan, and Kiangsi.[24] This seems highly improbable in view of Brandt's evidence of rising interprovincial rice shipments originating in the Yangtze area during the same period.[25] Even if rice production stagnated or declined slightly, milling output in the factory sector probably increased. I assume annual growth of 1 percent in rice milling activity between 1912 and 1936.

20. Ibid., 75–76, 100.
21. Estimates for 1933 show Shanghai contributing 49–54 percent of output in China proper, which in turn accounted for 87 percent of the national total. See *Chiu Chung-kuo chi chih mien fen kung yeh t'ung chi tzu liao* (Peking, 1966), 50–51 and Liu and Yeh, *Economy of the Chinese Mainland,* 428.
22. *Chiu Chung-kuo mien fen,* 53, 137. These are calculated from the initial and terminal years only. Using log-linear regressions (and supplying one missing entry by linear interpolation) produces growth rates of 7.0 and 6.7 percent respectively.
23. Perkins, *Agricultural Development,* 281, 283.
24. Ibid., 276.
25. Loren L. Brandt, Jr., "Population Growth, Agricultural Change and Economic Integration in Central and Eastern China: 1890's–1930's" (Ph.D. diss., University of Illinois, 1983), chap. 2.

It is now possible to derive an estimate of the long-term growth of Chinese manufacturing between 1912 and 1936. The results depend on a variety of assumptions, but are based on a far larger sample of industries than was used for earlier studies. In Table A.1, I combine the branch growth rates discussed above into a single estimate for the period 1912–36 using alternative weights taken from branch shares in 1933 value added and 1933 manufacturing employment. The resulting long-term growth rates of 8.1 percent using value-added weights or 4.9 percent using employment weights are derived from a sample that includes three-fourths of 1933 factory output. The value-added version provides better insight into the actual performance because employment weights incorrectly assume identical labor productivity across industries. In the present analysis, this exaggerates the relative importance of the stagnant silk industry and understates the contribution of the relatively capital-intensive cigarette industry. These biases explain most of the difference between the two overall growth rates.

These results rest on a substantial sample of industries. The excluded branches encompass a variety of small industries with different histories. Some, like chemicals, printing, apparel, and metal products, probably enjoyed rapid growth. Others, such as sugar refining, leather, and wood products, probably grew slowly. With wide variation in the fortunes of sectors excluded from our sample, it is unlikely that the unknown trends in these branches could pull the overall growth rate far from the range indicated by our results in Table A.1. I therefore conclude that the real output of factory industry in China (including Manchuria) grew at an average pace of approximately 8.1 percent per year between 1912 and 1936.

The Sectoral Composition of Chinese Manufacturing Output in 1933

This appendix contains data underlying the sectoral distribution of China's 1933 manufacturing output displayed in Table 2.6. The figures appear in Table B.1.

Table B.1
Sectoral Composition of Chinese Manufacturing Output in 1933
(million yuan, current prices)

Sector	Gross Output Value	Rate of Value Added	Gross Value Added
Food, beverage, tobacco	911.9	.206	187.6
Milled rice & grain	172.4	.083[a]	14.3
Wheat flour	194.9	.097[a]	18.9
Edible oil	155.5	.102[a]	15.9
Other food & beverages	121.2	.100[b]	12.1
Tobacco & cigarettes	267.9	.472[a]	126.4
Textiles	949.1	.264	250.2
Ginned cotton	15.3	.100[b]	1.5
Cotton yarn & cloth	780.5	.251[a]	195.9
Silk & silk goods	124.4	.344[a]	42.8
Wool, linen, hemp	28.9	.346[a]	10.0
Clothing & footwear	109.1	.384[a]	41.9
Lumber & wood products	24.2	.115[c]	2.8
Paper & printing	97.4	.410	40.0
Paper and products	26.0	.467[a]	12.1
Printing	71.4	.390[c]	27.8
Leather & rubber	84.5	.276	23.3
Leather & prods., glue	46.6	.280[c]	13.0
Rubber products	37.9	.270[c]	10.2

Table B.1, continued

Chemicals	123.0	.463	56.9
Matches	37.3	.540[a]	20.1
Dyes & paints	17.7	.420[c]	7.4
Soap & paraffin	15.2	.310[c]	4.7
Pharmaceuticals	13.4	.110[c]	1.5
Other chemical prods.	39.4	.588[c]	23.2
Nonmetallic minerals	64.6	.494	31.9
Cement	27.1	.518[a]	14.0
Glass & glassware	10.8	.540[c]	5.8
Other	26.7	.450[c]	12.0
Basic metals (iron & steel)	33.2	.559[a]	18.7
Metal products	185.9	.357	66.4
Coins	41.0	.250[c]	10.2
Machinery	36.3	.424[a]	15.4
Transport equipment	31.5	.420[c]	13.2
Misc. metal products	31.1	.300[c]	9.3
Electrical appliances	21.4	.420[c]	9.0
Shipbuilding	16.0	.360[c]	5.8
Other metal products	8.6	.400[b]	3.4
Other	62.3	.269	16.7
Oils, nonedible	45.2	.200[c]	9.0
Miscellaneous	17.1	.450[c]	7.7
Total	2645.4	.278	736.4

Note: Column subtotals may not check because of rounding error. "Other food & beverages" includes wine and liquor. "Clothing & footwear" consists of dyed cloth, clothing, and attire. "Other nonmetallic minerals" includes coke, charcoal, brick, and shingles. "Machinery," "transport equipment," and "shipbuilding" include repair work as well as manufacture.

[a]Ta-chung Liu and Kung-chia Yeh, The Economy of the Chinese Mainland: National Income and Economic Development.1933-1959 (Princeton, 1965), 146.

[b]Assumed.

[c]Estimated from ibid., table F-4, on the basis of figures given for similar products.

Source: The data on gross output value are from ibid., 426-28. The rates of value added for sectors with several components are quotients of sectoral gross output and value added. The value-added data are calculated from gross output and rates of value added.

Estimates of China's Money
Supply, 1910–36

Changes in the stock of money provide important insights into macro-economic trends. The existence of a substantial body of statistical informa-tion about currency conditions and the banking sector makes it possible to construct rough, but useful, estimates of changes in the national money stock during the prewar decades. The only previous effort in this direction appears to be that of Sueh-chang Yang, whose doctoral dissertation in-cludes the following estimates of the "total quantity of money in China":[1]

1931	6.315 billion yuan
1932	5.934
1933	6.062
1934	5.903
1935	6.588
1936	8.841

Yang's results are incomplete. They include no figures for copper coinage, for Manchuria, or for the deposits and note issue of foreign banks oper-ating in China proper. The purpose of this appendix is to produce more complete and better documented estimates of China's money supply dur-ing the 1930s and to extend the series backward in time to permit a quan-titative assessment of broad trends in the size and composition of China's money supply during the prewar decades of the present century.

China's prewar money supply included monetary metals, comprising

1. Sueh-chang Yang, "China's Depression and Subsequent Recovery, 1931–36" (Ph.D. diss., Harvard University, 1950), 58.

silver and copper; paper notes, including the issue of Chinese commercial and governmental banks, foreign commercial banks, the Japanese colonial authorities in Manchuria, and a variety of miscellaneous sources; and deposits held by Chinese and foreign banking institutions. A time series estimate of China's money stock will be derived in two steps. First, I review available data on each component of China's prewar money stock. These data are then combined to produce a time series of monetary growth for the entire period between 1910 and 1936. The data come from a variety of sources, some of which are undoubtedly open to question. Inevitably, data gaps must be filled by assumptions that may build further errors into the results. The derived monetary aggregates must therefore be seen as estimates rather than precise figures, but the underlying data appear sufficiently reliable to view the results obtained as indicating in general terms the size of the money stock and the direction and magnitude of changes in the national money supply during the prewar years. Readers should recall that China's currency was based on a silver standard until the monetary reform of November 1935. I use the terms "dollar" and "yuan" to refer to the standard (silver) dollar unit.

Monetary Metals

Monetary metals in prewar China included silver and copper but not gold. Despite the operation of an active gold exchange in Shanghai, gold did not "perform the function of currency" in prewar China; neither Chinese nor foreign gold coins circulated widely during the period under review.[2] Silver provided the chief medium of exchange, unit of account, and store of value in prewar China, while copper provided a parallel coinage used for small transactions and in many rural areas.

Silver

The estimation of the stock of monetary silver begins with the work of Eduard Kann, the well-known banker and scholar of Chinese monetary affairs. His detailed study of "How Much Silver Is There in China," published in 1931, concluded that "to-day there is a minimum silver money circulation in China of altogether silver dollars 2,200,000,000, comprising silver dollars, sycee [silver ingots cast in the form of 'shoes'] and subsidi-

2. Eduard Kann, *The Currencies of China*, 2d ed. (Shanghai, 1927), 276. Kann states (p. 264) that "apart from . . . isolated instances . . . China has been devoid of gold coins meant to act as legalised medium of circulation" throughout its modern history. The trade in gold bars is described in ibid., chaps. 12–14.

Appendix C

Table C.1
China's Stock of Silver, 1910-36
(Year-end total, million dollars)

Year	Year-end Silver Stock	
	A	B
1910	880	1905
1911	940	1965
1912	970	1995
1913	1000	2025
1914	1056	2081
1915	1035	2060
1916	1006	2031
1917	961	1986
1918	998	2023
1919	1081	2106
1920	1225	2250
1921	1276	2301
1922	1338	2363
1923	1443	2468
1924	1484	2509
1925	1581	2606
1926	1664	2689
1927	1765	2790
1928	1931	2956
1929	2096	3121
1930	2200	3225
1931	2271	3296
1932[a]	2289	3314
1933	2275	3300
1934	1995	3020
1935[a]	1703	2728
1936[a]	1391	2416

[a]The figures for these years are adjusted for reported net imports of silver coin and bullion into Manchoukuo from foreign countries other than China. The annual net imports are: for 1932, $29 million; for 1935, -$3 million; for 1936, -$22 million, (with a negative sign indicating net outflows). There were no significant net silver flows reported for 1933 or 1934. Trade data are from Annual Returns of the Foreign Trade of Manchoukuo (Dairen, annual), 1932 ed., 2-3; 1934 ed., 2-3; and 1936 ed., part 1, 2-3. The figures for 1932 were converted from Hai-kuan taels into Manchoukuo yuan using the rate of 1.55 yuan per tael given in ibid., 1934 ed., front matter. Manchoukuo yuan are converted into Chinese yuan using the Dairen-Shanghai exchange rates given in Table C.7.

continued...

Table C.1, continued

Sources: The figures are based on the estimated silver stock for 1930 (E. Kann "How Much Silver," 410, Version A) and for 1933 (Bank of China figure from Tang, China's New Currency System, 3, Version B) mentioned in the text of this Appendix. For other years, the data are derived from these benchmark figures using the standard conversion of $1.55 per tael together with the estimates of annual net imports of silver given in the following sources:

for 1910-16: Liang-lin Hsiao, China's Foreign Trade Statistics, 1864-1949 (Cambridge, 1974), 128.

for 1917-33: D. H. Leavens, "American Silver Policy and China," Harvard Business Review 14, no. 1 (1935):49.

for 1934-36: Bank of China, Report of the General Manager to the Annual Meeting of Shareholders, March 30, 1935 (Shanghai, 1935), 13; Report of the Chairman to the Annual Meeting of Shareholders, April 4, 1936 (Shanghai, 1936), 25 and Report of the Chairman to the Annual Meeting of Shareholders, April 3, 1937 (Shanghai, 1937), 18. Net imports for these years include estimates of clandestine exports.

ary coins."[3] In 1934, the Bank of China estimated "the total silver stocks in China at over 3,300 million dollars, including silver dollars, silver ingots ('sycee'), and subsidiary coins."[4] The Bank's total is very close to Kann's combined figure of $3.24 billion for monetary and nonmonetary silver stocks. Beginning with either Kann's or the Bank's estimate of silver stocks, one can derive totals for earlier and later years using the Maritime Customs figures for China's international trade in silver. Kann notes that, for the period 1890–1925, "these figures may be taken as fairly correct" because there was no evidence of substantial unrecorded flows across China's borders.[5] This favorable assessment of the customs data may be extended through 1933. For 1934–36, the customs data must be supplemented by estimates of clandestine silver export.[6]

3. Eduard Kann, "How Much Silver Is There in China?" *Chinese Economic Journal* 8 (1931):410. Kann also offered "a vague estimate of about 800,000,000 troy ounces," equivalent to 1.04 billion silver dollars of the quantity of silver used "for ornamental and household purposes" and in noncirculating hoards of wealth (p. 411).
4. Leang-li T'ang, *China's New Currency System* (Shanghai, 1936), 3.
5. Kann, *Currencies of China*, 277, which notes that the customs returns "do not include the considerable amounts of gold which reach" China without being declared at the customs. Sir Arthur Salter, *China and Silver* (New York, 1934), 25, refers to smuggling of gold, but not silver, from China.
6. T'ang, *Currency*, 67, dates the clandestine silver outflow from July 1934 and observes that the outflow of silver had "already reached enormous proportions" in the following month. Formal efforts to curb the silver drain came only

These adjustments are performed in Table C.1, in which I derive annual year-end estimates of China's silver stock for the period 1912–36. I present two variants of the time series, first using Kann's estimate of China's 1930 stock of monetary silver (Version A) and then using the larger Bank of China figure, which is taken as pertaining to the end of 1933, before the start of clandestine silver export (Version B). These results are not free of defects. The initial silver stock totals, the customs figures for 1912 to 1933, and especially the estimated volumes of smuggled exports during 1934–36 may contain errors. In addition, lack of data forces me to neglect possible transfers of silver between monetary and nonmonetary uses. Despite these weaknesses, the general picture shown in Table C.1 is clear. China's stock of monetary silver rose steadily and rapidly after World War I, with the 1931 peak surpassing the post–World War I level by more than 50 percent (Version B) or 100 percent (Version A). The years 1934–36 witnessed a massive silver outflow that lowered China's silver stocks to the level of the early 1920s.

Copper

The role and function of copper currency in China's economy were subjects of vigorous dispute during the 1930s. A report prepared by a distinguished group of bankers and economists concluded that "silver is the standard medium of exchange over practically all China" and that "coppers are now in most places merely a subsidiary currency, of use in small transactions."[7] These findings were attacked by K. Bloch, who produced a variety of evidence showing that despite the gradual expansion of the silver sector, copper coins and notes denominated in copper formed a separate and distinct monetary system linked with, but not subsidiary to, the silver currency that served the needs of large traders, industrialists, and financiers. Bloch insisted that "there is . . . much truth in the statement that the currency of the people in China is copper, for the people who live in the interior certainly use mostly copper coins and copper notes."[8]

Scattered information from several parts of China supports Bloch's

---

in October 1934, when the Chinese government imposed a 10 percent tax on silver exports. (Michael B. Russell, "American Silver Policy and China, 1933–1936" [Ph.D. diss., University of Illinois, 1972], 72).

7. K. Bloch, "On the Copper Currencies in China," *Nankai Social and Economic Quarterly* 8, no. 3 (1935):630, quoting *Silver and Prices in China (Report of the Committee for the Study of Silver Values and Commodity Prices)* (Shanghai, 1935).

8. Bloch, "Copper Currencies," 631.

view that copper remained in wide use. Residents of the largest cities used coppers to pay for newspapers, small personal services, tram rides, and hot water.[9] A Japanese village study in Ch'ang-shu county, part of the Lower Yangtze area of Kiangsu province near Shanghai, found that "in this village, daily [farm] wages routinely include a food supplement of 100 copper cash or about 3.3 *chiao*."[10] Wartime conditions in Szechwan, home of one-tenth of China's populace, point to a much greater role for copper. Writing in 1939, investigators found that "trade has been encumbered, and prices of many small articles have gone up rapidly" because of shortages of copper coins. In rural markets, where coppers were "more popular than [silver] yuan . . . rapid movement of prices in copper caused serious maladjustments in the rural price structure and made . . . economic condition[s] unstable."[11] Lists of currencies circulating in Kwangsi province include copper as well as silver-based units.[12]

The reports of major mints, painstakingly compiled by Eduard Kann, provide detailed information about the production of copper coins.[13] Unfortunately, figures on the number of coins struck offer no guide to the quantity in circulation because the mints often used existing coins as raw material.[14] Because of the constant melting of existing coins to facilitate the manufacture of inferior tokens and the consequent depreciation of the copper coinage relative to silver, the silver value of China's stock of copper coins reached only a small fraction of the enormous production totals reported by the mints.[15]

9. Kann, *Currencies of China*, 425–26; interview material.
10. This information refers to the period 1937–39. It is not clear whether the food supplement was paid in copper cash or converted to silver-based *chiao*, a unit equivalent to one-tenth of a yuan. See *Kōsōshō Jojukuken nōson jittai chōsa hōkokusho* (Shanghai, 1940), 101.
11. W. Y. Yang and Kwoh-hwa Hu, "Problem of Copper Dearth," *Economic Facts* 12 (1939):562, 570.
12. *I-pei hsien chih* (I-pei, 1937), 84 and Shen Yung-ch'un, *Kuang-hsi chih-nan* (Changsha, 1939), 148. I am indebted to Diana Lary for these references.
13. E[duard] Kann, *The History of Minting in China* (Shanghai, 1939).
14. There are numerous references to the melting of copper coins for resale or export (especially during World War I and the Sino-Japanese War) and for reminting. Bloch, "Copper Currencies," 623, notes that "even to-day [i.e., 1935] . . . the Kaifeng Mint still produces coppers by melting down good coppers and striking bad coppers containing less copper and more iron."
15. Kann's compilation of mint statistics, which he sees as an underestimate of actual output, includes 53 billion copper tokens (Kann, *Minting*, 47). At 100 copper cents (in principle equivalent to 1,000 of the traditional copper cash) to the silver dollar, the combined value of these coins would reach 9 billion silver dollars. However, by the mid-1930s, it took more than 300 copper cents to buy

Without the mint statistics, one must fall back on general and largely undocumented estimates of the stock of copper coins. Writing in 1936, T'ang Leang-li stated that, "The total value of . . . copper currency is at least 220 million . . . dollars. The amount of the old perforated 'hole cash,' which still circulates in some interior areas, reaches tens of millions, and its total brings the amount of copper [coins] in circulation to over half the value of the subsidiary silver circulating in the country." T'ang placed the latter total at a minimum of $450 million, implying a silver value of perhaps $250 million for China's stock of copper coinage, presumably for 1935.[16] Another figure for the same year is given by Wang Yeh-chien, who estimates the value of the copper coinage at $100 million for the same year.[17] For the early period, the only figure that I have found comes from discussions preceding the monetary reform proposals of 1910: "The treatment of the copper coinage the Board [of Finance] considered as the most difficult problem. The total value of these copper yuans in silver was estimated at 100,000,000 taels."[18] At the standard conversion of 72 Shanghai *taels* per 100 silver dollars, this amounts to $139 million. It is not clear whether this figure refers solely to minted copper coins, or whether copper-based paper notes or the traditional copper cash are included.

These figures offer poor raw material for monetary estimates. Since my results will emphasize the rapidity of monetary growth, the weakness of the data relating to copper coinage demands assumptions that will avoid the artificial inflation of monetary expansion. T'ang's 1935 figures suggest that perhaps 90 percent (by value) of copper coins in circulation were of the minted variety and only 10 percent were traditional cash. In 1910, the share of modern coins was surely smaller, although I have no specific figure. Even in the early period, the production of modern coins was not insignificant. The Canton mint produced 40 million copper cents, each equivalent to ten cash, and 695 million cash pieces between 1890 and 1901; thus even before the turn of the century, over one-third of this mint's output of copper currency by value consisted of coins rather than

---

a silver dollar in Shanghai. In Szechwan, where the mints poured out huge numbers of inferior copper coins with high nominal values, 1,560 copper cents were needed to obtain a silver dollar in 1931 (Bloch, "Copper Currencies," 620–23).

16. T'ang, *Currency*, 4.

17. Wang Yeh-chien, *Chung-kuo chin tai huo pi yü yin hang ti yen chin (1644–1937)* (Taipei, 1981), 49.

18. Wen Bin Wei, *The Currency Problem in China* (New York, 1914), 129.

cash.[19] With a number of other modern mints beginning operation around the turn of the century and issuing large numbers of new-style coppers, one may speculate that by 1910, this 1:3 ratio may have applied to the national stock of copper coins.[20] If the total of $139 million cited above is taken as excluding copper cash, a high maximum estimate of the 1910 copper currency stock may be derived at three times this figure, or approximately $420 million. I will use $420 million as a (high) estimate of the silver value of China's stock of copper coins at the end of 1909.

For 1935, there are alternative estimates of $100 million and roughly $250 million for the silver value of copper coinage. The former total appears unreasonably small. Even at 350 copper cents to the dollar, $100 million worth of coppers represents only seven ten-cent copper coins (the smallest denomination) for each of China's roughly 500 million people. Outside Manchuria, an area in which copper was scarce and had been replaced by small silver coins at an early date, and the largest cities, where industrial wages were paid in silver after 1928, all buyers and sellers held inventories of coppers.[21] Even in the Shanghai area copper coins were used for small purchases and financial intermediaries maintained copper accounts for thrifty children.[22] I therefore adopt T'ang's figure of $250 million for the estimated value of China's stock of copper coins in the mid-1930s.

My conclusion, then, is that the stock of copper coins declined from a possibly high initial figure of $420 million in 1909 to $250 million in 1935. Lacking detailed information about the pattern of change in the stock of copper coinage, I assume equal annual decrements of 6.3 million dollars in the silver value of China's copper coinage between these two dates; I assume an identical decline for 1935/36. The resulting series of copper currency values appears in Table C.16. Since the initial total may be too high, there is little chance that these crude figures conceal a major overstatement of monetary growth (or understatement of decline) in the copper sector. The small size of both the initial and the terminal figures means that broad conclusions about the size and growth of China's money stock do not depend critically on the accuracy of these weak estimates.

19. Kann, *Minting*, 10.
20. Kann, *Minting*, 6–7, lists twenty-two mints that were opened between 1887 and 1905, of which fifteen are specifically mentioned as producing copper cents before 1911.
21. Bloch, "Copper Currencies," notes the shift to silver payment for industrial wages.
22. Ibid., 628, which also notes the use of coppers as savings vehicles in Yunnan and Kweichow and in denominating mortgages and native bank loans in interior regions (p. 618).

Banknotes

Banknotes constitute the second major segment of China's prewar money supply. The volume of banknotes in circulation is most conveniently discussed under three headings: the issue of Chinese banks in China proper; the issue of domestic banks (including the Central Bank of Manchoukuo) in Manchuria; and the issue of foreign banks, including Japanese banks based outside China's boundaries but operating in Manchuria.

The Note Issue of Domestic Banks: *China Proper*

The available information on the note issue of Chinese banks in China proper is compiled in Table C.2. For 1934–36, I use figures produced by the Bank of China that were intended to be comprehensive. In view of the concentration of banking operations in major cities, especially Shanghai, and the considerable experience of the Bank of China in compiling monetary statistics, these figures may be accepted as reasonably accurate, although the relatively minor issue of institutions operated by provincial and county governments and purely local intermediaries is no doubt omitted from these totals. For the period 1923–34, I use figures, again compiled by the Bank of China, for the note issue of the major Shanghai banks and assume that these represent 80 percent of the total for Chinese institutions in China proper. Hsien K'o states that the figures for the principal Shanghai banks account for "over 80 percent" of the national total.[23] In 1934, the share of these major banks in estimated note issue was 77.4 percent. The data for the earlier years are probably less comprehensive and less reliable. However, figures for 1914 indicate that the Bank of China and the Bank of Communications dominated domestic note issue, accounting for 75.7 percent of the national total. I assume that these two institutions supplied 75 percent of combined note issue for all Chinese banks in China proper between 1915 and 1920.

The figures in Table C.2 fail to incorporate the activities of two groups of note issuers: traditional institutions, including native banks, exchange shops, and merchants; and modern-style financial intermediaries such as minor commercial banks and institutions sponsored by provincial and county governments. The number of traditional note-issuing institutions was large, even though the scale of issue by individual agents was small. A survey of parts of Shensi province found "not less than 37 different

23. Hsien K'o, *Chin pai nien lai ti kuo chu i tsai Hua yin hang fa hsing chih pi kai kuang* (Shanghai, 1958).

Table C.2
Note Issue of Chinese Banks in China Proper (1912-1936)
(Million dollars)

Year	Bank of China	Bank of Communications	Principal Banks	Total
1912	1.1[a]	0.8[a]	. . .	52.7[a]
1913	5.0[a]	4.5[a]	. . .	52.8[a]
1914	16.4[a]	6.0[a]	. . .	29.6[a]
1915	38.4[b]	24.9[a]	. . .	84.4[b]
1916	46.4[a]	21.3[a]	. . .	90.3[b]
1917	73.0[a]	28.6[c]	. . .	135.5[b]
1918	52.2[c]	34.1[c]	. . .	115.1[b]
1919	61.7[c]	29.3[c]	. . .	121.3[b]
1920	66.9[c]	30.9[d]	. . .	130.4[b]
1921	62.5[c]	32.5[e]	95.9[f]	147.1[e]
1922	77.8[e]	32.5[e]	115.0[f]	161.4[g]
1923	. . .	. . .	140.5[f]	175.6[h]
1924	. . .	. . .	151.5[f]	189.4[h]
1925	. . .	. . .	205.0[f]	256.2[h]
1926	. . .	. . .	229.0[f]	286.2[h]
1927	. . .	. . .	262.2[f]	327.8[h]
1928	. . .	. . .	308.8[f]	386.0[h]
1929	. . .	. . .	350.2[f]	437.8[h]
1930	. . .	. . .	413.0[f]	516.2[h]
1931	. . .	. . .	393.4[f]	491.8[h]
1932	184.4[f]	94.5[f]	430.5[f]	538.1[h]
1933	183.7[f]	93.0[f]	494.1[f]	617.6[h]
1934	204.7[f]	112.5[f]	578.8[f]	747.7[i]
1935	286.2[i]	180.8[i]	. . .	1032.6[i]
1936	465.7[i]	302.1[i]	. . .	1976.7[i]

[a]Hsien, <u>Ti kuo chu i tsai Hua yin hang</u>, 59.

[b]Calculated by assuming that the Bank of China and Bank of Communications accounted for 75 percent of the total. See the text of this appendix.

[c]<u>The China Yearbook</u> (Tientsin, annual), 1919/20 ed., 418; 1921/22 ed., 281, 284; 1923 ed., 729.

[d]Linear interpolation between the values for 1919 and 1921.

[e]<u>Shina kinyū jijō</u> (Tokyo, 1925), 34-35 and chart facing 190.

continued...

agencies issuing copper notes . . . and . . . this figure was not exhaustive."[24] Despite these omissions, which presumably lead to an underestimate of the stock of notes and may cause me to overstate the growth rate of note issue (if banknotes gradually replaced local notes, which are

24. Bloch, "Copper Currencies," 626.

Table C.2, continued

[f]An Analysis of the Accounts of the Principal Chinese Banks, 1934
(Shanghai, 1935), pp 2, 22.

[g]Linear interpolation between the values for 1921 and 1923.

[h]Calculated by assuming that the principal Shanghai banks
accounted for 80 percent of the total. See the text of this
Appendix.

[i]Ch'üan kuo yin hang nien chien, 1937 (Shanghai, 1937), 42, 71,
76, including notes issued on behalf of other institutions as well
as those of the issuing bank.

omitted from my totals), the figures compiled in Table C.2 probably give
a good approximation to actual trends in the stock of banknotes in
circulation.

The Note Issue of Domestic Banks: Manchuria

The available information on the note issue of domestic banks in Manchuria appears in Table C.3. These figures include the issue of Chinese institutions operating exclusively in the northeast, regional branches of Chinese intermediaries with offices elsewhere in China (for example, the
Bank of China), and foreign-controlled institutions such as the Central
Bank of Manchoukuo that operated only in Manchuria.[25] The note issue
of Japanese banks with headquarters outside the region is included along
with the notes of other foreign banks. The available data for Manchurian
banks resemble information on note issue in China proper in that the
figures for the 1930s appear both comprehensive and reliable, while those
for earlier years are clearly subject to wide margins of error. There may
be some double counting. It is possible that notes issued by the Manchurian branches of the Bank of China and the Bank of Communications are
included in both Tables C.2 and C.3. Even so, the possible scope of
double counting is very small.

The weakest data in Table C.3 are those for 1918, which come from a
study by the Bank of Chosen.[26] This study identifies several types of
notes, as summarized in Table C.4. The figures included in this survey

25. The Manchurian note issue of the Bank of China, the premier Chinese institution, was less than 3 million yuan around 1930. This bank, together with the
Bank of Communications, the second largest Chinese bank, and two regional
institutions issued notes jointly through the Joint Reserve Fund of Four Liaoning Banks, but the total reported as of September 1930 was only 10 million
yuan (*The Manchuria Year Book, 1932–33* [Tokyo, 1932], 407–8).
26. *Economic History of Manchuria* (Seoul, 1920), 250–62.

Table C.3
Note Issue of Domestic Institutions in Manchuria, 1918-36
(million dollars)

Year	Note Issue
1918	ca. 50
1927	173.2
1928	202.6[a]
1929	232.1
1930	181.2
1931	155.7
1932	149.6
1933	127.1
1934	164.1
1935	155.2
1936	249.2

[a]Linear interpolation between the 1927 and 1929 values.

Source: The text of this appendix.

amount to a combined total of roughly 50 million dollars. Lacking even the roughest figures for two of the currencies that circulated in parts of Manchuria, *kuan-t'ieh* and copper notes (*t'ung-yuan-p'iao*), this represents only a lower-bound figure for the actual total, which could perhaps have reached 100 million dollars.

Figures for the years 1927–31 are taken from compilations of Manchurian data that can be converted into *yin-p'iao* or *ch'ao-p'iao*, terms that refer to the silver yen notes issued by the Yokohama Specie Bank. These notes were very nearly equivalent to standard Chinese dollars, as can be seen by comparing exchange rates against the Shanghai *tael*, a popular silver accounting unit, shown in Table C.5. With the theoretical *tael/* dollar parity standing at approximately $1.40 per Shanghai *tael* or 0.714 Shanghai *taels* per standard dollar, it is reasonable to convert *yin-p'iao* or *ch'ao-p'iao* figures into standard dollars at a 1 : 1 ratio.[27] For the years 1927

27. Dollar/*tael* conversion based on Kann, *Currencies of China*, 168–71 and D. K. Lieu, *The Growth and Industrialization of Shanghai* (Shanghai, 1936), 92. Parity between *yin-p'iao* and standard Chinese dollars applies to the 1920s as well as the years covered in Table C.5.

Table C.4
Domestic Note Issue in Manchuria, 1919
(Million dollars)

Type of Note	Jan. 1919 Circulation
Kuan-t'ieh	no data
T'ung-yuan-p'iao	no data
Yang-ch'ien-p'iao	11.3[a]
Hui-tui-p'iao	20
Chai-chuan	3
T'ieh-tzu[b]	15

[a]Face value; these notes circulated at a 45 percent discount.

[b]Private notes issued by merchants and other nonbank agents.

Source: Economic History of Manchuria, 250-62.

Table C.5
Market Value of Ch'ao-p'iao Drafts in Shanghai Taels
(taels per 100 yen)

Year	Highest	Lowest
1927	74.475	69.975
1928	73.300	71.000
1929	72.750	71.525
1930	76.755	71.050
1931	75.500	71.200

Source: The Manchuria Year Book, 1932-33 (Tokyo, 1932), 399.

and 1929–31, we have detailed Japanese estimates of Manchurian currency circulation, with each type of note converted into a standard unit. The totals, omitting coins, silver ingots, and notes issued by foreign banks, are shown in Table C.6.

Finally, the figures for 1932–36 are based on the reports of the Central Bank of Manchoukuo, established in 1932, which gradually retired earlier currencies and replaced them with its own Manchoukuo yen. The bank's estimates of outstanding note issue, including the provision for older notes issued before the creation of the Japanese-controlled state of Man-

Table C.6
Domestic Note Circulation in Manchuria, 1927-31
(millions, year-end totals)

	1927	1929	1930	1931
1. Domestic note circulation	167.3	232.1	181.2	155.7
2. Currency unit	ta-yang ch'ien	hsien ta-yang	silver dollars	hsien ta-yang
3. Yin-p'iao per currency unit	1.035	1.000	1.000	1.000
4. Domestic note circulation (yin-p'iao or standard dollar)	173.2	232.1	181.2	155.7

Source: For 1927 and 1929, *The Manchuria Yearbook, 1931* (Tokyo, 1931), 254-55; for 1930, *Japan-Manchoukuo Year Book, 1934* (Tokyo, 1934), 676; for 1931, *The Manchuria Year Book, 1932-33*, 393-95.

Table C.7
Domestic Currency Circulation in Manchuria, 1932-36
(year-end data, in millions)

Year	Manchoukuo yen	Chinese dollars per yen	Chinese dollars
1932	151.9	0.9848	149.6
1933	129.2	0.9841	127.1
1934	168.3	0.9750	164.1
1935	178.6	0.8691	155.2
1936	254.2	0.9803	249.2

Source: *Manshū kaihatsu yonjū nenshi* (Tokyo, 1964-65), 2:850.

choukuo, appear in Table C.7, where they are also converted into standard dollars.

Foreign Banknotes

Several prewar studies include figures for the note issue of the various foreign banks in China. Unfortunately, most of these data represent the total note issue of these banks rather than the portion circulating in China. Since notes of the major foreign banks, including the Hong Kong and Shanghai Bank, the Bank of Chosen, the Bank of Taiwan, and the

Banque de L'Indochine, circulated outside China (in Hong Kong, Korea, Taiwan, and Indochina respectively) as well as within China's borders, these data are not suitable for estimating Chinese money supply totals.[28]

The only study that attempts to calculate the circulation of foreign banknotes within China is that of Hsien K'o, which is based on a careful review of a limited range of source materials. Hsien's estimate of the total issue of foreign banks circulating in China is derived as follows:[29]

Total note issue of foreign banks in China $=$	2/3 of the global issue of three British banks: Hong Kong and Shanghai, Chartered Bank, and Mercantile Bank of India

+ total note issue of three U.S. banks: International Banking Corp., American Oriental Banking Corp., and Asia Banking Corp.

+ total issue of the Yokohama Specie Bank together with 1/3 of the total issue of the Bank of Chosen and the Bank of Taiwan

+ total issue of the Banque de L'Indochine

+ total issue of several minor institutions of Dutch, Belgian, or mixed sino-foreign ownership.

Although Hsien gives few references, several checks show close correspondence between his data for individual banks and figures given in other sources.[30] The difficulty with Hsien's results is that his totals are

28. Materials suffering from this difficulty include *Jih-pen tui Hu t'ou tzu* (Shanghai, 1937), 19–20, 26–29, where the note issue "of Japanese banks in Shanghai" is identical with the total issue of the same banks as shown in *Hundred-Year Statistics of the Japanese Economy* (Tokyo, 1966), 167. *Shina kinyū jijō* (Tokyo, 1925), 40–41 and the table following 192, give figures for note issue "in China" that are identical or very close to global totals published elsewhere for the Hong Kong and Shanghai Bank, the Chartered Bank, the Mercantile Bank, the Bank of Taiwan, the Yokohama Specie Bank, and the International Banking Corp., among which only the last two issued most or all of their notes in China.
29. Hsien, *Ti kuo chu i tsai Hua yin hang*, 52–58.
30. The sole exception is Hsien's figure of 100.2 million yuan for the combined 1933 note issue of the International Banking Corp. and the American Oriental Banking Corp. (*Ti kuo chu i tsai Hua yin hang*, 52), which appears to be a misprint for 10.2 million yuan. The International Banking Corp., the largest American institution in China's banking community, reported US$1 million worth of notes circulating at the end of 1933, equivalent to 3.8 million Chinese yuan (*The Statist*, November 17, 1934, 780).

produced without regard for missing items. Furthermore, no explanation is given for the division of note circulation between China and other regions.

Beginning with the question of the geographic distribution of bank-notes, I have found no direct information concerning the notes of British banks. Hsien's assumption that two-thirds of their notes circulated in China may be too high. Japanese researchers assumed that the shares of China-based depositors in total deposits for the major British institutions were 60 percent for the Hong Kong and Shanghai Bank, 25 percent for the Chartered Bank, and 10 percent for the Mercantile Bank.[31] The importance of the Hong Kong and Shanghai Bank makes the totals quite sensitive to errors in apportioning its note issue between China and other territories. Hsien's assumption that the entire note issue of the U.S. banks circulated in China seems reasonable, as does his treatment of notes emanating from Japanese banks. The small volume of silver notes issued by the Yokohama Specie Bank circulated mainly, if not entirely, in Manchuria. Information about the Bank of Chosen confirms Hsien's assumptions: the share of its notes circulating in Manchuria ranged from 30 to 37 percent throughout 1919–30 with the exception of 1919 (23 percent) and 1929 (42 percent).[32] Hsien errs, however, in assuming that the entire issue of the Banque de L'Indochine circulated in China. This leads him to the unacceptable conclusion that the stock of this bank's notes exceeded comparable figures for any other foreign institution in China, a position surely occupied by the Hong Kong and Shanghai Bank in China proper and by the Bank of Chosen in Manchuria. Furthermore, a Japanese survey of the early 1920s reported that the Banque de L'Indochine did the largest portion of its business in Annam (Vietnam) and that its notes circulated "mainly in Annam," although they reached China's major cities as well as points along the railway linking Hanoi with Kunming (Yunnan).[33]

I propose to estimate the circulation of foreign banknotes in China on the basis of Hsien's first three components alone, those relating to the note issue of British, American, and Japanese banks. The resulting totals contain a downward bias in that the issue of French, Dutch, German, Belgian, and sino-foreign banks is excluded. These omissions, however, are small; they may be matched or surpassed by possible overestimation

31. *Shogaikoku no tai-Shi tōshi* (Tokyo, 1942–43) 1:facing p. 2. I am indebted to Professor Chang Chung-li for directing me to this source.
32. The Bank of Chosen note issue is from *Hundred-Year Statistics*, 166–67. The estimated circulation in Manchuria, "the result of careful calculation," is given in the *Japan Manchoukuo Year Book, 1934* (Tokyo, 1934), 682.
33. *Shina kinyū jijō*, 357.

Table C.8
Estimated Circulation of Foreign Banknotes in China, 1912-36
(million dollars)

Year	British Banks	U.S. Banks	Japanese Banks	Combined Total
1910	22.5	...	...	53.2[a]
1911	28.1	...	...	66.5[a]
1912	30.9	...	39.4	73.1[b]
1913	34.8	...	40.1	77.9[b]
1914	27.3	2.5	35.1	64.9
1915	27.6	3.0	52.4	83.0
1916	26.7	2.6	66.7	96.0
1917	18.6	2.9	72.6	94.1
1918	23.5	3.3	84.3	111.1
1919	26.2	4.5	49.2	79.9
1920	27.1	8.3	38.9	74.3
1921	45.1	14.8	61.3	121.2
1922	40.7	17.1	48.7	106.5
1923	49.9	13.3	42.6	105.8
1924	44.5	11.9	52.8	109.2
1925	44.3	13.4	63.8	121.5
1926	54.7	11.3	63.3	129.3
1927	55.3	10.6	69.6	135.5
1928	48.9	12.5	86.6	148.0
1929	66.9	12.0	105.2	184.1
1930	106.9	10.8	106.7	224.4
1931	124.4	14.7	77.6	216.7
1932	121.1	14.7	65.0	200.8
1933	124.5	6.8	61.6	192.9
1934	121.3	5.3	70.5	197.1
1935	121.9	5.0	98.8	225.7
1936	110.9	6.0	95.8	212.7

[a]Calculated from the following year's total by applying the percentage change in note issue of British banks to the total for all foreign banks.

[b]Calculated from the following year's total by applying the percentage change in note issue of British and Japanese banks to the total for all foreign banks.

Sources: See the text of this appendix.

of the share of notes issued by the British banks, especially the dominant Hong Kong and Shanghai Bank, that actually circulated in China. The data for individual banks come from more complete sources than were available to Hsien K'o. Results are summarized in Table C.8.

The annual year-end note issue of the three major British-controlled banks is given in the following issues of the *Statist*: for 1915–22, the issue of November 24, 1923, 248, 788, 792; for 1923–31, the issue of November 12, 1932, 672, 675, 735; for 1932–36, the issue of November 28, 1942, 26–28. The note issue for the Hong Kong and Shanghai Bank is given in terms of Hong Kong dollars. For 1933–36, these totals are converted to Chinese dollars or yuan using the rates shown in Liang-lin Hsiao, *China's Foreign Trade Statistics, 1864–1949* (Cambridge, 1974), 192. For 1923–32, Hong Kong dollars are converted into *Hai-kuan taels* at rates shown in Hsiao (ibid.) and then into yuan at the standard rate of $1.55 per *tael*. For 1910–22, Hong Kong dollar amounts are converted to pounds using the annual average of the first and last rates for each year quoted in the *Times* of London (for 1909–13 and December 1917) and the *Statist* (for the remaining years), then converted to *Hai-kuan taels* at rates shown in Hsiao, *Foreign Trade*, 190–91, and finally into dollars at the standard rate of $1.55 per *tael*. Figures for the Chartered Bank and the Mercantile Bank are given in pounds. These are converted to yuan (via *taels* before 1933) using the rates shown in Hsiao (ibid.).

The estimated note circulation for the three major U.S. banks is based on the figures for the International Banking Corporation (owned by National City Bank of New York) and on Hsien K'o's estimate that the combined note issue of American banks circulating in China in 1924 was 12.0 million yuan, which is equivalent to 6.23 million U.S. dollars.[34] The estimated note circulation of the U.S. banks in other years is based on Hsien's total for 1924 and the annual percentage changes in the reported issue of the International Banking Corp. to June 30 of the year in question (between 1914 and 1930; the figures for 1931–33 refer to December 31, with no change shown between June 30, 1930, and December 31, 1931). I find no data after 1933 and assume that the small total of note issue by U.S. banks remained unchanged through 1936. Figures for the International Banking Corp. come from the *Statist*: November 24, 1923, 877–78 (for 1914–23); November 12, 1932, 751 (for 1924–30); and November 17, 1934 (for year-end 1931–33).

The annual year-end note issue of the three large Japanese banks is recorded in *Hundred-Year Statistics of the Japanese Economy* (Tokyo, 1966), 166–67. Between 1913 and 1917 gold yen notes of the Yokohama Specie Bank are converted to silver yen at the rates given in *Mammō seiji keizai teiyō* (Tokyo, 1932), 471–72. Yen are converted to Chinese dollars using the rates shown in Hsiao, *Foreign Trade*, 191–92. For 1914–32, the rates link yen and *Hai-kuan taels*, and must be supplemented by the standard conversion factor of $1.55 per *Hai-kuan tael*.

34. Hsien, *Ti kuo chu i tsai Hua yin hang*, 54.

Table C.9
Estimated Banknote Circulation in China, 1914-36
(year-end data, million yuan)

Year	Domestic Banks		Foreign Banks	Total
	China Proper (1)	Manchuria (2)	(3)	(4)
1910	...	...	53.2	114.3[a]
1911	...	...	66.5	142.9[a]
1912	52.7	...	73.1	157.1[b]
1913	52.8	...	77.9	163.2[b]
1914	29.6	...	64.9	118.0[b]
1915	84.4	...	83.0	209.0[b]
1916	90.3	...	96.0	232.6[b]
1917	135.5	...	94.1	286.6[b]
1918	115.1	...	111.1	282.4[b]
1919	121.3	50.0	79.9	251.2
1920	130.4	...	74.3	281.2[c]
1921	147.1	...	121.2	368.6[c]
1922	161.4	...	106.5	368.0[c]
1923	175.6	...	105.8	386.6[c]
1924	189.4	...	109.2	410.2[c]
1925	256.2	...	121.5	518.9[c]
1926	286.2	...	129.3	570.8[c]
1927	327.8	173.2	135.5	636.5
1928	386.0	202.6	148.0	736.6
1929	437.8	232.1	184.1	854.0
1930	516.2	181.2	224.4	921.8
1931	491.8	155.7	216.7	864.2
1932	538.1	149.6	200.8	888.5
1933	617.6	127.1	192.9	937.6
1934	747.7	164.1	197.1	1108.9
1935	1032.6	155.2	225.7	1413.5
1936	1976.7	249.2	212.7	2438.6

[a]Calculated from the following year's figure by applying the percentage change in notes issued by foreign banks to the total for all banks.

[b]Calculated from the 1919 figure using an index of the combined annual total from Cols. 1 and 3, taking 1919 as 100.

[c]Calculated from the 1927 figure using an index of the combined annual total from Cols. 1 and 3, taking 1927 as 100.

Source: Tables C.2, C.3, and C.8.

These separate calculations of note totals for Chinese banks in China proper, domestic Manchurian banks, and foreign banks can be combined to yield estimates of national circulation of banknotes between 1914 and 1936. This is done in Table C.9.

Bank Deposits

Bank deposits form the third major component of estimated money stock. Lacking systematic information that would allow the separation of demand deposits and savings or time deposits, I focus initially on a broadly defined monetary aggregate corresponding roughly to M2 in contemporary American parlance. Incomplete data on the share of current deposits to the total (Table C.17) can be used to generate a tentative series for a narrowly defined monetary aggregate corresponding roughly to the M1 concept of money stock. I estimate separate deposit totals for four groups of institutions: Chinese banks throughout China (1913–31) and in China proper alone (1932–36); domestic institutions in Manchuria (including the Japanese-controlled Central Bank of Manchoukuo but excluding externally based Japan banks) during 1932–36; foreign banks (that is, institutions under foreign control and with headquarters outside China); and native banks or *ch'ien-chuang*.

The Deposits of Chinese Banks

Estimates of the deposits held by Chinese banks appear in Table C.10. The basic data come from a compendium entitled *An Analysis of the Accounts of the Principal Chinese Banks, 1934*, which provides annual data beginning in 1921 for twenty-nine Shanghai-based institutions. A comparison of the deposits reported by these "principal banks" with the estimated total deposits for 1932–34, years for which both figures are available, shows that the "principal banks" dominated China's banking industry. The concentration of banking activity in a relatively small number of Shanghai-based institutions and the long experience of the Bank of China's Shanghai branch in compiling banking statistics suggests that the figures in Table C.10 should be broadly accurate after 1921, even though our assumption of a constant share of the "principal banks" in total deposits throughout 1921–34 may lead to an understatement of actual deposit growth by ignoring the proliferation of new institutions in the later years of this period. The figures for 1913–20 inspire less confidence. As with the data for note issue, one suspects that the early entries may be too high, leading to an understatement of deposit growth.

The Deposits of Domestic Institutions in
Manchuria, 1932–36

Detailed information on Manchurian bank deposits appears in the publications of the Central Bank of Manchoukuo, but only for the 1930s. Be-

Table C.10
Deposits Held by Chinese Banks in China Proper, 1913-36
(million yuan)

Year	Bank of China	Bank of Communications	Principal Chinese Banks	Total
1912	. . .	. . .	. . .	497[a]
1913	17.0[b]	. . .	. . .	476.9[c]
1914	58.4[b]	. . .	. . .	456.8[c]
1915	. . .	. . .	. . .	436.8[c]
1916	. . .	. . .	. . .	416.7[c]
1917	145.9[b]	38.5[b]	. . .	396.6[d]
1918	147.2[b]	52.4[b]	. . .	429.2[d]
1919	181.5[b]	68.7[b]	. . .	538.1[d]
1920	190.3[b]	. . .	. . .	536.2[c]
1921	176.2[b]	52.6[e]	497.0[f]	534.4[g]
1922	187.0[e]	. . .	525.1[f]	564.6[g]
1923	. . .	. . .	551.4[f]	592.9[g]
1924	. . .	. . .	625.7[f]	672.8[g]
1925	. . .	. . .	783.3[f]	842.2[g]
1926	. . .	. . .	934.8[f]	1005.2[g]
1927	330.5[h]	158.3[h]	976.1[f]	1049.6[g]
1928	. . .	. . .	1123.5[f]	1208.1[g]
1929	. . .	. . .	1320.2[f]	1419.6[g]
1930	. . .	. . .	1620.3[f]	1742.2[g]
1931	. . .	. . .	1860.7[f]	2000.8[g]
1932	557.2[f]	214.3[f]	1974.0[f]	2115.7[i]
1933	648.7[f]	253.5[f]	2418.6[f]	2594.1[i]
1934	685.4[f]	293.2[f]	2751.4[f]	2997.8[j]
1935	. . .	. . .	. . .	3789.4[j]
1936	. . .	. . .	. . .	4551.3[j]

[a]Wang, Chung-kuo chin tai huo pi, 69.

[b]The China Year Book (Tientsin, annual), 1919/20, 418-19; 1921/22, 281, 284; 1923, 779.

[c]An arithmetic interpolation between the values for 1912 and 1917.

[d]In 1932-34, the principal banks accounted for between 92 and 93 percent of overall deposits by Chinese institutions in China proper. In 1927, the Bank of China and Bank of Communications accounted for 46.6 percent of total deposits in the principal Chinese banks. For 1917-19, I assume that these two banks held 0.5 x 0.93 or 46.5 percent of all deposits.

continued...

Table C.10, continued

ᵉThe data for 1921-22 are shown in Shina kinyū jijō, following 190.

ᶠAnalysis of Banks, 1934, 2, 18.

ᵍDerived by assuming that the principal banks accounted for 93 percent of total deposits, the actual ratio for 1932-34.

ʰKia-ngau Chang, "Toward Modernization of China's Currency and Banking, 1927-1937," in The Strenuous Decade: China's Nation-Building Efforts, 1927-1937, ed. Paul K. T. Sih (New York, 1970), 136-37.

ⁱFrank M. Tamagna, Banking and Finance in China (New York, 1942), 184.

ʲCh'üan kuo yin hang nien chien 1937 (Shanghai, 1937), 42.

Table C.11
Deposits of Domestic Banks in Manchuria, 1932-36
(year-end totals, millions)

Year	Central Bank of Manchoukuo (1)	Other (2)	Total (1)+(2) (yen) (3)	Exchange Rate (yuan/yen) (4)	Deposit Total (yuan) (5)
1932	50.291	2.854	53.145	.9848	52.3
1933	71.527	3.588	75.116	.9841	73.9
1934	103.117	20.153	123.270	.9750	120.2
1935	151.934	11.365	163.299	.8691	141.9
1936	222.731	13.042	235.773	.9803	231.1

Sources: For Lines 1-2, Manshū chūō ginkō jūnenshi (Hsinking, 1942), appendix, 8-9. For Col. 4, see Table C.7. Yen totals refer to Manchoukuo yen.

ginning in 1932, the Central Bank reported on its own deposits and those of Manchurian, Chinese, Japanese, and foreign banks as well as cooperatives and other financial institutions. The Manchurian deposits of Chinese banks may be included in the figures for 1932–36 shown in Table C.10. Since this study emphasizes the large size and rapid growth of national monetary aggregates, I shall assume that the Manchurian deposits of Chinese banks do appear in Table C.10 even after the Japanese seizure of Manchuria. In any case, the possible error is modest, for the size of these deposits falls steadily from 74.0 million yen in 1932 to only 25.9 million in 1936. The figures for the remaining categories of domestic deposits in Manchuria, those of the Central Bank of Manchoukuo and "domestic" (that is, indigenous to Manchuria) banks, are tabulated both in Manchoukuo yen and in Chinese yuan in Table C.11.

Prior to the creation of the Central Bank of Manchoukuo in 1932, banking was dominated by Chinese, Japanese, and foreign institutions the deposits of which, with the possible exception of those in Chinese banks, are counted elsewhere. Deposits in Manchurian banking institutions, which amounted to less than three million yuan in 1932 (Table C.11), are assumed to be negligible in all earlier years.

The Deposits of Foreign Banks

This is perhaps the most obscure component of China's prewar monetary aggregates. There are considerable data relating to the deposits held in Japanese banks, but the figures are often inconsistent. Other foreign banks rarely produced separate accounts for their Chinese operations. Pending archival research, the figures for these institutions must be viewed as highly speculative.

Japanese Banks. Information on deposits in Japanese banks is compiled in Table C.12. The best figures are for 1932–36, when Manchurian data are available from the Central Bank of Manchoukuo and the small deposits held by Japanese institutions in China proper can be estimated. For earlier years, Japan's Ministry of Finance issued regular reports of deposits held in China by Japanese banks, but as is evident in Table C.12, these figures are incomplete. The Ministry's totals are much lower than comparable figures prepared by the Tōa kenkyūjo in a report whose "top secret" label may be taken as indicative of careful research. Information in the Tōa kenkyūjo source is said to come from "data in the yearbook of the Finance Ministry's banking division, with ambiguities rectified with reference to reports of the Industry Ministry or by estimation."[35] Sakatani's deposit totals for four major institutions in Manchuria alone during the late 1920s are substantially above the supposedly more comprehensive Ministry of Finance totals.

The figures adopted for use in my broader compilation are indicated with asterisks in Table C.12. These include the national deposit totals calculated for 1918, 1927, and 1930 by the Tōa kenkyūjo, the Manchurian regional totals provided by Sakatani for 1918 and 1927, the *Manchuria Year Book* for 1930 and the Central Bank of Manchoukuo for 1932–36,

35. *Nihon no tai-Shi tōshi* (Tokyo, 1942), 63.

Table C.12
Reported Deposits of Japanese Banks In China, 1914-1936
(Million Chinese yuan)

Year	China and Manchuria		Manchuria Only		China Proper
	Finance Ministry (1)	Tôa kenkyûjo (2)	Sakatani (3)	Central Bank (4)	
1914	3.8	...	...	...	...
1918	...	86.0*	54.0*	...	32.0[a]
1922	...	...	109.1	...	...
1925	...	...	128.8	...	...
1926	...	...	135.5	...	...
1927	77.9	190.1*	168.1*	...	22.0*[a]
1928	88.9	253.9*[b]	162.7	...	...
1929	89.9	317.7*[b]	175.8	...	...
1930	76.5	381.5*	...	236.6*[c]	144.9*[a]
1931	372.0*[a]		...	254.0[d]	118.0*[e]
1932	362.4*[a]		...	271.4	91.0*[e]
1933	287.8*[a]		...	223.7	64.1*[e]
1934	315.4*[a]		...	278.3	37.1*[e]
1935	342.4*[a]		...	332.2	10.2*[f]
1936	445.4*[a]		...	435.4	10.2*[g]

*Indicates data that are chosen as representing the best available estimates in each category; only these figures are carried forward in the analysis.

[a]Calculated from other figures marked * pertaining to the same year.

[b]The 1928 and 1929 figures are obtained by linear interpolation between the values for 1927 and 1930.

[c]Manchurian deposits of Japanese banks for 1930 are given in The Manchuria Year Book, 1932-33, 413-14 as 125.2 million gold yen and 24.3 million silver yen. The latter are equivalent to the same quantity of silver yuan. The former are converted at the 1930 average rate of 0.92 gold yen per Hai-kuan tael (Annual Returns of the Foreign Trade of Manchoukuo 1932 [Dairen, 1933], 1) and $1.55 per Hai-kuan tael.

continued...

Table C.12, continued

^{d}The 1931 figure is a linear interpolation between the values for
1930 and 1932.

^{e}The figures for 1931-34 are linear interpolations between the
values for 1930 and 1935.

^{f}The 1935 issue of the yearbook published by Japan's Finance
Ministry reports deposits of Japanese banks in the Republic of China
(i.e., excluding Manchuria) amounting to 4.3 million gold yen, 0.7
million silver yen, and 0.9 million Chinese yuan (Ōkurasho nempō,
no. 60 [Tokyo, 1935], 323). Using the 1931 quotation of
approximately 2 yin-p'iao (or 2 Chinese yuan) per gold yen (The
Manchuria Year Book 1932-33, 398), the combined total comes to 10.2
million yuan.

^{g}Assumed identical with the figure for the previous year.

Sources: Col. 1: Ōkurasho nempō, no. 41 (1916), 304; no. 57
(1932), 283; and no. 60 (1935), 323. Small amounts in minor
currencies (other than gold and silver yen) are ignored.

Col. 2: Nihon no tai-Shi tōshi, 63.

Col. 3: Baron Y. Sakatani, Manchuria: A Survey of its Economic
Development (New York, 1980), 43.

Col. 4: Except as noted, Manshū chūō ginkō jūnenshi, appendix,
8-9.

Note: The underlying data for 1918-30 in Cols. 1 and 3 are in
gold and silver yen. All figures are converted to silver using the
annual rates given in Mammō seiji keizai teiyō (Tokyo, 1932), 471-
72. The resulting totals in "chao-p'iao" or silver yen issued by
the Yokohama Specie Bank are, as noted earlier in this appendix,
equivalent to Chinese (silver) dollars or yuan. The figures in Col.
2 are converted from Japanese yen to Chinese yuan (via Hai-kuan
taels) as described in conjunction with Table C.8. The data in Col.
4 are converted from Manchoukuo yen using the rates given in Table
C.7.

and the 1935 total for China proper issued by the Japanese Ministry of
Finance.

Non-Japanese Banks.   I have found two widely differing estimates of deposits held in the Chinese branches of non-Japanese foreign banks. T'an
Yü-tso cites Central Bank of China data showing the following structure
of bank deposits (presumably excluding Manchuria) for January 1937:[36]

Chinese modern banks   69.09%

Foreign banks   6.86

Native banks   21.40

36. T'an Yü-tso, *Chung-kuo chung yao yin hang fa chan shih* (Taipei, 1961), 13.
Note that the categories shown in this source add to only 99.02 percent.

Trust companies	1.67%
Unknown	0.98
Total	100.00

Using the 1936 year-end deposit total of 4,551.3 million yuan for Chinese banks shown in Table C.10, the January 1937 deposit figure for foreign banks in China proper may be derived as approximately 4,551.3 × 6.86/ 69.09 or 451.9 million yuan. Adding 12.4 million Manchoukuo yen, equivalent to 12.2 million Chinese yuan, to cover the reported deposits of European and American banks in Manchuria at the end of 1936 produces an approximate total of 464.2 million yuan worth of deposits held in the Chinese branches of non-Japanese foreign banks at the end of 1936.[37]

The second estimate comes from a Japanese wartime study of non-Japanese foreign investment in China. The authors present data on assets and deposits of twenty-three foreign banks and estimate the shares of assets and deposits located in China (excluding Hong Kong and presumably Manchuria as well), producing a combined deposit total of US$353.4 million at the end of 1936.[38] At the 1936 exchange rate of US$0.297 per yuan, this figure amounts to 1,189.9 million yuan, or more than 2.6 times the result obtained from the Chinese figures cited above.[39]

It is very difficult to choose between these figures. The validity of the higher figure produced by the Tōa kenkyūjo depends on the accuracy of the estimated shares of Chinese activity for various banks, especially the Hong Kong and Shanghai Bank, which accounts for 43 percent of the estimated total of non-Japanese foreign bank deposits in the higher variant. The Japanese study obtains this total by assuming that 60 percent of the Hong Kong Bank's global deposit total was held in China. But an earlier study by Wu Ch'eng-hsi noted that British banks, among which the Hong Kong Bank was by far the largest, "use about one-third of their total capital in China."[40] This raises the possibility that the Japanese researchers overstated the extent of the Hong Kong Bank's Chinese operations. The resolution of the inconsistency between these two estimates of foreign bank deposits must await archival research, particularly into the records of the Hong Kong and Shanghai Bank. To avoid exaggerating the size and growth of China's prewar banking system, I adopt the smaller figure of

37. Manchurian deposit data are from *Manshū chūō ginkō jūnenshi* (Hsinking, 1942), appendix, 8. The exchange rate between Manchoukuo yen and Chinese yuan is from Table C.7.
38. *Shogaikoku no tai-Shi tōshi*, 1:facing p. 2.
39. The exchange rate is from Liang-lin Hsiao, *China's Foreign Trade Statistics, 1864–1949* (Cambridge, 1974), 192.
40. Wu Ch'eng-hsi, *Chung-kuo ti yin hang* (Shanghai, 1934), 103.

Table C.13
Estimated Deposits of Foreign Banks, 1910-36
(million dollars)

| Year | Deposits in the Chinese and Manchurian Branches of | | | |
	Japanese Banks (1)	Other Foreign Banks Index (2)	Total (3)	All Foreign Banks (4)
1910	...	34.7	...	233.9
1911	...	32.4	...	218.4
1912	...	33.6	...	226.5
1913	...	35.6	...	240.0
1914	...	39.3	181.9	265.0
1915	...	39.4	182.0	265.6
1916	...	36.2	167.4	244.1
1917	...	37.5	173.4	252.8
1918	86.0	40.7	188.4	274.4
1919	...	40.3	186.2	301.3
1920	...	53.9	249.0	403.0
1921	...	57.4	265.5	429.1
1922	...	60.0	277.4	448.6
1923	...	60.2	278.2	450.0
1924	...	62.4	288.8	466.5
1925	...	65.8	304.0	491.9
1926	...	73.5	340.0	549.5
1927	190.1	66.6	307.8	497.9
1928	253.9	65.4	302.4	556.3
1929	317.7	78.2	361.4	679.1
1930	381.5	110.4	510.6	892.1
1931	372.0	92.3	426.9	798.9
1932	362.4	111.2	514.1	876.5
1933	287.8	104.3	482.3	770.1
1934	315.4	81.6	377.1	692.5
1935	342.4	92.6	428.4	770.8
1936	445.4	100.0	464.4	909.8

Note: Totals may not check because of rounding error.

Sources: Col. 1: Table C.12.

Col. 2: Index of year-end deposit totals, in Hong Kong dollars, for the Hong Kong and Shanghai Bank, with 1936 = 100. The data are from the same issues and pages of the Statist noted in the discussion following Table C.8.

Col. 3: The estimated year-end deposit totals for non-Japanese foreign banks are derived from the 1936 figure by assuming that the index of deposit growth in all banks was the same as for the Hong Kong and Shanghai Bank between 1914 and 1936.

Col. 4: For 1918 and 1927-36, the annual total is the sum of the components in Cols. 1 and 3. For other years, the annual total is derived from the total for the following year by assuming that the year-on-year change for all foreign bank deposits was identical with the change in the deposit index for the Hong Kong and Shanghai Bank shown in Col. 2.

$464.2 million as an estimate of year-end 1936 deposits in non-Japanese foreign banks.

The Combined Deposits of Foreign Banks in China and Manchuria.
Estimates for the combined deposits of foreign banks in all areas of China are derived in Table C.13. To obtain a time series estimate for total deposits of non-Japanese foreign banks, I use an index of year-end global deposit totals of the Hong Kong and Shanghai Bank, the largest and most influential foreign bank operating in China. The deposits of non-Japanese foreign banks, for which I have only a 1936 figure, are assumed to have grown in step with total deposits held by the Hong Kong and Shanghai Bank. The same assumption is applied to the deposits of all foreign banks for those years in which there is no information on annual deposit changes for Japanese or other foreign banks.

The Deposits of Native Banks

Information on the deposits of native banks or *ch'ien-chuang* is available for Shanghai and may be inferred for other regions by assuming a stable relation between capital and deposits. The data for Shanghai are as follows: [41]

	1932	*1934*
Number of native banks	62	60
Capital (million yuan)	24.4	17.2
Deposits (million yuan)	230.3	156.4
Ratio of deposits to capital	9.1	9.1

Since Tamagna observes that "a relation of 8 or 10 to 1 between deposits and capital of the native banks may probably be taken as a fairly general measure," I apply a deposit-capital ratio of 9:1 to estimates of paid-up native bank capital throughout China to obtain a rough approximation of the national deposit total. [42]

There are several surveys of native banks, all pointing to the conclusion

41. Data for 1932 are from *Shang-hai ch'ien chuang shih liao* (Shanghai, 1960), 270, with conversion from *taels* to yuan at the 1932 average of .70575 yuan per *tael* noted in *Chung-hua-min-kuo t'ung chi t'i yao, 1935* (Shanghai, 1936), 682. Data for 1934 are from Frank M. Tamagna, *Banking and Finance in China* (New York, 1942), 64.
42. Tamagna, *Banking*, 65, citing additional sources. Djang Siao-mei, "Banking, Currency and Credit," in *The Chinese Year Book, 1935–36* (Shanghai, 1935), 1447, applies a ratio of 8:1, as does Yeh-chien Wang, "The Growth and Decline of Native Banks in Shanghai," *Ching-chi lun-wen* 6, no. 1 (1978):131–32.

that their aggregate paid-up capital in the mid-1930s amounted to somewhat under $100 million. Tamagna's figures for 1934 (including 1932 data for Hangchow and 1937 figures for Tsingtao and Tientsin) include 1,185 establishments with a combined capital of $66 million, of which sixty-four Shanghai banks account for $20.5 million or 31.0 percent.[43] These results, however, exclude both the northeast and southwest regions. Djang Siao-mei shows a total of 1,127 banks in China proper (excluding Hong Kong) with total capital of $58.3 million and also notes a further 109 establishments in Manchuria. Djang's data, which refer, at least for Shanghai, to the end of June 1934, are also incomplete. The figures for Shanghai, and probably for other centers as well, cover only "first-class native banks" and exclude several categories of "secondary native banks" of lesser size and importance.[44] The most thorough study appears to be that of F. Y. Chang. Chang's figures cover all regions of China (excluding Hong Kong) and report a 1935 total of 1,296 native banks with aggregate capital of $84.2 million. Chang notes eighty banks in Shanghai, accounting for $25.4 million or 30.2 percent of total capital.[45] On the basis of this result, I conclude that in 1935 the deposits of native banks may have amounted to approximately 9 × $84.2 or $758 million, of which 30 percent, or $227 million, was held in Shanghai.

My estimate of deposit growth in the *ch'ien-chuang* sector, presented in Table C.14, is derived from the reported capitalization of native banks in Shanghai on the assumption that both the ratio between deposits and capital and Shanghai's 30 percent share of both totals did not change between 1914 and 1936. These assumptions produce a rapidly growing total. It is possible that the growth of native banking in Shanghai exceeded the national average because of Shanghai's role as China's financial center and because of the rapid expansion of industry and trade in the Lower Yangtze region of which Shanghai was the hub. At the same time, native banks in Shanghai faced strong rivalry from Chinese- and foreign-owned commercial banks. The resulting competition surely constrained deposit expansion to a greater degree than elsewhere in China.

It is possible that these estimates substantially underestimate the scale of the native banking sector in the 1930s. Data prepared by the Central Bank of China and cited above in connection with the estimation of deposits in the Chinese offices of foreign banks credit native banks with

43. Tamagna, *Banking*, 59–61, 64.
44. Djang, "Banking," 1444–47. The exclusion of secondary institutions is probably common to all the surveys mentioned in the text.
45. F. Y. Chang, "Banking and Currency," in *The Chinese Year Book, 1936–37* (Shanghai, 1936), 795–796.

Table C.14
Annual Deposits of Native Banks, 1912-36
(million yuan)

Year	Index of Paid-up Capital in Shanghai Native Banks (1935 = 100) (1)	National Deposits of Native Banks (million yuan) (2)
1912	8.3	62.9
1913	9.4	71.2
1914	10.6	80.3
1915	11.1	84.1
1916	14.6	110.7
1917	14.6	110.7
1918	22.6	171.3
1919	27.3	208.9
1920	40.1	304.0
1921	43.5	329.7
1922	55.7	422.2
1923	74.8	567.0
1924	85.8	650.4
1925	86.0	651.9
1926	96.8	733.7
1927	98.0	742.8
1928	92.8	703.4
1929	95.6	724.6
1930	100.0	758.0
1931	104.4	791.4
1932	110.3	836.0
1933	112.5	852.8
1934	106.8	809.5
1935	100.0	758.0
1936	92.9	704.2

Note: Totals may not check because of rounding error.

Sources: Col. 1: Calculated from Shang-hai ch'ien chuang shih liao, 191, 262, using data presented in terms of ".715 silver yuan."

Col. 2: For 1935, see the text. The figures for other years are derived from the 1935 total using the index in Col. 1.

21.40 percent of a 1937 deposit total within which the share of Chinese modern banks was 69.09 percent. If this proportion is applied to the year-end total of Chinese bank deposits for 1936 shown in Table C.10, native bank deposits at the end of 1936 may be calculated as 4,551.3 × 21.40/ 69.09 or 1,409.7 million yuan, or double the figure shown in Table C.14. I reject this alternative because it implies a deposit-capital ratio well outside the range described by well-informed contemporary accounts.

Appendix C

The Deposits of All Banks

It is now possible to derive the annual year-end estimates of the deposits in all banks, including domestic banks located in China proper and Manchuria, foreign banks, and *ch'ien-chuang*. The results appear in Table C.15.

Table C.15
Combined Yearend Deposits of All Banks in China, 1910-1936
(Million yuan)

Year	Domestic Modern Banks	Foreign Banks	Native Banks	Combined Total
1910	...	233.9	...	812.1[a]
1911	...	218.4	...	758.3[a]
1912	497.0	226.5	62.9	786.4
1913	476.9	240.0	71.2	788.1
1914	456.8	265.0	80.3	802.1
1915	436.8	265.6	84.1	786.5
1916	416.7	244.1	110.7	771.5
1917	396.6	252.8	110.7	760.1
1918	429.2	274.4	171.3	874.9
1919	538.1	301.3	206.9	1046.3
1920	536.2	403.0	304.0	1243.2
1921	534.4	429.1	329.7	1293.2
1922	564.6	448.6	422.2	1435.4
1923	592.9	450.0	567.0	1609.9
1924	672.8	466.5	650.4	1789.7
1925	842.2	491.9	651.9	1986.0
1926	1005.4	549.5	733.7	2288.6
1927	1049.6	497.9	742.8	2290.3
1928	1208.1	556.3	703.4	2467.8
1929	1419.6	679.1	724.6	2823.3
1930	1742.2	892.1	758.0	3392.3
1931	2000.8	798.9	791.4	3591.1
1932	2168.0[b]	876.5	836.0	3880.5
1933	2668.0[b]	770.1	852.8	4290.9
1934	3118.0[b]	692.5	809.5	4620.0
1935	3931.3[b]	770.8	758.0	5460.1
1936	4782.4[b]	909.8	704.2	6396.4

[a]The figures are derived from data for the following year by assuming the same percentage change recorded for deposits in foreign banks.

[b]The sum of deposits for Chinese modern banks (Table C.10) and domestic banks in Manchuria (Table C.11). The latter quantity is assumed to be subsumed in the former category in all prior years.

Source: Tables C.10, C.11, C.13, and C.14.

Estimates of China's Money Supply, 1910–36

With these preliminaries, I am finally in a position to derive the annual year-end estimates of the Chinese money supply for the years 1910–36. Separate results corresponding to broad (M2) and narrow (M1) money supply concepts appear in Tables C.16 and C.17. Each series includes silver coins, "shoes" (sycee) and bullion, copper coins, the note issue of Chinese and foreign banks, and the deposits held by Chinese and foreign commercial banks and by native banks (*ch'ien-chuang*). Two variants of each series are compiled, corresponding to the alternative estimates of China's monetary silver stock (Versions A and B) distinguished in Table C.1.

My calculation of the money stock totals includes two adjustments intended to exclude bank reserves and interbank deposits from the monetary aggregates. Chinese banks held a 60 percent reserve against note issue in the form of silver, foreign exchange, and government securities. Lacking information on the composition of these reserves, I assume that they consisted entirely of silver. Under this assumption, the silver component of the money supply is obtained by subtracting an amount equal to 60 percent of the estimated total of banknotes in circulation (Table C.9) from the estimated annual stocks of monetary silver (Table C.1). To the extent that the share of silver in these reserves stood below 100 percent and/or declined over time, this assumption may lead to an understatement of the size and/or rate of growth of the prewar money stock.[46] To adjust for interbank deposits, which are customarily excluded from monetary aggregates, I include only 96 percent of the estimated deposits in modern Chinese and foreign banks and 70 percent of the estimated native bank deposits in the monetary aggregates derived in Tables C.16 and C.17.[47]

The time series estimates for M2, a broadly defined monetary aggregate including currency (coin and notes) in circulation as well as current

46. Loren Brandt and Thomas J. Sargent, "Interpreting New Evidence About China and U.S. Silver Purchases" (Stanford, 1987), 12, report that, for two of the largest Chinese banks, the ratio of silver stocks to note issue dropped from 50 to 21 percent between 1932 and 1935. This suggests that the present estimates may understate both the level and growth rate of China's money supply during the early 1930s.
47. The estimated share of interbank holdings in deposit totals for modern banks (including foreign banks) is based on 1936 data reported in Brandt and Sargent, "Interpreting New Evidence About China and U.S. Silver Purchases," table 2. For native banks, extensive data from Tientsin for 1940 indicate that as much as 30 percent of overall deposits consisted of interbank holdings (*Tenshin no gingō* [Dairen, 1942], part 2, table 4). In both cases, I apply these figures to the entire period 1910–36.

Appendix C

Table C.16
Estimates of China's Money Supply, Broad Definition, 1910-36
(year-end totals, million yuan)

Year	Silver Version (1)		Copper (2)	Bank Notes (3)	Bank Deposits (4)	M2 Money Supply Version (5)	
	A	B				A	B
1910	880	1905	413.7	114.3	762.7	2102.2	3127.2
1911	940	1965	407.4	142.9	712.2	2116.7	3141.7
1912	970	1995	401.1	157.1	738.6	2172.5	3197.5
1913	1000	2025	394.8	163.2	738.1	2198.1	3223.1
1914	1056	2081	388.5	118.5	749.1	2240.8	3265.8
1915	1035	2060	382.2	209.7	733.2	2234.0	3259.0
1916	1006	2031	375.9	232.6	711.9	2186.8	3211.8
1917	961	1986	369.6	285.8	700.9	2146.2	3171.2
1918	998	2023	363.3	282.4	795.4	2269.6	3294.6
1919	1081	2106	357.0	251.2	950.7	2489.1	3514.1
1920	1225	2250	350.7	282.2	1114.4	2802.6	3827.6
1921	1276	2301	344.4	374.2	1155.8	2923.6	3948.6
1922	1338	2363	338.1	380.7	1268.2	3091.5	4116.5
1923	1443	2468	331.8	406.5	1398.1	3327.5	4352.5
1924	1484	2509	325.5	431.6	1549.0	3522.6	4547.6
1925	1581	2606	319.2	547.5	1737.1	3844.8	4869.8
1926	1664	2689	312.9	599.1	2006.3	4211.5	5236.5
1927	1765	2790	306.6	672.5	2005.6	4331.8	5356.8
1928	1931	2956	300.3	784.6	2186.2	4712.1	5737.1
1929	2096	3121	294.0	913.4	2522.0	5253.6	6278.6
1930	2200	3225	287.7	956.3	3059.5	5915.9	6940.9
1931	2271	3296	281.4	896.9	3241.7	6139.8	7164.8
1932	2289	3314	275.1	924.4	3507.9	6427.4	7452.4
1933	2275	3300	268.8	978.8	3897.5	6816.4	7841.4
1934	1995	3020	262.5	1108.9	4224.7	6925.8	7950.8
1935	1703	2728	256.2	1413.5	5044.6	7569.2	8594.2
1936	1391	2416	250.0	2438.6	5957.5	8573.8	9598.8

Sources: Col. 1: Monetary silver stock (Table C.1), less 60 percent of note issue (Table C.9).

Col. 2: Text of this appendix.   Col. 3: Table C.9.

Col. 4: The deposit total is from Table C.15, net of interbank deposits estimated at 4 percent of deposit total for modern banks (Chinese and foreign) and 30 percent of deposit total for native banks. The figures for 1910 and 1911 are derived from the data for the following year by assuming the same annual percentage change reported for foreign banks in Table C.15.

Col. 5: The sum of the components.

Table C.17
Estimates of China's Money Supply, Narrow Definition, 1910-36
(year-end totals, million yuan)

Year	Share of Current Deposits	M1 Money Supply Version	
		A	B
1910	0.7	1873.3	2898.3
1911	0.7	1903.1	2928.1
1912	0.7	1951.0	2976.0
1913	0.7	1976.7	3001.7
1914	0.7	2016.1	3041.1
1915	0.7	2014.0	3039.0
1916	0.7	1973.2	2998.2
1917	0.7	1935.9	2960.9
1918	0.7	2031.0	3056.0
1919	0.7	2203.9	3228.9
1920	0.7	2468.3	3493.3
1921	0.6951	2571.2	3596.2
1922	0.7253	2743.1	3768.1
1923	0.7036	2913.1	3938.1
1924	0.7207	3090.0	4115.0
1925	0.7236	3364.7	4389.7
1926	0.7035	3616.6	4641.6
1927	0.7173	3764.8	4789.8
1928	0.7195	4098.9	5123.9
1929	0.7252	4560.5	5585.5
1930	0.7339	5101.8	6126.8
1931	0.6521	5012.0	6037.0
1932	0.5932	5000.4	6025.4
1933	0.67	5530.2	6555.2
1934	0.67	5531.6	6556.6
1935	0.67	5904.5	6929.5
1936	0.67	6607.8	7632.8

Sources and Notes: The share of current deposits in the deposit
total is based on data for Chinese modern banks; it is assumed that
the share of current deposits is the same for interbank deposits as
for other deposits and that the share for Chinese modern banks is
valid for foreign and native banks as well. The data for 1912-20
are assumed; for 1921-32, from Wu Ch'eng-hsi, Chung-kuo ti yin hang
(Shanghai, 1934), 32; for 1934-36, based on Ch'üan kuo yin hang

continued...

and savings deposits, appear in Table C.16. Versions A and B are based
on alternative estimates of China's monetary silver stock. In Table C.17,
I use incomplete information on the composition of deposits in modern
Chinese banks to derive a rough division of bank deposits into current
accounts and time or savings accounts. With these results, it is possible

Table C.17, continued

<u>nien chien 1937</u>, 48. The estimated current deposits for 1910 and
1911 are each derived from the data for the following year by
assuming the same annual percentage change reported for foreign bank
deposits in Table C.15.

The narrowly defined money supply (M1, Version A or B) is
calculated as the sum of monetary silver (Version A or B) after
deducting 60 percent of total note issue, copper coinage, note
issue, and estimated current deposits (net of interbank deposits).
The latter figure is the product of deposit totals from Table C.16
(from which interbank holdings have been removed) and the current
deposit ratio given in Col. 1.

to construct time series estimates corresponding to a narrow definition of
money supply (M1) consisting of currency in circulation and current or
demand deposits (but not time or savings deposits). The results, compiled
in Table C.17, incorporate rather crude adjustments and should therefore
be considered as more tentative and less reliable than the M2 series presented in Table C.16.

Limitations of the Estimates

The results presented in Tables C.16 and C.17 incorporate a variety of
inevitably arbitrary procedures and often rely on weak sources, especially
for the early years and in relation to the activities of foreign banks in
China. I therefore can make no claim to precision. What is asserted, however, is that these data provide reasonable approximations of the size,
composition, and growth rate of China's money stock during the period
under review.

In addition to the general problems raised by the need to introduce
unverified assumptions to bridge data gaps and the shortcomings of certain sources, three monetary categories are entirely omitted from my calculations. These are the banknotes issued by the *ch'ien-chuang*, the
deposits of credit cooperatives, trust companies, and other institutions,
which might be described as "near-banks," and regional currencies, often
issued by provincial and local military governments, which flooded local
money markets in times of military emergency. The following brief observations suggest that none of these omissions is sufficiently large to
threaten the broad validity of my results.

Native banks issued notes directly and indirectly through the agency
of modern commercial banks. The notes issued indirectly are included in
Table C.2. I have, however, found no estimates of the direct note issue of

Table C.18
Bank, Cooperative and Postal Savings Deposits in Manchuria, 1932-36
(million Manchoukuo yen)

Year	Bank Deposits	Cooperative Deposits	Postal Savings	Total Deposits	Share of Bank Deposits
1932	432.5	2.3	29.8	464.7	93.0%
1933	390.3	2.8	32.9	426.0	91.6
1934	482.9	5.0	38.9	526.9	91.6
1935	580.9	9.6	46.8	637.3	91.2
1936	692.4	14.3	56.8	763.6	90.7

Source: <u>Manshû chûô ginkô jûnenshi</u>, appendix, 8-9.

the *ch'ien-chuang*. Tamagna makes the following comments about these notes:[48]

Notes [issued by native banks] in their own name consisted of local yuan bills, subsidiary currency and copper notes; these circulated only locally. . . . The most important . . . case of yuan bill issue by native banks was in Foochow . . . [where] the average amount in circulation was estimated at about 4 million local yuan [in 1932]. Subsidiary currency and copper notes were issued by native banks in various cities of Shantung . . . Kiangsi . . . Kiangsu . . . Kwangtung . . . Kwangsi, Shansi, Shensi, Chahar and Hopei. . . . Owing to their low face value, these notes circulated mostly among the poorest classes of the population.

These observations suggest that native banknotes served mainly to supplement or replace traditional copper currency in small retail transactions. If the "most important" instance of note issue by native banks involved no more than 4 million yuan, the impact of native banknotes on the size of the money stock (M2), which surpassed 10 billion yuan in 1936, or its composition and growth can only have been small.

The role of near-banks also appears minute in terms of national aggregates. Figures prepared by the Bank of China for January 1937 show that trust companies held only 1.67 percent of total deposits in China proper.[49] Table C.18 contains Manchurian data showing that bank deposits dominated regional deposit totals for the years 1932–36. On the basis of these figures, it seems safe to conclude that the omission of near-banks does not significantly affect my conclusions about the size, structure, and growth of China's prewar money stock.

48. Tamagna, *Banking*, 68–69.
49. T'an, *Chung-kuo chung yao yin hang*, 13.

A final omission concerns the note issue of regional military governments. There were numerous local currencies in Republican China, many
of which are omitted from the totals developed in Tables C.2 and C.3.
The question here is whether sudden increases in local note issue, which
often accompanied regional military conflicts, were sufficiently large to
affect the national currency picture. My approach is to consider the case
of the "Fengtien dollar," or *feng-p'iao*, issued in Manchuria between 1905
(or perhaps earlier) and the Japanese takeover in 1932. This case is significant because the *feng-p'iao* was among the most important regional currencies and also represents an instance of a massive overissue in response
to military emergency.[50]

The issue of *feng-p'iao* was centralized from 1924 in the provincially
controlled Official Bank of the Three Eastern Provinces. Soon thereafter,
Chang Tso-lin, the military ruler of Manchuria, became involved in large-
scale fighting in China proper. As Chang's spending plans rose, he began
to interfere in bank operations, forcing the bank to accelerate the growth
of note issue.[51] The result was a precipitous increase in the nominal value
of *feng-p'iao* in circulation together with an equally steep decline in the
market price of *feng-p'iao* notes. These developments are summarized in
Table C.19, which shows the size of the note issue and the exchange value
of *feng-p'iao* at six-month intervals from the beginning of 1925 to June
1929, when official action stabilized the *feng-p'iao* at a new rate of 60 per
yuan of *hsien ta-yang* or silver-backed currency.

The figures in Table C.19 offer convincing evidence that, even in what
may be the most significant instance, currency manipulation by military
governments failed to bring about large increases in the money supply.
Money markets, which Suleski scarcely mentions, reacted so quickly to
increases in the issue of *feng-p'iao* that the value in terms of standard
currency units of the total amount in circulation sometimes declined as
the nominal amount of note issue increased. Between January 1925 and
the peak of March 1928, the nominal amount of *feng-p'iao* in circulation
rose by a factor of nineteen, but market forces eroded the exchange value
of the Fengtien notes so quickly that the silver value of the total note
issue in March 1929 was less than 3 percent higher than at the beginning
of 1925.

This result suggests that a failure to account for the vagaries of depre-

---

50. For a summary, see Ronald Suleski, "The Rise and Fall of the Fengtien Dollar, 1917–1928: Currency Reform in Warlord China," *Modern Asian Studies*
13, no. 4 (1979) and the sources cited therein. "Fengtien" refers both to the
province of that name (now Liaoning) and the city also known as Mukden and
Shenyang.
51. Suleski, "Fengtien Dollar," 656–59.

Table C.19
Quantity and Value of Feng-p'iao in Circulation, 1925-1929

Date	Quantity in Circulation (million yuan) (1)	Feng-p'iao per Silver yuan (2)	Silver Value of Notes in Circulation (million yuan) (3)
January 1925	120	1.98	60.6
June 1925	100	2.20	45.4
December 1925	200	2.78	71.9
June 1926	200	4.66	42.9
December 1926	300	4.60	65.2
June 1927	400	10.66	37.5
December 1927	470	12.42	37.8
June 1928	610	25.00	24.4
December 1928	1260	28.60	44.0
March 1929	2270	36.40	62.3
June 1929	1580	62.70	25.2

Sources: Col. (1): The data are read from the graph shown in The Manchuria Year Book, 1932-33, 396.

Col. 2: Each figure shown is the arithmetic average of monthly high and low quotations of the number of feng-p'iao required to purchase one yuan of hsien ta-yang currency (equivalent to a standard Chinese yuan) from Manshû tsûka tôkei B: Kahei sôba hen (Dairen, 1932), 1.

Col. 3: In each row, the figure in Col. 3 is the quotient of the entries in Cols 1 and 2.

ciating local currencies is unlikely to affect the broad accuracy of the results outlined in Tables C.16. and C.17. The history of the *feng-p'iao* also shows why militarists hesitated to engage in currency manipulation and why those who did so quickly tumbled from positions of power. Historians have discovered instances in which soldiers forced merchants to accept debased currency at inflated values. But currency debasement quickly affected regional money markets. The figures in Table C.19 show that the exchanges often anticipated further debasement so that the silver value of the total note issue plummeted even as its nominal value increased. When this happened, the military governors and soldiers who held the largest quantities of debased notes were the biggest losers.

On the basis of these considerations, it appears reasonable to expect that a rectification of the omission of native banknotes, the deposits held by near-banks, and regional and local currency issues would not result in major changes in my findings about the size, composition, and growth of China's prewar money supply. Anticipating the conclusion that the growth of money supply was rapid and substantial, I have repeatedly avoided assumptions that might build an upward bias into the growth of the money stock estimates. For this reason, the present estimates are unlikely to overstate either the size of the money stock in the closing years of the period studied or the rate of growth of China's money supply between 1910 and 1936.

Appendix D

The Volume of Cargo Traffic in Prewar China

This appendix provides details of my estimates for the volume of cargo traffic carried by steam or motor vessel, junk, and traditional land carriers. The results are shown in Table 4.10.

Carriage by Steam or Motor Vessel

The figures for freight carriage by steam or motor vessel are based on Maritime Customs statistics for clearance of shipping in China's interport trade. These figures are given in registry tonnage. I estimate cargo weight at 70 percent of recorded tonnage on the basis of information from the port of Dairen for 1932–35, when the actual cargo weight of merchandise imports and exports amounted to 69.4 percent of registered tonnage of ships entered and cleared from the port.[1] In the absence of comparable figures for other years and ports, I cannot investigate possible changes across time and space in the ratio of cargo hauled to recorded tonnage entered and cleared.

The only available estimate of average length of haul for prewar steamship traffic is a figure of 1,015 kilometers implied by post-1949 estimates of the pre-1949 peak figure for tonnage carried and freight turnover produced by modern (that is, mechanized) ships and barges. This figure is far larger than comparable figures for the 1950s. Since other estimates for prewar transport magnitudes given in the same source are clearly erro-

1. *Manshūkoku gensei, 1937* (Hsinkyō, 1937), 363.

neous, I reject the 1,015 kilometer average.[2] Postwar estimates of the
average length of haul for mechanized shipping are as follows:[3]

1949	794 kilometers
1950	436 (?)
1951	713
1952	741
1953	675
1954	648
1955	685
1956	601
1957	640

With little reason to anticipate major differences in shipping patterns between the mid-1930s and the early post-1949 years, I assume an average
length of haul of 700 kilometers for the prewar period. Freight turnover
for various years between 1895 and 1936 is thus estimated from the
formula:

$$\text{Freight turnover} = \text{Tonnage cleared} \times 0.7 \times 700 \text{ km.}$$

where tonnage cleared is the Maritime Customs figure for shipping
cleared in interport trade, with modifications for 1933 and 1936 as described in Table D.1.

This procedure makes no allowance for the omission from the Maritime
Customs reports of steamship traffic between non-treaty ports, possibly
incomplete reportage of steamship traffic in the treaty ports, and changes
in the average length of haul and the degree of capacity utilization that no
doubt occurred during the period 1895–1936.

Carriage by Sailing Craft

My estimate of the freight turnover by sailing craft (junks) is derived from
a separate consideration of the following: the number of junks, the average annual distance traversed by junks, and the average size and payload
of junks. I use materials bearing on these subjects to construct an estimate

2. See *Ten Great Years: Statistics of the Economic and Cultural Achievements of
   the People's Republic of China* (Bellingham, 1974), 106–7. This source gives a
   prewar peak level of 40.4 billion ton-kilometers for railway freight turnover,
   impossibly larger than Huenemann's 1936 total of 14.6 billion ton-kilometers
   shown in Table 4.7, and an improbably low figure of 12.8 billion ton-kilometers
   for the prewar peak freight turnover by motorized shipping.
3. Calculated from *Ten Great Years*, 107. The 1950 figure for freight turnover
   appears to be a misprint in both the original and the translation.

Table D.1
Estimated Domestic Traffic and Freight Turnover for Steamships, 1895-1936

Year	Shipping Cleared For Domestic Trade (thousand tons) (1)	Freight Turnover (billion ton-km) (2)
1895	10669	5.2
1907	28033	13.7
1915	33195	16.3
1919	35372	17.3
1924	47992	23.5
1933	52912[a]	25.9
1936	54395[a]	26.6

[a]Excludes interport steamship traffic within Manchuria.

Sources: Col. 1: For 1895-1924, the figures shown are Maritime Customs figures for domestic interport shipping cleared at treaty ports as reported in Liang-lin Hsiao, China's Foreign Trade Statistics, 1864-1949 (Cambridge, 1974), 250-51. The figures for 1933 and 1936 are the sum of Hsiao's totals, which exclude traffic to and from Manchuria, and the Manchurian figures for shipping entered and cleared to or from Chinese ports. The latter data are from Annual Returns of the Foreign Trade of Manchoukuo, 1933 (Dairen, 1934), 7 and Annual Returns of the Foreign Trade of Manchoukuo, 1936 (Dairen, 1937), 1:8-9. For 1933, I assume that the share of shipping movements to and from Chinese ports is the same as in 1936.

Col. 2: Derived from Col. 1 as specified in the text of this Appendix.

of freight turnover by junks in 1936. The figures for prior years are based on an assumed 2 percent annual growth rate for junk traffic during the period 1895–1936.

The Number of Junks During the 1930s

Separate estimates by Wu Pao-san and Japanese occupation authorities place the number of junks in prewar China in the neighborhood of one million (Table D.2). I adopt Wu's results as an approximate but nonetheless carefully compiled estimate of the numbers of sailing vessels as of 1936.

Table D.2
Number of Junks in Pre-War China

Province	Wu Pao-san Estimate	Other Figures
Kiangsu	120,000	
Chekiang	100,000	300,000+[a]
Anhwei	50,000	
Kiangsi	40,000	
Hupei	100,000	
Hunan	150,000	
Szechwan	100,000	
Fukien	30,000	
Kwangtung	100,000	
Kwangsi	20,000	
Kweichow	8,000	
Yunnan	4,000	
Hopei	50,000	
Shantung	40,000	15,584[b]
Shansi	3,000	
Honan	30,000	
Shensi	10,000	
Northeast	30,000	
Northwest	3,000	
Total	988,000	over 1 million[c]

Source: Except as noted, Wu Pao-san, Chung-kuo kuo min so te, 1933 nien (Shanghai, 1947), 2:181.

[a]Chûshi no minsengyô (Tokyo, 1943), 36.

[b]Chang Hung-lieh, "Shantung Transport in the Past Year," Chiao t'ung tsa chih 3, no. 3-4 (1935):97, reporting results of a survey. Wu, Chung-kuo kuo min so te, 1933 nien, 2:180, notes the reported registration of 20,000 vessels for Shantung, but increases the total to 40,000 on account of the province's well-developed coastal as well as riverine trade.

[c]Shina no kôun (Tokyo, 1944), 52.

The Average Annual Distance Traveled by Junks

Peter Schran has compiled a number of reports showing daily distances covered by sailboats in various regions [(D) and (U) indicate downstream and upstream]:[4]

Szechwan	(D)	103–261 kilometers
	(U)	5–26
Yunnan	(D)	103
	(U)	35–43
Kwangsi	(D)	58–145
	(U)	22–58
Kiangsu		39–43

In estimating the volume of long-distance transport of farm products in 1893, Schran assumes daily travel of 45 kilometers.[5] Ernest Liang cites a figure showing daily travel of 48–96 kilometers.[6] A survey of China's northeastern region conducted during the 1920s reported that junks traveled an average of 20 miles or 32.2 kilometers each day.[7] The most detailed information comes from the Japanese survey conducted at Soochow in the spring of 1941, which included a thorough inquiry into the routes and frequency of travel of forty junks. In twenty-four instances, it is possible to calculate the annual travel distance implied by the survey results.[8] For these twenty-four cases, monthly travel ranged from a low of 192 to a high of 2,000 kilometers, with the average monthly distance traversed amounting to 578.5 kilometers or slightly under 20 kilometers daily.

4. Peter Schran, "A Much Neglected Source on Inland Communications in Late Ch'ing China" (Urbana, 1978), table 1.G.
5. Peter Schran, "Traditional Transportation and Railroad Development in China Since Late Ch'ing Times" (Urbana, 1984), table 2.
6. Ernest P. Liang, *China: Railways and Agricultural Development, 1875–1935* (Chicago, 1982), 20.
7. *North Manchuria and the Chinese Eastern Railway* (Harbin, 1924), 385–86.
8. The calculations are based on table 12 of the supplement to *Chūshi no minsengyō: Soshū minsen jittai chōsa hōkoku* (Tokyo, 1943). Omissions include cases 3, 8, 11, 12, 25, 26, 29, 31, 35, 39, and 40 (insufficient information to calculate monthly or annual distance traveled) and cases 9, 10, and 19 (unsatisfactory data, e.g., vessel no. 10 reportedly made 15 trips of 4–5 days duration each month). In calculating distances, midpoints were used when the number of journeys or the length of each trip is reported in interval form: e.g., a report of 2–3 monthly trips is recorded as 2.5 trips. Distances between ports are from p. 284 of *Chūshi no minsengyō*, from table 12 of the supplementary volume, and, for Shanghai-Nanking, from *Shina kaikōjōshi* (Tokyo, 1922–24), 2:871.

It is not easy to select an average from these figures, which show considerable variation. The Soochow data, which do not include junks participating in long-distance trade and were collected during a period of very low junk activity, probably understate average distances covered. If large junks moving upstream on the Yangtze between I-ch'ang and Chungking—a notoriously difficult passage—could cover as much as 26 kilometers per day (the Szechwan instance cited above refers to this route), it seems unreasonable to assume that the average vessel logged no more than 20 kilometers daily. The figures provided by Schran and Liang, however, may not take account of delays for loading and unloading, the existence of slack periods, and the need to tow junks upstream if prevailing winds were not favorable. Faced with this variety of alternatives, I assume that the average junk used year-round in regions with relatively favorable geographic and climatic conditions covered an average annual distance of 10,000 kilometers, which amounts to a daily average of 33.3 kilometers for vessels operated 300 days each year.

The Soochow survey included two vessels operated on a part-time basis. Vessel no. 23, reportedly "used only in the agricultural slack season," traveled 204 kilometers annually; vessel no. 38, used only in February and March, covered an annual distance of 838.4 kilometers. The average of these two figures, 521 kilometers or 7.5 percent of the distance traversed by vessels in full-time use that were included in the Soochow survey, is taken as an estimate of the annual distance logged by junks used on a part-time basis in the Lower Yangtze region and other areas with favorable conditions for junk traffic.

If junks in the Lower Yangtze region and other favorably endowed areas could travel 10,000 kilometers each year, vessels in regions where travel was hampered by winter weather, seasonal contraction of water flow, or swift currents and rapids undoubtedly covered smaller distances. In estimating the annual revenue earned by junks, Wu Pao-san assumes that junks operating in the northeast, where rivers freeze in winter, could earn only three-fifths as much as those in the Lower Yangtze region.[9] I assume that the same limitation applies to distance traveled so that the annual distance amounts to only $0.6 \times 10,000 = 6,000$ kilometers in the northeast and also in the following areas: Hupei, Szechwan, Hopei, Shansi, Honan, Shensi, and the northwest. I thus assume that 326,000 of Wu's estimated national total of 988,000 junks (Table D.2) are subject to this restriction.

9. Wu Pao-san, *Chung-kuo kuo min so te, 1933 nien* (Shanghai, 1947), 2:181.

Table D.3
Capacity of Junks in Prewar China

Region	Vessels	Tonnage	
		Total	Per Vessel
North China	20,760	199,705	9.6
Central China	15,167	197,389	13.0
Lower Yangtze	100,045	761,104	7.6
Kwangtung	7,862	75,061	9.5
Foochow-Amoy	15,500[a]	708,000[a]	45.7
Under Chungking government control	15,000	250,000	34.7
Shantung	15,584	260,253	16.7
Total	189,918	2,381,512	12.5

[a]Indicates mid-point of range given in the source.

Sources: The Shantung data are from Chang, "Shantung Transport," 97. Other figures are from Shina no kōun, 51-52.

The Size and Payload of Junks

Chinese junks take a variety of shapes and sizes ranging from small, flat-bottomed craft used in shallow creeks to large craft of 60–70 tons.[10] The largest body of data on average junk size comes from the efforts of the Japanese occupation authorities to register junks in regional organizations intended to control trade in various parts of occupied China during the late 1930s and early 1940s. Membership figures for these organizations provide most of the available information on junk size (see Table D.3). On the basis of these figures, I take 12.5 tons as the average capacity of Chinese junks in 1936.

The Japanese survey of 1941 notes that the normal carrying capacity of junks is approximately eight-tenths of the reported capacity.[11] The au-

10. Chūshi no minsengyō, 5, notes the construction of sixty-ton coal junks at Wusih during the 1940s; Schran, "A Much Neglected Source," notes the use of seventy-ton junks on the upper Yangtze in Szechwan (table 1.G).
11. Chūshi no minsengyō, 268.

thors also estimate total loadings by assuming that junks typically carry 90 percent of their normal capacity on each outward voyage and 50 percent of normal capacity on each return voyage (presumably reflecting the absence of prior information about demand for shipping services at the turn-around point). Under these assumptions, the average payload carried by a junk of capacity T tons becomes $0.5(0.9 + 0.5) \times 0.8T$ or 56 percent of the reported capacity. The average junk capacity of 12.5 tons implies an average payload of 56 percent of this amount or 7.0 tons.

A Time Series Estimate
of Freight Turnover by Junks

I can now estimate the volume of freight turnover by junks in the mid-1930s and, with an assumed growth rate of freight traffic, for earlier years as well. The estimation of freight turnover for 1936 is carried out in Table D.4. It is based on the foregoing discussion of the numbers of junks, the distances traveled, the average capacity, and the average payload. I assume that one-tenth of all vessels were used on a part-time basis and,

Table D.4
Estimate of Annual Freight Turnover by Junks, 1936

	Number of Vessels (thousands)	Annual Distance (kilometers)	Annual Freight Turnover	
			Million kilometers	Billion Ton-kilometers
Full distance				
Full Time	596	10000	5960	41.7
Part Time	66	750	50	0.3
Restricted distance				
Full Time	290	6000	1740	12.2
Part Time	36	450	16	0.1
Total	988	- -	7766	54.3

Source: The text of this appendix. The total number of junks (Table D.1) is separated into categories traveling a full annual distance and a restricted distance of three-fifths the full amount. Within each category, 10 percent of the vessels are assumed to be engaged in part-time traffic covering 7.5 percent of the distance associated with full-time operation in that category. The average vessel is assumed to carry a load of 7.0 tons.

following the Soochow study described above, that vessels in part-time use covered 7.5 percent of the distance traversed by junks in year-round use. The load factor of 7.0 tons per vessel is applied to all categories of sailing craft. This procedure yields an estimated 1936 turnover of 54.3 billion ton-kilometers for junk shipping.

The survey in Chapter 4 leaves little doubt that junk traffic increased during the prewar decades. The same materials, however, reveal a considerable dispersion of growth rates for various segments of the junk trade, making it difficult to select a reasonable estimate of the overall growth for the period 1895–1936. Despite occasional instances of negative growth, major segments of the junk trade (Tables 4.5 and 4.6) display long-term real growth rates clustering in the range of 1.5 to 7 percent per year, with traffic in some areas growing as rapidly as 10 percent or more. Faced with this complex mix of results, I assume long-term growth at an annual rate of 2 percent.

Unmechanized Land Carriage

There is little detailed information on unmechanized land carriage, but available data suffice to demonstrate the relatively small scale of overland traffic, which was severely restricted by its high cost. A review of anecdotal information about the capacity of various forms of overland carriage indicates its limited dimensions.

Human porters could carry 160 pound loads of cotton fifteen miles per day; at this rate, even assuming 300 annual workdays, the entire prewar labor force in old-fashioned transportation would only produce 6 billion ton-kilometers of haulage.[12] But with most of the estimated eleven million traditional transport workers working as boatmen, stevedores, or carters, porterage could hardly have amounted to more than a small fraction of this figure, in all likelihood well below one billion ton-kilometers.[13]

Unorganized local transport was also small. An output of one billion ton-kilometers would require each of 100 million rural households to haul two tons of produce to markets 5 kilometers away. But with the typical

12. Albert Feuerwerker, *Economic Trends in the Republic of China, 1912–1949* (Ann Arbor, 1977), 68. Ta-chung Liu and Kung-chia Yeh, *The Economy of the Chinese Mainland: National Income and Economic Development, 1933–1959* (Princeton, 1965), 596, give 1933 employment in traditional transport as 10.86 million persons.

13. The two Japanese-controlled junk associations established in the Lower Yangtze provinces in the late 1940s reported an average of 4.2 members for each registered junk at the end of 1941. On a national basis, this would imply a work force of approximately 4 million in sailboat transport alone. See *Chūshi no minsengyō*, 137, 145.

village community situated so that the least advantaged villager traveled only 4.5 kilometers to the nearest standard market and given the small scale of marketing activity by most farmers, it would appear that casual transport could not approach an annual volume of one billion ton-kilometers of freight turnover.[14]

Pack animals contributed only modestly to prewar freight traffic. Camels could carry up to 1,000 pounds as far as twenty miles per day, but at 300 annual workdays, China's entire camel population would contribute no more than 1.2 billion ton-kilometers per year.[15]

Carts probably contributed the largest volume of unmechanized land carriage. Large carts pulled by seven horses, used seasonally as freight vehicles in the north and northeast, could haul 2.5 tons up to thirty-five miles per day; assuming 100 annual workdays, China's entire horse population could account for no more than 1.3 billion annual ton-kilometers of freight haulage.[16] Small carts were also in wide use in the northern provinces; donkeys, mules, and oxen as well as horses were used for cartage. But with many of these animals in demand for farm work and with poor roads restricting cart traffic to the dry season, cartage probably contributed no more than one or perhaps two billion tons of freight turnover each year.

Despite the absence of detailed information, it is clear that under any realistic assumptions, the combined efforts of animal-drawn carts, porters, unorganized human carriage, and pack animals amounted to only a small fraction of the freight transported by sailing craft. On the basis of the limited data at hand, one may guess that unmechanized land carriage amounted to approximately 4 billion ton-kilometers during the mid-1930s. In view of the substantial commercialization of agriculture visible during the preceding decades and the role of unmechanized land carriers along ancillary routes serving expanding traffic streams hauled by other modes of transport, it appears likely that land carriage increased modestly during the prewar era. Lacking detailed information, I take 4 billion ton-kilometers as an estimate of land carriage in 1936 and assume a 1 percent annual growth rate between 1895 and 1936.

14. On farm to market distances, see G. William Skinner, "Marketing and Social Structure in Rural China," part 1, *Journal of Asian Studies* 24, no. 1 (1964):34.
15. Ming-ju Cheng, *The Influence of Communications Internal and External upon the Economic Future of China* (London, 1930), 32. The estimated camel population of 260,000 is from *Shina seihoku yōmō bōeki to kaikyōto no yakuwari* (Tokyo, 1940), 13.
16. Information on horse carts and horse population from Cheng, *The Influence of Communications*, 32 and Liu and Yeh, *Economy of the Chinese Mainland*, 135.

Bibliography

Note: The titles of Chinese- and Japanese-language articles are given in English translation only. The names of living authors resident in the People's Republic of China are cross-listed in *pinyin* romanization. "SMR" stands for Minami Manshū Tetsudo Kabushikigaisha [South Manchurian Railway Corporation].

Adshead, S. A. M. *The Modernization of the Chinese Salt Administration, 1900–1920.* Cambridge: Harvard University Press, 1970.

Allen, G. C. "The Heavy Industries." In *The Industrialization of Japan and Manchukuo, 1930–1940* edited by E. B. Schumpeter, 596–624. New York: Macmillan, 1940.

An Analysis of the Accounts of the Principal Chinese Banks, 1934. Shanghai: Bank of China, 1935.

Andersen, Meyer & Company Limited of China. Its History: Its Organization Today. Shanghai: Kelly and Walsh, 1931.

Annual Returns of the Foreign Trade of Manchoukuo. Dairen: Manchoukuo Department of Finance. 1932–36.

Archibald, Sandra O., and Loren Brandt. "A Flexible Model of Factor Biased Technological Change: An Application to Japanese Agriculture." Stanford: Stanford University Food Research Institute Working Paper Series, 1987.

Arnold, Julean. *Commercial Handbook of China.* 2 vols. Washington, D.C.: Government Printing Office, 1920. Reprint. San Francisco: Chinese Materials Center, 1975.

———. "How Low Silver Affects China's Trade." *China Weekly Review* 55, no. 1 (1930):16.

Ash, Robert. *Land Tenure in Pre-Revolutionary China.* London: Contemporary China Institute, 1976.

Baba Kuwatarō. *Shina no mengyō* [China's cotton industry]. Shanghai: Uiki Gakkai, 1924.

———. *Shina suiun ron* [On China's water transport]. Shanghai: Tōa Dōbun Shōin, 1936.

Bairoch, Paul. *The Economic Development of the Third World Since 1900.* Translated by Cynthia Postan. Berkeley and Los Angeles: University of California Press, 1977.

Bank of China. *Report of the Chairman to the Annual Meeting of Shareholders, April 4, 1936.* Shanghai: Bank of China, 1936.

———. *Report of the Chairman to the Annual Meeting of Shareholders, April 3, 1937.* Shanghai: Bank of China, 1937.

———. *Report of the General Manager to the Annual Meeting of Shareholders, March 19, 1932.* Shanghai: Bank of China, 1932.

———. *Report of the General Manager to the Annual Meeting of Shareholders, April 8, 1933.* Shanghai: Bank of China, 1933.

———. *Report of the General Manager to the Annual Meeting of Shareholders, March 30, 1935.* Shanghai: Bank of China, 1935.

Baster, A. S. J. *The International Banks.* London: P. S. King and Son, 1935.

Bloch, K. "On the Copper Currencies in China." *Nankai Social and Economic Quarterly* 8, no. 3 (1935):616–32.

Boorman, Howard L., ed. *Biographical Dictionary of Republican China.* 5 vols. New York: Columbia University Press, 1967–79.

Bordo, Michael D., and Lars Jonung. *The Long-run Behavior of the Velocity of Circulation: The international evidence.* Cambridge: Cambridge University Press, 1987.

Brandt, Loren. "Chinese Agriculture and the International Economy, 1870s–1930s: A Reassessment." *Explorations in Economic History* 22 (1985):168–93.

———. *Commercialization and Agricultural Development: Central and Eastern China, 1870s–1930s.* New York: Cambridge University Press, forthcoming.

———. "Farm Household Behavior, Factor Markets, and the Distributive Consequences of Commercialization in Early Twentieth-Century China." *Journal of Economic History* 47, no. 3 (1987):711–37.

———. "Population Growth, Agricultural Change and Economic Integration in Central and Eastern China: 1890's–1930's." Ph.D. diss., University of Illinois, 1983.

———. Review of *The Peasant Economy and Social Change in North China,* by Phillip C. C. Huang. *Economic Development and Cultural Change* 35, no. 3 (1987):670–82.

Brandt, Loren, and Thomas J. Sargent. "Interpreting New Evidence About China and U.S. Silver Purchases." Stanford: Hoover Institution Working Papers in Economics E-87-3, 1987.

Buck, David D. *Urban Change in China: Politics and Development in Tsinan, Shantung, 1890–1949.* Madison: University of Wisconsin Press, 1978.

Buck, John L. *Chinese Farm Economy: A Study of 2,866 Farms in Seventeen Localities and Seven Provinces in China.* Chicago: University of Chicago Press, 1930.

———. *Land Utilization in China.* Chicago: University of Chicago Press, 1937.

———. *Land Utilization in China, Atlas.* Nanking: University of Nanking, 1937.

———. *Land Utilization in China, Statistics.* Chicago: University of Chicago Press, 1937. Reprint. New York: Garland, 1982.

Bush, Richard C. "Industry and Politics in Kuomintang China." Ph.D. diss., Columbia University, 1978.

Carlson, Ellsworth C. *The Kaiping Mines, 1877–1912.* 2d ed. Cambridge: Harvard University East Asian Research Center, 1971.

Chan, Wellington K. K. *Merchants, Mandarins and Modern Enterprise in Late Ch'ing China.* Cambridge: Harvard University East Asian Research Center, 1979.

Chang Chia-ao. See Chang Kia-ngau.

Chang, C. M. "Local Government Expenditure in China." *Monthly Bulletin on Economic China* 7, no. 6 (1934):233–47.

Chang, F. Y. "Banking and Currency." In *The Chinese Year Book 1936–37,* 789–845. Shanghai: Commercial Press, 1936.

Chang, George H. "A Brief Survey of Chinese Native Banks." *Central Bank of China Bulletin* 4, no. 1 (1938):25–32.

———. "The Practice of Shanghai Native Banks." *Central Bank of China Bulletin* 4, no. 4 (1938):310–19 and 5, no. 2 (1939):134–42.

Chang Hung-lieh. "Shantung Transport in the Past Year." *Chiao t'ung tsa chih* 3, no. 3–4 (1935):95–98.

Chang, John K. *Industrial Development in Pre-Communist China: A Quantitative Analysis.* Chicago: Aldine, 1969.

Chang, Kia-ngau. "Chang Chia-ao." Manuscript. Columbia University Oral History Project, n.d.

———. "Toward Modernization of China's Currency and Banking, 1927–1937." In *The Strenuous Decade: China's Nation-Building Efforts, 1927–1937,* edited by Paul K. T. Sih, 129–65. New York: St. John's University Press, 1970.

Chang, Liang-jen. "Post Office." In *The Chinese Year Book, 1935–36.* Shanghai: Commercial Press, 1935. Reprint ed. Nendeln, Liechtenstein: Kraus-Thomson, 1968. Vol. 1:699–720.

Chang, L. L. "Farm Prices in Wuchin, Kiangsu, China." *Chinese Economic Journal* 10, no. 6 (1932):449–512.

Chang P'ei-kang and Chang Chih-i. *Che-chiang sheng shih liang chih yün hsiao* [Transport and sale of foodgrains in Chekiang province]. Changsha: Commercial Press, 1940.

Chang Sen. "Land Taxes and Regional Finance." *Ti cheng yüeh k'an* 4, no. 2–3 (1936):165–228.

Chang Yu-lan. *Chung-kuo yin hang fa chan shih* [Historical development of Chinese banks]. Shanghai: Shang-hai Jen Min Ch'u Pan She, 1957.

Chao, Kang. *Agricultural Production in Communist China, 1949–1965.* Madison: University of Wisconsin Press, 1970.

———. *The Development of Cotton Textile Production in China.* Cambridge: Harvard University East Asian Research Center, 1977.

———. *The Economic Development of Manchuria: The Rise of a Frontier Economy.* Ann Arbor: University of Michigan Center for Chinese Studies, 1983.

———. "The Growth of a Modern Cotton Textile Industry and the Competition with Handicrafts." In *China's Modern Economy in Historical Perspective,* edited by Dwight H. Perkins, 167–201. Stanford: Stanford University Press, 1975.

Ch'en Chen, comp. *Chung-kuo chin tai kung yeh shih tzu liao* [Materials on the history of China's modern industries]. Collection 4. Peking: San Lien Shu Tien, 1961.

Ch'en Chen and Yao Lo, comps. *Chung-kuo chin tai kung yeh shih tzu liao* [Materials on the history of China's modern industries]. Collection 1. Peking: San Lien Shu Tien, 1957.

Ch'en Chen, Yao Lo, and Feng Hsien-chih, comps. *Chung-kuo chin tai kung yeh shih tzu liao* [Materials on the history of China's modern industries]. Collection 2. Peking: San Lien Shu Tien, 1958.

Ch'en Cheng-mo. *Ko sheng nung kung ku yung hsi kuan chi hsü kung chuang k'uang* [Hiring practices for farm labor and its demand and supply in various provinces]. Nanking: Chung-shan Wen Hua Chiao Yü Kuan, 1935.

Chen, Han-seng. *Industrial Capital and Chinese Peasants.* Shanghai: Kelly and Walsh, 1939. Reprint. New York: Garland, 1980.

Ch'en, Jerome. *China and the West.* Bloomington: University of Indiana Press, 1979.

———. "Historical Background." In *Modern China's Search for a Politi-*

cal Form, edited by Jack Gray, 1–40. London: Oxford University Press, 1969.

———. "Local Government Finances in Republican China." *Republican China* 10, no. 2 (1985):42–54.

Chen, K. P. "The Reminiscences of Ch'en Kuang-fu (K. P. Chen) (December 20, 1881–July 1, 1976) as told to Julie Lien-ying How." Columbia University Oral History Project, 1960–61.

Chen, Nai-ruenn. "China's Balance of Payments: The Experience of Financing a Long-term Trade Deficit in the Twentieth Century." In *Modern Chinese Economic History*, edited by Chi-ming Hou and Tzong-shian Yu, 389–418. Taipei: Institute of Economics, Academia Sinica, 1979.

———. *Chinese Economic Statistics: A Handbook for Mainland China.* Chicago: Aldine, 1967.

Ch'en Po-chuang. *Hsiao mai chi mien fen* [Wheat and wheat flour]. Shanghai: Chiao-t'ung Ta-hsüeh Yen Chiu So, 1936.

Ch'en Ta. *Chung-kuo lao kung wen t'i* [China's labor problems]. Shanghai: Commercial Press, 1929.

Ch'en T'ing-hsüan. "The Feudal Nature of Farm Employment Relations in Modern China." *Chung-kuo ching chi shih yen chiu* 3 (1987): 121–32.

Chen Tingxuan. See Ch'en T'ing-hsüan.

Ch'en Wen-lu. "Minimum Wages and the Living Standards of Chinese Workers." *Lao tung chi pao* 3 (1934):65–97.

Chen Zhen. See Ch'en Chen.

Chenery, Hollis, Montek S. Ahluwalia, C. L. G. Bell, John H. Duloy, and Richard Jolly. *Redistribution with Growth.* London: Oxford University Press, 1974.

Cheng, Ming-ju. *The Influence of Communications Internal and External upon the Economic Future of China.* London: Routledge, 1930.

Cheng, Ying-wen. *Postal Communication in China and Its Modernization, 1860–1896.* Cambridge: Harvard University East Asian Research Center, 1970.

Cheng, Yu-kwei. *Foreign Trade and Industrial Development of China.* Washington, D.C.: The University Press of Washington, 1956.

Chi Ch'a tiao ch'a t'ung chi ts'ung k'an [Compendium of survey data on Hopei and Chahar]. Peiping. Vols. 1–2. 1936–37.

Ch'i, Hsi-sheng. *Warlord Politics in China, 1916–1928.* Stanford: Stanford University Press, 1976.

Chiang-su ch'eng shih li shih ti li [Historical geography of cities in Kiangsu]. Huai-yin: Chiang-su K'o Hsüeh Chi Shu Ch'u Pan She, 1982.

Chiang-su shih nien, 1949–1959 [Kiangsu province's ten years]. Nanking: Chiang-su Jen Min Ch'u Pan She, 1959.

Chiao t'ung nien chien, 1935 [Transport yearbook, 1935]. Shanghai: Chiao T'ung Pu Tsung Wu Ssu, 1935.

Chiao t'ung shih [History of communications]. 37 vols. Nanking: Ministry of Communications, 1930–37.

Chih-li sheng shang p'in ch'en lieh so ti i tz'u shih yeh tiao ch'a [First economic survey by the commercial exposition of Chihli province]. Tientsin: Chih-li Sheng Shang P'in Ch'en Li So, 1917.

Chin Chi-shuo. "Shanghai's Changing Economic Position and Role Before and After Liberation." *She hui k'o hsüeh* 10 (1984):14–19.

China. The Maritime Customs. See *The Foreign Trade of China, Returns of Trade and Trade Reports*, and *The Trade of China*.

China Industrial Handbooks: Chekiang. Shanghai: Bureau of Foreign Trade, 1935. Reprint. Taipei: Ch'eng Wen, 1973.

China Industrial Handbooks: Kiangsu. Shanghai: Bureau of Foreign Trade, 1933.

China Proper. 3 vols. Cambridge: Naval Intelligence Division, 1945.

China: Socialist Economic Development. 3 vols. Washington D.C.: The World Bank, 1983.

China Weekly Review. Shanghai: Millard, 1926–35.

The China Year Book. Tientsin and Shanghai: North China Daily News and Standard, 1919–39.

Chin-ch'eng yin hang shih liao [Historical materials on the Kincheng bank]. Shanghai: Shang-hai Jen Min Ch'u Pan She, 1983

Chinese Economic Bulletin. Peking: Chinese Government Bureau of Economic Information, 1927–34.

Ch'iu Ch'i-hua. *Wo kuo fa chan yün shu ho yu tien ti ti i ko wu nien chi hua* [China's first five-year plan for developing transport and postal communications]. Peking: Jen Min Ch'u Pan She, 1956.

Chiu Chung-kuo chi chih mien fen kung yeh t'ung chi tzu liao [Statistical materials on the flour industry in old China]. Peking: Chung Hua Shu Chü, 1966.

Chiu Chung-kuo K'ai-luan mei k'uang ti kung tzu chih tu ho pao kung chih tu [Wage and contract labor systems at the K'ai-luan coal mine to 1949]. Tientsin: T'ien-chin Jen Min Ch'u Pan She, 1983.

Chou Hsiu-luan, *Ti i tzu shih chieh ta chan shih ch'i Chung-kuo min tsu kung yeh ti fa chan* [Development of Chinese private industry during World War I]. Shanghai: Shang-hai Jen Min Ch'u Pan She, 1958.

Chou, Shun-hsin. "Railway Development and Economic Growth in Manchuria." *China Quarterly* 45 (1971):57–84.

Chu, T. S., and T. Chin. *Marketing of Cotton in Hopei Province*. Peiping: Institute of Social Research, 1929.

Ch'u Yü-ju. "Survey Report on the Yen-fu Cotton District [in North Kiangsu]." *Nung hang yüeh k'an* 1, no. 4 (1934):35–42.

Chuan, Han-sheng, and Richard A. Kraus. *Mid-Ch'ing Rice Markets and Trade: An Essay in Price History*. Cambridge: Harvard University Press, 1975.

Ch'üan kuo kung jen sheng huo chi kung yeh sheng ch'an tiao ch'a t'ung chi pao kao shu [Statistical report of the national survey of workers' living conditions and industrial production]. 3 vols. Nanking: Kung Shang Pu, 1930.

Ch'üan kuo t'u ti tiao ch'a pao kao kang yao [Outline report of the national land survey]. Nanking: T'u Ti Wei Yuan Hui, 1937.

Ch'üan kuo yin hang nien chien, 1937 [Chinese banking yearbook, 1937]. Shanghai: Chung-kuo Yin Hang, 1937. Reprint. Washington, D.C.: Center for Chinese Research Materials, 1971.

Chūka minkoku oyobi Manshūkoku bōeki tōkeihyō [Statistical tables of trade for the Republic of China and Manchoukuo]. Tokyo: Tōkyō Shōkō Kaigisho, 1939.

Chung-hua-min-kuo t'ung chi t'i yao, 1935 [Statistical abstract of the Republic of China, 1935]. Shanghai: Commercial Press, 1936.

Chung-kuo ching chi nien chien, 1981 [Economic almanac of China, 1981]. Peking: Ching Chi Kuan Li Tsa Chih She, 1981.

(Ti i tz'u) Chung-kuo lao tung nien chien [The first China labor yearbook]. Peking: Pei-p'ing She Hui Tiao Ch'a Pu, 1928.

Chung-kuo min tsu huo ch'ai kung yeh [China's private-sector match industry]. Peking: Chung-hua Shu Chü, 1963.

Chung-kuo nung yeh chin jung kai yao [Outline of China's agricultural finance]. Shanghai: Commercial Press, 1936

Chung-kuo t'ung chi chai yao, 1987 [Statistical abstract of China, 1987]. Peking: Chung-kuo T'ung Chi Ch'u Pan She, 1987.

Chung-kuo t'ung chi nien chien [Statistical yearbook of China]. Peking: Chung-kuo T'ung Chi Ch'u Pan She, 1981, 1984.

Chūshi no minsengyō: Soshū minsen jittai chōsa hōkoku [The junk trade of Central China: Survey report on junk conditions at Soochow]. 2 vols. Tokyo: Hōbunkan, 1943.

Clark, Grover. *Economic Rivalries in China*. New Haven: Yale University Press, 1932.

Clark, M. Gardner. *The Development of China's Steel Industry and Soviet Technical Aid*. Ithaca: New York State School of Industrial and Labor Relations, 1973.

Coble, Parks M. *The Shanghai Capitalists and the Nationalist Government, 1927–1937.* Cambridge: Harvard University Council on East
Asian Studies, 1980.

Cochran, Sherman. *Big Business in China: Sino-Foreign Rivalry in
the Cigarette Industry, 1890–1930.* Cambridge: Harvard University
Press, 1980.

————. "Controlling a National Market in China: Interregional Trade in
Tobacco Products and Cotton Textiles, 1850–1984." Ithaca, 1984.
Paper presented at a conference on Spatial and Temporal Trends and
Cycles in Chinese Economic History, Bellagio, Italy.

Collis, Maurice. *Wayfoong: The Hongkong and Shanghai Banking Corporation.* London: Faber and Faber, 1965.

"Consignment Trading." In British Broadcasting Corporation, *Summary
of World Broadcasts: Part 3, The Far East, Weekly Economic Report,*
W1098 (1980):A2.

"Cotton Cultivation in Shensi." *Chinese Economic Monthly* 3, no. 5
(1926):200–201.

Crawcour, E. S. "The Tokugawa Heritage." In *The State and Economic
Enterprise in Japan,* edited by William W. Lockwood, 17–44. Princeton: Princeton University Press, 1965.

Crawcour, E. S., and Kozo Yamamura. "The Tokugawa Monetary System:
1767–1868." *Economic Development and Cultural Change* 18, no. 4
(1970): part 1, 489–518.

Delfs, Robert. "Lesson from Sunan." *Far Eastern Economic Review,*
June 4, 1987, 78–79.

Dernberger, Robert F. "The Role of the Foreigner in China's Economic
Development, 1840–1949." In *China's Modern Economy in Historical
Perspective,* edited by Dwight H. Perkins, 19–48. Stanford: Stanford
University Press, 1975.

Dietrich, Craig. "Cotton Manufacture and Trade in China (ca. 1500–
1800)." Ph.D. diss., University of Chicago, 1970.

Ding Changqing. See Ting Ch'ang-ch'ing.

Ding Richu. See Ting Jih-ch'u.

Dittrich, Scott R., and Ramon H. Myers. "Resource Allocation in Traditional Agriculture: Republican China, 1937–1940." *Journal of Political
Economy* 79, no. 4 (1971):887–96.

Djang, Siao-mei. "Banking, Currency and Credit." In *The Chinese Year
Book, 1935–36,* 1429–1509. Shanghai: Commercial Press, 1935.

Duara, Prasenjit. "State Involution: A Study of Local Finances in North
China, 1911–1935." Berkeley, 1986. Paper presented at the Regional
Seminar in Chinese Studies, University of California, Berkeley.

Eastman, Lloyd E. *The Abortive Revolution: China Under Nationalist Rule, 1927–1937.* Cambridge: Harvard University Press, 1974.

Eckstein, Alexander, Kang Chao, and John K. Chang. "The Economic Development of Manchuria: The Rise of a Frontier Economy." *Journal of Economic History* 34, no. 1 (1974):239–64.

Economic History of Manchuria. Seoul: Bank of Chosen, 1920.

Emi, Koichi. *Government Fiscal Outlays and Economic Growth in Japan, 1868–1960.* Tokyo: Kinokuniya, 1963.

Eng, Robert Y. "Chinese Entrepreneurs, the Government and the Foreign Sector: The Canton and Shanghai Silk-Reeling Enterprises, 1861–1932." *Modern Asian Studies* 18, no. 3 (1984):353–70.

"Explanation of Table Showing Trends in Major Wages and Prices for Shanghai in the Past Ten Years." *Chiao yü yü chih yeh* 22 (1920).

Fairbank, John K. *Trade and Diplomacy on the China Coast.* Stanford: Stanford University Press, 1953.

Fairbank, John K., and Albert Feuerwerker, eds. *The Cambridge History of China.* Vol. 13, *Republican China, 1912–1949, Part 2.* Cambridge: Cambridge University Press, 1986.

Faure, David W. "Local Political Disturbances in Kiangsu Province, China, 1870–1911." Ph.D. diss., Princeton University, 1976.

————. "The Plight of the Farmers: A Study of the Rural Economy of Jiangnan and the Pearl River Delta, 1870–1937." *Modern China* 11, no. 1 (1985):3–37.

————. "The Rural Economy of Kiangsu Province, 1870–1911." *The Journal of the Institute of Chinese Studies of the Chinese University of Hong Kong* 9, no. 2 (1978):365–471.

Fei, Hsiao-t'ung, and Chih-i Chang. *Earthbound China: A Study of Rural Economy in Yunnan.* Chicago: University of Chicago Press, 1945. Reprint. Chicago: University of Chicago Press, 1975.

Feng Ho-fa. *Chung-kuo nung ts'un ching chi tzu liao* [Materials on China's village economy]. 2 vols. Shanghai: Li–ming Shu Chü, 1935.

Feng Liu-t'ang, ed. *Shang-hai min shih wen t'i* [Problems of feeding Shanghai's populace]. Shanghai: Shang-hai Shih She Hui Chü, 1931.

Feuerwerker, Albert. *China's Early Industrialization: Sheng Hsüan-huai (1844–1916) and Mandarin Enterprise.* Cambridge: Harvard University Press, 1958.

————. *The Chinese Economy, 1912–1949.* Ann Arbor: University of Michigan Center for Chinese Studies, 1968.

————. *Economic Trends in the Republic of China, 1912–1949.* Ann Arbor: University of Michigan Center for Chinese Studies, 1977.

————. "Handicraft and Manufactured Cotton Textiles in China, 1871–1910." *Journal of Economic History* 30, no. 2 (1970):338–78.

Finance and Commerce. Shanghai. 1927–35.

"Finance Minister's Second Annual Report." *Chinese Economic Journal* 8, no. 4 (1931):325–45.

Fleisig, Heywood. "The United States and the Non-European Periphery During the Early Years of the Great Depression." In *The Great Depression Revisited,* edited by Herman van der Wee, 145–81. The Hague: Martinus Nijhoff, 1972.

Fong, H. D. *Cotton Industry and Trade in China.* 2 vols. Tientsin: Nankai Institute of Economics, 1932.

―――. "Industrial Capital in China." *Nankai Social and Economic Quarterly* 9, no. 1 (1936):27–94.

Fong, H. D., and H. H. Pi. "The Growth and Decline of Rural Industrial Enterprise in North China: A Case Study of the Cotton Handloom Weaving Industry in Paoti." *Nankai Social and Economic Quarterly* 8, no. 3 (1936):691–772.

"Foreign Banks in Shanghai." *Shang-hai shih t'ung chih kuan ch'i k'an* 2, no. 2 (1934):547–602.

The Foreign Trade of China. Shanghai: Inspectorate General of Customs. 1920–31.

Friedman, Milton, and Anna Jacobson Schwartz. *A Monetary History of the United States, 1867–1960.* Princeton: Princeton University Press, 1963.

Fujino Shōzaburō, Fujino Shirō, and Ono Akira. *Sen'igyō* [Textiles]. Tokyo: Tōyō Keizai Shimpōsha, 1979.

Gamble, Sidney D. *Ting Hsien: A North China Rural Community.* New York: Institute of Pacific Relations, 1954. Reprint. Stanford: Stanford University Press, 1968.

Gibb, George S. *The Saco-Lowell Shops: Textile Machinery Building in New England, 1813–1949.* Cambridge: Harvard University Press, 1950.

Gillin, Donald G. "China's First Five-Year Plan." *Journal of Asian Studies* 24, no. 2 (1965):245–59.

―――. *Warlord: Yen Hsi-shan in Shansi Province, 1911–1949.* Princeton: Princeton University Press, 1967.

Gillis, Malcolm, Dwight H. Perkins, Michael Roemer, and Donald R. Snodgrass. *Economics of Development.* New York: Norton, 1983.

Gottschang, Thomas R. "Economic Development in Northeast China." Worcester, 1984. Paper presented at a conference on Spatial and Temporal Trends and Cycles in Chinese Economic History, Bellagio, Italy.

―――. "Migration from North China to Manchuria: An Economic History, 1891–1942." Ph.D. diss., University of Michigan, 1982.

―――. "Structural Change, Disasters, and Migration: The Historical Case of Manchuria." *Economic Development and Cultural Change* 35, no. 3 (1987):461–90.

Great Britain. Department of Overseas Trade. *The Commercial, Industrial and Economic Situation in China to September 1st, 1928.* London: HMSO, 1928.

———. *Economic Conditions in China to September 1st, 1929.* London: HMSO, 1930.

———. *Economic Conditions in China to August 20th, 1930.* London: HMSO, 1930.

Hall, Ray O. *Chapters and Documents on Chinese National Banking.* Shanghai: author, 1920.

Hamilton, Gary C. "Nineteenth Century Chinese Merchant Associations: Conspiracy or Combination?" *Ch'ing-shih wen-t'i* 3, no. 8 (1977): 50–71.

Hancock, Charles F. "Introduction and Influence of Modern Machinery in China." M.A. thesis, University of Texas, 1926.

Hanley, Susan B., and Kozo Yamamura. *Economic and Demographic Change in Preindustrial Japan, 1600–1868.* Princeton: Princeton University Press, 1977.

Hanley, Susan B., and Kozo Yamamura. "A Quiet Transformation in Tokugawa Economic History." *Journal of Asian Studies* 30, no. 2 (1971):373–84.

Hao, Yen-p'ing. *The Commercial Revolution in Nineteenth-Century China: The Rise of Sino-Western Mercantile Capitalism.* Berkeley and Los Angeles: University of California Press, 1986

———. *The Compradore in Nineteenth Century China.* Cambridge: Harvard University Press, 1970.

Hauser, William B. *Economic Institutional Change in Tokugawa Japan: Osaka and the Kinai Cotton Trade.* Cambridge: Cambridge University Press, 1974.

Hermann, Albert. *An Historical Atlas of China.* Chicago: Aldine, 1966.

Hershatter, Gail. *The Workers of Tianjin, 1900–1949.* Stanford: Stanford University Press, 1986.

Hinrichs, Harley H. "Determinants of Government Revenue Shares Among Less-Developed Countries." *Economic Journal* 75 (1965): 546–56.

Ho, Franklin L. *Index Numbers of the Quantities and Prices of Imports and Exports and of the Barter Terms of Trade in China, 1867–1928.* Tientsin: Nankai University Committee on Social and Economic Research, 1930.

Ho, Ping-ti. *Studies on the Population of China, 1368–1953.* Cambridge: Harvard University Press, 1959.

Hokushi shōhin sōran [Guide to commercial products of North China]. Tokyo: Nihon Hyōronsha, 1943.

Holmes, Gordon O. "U.S. Transport Intensity, ca. 1860–1870." Toronto,

1981. Research report, University of Toronto Department of Economics. Photocopy.

Honig, Emily. "The Contract Labor System and Women Workers: Pre-Liberation Cotton Mills of Shanghai." *Modern China* 9, no. 4 (1983): 421–54.

Horiuchi Sumiyo. "Conditions of the Junk Trade Around Tsingtao." *Mantetsu chōsa geppō* 22, no. 9 (1942):115–37.

Hotchi Zenjirō. "The Present Situation of China's Cotton Textile Industry." *Mantetsu chōsa geppō* 15, no. 12 (1935):1–41.

Hou, Chi-ming. *Foreign Investment and Economic Development in China, 1840–1937.* Cambridge: Harvard University Press, 1965.

Houthakker, H. S. "An International Comparison of Household Expenditure Patterns, Commemorating the Centenary of Engel's Law." *Econometrica* 25, no. 4 (1957):532–51.

Howard, C. W. *The Sericulture Industry of South China.* Canton: Lingnan University, 1923.

Hsia Lin-ken. "On the Transformation of Cotton Textile Handicraft Industry in the Modern Shanghai Region." *Chung-kuo she hui ching chi shih yen chiu* 3 (1984):24–31.

Hsiao, Liang-lin. *China's Foreign Trade Statistics, 1864–1949.* Cambridge: Harvard University Press, 1974.

Hsien K'o. *Chin pai nien lai ti kuo chu i tsai Hua yin hang fa hsing chih pi kai k'uang* [Issue of paper currency by imperialist banks in China during the past century]. Shanghai: Shang-hai Jen Min Ch'u Pan She, 1958.

Hsü, Immanuel C. Y. "The Great Debate in China, 1874: Maritime Defense vs. Frontier Defense." *Harvard Journal of Asiatic Studies* 25 (1964–65):212–28.

Hsü Tao-fu. *Chung-kuo chin tai nung yeh sheng ch'an chi mao i t'ung chi tzu liao* [Statistical materials on agricultural production and trade in modern China]. Shanghai: Shang-hai Jen Min Ch'u Pan She, 1983.

Hsüeh Mu-ch'iao. "Some Opinions on Reforming the Economic System." In U.S. Foreign Broadcast Information Service. *Daily Report: China,* June 25, 1980, L13-L18.

Hu-pei shih hsien kai k'uang [Conditions in cities and counties of Hupeh]. Wuhan: Hu-pei Sheng Ti Fang Chih Pien Hsüan Wei Yuan Hui, 1984.

Huang Han-min. "Analysis of Pre-Liberation Wage Levels for Shanghai Workers." *Shang-hai ching chi k'o hsüeh* 3 (1984):51–58.

———. "Brief Analysis of Annual Fluctuations in Nominal Wage Income of Shanghai Workers, 1927–1936." *Shang-hai ching chi k'o hsüeh* 1 (1985):42–47.

Huang, Philip C. C. *The Peasant Economy and Social Change in North China.* Stanford: Stanford University Press, 1985.

Hubbard, G. E. *Eastern Industrialization and Its Effect on the West, with Special Reference to Great Britain and Japan.* London: Oxford University Press, 1935.

Huber, J. Richard. "Effect on Prices of Japan's Entry into World Commerce After 1858." *Journal of Political Economy* 79, no. 3 (1971): 614–28.

Huenemann, Ralph W. "The Dragon and the Iron Horse: The Economics of Railroads in China, 1876–1937." Ph.D. diss., Harvard University, 1981.

————. *The Dragon and the Iron Horse: The Economics of Railroads in China, 1876–1937.* Cambridge: Harvard University Press, 1984.

Hundred-Year Statistics of the Japanese Economy. Tokyo: Bank of Japan, 1966.

I-pei hsien chih [Gazetteer of I-pei county, Kwangsi]. I-pei, 1937. Reprint. Taipei: Ch'eng Wen, 1968.

Ishikawa, Shigeru. "The Development of Capital Goods Sector: Experience of Pre-PRC China." World Employment Programme Research Working Paper. Geneva: International Labor Organization, 1985.

Japan Manchoukuo Year Book, 1934. Tokyo: Japan-Manchoukuo Year Book Company, 1934.

Jih-pen tui Hu t'ou tzu [Japanese investment in Shanghai]. Shanghai: Commercial Press, 1937.

Jones, Susan Mann. See Mann, Susan.

Jung chia ch'i yeh shih liao [Historical materials on the Jung family enterprises]. 2 vols. Shanghai: Shang-hai Jen Min Ch'u Pan She, 1980.

Kahoku ni okeru kōtsū unyu rōdōsha chōsa [Survey of transport laborers in North China]. Peking: Zai Pekin Dai Nippon Teikoku Taishikan, 1942.

Kairan tankō rōdō chōsa hōkoku [Survey report on labor at the K'ai-luan coal mines]. 2 vols. Perking: Kahoku Sōgō Chōsa Kenkyūjo, 1943.

Kann, Eduard. *The Currencies of China.* 2d ed. Shanghai: Kelly and Walsh, 1927.

————. *The History of Minting in China.* Shanghai: Numismatic Society of China, 1939.

————. "How Much Silver Is There in China?" *Chinese Economic Journal* 8 (1931):410–21.

————. "Modern Banknotes in China (1931 to end of 1936)." *Central Bank of China Bulletin* 3, no. 1 (1937):27–56.

————. "What Is a Shanghai Tael?" *Chinese Economic Journal* 1 (1927): 769–72.

Kapp, Robert A. *Szechwan and the Chinese Republic: Provincial Militarism and Central Power, 1911–1938.* New Haven: Yale University Press, 1973.

Kavic, Lorne J. *India's Quest for Security.* Berkeley and Los Angeles: University of California Press, 1967.

Kennedy, Thomas L. *The Arms of Kiangnan: Modernization in the Chinese Ordnance Industry, 1860–1895.* Boulder, Colo.: Westview, 1978.

Kindleberger, Charles P. *The World in Depression, 1929–1939.* Berkeley and Los Angeles: University of California Press, 1973.

King, Paul. *In the Chinese Customs Service: A Personal Record of Forty-seven Years.* London: Heath Cranton, 1924.

Kirby, William C. *Germany and Republican China.* Stanford: Stanford University Press, 1984.

—————. "Kuomintang China's 'Great Leap Outward': The 1936 Three-Year Plan for Industrial Development." *Illinois Papers in Asian Studies* 2 (1983):43–66.

Kita Shina ni okeru mensakuchi nōson jijō (Kahokushō Tsūken Kokaison) [Farm village conditions in the cotton districts of North China, Hsiao-chieh village, T'ung county, Hopei]. Tientsin: SMR Tenshin Jimusho, 1936.

Knight, Frank H. *On the History and Method of Economics.* Chicago: University of Chicago Press, 1956.

Kong Jingwei. See K'ung Ching-wei.

Kōsōshō Jōjukuken nōson jittai chōsa hōkokusho [Survey report on rural village conditions in Ch'ang-shu county, Kiangsu]. Shanghai: SMR Shanhai Jimusho, 1940.

Kōsōshō Sōkōken nōson jittai chōsa hōkokusho [Survey report on rural village conditions in Sung-chiang county, Kiangsu]. Shanghai: SMR Shanhai Jimusho, 1940.

Kraus, Richard A. "Cotton and Cotton Goods in China, 1918–1936: The Impact of Modernization on the Traditional Sector." Ph.D. diss., Harvard University, 1968.

Kraus, Willy. *Economic Development and Social Change in the People's Republic of China.* Translated by E. M. Holz. New York: Springer-Verlag, 1979.

Kuang-hsi sheng ko hsien ch'u ju ching ta tsung huo wu kai k'uang [Conditions for major categories of merchandise entering and leaving various Kwangsi counties]. Kuang-hsi t'ung chi ts'ung shu, item 8. N.p.: Kuang-hsi T'ung Chi Chü, 1934.

Kuhn, Philip A. "Local Taxation and Finance in Republican China." In *Select Papers for the Center for Far Eastern Studies,* edited by Susan Mann Jones, 100–136. Chicago: University of Chicago Center for Far Eastern Studies, 1979.

—————. *Rebellion and Its Enemies in Late Imperial China.* Cambridge: Harvard University Press, 1970.

K'ung Ching-wei. *Chung-kuo chin pai nien ching chi shih kang* [Outline of China's economic history in the past hundred years]. Changchun: Chi-lin Jen Min Ch'u Pan She, 1980.

Kung Chün. *Chung-kuo hsin kung yeh fa chan shih ta kang* [Outline history of China's new industrial development]. Shanghai: Commercial Press, 1933.

Kuznets, Simon. *Modern Economic Growth: Rate, Structure, and Spread.* New Haven: Yale University Press, 1966.

Kyi, Z. T. "Match-making Industry." *Chinese Economic Journal* 4 (1929): 305–11.

Lamson, H. D. "The Effect of Industrialization upon Village Livelihood." *Chinese Economic Journal* 9, no. 4 (1931):1025–82.

Lardy, Nicholas R. "Consumption and Living Standards in China, 1978–83." *China Quarterly* 100 (1984):849–65.

———. *Economic Growth and Distribution in China.* New York: Cambridge University Press, 1978.

———. "Regional Growth and Income Distribution in China." In *China's Development Experience in Comparative Perspective*, edited by Robert F. Dernberger, 153–90. Cambridge: Harvard University Press, 1980.

Lary, Diana. *Region and Nation: The Kwangsi Clique in Chinese Politics, 1925–1937.* Cambridge: Cambridge University Press, 1974.

———. *Warlord Soldiers: Chinese Common Soldiers.* Cambridge: Cambridge University Press, 1985.

Leavens, D. H. "American Silver Policy and China." *Harvard Business Review* 14, no. 1 (1935):45–58.

Leff, Nathaniel H. *Underdevelopment and Development in Brazil.* Vol. 1, *Economic Structure and Change, 1822–1947.* London: Allen and Unwin, 1982.

Leung, Chi-Keung. *China: Railway Patterns and National Goals.* Chicago: University of Chicago Department of Geography, 1960.

Lewis, A. B., and Lien Wang. "Farm Prices in Wuchin, Kiangsu." *Economic Facts* 2 (1936):73–91

Lewis, W. Arthur. *Growth and Fluctuations, 1870–1913.* London: Allen and Unwin, 1978.

———. *The Theory of Economic Growth.* Homewood, Ill.: Irwin, 1955.

Li Ch'eng-jui. *Chung-hua jen-min kung-ho-kuo nung yeh shui shih kao* [Draft history of agricultural taxation in the People's Republic of China]. Peking: Ts'ai Cheng Ch'u Pan She, 1959.

Li, Chien-ming. *The Accounting System of Native Banks in Peking and Tientsin.* Tientsin: Institut des Hautes Etudes Industrielles et Commerciales, 1941.

Li Hsiao-yung, "Development of Highway Transport in Republican Fukien." *Chung-kuo she hui ching chi shih yen chiu* 2 (1986):93–99.

Li, Lillian M. *China's Silk Trade: Traditional Industry in the Modern*

World, 1842–1937. Cambridge: Harvard University Council on East Asian Studies, 1981.

Liang, Ernest P. *China: Railways and Agricultural Development, 1875–1935.* Chicago: University of Chicago Department of Geography, 1982.

Lieu, D. K. [Liu Ta-chün]. *China's Industries and Finance.* Peking: Chinese Government Bureau of Economic Information, 1927.

———. *The Growth and Industrialization of Shanghai.* Shanghai: China Institute of Pacific Relations, 1936.

Lindstrom, Diane. *Economic Development in the Philadelphia Region, 1810–1850.* New York: Columbia University Press, 1978.

Lippit, Victor D. *The Economic Development of China.* Armonk, N.Y.: M. E. Sharpe, 1987.

———. *Land Reform and Economic Development in China: A Study of Institutional Change and Development Finance.* White Plains, N.Y.: International Arts and Sciences Press, 1974.

Liu, F. F. *A Military History of Modern China.* Princeton: Princeton University Press, 1956.

Liu Hung-sheng ch'i yeh shih liao [Historical materials on Liu Hung-sheng's enterprises]. 3 vols. Shanghai: Shang-hai Jen Min Ch'u Pan She, 1981.

Liu Ta-chün [see also D. K. Lieu]. *Chung-kuo kung yeh tiao ch'a pao kao* [Survey report on Chinese industry]. 3 vols. Shanghai: Ching Chi T'ung Chi Yen Chiu So, 1937.

Liu, Ta-chung. "Quantitative Trends in the Economy." In *Economic Trends in Communist China,* edited by Alexander Eckstein, Walter Galenson, and Ta-chung Liu, 87–182. Chicago: Aldine, 1968.

Liu, Ta-chung, and Kung-chia Yeh. *The Economy of the Chinese Mainland: National Income and Economic Development, 1933–1959.* Princeton: Princeton University Press, 1965.

Liu Yen-nung. "Shipping Conditions in the Port of Wenchow." *Chiao t'ung tsa chih* 3, no. 3 (1935):53–62.

Lo Chieh-fu. *Chung-kuo ts'ai cheng wen t'i* [China's fiscal problem]. Shanghai: T'ai P'ing Yang Shu Tien, 1933.

Mallory, Walter H. *China: Land of Famine.* New York: American Geographical Society, 1926.

Mammō seiji keizai teiyō [Outline of political economy of Manchuria and Mongolia]. Tokyo: Kaizōsha, 1932.

The Manchoukuo Year Book, 1934. Tokyo: Tōa Keizai Chōsakyoku, 1934.

The Manchuria Year Book. Tokyo: Tōa Keizai Chōsakyoku. 1931, 1932–33.

Mann, Susan. "The Ningpo Pang and Financial Power at Shanghai." In *The Chinese City Between Two Worlds,* edited by Mark Elvin and

G. William Skinner, 73–96. Stanford: Stanford University Press, 1974.

Manshū chūō ginkō jūnenshi [Ten-Year history of the Central Bank of Manchoukuo]. Hsinking: Manshū Chūō Ginkō, 1942.

Manshū kaihatsu yonjū nenshi [Forty-Year history of development in Manchuria]. 3 vols. Tokyo: Manshū Kaihatsu Yonjū Nenshi Kankō Kai, 1964–65.

Manshū kayakurui tōsei oyobi matchi kōgyō hōsaku [Regulation of explosives and policy for the match industry in Manchuria]. N.p.: SMR Keizai Chōsabu, 1935.

Manshū kōjō tōkei B, 1934 [Manchurian factory statistics B, 1934]. Dairen: SMR, 1937.

Manshū sangyō tōkei, 1932 [Industrial statistics of Manchuria, 1932]. Dairen: SMR Keizai Chōsakai, 1933.

Manshū tsūka tōkei B: Kahei sōba hen [Statistics of Manchurian currency, B: Money market section]. Dairen: SMR Keizai Chōsakai, 1932.

Manshūkoku gensei, 1937 [Current situation in Manchoukuo, 1937]. Hsinkyō: Manshū Kōhō Kyōkai, 1937.

"Match Industry in China." *Chinese Economic Journal* 10, no. 3 (1932): 197–211.

Matchi kōgyō hōkokusho [Report on the match industry]. Japanese version of Chinese original *Lin ts'un kung yeh pao kao shu*. Nanking: Ch'üan Kuo Ching Chi Wei Yuan Hui, 1935. Translation. Nanking: Chūshi Kensetsu Shiryō Seibi Iinkai, 1940.

McDonald, Angus, Jr. *The Urban Origins of Rural Revolution: Elites and the Masses in Hunan Province, China, 1911–1927*. Berkeley and Los Angeles: University of California Press, 1978.

McElderry, Andrea L. *Shanghai Old-Style Banks (Ch'ien-Chuang), 1800–1935*. Ann Arbor: University of Michigan Center for Chinese Studies, 1976.

Mien? [Cotton?]. Shanghai: Shanghai Commercial and Savings Bank, 1931.

Min-sheng shih-yeh kung-ssu shih i chou nien chi nien k'an [Yearbook commemorating the eleventh anniversary of the Min-sheng company]. Chungking: Min-sheng Shih Yeh Kung Ssu, 1937.

Minami, Ryoshin. "The Introduction of Electric Power and Its Impact on the Manufacturing Industries: With Special Reference to Smaller Scale Plants." In *Japanese Industrialization and Its Social Consequences*, edited by Hugh T. Patrick, 299–325. Berkeley and Los Angeles: University of California Press, 1976.

Mitchell, B. R. *European Historical Statistics, 1750–1970*. Abridged ed. New York: Columbia University Press, 1978.

Morikawa Tetsurō. *Nihon gigokushi* [History of political corruption in Japan]. Tokyo: Sanichi Shobō, 1976.

Moulder, Frances V. *Japan, China and the Modern World Economy: Toward a Reinterpretation of East Asian Development, ca. 1600 to ca. 1918.* Cambridge: Cambridge University Press, 1977.

Murphey, Rhoads. *The Outsiders: The Western Experience in India and China.* Ann Arbor: University of Michigan Press, 1977.

—————. *Shanghai: Key to Modern China.* Cambridge: Harvard University Press, 1953.

Myers, Ramon H. "The Agrarian System." In *The Cambridge History of China.* Vol. 13, *Republican China, 1912–1949, Part 2,* edited by John K. Fairbank and Albert Feuerwerker, 230–69. Cambridge: Cambridge University Press, 1986.

—————. *The Chinese Peasant Economy: Agricultural Development in Hopei and Shantung, 1890–1949.* Cambridge: Harvard University Press, 1970.

—————. "The Commercialization of Agriculture in Modern China." In *Economic Organization in Chinese Society,* edited by W. E. Willmott, 173–91. Stanford: Stanford University Press, 1972.

—————. "Wheat in China—Past, Present and Future." *China Quarterly* 74 (1978):297–333.

—————. "The World Depression and the Chinese Economy." Stanford: Hoover Institution, 1986. Photocopy.

Namboku Manshū no shuyō kaikō kakō [Important ocean and river ports of south and north Manchuria]. Dairen: SMR Sōmubu Chōsaka, 1927.

Nan-k'ai chih shu tzu liao hui pien, 1913–1952 [Compendium of Nan-k'ai index number materials, 1913–1952]. Peking: T'ung Chi Ch'u Pan She, 1958.

Negishi Tadashi. *Baiben seido no kenkyū* [Studies on the compradore system]. Tokyo: Nihon Tosho Kabushikigaisha, 1948.

Nieh Pao-chang. *Chung-kuo mai pan tzu ch'an chieh chi ti fa sheng* [The emergence of China's compradore bourgeoisie]. Peking: Chung-kuo She Hui K'o Hsüeh Ch'u Pan She, 1979.

Niemi, Albert W., Jr. *State and Regional Patterns in American Manufacturing, 1860–1900.* Westport, Conn.: Greenwood Press, 1974.

Nihon no tai-Shi tōshi [Japan's investment in China]. Tokyo: Tōa Kenkyūjo, 1942.

The North China Famine of 1920–1921 with Special Reference to the West Chihli Area. Peking: Peking United International Famine Relief Committee, 1922.

North Manchuria and the Chinese Eastern Railway. Harbin: C.E.R. Printing Office, 1924. Reprint. New York: Garland, 1982.

(Ti chiu tz'u) nung shang t'ung chi piao [Ninth table of agricultural and commercial statistics]. Peking: Nung Shang Pu Tsung Wu T'ing T'ung Chi K'o, 1924.

Ohkawa, Kazushi. "Aggregate Growth and Product Allocation." In *Patterns of Japanese Economic Development*, edited by Kazushi Ohkawa and Miyohei Shinohara, 3–33. New Haven: Yale University Press, 1979.

———. "Phases of Agricultural Development and Economic Growth." In *Agriculture and Economic Growth: Japan's Experience*, edited by Kazushi Ohkawa, Bruce F. Johnston, and Hiromitsu Kaneda, 3–36. Princeton: Princeton University Press, 1970.

———. "Production Structure." In *Patterns of Japanese Economic Development*, edited by Kazushi Ohkawa and Miyohei Shinohara, 34–58. New Haven: Yale University Press, 1979.

Ohkawa, Kazushi, and Henry Rosovsky. *Japanese Economic Growth: Trend Acceleration in the Twentieth Century*. Stanford: Stanford University Press, 1973.

Ohkawa, Kazushi, and Miyohei Shinohara, eds. *Patterns of Japanese Economic Development*. New Haven: Yale University Press, 1979.

Ohkawa Kazushi, Takamatsu Nobukiyo, and Yamamoto Yuzo. *Kokumin shotoku* [National income]. Tokyo: Tōyō Keizai Shimpōsha, 1974.

Ōkurasho nempō [Ministry of Finance yearbook]. Tokyo: Ōkurasho Kambō Bunshoka. No. 41 (1916)–60 (1935).

Onoe Etsuzō. *Chūgoku no sangyō ritchi ni kansuru kenkyū* [Studies in the location of Chinese industry]. Tokyo: Ajia Keizai Kenkyūjo, 1971.

Osterhammel, Jürgen. "Imperialism in Transition: British Business and the Chinese Authorities, 1931–37." *China Quarterly* 98 (1984): 260–86.

Ou, Pao-san [see also Wu Pao-san]. *National Income of China, 1933, 1936 and 1946*. Nanking: Academia Sinica Institute of Social Sciences, 1947.

Pearse, Arno S. *The Cotton Industry of Japan and China*. Manchester: International Federation of Master Cotton Spinners and Manufacturers, 1929.

Perkins, Dwight H. *Agricultural Development in China, 1368–1968*. Chicago: Aldine, 1969.

———. "Government as an Obstacle to Industrialization: The Case of Nineteenth-Century China." *Journal of Economic History* 27, no. 4 (1967):478–92.

———. "Growth and Changing Structure of China's Twentieth-Century Economy." In *China's Modern Economy in Historical Perspective*, edited by Dwight H. Perkins, 115–65. Stanford: Stanford University Press, 1975.

———. "Introduction: The Persistence of the Past." In *China's Modern Economy in Historical Perspective*, edited by Dwight H. Perkins, 1–18. Stanford: Stanford University Press, 1975.

Pi Hsiang-hui. "Forms of Financial Flows in Pao-ti County, Hopei." In *Chung-kuo ching chi yen chiu* [Studies on China's economy], edited by Fang Hsien-t'ing, Vol. 2:839–43. Changsha: Commercial Press, 1938.

Pomeranz, Kenneth. "Local Interest Story: Political Conflict and Regional Differences in the Shandong Capital Market, 1900–1937." New Haven, 1988. Paper presented at a conference on Economic Methods for Chinese Historical Research, Oracle, Ariz.

Potter, Jack M. *Capitalism and the Chinese Peasant.* Berkeley and Los Angeles: University of California Press, 1968.

Pred, Allan R. *The Spatial Dynamics of U.S. Urban-Industrial Growth, 1800–1914.* Cambridge: MIT Press, 1966.

———. *Urban Growth and the Circulation of Information: The United States System of Cities, 1790–1840.* Cambridge: Harvard University Press, 1973.

Pu? Shang-hai chih mien pu yü mien pu yeh [Cloth? Shanghai's cotton cloth and cotton cloth industry]. Shanghai: Shanghai Commercial and Savings Bank, 1932.

Rawski, Evelyn S. *Agricultural Change and the Peasant Economy of South China.* Cambridge: Harvard University Press, 1972.

———. *Education and Popular Literacy in Ch'ing China.* Ann Arbor: University of Michigan Press, 1979.

Rawski, Thomas G. "China's Republican Economy: An Introduction." Toronto: Joint Centre on Modern East Asia, Discussion Paper #1, 1978.

———. *China's Transition to Industrialism: Producer Goods and Economic Development in the Twentieth Century.* Ann Arbor: University of Michigan Press, 1980.

———. "Chinese Dominance of Treaty Port Commerce and Its Implications, 1860–1875." *Explorations in Economic History* 7, no. 4 (1970): 451–73.

———. "Economic Growth and Integration in Prewar China." Toronto: Joint Centre on Modern East Asia, Discussion Paper #5, 1982.

———. "The Economy of the Lower Yangtze Region, 1850–1980." Toronto, 1984. Paper presented at a conference on Spatial and Temporal Trends and Cycles in Chinese Economic History, Bellagio, Italy.

Rebick, Mark. "Labour-Tying in Japanese Agriculture, 1894–1940." Toronto: University of Toronto seminar paper, 1984. Typescript.

Reder, Melvin W. "Chicago and Economics: Permanence and Change." *Journal of Economic Literature* 20, no. 1 (1982):1–38.

Remer, C. F. *Foreign Investments in China.* New York: Macmillan, 1933. Reprint. New York: Howard Fertig, 1968.

Returns of Trade and Trade Reports. Shanghai: Inspectorate General of Customs, 1900–1919.

Reubens, Edwin P. "Opportunities, Governments and Economic Development in Manchuria, 1860–1940." In *The State and Economic Growth: Papers of a Conference Held on October 11–13, 1956,* edited by Hugh G. J. Aitken, 148–88. New York: Social Science Research Council, 1959.

Reynolds, Bruce L. "The Impact of Trade and Foreign Investment on Industrialization: Chinese Textiles, 1875–1931." Ph.D. diss., University of Michigan, 1975.

———. "Weft: The Technological Sanctuary of Chinese Handspun Yarn." *Ch'ing-shih wen-t'i* 3, no.2 (1974):1–18.

Reynolds, Lloyd G. *Economic Growth in the Third World, 1850–1980.* New Haven: Yale University Press, 1985.

Richardson, Harry W. *Regional Economics.* Urbana: University of Illinois Press, 1978.

Riskin, Carl. *China's Political Economy: The Quest for Development Since 1949.* Oxford: Oxford University Press, 1987.

Rōdōsha o chūshin to shite mitaru Hokuman nōson no nōgyō keiei jijō [Conditions of farm management in North Manchurian villages viewed from the standpoint of labor]. 2 vols. Harbin: SMR Hokuman Keizai Chōsajo, 1939.

"Role of Major Ports in Foreign Trade Viewed." In U.S. Foreign Broadcast Information Service. *Daily Report: China,* August 2, 1982, K13–K14.

Roll, Charles R. *The Distribution of Rural Incomes in China.* New York: Garland, 1980.

Rosenbaum, Arthur. "Railway Enterprise and Economic Development: The Case of the Imperial Railways of North China, 1900–1911." *Modern China* 2, no. 2 (1976):227–72.

Rosenberg, Nathan, ed. *The American System of Manufactures.* Edinburgh: Edinburgh University Press, 1969.

Rosovsky, Henry. "Japan's Transition to Modern Economic Growth." In *Economic Growth in Two Systems,* edited by Henry Rosovsky, 91–139. New York: Wiley, 1966.

Rostow, W. W. *The Stages of Economic Growth: A Non-Communist Manifesto.* Cambridge: Cambridge University Press, 1965.

Rowe, William T. *Hankow: Commerce and Society in a Chinese City, 1796–1889.* Stanford: Stanford University Press, 1984.

———. "Urban Society in Late Imperial China: Hankow, 1796–1889." Ph.D. diss., Columbia University, 1980.

Rozman, Gilbert. *Urban Networks in Ch'ing China and Tokugawa Japan.* Princeton: Princeton University Press, 1973.

Russell, Michael B. "American Silver Policy and China, 1933–1936." Ph.D. diss., University of Illinois, 1972.

Sakatani, Baron Y. *Manchuria: A Survey of Its Economic Development.* New York: Carnegie Endowment for International Peace, 1932. Reprint. New York: Garland, 1980.

Salter, Sir Arthur. *Silver and China.* New York: Economic Forum, 1934.

Sands, Barbara N. "Agricultural Decisionmaking Under Uncertainty: The Case of the Shanxi Farmers, 1931–36." Tucson: University of Arizona, 1987. Photocopy.

Sands, Barbara N., and Ramon H. Myers. "The Spatial Approach to Chinese History: A Test." *Journal of Asian Studies* 45, no. 4 (1986): 721–43.

Santō kenkyū shiryō [Research materials on Shantung]. 2 vols. Tsingtao: Chintao Shubigun Minseibu, 1920.

Schran, Peter. "China's Demographic Evolution 1850–1953 Reconsidered." *China Quarterly* 75 (1978):638–46.

————. *Guerrilla Economy: The Development of the Shensi-Kansu-Ninghsia Border Region, 1937–1945.* Albany: State University of New York Press, 1976.

————. "A Much Neglected Source on Inland Communications in Late Ch'ing China." Urbana: University of Illinois, 1978. Photocopy.

————. "Traditional Transportation and Railroad Development in China Since Late Ch'ing Times." Urbana, 1984. Paper presented at a conference on Spatial and Temporal Trends and Cycles in Chinese Economic History, Bellagio, Italy.

————. "What Can Prices Tell Us About China's Modern Economic History?" Urbana: University of Illinois, 1988. Photocopy.

"Selected Documents and Telegrams on the Commercial and Financial Crises at Ningpo and Shanghai During the Hsüan-t'ung Reign (1908–1911)." *Li shih tang an* 3 (1984):36–41.

Sha? Shang-hai chih mien shao yü sha yeh [Yarn? Shanghai's cotton yarn and yarn trade]. Shanghai: Shanghai Commercial and Savings Bank, 1931.

Shan-hsi k'ao ch'a pao kao shu [Investigation report on Shansi]. Shanghai: Ch'üan Kuo Ching Chi Wei Yüan Hui, 1936.

Shang-hai chieh fang ch'ien hou wu chia tzu liao hui pien, 1921–1957 [Collection of pre- and post-liberation Shanghai price materials]. Shanghai: Shang-hai Jen Min Ch'u Pan She, 1958.

Shang-hai ch'ien chuang shih liao [Historical materials on Shanghai's native banks]. Shanghai: Shang-hai Jen Min Ch'u Pan She, 1960.

Shang-hai mai fen shih ch'ang tiao ch'a [Survey of Shanghai's wheat and flour markets]. Shanghai: Institute of Social and Economic Research, 1935.

Shang-hai min tsu hsiang chiao kung yeh [Shanghai's private-sector rubber industry]. Peking: Chung Hua Shu Chü, 1979.

Shang-hai shih ssu li ch'ien yeh ch'u chi chung hsüeh, hsiao hsüeh shih chou nien chi nien k'an [Tenth anniversary commemorative volume for the elementary and junior middle schools of the Shanghai private money-shop trade]. N.p., preface dated 1935.

Shanhai tokubetsushi Kateiku nōson jittai chōsa hōkokusho [Survey report on rural village conditions in Chia-ting district, Shanghai special municipality]. Shanghai: SMR Shanhai Jimusho, 1940.

Shen Yung-ch'un. *Kuang-hsi chih-nan* [Guide to Kwangsi]. Changsha: Commercial Press, 1939.

Sheridan, James E. *China in Disintegration: The Republican Era in Chinese History, 1912–1949.* New York: Free Press, 1975.

―――. *Chinese Warlord: The Career of Feng Yü-hsiang.* Stanford: Stanford University Press, 1966.

Shih Yü-shou and Liu Hsin-ch'üan. "Survey of Workers at the Chunghsing Coal Mine in Shantung." *She hui k'o hsüeh tsa chih* 3, no. 1 (1932):35–93

Shima Ichirō. *Chūgoku minzoku kōgyō no tenkai* [Development of private-sector industry in China]. Tokyo: Minerva, 1978.

Shina kaikōjōshi [Gazetteer of Chinese treaty ports]. 2 vols. Tokyo: Tōa Dōbunkai Hensanbu, 1922–24.

Shina kinyū jijō [Financial conditions in China]. Tokyo: Gaimusho Tsūshōkyoku Dainika, 1925.

Shina kōkōgyō ni kansuru shuyō bunken mokuroku [Index of important materials on Chinese industry and mining]. 3 vols. Kyoto: Kyoto Teikoku Daigaku, Keizai Gakubu, Shina Keizai Kanko Chōsabu, 1940.

Shina matchi kōgyō jōtai shisatsu hōkoku [Report on conditions in China's match industry]. Osaka: Nihon Ōrin Matchi Dogyō Kumiai, 1913.

Shina no janku to Nanman no sankō [Chinese junks and the three ports of Southern Manchuria]. Dairen: SMR Sōmubu Chōsaka, 1927.

Shina no kōun [China's shipping]. Tokyo: Tōa Kaiun Kabushikigaisha, 1944.

Shina seihoku yōmō bōeki to kaikyōto no yakuwari [The wool trade in northwest China and the role of Muslims]. Tokyo: Tōa Kenkyūjo, 1940.

Shina shōbetsu zenshi [Provincial gazetteer of China]. Vol. 9. Tokyo: Tōa Dōbunkai, 1918.

Shinohara Miyohei. *Kōkōgyō* [Mining and manufacturing]. Tokyo: Tōyō Keizai Shimpōsha, 1972.

―――. "Manufacturing." In *Patterns of Japanese Economic Development*, edited by Kazushi Ohkawa and Miyohei Shinohara, 104–21. New Haven: Yale University Press, 1979.

Shogaikoku no tai-Shi tōshi [Investments by various foreign nations in China]. 3 vols. Tokyo: Tōa Kenkyūjo, 1942–43.

Skinner, G. William. "Chinese Peasants and the Closed Community: An Open and Shut Case." *Comparative Studies in Society and History* 13, no. 3 (1971):270–81.

———. "Cities in the Hierarchy of Local Systems." In *The City in Late Imperial China*, edited by G. William Skinner, 275–351. Stanford: Stanford University Press, 1977.

———. "Marketing and Social Structure in Rural China." Parts 1, 2. *Journal of Asian Studies* 24 (1964–65):3–43, 195–228.

———. "Regional Urbanization in Nineteenth-Century China." In *The City in Late Imperial China*, edited by G. William Skinner, 211–49. Stanford: Stanford University Press, 1977.

———, ed. *Modern Chinese Society: An Analytical Bibliography.* Vol. 1, *Publications in Western Languages, 1644–1972.* Stanford: Stanford University Press, 1973.

Smith, Thomas C. *Political Change and Industrial Development in Japan: Government Enterprise, 1868–1880.* Stanford: Stanford University Press, 1955.

Spalding, William F. *Eastern Exchange, Currency and Finance.* 2d ed. London: Pitman, 1917.

Standard of Living of Shanghai Laborers. Shanghai: Bureau of Social Affairs, 1934.

The Statist. London. 1914–42.

The Statistical History of the United States from Colonial Times to the Present. Stamford, Conn.: Fairfield Publishers, 1965.

Stauffer, Milton T. *The Christian Occupation of China.* Shanghai: China Constitution Committee, 1922.

Suleski, Ronald. "The Rise and Fall of the Fengtien Dollar, 1917–1928: Currency Reform in Warlord China." *Modern Asian Studies* 13, no. 4 (1979):643–60.

"Survey Report on Routes and Quantities of Raw Material Shipments in Central China." *Chōsa geppō* 2, no. 6 (1941):113–256.

Sutton, Donald S. "Reflections on the Economic Effects of the Haiphong-Kunming Railway, 1910–1940." Pittsburgh: Carnegie-Mellon University, 1978. Photocopy.

Suzuki, Tomoo. "The Shanghai Silk-Reeling Industry During the Period of the 1911 Revolution." In *The 1911 Revolution in China: Interpretive Essays*, edited by Shinkichi Etō and Harold Z. Schiffrin, 49–59. Tokyo: University of Tokyo Press, 1984.

Svennilson, Ingvar. *Growth and Stagnation in the European Economy.* Geneva: U.N. Economic Commission for Europe, 1954.

Swen, W. Y. "Types of Farming, Costs of Production and Annual Labor Distribution in Weihsien County, Shantung, China." *Chinese Economic Journal* 3, no. 2 (1928):642–80.

Swisher, Earl. *Canton in Revolution: The Collected Papers of Earl Swisher, 1925–1928*, edited by Kenneth W. Rea. Boulder, Colo.: Westview, 1977.

Ta-lung chi ch'i ch'ang ti fa sheng fa chan yü kai tsao [Origin, development, and transformation of the Ta-lung machinery works]. Shanghai: Shang-hai Jen Min Ch'u Pan She, 1959.

Takemoto Akira. "Development of Japanese Textile Firms in China and Its Background, 1914–1937." *Rokkadai ronshū* 24, no. 2 (1977):55–69.

Tamagna, Frank M. *Banking and Finance in China*. New York: Institute of Pacific Relations, 1942.

T'an Yü-tso. *Chung-kuo chung yao yin hang fa chan shih* [Historical development of China's major banks]. Taipei: Chung-kuo Hsin Wen Ch'u Pan Kung Ssu, 1961.

T'ang, Leang-li. *China's New Currency System*. Shanghai: China United Press, 1936.

Tao, L. K. *Livelihood in Peking: An Analysis of the Budgets of Sixty Families*. Peking: China Foundation for the Promotion of Education and Culture, 1928.

Tawney, R. H. *Land and Labor in China*. Boston: Beacon, 1966.

Ten Great Years: Statistics of the Economic and Cultural Achievements of the People's Republic of China. Peking: State Statistical Bureau, 1959. Translation. Bellingham, Wash.: Western Washington State College Program in East Asian Studies, 1974.

Tenshin no gingō [The silver shops of Tientsin]. Dairen: SMR Chōsabu, 1942.

Tezuka Masao. *Shina jūkōgyō hattatsushi* [History of China's development of heavy industry]. Kyoto: Taigadō, 1944.

Tezuka Masao and Maeda Takahisa. *Shina shotankō jittai chōsa hōkoku: Santōsho Hakuzan dohō tankō o chūshin toshite* [Report on conditions at small coal mines in China: Particularly the native mines at Po-shan, Shantung]. Tokyo: Tōa Kenkyūjo, 1943.

Tien, Hung-mao. *Government and Politics in Kuomintang China, 1927–1937*. Stanford: Stanford University Press, 1972.

T'ien-chin mien hua yün hsiao kai k'uang [Transport and sales conditions for cotton in Tientsin]. Peking: Hua-pei Nung Ch'an Yen Chiu Kai Chin She, 1934.

The Times. London. 1909–17.

Ting Ch'ang-ch'ing, Yen Kuang-hua, and Liu Fo-ting. "Views on the Problem of Working Class Impoverishment in Old China: Analysis of the

Level and Trend of K'ai-luan Coal Miners' Wages." *Nan-kai ching-chi yen-chiu-so nien k'an* (1984):297–310.

Ting Jih-ch'u and Tu Hsün-ch'eng. "A Brief Account of Yü Hsia-ch'ing." *Li shih yen chiu* 3 (1981):145–66.

Ting, Leonard G. "Chinese Modern Banks and the Finance of Government and Industry." *Nankai Social and Economic Quarterly* 8, no. 3 (1935):578–616.

The Trade of China. Shanghai: Inspectorate General of Customs. 1932–36.

Tsha, T. Y. "A Study of Wage Rates in Shanghai, 1930–34." *Nankai Social and Economic Quarterly* 8, no. 3 (1935):459–510.

Tung fang tsa chih [Eastern miscellany]. Shanghai. 1928–33.

Umemura Mataji. *Nōringyō* [Agriculture and forestry]. Tokyo: Tōyō Keizai Shimpōsha, 1966.

U.S. Department of State. *Records of the Department of State Relating to Internal Affairs of China, 1910–29.* Washington, D.C.: National Archives and Records Service, 1973.

Wage Rates in Shanghai. Shanghai: Commercial Press, 1935.

"Wages of Farm Labor in Different Provinces." *T'ung chi yüeh pao* 13 (1933):99–106.

Wang Chi-shen, ed. *Chan shih Shang-hai ching chi* [Shanghai's wartime economy]. Shanghai: Shang-hai Ching Chi Yen Chiu So, 1945.

Wang Ching-yü. "Shareholdings of Chinese Merchants in Nineteenth-Century Foreign Enterprise in China." *Li shih yen chiu* 4 (1965): 39–74.

Wang Hai-po [Wang Haibo]. "Proportional Relations Between Accumulation and Consumption." In *Chung-kuo ching chi chieh kou wen t'i yen chiu* [Research on problems of Chinese economic structure], edited by Ma Hung and Sun Hsiang-ch'ing, Vol. 2:562–600. Peking: Jen Min Ch'u Pan She, 1981.

Wang, Lien. "Farm Prices in Szechwan, 1910–1934." *Economic Facts* 9 (1938):412–19.

Wang, Shu-hwai. "China's Modernization in Communications, 1860–1916: A Regional Comparison." In *Modern Chinese Economic History*, edited by Chi-ming Hou and Tzong-shian Yu, 335–51. Taipei: Institute of Economics, Academia Sinica, 1979.

———. "The Effect of Railroad Transportation in China, 1912–1927." *Chung-yang yen-chiu-yuan chin tai shih yen chiu so chi k'an* 12 (1983):301–62.

Wang Yeh-chien. *Chung-kuo chin tai huo pi yü yin hang ti yen chin (1644–1937)* [Development of money and banking in China, 1644–1937]. Taipei: Chung-yang Yen Chiu Yuan Ching Chi Yen Chiu So, 1981.

————. "Evolution of the Chinese Monetary System, 1644–1850." In *Modern Chinese Economic History*, edited by Chi-ming Hou and Tzong-shian Yu, 425–52. Taipei: Institute of Economics, Academia Sinica, 1979.

————. "The Growth and Decline of Native Banks in Shanghai." *Ching-chi lun-wen* 6, no. 1 (1978):111–42.

————. *Land Taxation in Imperial China, 1750–1911*. Cambridge: Harvard University Press, 1973.

————. "Spatial and Temporal Patterns of Grain Prices in China, 1740–1910." Kent, 1984. Paper presented at a conference on Spatial and Temporal Trends and Cycles in Chinese Economic History, Bellagio, Italy.

Wei, Wen Bin. *The Currency Problem in China*. New York: Columbia University Faculty of Political Science, 1914.

Weidner, Terry M. "Rural Economy and Local Government in Nationalist China: Chekiang Province, 1927–1937." Ph.D. diss., University of California, Davis, 1980.

Wen, Yu-ching. "Electrical Communications." In *The Chinese Year Book, 1936–37*, vol. 2:1082–1125. Shanghai: Commercial Press, 1936. Reprint. Nendeln, Liechtenstein: Kraus-Thomson, 1968.

Whitney, J. B. R. *China: Area, Administration, and Nation Building*. Chicago: University of Chicago, Department of Geography, 1970.

Wiens, Thomas B. *The Microeconomics of Peasant Economy in China, 1912–1940*. New York: Garland, 1982.

Wright, Stanley F. *The Collection and Disposal of the Maritime and Native Customs Revenue Since the Revolution of 1911*. Shanghai: Inspector General of Customs, 1927.

————. *Kiangsi Native Trade and Its Taxation*. Shanghai, 1920. Reprint. New York: Garland, 1980.

Wright, Tim. *Coal Mining in China's Economy and Society, 1895–1937*. Cambridge: Cambridge University Press, 1984.

————. "Entrepreneurs, Politicians and the Chinese Coal Industry, 1895–1937." *Modern Asian Studies* 14, no. 4 (1980):579–602.

————. "Growth of the Modern Chinese Coal Industry: An Analysis of Supply and Demand." *Modern China* 7, no. 3 (1981):317–50.

————. "A New Series for Electric Power Production in Pre-1937 China." Murdoch, Australia: Murdoch University, n.d. Photocopy.

Wrigley, E. A. "A Simple Model of London's Importance in Changing English Society and Economy, 1650–1750." *Past and Present* 37 (1967):44–70.

Wu Ch'eng-hsi. *Chung-kuo ti yin hang* [China's banks]. Shanghai: Commercial Press, 1934.

Wu Ch'eng-ming. *Chung-kuo tzu pen chu i yü kuo nei shih ch'ang* [Chinese capitalism and the domestic market]. Peking: Chung-kuo She Hui K'o Hsüeh Ch'u Pan She, 1985.

Wu Pao-san [see also Pao-san Ou]. *Chung-kuo kuo min so te, 1933 nien* [China's national income for 1933]. 2 vols. Shanghai: Chung-hua Shu Chü, 1947.

Wu, Yuan-li. *The Spatial Economy of Communist China: A Study on Industrial Location and Transportation.* New York: Praeger, 1967.

Xia Lingen. See Hsia Lin-ken.

Xian Ke. See Hsien K'o.

Xue Muqiao. See Hsüeh Mu-ch'iao.

Yamamura, Kozo. "Success Illgotten? The Role of Meiji Militarism in Japan's Technological Progress." *Journal of Economic History* 37, no. 1 (1977):113–35.

Yan Guanghua. See Yen Kuang-hua.

Yan Xuexi. See Yen Hsüeh-hsi.

Yan Zhongping. See Yen Chung-p'ing.

Yang, Ch'ing-k'un [C. K. Yang]. "The Contraction of Space in Modern China." *Ling-nan hsüeh pao* 12, no. 1 (1949):151–61.

———. *A North China Local Market Economy: A Summary of a Study of Periodic Markets in Chowping Hsien, Shantung.* New York: Institute of Pacific Relations, 1944.

———. "Some Preliminary Statistical Patterns of Mass Actions in Nineteenth-Century China." In *Conflict and Control in Late Imperial China,* edited by Frederic Wakeman and Carolyn Grant, 174–210. Berkeley and Los Angeles: University of California Press, 1975.

Yang, Sueh-chang. "China's Depression and Subsequent Recovery, 1931–36." Ph.D. diss., Harvard University, 1950.

Yang, W. Y., and Kwoh-hwa Hu. "Problem of Copper Dearth." *Economic Facts* 12 (1939):561–84.

Yao, S. K. "Aviation." In *The Chinese Year Book, 1935–36,* vol. 1: 593–609. Shanghai: Commercial Press, 1935. Reprint. Nendeln, Liechtenstein: Kraus-Thomson, 1968.

Yeh Ch'ien-chi. "Production, Transport, and Marketing for Hsi-ho Cotton." In *Chung-kuo ching chi yen chiu* [Studies on China's economy], edited by Fang Hsien-t'ing, vol. 1: 195–224. Changsha: Commercial Press, 1938.

Yeh, K[ung] C[hia]. "Capital Formation." In *Economic Trends in Communist China,* edited by Alexander Eckstein, Walter Galenson, and Ta-chung Liu, 509–48. Chicago: Aldine, 1968.

———. "Capital Formation in Mainland China: 1931–36 and 1952–57." Ph.D. diss., Columbia University, 1964.

———. "China's National Income, 1931–36." In *Modern Chinese Economic History*, edited by Chi-ming Hou and Tzong-shian Yu, 95–128. Taipei: Institute of Economics, Academia Sinica, 1979.

Yen Chung-p'ing, comp. *Chung-kuo chin tai ching chi shih t'ung chi tzu liao hsüan chi* [Selected statistical materials on China's modern economic history]. Peking: K'o Hsüeh Ch'u Pan She, 1955.

———. *Chung-kuo mien fang chih shih kao* [Draft history of China's cotton textile industry]. Peking: K'o Hsüeh Ch'u Pan She, 1963.

Yen Hsüeh-hsi. *Chiang-su chin hsien tai ching chi shih wen chi* [Essays on modern economic history of Kiangsu province]. Nanking: Chiang-su Sheng Chung-kuo Hsien Tai Shih Hsüeh Hui, 1983.

Yen, Jen-kuang. "Telecommunications." In *The Chinese Year Book, 1935–36*, vol. 1:673–98. Shanghai: Commercial Press, 1935. Reprint. Nendeln, Liechtenstein: Kraus-Thomson, 1968.

Yen Kuang-hua and Ting Ch'ang-ch'ing. "The Level of Workers' Wages at the Old K'ai-luan Coal Mines." *Nan-k'ai ching-chi yen-chiu-so chi k'an* 2 (1982):36–46, 18.

Yen Mu-yu. "Amount of Bank Lending to Agriculture in China, 1931–37." *Yen-ching ta-hsüeh ching chi hsüeh pao* 2 (1941):193–224.

Yokoyama Suguru. "Establishment of Match Manufacturing in China." *Hiroshima daigaku bungakubu kiyō* 25, no. 1 (1965):262–82.

———. "On the Relation Between Private Chinese Industrial Capital and the Native Banks." *Shakai keizai shigaku* 27, no. 3 (1961):224–38.

Yoshida Kōichi. "Cotton Marketing in One Locality in China During the First Half of the Twentieth Century." *Shirin* 60, no. 2 (1977):171–205.

Young, Arthur N. *China's Nation-Building Effort, 1927–1937: The Financial and Economic Record*. Stanford: Hoover Institution, 1971.

———. *China's Wartime Finance and Inflation, 1937–1945*. Cambridge: Harvard University Press, 1965.

Yü T'ao. "Currency Circulation in Base Areas During the Period of the Land Revolution." *Chung-kuo ch'ien pi* 1 (1983):41–43.

Yün-nan kung shang yeh kai k'uang [Commercial and industrial conditions in Yunnan]. Kunming: Yün-nan Shih Yeh Ssu Kung Shang K'o, 1924.

INDEX

441

Compositor: G & S Typesetters, Inc.
Text: 11/13 Caledonia
Display: Caledonia
Printer: Braun-Brumfield, Inc.
Binder: Braun-Brumfield, Inc.